PRIMARY SOURCE DOCUMENTS

Susan Rimby
Shippensburg University

Pamela Marquez
Community College of Aurora

Katie Janssen

WOMEN AND THE MAKING OF AMERICA

Mari Jo Buhle
Brown University

Teresa Murphy
George Washington University

Jane Gerhard
Holyoke College

PEARSON

Upper Saddle River, New Jersey 07458

© 2009 by PEARSON EDUCATION, INC.
Upper Saddle River, New Jersey 07458

ISBN 10:   0-13-227842-1
ISBN 13: 978-0-13-227842-3

Introduction

Chapter 1

Chapter 2

Chapter 3

Chapter 4

Chapter 5

Chapter 10

Chapter 11

Chapter 12

Chapter 13

Chapter 14

Chapter 15

Chapter 16

Chapter 17

Chapter 18

Chapter 19

Chapter 20

20-1 Postwar Unionism and Feminism
20-2 The Civil Rights Act of 1964
20-3 Sex and Caste
20-4 Sit-In
20-5 Voting Rights in Mississippi
20-6 The Birth of NOW
20-7 NOW Statement of Purpose
20-8 Womanpower

Chapter 21

21-1 SNCC Position Paper
21-2 Black, Feminist, and Lesbian
21-3 The Equal Rights Amendment (1972)
21-4 Women's Shitwork
21-5 The Personal is Political
21-6 *Roe v. Wade* (1973)
21-7 Mirta Vidal: New Voice of La Raza

Chapter 22

22-1 Defining Feminist Activism
22-2 Asma Gull Hasan: American Muslim Women, Between Two Worlds
22-3 From the Consciousness-Raising Group to the Women's Studies Classroom
22-4 Restaurant Worker
22-5 If I Stop Trying, I Will be Deaf
22-6 Crossing the Rio Grande
22-7 Comparable Worth

I-1 From Challenging Dichotomies: Perspectives on Women's History
Gisela Bock

Gisela Bock is a German feminist historian perhaps best known as the leader of a group calling for women to be paid for housework. Her best known work, Compulsory Sterilization in National Socialism *is the study of hundreds of thousands of forced sterilizations in Nazi Germany during the 1930s and 1940s due to the antinatalist policies of the Third Reich that punished those women not fortunate enough to give birth to "racially pure" children. The following extract is the first section of her work "Challenging Dichotomies: Perspectives on Women's History."*

Source: Bock, Gisela. "Challenging Dichotomies in Women's History." *Writing Women's History: International Perspectives.* Karen Offen, Ruth Roach Pierson, and Jane Renall, editors. Indiana University Press, 1991. pp 1-7.

Women's history has come a long way. Some twenty years ago, Gerda Lerner wrote that 'the striking fact about the historiography of women is the general neglect of the subject by historians'. Historical scholarship was far from 'objective' or 'universal', because it was based on male experience, placed men at the centre and as a measure of all things human, thereby leaving out half of humankind. In the past two decades, the situation has changed considerably. In an enormous (and enormously growing) body of scholarship women have been rendered visible. They have been placed at the centre, and what women do, have to do, and want to do has been re-evaluated in view of social, political and cultural change, of an improvement in women's situations and, more generally, in terms of a change towards more freedom and justice. More precisely, what has been rendered historically visible by making women a subject of research was, in the first place, their subjection. In the second place, however, it was their subjectivity - because women are not only vic-tims, but also actively shape their own lives, society and history.

Much of this research was carried out in the context of three conceptual or theoretical frameworks that have been used by many feminist scholars, particularly historians, in the past two decades and which will be outlined in the first section of this paper. These frameworks point to three dichotomies in traditional thought on gender relations, and all of them have been not only used, but also profoundly challenged. The second section will illustrate three further dichotomies which, in the development of modern women's history, have emerged more recently and which presently seem to dominate and direct women's studies. All. of these dichotomies have been discussed, to a greater or lesser degree, internationally, but there are some interesting national differences in the debates themselves as well as in their sequence over time. Particularly noteworthy are certain changes in language brought about in this context. These are, of course, nationally different, but they also indicate to what extent women's history and women's studies have succeeded in crossing national boundaries.

Women as subject, the subjection of women and women's subjectivity

1. Nature versus culture. It was mainly in the United States in the early 1970s that the relation of the sexes was discussed in terms of the relation, or rather dichotomy, between 'nature and nurture' or 'nature and culture', Men and their activities had been seen as culture and of cultural value, whereas women and their activities had been seen as natural, outside of history and society, always the same and therefore not worthy of scholarly, political or theoretical interest and inquiry. Moreover, it was the relations between the sexes, and most particularly their relations of power and subjection, that had been attributed to nature. 'Nature', in this context, most often meant sexuality between men and women, women's bodies and their capacity for pregnancy and motherhood. Fatherhood, however, was usually seen not as natural but as 'social'. Female scholars challenged this traditional dichotomy. They argued that what 'nature' really meant in this discourse was a devaluation of everything that women stood for, that '"nature" always has a social meaning', that both 'nature' and 'culture' meant different things at different times, in different places and to the different sexes, and that women's bodies and bodily capacities were not always and everywhere seen as disabilities, but also as a basis for certain kinds of informal power and public activities. The nature/culture dichotomy was recognised as a specific and perhaps specifically Western way of expressing the hierarchies between the sexes. The binary terms of this dichotomy only apparently refer to antagonistic and independent terms; but in fact, they refer to a hierarchy of social realities and cultural meanings, between strongly interdependent terms. In other words: no such nature without such culture, and no such culture without such nature. One of the linguistic results of such insights in women's history is that the term 'nature' is now almost always placed in quotation marks.

The study of women's identification with nature, of their embodiment and their body-related activities, such as motherhood, nursing and caring, has resulted in a number of important works which deal with these distinctively female domains. Early works on the history of motherhood were written by French scholars. More recently, research on the female body has shown to what degree it is historically conditioned and dependent on the cultural context. Feminist philosophers, particularly in France, are building theoretical frameworks precisely around the distinctive female experience, and this approach is currently arousing great and controversial interest in the United States. On the other hand, French and other historians argue that this focus on women's 'nature' may be politically counterproductive because it seems to confirm traditional stereotypes according to which women seem to be exclusively defined by their body, by motherhood and by their sex, and to overlook the more important political dimensions of women's history.

2. Work versus family. A second theoretical framework for rendering women visible, and for dismantling their identification with the merely natural, unchanging and therefore uninteresting, was the issue of their distinctive patterns of work. The discussion around it had its origins more in the European than in the American context, particularly in Italy, Britain, Germany and France. What had been seen as nature was now seen as work: bearing, rearing and caring for children, looking after the breadwinner-husband and after other family members. To call this activity 'work' meant to challenge the dichotomy 'work and family' (because the family may mean work to women), but also 'work and leisure' (because men's leisure may be women's work), and 'working men and supported wives' (because wives support men through their work). It meant questioning the view that work is only that which is done for pay. Women have always worked, and unpaid work was and is women's work. Obviously, men's work is valued more highly than women's work. In theoretical and economic terms, it has been demonstrated that women's work was overlooked by male theoreticians of work and the economy and why this happened; accordingly the value or 'productivity' of domestic work came to be discussed. In historical terms, it has been shown how strongly this work changed over time and cross-culturally. For example, in Britain and Australia, housewives were counted among the 'occupied' categories in the census up to the end of the nineteenth century, when they were excluded from them; around the same time, radical feminists in Germany and elsewhere were demanding that their work be included in the measurement of the Gross National Product.

The sexual division of labour was found to be not just a division, but a hierarchy of labour; and not just one of labour but, primarily, a sexual division of value and rewards. The lower value of women's work continues - through economic and cultural mediation - in employment outside the home. Here, where women have always worked, they earned only 50 per cent to 80 per cent of men's earnings in the nineteenth and twentieth centuries in western countries, with variations over time and space. Women's employment in the caring and nursing professions, where they are the overwhelming majority, usually does not guarantee them a decent survival income, the 1989 nurses' strike in West Germany being just one example. The recent international increase in the number of single mothers has led to a 'feminisation of poverty', even beyond the traditionally high level of female poverty.

The apparent dichotomy between 'work and family', between men as workers and women as 'non-workers', turns out to be one between paid and unpaid work, between underpaid and decently paid work, between the superior and inferior value of men's and women's work respectively. The underlying assumption of mutually exclusive superiority and inferiority seems to be another common feature of such gender-linked dichotomies. The challenge posed by women's studies to this opposition is obviously linked to political and economic challenges to pay women's as yet unpaid work, to raise their earnings in low-pay jobs, and to admit more women to well-paid professions. It has also led to some linguistic changes. Even though, in the English language, the terms 'working women' and 'working mothers' are still reserved for employed women only, and non-employed women are still often called 'non-working', the terms 'work and family' are now often replaced by 'paid and unpaid work'. In German, women's historians distinguish consistently between 'work' and 'employment', Arbeit [work] and Erwerbstlltigkeit [income-earning], and Arbeitslosigkeit [unemployment, literally 'worklessness'] has been replaced by Erwerbs losigkeit ['incomelessness '].

3. Public versus private. A third conceptual framework of women's history has been the relation between the public and the private, or the political and the personal, or the sphere of power and the domestic sphere. Traditional political theory has seen them, again, as a dichotomy of mutually exclusive terms, identified with women's 'sphere' and men's 'world'. Women's studies have profoundly challenged this view, pointing out its inadequacy for understanding politics and society, The slogan 'the personal is political' indicated that the issue of power is not confined to 'high politics', but also appears in sexual relations. Men inhabit, and rule within both spheres, whereas women's proper place was seen to be only in the domestic sphere and in her subjection to father or husband. This means, on the one hand, the dichotomy is not one between two autonomous, symmetrical and equivalent spheres, but rather a complex relation between domination and subordination, between power and powerlessness. On the other hand, women's studies have shown that the public 'world' was essentially based on the domestic 'sphere'. Male workers, male politicians and male scholars perform their tasks only because they are born, reared and cared for by women's labour. The boundaries between public and private shift significantly over time and cross-culturally, as in the historical transition between private charity and public assistance, in both of which women played important roles. State policy has not left women out, but has shaped their personal circumstances by public intervention in, for instance, legislation on rape and abortion, and by the absence of legislation. The modern welfare states have discriminated against women in old age pensions and unemployment benefits; they have introduced maternity leave for employed women without replacing their loss of income - in Europe, this was changed mainly through the struggles of the women's movements since around 1900 - and income tax reforms have supported husbands and fathers, but not wives and mothers. The welfare state has not excluded women's sphere but included it as private, implying that it is under the rule of the husband. The Nazi regime went much beyond this, because its intervention tended to destroy the private sphere; not however, as is often said, by promoting motherhood, but by promoting precisely the opposite: a policy of mass compulsory sterilisation for women and men who were considered 'racially inferior'. This antinatalist policy was explicitly based on the doctrine that 'the private is political' and that the definition of the boundaries between the political and the private is a political act; according to the National Socialists, it was the sterilisation policy which established and asserted 'the primacy of the state in the field of life, marriage and the family'.

Women's history has also discovered that what is perceived as 'private' by some may be seen as 'public' by others. The domestic tasks of bearing and rearing children, for instance, were proclaimed as being of public importance by many women in the early women's movement. They requested that it be re-evaluated, and many of them based their demand for equal political citizenship precisely on this vision of the 'separate sphere', understood not as a dichotomy of mutually exclusive and hierarchical terms, but as a source of equal rights and responsibilities of the female sex in respect to civil society. On this basis, they did not so much challenge the sexual division of labour, as the sexual division of power. In this sense, the late anthropologist Michelle Zimbalist Rosaldo argued that women could, and did, challenge male rule either by seeking to enter the distinctively male sphere, or by stressing the value of their own sphere; sometimes they attempted to combine both. Women's historians have also pointed out that the traditional nineteenth-century or Victorian version of the female separate sphere was not oppressive in a simple way, but left considerable space for female bonding and the development of a women's culture as an expression of women's subjectivity.

* * * * *

These three dichotomies seem to have some important characteristics in common. They are eminently gender-linked, and as such they have distant roots in European and western traditions of gender perception. They have been taken up and used as crucial conceptual frameworks in the newly emerging women's history of the past decades, and simultaneously their long-standing apparent validity for the perception of gender relations has been thoroughly challenged. This challenge concerned the analysis, historicisation and deconstruction of the character and meaning of these three dual categories, as well as the links between them, and it questioned the traditional assumption that these dichotomies were expressions natural and necessary expressions - of sexual difference.

The question has been raised as to whether these dichotomies are just a few examples among many similar binary oppositions and dualistic modes of western thought in general, or whether their gender-linked character makes them very special. (Of course, other classic dichotomies, such as 'subjective/objective', 'rational/emotional', have also assumed gender-linked meanings, even though not all of them have been equally central to historical analytical frameworks; on the other hand, the dichotomies discussed above have also been studied in contexts which were not primarily gender-linked.) But it seems that, whenever they are used for describing gender relations, they do not refer so much to separate, autonomous, independent, equivalent dual spheres, as to relations of hierarchy: hierarchies of spheres, meanings, values, of inferiority and superiority, of subordination and power; in other words, to relations where 'culture' subjects 'nature', the world of 'work' reigns over that of the 'family', the 'political' dominates the 'private'.

In terms of logical rules, these apparent dichotomies are not mutually exclusive contradictories, as in A is not B, B is not A (woman is not man and vice versa). Rather these apparent dichotomies are (really) contraries, for they may coexist freely, and/or coexist with C (as alternatives to the dichotomous attributions) and all of them may have a positive reality.

Patriarchal theorists have constituted these dualisms on the model of logically contradictory opposites, as in the impossible combination of A and Not-A, in which what defines Not-A is its privation with respect to A, that is, its lack of A. These contradictory opposites in their rigidity, allow for neither alternatives (tertium non datur) [no third value is given]; nor reversals, as in Not-A being attributed to men and A to women. When, for instance, gender is constructed on a model of mutually exclusive, binary opposites, if men are defined as rational, then women are defined by an absence of rationality. In this construction, for the woman to take on rationality is for her to begin to assimilate to the male norm and thus to begin to cease to be a woman. Contraries, in contrast, allow for a multiplicity of alternatives. Feminists have argued that 'mere contrary distinctions are not eternally tied to dichotomous structure, and as dichotomies they are limited in scope'. Therefore, it might be useful to distinguish more clearly between dichotomies of mutual exclusion and hierarchy on one side, and contraries, distinctions or differences, on the other, which are neither hierarchical nor mutually exclusive. Above all, sensitivity to the prevalence of binary oppositions of a dichotomous kind in discourses of gender has taught us to beware of their historical and political pitfalls.

Focus Questions:

1. Do you see any of the traditional dichotomies described above at work in today's society? Are they more or less prevalent?

2. Are women-only spheres always necessarily oppressive? Why or why not?

I-2 From Gender, Race, and Culture: Spanish-Mexican Women in the Historiography of Frontier California

Antonia I. Castañeda teaches in the Department of History at St. Mary's University. Her writing focuses on gender, sexuality, and women of color in California and the Borderlands from the 16th century to the present. This portion of her essay is a critique of the contemporary travel writers and historians whose erroneous and often prejudiced work influenced future writers over the next century.

Source: Castanieda Antonia I., *Frontiers: A Journal of Women Studies,* Vol. 11, No. 1, Las Chicanas, (1990), pp. 8-10

Historians, whether writing for a popular or a scholarly audience, reflect contemporary ideology with respect to sex, race, and culture. Until the mid-1970s, when significant revisionist work in social, women's, and Chicano history began to appear, the writing of California history reflected an ideology that ascribed racial and cultural inferiority to Mexicans and sexual inferiority to women.' Not only do ideas about women form an integral part of the ideological universe of all societies, but the position of women in society is one measure by which civilizations have historically been judged. Accordingly, California historians applied Anglo, middle-class norms of women's proper behavior to Mexican women's comportment and judged them according to their own perceptions of Mexican culture and of women's positions within that culture.

This essay pays a good deal of attention to the popular histories of frontier California because of the inordinate influence they have had on the more scholarly studies. In particular, the factual errors and stereotypes in the work of Hubert Howe Bancroft, Theodore H. Hittell, and Zoeth Skinner Eldredge have been propagated not only by other nineteenth- and twentieth-century popularizers but also by scholars-in the few instances where they include women at all. Although historians of the Teutonic, frontier hypothesis, and Spanish borderlands schools barely mention women, an implicit gender ideology influences their discussions of race, national character, and culture. The more recent literature in social, women's, and Chicano history breaks sharply with the earlier ideology and corollary interpretations with respect to race and culture or gender and culture, but it has yet to construct an integrative interpretation that incorporates sex-gender, race, and culture.

The Popular Histories of the Late Nineteenth Century

Women were not treated with the greatest respect: in Latin and in savage countries they seldom are; hence, as these were half Latin and half savage, we are not surprised to learn that the men too often idled away their time, leaving the women to do all the work and rear the family.

Written by lawyers, bankers, and other prominent men who came to California in the aftermath of the Mexican War and the gold rush, the multivolume popular histories of the late nineteenth century provide the first composite description and interpretation of Spanish-Mexican California. These histories fundamentally reflect the political and socioracial ideology that informed both the war with Mexico and the subsequent sociopolitical and economic marginalization of Mexicans in California. With respect to women, they reaffirm the contradictory but stereotypic images found in the travel journals and other documents written by entrepreneurs, merchants, adventurers, and other members of the advance guard of Euro-American expansion between the 1820s and 1840s.

In the tradition of the patrician historians whose romantic literary style set the standards and popular patterns from the end of the nineteenth century until well into the twentieth, Bancroft, Hittell, and other popularizers intersperse their voluminous histories of California with musings about race, religion, national character, savagery, and civilization. Riddled with the

nationalistic fervor of the post-Civil War decades and with an unquestioning belief in Nordic racial superiority, these historians predictably conclude that the Anglo-Saxon race and civilization are far superior to the Latin race and Spanish-Mexican civilization that had produced in California, according to Bancroft, "a race halfway between the proud Castillian and the lowly root digger," existing "halfway between savagery and civilization." Only Amerindians ranked lower than the minions of Spain.

In the works on early colonial development, the discussion of women is only incidental to the larger consideration of specific institutions-the mission, presidio, and pueblo-or of great men-the governors. Thus, for example, a brief discussion of the maltreatment of Amerindian women in the mission system has no importance beyond its illustration of institutional development and Spanish brutality, which, in the tradition of the "Black Legend," spared not even women. Similarly, Bancroft treats sexual and other violence against native women primarily in relation to the bitter conflict between the institutions of church and state, and attributes it to the moral degeneration of the racially mixed soldier-settler population.

Bancroft and his colleagues also introduce individual elite women to their readers. The portraits of two in particular set the tone for the consistent romanticization of "Spanish" as opposed to "Mexican" women. A prototype of the tempestuous Spanish woman, Eulalia Callis, high-born Catalan wife of the doughty Governor Fages, was dubbed the "infamous gobernadora" (governor's wife) for refusing Fages her bed upon his refusal to relinquish the governorship and return the family to Mexico.

Even more important in the development of the "Spanish" stereotype was Concepción Arguello, the young daughter of Don Jose Arguello, Commandant at the Presidio of San Francisco. Prototype of the tragic maiden, Dona Concepcion became betrothed to the Russian ambassador and chamberlain, Nickolai Petrovich Resanov, in 1806. Resanov had sailed to California from Alaska aboard the brig Juno, seeking to trade the ship's entire cargo for foodstuffs desperately needed to stave off starvation and mass desertions in Sitka. But Governor Arrillaga, bound by Spain's policy of prohibiting trade with foreigners, refused to negotiate. Undaunted, Resanov wooed the young Concepcion and, upon her acceptance of his proposal of marriage persuaded her father to intercede with the governor, who finally agreed to the trade.

Resanov left for Alaska and thereafter for Russia,

promising to return as soon as he had the Czar's permission to marry, but he died while in Russia. Dofia Concepción continued to await his return, for she did not learn of his death until many years later. After a life spent in nursing and charitable work, she became, in 1851, the first novice in the newly established Dominican convent in Monterey. She took her vows as Sister Maria Dominica in 1852 and died five years later at age sixty-six.

Bancroft's commentary addresses not only the diplomatic and political strategy evident in Resanov's courtship and proposal of marriage but also the character of the Californians, both male and female: "What wonder that court life at St. Petersburg was fascinating, or that this child, weary of the sun-basking indolence of those about her, allowed her heart to follow her ambitions." This aura of exotic drama and romance informs all later descriptions of "Spanish" women, in popular and scholarly works alike.

Bancroft also briefly discusses women in the context of colonial settlement and the family. He records the arrival of the first group of Spanish-Mexican women and families in 1774 and the overland journeys of the Anza and Rivera soldier-settler families in 1775-1776 and 1781 respectively. He also comments on Governor Borica's efforts to attract single women to the distant frontier and on the arrival of the ninas de cuna, the ten orphan girls brought to Alta California in 1800 as future marriage partners for single presidial soldiers.

In general, the popular historical accounts of the Spanish period (1769-1821) are notable for their absence of pejorative gender-specific sexual stereotypes. Instead, pejorative stereotypes are generalized to the entire group and focus on race. In accounts of Mexican California (1822-1846), the popular historians divide women into two classes: "Spanish" and "Mexican." Although the vast majority of Californians, including the elite, were mestizo or mulato and Mexican, not Spanish, in nationality, women from long-time Californian elite, land-owning families, some of whom married Europeans or Euro-Americans, were called "Spanish." Women from more recently arrived or non-elite families were called "Mexican." "Spanish" women were morally, sexually, and racially pure; "Mexican" women were immoral and sexually and racially impure. These sexual stereotypes not only reveal the convergence of contemporary political and social ideological currents but also underscore the centrality of the politics of sex to the ideological justification of expansion, war, and conquest. The dominant social Darwinism of the late nineteenth century, which used scientific theory to rationalize Nordic racial superiority and male sexual supremacy, also held that a society's degree of civilization could be judged by the status and character of its women. The Victorian True Woman, like her predecessor the Republican Mother, represented the most advanced stage of civilized society. Physically and mentally inferior to men but possessed of the cardinal female virtues-piety, purity, submissiveness, and domesticity-she was confined to the home, where she could neither threaten nor challenge the existing order. She was the norm by which historians judged Mexican women, individually and collectively, and thus one of the norms by which they judged Mexican society. Like other reductionist representations of Mexicans in the literature that treats the Mexican period as a "backdrop to the coming of Old Glory," pejorative stereotypes of Mexicanas thus served a political purpose. The worst stereotypes of women appeared in the histories of the Mexican rather than the Spanish period not just because the primary sources were written largely by white men who visited and/or lived in Mexican, not Spanish, California, but because the war was fought with Mexico.

The most extensive treatment of Mexican women appears in Bancroft's interpretative social history, California Pastoral, in which he devotes an entire chapter to "Woman and Her Sphere." By virtue of publishing the earliest work of this genre, Bancroft became the main source for the stereotypes of women in Mexican California in subsequent histories.

In the work of Bancroft, Hittell, and their modern successors, the portrayals of Mexican men, the wartime foes, are uniformly stereotypic and pejorative, focusing both on their racial origins and on a national character formed by Spanish tyranny, absolutism, and fanaticism. Bancroft describes Mexicans as "droves of mongrels" deriving from a "turgid racial stream" and concludes that they were "not a strong community either physically, morally, or politically." He depicts life in Mexican California as a long, happy holiday in a lotus land where "to eat, to drink, to make love, to smoke, to dance, to ride, to sleep seemed the whole duty of man."

His stereotypes of women, however, are contradictory and reveal greater gradation. Women's position in Mexican society, especially, is treated contradictorily. "The Californians, violent exercise and lack of education makes them rough and almost brutal. They have little regard for their women, and are of a jealous disposition ... they are indifferent husbands, faithless and exacting and very hard taskmasters," Bancroft says at one point. Yet several pages later he comments, "there was strong affection and never a happier family than when a ranchero, dwelling in pastoral simplicity saw his sons and his sons' sons bringing to the paternal roof their wives and seating them at the ever-lengthening table."

Bancroft's Mexican women are dunces and drudges. They work laboriously and continuously; bear twelve, fifteen, and twenty children; and are subject to being prostituted by their husbands, who "wink at the familiarity of a wealthy neighbor who pays handsomely for his entertainment." Women have no recourse to laws, which men make and women obey. At the same time, however, Bancroft quotes earlier writers to the effect that "the women are pretty, but vain, frivolous, bad managers, and extravagant. They are passionately fond of fine, showy dresses and jewelry ... their morality is none of the purest; and the coarse and lascivious dances show the degraded tone of manners that exist." Nevertheless, infidelity is rare because Califomianas fear the swift and deadly revenge exacted by jealous husbands.

Bancroft based his negative images of Mexican women on the accounts of Richard Henry Dana and others who visited California in the 1840s, on the eve of the war with Mexico. But he also recorded a positive image derived from the writings of Alfred Robinson and other Euro-Americans who traveled to California in the 1820s and 1830s to ply the hide and tallow trade and who married elite Californianas and settled there.

Robinson's accounts expressed similar negative stereotypes of men but presented positive portrayals of "Spanish" or "Californio" women. Robinson, who married Maria Teresa de la Guerra y Noriega, wrote that "the men are generally indolent and addicted to many vices ... yet... in few places of the world ... can be found more chastity, industrious habits and correct deportment than among the women." Similar images appeared in literary pieces written on the eve of the Mexican War by individuals who had no firsthand experience of California. In this literature, Spanish-speaking women invited the advances of Euro-American men whom they anxiously awaited as their saviors from Mexican men. For example, "They Wait for Us," published in Boston at the time that John C. Fremont's outlaw band was raising the Bear Flag at Sonoma in June 1846, treats Mexican women as the symbol for the country about to be conquered:

They Wait for Us

The Spanish maid, with eyes of fire
At balmy evening turns her lyre,
And, looking to the Eastern sky,
Awaits our Yankee Chivalry
Whose purer blood and valiant arms,
Are fit to clasp her budding charms.
The man, her mate, is sunk in sloth-
To love, his senseless heart is loth:
The pipe and glass and tinkling lute,
A sofa, and a dish of fruit;
A nap, some dozen times by day;
Sombre and sad, and never gay.

The meaning is clear-Mexicans cannot appreciate, love, direct, or control their women/country.

Forty years later, Bancroft and Hittell underscored this theme in the primary sources. "It was a happy day," writes Bancroft, "for the California bride whose husband was an American." According to Hittell, Californian senoritas eagerly sought American husbands, who "might not touch the guitar as lightly," but "made better husbands than those of Mexican blood." The chaste, industrious Spanish beauty who forsook her inferior man and nation in favor of the superior Euro-American became embedded in the literature. The negative image that Bancroft et al. picked up from the English-language primary sources was reserved for Mexican women: fandango-dancing, monte-dealing prostitutes, the consorts of Mexican bandits. These dual stereotypes became the prototypic images of Spanish-speaking women in California. They were the grist of popular fiction and contemporary newspapers through-out the latter part of the nineteenth and early twentieth centuries, and they resurfaced in the popular historical literature of the twentieth century, including the few works that focused specifically on women of Spanish California.

FOCUS QUESTIONS:

1. Highlight some of the differences in the portrayal of Spanish and Mexican women by contemporary historians and travel writers.

2. By what standards did writers base their judgment of Mexican women? How did this influence their attitude toward Mexican society as a whole?

I-3 From Beyond the Search for Sisterhood: American Women's History in the 1980s

Nancy A. Hewitt is a professor of History and Women's Studies at Rutgers University and has written on a number of articles on women's activism. This essay, written in 1985, examines the relationship between the feminist movement of the 1980s and the history of the 1960s and 1970s that immediately preceded it.

Source: Hewitt, Nancy A., *Social History,* Vol. 10, No. 3, North American Issue, (Oct., 1985), pp. 299-321

I

One of the principal projects of the contemporary feminist movement in the United States has been the development of a sense of community among women, rooted in their common oppression and expressed through a distinctive women's culture. This project is premised on the patriarchal assumptions accepted by the majority of North America's early feminist leaders: that gender is the primary source of oppression in society and is the model for all other forms of oppression. American women's historians of the 1960s and 1970s not only accepted the premises and projects of the women's movement but also helped to establish them. The bonds that encircled past generations of women were initially perceived as restrictive, arising from female victimization at the hands of patriarchs in such institutions as medicine, education, the church, the state, and the family. Historians soon concluded, however, that oppression was a double-edged sword; the counterpart of subordination in or exclusion from male-dominated domains was inclusion in an all-female enclave. The concept of womanhood, it soon appeared, bound women together even as it bound them down. The formative works in American women's history have focused on the formation of these separate sexual spheres, particularly among the emerging urban bourgeoisie in the first half of the nineteenth century. Reified in prescriptive literature, realized in daily life, and ritualized in female collectivities, this 'woman's sphere' came to be seen as the foundation of women's culture and community in antebellum America.

Though feminists, including scholars, have perceived community as a source of support and solidarity for women, both history and politics affirm that a strong sense of community can also be a source of exclusion, prejudices, and prohibitions. For the past decade, the women's movement itself has been accused of forming its own exclusive community, characterized by elitism, ethnocentrism, and a disregard for diversity. At the same time, students of black and working-class women's lives have argued that the notion of a single women's community rooted in common oppression denies the social and material realities of caste and class in America. Yet as the concept of community has become increasingly problematic for women's historians, it has also become increasingly paradigmatic. This article will evaluate the current paradigm in American women's history - premised on patriarchy and constructed around community - by comparing the creation, conditions and practices of communal life among black and white working-class women with that among the white bourgeoisie in the nineteenth and early twentieth centuries.

The community that has become the cornerstone of North American women's history was discovered within the Victorian middle class. There a 'rich female subculture' flourished 'in which women, relegated to domesticity, constructed powerful emotional and practical bonds with each other. Three distinct but related investigations converged to illuminate this enclave of sisterhood. Barbara Welter first identified the construction of a new ideology of gender in the years 1820 to 1860 that defined the 'true woman' as pious, pure, domestic, and submissive. Nancy Cott correlated this ideology with a separation of women and men into distinct spheres of activity, at least among New England's middling classes. For this group, commercial and industrial developments in the late eighteenth and early nineteenth centuries simultaneously consigned married women to domesticity and launched men on public careers. Carroll Smith-Rosenberg then discovered within the private domain a dynamic 'world of love and ritual' in which a distinct set of values was elaborated into a richly textured women's culture.

Though each of these authors regarded her work as speculative and carefully noted parameters of time, region, and class, the true woman/separate spheres/woman's culture triad became the most widely used framework for interpreting women's past in the United States. The articles and arguments presented by the architects of the paradigm are widely quoted, reprinted frequently, summarized in textbooks and popular histories, reproduced in curriculum packets, and elaborated upon in an array of scholarly studies. By gendering the Victorian landscape and evaluating historical patterns and processes in women's own terms, the historians of bourgeois womanhood have established concepts and categories that now shape the analysis of all groups of American women.

Historians soon traced the bonds of womanhood into public arenas and across race and class barriers. According to Cott, the 'doctrine of woman's sphere opened to women (reserved for them) the avenues of domestic influence, religious morality, and child nurture. It articulated a social power based on their special female qualities. That social power was first revealed in church and charitable societies and in educational missions, then was gradually expanded into campaigns for moral reform, temperance, the abolition of slavery, and even women's rights. By the late nineteenth century, domestic skills and social power would converge in 'social housekeeping', embracing and justifying women's participation in urban development, social welfare programs, social work, the settlement house movement, immigrant education, labor reform, and electoral politics.

At the same time that middle-class wives reached across the domestic threshold, they also apparently, though more haltingly, stepped across the moat dividing them from women of other classes and races. Some plantation mistresses, for instance, decried, at least in their private diaries, the sexual double standard reflected in white men's abuse of slave women. In at least one southern town, free black and white women seemed to adopt a common set of values grounded in personalism: both races were more attuned to the needs and interests of other women, more concerned with economic security, more supportive of organized charity, and more serious about the spiritual life than men'." White working-class women were also soon caught in the web of womanhood. One historian noted that this web could be paralyzing for an individual working woman, but added that 'when a strong enough wind is blowing, the whole web and all the women in it can be seen to move and this is a new kind of movement, a new source of power and connectedness. Those connections, moreover, stretched across economic strata as industrialization created 'an oppressive leisure life' for affluent women and 'an oppressive work life' for their laboring sisters, forging a 'bond of sisterhood 'across classes.

Elaborations on and extensions of female community multiplied rapidly. Women on wagon trains heading west, worshippers in evangelical revivals and in Quaker meeting houses, prostitutes on the Comstock Lode, mill workers in Lowell boarding houses, and immigrants on the streets of Lawrence and the stoops of Providence loved and nurtured one another, exchanged recipes, gossip, and herbal remedies, swapped food and clothing, shared childrearing and domestic chores, covered for each other at work, protected one another from abusive fathers, husbands,

lovers, and bosses, and supported each other in birth and death. For each group, these 'friendship and support networks' could also become 'crucibles in which collective acts of rebellion were formed. Middle-class 'rebels' formed single-sex public associations to ameliorate social ills and eradicate social evils. Quaker farm wives, in Seneca Falls, Waterloo, and Rochester, New York, attacked the 'repeated injuries and usurpations on the part of man toward woman. Lowell mill operatives on strike for higher wages vowed that 'none will go back, unless they receive us all as one'." In Lawrence, New York's Lower East Side, Cripple Creek, Colorado, and Tampa, Florida, immigrant women - as wives and wage-earners - united shop-floor struggle with neighborhood discontent and employed the resources of their everyday life as weapons in the class struggle.

How could the bonds of womanhood, first forged in the domestic enclaves of the Victorian bourgeoisie, have filtered through the walls dividing private and public domains, affluent and poor, native-born and immigrant, black and white? The answer provided by the authors of the woman's community construct was a combination of patriarchy and modernization. Patriarchy explained what women held in common - sexual vulnerability, domestic isolation, economic and educational deprivation, and political exclusion. Modernization served as the causal mechanism by which the ideology of separate spheres and the values of 'true womanhood' were dispersed throughout the society. Employing modernization as the mechanism of change allowed North American scholars to recognize broad forces - industrialization, urbanization and class stratification - and collective psychological developments - the growth of individualism and the search for autonomy - while maintaining the primacy of gender. In addition, the 'trickle down' method by which societies supposedly become modern suggested that the analysis of elite women could provide an appropriate framework for understanding and predicting the experiences of all women. Finally, the teleological bent of modernization obscures conflict and thereby reinforced the notion that bonds among women based on gender are stronger than barriers between women based on class or race.

The adoption of modernization by leading social, including women's, historians has carried us a great distance from Jesse Lemisch's early plea for a history written 'from the bottom up '. As more feminist scholars pursued studies of black and white working-class life, however, they demanded renewed attention to the complexity of women's experience and recognition of the conflict that it engenders. At the same time, students of bourgeois women began debating woman's specific role in modernization: was she the repository of traditional values, the happy humanizer of modernity, a victim of male-dominated forces, or an eager agent of Progress? Those who compared the experiences of privileged and poor women in the Victorian era concluded that, if modernization occurred, it led not to the inclusion of women in a universal sisterhood but rather to the dichotomization of women along class lines into the pious and pure 'modern' woman and the prurient and parasitical 'pre-modern' woman. Students of the Third World were even more adamant that women, rather than gaining by the development of a new domesticated ideal, lost 'traditional forms of power and authority on the road to "emancipation" from premodern lifeways.

In addition, some women's historians attacked the concept of modernization itself as vague, untested, 'nebulous', 'both one-dimensional and elastic', or as 'a piece of post-capitalist ideology'. This last criticism focused on the corner-stone of the current paradigm - the separation of spheres - suggesting that it may have been culturally prescribed by dominant sectors of society to divide classes against themselves. It is not clear, however, that either the working classes or the bourgeoisie itself actually patterned their lives according to

such prescriptions. Certainly bourgeois women were not so separated from same-class men as to disengage them from the prejudices and power inherent in their class position. Evidence of this appears in white suffragists' use of racist rhetoric, Protestant charitable ladies' denial of aid to Catholics, affluent women's refusal to support working women's strikes, moral reformers' abhorrence of working-class sexual mores, and settlement house educators' denigration of immigrant culture. Finally, students of black women's history reject the teleological design of modernization. Like contemporary black feminists, they argue that the concept of a woman's community derived from white women's experience distorts the reality of black lives and ignores the ways that white solidarity, including sisterhood, has served to deny rights to blacks, including women.

FOCUS QUESTIONS:

1. What are some of the drawbacks of a community created from the foundation of a "woman's sphere"?

2. In what ways did duties traditionally relegated to the "woman's sphere" evolve and expand into the public sphere?

3. What are some of the criticisms women's historians have of modernization?

I-4 From African-American Women's History and the Metalanguage of Race

Evelyn Brooks Higginbotham is chair of the Department of African and African American Studies at Harvard University. This essay won the prize for Best Article at the 1993 Berkshire Conference of Women Historians.

Source: Higginbotham, Evelyn Brooks, *Signs,* Vol. 17, No. 2, (Winter, 1992), pp. 251, 262-266, 273-274

THEORETICAL DISCUSSION in African-American women's history begs for greater voice. I say this as a black woman who is cognizant of the strengths and limitations of current feminist theory. Feminist scholars have moved rapidly forward in addressing theories of subjectivity, questions of difference, the construction of social relations as relations of power, the conceptual implications of binary oppositions such as male versus female or equality versus difference-all issues defined with relevance to gender and with potential for intellectual and social transforma-

tions. Notwithstanding a few notable exceptions, this new wave of feminist theorists finds little to say about race. The general trend has been to mention black and Third World feminists who first called attention to the glaring fallacies in essentialist analysis and to claims of a homogeneous "womanhood," "woman's culture," and "patriarchal oppression of women." Beyond this recognition, however, white feminist scholars pay hardly more than lip service to race as they continue to analyze their own experience in ever more sophisticated forms.

This narrowness of vision is particularly ironic in that these very issues of equality and difference, the constructive strategies of power, and subjectivity and consciousness have stood at the core of black scholarship for some half-century or more. Historian W. E. B. Du Bois, sociologist Oliver Cox, and scientist Charles R. Drew are only some of the more significant pre-1950s contributors to the discussion of race as a social category and to the refutation of essentialist biological and genetic explanations. These issues continue to be salient in our own time, when racism in America grows with both verve and subtlety and when "enlightened" women's historians witness, as has been the case in recent years, recurrent racial tensions at our own professional and scholarly gatherings.

Feminist scholars, especially those of African-American women's history, must accept the challenge to bring race more prominently into their analyses of power. The explication of race entails three interrelated strategies, separated here merely for the sake of analysis. First of all, we must define the construction and "technologies" of race as well as those of gender and sexuality. Second, we must expose the role of race as a metalanguage by calling attention to its powerful, all-encompassing effect on the construction and representation of other social and power relations, namely, gender, class, and sexuality. Third, we must recognize race as providing sites of dialogic exchange and contestation, since race has constituted a discursive tool for both oppression and liberation. As Michael Omi and Howard Winant argue, "the effort must be made to understand race as an unstable and 'decentered' complex of social meanings constantly being transformed by political struggle." Such a three-pronged approach to the history of African-American women will require borrowing and blending work by black intellectuals, white feminist scholars, and other theorists such as white male philosophers and linguists. Indeed, the very process of borrowing and blending speaks to the tradition of syncretism that has characterized the Afro-American experience.

Racial constructions of gender

To understand race as a metalanguage, we must recognize its historical and material grounding-what Russian linguist and critic M. M. Bakhtin referred to as "the power of the word to mean." This power evolves from concrete situational and ideological contexts, that is, from a position of enunciation that reflects not only time and place but values as well. The concept of race, in its verbal and extraverbal dimension, and even more specifically, in its role in the representation as well as self-representation of individuals in American society (what psychoanalytic theorists call "subjectification"), is constituted in language in which (as Bakhtin points out) there have never been" 'neutral' words and forms-words and forms that can belong to 'no one'; language has been completely taken over, shot through with intentions and accents."

The social context for the construction of race as a tool for black oppression is historically rooted in the context of slavery. Barbara Fields reminds us: "The idea one people has of another, even when the difference between them is embodied in the most striking physical characteristics, is always mediated by the social context within which the two come in contact." Race

came to life primarily as the signifier of the master/slave relation and thus emerged superimposed upon class and property relations. Defined by law as "animate chattel," slaves constituted property as well as a social class and were exploited under a system that sanctioned white ownership of black bodies and black labor. Studies of black women in slavery, however, make poignantly clear the role of race not only in shaping the class relations of the South's "peculiar institution," but also in constructing gender's "power to mean." Sojourner Truth's famous and haunting question, "Ar'n't I a Woman?" laid bare the racialized configuration of gender under a system of class rule that compelled and expropriated women's physical labor and denied them legal right to their own bodies and sexuality, much less to the bodies to which they gave birth. While law and public opinion idealized motherhood and enforced the protection of white women's bodies, the opposite held true for black women's. Sojourner Truth's personal testimony demonstrated gender's racial meaning. She had "ploughed, and planted, and gathered into barns," and no male slave had outdone her. She had given birth to thirteen children, all of whom were sold away from her. When she cried out in grief from the depths of her motherhood, "none but Jesus heard."

Wasn't Sojourner Truth a woman? The courts answered this question for slavewomen by ruling them outside the statutory rubric "woman." In discussing the case of *State of Missouri v. Celia*, A. Leon Higginbotham, Jr., elucidates the racial signification of gender. Celia was fourteen years old when purchased by a successful farmer, Robert Newsome. During the five years of his ownership, Newsome habitually forced her into sexual intercourse. At age nineteen she had borne a child by him and was expecting another. In June 1855, while pregnant and ill, Celia defended herself against attempted rape by her master. Her testimony reveals that she warned him she would hurt him if he continued to abuse her while sick. When her threats would not deter his advances, she hit him over the head with a stick, immediately killing him. In an act presaging Richard Wright's *Native Son*, she then burned his body in the fireplace and the next morning spread his ashes on the pathway. Celia was apprehended and tried for first-degree murder. Her counsel sought to lower the charge of first degree to murder in self-defense, that Celia had a right to resist her master's sexual advances, especially because of the imminent danger to her health. A slave master's economic and property rights, the defense contended, did not include rape. The defense rested its case on Missouri statutes that protected women from attempts to ravish, rape, or defile. The language of these particular statutes explicitly used the term "any woman," while other unrelated Missouri statutes explicitly used terms such as "white female" and "slave" or "negro" in their criminal codes. The question centered on her womanhood. The court found Celia guilty: "If Newsome was in the habit of having intercourse with the defendant who was his slave, . . . it is murder in the first degree." Celia was sentenced to death, having been denied an appeal, and was hanged in December 1855 after the birth of her child.

Since racially based justifications of slavery stood at the core of Southern law, race relations, and social etiquette in general, then proof of "womanhood" did not rest on a common female essence, shared culture, or mere physical appearance. (Sojourner Truth, on one occasion, was forced to bare her breasts to a doubting audience in order to vindicate her womanhood.) This is not to deny gender's role within the social and power relations of race. Black women experienced the vicissitudes of slavery through gendered lives and thus differently from slave men. They bore and nursed children and performed domestic duties-all on top of doing fieldwork. Unlike slave men, slave women fell victim to rape precisely because of their gender. Yet gender itself was both constructed and fragmented by race. Gender, so colored by race, remained from birth until death inextricably linked to one's personal identity and social status. For black and white women, gendered identity was reconstructed and represented in very different, indeed antagonistic, racialized contexts.

Racial constructions of sexuality

The exclusion of black women from the dominant society's definition of "lady" said as much about sexuality as it did about class. The metalanguage of race signifies, too, the imbrication of race within the representation of sexuality. Historians of women and of science, largely influenced by Michel Foucault, now attest to the variable quality of changing conceptions of sexuality over time-conceptions informed as much by race and class as by gender. Sexuality has come to be defined not in terms of biological essentials or as a universal truth detached and transcendent from other aspects of human life and society. Rather, it is an evolving conception applied to the body but given meaning and identity by economic, cultural, and historical context.

In the centuries between the Renaissance and the Victorian era, Western culture constructed and represented changing and conflicting images of woman's sexuality, which shifted diametrically from images of lasciviousness to moral purity. Yet Western conceptions of black women's sexuality resisted change during this same time. Winthrop Jordan's now classic study of racial attitudes toward blacks between the sixteenth and nineteenth centuries argues that black women's bodies epitomized centuries-long European perceptions of Africans as primitive, animal-like, and savage. In America, no less distinguished and learned a figure than Thomas Jefferson conjectured that black women mated with orangutans. While such thinking rationalized slavery and the sexual exploitation of slave women by white masters, it also perpetuated an enormous division between black people and white people on the "scale of humanity": carnality as opposed to intellect and/or spirit; savagery as opposed to civilization; deviance as opposed to normality; promiscuity as opposed to purity; passion as opposed to passionlessness. The black woman came to symbolize, according to Sander Gilman, an "icon for black sexuality in general." This discursive gap between the races was if anything greater between white and black women than between white and black men.

Violence figured preeminently in racialized constructions of sexuality. From the days of slavery, the social construction and representation of black sexuality reinforced violence, rhetorical and real, against black women and men. That the rape of black women could continue to go on with impunity long after slavery's demise underscores the pervasive belief in black female promiscuity. This belief found expression in the statement of one Southern white woman in 1904: "I cannot imagine such a creation as a virtuous black woman."

The lynching of black men, with its often attendant castration, reeked of sexualized representations of race. The work of black feminists of the late nineteenth century makes clear that lynching, while often rationalized by whites as a punishment for the rape of white women, more often was perpetrated to maintain racial etiquette and the socioeconomic and political hegemony of whites. Ida Wells-Barnett, Anna J. Cooper, Mary Church Terrell, and Pauline Hopkins exposed and contrasted the specter of the white woman's rape in the case of lynching and the sanctioned rape of black women by white men. Hazel Carby, in discussing these black feminist writers, established their understanding of the intersection of strategies of power with lynching and rape:

Their legacy to us is theories that expose the colonization of the black female body by white male power and the destruction of black males who attempted to exercise any oppositional patriarchal control. When accused of threatening the white female body, the repository of heirs to property and power, the black male, and his economic, political, and social advancement, is lynched out of existence. Cooper, Wells, and Hopkins assert the necessity of seeing the relation between histories: the rape of black women in the nineties is directly linked to the rape of the female slave. Their analyses are dynamic and not limited to a parochial understanding of "women's issues"; they have firmly established the dialectical relation between economic/political power and economic/sexual power in the battle for control of women's bodies.

Through a variety of mediums-theater, art, the press, and literature-discourses of racism developed and reified stereotypes of sexuality. Such representations grew out of and facilitated the larger subjugation and control of the black population. The categorization of class and racial groups according to culturally constituted sexual identities facilitated blacks' subordination within a stratified society and rendered them powerless against the intrusion of the state into their innermost private lives.

This intrusion went hand in hand with the role of the state in legislating and enforcing racial segregation, disfranchisement, and economic discrimination.

James Jones's *Bad Blood: The Tuskegee Syphilis Experiment* provides us with a profoundly disturbing example of such intrusion into blacks' private lives. Jones recounts how a federal agency, the Public Health Service, embarked in 1932 upon decades of tests on black men with syphilis, denying them access to its cure in order to assess the disease's debilitating effects on the body. The federal agency felt at liberty to make the study because of its unquestioning acceptance of stereotypes that conflated race, gender, and class. By defining this health problem in racial terms, "objective scientific researchers" could be absolved of all responsibility. Some even posited that blacks had "earned their illness as just recompense for wicked life-styles."

The Public Health Service's willingness to prolong syphilis despite the discovery of penicillin discloses not only the federal government's lack of concern for the health of the men in its study, but its even lesser concern for black women in relationships with these men. Black women failed to receive so much as a pretense of protection, so widely accepted was the belief that the spread of the disease was inevitable because black women were promiscuous by nature. This emphasis on black immorality precluded any sensitivity to congenital syphilis; thus innocent black babies born with the disease went unnoticed and equally unprotected. Certainly the officials of the Public Health Service real-ized that blacks lived amid staggering poverty, amid a socioeconomic environment conducive to disease. Yet these public servants encoded hegemonic articulations of race into the language of medicine and scientific theory. Their perceptions of sexually transmitted disease, like those of the larger society, were affected by race. Jones concludes:

The effect of these views was to isolate blacks even further within American society-to remove them from the world of health and to lock them within a prison of sickness. Whether by accident or design, physicians had come dangerously close to depicting the syphilitic black as the representative black. As sickness replaced health as the normal condition of the race, something was lost from the sense of horror and urgency with which physicians had defined disease. The result was a powerful rationale for inactivity in the face of disease, which by their own estimates, physicians believed to be epidemic.

In response to assaults upon black sexuality, according to Darlene Clark Hine, there arose among black women a politics of silence, a "culture of dissemblance." In order to "protect the sanctity of inner aspects of their lives," black women, especially those of the middle class, reconstructed and represented their sexuality through its absence- through silence, secrecy, and invisibility. In so doing, they sought to combat the pervasive negative images and stereotypes. Black clubwomen's adherence to Victorian ideology, as well as their self-representation as "super moral," according to Hine, was perceived as crucial not only to the protection and upward mobility of black women but also to the attainment of respect, justice, and opportunity for all black Americans.

Conclusion

By analyzing white America's deployment of race in the construction of power relations, perhaps we can better understand why black women historians have largely refrained from an analysis of gender along the lines of the male/female dichotomy so prevalent among white feminists. Indeed, some black women scholars adopt the term womanist instead of feminist in rejection of gender-based dichotomies that lead to a false homogenizing of women. By so doing they follow in the spirit of black scholar and educator Anna J. Cooper, who in *A Voice from the South* (1892) inextricably linked her racial identity to the "quiet, undisputed dignity" of her womanhood. At the threshold of the twenty-first century, black women scholars continue to emphasize the inseparable unity of race and gender in their thought. They dismiss efforts to bifurcate the identity of black women (and indeed of all women) into discrete categories-as if culture, consciousness, and lived experience could at times constitute "woman" isolated from the contexts of race, class, and sexuality that give form and content to the particular women we are.

On the other hand, we should challenge both the overdeterminancy of race vis-a-vis social relations among blacks themselves and conceptions of the black community as harmonious and monolithic. The historic reality of racial conflict in America has tended to devalue and discourage attention to gender conflict within black communities and to tensions of class or sexuality among black women. The totalizing tendency of race precludes recognition and acknowledgment of intragroup social relations as relations of power. With its implicit understandings, shared cultural codes, and inchoate sense of a common heritage and destiny, the metalanguage of race resounds over and above a plethora of conflicting voices. But it cannot silence them.

Black women of different economic and regional backgrounds, of different skin tones and sexual orientations, have found themselves in conflict over interpretation of symbols and norms, public behavior, coping strategies, and a variety of micropolitical acts of resistance to structures of domination. Although racialized cultural identity has clearly served blacks in the struggle against discrimination, it has not sufficiently addressed the empirical reality of gender conflict within the black community or class differences among black women themselves. Historian E. Frances White makes this point brilliantly when she asserts that "the site of counter-discourse is itself contested terrain." By fully recognizing race as an unstable, shifting, and strategic reconstruction, feminist scholars must take up new challenges to inform and confound many of the assumptions currently underlying Afro-American history and women's history. We must problematize much more of what we take for granted.

We must bring to light and to coherence the one and the many that we always were in history and still actually are today.

Department of History
University of Pennsylvania

FOCUS QUESTIONS:

1. Higginbotham writes that current theorists "find little to say about race". Why is that omission ironic? How can feminist scholars address this omission?

2. How is the construction of race used as a tool for black oppression? Can this be applied to gender as well?

3. What effect did the unchallenged racialized construction of sexuality have on black women both during slavery and after its abolition?

I-5 From Placing Women in History: Definitions and Challenges

Both a writer and historian, Gerda Lerner was instrumental in helping to establish fields of study in women's and African-American history. Born in Austria, she escaped Nazi persecution and immigrated to the United States where she was an active member of the Communist Party USA. She earned her Ph.D in her mid-40s and went on to develop the curriculum for women's studies programs at Long Island University and Sarah Lawrence College.

Source: Lerner, Gerda, *Feminist Studies*, Vol. 3, No. 1/2, (Autumn, 1975), pp. 5-14

In the brief span of five years in which American historians have begun to develop women's history as an independent field, they have sought to find a conceptual frame-work and a methodology appropriate to the task.

The first level at which historians, trained in traditional history, approach women's history is by writing the history of "women worthies" or "compensatory history." Who are the women missing from history? Who are the women of achievement and what did they achieve? The resulting history of "notable women" does not tell us much about those activities in which most women engaged, nor does it tell us about the significance of women's activities to society as a whole. The history of notable women is the history of exceptional, even deviant women, and does not describe the experience and history of the mass of women. This insight is a refinement of an awareness of class differences in history: Women of different classes have different historical experiences. To comprehend the full complexity of society at a given stage of its development, it is essential to take account of such differences.

Women also have a different experience with respect to consciousness, depending on whether their work, their expression, their activity is male-defined or woman-oriented. Women, like men, are indoctrinated in a male-defined value system and conduct their lives accordingly. Thus, colonial and early nineteenth-century female reformers directed their activities into channels which were merely an extension of their domestic concerns and traditional roles. They taught school, cared for the poor, the sick, the aged. As their consciousness developed, they turned their attention toward the needs of women. Becoming woman-oriented, they began to "uplift" prostitutes, organize women for abolition or temperance and sought to upgrade female education, but only in order to equip women better for their traditional roles. Only at a later stage, growing out of the recognition of the separate interests of women as a group, and of their subordinate place in society, did their consciousness become woman-defined. Feminist thought starts at this level and encompasses the active assertion of the rights and grievances of women. These various stages of female consciousness need to be considered in historical analysis.

The next level of conceptualizing women's history has been "contribution history": describing women's contribution to, their status in, and their oppression by male-defined society. Under this category we find a variety of questions being asked: What have women contributed to abolition, to reform, to the Progressive movement, to the labor movement, to the New Deal? The movement in question stands in the foreground Placing Women in History of inquiry; women made a "contribution" to it; the contribution is judged first of all with respect to its effect on that movement and secondly by standards appropriate to men.

The ways in which women were aided and affected by the work of these "great women," the ways in which they themselves grew into feminist awareness, are ignored. Jane Addams' enormous contribution in creating a supporting female network and new structures for living are subordinated to her role as a Progressive, or to an interpretation which regards her as merely representative of a group of frustrated college-trained women with no place to go. In other words, a deviant from male-defined norms. Margaret Sanger is seen merely as the founder of the birth control movement, not as a woman raising a revolutionary challenge to the centuries-old practice by which the bodies and lives of women are dominated and ruled by man-made laws. In the labor movement, women are described as "also there" or as problems. Their essential role on behalf of themselves and of other women is seldom considered a central theme in writing their history. Women are the outgroup, Simone de Beauvoir's "other."

Another set of questions concern oppression and its opposite, the struggle for woman's rights. Who

oppressed women and how were they oppressed? How did they respond to such oppression?

Such questions have yielded detailed and very valuable accounts of economic or social oppression, and of the various organizational, political ways in which women as a group have fought such oppression. Judging from the results, it is clear that to ask the question-why and how were women victimized-has its usefulness. We learn what society or individuals or classes of people have done to women, and we learn how women themselves have reacted to conditions imposed upon them. While inferior status and oppressive restrains were no doubt aspects of women's historical experience, and should be so recorded, the limitation of this approach is that it makes it appear either that women were largely passive or that, at the most, they reacted to male pressures or to the restraints of patriarchal society. Such inquiry fails to elicit the positive and essential way in which women have functioned in history. Mary Beard was the first to point out that the ongoing and continuing contribution of women to the development of human culture cannot be found by treating them only as victims of oppression. I have in my own work learned that it is far more useful to deal with this question as one aspect of women's history, but never to regard it as the central aspect of women's history. Essentially, treating women as victims of oppression once again places them in a male-defined conceptual framework: oppressed, victimized by standards and values established by men. The true history of women is the history of their ongoing functioning in that male-defined world, on their own terms. The question of oppression does not elicit that story, and is therefore a tool of limited usefulness to the historian.

A major focus of women's history has been on women's-rights struggles, especially the winning of suffrage, on organizational and institutional history of the women's movements, and on its leaders. This, again, is an important aspect of women's history, but it cannot and should not be its central concern.

Some recent literature has dealt with marriage and divorce, with educational opportunities, and with the economic struggles of working women. Much of recent work has been concerned with the image of women and "woman's sphere," with the educational ideals of society, the values to which women are indoctrinated, and with gender role acculturation as seen in historical perspective. A separate field of study has examined the ideals, values, and prescriptions concerning sexuality, especially female sexuality. Ron Walters and Ben Barker-Benfield has tended to confirm traditional stereotypes concerning Victorian sexuality, the double standard, and the subordinate position of women. Much of this material is based on the study of such readily available sources as sermons, educational tracts, women's magazines, and medical textbooks. The pitfall in such interpretation, as Carl Degler has pointed out in his recent perceptive article, is the tendency to confuse prescriptive literature with actual behavior. In fact, what we are learning from most of these monographs is not what women did, felt, or experienced, but what men in the past thought women should do. Charles Rosenberg, Carroll Smith-Rosenberg, and Carl Degler have shown how to approach the same material and interpret it from the new perspective of women's history. They have sharply distinguished between prescription and behavior, between myth and reality.

Other attempts to deduce women's status from popular literature and ideology demonstrate similar difficulties. Barbara Welter is an early and highly influential article, found the emergence of "the cult of true womanhood" in sermons and periodicals of the Jacksonian era. Many historians, feminists among them, have deduced from this that Victorian ideals of woman's place pervaded the society and were representative of its realities. More detailed analysis reveals that this mass media concern with woman's domesticity was, in fact, a response to the opposite trend in society. Lower-class women were entering the factories, middle-class women were discontented with their accustomed roles, and the family, as an institution, was experiencing turmoil and crisis. Idealization is very frequently a defensive ideology and an expression of tension within society. To use ideology as a measure of the shifting status of women, it must be set against a careful analysis of social structure, economic conditions, institutional changes, and popular values. With this caution society's attitudes toward women and toward gender role indoctrination can be usefully analyzed as manifestations of a shifting value system and of tensions within patriarchal society.

"Contribution" history is an important stage in the creation of a true history of women. The monographic work which such inquiries produce is essential to the development of more complex and sophisticated questions, but it is well to keep the limitations of such inquiry in mind. When all is said and done, what we have mostly done in writing contribution history is to describe what men in the past told women to do and what men in the past thought women should be. This is just another way of saying that historians of women's history have so far used a traditional conceptual framework. Essentially, they have applied questions from traditional history to women, and tried to fit women's past into the empty spaces of historical scholarship. The limitation of such work is that it deals with women in male-defined society and tries to fit them into the categories and value systems which consider man the measure of significance. Perhaps it would be useful to refer to this level of work as "transitional women's history," seeing it as an inevitable step in the development of new criteria and concepts.

Another methodological question which arises frequently concerns the connection between women's history and other recently emerging fields. Why is women's history not simply an aspect of "good" social history? Are women not part of the anonymous in history? Are they not oppressed the same way as racial or class or ethnic groups have been oppressed? Are they not marginal and akin in most respects to minorities? The answers to these questions are not simple. It is obvious that there has already been rich cross-fertilization between the new social history and women's history, but it has not been nor should it be a case of subsuming women's history under the larger and already respectable field of social history.

Yes, women are part of the anonymous in history, but unlike them, they are also and always have been part of the ruling elite. They are oppressed, but not quite like either racial or ethnic groups, though some of them are. They are subordinate and exploited, but not quite like lower classes, though some of them are. We have not yet really solved the problems of definition, but it can be suggested that the key to understanding women's history is in accepting-painful though that may be-that it is the history of the majority of mankind. Women are essentially different from all the above categories, because they are the majority now and always have been at least half of mankind, and because their subjection to patriarchal institutions antedates all other oppression and has outlasted all economic and social changes in recorded history.

Social history methodology is very useful for women's history, but it must be placed within a different conceptual framework. For example, historians working in family history ask a great many questions pertaining to women, but family history is not in itself women's history. It is no longer sufficient to view women mainly as members of families. Family history has neglected by and large to deal with unmarried and widowed women. In its applications to specific monographic studies, such as the work of Philip Greven, family history has been used to describe the relationships of fathers and sons and the property arrangements between them. The relationships of fathers to daughters and mothers to their children have been ignored. The complex family-support patterns, for example, whereby the work and wages of daughters are used to support the education of brothers and to maintain aged parents, while that of sons is not so used, have been ignored.

Another way in which family history has been interpreted within the context of patriarchal assumptions is by using a vaguely defined "domestic power" of women, power within the family, as a measure of the societal status of women. In a methodologically highly sophisticated article, Daniel Scott Smith discovers in the nineteenth century the rise of something called "domestic feminism," expressed in a lowered birth rate from which he deduces an increasing control of women over their reproductive lives. One might, from similar figures, as easily deduce a desire on the part of men to curb their offspring due to the demands of a developing industrial system for a more highly educated labor force, hence for fewer children per family. Demographic data can indeed tell us something about female as well as male status in society, but only in the context of an economic and sociological analysis. Further, the status of women within the family is something quite different and distinct from their status in the society in general.

I learned in studying the history of black women and the black family that relatively high status for women within the family does not signify "matriarchy" or "power for women," since black women are not only members of families, but persons functioning in a larger society. The status of persons is determined not in one area of their functioning, such as within the family, but in several. The decisive historical fact about women is that the areas of their functioning, not only their status within those areas, have been determined by men. The effect on the consciousness of women has been pervasive. It is one of the decisive aspects of their history, and any analysis which does not take this complexity into consideration must be inadequate.

Then there is the impact of demographic techniques, the study of large aggregates of anonymous people by computer technology based on census data, public documents, property records. Demographic techniques have led to insights which are very useful for women's history. They have yielded revealing data on fertility fluctuations, on changes in illegitimacy patterns and sex ratios, and aggregate studies of life cycles. The latter work has been done very successfully by Joseph Kett, Robert Wells, Peter Laslett and Kenneth Keniston. The field has in the United States been largely dominated by male historians, mostly through self-imposed sex-role stereotyping by women historians who have shared a prejudice against the computer and statistics. However, a group of younger scholars, trained in demographic techniques, have begun to research and publish material concerning working-class women. Alice Harris, Virginia McLaughlin, Judith and Daniel Walkowitz, Susan Kleinberg and Tamara Hareven are among those who have elicited woman-oriented interpretations from aggregate data. They have demonstrated that social history can be enriched by combining cliometrics with sophisticated humanistic and feminist interpretations. They have added "gender" as a factor for analysis to such familiar concepts as class, race and ethnicity.

The compensatory questions raised by women's history specialists are proving interesting and valuable in a variety of fields. It is perfectly understandable that after centuries of neglect of the role of women in history, compensatory questions and those concerning woman's contribution will and must be asked. In the process of answering such questions it is important to keep in mind the inevitable limitation of the answers they yield. Not the least of these limitations is that this approach tends to separate the work and activities of women from those of men, even where they were essentially connected. As yet, synthesis is lacking. For example, the rich history of the abolition movement has been told as though women played a marginal, auxiliary, and at times mainly disruptive role in it. Yet female antislavery societies outnumbered male societies; women abolitionists largely financed the movement with their fundraising activities, did much of the work of propaganda-writing in and distribution of newspapers and magazines. The enormous political significance of women-organized petition campaigns remains unrecorded. Most importantly, no historical work has as yet taken the organizational work of female abolitionists seriously as an integral part of the antislavery movement.

Slowly, as the field has matured, historians of women's history have become dissatisfied with old questions and old methods, and have come up with new ways of approaching historical material. They have, for example, begun to ask about the actual experience of women in the past. This is obviously different from a description of the condition of women written from the perspective of male sources, and leads one to the use of women's letters, diaries, autobiographies, and oral history sources. This shift from male-oriented to female-oriented consciousness is most important and leads to challenging new interpretations.

Historians of women's history have studied

female sexuality and its regulation from the female point of view, making imaginative use of such sources as medical textbooks, diaries, and case histories of hospital patients. Questions concerning women's experience have led to studies of birth control, as it affects women and as an issue expressing cultural and symbolic values; of the physical conditions to which women are prone, such as menarche and pregnancy and women's ailments; of customs, attitudes, and fashions affecting women's health and women's life experience. Historians are now exploring the impact of female bonding, of female friendship and homosexual relations, and the experience of women in groups, such as women in utopian communities, in women's clubs and settlement houses. There has been an interest in the possibility that women's century-long preoccupation with birth and with the care of the sick and dying have led to some specific female rituals.

Women's history has already presented a challenge to some basic assumptions historians make. While most historians are aware of the fact that their findings are not value-free and are trained to check their biases by a variety of methods, they are as yet quite unaware of their own sexist bias and, more importantly, of the sexist bias which pervades the value system, the culture, and the very language within which they work.

Women's history presents a challenge to the periodization of traditional history. The periods in which basic changes occur in society and which historians have commonly regarded as turning points for all historical development, are not necessarily the same for men as for women. This is not surprising when we consider that the traditional time frame in history has been derived from political history. Women have been the one group in history longest excluded from political power as they have, by and large, been excluded from military decision making. Thus the irrelevance of periodization based on military and political developments to their historical experience should have been predictable.

Renate Bridenthal's and Joan Kelly-Gadol's articles in this volume confirm that the history of women demands different periodization than does political history. Neither the Renaissance, it appears, nor the period during which women's suffrage was won, were periods in which women experienced an advance in their status. Recent work of American historians of women's history, such as Linda Kerber's work on the American Revolution and my own work, confirms this conclusion. For example, neither during nor after the American Revolution nor in the age of Jackson did

women share the historical experience of men. On the contrary, they experienced in both periods status loss, a restriction of options as to occupations and role choices, and certainly in Jacksonian America, there were restrictions imposed upon their sexuality, at least in prescriptive behavior. If one applies to both of these cases the kind of sophisticated and detailed analysis Kelly-Gadol attempts-that is, differentiations between women of different classes and comparisons between the status of men of a given class and women of that class-one finds the picture further complicated. Status loss in one area-social production-may be offset by status gain in another-access to education.

What kind of periodization might be substituted for the periodization of traditional history, in order for it to be applicable to women? The answer depends largely on the conceptual framework in which the historian works. Many historians of women's history, in their search for a unifying framework, have tended to use the Marxist or neo-Marxist model supplied by Juliet Mitchell and recently elaborated by Sheila Row-Botham. The important fact, says Mitchell, which distinguished the past of women from that of men is precisely that until very recently sexuality and reproduction were inevitably linked for women, while they were not so linked for men. Similarly, child-bearing and child-rearing were inevitably linked for women and still are so linked. Women's freedom depends on breaking those links. Using Mitchell's categories we can and should ask of each historical period: What happened to the link between sexuality and reproduction? What happened to the link between child-bearing and child-rearing? Important changes in the status of women occur when it becomes possible through the availability of birth control information and technology to sever sexuality from inevitable motherhood. However, it may be the case that it is not the availability and distribution of birth control information and technology so much as the level of medical and health care which are the determinants of change. That is, when infant mortality decreases, so that raising every child to adulthood becomes the normal expectation of parents, family size declines.

The above case illustrates the difficulty that has vexed historians of women's history in trying to locate a periodization more appropriate to women. Working in different fields and specialities, many historians have observed that the transition from agricultural to industrializing society and then again the transition to fully developed industrial society entails important changes affecting women and the family. Changes in relations of production affect women's status as family members and as workers. Later, shifts in the mode of production affect the kinds of occupations women can enter and their status within them. Major shifts in health care and technological development, related to industrialization, also affect the lives of women. It is not too difficult to discern such patterns and to conclude that there must be a causal relationship between changes in the mode of production and the status of women. Here, the Marxist model seems to offer an immediately satisfying solution, especially if, following Mitchell, "sexuality" as a factor is added to such factors as class. But in the case of women, just as in the case of racial castes, ideology and prescription internalized by both women and men, seem to be as much a causative factor as are material changes in production relations. Does the entry of lower-class women into industrial production really bring them closer to "liberation"? In the absence of institutional changes such as the right to abortion and safe contraception, altered child-rearing arrangements, and varied options for sexual expression, changes in economic relations may become oppressive. Unless such changes are accompanied by changes in consciousness, which in turn result in institutional changes, they do not favorably affect the lives of women.

Is smaller family size the result of "domestic freedom" of choice exercised by women, the freedom of choice exercised by men, the ideologically buttressed coercion of institutions in the service of an economic class? Is it liberating for women, for men, or for corporations? This raises another difficult question: What about the relationship of upper-class to lower-class women? To what extent is the relative advance in the status of upper-class women predicated on the status loss of lower-class women? Examples of this are: the liberation of the middle-class American housewife in the mid-nineteenth century through the availability of cheap black or immigrant domestic workers; the liberation of the twentieth-century housewife from incessant drudgery in the home through agricultural stoop labor and the food-processing industry, both employing low paid female workers.

Is periodization then dependent as much on class as on gender? This question is just one of several which challenge the universalist assumptions of all previous historical categories. I cannot provide an answer, but I think the questions themselves point us in the right direction.

It appears to me that all conceptual models of history hitherto developed have only limited usefulness for women's history, since all are based on the assumptions of a patriarchal ordering of values. The structural-functionalist framework leaves out class and sex factors, the traditional Marxist framework leaves out sex and race factors as essentials, admitting them only as marginal factors. Mitchell's neo-Marxist model includes these, but slights ideas, values, and psychological factors. Still, her four-structures model and the refinements of it proposed by Bridenthal, are an excellent addition to the conceptual working tools of the historian of women's history. They should be tried out, discussed, refined. But they are not, in my opinion, the whole answer.

Kelly-Gadol offers the useful suggestion that attitudes toward sexuality should be studied in each historical period. She considers the constraints upon women's sexuality imposed by society a useful measure of women's true status. This approach would necessitate comparisons between prescribed behavior for women and men as well as indications of their actual sexual behavior at any given time. This challenging method can be used with great effectiveness for certain periods of history and especially for upper- and middle-class women. I doubt that it can be usefully employed as a general criterion, because of the difficulty of finding substantiating evidence, especially as it pertains to lower classes.

I raised the question of a conceptual framework for dealing with women's history in 1969, reasoning from the assumption that women were a subgroup in history. Neither caste, class, nor race quite fit the model for describing us. I have now come to the conclusion that the idea that women are some kind of a subgroup or particular is wrong. It will not do-there are just too many of us. No single framework, no single factor, four-factor or eight-factor explanation can serve to contain all that the history of women is. Picture, if you can, an attempt to organize the history of men by using four factors. It will not work; neither will it work for women.

Women are and always have been at least half of mankind and most of the time have been the majority of mankind. Their culturally determined and psychologically internalized marginality seems to be what makes their historical experience essentially different from that of men. But men have defined their experience as history and have left women out. At this time, as during earlier periods of feminist activity, women are urged to fit into the empty spaces, assuming their traditional marginal, "sub-group" status. But the truth is that history, as written and perceived up to now, is the history of a minority, who may well turn out to be the "subgroup." In order to write a new history worthy of the name, we will have to recognize that no single methodology and conceptual framework can fit the complexities of the historical experience of all women.

The first stage of "transitional history" may be to add some new categories to the general categories by which historians organize their material: sexuality, reproduction, the link between child-bearing and child-rearing; role indoctrination; sexual values and myths; female consciousness. Further, all of these need to be analysed, taking factors of race, class, ethnicity and, possibly, religion into consideration. What we have here is not a single framework for dealing with women in history, but new questions to all of universal history.

The next stage may be to explore the possibility that what we call women's history may actually be the study of a separate women's culture. Such a culture would include not only the separate occupations, status, experiences, and rituals of women but also their consciousness, which internalizes partiarchal assumptions. In some cases, it would include the tensions created in that culture between the prescribed patriarchal assumptions and women's efforts to attain autonomy and emancipation.

The questions asked about the past of women may demand interdisciplinary approaches. They also may demand broadly conceived group research projects that end up giving functional answers; answers that deal not with slices of a given time or society or period, but which instead deal with a functioning organism, a functioning whole, the society in which both men and women live.

A following stage may develop a synthesis: a history of the dialectic, the tensions between the two cultures, male and female. Such a synthesis could be based on close comparative study of given periods in which the historical experience of men is com- pared to that of women, their tensions and interactions being as much the subject of study as their differences. Only after a series of such detailed studies can we hope to find the parameters by which to define the new universal history. My guess is that no one conceptual framework will fit so complex a subject.

Methods are tools for analysis-some of us will stick with one tool, some of us will reach for different tools as we need them. For women, the problem really is that we must acquire not only the confidence needed for using tools, but for making new ones to fit our needs. We should do so relying on our learned skills and our rational scepticism of handed-down doctrine. The recognition that we had been denied our history came to many of us as a staggering flash of insight, which altered our consciousness irretrievably. We have come a long way since then. The next step is to face, once and for all and with all its complex consequences, that women are the majority of mankind and have been essential to the making of history. Thus, all history as we now know it, is merely prehistory. Only a new history firmly based on this recognition and equally concerned with men, women, the establishment and the passing away of patriarchy, can lay claim to being a truly universal history.

FOCUS QUESTIONS:

1. What does Lerner seem to be saying about women as victims of oppression? What do women sacrifice by accepting this?

2. What is the greatest threat to the role women play in history "on their own terms"? What can be done to overcome this threat?

I-6 From Subject to Change: Theories and Paradigms of U.S. Feminist History

This essay discusses the development of theoretical debates within U.S. women's history arguing that a diversity of approaches and topics would be useful for the field.

Source: Thurner, Manuela. "Subject to Change: Issues and Paradigms of U.S. Feminist History." *Journal of Women's History* 9 (Summer 1997): 122-146.

A History of Their Own

Emerging out of the women's liberation movement of the 1960s and 1970s, women's history has always been linked to an avowedly political agenda. This agenda, in short, was to denounce sexism and discrimination against women, to expose the origins, foundations, and workings of patriarchy, and subsequently to formulate and implement strategies for its eventual demolition. Due to the fact that the second-wave women's rights movement shared historical space and cultural momentum with, among others, the antiwar, civil rights, and gay liberation movements, attention was also paid to other forms of inequality and discrimination, variously seen to be independent of or related to the patriarchal oppression of women. History was considered to be an especially relevant and important helpmate in this enterprise, both because of its potential to create and sustain a community through a sense of a shared past, and through its promise to provide a more precise map of the varieties, limitations of, as well as possible alternatives to patriarchal structures and power. Although or maybe because they were not yet bound by institutionalized structures, women's historians in the 1960s and early 1970s were a varied group, buoyed by a sense that by (re)writing history they were in fact making history.

Those working from within academic institutions, while freely borrowing from and communicating with other disciplines, found an especially helpful ally in the new social history which shared their ambition to rewrite history "from the bottom Up." Documenting the variety and diversity of women's activities and lives in the past, historians set out to make visible those "hidden from history" and to rectify images of women as promulgated in "male-stream" studies of American history. In the words of Joan Kelly, one of the pioneers of the field, the goal was "to restore women to history, and to restore our history to women." To that end, it was seen as essential to keep in mind both Simone de Beauvoir's view of women at the mercy of economic, political, social, and ideological processes as well as Mary Ritter Beard's perspective on women as a "force in history." Women's historians also were confronted with the need to strike another balance: while they were particularly and sometimes painfully aware of the "fact" that all narratives of the human past were fundamentally subjective, incomplete, and mythologizing readings and writings, they also had to believe in the empirical promise of history, i.e., to be able to assert that one could make "true" statements about the female past. Reminding her colleagues that the impossibility of objective truths did not mean that there were no objective lies, the goal for women's historians was, in the words of Linda Gordon, "to maintain this tension between accuracy and mythic power."

Thus faced with a daunting array of tasks and challenges, both empirical and theoretical, early women's history comprised an immense and eclectic variety of approaches and concerns. Yet according to many contemporary and later accounts of the development and state of women's history up to the mid-1970s, the field's concentration was seen to be in three major areas: first, in the research into historical ideals of femininity, culled from all kinds and genres of writing; second, in biographies of extraordinary women, the so-called" great women" or "women worthies"; and, finally, in studies and analyses of feminist and collective women's movements, especially the women's suffrage movements Extremely self-conscious and self-critical both vis-a.-vis their scholarly colleagues as well as their broader feminist constituency, women's historians soon recognized and criticized the fact that,

by and large, these approaches were imitating the parameters and categories of traditional "patriarchal history." Analyses of prescriptive writings, in addition to providing little insights into women's "real" lives, often served to underwrite further the canonical status of the texts under scrutiny, most of them authored by men. While histories of great women copied the elitist and exclusivist "great men of history paradigm," analyses of "organized womanhood," facilitated by the richness of sources, were seen to imply that analyses of female activities were worthy of historical attention only if set in the public arena of electoral politics. In addition, many studies of single or collective womanhood were seen to follow a teleological narrative pattern, bolstered by the "whiggish" belief in a steadily progressive democratization and modernization of U.S. society. Inquiries into the status of women, which could perhaps be called the fourth major topic of early women's history, also served to call into question traditional historical periodization. Realizing that it was not enough simply to add women to the historical record on terms not their own, women's historians increasingly became interested in devising new methodologies and conceptual models more specific to their questions and concerns.

Since it accomplished just that, Carroll Smith-Rosenberg's 1975 essay, "The Female World of Love and Ritual," quickly became a model for women's historians Analyzing nonelite white women's correspondence of 35 families between circa 1760 and 1880, Smith-Rosenberg drew a picture of a specifically middle-class female (sub)culture with its own rituals, values, and ways of communicating, thus lending credence to Barbara Welter's 1966 postulation of the existence of "separate spheres" for Victorian men and women. In contrast to Welter's interpretation, which was based on male-authored prescriptive writings, Smith-Rosenberg's reading of the female sphere did not make it out to be a highly restrictive and crippling realm; rather, she imagined it as a social space that offered women many opportunities for autonomy, agency, and a variety of activities. In subsequent years, this idea of a woman's sphere and a women's culture grounded in this sphere arguably became the major subject of U.S. women's history. Not the least of its attractions was the fact that it opened up a vast space for research, discovery, and interpretation, a space, moreover, in which women wielded power and enjoyed their lives. Wherever women lived and worked together, whether at home, work, or church, under ordinary or extraordinary circumstances, a specific women's culture was seen to form and function.

While the idea of separate spheres was, on the one

hand, clearly a subject of empirical investigation and analysis, its power to produce new perspectives and knowledge made it as much an analytical tool as a topic of women's history.14 The paradigm's appeal was such that it was adapted and adopted by feminist historians specializing in a variety of areas. Since it portrayed a world where women's intense homosocial bonding may have included more explicitly homosexual activities, historians of lesbian women, eager to find foremothers and historical antecedents for their experiences and struggles, greeted Smith-Rosenberg's article as a groundbreaking piece. Labor historians' analyses of women's work throughout the centuries-from the midwives of colonial times to the factory girls of the early nineteenth century and the saleswomen of the turn of the century-furnished further evidence of a female culture outside the private sphere of the home. Historians of feminism came to see woman's sphere, which encompassed religious, social, and charitable work, as the birthplace of both feminist activists and ideology. Throughout the nineteenth century, Paula Baker saw an increasing "domestication of American politics," which found its logical and timely consequence in the granting of women's suffrage in 1920. The postulation of a "separate, public female sphere" thus opened a path for a variety of analyses into the relationship between the private and the public; the subsequent redefinitions of the political arguably' are among the most far-reaching reformulations and revisions of u.s. history. Generating insights and debates that not only expanded the boundaries of women's history but changed the face of much received historical wisdom, the separate spheres paradigm thus achieved theoretical as well as topical prominence.

The concept of a women's culture found support from two very different theoretical schools, whose appeals within and outside of academic circles further contributed to its popularity. E. P. Thompson's 1966 neo-Marxist classic, The Making of the English Working Class, exerted much influence on women's historians' thinking about the role of cultural factors in the development of a group-based consciousness. Moreover, for Marxist historians, the separate spheres paradigm sat well with Friedrich Engels's observations regarding the division and interdependence of public (productive) and private (reproductive) spheres in capitalist societies, a division that was taken to be in the interest of the dominant class and thus central to capitalist ideology and social structure. While Joan Kelly called for a "doubled vision" that would bring the areas of production and reproduction into the same historical picture, other feminist scholars formulated the so-called dual systems theory, which analyzed patriarchy and capitalism as coexisting, separate but equal mechanisms of oppression. As far as the inner life of these gender-divided spheres was concerned, psychological literature, most especially Carol Gilligan's influential In a Different Voice (1982), was sometimes referenced to bolster the concept of women's culture. Some feminists and historians-cultural feminists and historians of difference, as they came to be called-considered Gilligan's observation that women, in contrast to men, based their decisions and opinions on a "standard of relationship, an ethic of nurturance, responsibility, and care," to be further evidence for the historical and possibly cross-cultural existence of a separate women's culture. While Linda Kerber strongly condemned historians' employment of ahistorical psychoanalytic theories, others pointed out the historical failure or at least janus-faced nature of a feminism that grounded itself in those values that societies and cultures have termed to be traditionally and "naturally" female. As "a Marxism you can take home to mother," in the words of Joan Williams, the "ideology of domesticity" was, in the final analysis, seen to be not very effective when it came to analyzing and addressing patriarchal structures of inequality and oppression.

Historians from racial and ethnic minorities charged that the concept of women's separate sphere was basically restricted to white, middle-class Protestant women and thus held little promise to explain African-American or immigrant women's experiences. Historians of lesbian women soon saw the need for a more accurate definition of the female networks and relationships constituting this homosocial sphere, and historians of periods other than the nineteenth century asked for an increasing historicization of the paradigm, questioning its usefulness to explain women's lives beyond a specific moment in history and location in culture. Others disliked the too positive portrayal and romanticization of a female world and warned against forgetting that this female sphere existed in amen's world that largely determined its contours. Over and against an increasing" culturalization" of women's history, they demanded that an analysis of patriarchy had to be the central concern of women's history, that the emphasis had to be on analyses of the inequalities and hierarchical interdependency of those two separate, but hardly equal spheres.

These historians' exhortation to keep in mind "the social relation of the sexes" was certainly not a new idea. With Smith-Rosenberg's article not yet off the press, Natalie Zeman Davis, at the second Berkshire Conference in 1975, pointed out the shortcomings of a history that focused exclusively on women:

It seems to me that we should be interested in the history of both women and men, that we should not be working only on the subjected sex any more than an historian of class can focus entirely on peasants. Our goal is to understand the significance of the sexes, of gender groups in the historical past.

The following year, three historians emphasized that it was "precisely the interactions between women's sphere(s) and the 'rest' of history that enable us to discover women's contributions to world history and the meaning of their subjection." And in 1977, Gerda Lerner voiced her opinion that women's history as herstory would necessarily be only the first step on the way to a truly "universal history" that would take into account the perspectives of both men and women.

Deconstructing Discourses

In the mid-1980s, the linguistic turn in the social sciences and the reception of poststructuralist theories of French provenance coincided with growing uneasiness with a variety of herstory approaches, leading to a new model for historical scholarship-gender history. According to Joan Scott, who has in the meantime come to be designated the primary spokesperson for this paradigm, women's history, by adhering too closely to the methodology of social history, was either too integrationist or, by imagining a history of their own, too separatist fundamentally and lastingly to transform the discipline of history. Thus, in 1986, Scott introduced" gender" as a new and "useful category of historical analysis" and thus initiated a new phase in U.S. women's history, even, as Barbara Melosh put it, "a departure from women's history."

When the term" gender" began to be more frequently used in the 1980s, it was initially taken to be a substitute for "women." As a neutral, euphemistic term, it did not immediately conjure up visions of radical feminism and thus helped women's history to win a broader acceptance within academic structures. Gender also came to be a virtual synonym for the "social relations of the sexes" as understood by Natalie Zeman Davis and Joan Kelly or by anthropologist Gayle Rubin who, in 1975, had coined the term "sex/ gender system" to denote the cross-cultural variability of men's and women's roles and functions based on their perceived biological differences. Finally, gender became a major term in psychoanalytic explanations of the constitution of the subject's identity. Finding fault with all these various definitions and usages, Scott proposed a definition of gender that drew heavily on the theories of Michel Foucault and Jacques Derrida.

Gender, according to Scott, is the "knowledge about sexual difference," with knowledge, in a Foucauldean sense, defined not only as ideas and insights, but denoting all the institutions, structures, daily practices, and rituals by which and through which a society organizes and understands itself. Thus, gender is "the social organization of sexual difference," "the knowledge that assigns meaning to bodily difference." Meaning, according to Derrida, is necessarily grounded in difference: something/somebody is black, since he/she/it is not white; somebody is a foreigner / outsider, since he / she is not a native f insider; somebody is male, since he is not female. Although or because this meaning is always based on and dependent on the existence of an Other which it needs to repress in order to assert itself, the production of meaning is necessarily based on an unstable hierarchy. Gender and race, since seemingly rooted in immutable, "natural," biological facts, are metaphors of difference par excellence; as discursive constructs, however, meaning and power produced through reference to gender can be" deconstructed," demystified, and thus made open to change. Deconstructing gender, which is according to Scott, "a primary way of signifying relationships of power," thus constitutes a highly political enterprise.

Since meaning is produced through and in language, this approach to gender takes leave of a belief in "material" experiences of "real men and women," and instead takes discourse, rhetoric, and representation to be the subject thatreally matters. Not supposedly objective or natural realities are at the center of Scott's theory, but epistemological categories:

The story is no longer about the things that have happened to women and men and how they have reacted to them; instead it is about how the subjective and collective meanings of women and men as categories of identity have been constructed.36

As an exemplary discipline for the creation, construction, and perpetuation of discourses and knowledges of gender, history is not merely descriptive of the past, but operates to produce, support, and legitimize hierarchies of gender. History as a discipline thus no longer serves as an instrument of, but becomes a subject of feminist inquiry and criticism. By using gender as an analytical tool, one can uncover the" deeply gendered nature of history itself":

Feminist history then becomes not just an attempt to correct or supplement an incomplete record of the past but a way of critically understanding how history operates as a site of the production of gender knowledge.

In Scott's view, herstorians fail to address or, even worse, frustrate this agenda by simply accepting the category "women" as well as other historical terminology instead of questioning the very production and workings of these categories. As long as historians take their task to be writing the history of "women" and their "experiences," she sees them as contributing to the further consolidation of an epistemology which always constructs women as the Other and thus as deviant of and secondary to a male norm. The only strategy to break free of the vicious circle. of tautological arguments of women's discrimination based on specifically female experiences, Scott argues, is to change the very subject of historical inquiry. Only "when historians take as their project not the reproduction and transmission of knowledge, but the analysis of the production of knowledge itself," can feminist history redeem its promise to change the way history is written and perceived by a larger public.

According to Scott, this perspective also manages to make visible the gendered nature of areas in which women do not make an appearance as historical agents as, for example, in such male-dominated domains as international diplomacy and the military, fields that traditionally have been the most privileged areas of historical scholarship:

High politics itself is a gendered concept, for it established its crucial importance and public power, the reasons for and the facts of its highest authority, precisely in its exclusion of women from its work. Gender is one of the recurrent references by which political power has been conceived, legitimated, and criticized.

Therefore, gender as a category for historical analysis has to be taken into account even by specialists in areas where women's historians, looking for women, search in vain. Gender thus becomes a truly ubiquitous and universal category; since it is integral to all areas of historical inquiry, there remains no "gender-free zone."

Probably partly because Scott herself has demonstrated the applicability of her theory through an analysis of primary and secondary literature in the field of labor history, and maybe also because the field's historical relation to Marxist theory has accustomed them to theoretical rigor, a number of labor historians have been particularly drawn to Scott's approachY Yet while women's historians generally agree on the significance as well as usefulness of gender as a category for historical analysis, Joan Scott's theoretical tour de force has started a lively debate among historians. Discomfort with what some take to be an elitist, near unintelligible

vocabulary of poststructuralist theorizing constitutes the least important critique. More frequently, critics contend that poststructuralist gender theory often claims to be the one and only theory by criticizing all other approaches as naive, inappropriate, or ineffective. Others argue that most insights that are now couched and reified in poststructuralist terms of Foucauldean or Derridean origins have already been articulated over the years by a variety of scholars. For scholars of gay and lesbian history, for example, the interrogation of historical categories was certainly not a new concept; they, after all, had claimed Foucault as one of their own long before others began to subsume his concern with sexuality under a broader discussion of deviancy and discourses. Moreover, the difficulty of establishing the proper subject for gay and lesbian history, i.e., to find "real" lesbians and gays throughout history, led lesbian historians early on to investigate the historical contingency and constructedness of such categories as homosexuality and heterosexuality and to question the ideology of gender dualism characteristic of most contemporary societies.

Other critics of Scott's poststructuralist approach worry that the abstract debates about discourse, language, and gender as a metaphor of difference are of little help when it comes to the description of and the attack on real, material inequalities within and without academic circles. Joan Hoff, who for many years has probably been the harshest critic of poststructuralist theory, perceives gender history to be a symbol and symptom of a dangerous indifference and apolitical relativism, even a "deliberate depoliticization of power through representations of the female self as totally diffuse and decentered." She deplores poststructuralism's abstract theorizing, its emphasis on intertextuality rather than on human interrelationships, and castigates it for being ethnocentric, sexist, and thus profoundly antifeminist. In her worst-case scenario, the price paid for a deconstructivist approach is not only the very subject women's historians and women's activists have been concerned with women-but even history itself. While Judith Newton has labeled poststructuralist gender theory a "scholarship you can bring home to dad," Joan Hoff even suggested that it was "the patriarchal ideology for the end of the twentieth century." Was Scott's theory of gender a sign of the fact that the old fathers Marx and Freud had been supplanted by new ones, including Foucault and Derrida? Somewhat more moderate in her criticism than Hoff, setting herself apart from both hers tory and poststructuralist approaches, Judith Bennett has also called for a repoliticization of women's history, i.e., a return to patriarchy as the central subject of their inquiry. And even those historians who generally acknowledge the relevance and the significance of deconstructionist methods for women's history point out that the destabilization and demystification of certain categories could indeed be inimical or damaging to the feminist agenda.

Arguing over the issue of whether women's history or gender history is the better feminist history, Joan Scott and Linda Gordon, in the summer 1990 issue of Signs, have laid bare the essentials of the debate.51 Is all history only text, discourse, and representation, or can historians get at the materiality of the past, a "reality behind language," in order to record the experiences and activities of men and women? Is individual or collective action based in concrete, material experiences or is it, according to Scott, purely a "discursive effect"? Does the emphasis on language and discourse deflect attention from issues of power, oppression, and discrimination or is discourse the central, maybe even the only, area through which struggles for power are articulated and consequently the arena in which those struggles need to be fought? Is it sufficient to define gender as a metaphor of sexual difference if it needs to be understood as a system or structure of oppression?

Stimulated by these sometimes quite acerbic debates about the uses and abuses of gender history, some have tried to make concrete proposals for the integration of poststructuralist approaches into their analyses of male and female identities and subjectivities. Lesbian and gay history has been a field that, for many years, has debated and successfully practiced a combination of essentialist and de constructivist approaches, always aware of the interplay between the construction of social categories and the formation of subjective identities. In addition, gender as a category of analysis holds special promise for those interested in the construction of masculinities and the history of men qua men. Although, as Nancy Cott has argued, there is no dearth of information about men, it has now become possible and necessary to analyze their history from the perspective of gender: "Since we know so little about men as gendered beings, 'men's history' must be about the social construction of masculinity and manhood rather than simply about men as a group." The delineations between the public and private sphere, the relationship between individual and society, and other leitmotifs of U.S. history and Western civilization could then be identified as being grounded in a specifically male discourse.

Postulating "that real historical women do exist and share certain experiences and that deconstruction's demystification makes theoretical sense," both Mary Poovey and Louise Newman have argued for the possibility of a synthesis of the approaches used by what Newman has called "historians of experience" and "historians of representation." While acknowledging the usefulness of gender history, Poovey cautions against "consolidating all women into a falsely unified 'woman/If if the concept of gender were to be reified as the "social organization of sexual difference." Moreover, Poovey points out that poststructuralist gender history, not least by its own logic, needs to subject itself to the same deconstructive criticism that it brings to all other discourses. Especially women's historians are, after all, hardly in a position to forget that their paradigms, premises, and interpretations are products of a specific historical moment, cultural location, and individual standpoint, and thus not only representative of a certain politics and polemics, but also constantly subject to change.s6

Difference and Dominance

Most critically, historians of minority groups often perceive themselves to be marginalized within these debates; once again, women's history's dominant paradigm seems to ignore their theoretical and empirical contributions to women's history as well as fail to explain their history to women of color. Prom the perspective of historians of race and ethnicity, it has been obvious that Marxist categories of analysis were not only "sex-blind," but also deficient to explain why certain racial and ethnic groups were the most discriminated against within a class-based hierarchy. The conceptual analogy between race and gender, introduced by Simone de Beauvoir and very popular in the 1960s and 1970s, when activists tried to intensify the collaboration between the civil rights and the women's liberation movements, was hardly acceptable for black women, since it ran the danger of disregarding black women altogether, as is illustrated by the title of a 1982 anthology, All the Women Are White, All the Blacks Are Men, But Some of Us Are Brave. The propagation of a woman's culture historically and ideologically rooted in middle-class domesticity, and frequently claimed to be morally superior to men's, was hardly convincing to African-American women, given their specific history of slavery, physical and psychological violence, urban poverty, and their oppression at the hands of white women as well as white men. Similarly, many perceived the poststructuralist concept of gender, with its emphasis on race, class, and gender as metalanguages of difference, to be equally inadequate to grasp their specific experiences of oppression and resistance.

In her 1987 essay, "The Race for Theory," literary theorist Barbara Christian criticized the hegemony of certain theoretical approaches and the fact that most of them have been authored by whites. Against this theoretical monism and a "grand feminist theory," claiming to be universally applicable and valid, she argued for a pluralism of voices and approaches and thus a broader definition of theory, which would also, for example, make room for narrative strategies and elements. Nancy Hewitt also warned her colleagues against denouncing the voices from the margins as theoretically naive or unimportant. Not only would it be a serious mistake to overlook the variety and diversity of positions within women's history, but such an attitude would only replicate the imperialist attitudes feminist historians had, after all, set out to dismantle. No longer concerned to present a united front against mom and/ or dad, "sibling rivalry" was now seen to be as central to historical and theoretical debates and developments as a collective critique of authority.

Amidst recent debates about multiculturalism, this renewed emphasis on difference among women is especially pertinent to and propagated by historians of ethnic minorities. Analogous to women's history's original agenda to dethrone the "universal man of American history," it is now seen as necessary to topple the "uniracial universal woman" from the pedestal she has come to occupy in historical scholarship-thus the avowed motivation behind the first Multicultural Reader in U.S. Women's History. Also seconding the effort to move marginal subjects center-stage, lesbian theorists and historians are increasingly being heard again in their attempt "to bring the lesbian subject out of the closet of feminist history." Citing the lack of analyses of heterosexist oppression even within" difference-sensitive" frameworks, Cheshire Calhoun has recently suggested that feminist theory and history as currently conceived do not make room for the lesbian, that, in fact, "lesbian representation cannot be accomplished under the sign 'women.' Last but certainly not least, Phyllis Palmer and Nancy Hewitt have reminded us that it needs to be shown that whites, capitalists, and men also "have a race, class, and gender" and that these factors are equally determinant of their lives as of the lives of those belonging to the so-called "marked groups."

While these critiques and perspectives promise a host of new insights and major revisions of traditional concepts and paradigms of U.S. historiography, the question of how to conceptualize such inquiries is again at the forefront of scholars' debates. How is one to do justice to the coexistence, collaboration, or confrontation of different groups within a certain histori-cal and geographical context and to the complexity of individual lives? Historians wonder how the manifold stories of "race/ class/ sex/ sexual/ regional/generational/national/religious subgroup[s] -thus the certainly incomplete list compiled by Nancy Hewitt-can be brought together into one narrative, how these parts can be put together to form a new whole. How is one to determine, especially in hindsight, whether a married Cuban-born tobacco fieldworker and mother of two in Florida or a single, bisexual, WASP female lawyer in Massachusetts have acted and reacted in certain contexts because of their skin color, ethnic identification, sexual orientation, economic positioning, religious convictions, marital or life-cycle status, or any mixture of the above? How is one to write history, if the subject of history-be it the nation-state or the individual-is, so to speak, falling into pieces? Or if he / she is reassembling himself/herself in hitherto unknown combinations, as is suggested by recent propositions of "cyborgs," "queer straights," or the "male lesbian" as legitimate subjects for feminist (historical) analysis?

Warning against too vague a definition of difference that potentially leaves the historian floundering in a sea with too many fish to catch, Linda Gordon argues that the difference paradigm needs to be translated "into a more relational, power-conscious, and subversive set of analytic premises and questions." In the formulation of Elsa Barkley Brown, the primary goal for feminist historians needs to be to analyze the interdependencies and inequalities between these differences, to investigate "the relational nature of these differences." Once again, these are not necessarily new insights. Bonnie Thornton Dill and Deborah King, in 1979 and 1983 respectively, have argued for a conceptualization showing racism, sexism, and capitalism to be integrally related mechanisms of oppression. A focus on patriarchy and gender differences alone cannot explain, for example, African-American women's specific oppression and thus no longer suffices to redeem women's and gender history's radical potential. Maintaining that an "unquestioning application of liberal doses of Eurocentricity can completely distort and transform herstory into history," Hazel Carby points out that no history has the right to call itself feminist or revolutionary if it were to "reproduc[e] the structural inequalities that exist between the 'metropoles' and the 'peripheries', and within the 'metropoles' between black and white women."

One possibility for accepting this challenge to interrogate critically the concept of difference and to pay attention to the various forms of oppression and discrimination is to take a broad view and to attempt a grand narrative. Setting out to write the world history of patriarchy and feminism, Gerda Lerner defines" difference" as the crucial element of all structures of inequality:

When men discovered how to turn" difference" into dominance they laid the ideological foundation for all systems of hierarchy, inequality, and exploitation .... This "invention of hierarchy" can be traced and defined historically: it occurs everywhere in the world under similar circumstances, although not at the same time?

According to Lerner, sexism, racism, and classism are thus merely variations of the same structure of power of a hegemony Lerner calls "patriarchy," by which term she means all structures of inequality that define and legitimize themselves through difference.

However, many scholars argue against such encyclopedic synthesis, questioning not only its feasibility, but even more strongly its desirability. Thus, Jacqueline Dowd Hall announced at the "First Southern Conference on Women's History" in 1988:

Our purpose, in any case, should not be to replace one model or agreed-upon fiction with another. Rather than seeking some new "centered structure," I would call for an historical practice that turns on partiality, that is self-conscious about perspective, that releases multiple voices rather than competing orthodoxies, and that, above all, nurtures an "internally differing but united political community."

Diane Elam, from a deconstructionist perspective, has called for a history "written in the future anterior," by which she means a history that" doesn't claim to know in advance what it is women can do and be," a history "that is a rewriting, yet is itself always ready to be rewritten."

African-American historians, for many years, have suggested new techniques and methodologies to accommodate the voices and stories of a variety of historical actors and groups. According to Bettina Aptheker and Elsa Barkley Brown, a historian's goal and ambition should be neither to establish herself at the center nor to negotiate a standpoint outside of or marginal to the reigning orthodoxies. Historians should be able "to pivot the center," i.e., to assume different standpoints and to acknowledge them to be the center and starting points for their observations and interpretations. In contrast to linear, logical, well-ordered Western epistemology, Elsa Barkley Brown calls this method nonlinear and polyrhythmic. For her, history is not a clearly and orderly structured textile, a classical concert, or an isolated monologue that requires an awestruck, passive audience; rather, it is comparable to a quilt, jazz, or "gumbo ya ya," a Creole

expression for the simultaneous talking of various people. According to Brown, history deals with structures, rhythms, and voices, which only in their synchronous interplay make for a more complete and complex picture of the past. By using terms and metaphors from the field of cultural aesthetics in order to illustrate her philosophy of history, she also suggests that the cultural forms characteristic of certain groups offer us insights into their epistemologies.

Conclusion

It seems to me that two caveats are in order at this point. First, one would do well to remember that the theoretical debates among feminist historians, prone to develop a dynamic of their own, can hardly do justice to the heterogeneity and diversity of approaches employed by historians when they embark upon their empirical studies. While the focus of this, as of any, article is necessarily exclusionary and limited, I would venture to justify my choice of themes by arguing that they, more than any other paradigms and positions, have constituted the pivots of extremely far-reaching and fundamental debates among women's historians; as such, their significance lies as much in the criticism and commentary they have sparked as in the insights they have produced. Second, if my attempt to summarize the debates within women's history has created the impression that I have argued for a progressive evolution within the discipline, which permits new formulations and explanations to discard their predecessors as outdated or obsolete, this impression would be very unfortunate. Not only has a critique of the notion of progressive evolution been one of the earliest and central insights of women's history; more important, the three paradigms I have chosen as organizing principles cannot be separated as neatly-both for their chronological sequence as well as their contents-as I have done here for analytical and presentational reasons. (This probably goes to show how difficult it is to adopt a presentational mode that does justice to the complexity and simultaneity of the dialogue among women's historians.)

On the other hand, it would be equally wrong to minimize the fact that certain viewpoints become and are more pronounced and prominent at one time rather than another. My suggestion is that this has as much or even more to do with who is doing the talking and in what context, than with what she is saying; the higher and more exposed the podium from which one is speaking, the more clearly and widely one is heard. It does make a difference, after all, whether one's ideas are published in the first issue of a journal that goes on to become a major player in the field, whether one formulates one's ideas in Princeton's Institute of Advanced Studies, or whether one is somebody" daring" to comment upon historical research from outside the hallowed walls of academia. The fact that the voices of minority women's historians are only recently being given more attention does not mean that they had not been raised before. Yet their ideas and insights frequently lacked-and continue to lack-the authority that is, within the academy, conferred by a variety of factors such as the access of women of color to institutional resources, academic networks, and major journals, and their representation among student bodies and faculty at colleges and universities. The larger the representation of "alternative standpoints" at renowned universities, the academic "metropoles," the better the preconditions for a wider dissemination and acceptance of what may otherwise forever remain "peripheral" ideas. At a time when one wonders how to do justice to the multiple voices from the past, one equally has to interrogate today's politics of the profession to accommodate a variety of perspectives.

If one were to try to find a common theme among the debates presented here, it could be the issue of who and what constitutes the appropriate subject of (feminist) history. Initially, the agenda was to retrieve women, individually and collectively, as historical agents and subjects. Yet if women's historians were writing about women, which women were we going to talk about and what were we going to call them? While historians of feminism and lesbian historians debated definitions, historians of women of color argued that one, after all, was not simply woman and thus questioned the usefulness of a subject identified exclusively through her sex or gender.s1 The poststructuralist insight that the very "notion of what a woman is" changes historically and cross-culturally and that "woman" was thus a discursive construct led to a focus on the production of categories and discourse as a subject for historical analysis. And with feminist theory voluminously debating the issue of "difference," there is a feeling that" a debate about difference seems to have replaced the debate about women." Yet I would argue that there has been not so much a shift as a multiplication of subjects that allows feminist history not only to reach a broader constituency both within and outside the academy, but also makes for a more complex, colorful, and thus credible picture of the past.

As a key concept of postmodern thought, it is not surprising that "difference" is one of the main t~rms and concerns of late twentiethcentury feminist theorists and historians. On the conceptual level, the necessity to be attentive to and adequately to represent difference poses enormous difficulties and challenges for historians. Women's historians, it seems, are particularly aware of the predicament that legal theorist Martha Minow has called "the dilemma of difference," and that Elizabeth Spelman has defined as the paradox that "both the assertion of difference and the denial of difference can operate on behalf of domination." Yet instead of turning the debate on difference into the scapegoat for feminist disillusionment in the 1990s, it might be well to remember "the productive aspects" of boundary drawings, differentiations, and classifications. A perspective that recognizes and accommodates differences only creates the preconditions and the framework for new insights and new knowledge. Similarly, the heterogeneity and the variety of standpoints assumed in the debate over what constitutes feminist history should be no cause for alarm. Arguing that it is "not difference which immobilizes us, but silence," Audre Lorde suggests that difference "must be not merely tolerated, but seen as a fund of necessary polarities between which our creativity can spark like a dialectic."

Thus, it seems to me that a "grand theory" cannot be a realistic option nor should it be the ultimate goal of women's history, even if such holistic stringency and logic can, in theory, be achieved. Instead of every approach claiming to be more feminist and more effective than the one it criticizes yet builds upon, one should keep in mind that the more varied the theories and tactics, the better the chance eventually to bring about a lasting transformation of academic and social structures. Rather than signifying a dissipation or even paralysis of its radical potential or energies, the diversity of approaches and subjects of U.S. women's history bespeaks its vigor and strength. This becomes especially apparent when one looks to and out from countries where women's history has not yet achieved the degree of prominence and acceptance it now takes for granted in the United States. Thus, amidst their internal squabbles, U.S. women's historians might do well to look abroad, not in order to export their paradigms and insights wholesale to other countries and cultures, but in order for all sides to profit from a dialogue that will enrich U.S. theoretical debates as much as it might empower those struggling to write and institutionalize women's history elsewhere.

FOCUS QUESTIONS:

1. Why was the concept of "separate spheres" appealing to feminist historians? What were its drawbacks?

2. According to Thurner, how did Joan Scott help to redefine the term "gender"? What was her proposal? How did critics of her approach feel?

WORLDS APART, to 1700

1-1 Excerpts from the Florentine Codex

The Florentine Codex is the primary record of Aztec life before the Spanish conquest. Over a period of approximately forty years, Bernadinao DeSahagun had the original source material transcribed into a set of 12 books. The two selections below are taken from the tenth book and describe how newborn children are received and descriptions of various attributes (both positive and negative) of women in the society.

Source: DeSahagun, Fr. Bernadino. *The Florentine Codex: General History of the Things of New Spain,* vol. 10, Arthur J.O. Anderson and Charles E. Dibble, translators. Sante Fe: The School of American Research and the University of Utah Press, 1960. pp. 46-53, 171-172.

"Aztec Greetings to Newborn Babies" – Part IV

Thirty-fourth Chapter, in which are told and mentioned what they did when they visited women recently delivered, and other things which were done where a woman recently delivered dwelt.

And here it is told that when a child was born, and when [the mother's] relatives knew of it, and it was known and the news spread and was noised abroad, her family and blood relations were assembled and brought together. They set forth, and came and proceeded to visit the much revered child.

When they entered, at the very first, they took ashes; they anointed their knees with ashes; they rubbed themselves. And also they put ashes on the knees of their children yet in the cradles; or those still crawling, going on all fours; those who stood, who already took to their feet; the boys, girls, youths, young men, unmarried girls, and young women. Everywhere, on all parts of the body they placed ashes; on every joint and articulation: their ankles, their elbows, their buttocks, over the kidneys, the napes of their necks, their shoulders, but especially their knees . . .

And it was so said and averred that thereby they would not become lame. But if this were not so done, they would become lame, and all the joints, in every place, would creak.

And also for four days they carefully watched the fire. It never went out. It continued to flare up, to grow and increase, to flare red. They thus carefully started it; it was well set. And no one might take the fire. And if anyone wished to take the fire, or a light, they would not give it to him, lest he take renown from the child who had been born, until the four days had ended, or for still a few days, when they bathed him.

Thirty-fifth Chapter. Here is told what was done when they bathed their children, and how food was eaten when they gave them their names; and the discourse which the old people gave when they addressed the child and the mother.

And when he was bathed, quite early in the morning, in the morning light, when the sun appeared, they had the small children perform the naming ceremony. They went out shouting and panting on the roads; to the. entrances they ran. Thus they went calling out what he had been given as a name, as hath already been mentioned, in a certain place. They took the naming ceremony gift, parched maize toasted with beans. They provided it with beans, many beans, offered in a vessel.

And it is said that so was the custom if someone were born on a day sign beginning in the first position (as hath been said in many places). If it were a good time, then at once they quickly bathed him. Or later, they set it aside and skipped a day, so that they could make good the feasting and drinking for the child.

But if they could not do so then, they bathed him later, on the third day sign. As here it appeareth in [the series of] One Eagle, the one perhaps then born they would bathe later, on Three Motion.

Those whose fathers and mothers were poor, the indigent, who were in misery, and had nothing to use, with which to gather together and assemble people, only with affliction, sickness, and misery bathed their child. For they only aggravated and worsened it when they did not delay, defer, retard, procrastinate, or postpone [the day of bathing].

But if the fathers were rich and prosperous, if there was wherewith to eat, they selected for one a later date, on the seventh day sign; at that time they bathed the child and placed him in the cradle. This was because, as hath been said, they always considered the seventh day sign good. At that time they held an important banquet. There was drink and food. From all parts Rowers were taken; all the Rower bearers came. There was jostling and crowding. And the old men and old women greeted the small boy and his newly delivered mother. They said:

"O my beloved grandson, thou hast endured suffering and fatigue. For thou hast come here to earth; thou hast appeared on earth. Thou shalt behold, come to know, and feel pain, affliction, and suffering. It is a place of torment and affliction; of constant torment and affliction; a time of torment and a time of affliction to which thou hast corne; a place of bitterness, a place of much work and affliction. Perhaps we shall receive as merits and as good deserts that for a short time thou shalt be lent to us. For thou art the living image, the likeness, the noble child, anet the offspring of thy ancestors, thy beloved grandsires, thy great-grandsires, thy great grandmothers, the grandfathers of thy nephews, who already have gone beyond, who a short time ago came to stand guard for a little while, here where thou liest and hast endured suffering and fatigue, o my beloved grandson. For our lord hath sent thee."

Forthwith they petted him and stroked him with their hands, to show that they loved the child. Also at once they addressed. and greeted his newly delivered mother. They said:

"O my daughter, O my beloved daughter, my lady, my beloved lady, thou hast endured suffering and fatigue. For in some way thou hast separated thyself from and left the jeweled necklace, the precious feather which was within thee. Now that he is come forth on earth, you are not indivisible; you will not be joined together, for you are separated. What will our lord require? Perhaps for a little day we shall take him as lent to us. We shall love him like a precious necklace or a precious stone bracelet. Be calm and modest; take care. Do not relapse into sickness nor let accident befall thee. Do not try to be up and about. Be careful, in convalescing, when they place thee in the sweatbath. And

do not neglect the child. Take care of him. Even in thy sleep, be fearful for him. Do not pierce his palate, [in nursing him]; do not crush him in thy sleep; do not let him sleep unwatched, so that thou nowhere mayest bring mishap to him. Do not do so intentionally; for our lord hath given him."

Thus only briefly they greeted her, lest they tire her by useless talk.

"Aztec Women's Careers and Character" Part XI

Thirteenth Chapter, which telleth of the noblewomen.

A NOBLEWOMAN

A noble person [is] wonderful, revered, esteemed, respected; a shelter.

The good noblewoman [is] a protector - one who loves, who guards people. She protects, loves, guards one.

The bad noblewoman [is] violent, furious, savage, revolting - a respecter of no one. She respects no one; she belittles, brags, becomes presumptuous; she takes things in jest and keeps them; she appropriates things; she deceives herself.

[ANOTHER] NOBLEWOMAN

The noblewoman [is] esteemed, lovely - an esteemed noble, respected, revered, dignified.

The good noblewoman [is] a protector. She shows love, she constantly shows love. She loves people. She lives as a noblewoman.

The bad noblewoman [is] savage, wrathful, spiteful, hateful, reserved; [she is] one who is enraged, unjust, disturbed, troubled. She becomes troubled, disturbed, enraged, over-demanding.

[ANOTHER] NOBLEWOMAN

The noblewoman [is] one who merits obedience; [she is] honorable, of high standing - to be heeded. A modest woman, a true woman, accomplished in the ways of women, she is also vigorous, famed, esteemed, fierce, stern.

The good noblewoman is venerable, respectable, illustrious, famed, esteemed, kind, contrite. [She is] one who belittles no one, who treats others with tenderness.

The bad noblewoman [is] wrathful, an evildoer. [She is] one who is overcome with hatred - pugnacious, revolting, hateful - who wishes to trouble, who wishes to cause worry; irresponsible, irritable, excitable - one who is disturbed. She becomes disturbed, troubled; she does evil; she becomes overwrought with hatred.

[ANOTHER] NOBLEWOMAN

The noblewoman [is] a protector, meritorious of obedience, revered, worthy of being obeyed; a taker of responsibilities, a bearer of burdens - famed, venerable, renowned.

The good noblewoman [is] patient, gentle, kind, benign, hard-working, resolute, firm of heart, willing as a worker, well disposed, careful of her estate. She governs, leads, provides for one, arranges well, administers peacefully.

The bad noblewoman [is] one who is rash, who is fitful. She incites riots; she arouses fear, implants fear, spreads fear; she terrorizes [as if] she ate people. She impels flight - causes havoc - among people. She squanders.

[ANOTHER] NOBLEWOMAN

The noblewoman [is] a woman ruler, governor, leader - a provider, an administrator.

The good woman ruler [is] a provider of good conditions, a corrector, a punisher, a chastiser, a reprimander. She is heeded, obeyed; she creates order; she establishes rules.

The bad noblewoman [is] unreliable, negligent, overbearing - one who mistreats others. She is overbearing; she mistreats one, is given to vice, drinking, drunkeness. She leads one into danger; she leads, she introduces one into error. She is troubled; she confounds one.

THE MAIDEN

The maiden is noble, a noble among nobles, a child of nobility. [She is one] from whom noble lineage issues, or she is of noble birth, worthy of being loved, worthy of preferred treatment.

The good maiden is yet a virgin, mature, clean, unblemished, pious, pure of heart, benign, chaste, candid, well disposed. She is benign; she loves; she shows reverence; she is peaceful; she bows in reverence; she is humble, reserved; she speaks well, calmly.

The bad maiden [is] a descendant of commoners - a belittler, a rude person, of lowly birth. She acts like a commoner; she is furious, hateful, dishonored, dis-

solute, given to carnal pleasure, impetuous.

THE GIRL, THE LITTLE GIRL

The little girl is a noble, an esteemed noble, a descendant of nobles.

A good little girl [is] of good, clean life - a guardian of her honor. [She is] self-respecting, energetic, deliberating, reflective, enterprising. She is selfrespecting, energetic, patient when reprimanded, humble.

The bad little girl [is] an evil talker, a belittler inconsiderate, perverse, impetuous, lewd. She shows disrespect; she detests, she shows irreverence, she belittles, she presumes.

THE MAIDEN

The maiden [is] of the nobility - courteous, loved, esteemed, beloved.

The good maiden [is] loving, pleasing, reverent, respectful, retiring. She is pleasing, appreciative, admiring of things.

The bad maiden [is] corrupt, incorrigible, rebellious - a proud woman, shameless, brazen, treacherous, stupid. She is inconsiderate, imbecile, stupid; she brings dishonor, disgrace.

[ANOTHER] NOBLEWOMAN

The noblewoman - the courteous, illustrious noble.

The good noblewoman [is] a child of lineage, of noble lineage. She brings fame to others, honors her birthright, causes one to be proud of her.

The bad noblewoman [is] a gluttonous noble, a noble completely dishonored, of little value - a fool, impudent - a consumer of her inner substance, a drunkard. She shows concern for none but herself; she lives completely for herself; she governs her own conduct, assumes her own burdens; she is disrespectful.

[ANOTHER] NOBLEWOMAN

The noblewoman [is] esteemed - an esteemed noble, a legitimate child.

The good noblewoman [is] one who is exemplary, who follows the ways of her parents, who gives a good, sound example. She is of the chosen; she is one of the chosen few.

The bad noblewoman [is] one who degrades herself, who lives in filth and corruption - detestable, slobbering, false. She degrades herself, brings herself to ruin, hurls - places - herself in filth and corruption.

[ANOTHER] NOBLEWOMAN

The noblewoman is a descendant of noble ancestors; [she is] of noble rearing.

The good noblewoman [is] tranquil, quiet, peaceful, modest, dignified. She honors, she respects all people. She shows respect, consideration, veneration.

The bad noblewoman [is] daring, overbearing toward others - a scatterer, a spreader of hatred. She scatters hatred, shows effrontery, is rude, becomes brazen, lifts her head in pride, exhibits vanity.

[ANOTHER] NOBLEWOMAN

The noblewoman is of noble rearing - a meritorious noble.

The good noblewoman is peaceful, kind, gentle.

The bad noblewoman [is] inflated; a consumer of her inner substance, decrepit. She is presumptuous; she acts in haste; she is impetuous.

[ANOTHER] NOBLEWOMAN

The noblewoman [is] the child of nobles, a true noble. She is worthy thereof. She realizes the estate of nobility; she participates in and is suited to it.

The bad noblewoman [is] common, dull - descended from commoners, irritating. She brags; she presumes; she understands things backwards; she does things backwards; she causes irritation.

[ANOTHER] NOBLEWOMAN

The noblewoman [is] completely good, just, pure, respectable.

The good noblewoman [is] one who humbles herself, who bows in reverence. Gracious, kind, she is benign, persuasive; she bows in reverence; she is humble, appreciative.

The bad noblewoman [is] untrained, deranged, disobedient, pompous. She goes about dissolute, brazen. She is gaudy; she goes about in gaudy raiment - rude, drunk.

[ANOTHER] NOBLEWOMAN

The noblewoman through her is nobility engendered. [She is] of the nobility.

The good noblewoman [is] retiring, submissive, humble, desirous of no praise.

The bad noblewoman [is] boastful, vainglorious, desirous of being known. She is vainglorious, desirous of being known; she boasts, brags, boasts.

[ANOTHER] NOBLEWOMAN

The noblewoman is famed, venerable, esteemed, honored.

The good noblewoman [is] one who weeps, who is compassionate, concerned; one who admires, who shows veneration, who reveres things, who reveres people. She shows understanding of the poor; she reveres things, she reveres people.

The bad noblewoman [is] proud, ... , inflated; she acts superior. ...

[ANOTHER] NOBLEWOMAN

The noblewoman [is] of noble heart, of nobility. The good noblewoman [is] of elegant speech, softspoken - a gentle person, peaceful, refined. She speaks with elegance; she acts with refined modesty.

The bad noblewoman [is] like a field worker brutish, a great field worker, a great commoner; a glutton, a drinker, an eater - a glutton, incapable, useless, time-wasting ....

[ANOTHER] NOBLEWOMAN

The noblewoman [is] of nobility, belongs to the order of rulers, comes from rulership whether she is legitimate or a bastard child.

The good noblewoman [is] one who is bashful, ashamed [of evil], who does things with timidity, who is embarrassed [by evil]. She is embarrassed [by evil]; she works willingly, voluntarily.

The bad noblewoman [is] infamous, very audacious, stern, proud, very stupid, brazen, besotted, drunk. She goes about besotted; she goes about demented; she goes about eating mushrooms ...

[ANOTHER] NOBLEWOMAN

The noblewoman is a noble, a noble ruler, an esteemed noble - esteemed, lovely, worthy of being loved, worthy of preferred treatment, worthy of veneration, deserving of honor, enjoying glory; good, modest, respected, self-respecting. [She is like something] white - refined; like a pillar; like a wooden beam, slender, of medium stature. [She is] valiant, having valor, bravery, courage. [She is] esteemed, famed, precious, beautiful.

THE GOOD NOBLEWOMAN

The good noblewoman, the beloved noblewoman [is] highly esteemed, good, irreproachable, faultless, dignified, brave; [like] a quetzal feather, a bracelet, a green stone, a turquoise. Very much hers are goodness, humanity, humaneness, the human way of life, excellence, modesty, the fullness of love. Completely hers are the sources of goodness, of grace, of humaneness as to body and soul [She is] perfect, faultless.

The bad noblewoman [is] bad, wicked, evil, ill, incorrigible, disloyal, full of affliction, quite besmirched, quite dejected. [She is] haughty, presumptuous, arrogant, unchaste, lewd, debauched. She is given to drunkenness, to drinking; she goes about being rude; she goes about telling tales. [She is] vain, petty, given to bad conduct; a drunkard, savage, torpid, [like] a foreigner, an imbecile - stupid, feeble .... , ... ; she is oblivious of what all know of her. [She is] a sleepy-head, a dried-out sleepy-head, an oversleeping woman; a pervert, a perverted woman, perverse.

Fourteenth Chapter, which telleth of the nature, the condition of the common women.

THE ROBUST WOMAN

The robust woman, the middle-aged woman [is] strong, rugged, energetic, wiry, very tough, exceedingly tough, animated, vigorous; a willing worker, long-suffering.

The good robust woman [is] pious, chaste, careful of her honor; not unclean; unblemished; one who is irreproachable - like a bracelet, like a green stone, like fine turquoise.

The evil robust woman [is] belittling and offensive to others - belittling to others; disgusting. She is ill bred, incompatible; she does not work in calm; she acts fitfully, without consideration; she is impetuous.

THE MATURE WOMAN

The mature woman [is] candid.

The good mature woman [is] resolute, firm of heart; constant - not to be dismayed; brave, like a man; vigorous, resolute; persevering - not one to falter; a steadfast, resolute worker. She is long-suffering; she accepts reprimands calmly - endures things like a man. She becomes firm - takes courage. She is intent. She gives of herself. She goes in humility. She exerts herself.

The bad mature woman [is] thin, tottering, weak - an inconstant companion, unfriendly. She annoys others, chagrins them, embarrasses, shames, oppresses one. Extremely feeble, impatient, chagrined, exhausted, fretful, she becomes impatient, loses hope, becomes embarrassed - chagrined. She goes about in shame; she persists in evil. Evil is her life. She lives in vice.

THE WEAVER OF DESIGNS

The weaver of designs is one who concerns herself with using thread, who works with thread.

The good weaver of designs is skilled - a maker of varicolored capes, an outliner of designs, a blender of colors, a joiner of pieces, a matcher of pieces, a person of good memory. She does things dexterously.

She weaves designs. She selects. She weaves tightly. She forms borders. She forms the neck. She uses an uncompressed weave. She makes capes with the ballcourt and tree design. She weaves loosely - a loose, thick thread. She provides a metal weft. She forms the design with the sun on it.

The bad weaver of designs is untrained - silly, foolish, unobservant, unskilled of hand, ignorant, stupid. She tangles [the thread] ; she harms [her work] - she spoils it. She ruins things scandalously; she scandalously ruins the surface of things.

THE SPINNER

The spinner [is] one who combs, who shakes out [the cotton].

The good spinner [is] one who handles things delicately, who forms an even thread. [She is J soft, skilled of hand - of craftsman's hands. She puts [the thread J in her lap; she fills the spindle; she makes a ball [of thread] ; she takes it into her hand - winds it into a skein in her hands. She triples [the thread]. She spins a loose, thick thread.

The bad spinner pulls [threads], leaves lumps, moistens what she grasps with her lips, twists incompletely. [She is] useless - of useless hands, negligent, slothful, neglectful- a neglectful one, lazy.

THE SEAMSTRESS

The seamstress is one who uses the needle, a needle worker. She sews; she makes designs.

The good seamstress [is] a craftsman, of craftsman's hands, of skilled hands ~ a resourceful, meditative woman. She makes designs; she sews.

The bad seamstress [is] one who bastes, who tangles [thread]. She tangles [thread]; she bastes; she tangles the sewing. She deceives one; she ridicules one.

THE COOK

The cook is one who makes sauces, who makes tortillas; who kneads [dough]; who makes things acid, who leavens. [She is] wiry, energetic. [She is] a maker of tortillas - a tortilla-maker; she makes them disc-shaped, thin, long. . . . She makes them into balls; twisted tortillas - twisted about chili; she uses grains of maize. She makes tamales - meat tamales; she makes cylindrical tortillas; she makes thick, coarse ones. She dilutes sauces; she cooks; she fries; she makes juices.

The good cook is honest, discreet; [she is] one who likes good food - an epicure, a taster [of food. She is] clean, one who bathes herself; prudent; one who washes her hands, who washes herself; who has good drink, good food.

The bad cook [is] dishonest, detestable, nauseating, offensive to others - sweaty, crude, gluttonous, stuffed, distended with food — much distended, acquisitive. As one who puts dough into the oven, she puts it into the oven. She smokes the food; she makes it very salty, briny; she sours it. She is a field hand very much a field hand, very much a commoner.

THE PHYSICIAN

The physician [is] a knower of herbs, of roots, or trees, of stones; she is experienced in these. [She is] one who has [the results of] examinations; she is a woman of experience, of trust, of professional skill: a counselor.

The good physician is a restorer, a provider of health, a reviver, a relaxer - one who makes people feel well, who envelopes one in ashes. She cures people; she provides them health; she lances them, she bleeds them - bleeds them in various places, pierces them with an obsidian lancet. She gives them potions, purges them, gives them medicine. She cures disorders or the anus. She anoints them; she rubs, she massages them. She provides them splints; she sets their bones - she sets a number of bones. She makes incisions, treats one's festering, one's gout, one's eyes. She cuts [growths from] one's eyes.

The bad physician [pretends to be] a counselor, advised, a person of trust, of professional knowledge. She has a vulva, a crushed vulva, a friction-loving vulva. [She is] a doer of evil. She bewitches - a sorceress, a person of sorcery, a possessed one. She makes one drink potions, kills people with medications, causes them to worsen, endangers them, increases sickness, makes them sick, kills them. She deceives people, ridicules them, seduces them, perverts them, bewitches them, blows [evil] upon them, removes an object from them, sees their fate in water, reads their fate with cords, casts lots with grains of maize, draws worms from their teeth. She draws paper - flint - obsidian - worms from them; she removes these from them. She deceives them, perverts them, makes them believe.

FOCUS QUESTIONS:

1. How are aggressive women looked upon in Aztec society? Does it seem to be a favorable trait for women?

2. What types of occupations are available to Aztec women? Are there any opportunities beyond domestic ones?

3. What do these excerpts tell you about who DeSahagun was speaking to when compiling these codices?

1-2 The "Man-Woman" Role: An Overview

Liminality is often described as the threshold between to planes of existence. The man-woman of Amerindian culture occupies such a space, usually a male able to occupy a traditionally female role, yet be crucial to the military success of some tribes. This excerpt provides a brief overview of this phenomenon as observed by anthropologists.

Source: Fulton and Anderson, "The Amerindian 'Man-Woman': Gender, Liminality, and Cultural Continuity,"

Current Anthropology, vol 3 No 5 (Dec 1992), 606-607.

Writing in the American Anthropologist in 1955, Angelino and Shedd observed that, although Kroeber had called for "a synthetic work on the subject" of the "manwoman" 5 years earlier, the task had not yet been undertaken. They argued that "if progress is to be made in comparing various cultural groups so that general principles may be arrived at, and if the concept is to be generally usable, some order must be evoked" (p. 125). Answering their call a decade later, Jacobs (1968) made an initial attempt at reviewing the data, citing over 60 sources which made reference to the role and cataloging the tribes in which it was reported present or absent. She further identified 21 tribes that reported a female "man-woman." Moreover, she made a first effort to interpret the phenomenon objectively. Katz (1976) compiled nearly 50 documents which made reference to the "man-woman" role, commenting that the references "tell as much, and often more, about the commentator's sentiments about Native homosexuality than they do about its actual historical forms" (p. 181). For instance, he quoted the Spanish explorer Alvar Nunez Cabeza de Vaca, who, exploring Florida between 1528 and 1533, wrote: "During the time that I was thus among these people I saw a devilish thing, and it is that I saw one man married to another, and these are impotent, effeminate men [amariconados] and they go about dressed as women, and do women's tasks" (p. 285). It was not until 1983, however, with the publication of Callender and Kochems's "The North American Berdache," that a comprehensive synthesis of the available literature was realized.

Callender and Kochems find the evidence reasonably good that the "man-woman" status existed in 113 tribal communities, from "California to the Mississippi Valley and Upper Great Lakes, with scattered occurrences beyond," and "seems to have been surprisingly absent, undeveloped, or very obscure throughout the East except for its southern fringe" (pp. 444-46). They argue that while the role has been described as "rare or uncommon," earlier accounts suggest that it was more unexceptional-except that female "men-women" "tended to be much rarer than their male counterparts"-and that their numbers greatly decreased following contact with white culture (pp. 446-471).

The adoption of female accoutrements by the "manwoman" was "widespread and significant" although "neither universal nor invariable" (p. 447). Transvestism and occupation were closely linked: tasks identified as female were a prominent feature of the role, and "male berdaches [were] consistently described as exceptionally skilled in women's work." Two features of the role-the "supernatural powers often ascribed to it" and "the intermediate nature of [its] gender status"-reportedly allowed for this occupational skill and accounted for their economic success. The "man-woman" also provided services, including giving secret names to newborns, acting as go-between, and participating in burial and mourning rituals, that produced additional income (pp. 447-48).

The "man-woman" was frequently prohibited from participating in warfare, although in some societies the "man-woman" fought but was forbidden to use "male" weapons. In others the incumbent of the role was a noncombatant participant-treating the wounded, car-

rying supplies, and attending to the horses. The "man-woman" was also custodian of the scalps taken in battle and responsible for the dance that was held upon the successful warriors' return. The incumbent of the role was perceived to be central to a successful military engagement in a number of societies and overall played a crucial role in the "war complex" (pp. 448-491).

With regard to the "homosexuality" of the role, Callender and Kochems consider it "possible that if some cultures considered homosexual activity a significant aspect of this status, others did not." They observe, however, that most descriptions stressed its homosexual component and that "man-woman" sexual relationships ranged from "casual promiscuity to stable marriages." It is apparently nowhere reported that the "man-woman" had sexual relations with another "manwoman" (pp. 449-51). -

Recruitment into the "man-woman" role was accounted for by a childhood proclivity for the social functions of the other gender or by a vision or some other supernatural validation. Callender and Kochems note "that secular and supernatural views of the processes leading to berdachehood are inherently neither contradictory nor mutually exclusive." Finally, they call attention to a neglected aspect of the selection process, namely, that "only members of certain social groups could become berdaches" (pp. 446-47). They report that attitudes toward the "man-woman" ranged from "awe and reverence through indifference to scorn and contempt" and that in some societies the community's very existence was believed to depend upon the role (p. 453) ...

Why did aboriginal cultures give formal recognition to this status, and why did anyone assume the "manwoman" role? Callender and Kochems reject the hypotheses of "institutionalized homosexuality" and an alternative to the "traditional" aggressive "male" role and express some reservations about the idea that the role is primarily a religious one and part of a global pattern of shamanism. They agree with Whitehead that assumption of the role was motivated primarily by the opportunity it provided for prestige, though they question whether men were considered superior to women throughout aboriginal North America and how primary they were in determining cultural practices (pp. 453- 56).

FOCUS QUESTIONS:

1. Does a role for the man-woman exist in society today? Why or why not?

1-3 The Work of Gender in the Discourse of Discovery

Amerigo Vespucci is credited with determining that the land "discovered" by Columbus was not an extension of India but, in fact, a separate continent. Implicit in the grandeur of the European ideology of conquest was the latent fear of the savage—particularly the female savage, who, like the unexplored continent represented something to be both desired and feared.

Source: Louis Montrose, *Representations*, No. 33, Special Issue: The New World. (Winter, 1991), pp. 3-7.

By the 1570s, allegorical personifications of America as a female nude with feathered headdress had begun to appear in engravings and paintings, on maps and title pages, throughout Western Europe. Perhaps the most resonant of such images is Jan van der Straet's drawing of Vespucci's discovery of America, widely disseminated in print in the late sixteenth century by means of Theodor Galle's engraving (fig. Here a naked woman, crowned with feathers, upraises herself from her hammock to meet the gaze of the armored and robed man who has just come ashore; she extends her right arm toward him, apparently in a gesture of wonder-or, perhaps, of apprehension. Standing with his feet firmly planted upon the ground, Vespucci observes the personified and feminized space that will bear his name. This recumbent figure, now discovered and roused from her torpor, is about to be hailed, claimed, and possessed as America. As the motto included in Galle's engraving puts it, "Americen Americus retexit, &Semel inde semper excitam" Americus rediscovers America; he called her once and thenceforth she was always awake."This theme is discreetly amplified by the presence of a sloth, which regards the scene of awakening from its own shaded spot upon the tree behind America. Vespucci carries with him the variously empowering ideological and technological instruments of civilization, exploration, and conquest: a cruciform staff with a banner bearing the Southern Cross, a navigational astrolabe, and a sword-the mutually reinforcing emblems of belief, empirical knowledge, and violence. At the left, behind Vespucci, the prows of the ships that facilitate the expansion of European hegemony enter the pictorial space of the New World; on the right, behind America, representatives of the indigenous fauna are displayed as if emerging from an American interior at once natural and strange.

Close to the picture's vanishing point-in the distance, yet at the center-a group of naked savages, potential subjects of the civilizing process, are preparing a cannibal feast. A severed human haunch is being cooked over the fire; another, already spitted, awaits its turn. America's body pose is partially mirrored by both the apparently female figure who turns the spit and the clearly female figure who cradles an infant as she awaits the feast. Most strikingly, the form of the severed human leg and haunch turning upon the spit precisely inverts and miniaturizes America's own. In terms of the pictorial space, this scene of cannibalism is perspectively distanced, pushed into the background; in terms of the pictorial surface, however, it is placed at the center of the visual field, between the mutual gazes of Americus and America, and directly above the latter's outstretched arm.

I think it possible that the represented scene alludes to an incident reported to have taken place during the third of Vespucci's alleged four voyages, and recounted in his famous letter of 1504. I quote from the mid-sixteenth-century English translation by Richard Eden:

At the length they broughte certayne women, which shewed them selves familier towarde the Spaniardes: Whereupon they sent forth a young man, beyng very strong and quicke, at whom as the women wondered, and stode gasinge on him and feling his apparell: there came sodeynly a woman downe from a mountayne, bringing with her secretly a great stake, with which she gave him such a stroke behynde, that he fell dead on the earth. The other wommene foorthwith toke him by the legges, and drewe him to the mountayne, whyle in the mean tyme the men of the countreye came foorth with bowes and arrowes, and shot at oure men. ...The women also which had slayne the yong man, cut him in pieces even in the sight of the Spaniardes, shewinge them the pieces, and rosting them at a greate.

The elements of savagery, deceit, and cannibalism central to the emergent European discourse on the inhabitants of the New World are already in place in this very early example. Of particular significance here is the blending of these basic ingredients of protocolonialist ideology with a crude and anxious misogynistic fantasy, a powerful conjunction of the savage and the feminine.'

This conjunction is reinforced in another, equally striking Vespuccian anecdote. Vespucci presents a different account of his third voyage in his other extant letter, this one dated 1503 and addressed to Lorenzo Piero Francesco de Medici. Like the previous letter, this one was in wide European circulation in printed translations within a few years of its date. Here Vespucci's marvelous ethnography includes the following observation:

Another custom among them is sufficiently shameful, and beyond all human credibility. Their women, being very libidinous, make the penis of their husbands swell to such a size as to appear deformed; and this is accomplished by a certain artifice, being the bite of some poisonous animal, and by reason of this many lose their virile organ and remain eunuchs.

The oral fantasy of female insatiability and male dismemberment realized in the other letter as a cannibalistic confrontation of alien cultures is here translated into a precise genital and domestic form. Because the husband's sexual organ is under the control of his wife and is wholly subject to her ambiguous desires, the very enhancement of his virility becomes the means of his emasculation.

In the light of Vespucci's anecdotes, the compositional centrality of van der Straet's apparently incidental background scene takes on new significance: it is at the center of the composition in more ways than one, for it may be construed as generating or necessitating the compensatory foreground scene that symbolically contains or displaces it. In van der Straet's visualization of discovery as the advance of civilization, what is closer to the horizon is also closer to the point of origin: it is where we have come from-a prior episode in the history of contacts between Europeans and native Americans, and an earlier episode in the history of human society; and it is now what we must control-a cultural moment that is to be put firmly, decisively, behind us. In the formal relationship of proportion and inversion existing between America's leg and what I suppose to be that of the dismembered Spanish youth, I find a figure for the dynamic of gender and power in which the collective imagination of early modern Europe articulates its confrontation with alien cultures. The supposed sexual guile and deceit that enable the native women to murder, dismember, and eat a European man are in a relationship of opposition and inversion to the vaunted masculine knowledge and power with which the erect and armored Vespucci will master the prone and naked America. Thus, the interplay between the foreground and background scenes of the van der Straet-Galle composition gives iconic form to the oscillation characterizing Europe's ideological encounter with the New World: an oscillation between fascination and repulsion, likeness and strangeness, desires to destroy and to assimilate the Other; an oscillation between the confirmation and the subversion of familiar values, beliefs, and perceptual norms.

Michel de Certeau reproduces the engraving of Vespucci's discovery of America as the frontispiece of his book *The Writing of History.* As he explains in his preface, to him this image is emblematic of the inception of a distinctively modern discursive practice of historical and cultural knowledge; this historiography subjects its ostensible subject to its own purportedly objective discipline; it ruptures the continuum "between a subject and an object of the operation, between a *will to write* and a *written body* (or a body to be written)." For de Certeau, the history of this modern writing of history begins in the sixteenth century with "the 'ethnographical' organization of writing in its relation with 'primitive,' 'savage,' 'traditional,' or 'popular' orality that it establishes as its other." Thus, for , the tableau of Vespucci and America is

an inaugural scene. . . . The conqueror will write the body of the other and trace there his own history. From her he will make a historied body-a blazon-of his labors and phantasms. . . . What is really initiated here is a colonization of the body by the discourse of power. This is writing that conquers. It will use the New World as if it were a blank, "savage" page which Western desire will be written.

"America" awakens to discover herself written into a story that is not of her own making, to find herself a figure in another's dream. When called by Vespucci, she is interpellated within a European history that identifies itself simply as History, single and inexorable; this history can only misrecognize America's history as sleep and mere oblivion. In 1974, when a speaker at the first Indian Congress of South America declared, "Today, at the hour of our awakening, we must be our own historians," he spoke as if in a long suppressed response to the ironic awakening of van der Straet's America, her awakening to the effacement of her own past and future.

Although applied here to a graphic representation that is iconic rather than verbal, de Certeau's reflections suggestively raise and conjoin issues that I wish to pursue in relation to Sir Walter Ralegh's *The Discoverie of the large, rich, and beautfull Empire of Guiana* (1596) and some other Elizabethan examples of "writing that conquer." These issues include consideration of the writing subject's textualization of the body of the Other, neither as mere description nor as genuine encounter but rather as an act of symbolic violence, mastery, and self-empowerment; and the tendency of such discursive representation to assume a narrative form, to manifest itself as "a historied body-in particular, as a mode of symbolic action whose agent is gendered masculine and whose object is gendered feminine. Rather than reduce such issues to the abstract, closed, and static terms of a binary opposition-whether between European and Indian, Culture and Nature, Self and Other, or, indeed, Male and

Female-I shall endeavor to discriminate among various sources, manifestations, and consequences of what de Certeau generalizes as the "Western desire" that is written upon the putatively "blank page" of the New World, and to do so by specifying the ideological configurations of gender and social estate, as well as national, religious, and/or ethnic identities, that are brought into play during any particular process of.

FOCUS QUESTIONS:

1. Why do you think America is portrayed as female in the van der Straet's painting?

1-4 Ballad of a Tyrannical Husband

Ballad of a Tyrannical Husband is a fifteenth century didactic verse portraying an argument between a husband and wife over household duties and how men should value their wives more. It also gives some insight to the workings of the peasant class.

Source: Ed. John Harland, F.S.A., *Ballads and Songs of Lancashire: Ancient and Modern*, Second Edition, London: George Routledge and Sons and L.C. Gent, 1875. pp. 2-7.

O thou that art gentle, for joy of thy dame,
As thou wrought this wide world, in heav'n is thy hame;
Save all this company, and shield them from shame,
That will listen to me, and 'tend to this game.

God keep all women that to this town 'long,
Maidens, and widows, and eke wives among,
For much they are blamed, and sometimes with wrong,
I take witness of all folk that heareth this song.

Listen, good sirs, both young and old;
Of a good husband this tale shall be told;
He wedded a woman that was fair and bold,
And had goods enow to wend as they wold."

She was a good housewife, courteous and kind,
And he was an angry man, and soon would be tined
Chiding and brawling, and fared like a fiend,
As one that oft will be wroth with his best friend.

The goodman and his lad to the plough are gone,
The goodwife had much to do, and servant had she none,
Many small children to look after beside herself alone,
She did more than she could inside her o'wn house.
Home came the goodman early in the day

To see that everything was according to his wishes.
'Dame,' he said, 'is our dinner ready?' 'Sir,' she said, 'no.
How would you have me do more that 1 can?'

Then he began to chide and said, 'Damn you!
I wish you would go all day to plough with me,
To walk in the clods that are wet and boggy,
Then you would know what it is to be a ploughman.

Then the goodwife swore, and thus she said,
'I have more to do than I am able to do.
If you were to follow me for a whole day,
You would be weary of your part, I dare bet my head.'

'Blast! In the devil's name!' said the goodman,
'What. have you to do, but sit here at home?
You go to your neighbour's house, one after the other,
And sit there chattering with Jack and with Jane.'

Then said the goodwife, 'May you rot!
I have more to do, if everything were known; When I lie in my bed, my sleep is but small,
Yet early in the morning you will call me to get up.

'When I lie all night awake with our child,
I rise up in the morning and find our house chaotic.
Then I milk our cows and turn them out in the field,
While you sleep quite soundly, Christ protect me!

'Then I make butter later on in the day.
Afterwards I make cheese - these you consider a joke
Then our children will weep and they must get up,
Yet you will criticise me if any of our produce isn't there.

'When I have done this, yet there comes even more:
I give Our chickens food or else they will be lean;

Our hens, our capons, and our ducks all together,
Yet I tend to our gosling that go on the green.

'I bake, 1 brew, it will not otherwise be well,
I beat and swingle flax, so help me God,
I heckle the tow, I warm up and cool down [or I winnow and ruddle [sheep]],
I tease wool and card it and spin it on the wheel.

'Dame,' said the goodman, 'the devil have your bones!
You do not need to bake or brew more than once a fortnight.
I see no good that you do within this big house,
But always you excuse yourself with grunts and groans.'

'Either I make a piece of linen and woollen cloth once a year,
In order to clothe ourselves and our children in together,
Or else we should go to the market and buy it very dear;
I am as busy as I may every year.

'When I have done this, I look at the sun,
I prepare food for our beasts before you come home,
And food for ourselves before it is noon,
Yet 1 don't get a fair word when I have done

So I look to our good without and within,
"That there be none away, neither more nor min,
"Glad to please you to pay, lest any bats" begin,"
And for to chide thus with me, i' faith you be in sin."

Then said the goodman in a sorry time,
"All this would a good housewife do long ere it were prime,
" And sene [since] the good we have is half deal thine,
"Thou shalt labour for thy part as I do for mine.

"Therefore, dame, make thee ready, I warn thee anon,
"To-morrow with my lads to the plough thou shalt gone;
"And I will be housewife, and keep our house at home,
"And take mine ease as thou hast done, by God and St. John !"

Ay, grant," quoth the goodwife, "as I understand.
"To-morrow in the morning I will be walkande,
"Yet will I rise, while ye be sleepand,
"And see that all things be ready laid to your hand.'

So it pass'd all to the morrow that it was daylight.
The goodwife thought over her deeds and up she rose right.
"Dame!" said the goodman. "I swear by God's might,
"I will fette home our beasts, and help that they were dight."

The goodman to the field hied him full yarne;
The goodwife made butter, her deed were full derne;
She took again the butter-milk and put it in the churn,
And said, "Yet of one point our Sire shall be to learn."

Home came the goodman and took good keep
How the wife had laid her flesh for to steep.
She said, "Sir, all this day, ye need not to sleep,
"Keep well our children, and let them not weep.

"If you go to the kiln, malt for to make,
"Put small fire underneath, Sir, for God his sake.
The kiln is low and dry, good tend" that ye take.
"For an it fasten on a fire, it will be evil to slake.

"Here sit two geese abroad ; keep them well from woo,
"And they may come to good, or you'll work sorrow enow."
"Dame," said the goodman, "hie thee to the plough,
"Teach me no more housewifery, for I can" enow.

"Forth went the goodwife, courteous and hend,
"She call'd to her lad, and to the plough they wend ?
'They were busy all day.—A fytte here I find,
An I had drunk once, ye shall hear the best behind.

A FYTTE.

FOCUS QUESTIONS:

1. How is labor divided in this particular family?
2. Do the problems they encounter still exist today?

1-5 Two Views of Maria Theresa

Maria Theresa (1717 – 1780) was the Archduchess regnant of Austria, Queen regnant of Hungary, Croatia and Bohemia, and a Holy Roman Empress by marriage. Frederick the Great became her rival when Prussia attacked Silesia, starting the War of Austrian Succession. Otto Christopher Podewils was Prussian envoy to Austria during this war.

Source: Roider, Karl A., Jr. translator and editor. *Maria Theresa.* Englewood Cliffs, N.J: Prentice-Hall, 1973. pp 34-35, 115-117.

Frederick the Great

In 1755 the king [Frederick II sometimes refers to himself in the third person] augmented the regiments of the garrisons: those of Silesia were increased by eight, those of Prussia by three, those of Brandenburg by two; that made thirty battalions in all. In a poor country a sovereign does not find his resources in the bank accounts of his subjects, and his duty is to cover extraordinary but necessary expenses by his prudence and good economy. Supplies collected in the summer are consumed during the winter. It is just as necessary to use our funds economically in peace as it is in war. This point, unfortunately so important, was not forgotten, and Prussia was prepared to conduct a few campaigns with its own funds; in one word, we were ready to enter the arena at the first moment and to test our steel with the enemy's. In the following you will see how useful was this precaution, and why the king found it necessary, by the unusual situation of his provinces, to be armed and ready for all possibilities in order not to serve as a plaything for his country's neighbors and enemies. On the contrary, it was possible to win victories, if the resources of the state permitted it.

The king had in the person of the empress-queen an ambitious and vindictive enemy, even more dangerous because she was a woman, obstinate in her opinions and implacable. This was so true that, in the secrecy of her dressing room, the empress-queen prepared the grand projects that burst forth later on. This superb woman, devoured by ambition, wanted to travel all roads gloriously; she put her finances into an order unknown to her ancestors and not only utilized reforms to make up for the revenues lost when she ceded lands to the king of Prussia and king of Sardinia, but actually increased her overall income. Count Haugwitz became controller general of finances, and under his administration income rose to 36 million

gulden or 48 million ecus. Her father, Emperor Charles VI, who had even possessed the kingdom of Naples, Serbia, and Silesia, never received that much. Her husband, the emperor, who dared not interfere in affairs of state, threw himself into business ventures; each year he extracted enormous sums from his revenues in Tuscany and invested them in commerce. He established manufacturing companies, lent money, supervised the delivery of uniforms, arms, horses, and weapons for the entire imperial army. Associated with a Count Bolza and a merchant named Schimmelmann, he won the contract to farm the taxes of Saxony and in 1756 even provided the forage and flour to the army of the king of Prussia, who was engaged in war with his wife, the empress. During the war the emperor advanced considerable sums to this princess as good credit: in short, he was the banker of the court, and in character with his title of king of Jerusalem, he conformed to the immemorial profession of the Jewish nation.

In preceding wars the empress had sensed the need of improving discipline in her army. She chose generals who were both hard working and capable of introducing discipline among the troops. She also put old officers, little able to do their proper jobs, on pensions and replaced them with young men, who were full of enthusiasm and love for the business of war. The empress herself appeared frequently in the camps of Prague and Olomouc in order to inspire the troops by her presence and gifts. Better than any other prince, she knew how to use those distinctive flatteries which subjects love so much. She rewarded those officers who were recommended by their generals, and above all she excited their devotion, talents, and desire to please her. At the same time she formed a school of artillery under the direction of Prince Liechtenstein; he increased this corps to six battalions, and utilized cannon to a degree unprecedented in our day. Because of his ardor for the empress, he contributed 100,000 ecus to the school out of his own pocket. Finally, in order to neglect nothing that would improve the military, the empress founded near Vienna a college to instruct the young nobility in the arts of war; it includes able professors of geometry, fortification, geography, and history, which constitute the appropriate subjects. This school serves as a seedbed of officers for her army. Owing to all these efforts, the military in this country has achieved a degree of perfection it had never reached under the emperors of the house of Austria, and it was a woman who realized the plans worthy of a great man.

This princess, little satisfied with the manner in

which foreign and domestic affairs were treated and able to impress her opinions on all areas of administration, selected Count Kaunitz to serve her at the end of 1755. She awarded him the office of first minister so that his one head could encompass all the branches of government. We have had the opportunity to become especially acquainted with this man who plays such an important role. He possesses all the sentiments of his sovereign, and he knows how to flatter her passions and win her confidence. As soon as he entered the ministry, he worked to create that alliance system that would isolate the king of Prussia and prepare the way for the empress to achieve her dearest ambitions: the conquest of Silesia and the humiliation of the Prussian monarch. But that is the proper story of the following chapters, so we will not speak further of it here.

That is how these two powers used the peace to prepare for war -like two wrestlers flexing their muscles and burning with desire to grapple with each other.

Upon hearing the news of Maria Theresa's death, Frederick the Great, himself sixty-eight years old at the time, wrote a brief letter to a friend in which, after philosophizing a bit on death in general, he paid the highest compliment he could to his worthy rival.

For my part I am becoming increasingly apathetic, a condition to which age leads the senile chatterer. Without becoming disturbed, I see dying and being born as dependent on when the command comes for one to enter the world or leave it. In this way I accepted the death of the empress-queen. She did honor to her throne and to her sex: I fought wars with her, but never was I her enemy.

Count Otto Podewils

As ordered by Your Majesty, I hereby provide the characteristics of the most important personages of the court, as I have observed them.

I am not so conceited as to believe that the impressions I send you will be completely correct. It requires greater insight than I, as I know, possess. Furthermore, the condition in which I find myself [a recent enemy of Austria] forms an almost insurmountable barrier to acquiring a complete knowledge of the personalities of those individuals whom I have undertaken to describe ....

I begin with a portrait of the empress-queen, as the principal subject of my painting.

She is somewhat over medium height. Before her marriage, she was very beautiful, but the numerous births she has endured [at this time she had borne six daughters and two sons] have left her quite heavy. Nonetheless, she has a sprightly gait and a majestic bearing. Her appearance is pleasant, although she spoils it by the way she dresses, particularly by wearing the small English crinolines, which she likes.

She has a round, full face and a bold forehead. Her pronounced eyebrows are, like her hair, blond without any touch of red. Her eyes are large, bright, and at the same time full of gentleness, all accented by their light-blue color. Her nose is small, neither hooked nor turned up, the mouth a little large, but still pretty, the teeth white, the smile pleasant, the neck and throat well formed, and the arms and hands beautiful. She still retains her nice complexion, although she devotes little time to it. She has much color. Her expression is open and bright, her conversation friendly and charming. No one can deny that she is a lovely person.

When she became ruler, she knew the secret of winning everyone's love and admiration. Her sex, her beauty, and her misfortune helped in no small measure. The exaltations of praise issued in abundance by the officially subsidized journalists were believed by all. By showing only her good side-innocent, generous, charitable, popular, courageous, and noble-she quickly won the hearts of her subjects and convinced·· them that, as she had believed from the beginning, the late Emperor Charles VII was a criminal. She granted everyone an audience; personally read petitions; concerned herself with the administration of justice; accepted willingly the chores of government; rewarded one person with a kind word, another with a smile or courteous sign; made her negative replies bearable; gave splendid promises; and publicly displayed the greatest piety, remarking often that she would trust everything to God. She honored the clergy, displayed much reverence for religion, expressed her love for the poor, founded hospitals, divided money among the soldiers, sponsored ceremonies, allowed plays to run, and personally addressed the landed Estates, to whom she described in exalted and moving terms her situation and bewailed the misfortune into which her enemies had thrust her. She called herself disconsolate to be forced against her will to share her calamities with her loyal subjects and promised at the first opportunity to reward the ardor of each. She promised the Hungarians to reestablish and confirm their old privileges and told them she wanted to remedy their old grievances. She publicly displayed her spiritual strength, showed defiance to her misfortune, and tried to instill her own courage into her subjects.

I heard only words of praise for this empress. People extolled her to the clouds. Everyone considered himself fortunate. The landed Estates paid to her all that they could. The people bore their taxes without murmuring. The nobility offered her money, often without waiting to be asked. The Hungarians insisted they would fight for her; the officers served happily for half-pay because she had convinced them that it was not her fault she could not give them more. Full of enthusiasm, everyone stood by her and rushed to sacrifice himself for this best of all princesses. People deified her. Everybody wanted to have her picture. She never appeared in public without being greeted with applause.

A more pleasant personality was hard to imagine. Perhaps it would have been less difficult to acquire it than to display it in public. The queen could do so only a short time. Misfortune increases her delight in being loved and increases her desire to be loved. The reversals which she suffered at the beginning of her reign brought out this desire, but the success of her policies after the Treaty of Breslau [1742] reduced it somewhat. Slowly but surely, however, she has again assumed her natural character. The effort to hide her spirit under the veil of misfortune has now disappeared. I begin to notice that she, less motivated by the difficulties of her people than by the thought of increasing her power, prosecutes the war without aversion [Although at peace with Prussia, Austria was still at war with France]. The exaltations which everyone had showered upon her, and her own egotism have given her a high opinion of her talent and her ability, and have made her domineering. She listens to advice only grudgingly, allows no contradiction, tries to arouse fear rather than love, fancies herself as proud as her ancestors, treats many with arrogance, and shows herself vengeful and intransigent. She hears impatiently the petitions brought to her, tries to encroach upon the privileges of the Hungarians, oppresses the Protestants by relieving almost none of their grievances, and gives a bad impression of her piety, in which she displays so little respect for religion that one day she went to church on a horse, prompting the clergy to decry such an act as a great scandal and to voice their public disapproval.

So great a change in her character elicited considerable reaction among her subjects who began to protest the taxes they had to pay and expressed great discontent over them. They no longer wished to see her on the streets or to possess her picture. Almost everyone believed he had grounds for complaint.

Nevertheless, I must add: much else contributed to the general unhappiness. It was impossible for the queen to satisfy everyone, to keep all the promises she had made, and to fulfill in every case the high opinion which she had given of her personality and talents. The more complete the good fortune that each one promised himself during her reign, the more he believed he had reason to complain that his expectations were not realized.

One can also not deny: if the queen does not possess all the qualities that she at first displayed to a degree that won for her the admiration of all, she still deserves great praise. She apparently recognized the damage she had done to herself and tried to correct it, although I doubt if she will again be as popular as she once was.

Her spirit is lively, masterful, and capable of dealing with affairs of state. She possesses an excellent memory and good judgment. She has such good control of herself that it 'is very difficult to judge from her appearance and behavior what she really thinks.

Her conversation is almost always friendly and gracious, and displays the coyest courage. Her behavior is easy and captivating, and appears even more so to her subjects, who are accustomed to regarding pride and arrogance as qualities inseparable from their monarchs. She speaks well, expresses herself gracefully, and appears to listen attentively. It is still easy to gain an audience with her, although somewhat less so than at the beginning of her reign, when anyone could speak with her. In order to win an audience now, we must go to the court lady who supervises the calendar. Seldom has the empress refused one, however; she listens with patience and good will to those who address her and personally replies to the petitions that reach her. On days at home she spends the greater part of the time, whenever she has the chance, in granting audiences. When she is in the city, the same thing happens while everyone attends court. In the garden she usually grants audiences while walking. She gives almost no audiences in circumstances where one is displeased. A short time ago she had told a Hungarian general who had requested an audience that she would see him the next day during a reception. He heatedly replied that he had no wish to be seen and scrutinized by everyone, and, if she was not willing to see him in private, as the dead emperor and she herself had done earlier, then he would rather not see her at all. At first she was quite enraged, but necessity demanded that she grant his wish.

She spends a great deal of time with affairs of state and seems to have an excellent knowledge of them.

She reads most of the reports from her ambassadors at foreign courts or has them read to her, examines the rough drafts of important documents before they are written in final form, converses often with her ministers, and attends the conferences which concern state business of some magnitude. Above all she wants to be thoroughly instructed about matters concerning the army. She tries with some success to penetrate the personalities and talents of the generals. She herself chose all of those who served in the last Italian campaign, and everyone agreed they were the best of her officers.

Her ambition cherishes the wish to rule personally. She enjoys more success at it than most of her ancestors, but the personal interests of her ministers and her court inspire them to prevent or hinder her from having an exact knowledge of her business, so that she will not remedy those abuses of which they and their families take so much advantage. This resistance makes her efforts, if not completely useless, for the most part unfruitful. She knows people deceive her, but she can do nothing about it. Often she expresses her impatience and has more than once said that she wishes God would open her eyes to the corruption in the government.

Nonetheless, she has ended many abuses and cut unnecessary expenses. She plans to undertake still more reforms in finances and the army, and concerning both, she suggests to her ministers Your Majesty's system as a model. She sometimes shows them the remarkable difference between the revenues which Your Majesty extracts from Silesia and those which she and her ancestors received, and refuses to accept their excuses that this province is being oppressed.

She also envisions one day reordering the condition of the army, especially establishing its wages on the same system as Your Majesty's. It is unlikely, however, that she will ever succeed. The generals and ministers have too many interests not to oppose these changes, and they do so by creating insurmountable obstacles and difficulties in her path. Only those officers who have no connections would gain advantages from a regularizing of wages. But those who have influence at court, either themselves or through their parents, would continue to receive far greater rewards in the disorder that now prevails.

In order to forestall these reforms, the ministers and generals have already posed a thousand difficulties regarding even the minimal changes the empress wants to introduce. I recall that, one day when she stopped a regiment during a parade, she commented that she found their overcoats too long and suggested

that they must be troublesome to soldiers during marches in great heat or rain. She added that they should change to the Prussian model. Instantly the officers argued that the troops needed these long coats to cover them at night, whereas the Prussians did not need them because every Prussian tent had blankets. She replied that each of her soldiers should have a blanket too. The next day she received an estimate of the cost. Someone had so exaggerated the expense for the blankets, the packhorses to carry them, and the people to care for them, that the total came to an enormous sum, which easily convinced the empress to abandon the idea.

She tries to praise the military, which now enjoys greater respect than under the late emperor. Repeatedly she has said that under her reign a man could make his fortune with his dagger only. She allows officers in her service to eat at her table regardless of their birth. Such a policy greatly displeases the high nobility, which is already quite offended that the empress has abolished many traditional court practices that in general she hates passionately.

She goes to some lengths to win the soldiers by her generosity, often permitting money to be divided among them and seldom passing by the life guards without giving them a few ducats. By doing so she has become beloved by the troops, whose admiration she has also won by the determination she has demonstrated during the most serious defeats. It is certain that she has intended for a long time to assume command of the army herself.

She especially tries to belie the weaknesses of her sex and to strive for virtues which are least suitable to her and which few women possess. She even seems angry to have been born a woman. She spends little time caring for her beauty; she exposes herself without consideration to the vagaries of the weather, strolls many hours in the sun and in the cold, which she tolerates much better than heat. She cares little about her attire and, aside from ceremonial days, dresses very simply, as does the whole court now after her example.

One could never accuse her of coquetry. In this respect, she has never given one hint of infidelity. She loves the emperor dearly, but also demands great devotion from him. People claim that her love for this prince is caused partly by her temperament and the good qualities with which he can satisfy it. Among other things they emphasize the little influence which he, despite her love for him, has on her spirit. I have it on good authority that one day during a conference in which the empress had heatedly defended a position against the views of her ministers, she in very sharp words told the emperor, as he made known his opinion, that he should not mix in business he did not understand. The emperor grumbled about this treatment for a few days and complained about it to one of his favorites, a Lorraine colonel by the name of Rosieres. This man answered, "Sire, permit me to say that you have handled the empress the wrong way. Had I been in your position, I would have forced her to treat me better, and I would have received her as limp as a glove." "Why should I?" asked the emperor. "I wouldn't be able to sleep," answered the colonel. "Believe me, she loves you in this way, and by refusing her, you could achieve everything." This conversation was reported to the empress, who hounded this officer so unmercifully that he decided to leave the service, despite all the emperor's efforts to get him to stay.

Without doubt she is very jealous of the emperor and does everything possible to prevent him from establishing a liaison. To the few women whom the emperor ,had begun to notice, she has thrown very grim looks. She would like to forbid all gallantry at her court, and shows great contempt for women who have love affairs and just as much for the men who court them. I know that one day she had a vehement argument with Count Esterhazy-for whom, incidentally, she has much respect and who always attends her card parties -concerning a love affair that he has openly enjoyed with the wife of Count Althann. She tries to keep the emperor from everyone inclined to such adventures, and people say that Count [Rudolph Joseph] Colloredo, who makes no secret of his liaisons, will never win her good will. For some time he has been in a form of disgrace because he took the emperor on a few pleasure trips. The same thing has happened to a few others. She wants to live a middle-class marriage with the emperor.

She dearly loves her children, who are always around her on holidays. She used to love the oldest archduchess [Archduchess Elizabeth who died in June, 1740, at the age of three] the most, but she has died. Now she prefers Archduke Joseph. She lets him get into many things for which she must reprimand him. Sometimes she assumes an appearance of strictness toward him and vows not to spoil him. One day she wanted to have him whipped. Someone remonstrated with her that there was no precedent for anyone acting in such a way towards an archduke. "I believe it," she replied, "and look at how they turned out." She loves her mother very much but allows her no participation in affairs of government.

She enjoys entertainment, without depending on it too much.

Earlier she had more love for dances and masked balls than now. She dances with enthusiasm and, for her figure, with agility. She loves gambling and plays cards quite boldly but appears sensitive about it. Once she lost more than one hundred thousand ducats. It was rumored that Sir [Thomas] Robinson [the British ambassador] received orders from his court to reproach her for it.

Although she plays the harpsichord, and that quite well, and apparently understands much about music, she makes very little of it.

One of her greatest pleasures is to go for walks and, above all, to ride horseback. She rides fearfully fast. The emperor and others have tried vainly to slow her down. She first learned to ride in preparation for the Hungarian coronation. She believed it politically sound because she had noticed that the Hungarians expressed much enthusiasm upon seeing her on horseback. She discovered such fervent pleasure in this recreation that it has become her fondest enjoyment. Sometimes she rides on _ an estate, at other times to private houses to eat breakfast or drink coffee. She also goes on many walks, sometimes three to four hours at a time.

She seldom hunts and does so only to please the emperor.

She loves architecture, without understanding it very well, as her house in Schon brunn, built according to her taste, testifies.

By nature she is happy, but it appears that the disappointments she has. had to bear have embittered her, and now she is somewhat harsh. Apparently she has taken her misfortunes extraordinarily to heart, and one day I heard her say that she would not begin her life over again for anything in the world.

People call her fickle, and it is certain that her favorites do not enjoy their positions long. Countess Fuchs and her daughters, Countesses Logier and Daun, have generally stood out, but all three, especially the mother, were more than once on the verge of seeing their favor disappear had not the emperor troubled to reconcile them with the empress. They have, after all, little influence and even then only indirectly and in roundabout ways. The only person most noticeably in favor is one of her chamber ladies called Fritz [Elisabeth von Fritz]; Maria Theresa just married her to a Hungarian nobleman named Petrach, to whom she has given a present of twelve thousand gulden and appointed to the bodyguards with the rank of lieutenant colonel. People say that this woman, who still attends the empress, offers her advice even on affairs of state. I have doubts about this last rumor because it accords neither with the spirit of the empress to rule by her own will and to see and do everything personally, nor with her care to eliminate the slightest doubt that she herself rules.

The empress has never renounced her own generosity. She is by nature benevolent and likes to make everyone happy. She makes a little too much of her gratitude and displays it openly at frequent opportunities.

Her habits are well ordered. In the winter she rises at 6:00 A.M., in the summer at 4:00 or 5:00 and devotes the whole morning to affairs of state, reading reports, signing documents, and attending conferences. She eats lunch around 1:00 P.M., rarely spending more than a half an hour at the table. Often she eats alone. In summer and even sometimes in winter she goes for a walk after lunch, often alone, and spends most of the rest of the afternoon reading reports. From 7:00 to 8:30 P.M. she usually plays faro. In the evening she eats little, most often only a broth, sometimes goes for a walk after dinner, and usually goes to bed before 10:00 P.M.

She takes little medicine, relying instead upon her healthy constitution. When she feels hot, even in the middle of winter, she often sits at an open window in the room in which she eats, which annoys everyone but herself. Her doctors repeatedly tell her that she will regret this practice, but she only laughs at them.

Her method of judging affairs of state I have already had the honor of presenting to Your Majesty in my regular reports. She possesses extraordinary ambition and would like to make the house of Austria more glorious than it was under her ancestors.

She has had the joy of reaching one of her ambitious goals, the return of the imperial crown to her house.

She seems to have inherited from her ancestors the traditional hatred of France, with whom, I believe, she will never have good relations, although she has sufficiently mastered her passions, should her interests demand it.

She does not like Your Majesty, but she respects you. She will he unable to forget the loss of Silesia, which grieves her all the more, I hear from good sources, because at the same time her troops lost their honor. In general, she regards Your Majesty as a hindrance to the growth of her power and above all to her influence in the [Holy Roman] Empire, which she would like to expand as did her ancestors.

These are, Majesty, the main points which I have been able to collect regarding the personality of the queen-empress. I intend to send to Your Majesty the portraits of the other members of the court, as soon as my business permits me. I beg Your Majesty's pardon in advance if I do not reply to your orders as quickly as I would like. Because I personally cipher and decipher all messages in the interests of greater security, Your Majesty will realize that I have little leisure time left to me.

FOCUS QUESTIONS:

1. Frederick describes Maria Theresa as being more dangerous because she is a woman. What do you think he means by that?

2. What is the "weakness of her sex" that Podewils refers to?

1-6 Witches at Windsor (1579)

In Windsor, England in January 1579, four women were condemned as witches and executed on February 26, 1579. Mother Dutton, Mother Devell, Mother Margaret, and Elizabeth Stile, alias Rockingham were accused of causing the deaths of a number of people through their "Sorceries and Inchauntementes."

Source: A Rehearsall both straung and true, of hainous and horrible actes committed by Elizabeth Stile, Alias Rockingham, Mother Dutten, Mother Devell, Mother Margaret, Power notorious Witches, apprehended at winsore in the Countie of Barks. and at Abbington arraigned, con-

demned, and executed on the 26 daye of Februarie laste Anno. 1579. (London, 1579) modernized and reprinted in Barbara Rosen. *Witchcraft*. London, 1969, 83-91.

The Reader

Among the punishments which the Lord God hath laid upon us, for the manifest impiety and careless contempt of His word abounding in these our desperate days, the swarms of witches and enchanters are not the last nor the least. For that old serpent Satan, suffered to be the scourge for our sins, hath of late years greatly multiplied the brood of them and much increased their malice. Which practice he hath the more easily performed for that wholesome remedies, provided for the curing of such cankers, are either never a whit, or not rightly applied. For albeit the justices be severe in executing of the laws in that behalf, yet such is the foolish pity, or slackness, or both, of the multitude and under-officers that they most commonly are winked at, and so escape unpunished, to the dishonour of God and imminent danger on her Majesty's liege people. Nay, the fondness and ignorance of many is such that they succour those devilish imps, have recourse to them for the health of themselves or others, and for things lost, calling them by the honorable name of 'wise women'. Wherein they know not what honour they do to the devil.

For it is Satan that doeth all, that plagueth with sickness, that maimeth, murdereth, and robbeth, and at his lust restoreth. The witch beareth the name, but the devil dispatcheth the deeds-without him the witch can contrive no mischief. He without the witch can work treason too much, too oft, and too soon.

If then by the law of the Lord of life witches and enchanters are accounted unworthy to live; if by the law of this land they are to be done to death, as traitors to their prince, and felons in respect of her Highness' subjects-whosoever thou be, beware of aiding them! Go not with Saul the reprobate to ask council of them, neither, for Christianity sake, seem to be more slack in a good purpose than Cicero the Ethnic, who plainly adviseth that witches, poisoners etc. are to be rather shut up in prison and tied with fetters, than moved to amend with council and persuasions, only afterwards suffered to escape, whereby they may renew their malicious and treasonable drifts.

1579 January the 28 day

The true examination and confession of Elizabeth Stile, alias Rockingham, uttered at the Jail of Reading, in the county of Barks. immediately after her apprehension in the presence of the persons hereafter mentioned.

Elizabeth Stile alias Rockingham, late of Windsor, widow, of the age of 65 years or thereabout, being apprehended at Windsor aforesaid and brought personally before the right worshipful Sir Henry Neville, knight, being by him examined and found by manifest and undeniable proofs of her honest neighbours to be a lewd, malicious and hurtful woman to the people and inhabitants thereabouts, was thereupon committed to the common jail of Reading, there to remain until the next great assizes there to be holden, that her offence might be more straitly sifted, and she the offender to receive the guerdon due for her demerits.

Whither when she was come and moved by the jailor there named Thomas Rowe to turn herself to God, from whom she had notoriously fallen, and mildly to bear the punishment belonging to her deeds past; and therewithal urged in sign of her repentance to confess her former follies and facts, she seemed to have some remorse in conscience and desired to have some talk with the said Thomas Rowe. To whom with one John Knight the constable, John Griffith an innholder, and one William Printall, being all four present, she confessed as followeth.

And first concerning those persons that practise the damnable art of witchcraft, sorcery or enchantment, of her own certain knowledge and 'Voluntary motion she uttered to this effect ensuing.

Imprimis: that one Father Rosimond dwelling in Farnham parish, being a widower, and also a daughter of his, are both witches or enchanters, which Rosimond she saith hath and can transform himself by devilish means into the shape and likeness of any beast whatsoever he will.

2. Item: that one Mother Dutten dwelling within one Hoskins' in Clewer parish can tell everyone's message as soon as she seeth them approach near to the place of her abode and further, she keepeth a spirit or fiend in the likeness of a toad, and feedeth the same fiend (lying in a border of green herbs within her garden) with blood which she causeth to issue from her own flank.

3. Item: that one Mother Devell, dwelling nigh the pond in Windsor aforesaid, being a very poor woman, hath a spirit in the shape of a black cat and calleth it Jill, whereby she is aided in her witchcraft; and daily feedeth it with milk, mingled with her own blood.

4. Item: that one Mother Margaret dwelling in the almshouse at Windsor goeth with two crutches, doth feed a kitling or fiend by her named Jenny with crumbs of bread and her own blood.

5. Item: the said Elizabeth Stile, alias Rockingham, of herself confesseth that she the same Elizabeth until the time of her apprehension kept a rat (being in very deed a wicked spirit) natning it Philip; and that she fed the same rat with blood issuing from her right-hand wrist, the marks whereof evidently remain, and also that she gave her right side to the devil, and so did the residue of the witches before named.

And thus far forth touching the persons aforementioned in general, now resteth her declaration of their detestable drifts and devices in particular.

6. Furthermore, she confesseth that when she was apprehended Mother Margaret came to her and gave her money, charging her in any wise not to detect their secrets; which if she this prisoner did, the said Mother Margaret threatened that she should be hardly entreated.

7. And moreover, she saith that Father Rosimond with his daughter, Mother Dutten, Mother Devell, Mother Margaret, and herself the said Elizabeth Hockingham, did accustom to meet within the backside of Master Dodge's, in the pits3 there, and did in that place conclude upon heinous and villainous practices, such as by them or any of them, before had been devised or determined.

8. Also she saith and confesseth that they all purposed and agreed, by their sorceries and enchantments to despatch privily one Langford a farmer, dwelling in Windsor by the Thames side, and that they murdered him accordingly.

9. They also by their devilish art killed one Master Gallis who in times past had been Mayor of Windsor.

10. The like they practised against one of the said Langford's maids, whom by the mischievous means above expressed they bereft of life.

11. Likewise a butcher named Switcher escaped not their treachery but was by their witchcraft brought to his grave.

12. Another butcher named Mastlin was by them handled in such sort that he consumed away.

13. The manner of their enchantments, whereby four of the persons aforenamed were murdered, was thus: Mother Dutten made four pictures of red wax, about a span long, and three or four fingers broad, for Langford, for his maid, for Master Gallis, and for Switcher; and the said Mother Dutten, by their council and consent, did stick an hawthorn prick against the left sides of the breasts of the images, directly there where they thought the hearts of the persons to be set whom the same pictures did represent, and thereupon within short space, the said four persons, being suddenly taken, died.

14. As for Mastlin the fifth man, she confesseth that he was bewitched, but how or whether he died or no, she uttereth not.

15. Further, the same Elizabeth saith that herself did kill one Saddock with a clap on the shoulder, for not keeping his promise for an old cloak to make her a safeguard, who presently went home and died.

16. Further she saith, that she and every of them did overspeak one Humphrey Hosey and his wife, and one Richard Mills, and one John Mathiriglise, that they lay sick in a strange order a long time, but they were recovered again.

17. Further she saith, that Mother Devell did overspeak one William Foster, a fisher, and one Willis' wife, a baker.

18. Further she saith, that Mother Dutten did give one picture, but she knoweth not whether it was of a man or of a woman; and the man that had it of her she thinketh to be dead, but she knoweth not his name.

19. Further she saith, that one George Whitting, servant to Matthew Glover ofEton, had one picture of herself for one Foster, for that the said George and Foster fell out at variance; and the picture was made in Mother Dutten's house and that Mother Dutten, Mother Devell and herself were at the making; and that Mother Devell did say to her Bun or evil spirit 'Plague him and spare him not!' and she did thrust a hawthorn prick against the heart of him, and so he lay at the point of death a long time, but Mother Dutten recovered him again.

20. And in the end they killed a cow of his by their witchcraft.

21. And further she saith, that they and every of them, if any had angered them, they would go to their spirits and say 'Such-a-one hath angered me, go do them this mischief' and for their hire would give them a drop of their own blood; and presently the party was plagued by some lamentable casualty.

22. Elizabeth Stile also confesseth that she herself hath gone to Old Windsor, to the bedmakers there, to beg a mess of milk, which she could not have for that the maid was then milking, but her rat had provided for her both milk and cream against her coming home.

23. Elizabeth Stile, touched with more remorse, saith that Mother Dutten and Mother Devell were her first enticers to folly; and that she and every of them did meet sometimes in Master Dodge's pits, and sometime about eleven of the clock in the night at the pound, and that Mother Dutten and Mother Devell did persuade her to do as they had done in forsaking God and His works and giving herself to the devil.

24. Elizabeth Stile confesseth herself often times to have gone to Father Rosimond's house, where she found him sitting in a wood not far from thence, under the body of a tree, sometimes in the shape of an ape and otherwhiles like an horse. She also confesseth her-

self to have turned a child's hand in Windsor clean backwards, which was returned to the right place by Mother Dutten.

25. Further she saith, that she will stand unto her death to all and every article before rehearsed, and that Father Rosimond can transform himself into the likeness of an ape or a horse, and that he can help any man so bewitched to his health again, as well as to bewitch.

26. Further she saith, that Mother Seder dwelling in the almshouse was the mistress witch of all the rest, and she is now dead.

27. Further she saith, that if she had been so disposed, four or five or more of the best men in Windsor should not have brought her to the jail, but that she came of her own accord; and by the way as she came with John Brame, who brought her to the jail, her Bun or familiar came to her in the likeness of a black cat and would have had her away, but she banished him, hoping for favour.

Memorandum, that besides the examination and confession aforesaid, there was given in evidence viva voce at the arraignment of the said witches, one special matter by an ostler of Windsor, who affirmeth upon his oath that the said Mother Stile, using to come to his master's house, had oftentimes relief given her by him. And on a time not long since she coming to his master's house when there was little left to be given her, for that she came somewhat late, yet he giving her also somewhat at that time, she therewith not contented went her ways in some anger and, as it seemed, offended with the said ostler for that she had no better alms; and by the sequel, so it appeared.

For not long after, he had a great ache in his limbs that he was not able to take any rest nor to do any labour, and having sought many means for remedy thereof, could find none. At the last he went to a wiseman, named Father Rosimond, alias Osborne, who told him that he was bewitched and that there was many ill women in Windsor, and asked him whom he did mistrust, and the said ostler answered 'One Mother Stile,' one of the witches aforesaid. 'Well,' said the wiseman, 'if you can meet her, and all to-scratch her so that you draw blood of her, you shall presently mend.' And the said ostler upon his oath declared that he watching her on a time did all to-scratch her by the face, that he made the blood come after, and presently his pain went away so that he hath been no more

grieved since.

Moreover, on a time a man's son of Windsor coming to fetch water at a well which was by the door of the said Mother Stile, and by chance hurling a stone upon her house, she was therewithal much grieved, and said 'she would be even with him', and took his pitcher which he had brought from him. The boy, coming homewards, happened to meet with his father, and told him how that Mother Stile had taken away his pitcher from him.

'Well,' said his father 'you have done her some unhappiness; come on with me and I will go speak with her.' And so the boy going with his father towards her house did suddenly cry out 'Oh, my hand, my hand!' His father therewithal looking back and seeing his son's hand to turn and wend backwards, laid hold thereupon, but he was not able to stay the turning thereof. Besides, a neighbour of his being in his company at that time did also lay hold thereon, and notwithstanding both their strengths, the child's hand did turn backwards, and the palm thereof did stand where the back did, to the grievous torment of the said child and vexation of his father. The which hand was turned again to his right place either by the said Father Rosimond or the said Mother Devell.

Also this is not to be forgotten, that the said Mother Stile, being at the time of her apprehension so well in health of body and limbs that she was able, and did, go on foot from Windsor unto Reading unto the jail, which are twelve miles distant; shortly after that she had made the aforesaid confession, the other witches were apprehended and were brought to the said jail, [where] the said Mother Devell did so bewitch her and others (as she confessed unto the jailer) with her enchantments, that the use of all her limbs and senses were taken quite from her, and her toes did rot off her feet, and she was laid upon a barrow, as a most ugly creature to behold, and so brought before the judges at such time as she was arraigned.

Finis.

FOCUS QUESTIONS:

1. Why do you think Father Rosimond escaped punishment? What does that say about who was or wasn't punished in similar trials?

CONTACT AND CONQUEST, 1500-1700

2-1 The Trial of Anne Hutchinson (1638)

Anne Hutchinson, the articulate and resolute wife of a prominent New England merchant, was placed on trial before the General Court in 1637 for challenging the authority of the ministry and promoting individualism—provocative issues in Puritan society. During the first two days of examination she defended her position well, frustrating the best efforts of Governor Winthrop and others to convict her. Finally, her claim of direct divine inspiration brought her a conviction on the grounds of blasphemy. She was banished from the colony in 1638.

Source: The American Colonist's Library, Primary Source Documents Pertaining to Early American History, http://personal.pitnet.net/primarysources/hutchinson.html

MR. [JOHN] WINTHROP, GOVERNOR: Mrs Hutchinson, you are called here as one of those that have troubled the peace of the commonwealth and the churches here; you are known to be a woman that hath had a great share in the promoting and divulging of those opinions that are the cause of this trouble, and to be nearly joined not only in affinity and affection with some of those the court had taken notice of and passed censure upon, but you have spoken diverse things, as we have been informed, very prejudicial to the honour of the churches and ministers thereof, and you have maintained a meeting and an assembly in your house that hath been condemned by the general assembly as a thing not tolerable nor comely in the sight of God nor fitting for your sex, and notwithstanding that was cried down you have continued the same. Therefore we have thought good to send for you to understand how things are, that if you be in an erroneous way we may reduce you that so you may become a profitable member here among us. Otherwise if you be obstinate in your course that then the court may take such course that you may trouble us no further. Therefore I would intreat you to express whether you do assent and hold in practice to those opinions and factions that have been handled in court already, that is to say, whether you do not justify Mr. Wheelwright's sermon and the petition.

MRS. HUTCHINSON: I am called here to answer before you but I hear no things laid to my charge.

GOV.: I have told you some already and more I can tell you.

MRS. H.: Name one, Sir.

GOV.: Have I not named some already?

MRS. H.: What have I said or done?

GOV.: Why for your doings, this you did harbor and countenance those that are parties in this faction that you have heard of.

MRS. H.: That's matter of conscience, Sir.

GOV.: Your conscience you must keep, or it must be kept for you.

MRS. H.: Must not I then entertain the saints because I must keep my conscience.

GOV.: Say that one brother should commit felony or treason and come to his brother's house, if he knows him guilty and conceals him he is guilty of the same. It is his conscience to entertain him, but if his conscience comes into act in giving countenance and entertainment to him that hath broken the law he is guilty too. So if you do countenance those that are transgressors of the law you are in the same fact.

MRS. H.: What law do they transgress?

GOV.: The law of God and of the state.

MRS. H.: In what particular?

GOV.: Why in this among the rest, whereas the Lord doth say honour thy father and thy mother.

MRS. H.: Ey Sir in the Lord.

GOV.: This honour you have broke in giving countenance to them.

MRS. H.: In entertaining those did I entertain them against any act (for there is the thing) or what God has appointed?

GOV.: You knew that Mr. Wheelwright did preach this sermon and those that countenance him in this do break a law.

MRS. H.: What law have I broken?

GOV.: Why the fifth commandment.

MRS. H.: I deny that for he [Mr. Wheelwright] saith in the Lord.

GOV.: You have joined with them in the faction.

MRS. H.: In what faction have I joined with them?

GOV.: In presenting the petition.

MRS. H.: Suppose I had set my hand to the petition. What then?

GOV.: You saw that case tried before.

MRS. H.: But I had not my hand to [not signed] the petition.

GOV.: You have councelled them.

MRS. H.: Wherein?

GOV.: Why in entertaining them.

MRS. H.: What breach of law is that, Sir?

GOV.: Why dishonouring the commonwealth.

MRS. H.: But put the case, Sir, that I do fear the Lord and my parents. May not I entertain them that fear the Lord because my parents will not give me leave?

GOV.: If they be the fathers of the commonwealth, and they of another religion, if you entertain them then you dishonour your parents and are justly punishable.

MRS. H.: If I entertain them, as they have dishonoured their parents I do.

GOV.: No but you by countenancing them above others put honor upon them.

MRS. H.: I may put honor upon them as the children of God and as they do honor the Lord.

GOV.: We do not mean to discourse with those of your sex but only this: you so adhere unto them and do endeavor to set forward this faction and so you do dishonour us.

MRS. H.: I do acknowledge no such thing. Neither do I think that I ever put any dishonour upon you.

GOV.: Why do you keep such a meeting at your house as you do every week upon a set day?

MRS. H.: It is lawful for me to do so, as it is all your practices, and can you find a warrant for yourself and condemn me for the same thing? The ground of my taking it up was, when I first came to this land because I did not go to such meetings as those were, it was presently reported that I did not allow of such meetings but held them unlawful and therefore in that regard they said I was proud and did despise all ordinances. Upon that a friend came unto me and told me of it and I to prevent such aspersions took it up, but it was in practice before I came. Therefore I was not the first.

GOV.: . . . By what warrant do you continue such a course?

MRS. H.: I conceive there lies a clear rule in Titus that the elder women should instruct the younger and then I must have a time wherein I must do it.

GOV.: All this I grant you, I grant you a time for it, but what is this to the purpose that you Mrs. Hutchinson must call a company together from their callings to come to be taught of you? . . .

MRS. H.: If you look upon the rule in Titus it is a rule to me. If you convince me that it is no rule I shall yield.

GOV.: You know that there is no rule that crosses another, but this rule crosses that in the Corinthians. But you must take it in this sense that elder women must instruct the younger about their business and to love their husbands and not to make them to clash . . .

MRS. H.: Will it please you to answer me this and to give me a rule for then I will willingly submit to any truth. If any come to my house to be instructed in the ways of God what rule have I to put them away? . . . . Do you think it not lawful for me to teach women and why do you call me to teach the court?

GOV.: We do not call you to teach the court but to lay open yourself. . . .

[They continue to argue over what rule she had broken]

GOV.: Your course is not to be suffered for. Besides that we find such a course as this to be greatly prejudicial to the state. Besides the occasion that it is to seduce many honest persons that are called to those meetings and your opinions and your opinions being known to be different from the word of God may seduce many simple souls that resort unto you. Besides that the occasion which hath come of late hath come from none but such as have frequented your meetings, so that now they are flown off from magistrates and ministers and since they have come to you. And besides that it will not well stand with the commonwealth that families should be neglected for so many neighbors and dames and so much time spent. We see no rule of God for this. We see not that any should have authority to set up any other exercises besides what authority hath already set up and so what hurt comes of this you will be guilty of and we for suffering you.

MRS. H.: Sir, I do not believe that to be so.

GOV.: Well, we see how it is. We must therefore put it away from you or restrain you from maintaining this course.

MRS. H. If you have a rule for it from God's word you may.

GOV.: We are your judges, and not you ours and we must compel you to it.

MRS. H.: If it please you by authority to put it down I will freely let you for I am subject to your authority.. . .

DEPUTY GOVERNOR, THOMAS DUDLEY: I would go a little higher with Mrs. Hutchinson. About three years ago we were all in peace. Mrs Hutchinson, from that time she came hath made a disturbance, and some that came over with her in the ship did inform me what she was as soon as she was landed. I being then in place dealt with the pastor and teacher of Boston and desired them to enquire of her, and then I was satisfied that she held nothing different from us. But within half a year after, she had vented divers of her strange opinions and had made parties in the country, and at length it comes that Mr. Cotton and Mr. Vane were of her judgment, but Mr. Cotton had cleared himself that he was not of that mind. But now it appears by this woman's meeting that Mrs. Hutchinson hath so forestalled the minds of many by their resort to her meeting that now she hath a potent party in the country. Now if all these things have endangered us as from that foundation and if she in particular hath disparaged all our ministers in the land that they have preached a covenant of works, and only Mr. Cotton a covenant of grace, why this is not to be suffered, and therefore being driven to the foundation and it being found that Mrs. Hutchinson is she that hath depraved all the ministers and hath been the cause of what is fallen out, why we must take away the foundation and the building will fall.

MRS. H.: I pray, Sir, prove it that I said they preached nothing but a covenant of works.

DEP. GOV.: Nothing but a covenant of works. Why a Jesuit may preach truth sometimes.

MRS. H.: Did I ever say they preached a covenant of works then?

DEP. GOV.: If they do not preach a covenant of grace clearly, then they preach a covenant of works.

MRS. H.: No, Sir. One may preach a covenant of grace more clearly than another, so I said. . . .

DEP. GOV.: When they do preach a covenant of works do they preach truth?

MRS. H.: Yes, Sir. But when they preach a covenant of works for salvation, that is not truth.

DEP. GOV.: I do but ask you this: when the ministers do preach a covenant of works do they preach a way of salvation?

MRS. H.: I did not come hither to answer questions of that sort.

DEP. GOV.: Because you will deny the thing.

MRS. H.: Ey, but that is to be proved first.

DEP. GOV.: I will make it plain that you did say that the ministers did preach a covenant of works.

MRS. H.: I deny that.

DEP. GOV.: And that you said they were not able ministers of the New Testament, but Mr. Cotton only.

MRS. H.: If ever I spake that I proved it by God's word.

COURT: Very well, very well.

MRS. H.: If one shall come unto me in private, and desire me seriously to tell them what I thought of such an one, I must either speak false or true in my answer.

DEP. GOV.: Likewise I will prove this that you said the gospel in the letter and words holds forth nothing but a covenant of works and that all that do not hold as you do are in a covenant of works . . .

MRS. H.: I deny this for if I should so say I should speak against my own judgment. . . .

MR. HUGH PETERS: That which concerns us to speak unto, as yet we are sparing in, unless the court command us to speak, then we shall answer to Mrs. Hutchinson notwithstanding our brethren are very unwilling to answer. [The Governor says to do so. Six ministers then testify to the particular charges and that she was "not only difficult in her opinions, but also of an intemperate spirit"]

MR. HUGH PETERS: . . . . [I asked her] What difference do you conceive to be between your teacher and us?...

Briefly, she told me there was a wide and broad difference. . . . He preaches the covenant of grace and you the covenant of works, and that you are not able ministers of the New Testament and know no more than the apostles did before the resurrection of Christ. I did then put it to her, What do you conceive of such a brother? She answered he had not the seal of the spirit.

MRS. H.: If our pastor would shew his writings you should see what I said, and that many things are not so as is reported.

MR. WILSON: . . . what is written [here now] I will avouch.

MR. WELD: [agrees that Peters related Hutchinson's words accurately]

MR. PHILLIPS: [agrees that Peters related Hutchinson's words accurately and added] Then I asked her of myself (being she spake rashly of them all) because she never heard me at all. She likewise said that we were not able ministers of the New Testament and her reason was because we were not sealed.

MR. SIMMES: Agrees that Peters related Hutchinson's words accurately

MR. SHEPHARD: Also to Same.

MR. ELIOT: [agrees that Peters related Hutchinson's words accurately]

DEP. GOV.: I called these witnesses and you deny them. You see they have proved this and you deny this, but it is clear. You say they preached a covenant of works and that they were not able ministers of the New Testament; now there are two other things that you did affirm which were that the scriptures in the letter of them held forth nothing but a covenant of works and likewise that those that were under a covenant of works cannot be saved.

MRS. H.: Prove that I said so.

GOV.: Did you say so?

MRS. H.: No, Sir, it is your conclusion.

DEP. GOV.: What do I do charging of you if you deny what is so fully proved?

GOV.: Here are six undeniable ministers who say it is true and yet you deny that you did say that they preach a covenant of works and that they were not able ministers of the gospel, and it appears plainly that you have spoken it, and whereas you say that it was drawn from you in a way of friendship, you did profess then that it was out of conscience that you spake . . .

MRS. H.: . . . . They thought that I did conceive there was a difference between them and Mr. Cotton. . . . I might say they might preach a covenant of works as did the apostles, but to preach a covenant of works and to be under a covenant of works is another business.

DEP. GOV.: There have been six witnesses to prove this and yet you deny it. [and then he mentions a seventh, Mr. Nathaniel Ward]

MRS. H.: I acknowledge using the words of the apostle to the Corinthians unto him, [Mr. Ward] that they that were ministers of the letter and not the spirit did preach a covenant of works.

GOV.: Mrs. Hutchinson, the court you see hath laboured to bring you to acknowledge the error of your way that so you might be reduced, the time grows late, we shall therefore give you a little more time to consider of it and therefore desire that you attend the court again in the morning. [The next morning]

GOV.: We proceeded . . . as far as we could . . . There were divers things laid to her charge: her ordinary meetings about religious exercises, her speeches in derogation of the ministers among us, and the weakening of the hands and hearts of the people towards them. Here was sufficient proof made of that which she was accused of, in that point concerning the ministers and their ministry, as that they did preach a covenant of works when others did preach a covenant of grace, and that they were not able ministers of the New Testament, and that they had not the seal of the spirit, and this was spoken not as was pretended out of private conference, but out of conscience and warrant from scripture alleged the fear of man is a snare and seeing God had given her a calling to it she would freely speak. Some other speeches she used, as that the letter of the scripture held forth a covenant of works, and this is offered to be proved by probable grounds. ... Controversy—should the witnesses should be recalled and made swear an oath, as Mrs. Hutchinson desired, is resolved against doing so.

GOV.: I see no necessity of an oath in this thing seeing it is true and the substance of the matter confirmed by divers, yet that all may be satisfied, if the elders will take an oath they shall have it given them . . .

MRS. H.: After that they have taken an oath I will make good what I say.

GOV.: Let us state the case, and then we may know what to do. That which is laid to Mrs. Hutchinson charge is that, that she hath traduced the magistrates and ministers of this jurisdiction, that she hath said the ministers preached a covenant of works and Mr.

Cotton a covenant of grace, and that they were not able ministers of the gospel, and she excuses it that she made it a private conference and with a promise of secrecy, &c. Now this is charged upon her, and they therefore sent for her seeing she made it her table talk, and then she said the fear of man was a snare and therefore she would not be affeared of them . . .

DEP. GOV.: Let her witnesses be called.

GOV.: Who be they?

MRS. H.: Mr. Leveret and our teacher and Mr. Coggeshall.

GOV.: Mr. Coggeshall was not present.

MR. COGGESHALL: Yes, but I was. Only I desired to be silent till I should be called.

GOV.: Will you, Mr. Coggeshall, say that she did not say so?

MR. COGGESHALL: Yes, I dare say that she did not say all that which they lay against her.

MR. PETERS: How dare you look into the court to say such a word?

MR. COGGESHALL: Mr. Peters takes upon him to forbid me. I shall be silent.

MR. STOUGHTON [ASSISTANT OF THE COURT]: Ey, but she intended this that they say.

GOV.: Well, Mr. Leveret, what were the words? I pray, speak.

MR. LEVERET: To my best remembrance when the elders did send for her, Mr. Peters did with much vehemency and intreaty urge her to tell what difference there was between Mr. Cotton and them, and upon his urging of her she said "The fear of man is a snare, but they that trust upon the Lord shall be safe." And being asked wherein the difference was, she answered that they did not preach a covenant of grace so clearly as Mr. Cotton did, and she gave this reason of it: because that as the apostles were for a time without the spirit so until they had received the witness of the spirit they could not preach a covenant of grace so clearly.

GOV.: Don't you remember that she said they were not able ministers of the New Testament?

MRS. H.: Mr. Weld and I had an hour's discourse at the window and then I spake that, if I spake it.. . .

GOV.: Mr Cotton, the court desires that you declare what you do remember of the conference which was at the time and is now in question.

MR. COTTON: I did not think I should be called to bear witness in this cause and therefore did not labor to call to remembrance what was done; but the greatest passage that took impression upon me was to this purpose. The elders spake that they had heard that she had spoken some condemning words of their ministry, and among other things they did first pray her to answer wherein she thought their ministry did differ from mine. How the comparison sprang I am ignorant, but sorry I was that any comparison should be between me and my brethren and uncomfortable it was. She told them to this purpose that they did not hold forth a covenant of grace as I did. But wherein did we differ? Why she said that they did not hold forth the seal of the spirit as he doth. Where is the difference there? Say they, why saith she, speaking to one or other of them, I know not to whom. You preach of the seal of the spirit upon a work and he upon free grace without a work or without respect to a work; he preaches the seal of the spirit upon free grace and you upon a work. I told her I was very sorry that she put comparisons between my ministry and theirs, for she had said more than I could myself, and rather I had that she had put us in fellowship with them and not have made that discrepancy. She said she found the difference . . .

This was the sum of the difference, nor did it seem to be so ill taken as it is and our brethren did say also that they would not so easily believe reports as they had done and withal mentioned that they would speak no more of it, some of them did; and afterwards some of them did say they were less satisfied than before. And I must say that I did not find her saying that they were under a covenant of works, nor that she said they did preach a covenant of works. [more back and forth between Rev. John Cotton, trying to defend Mrs. Hutchinson, and Mr. Peters, about exactly what Mrs. Hutchinson said]

MRS. H.: If you please to give me leave I shall give you the ground of what I know to be true. Being much troubled to see the falseness of the constitution of the Church of England, I had like to have turned Separatist. Whereupon I kept a day of solemn humiliation and pondering of the thing; this scripture was brought unto me—he that denies Jesus Christ to be come in the flesh is antichrist. This I considered of and in considering found that the papists did not deny him to be come in the flesh, nor we did not deny him—who then was antichrist? Was the Turk antichrist only? The Lord knows that I could not open scripture; he must by his prophetical office open it unto me. So after that being unsatisfied in the thing, the Lord was pleased to bring this scripture out of the Hebrews. he that denies the testament denies the testator, and in this did open unto me and give me to see that those which did not teach the new covenant had the spirit of antichrist, and upon this he did discover the ministry unto me; and ever since, I bless the Lord, he hath let me see which was the clear ministry and which the wrong. Since that time I confess I have been more choice and he hath left me to distinguish between the voice of my beloved and the voice of Moses, the voice of John the Baptist and the voice of antichrist, for all those voices are spoken of in scripture. Now if you do condemn me for speaking what in my conscience I know to be truth I must commit myself unto the Lord.

MR. NOWEL [ASSISTANT TO THE COURT]: How do you know that was the spirit?

MRS. H.: How did Abraham know that it was God that bid him offer his son, being a breach of the sixth commandment?

DEP. GOV.: By an immediate voice.

MRS. H.: So to me by an immediate revelation.

DEP. GOV.: How! an immediate revelation.

MRS. H.: By the voice of his own spirit to my soul. I will give you another scripture, Jer[emiah] 46: 27–28—out of which the Lord showed me what he would do for me and the rest of his servants. But after he was pleased to reveal himself to me I did presently, like Abraham, run to Hagar. And after that he did let me see the atheism of my own heart, for which I begged of the Lord that it might not remain in my heart, and being thus, he did show me this (a twelvemonth after) which I told you of before.... Therefore, I desire you to look to it, for you see this scripture fulfilled this day and therefore I desire you as you tender the Lord and the church and commonwealth to consider and look what you do. You have power over my body but the Lord Jesus hath power over my body and soul; and assure yourselves thus much, you do as much as in you lies to put the Lord Jesus Christ from you, and if you go on in this course you begin, you will bring a curse upon you and your posterity, and the mouth of the Lord hath spoken it.

DEP. GOV.: What is the scripture she brings?

MR. STOUGHTON [ASSISTANT TO THE COURT]: Behold I turn away from you.

MRS. H.: But now having seen him which is invisible I fear not what man can do unto me.

GOV.: Daniel was delivered by miracle; do you think to be deliver'd so too?

MRS. H.: I do here speak it before the court. I look that the Lord kshould deliver me by his providence.. . . [because God had said to her] though I should meet with affliction, yet I am the same God that delivered Daniel out of the lion's den, I will also deliver thee.

MR. HARLAKENDEN [ASSISTANT TO THE COURT]: I may read scripture and the most glorious hypocrite may read them and yet go down to hell.

MRS. H.: It may be so.. . .

GOV.: I am persuaded that the revelation she brings forth is delusion.

[The trial text here reads:] All the court but some two or three ministers cry out, we all believe it—we all believe it. [Mrs. Hutchinson was found guilty]

GOV.: The court hath already declared themselves satisfied concerning the things you hear, and concerning the troublesomeness of her spirit and the danger of her course amongst us, which is not to be suffered. Therefore if it be the mind of the court that Mrs. Hutchinson for these things that appear before us is unfit for our society, and if it be the mind of the court that she shall be banished out of our liberties and imprisoned till she be sent away, let them hold up their hands. [All but three did so]

GOV.: Mrs. Hutchinson, the sentence of the court you hear is that you are banished from out of our jurisdiction as being a woman not fit for our society, and are to be imprisoned till the court shall send you away.

MRS. H.: I desire to know wherefore I am banished?

GOV.: Say no more. The court knows wherefore and is satisfied.

FOCUS QUESTIONS:

1. How was Anne Hutchinson able to frustrate the best efforts of the court to find her guilty during the early stages of the trial?

2. Aggravating the situation at the General Court was the fact that the authority of the ministry was being challenged by a woman. How do you think other women of similar status in New England society viewed Anne Hutchinson? Was she inspirational or foolish?

3. To what extent is this trial about gender? In your interpretation, what were Hutchinson's most serious offenses?

2-2 Juan Sanz De Lezaún, "An Account of Lamentable Happenings in New Mexico."

In this document, DeLezaún, a Franciscan missionary, recounts two events—the attack by a group of Comanches on a small town leading to the deaths of a girl and an old woman, and an uprising caused by the death of a Zuma Indian caught stealing corn.

Source: In *Historical Documents Relating to New Mexico, Nueva Viscaya and Approaches Thereto.* Charles Wilson Hackett et al, editors. Washington, D.C.: Carnegie Institution, 1923, 476-477.

An account of lamentable happenings in New Mexico, and of losses experienced daily in affairs spiritual and temporal; written by Reverend Father Fray Juan Sanz de Lezaún, in the year 1760

. . . The fathers receive no credit whatever for their service to God or to our king. Evidence of this is the invasion of the enemy into the town of Habiquiú in August 1747, when they carried off twenty-three women and children, besides killing a girl and an old woman for having defended themselves. Reverend Mirabel, who was custodian and lived in the mission of San Juan, immediately reported this to the governor, who at the time was Don Joaquín Codallos. The governor paid no attention until the reverend father, moved by the unrest of all his neighbors, again wrote, and, as the affair was now public knowledge in the entire kingdom, the governor gave orders after four days, and they went out in pursuit of the enemy, but accomplished nothing because the latter had had plenty of time to get ahead of them. A few settlers went out to follow their trail and found three women dead and a new-born child; the rest had all been carried off. One of them was brought back at the end of seven years by the Comanches, they having been the ones responsible for this misdeed, while the poor heathen Yutas paid for it. At the time when they brought this woman the governor was Don Tomás Vélez Cachupín. This being the situation, what can the poor religious do about it all, burdened as they are with sorrows, unable to defend any one, and seeing so many souls lost without being able to find a means of proving all these things?

****

In El Paso del Rio del Norte, in the year 1752, the captain ordered a Zuma Indian killed on account of five ears of corn. The Indian had been his weekly servant, and on the day when he finished his week he was carrying the ears away tied up in his blanket. A servant of the captain seeing the bundle went to feel of it; the Indian, fearing that they would whip him, threw off his blanket and started to run. The sergeant, some soldiers, and some settlers followed him, and he took refuge on a little hill back of the mission of El Paso. They got him to come down by trickery, tied him, and the sergeant ordered the soldiers to beat him. The miserable Indian cried out saying he was a Christian, and they should allow him to confess, and that they should call the white missionary father from El Paso. This was denied him; but the soldiers were unwilling to obey the sergeant, so he commanded a settler to shoot the Indian, which the perverse fellow did. After the miserable Indian was dead, the sergeant ordered him hung up on a plain, where he stayed until the fathers came to take the body down and give it sepulture.

From this occurrence came the uprising of the Zumas, concerning which all the residents of El Paso can give full information. Very serious losses resulted from this uprising. The Zumas united with the Apaches, and they harried all the roads with armed bands which could not be exterminated. Let the people of New Mexico tell how, on their return to their houses, having stopped near the hacienda of Ojo Caliente, they were fallen upon by the Zumas so suddenly that they did not even have time to take up their arms; but, leaving all their loads and their mules, had to take refuge in the house. The Zumas carried off all the mule and horse droves, the bales of clothing, and many other things which they were taking for their houses. The Spaniards were all left afoot, though some received relief in the form of assistance from El Paso.

FOCUS QUESTIONS:

1. What does the first passage tell you about the Comanche attitude toward women and children? Why would they take some and kill others?

2. Compare the reaction of Codallos in the first passage to the reaction of the captain in the second passage. Is there an implicit statement about the value of women vs. the value of material goods?

3. What is the position of de Lezaún? How does he view these events?

2-3 Experience Mayhew Describes the Pious Wampanoag Women of Martha's Vineyard (1727)

This description of Wampanoag women by a white colonist gives us insight into both cultures.

Source: In *Major Problems in American Women's History.* 2ⁿᵈ edition. Mary Beth Norton and Ruth M. Alexander, editors. Lexington, MA: D.C. Heath and Company, 1996, 23-24.

The number of Women truly fearing God, has by some been thought to exceed that of Men so doing; but whether the Observation will generally hold true or not, I shall not now inquire. However, it seems to be a Truth with respect to our Indians, so far as my Knowledge of them extends, that there have been, and are a greater number of their Women appearing pious than of the Men among them ....

[Rebeccah Sissetom] appeared sober, and well disposed from her very Childhood, was obedient to her Parents, and not so much given to Vanity as most Children are.

Having been taught to read while she was young, she appeared to delight in her Book. She seemed also to delight in going to Meetings; and, being about ten Years old when her Mother was admitted to full Communion in the Church of Christ, she her self manifested a Desire of being baptized before the same was proposed to her, and was accordingly admitted to the Privilege, being first examined, and found to understand the Nature of the baptismal Covenant, as well as willing to give her Consent to it.

After this she frequently discoursed of the things of God and another Life, and this in such a manner as shewed a becoming Seriousness, and manifested a Desire of obtaining that Knowledge which is necessary to Salvation, and also a great Concern that she might not fall short of eternal Life ....

[Hannah Nohnosoo] join'd early to the Church already mentioned, and was a Member of it in full Communion, I suppose, at least forty Years before she died; in all which time, I cannot learn that she was ever guilty of any scandalous Evil whatsoever, but constantly behav'd her self as became a good Christian, so as to adorn the Doctrine of God her Saviour in all things.

She was really, and not by Profession only, a praying Woman, praying always when there were proper Occasions for it; as in her own Family when she was a Widow and her Children lived with her; and afterwards in the Houses wherein she lived with others, when there were none present for whom it might be more proper. And she always manifested a Love and Zeal for the House and Ordinances of God, not in her Discourses only, but in her constant and serious Attendance on them ....

Having very considerable Skill in some of the Distempers to which human Bodies are subject, and in the Nature of many of those Herbs and Plants which were proper Remedies against them, she often did good by her Medicines among her Neighbours, especially the poorer sort of them, whom she readily served without asking them any thing for what she did for them .... Several Women, some English and some Indians, being divers Years after Marriage without the Blessing of Children, having barren Wombs and dry Breasts, which Persons in a married State are scarce ever pleased with, some of these Women applying themselves to the good old Hannah of whom I am now speaking, for help in Case that thus afflicted them, have soon after become joyful Mothers of Children; for which Comfort, under God, they have been oblig'd to her. ...

[Jerusha Ompan] seemed to have the Fear of God in her Heart, while she was but a young Girl, was very dutiful to her Parents, and was not known to be given to any Vice. She never much affected going to Huskings and Weddings, and if at any time she went to them, she would be sure to come home seasonably, not tarrying too long, as the Generality of Persons did ....

She was about 29 Years old before she dy'd; and tho she had had some Offers of Marriage made to her, yet she would accept none of them, alledging to her Friends as the reason of her Refusal, that of the Apostle in the first Epistle to the Corinthians, Chap. vii. The unmarried Woman careth for the Things of the Lord, &c ....

[Hannah Tiler] was as bad by Nature as any others, so the former part of her Life was no better ordered than the Lives of Persons in a State of Nature generally be .... [Her husband] lived but viciously before he married her, and continued so to do for some Years afterward. He would frequently have his drunken Fits...

But the Woman being at length convinced of the great Evil there is in the Sin of Drunkenness, resolved that she would forsake it, and God helped her so to do; so that she overcame her Temptations to that Vice, and lived in that regard very temperately: but being her self in that Particular reformed, and Drunkenness now becoming exceeding offensive to her, she could not bear with it in others, and therefore could not forbear talking too angrily to her Husband when she saw him guilty of that Crime; and this was an Occasion of sore Contentions betwixt them ....

Being thus reform'd in her Life, she made a publick Profession of Religion, and joined her self to the Church of Christ about nine or ten Years before that wherein she died; during all which time, she walked, as far as I can understand, very blamelessly, ordering her Conversation as did become the Gospel. ...

Accordingly she, after some time, did so far overcome his Evil by her Goodness, that he carried himself more kindly to her than formerly he had done; and appeared to become religious, took some care about the Instruction of his Children, and made a publick Profession of Faith and Repentance, joining himself to the Church of Christ. ...

FOCUS QUESTIONS:

1. What does Prudence Mayhew find most praiseworthy and most reprehensible about the women she describes?

2. Hannah Tiler is described as being in a "State of Nature". What does Mayhew mean by this?

3. What do you infer is Mayhew's main purpose in writing about these women? Is her purpose to teach, to condemn, or something else?

2-4 Native Women Resist the Jesuits (1640)

This passage describes the conversion of Native American women to Christianity. This brief document provides a glimpse of a moment in time, and informs us of the gendered nature of this three-way interaction, between the Christian fathers, and the Native American men and women. Although the passage is short, much can be gleaned about the shifting relationships within Native American society.

Source: In *Countering Colonization: Native American Women and Great Lakes Missions, 1630-1900.* by Carol Devens. Berkeley: University of California Press, 1992, 22.

They [Native American men] resolved to call together the women, to urge them to be instructed and to receive holy Baptism. Accordingly, they were brought together, and the young people also. The best of it was that they preached to them so well that the following day some of these poor women, encountering Father de Quen, said to him, "Where is such a Father? we have come to beg him to baptize us. Yesterday the men summoned us to a Council, the first time that women have ever entered one; but they treated us so rudely that we were greatly astonished.'It is you women,'they said to us,'who are the cause of all our misfortunes, - it is you who keep the demons among us. You do not urge to be baptized; you must not be satisfied to ask this favor only once from the Fathers, you must importune them. You are lazy about going to prayers; when you pass before the cross, you never salute it; you wish to be independent. Now know that you will obey your husbands; and you young people, you will obey your parents and our Captains; and, if any fail to do so, we have concluded to give them nothing to eat.'" This is a part of the sermon of these new Preachers, who, in my opinion, are so much the more wonderful as they are new and very far removed from the Savage methods of action. I believe, indeed, that they will not all at once enter into this great submissiveness that they promise themselves; but it will be in this point as in others, they will embrace it little by little. A young woman having fled, shortly after these elections, into the woods, not wishing to obey her husband, the Captains had her searched for, and came to ask us, if, having found her, it would not be well to chain her by one foot; and if it would be enough to make her pass four days and four nights without eating, as penance for her fault.

FOCUS QUESTIONS:

1. What was the role of the three parties in these events?

2. What kinds of changes are reflected in this excerpt?

2-5 Father Le Jeune on the Importance of Native American Women (1633)

Like the previous source, this one also views Native American women through the eyes of a Christian missionary. Again, the main concern is conversion and baptism, so that our perspective of these events is necessarily narrow.

Source: In *Major Problems in American Women's History.* 2nd edition. Mary Beth Norton and Ruth M. Alexander, editors. Lexington, MA: D.C. Heath and Company, 1996, 21.

I see that it is absolutely necessary to teach the girls as well as the boys, and that we shall do nothing or very little, unless some good household has the care of this sex; for the boys that we shall have reared in the knowledge of God, when they marry Savage girls or women accustomed' to wandering in the woods, will, as their husbands, be compelled to follow them and thus fall back into barbarism, or to leave them, another evil full of danger.

On the first day of April, the Captain of the Algonquains came to see us.

. . . I asked him if he had a son, and if he would not give him to us to be educated. He asked me how many children I wanted, and [said] that I already had two. I told him that in time I should perhaps feed twenty. He was astonished. "Wilt thou clothe so many as well?" asked he. I answered him that we would not take them until we had the means to clothe them. He replied that he would be very glad to give us his son, but that his wife did not wish to do so. The women have great power here. A man may promise you something, and, if he does not keep his promise, he thinks he is sufficiently excused when he tells you that. his wife did not wish to do it. I told him then that he was the master, and that in France women do not rule their husbands.

FOCUS QUESTIONS:

1. In primary sources such as this one, our information is highly colored by the perspective of the writer. In such cases, sources may tell us much more about the author than the subject. What cultural assumptions affect the author's understanding of the culture he describes?

2. As in the previous source, a three-way struggle is involved here. Why do you think this conflict results in missionaries and American men allied against Native American women?

2-6 Benjamin Wadsworth, A Well-Ordered Family (1712)

Benjamin Wadsworth was a Harvard-trained minister who published various sermons and essays throughout his lifetime. He is perhaps most famous for his tenure as Harvard's president from 1725 until his death in 1737. He was apparently considered a better minister than college president. The excerpt below gives us a glimpse, though probably idealized, of marital relations in New England in the early 18th century.

Christians should endeavor to please and glorify God, in whatever capacity or relation they sustain.

Under this doctrine, my design is (by God's help) to say something about relative duties, particularly in families. I shall therefore endeavor to speak as briefly and plainly as I can about: (1) family prayer; (2) the duties of husbands and wives; (3) the duties of parents and children; (4) the duties of masters and servants. . . .

About the Duties of Husbands and Wives

Concerning the duties of this relation we may assert a few things. It is their duty to dwell together with one another. Surely they should dwell together; if one house cannot hold them, surely they are not affected to each other as they should be. They should have a very great and tender love and affection to one another. This is plainly commanded by God. This duty of love is mutual; it should be performed by each, to each of them. When, therefore, they quarrel or disagree, then they do the Devil's work; he is pleased at it, glad of it. But such contention provokes God; it dishonors Him; it is a vile example before inferiors in the family; it tends to prevent family prayer.

As to outward things. If the one is sick, troubled, or distressed, the other should manifest care, tenderness, pity, and compassion, and afford all possible relief and succor. They should likewise unite their prudent counsels and endeavors, comfortably to maintain themselves and the family under their joint care.

Husband and wife should be patient one toward another. If both are truly pious, yet neither of them is perfectly holy, in such cases a patient, forgiving, forbearing spirit is very needful. . . .

The husband's government ought to be gentle and

easy, and the wife's obedience ready and cheerful. The husband is called the head of the woman. It belongs to the head to rule and govern. Wives are part of the house and family, and ought to be under the husband's government. Yet his government should not be with rigor, haughtiness, harshness, severity, but with the greatest love, gentleness, kindness, tenderness that may be. Though he governs her, he must not treat her as a servant, but as his own flesh; he must love her as himself.

Those husbands are much to blame who do not carry it lovingly and kindly to their wives. O man, if your wife is not so young, beautiful, healthy, well-tempered, and qualified as you would wish; if she did not bring a large estate to you, or cannot do so much for you, as some other women have done for their husbands; yet she is your wife, and the great God commands you to love her, not be bitter, but kind to her. What can be more plain and expressive than that?

Those wives are much to blame who do not carry it lovingly and obediently to their own husbands. O woman, if your husband is not as young, beautiful, healthy, so well-tempered, and qualified as you could wish; if he has not such abilities, riches, honors, as some others have; yet he is your husband, and the great God commands you to love, honor, and obey

him. Yea, though possibly you have greater abilities of mind than he has, was of some high birth, and he of a more common birth, or did bring more estate, yet since he is your husband, God has made him your head, and set him above you, and made it your duty to love and revere him.

Parents should act wisely and prudently in the matching of their children. They should endeavor that they may marry someone who is most proper for them, most likely to bring blessings to them.

FOCUS QUESTIONS:

1. Although this excerpt focuses on the respective duties of husbands and wives, can you discern which behaviors Wadsworth believes most commonly plague marriages?

2. How does Wadsworth define the relationship between husband and wife? Who has power? How should that power be used?

3. What duties are described as belonging to one partner or the other? What duties are the responsibility of both?

4. How do Wadsworth's views concerning marriage reflect his religious beliefs?

2-7 Laws on Female Slaves— Seventeenth-Century Virginia

The following two sections from colonial codes of law demonstrate the value of female slaves, both as a taxable commodity and as a litmus test of whether a biracial individual would be a slave or free.

Source: Henning, William Waller. Editor. *The Statutes at Large, Being a Collection of All the Laws of Virginia.* Charlottesville: University of Virginia Press, 1969. Reprinted in DuBois and Dumenil, 64.

Laws of Virginia (1643)

Be it further enacted and confirmed That there be tenn pounds of tob'o. per poll and a bushell of corne per poll paid to the ministers within the servall parishes of the collony for all titheable persons, that is to say, as well for all youths of sixteen years of age as upwards, as also for all negro women at the age of sixteen years.

Laws of Virginia (1662)

WHEREAS some doubts have arrisen whether children got by any Englishman upon a negro woman should be slave or free, Be it therefore enacted and declared by this present grand assembly, that all children borne in this country shalbe held bond or free only according to the condition of the mother. And that if any christian shall commit fornication with a negro man or woman, hee or shee soe offending shall pay double the fines imposed by the former act.

FOCUS QUESTIONS:

1. Why would Virginia consider female slaves titheable (or taxable)? What value did they provide to their owners?

2. What reasons can you postulate for assigning a mother's status to her children, as in the 1662 law code?

3. Can you think of any other examples where a mother's identity dictates the upbringing of her children?

2-8 Anne Bradstreet on Queen Elizabeth

Anne Bradstreet was one of the first American poets. She wrote this poem in honor of Elizabeth I, Queen of England. Written in a style unusual for Bradstreet, this poem is written in an elevated, archaic style, full of historical, mythological and Biblical allusions.

Source: John Harvard Ellis, ed., *The Works of Anne Bradstreet in Prose and Verse*, Charlestown: Abraham E. Cutter, 1867. pp. 357-362.

In Honour of that High and Mighty Princess, Queen Elizabeth

The Proem.

1 Although great Queen, thou now in silence lie,
2 Yet thy loud Herald Fame, doth to the sky
3 Thy wondrous worth proclaim, in every clime,
4 And so has vow'd, whilst there is world or time.
5 So great's thy glory, and thine excellence,
6 The sound thereof raps every human sense
7 That men account it no impiety
8 To say thou wert a fleshly Deity.
9 Thousands bring off'rings (though out of date)
10 Thy world of honours to accumulate.
11 'Mongst hundred Hecatombs of roaring Verse,
12 'Mine bleating stands before thy royal Hearse.
13 Thou never didst, nor canst thou now disdain,
14 T' accept the tribute of a loyal Brain.
15 Thy clemency did yerst esteem as much
16 The acclamations of the poor, as rich,
17 Which makes me deem, my rudeness is no wrong,
18 Though I resound thy greatness 'mongst the throng.

The Poem.

19 No Ph{oe}nix Pen, nor Spenser's Poetry,
20 No Speed's, nor Camden's learned History;
21 Eliza's works, wars, praise, can e're compact,
22 The World's the Theater where she did act.
23 No memories, nor volumes can contain,
24 The nine Olymp'ades of her happy reign,
25 Who was so good, so just, so learn'd, so wise,
26 From all the Kings on earth she won the prize.
27 Nor say I more than truly is her due.
28 Millions will testify that this is true.

29 She hath wip'd off th' aspersion of her Sex,
30 That women wisdom lack to play the Rex.
31 Spain's Monarch sa's not so, not yet his Host:
32 She taught them better manners to their cost.
33 The Salic Law had not in force now been,
34 If France had ever hop'd for such a Queen.
35 But can you Doctors now this point dispute,
36 She's argument enough to make you mute,
37 Since first the Sun did run, his ne'er runn'd race,
38 And earth had twice a year, a new old face;
39 Since time was time, and man unmanly man,
40 Come shew me such a Ph{oe}nix if you can.
41 Was ever people better rul'd than hers?
42 Was ever Land more happy, freed from stirs?
43 Did ever wealth in England so abound?
44 Her Victories in foreign Coasts resound?
45 Ships more invincible than Spain's, her foe
46 She rack't, she sack't, she sunk his Armadoe.
47 Her stately Troops advanc'd to Lisbon's wall,
48 Don Anthony in's right for to install.
49 She frankly help'd Franks' (brave) distressed King,
50 The States united now her fame do sing.
51 She their Protectrix was, they well do know,
52 Unto our dread Virago, what they owe.
53 Her Nobles sacrific'd their noble blood,
54 Nor men, nor coin she shap'd, to do them good.
55 The rude untamed Irish she did quell,
56 And Tiron bound, before her picture fell.
57 Had ever Prince such Counsellors as she?
58 Her self Minerva caus'd them so to be.
59 Such Soldiers, and such Captains never seen,
60 As were the subjects of our (Pallas) Queen:
61 Her Sea-men through all straits the world did round,
62 Terra incognitæ might know her sound.
63 Her Drake came laded home with Spanish gold,
64 Her Essex took Cadiz, their Herculean hold.
65 But time would fail me, so my wit would too,
66 To tell of half she did, or she could do.
67 Semiramis to her is but obscure;
68 More infamy than fame she did procure.
69 She plac'd her glory but on Babel's walls,
70 World's wonder for a time, but yet it falls.
71 Fierce Tomris (Cirus' Heads-man, Sythians' Queen)
72 Had put her Harness off, had she but seen

73 Our Amazon i' th' Camp at Tilbury,

74 (Judging all valour, and all Majesty)

75 Within that Princess to have residence,

76 And prostrate yielded to her Excellence.

77 Dido first Foundress of proud Carthage walls

78 (Who living consummates her Funerals),

79 A great Eliza, but compar'd with ours,

80 How vanisheth her glory, wealth, and powers.

81 Proud profuse Cleopatra, whose wrong name,

82 Instead of glory, prov'd her Country's shame:

83 Of her what worth in Story's to be seen,

84 But that she was a rich Ægyptian Queen.

85 Zenobia, potent Empress of the East,

86 And of all these without compare the best

87 (Whom none but great Aurelius could quell)

88 Yet for our Queen is no fit parallel:

89 She was a Ph{oe}nix Queen, so shall she be,

90 Her ashes not reviv'd more Ph{oe}nix she.

91 Her personal perfections, who would tell,

92 Must dip his Pen i' th' Heliconian Well,

93 Which I may not, my pride doth but aspire

94 To read what others write and then admire.

95 Now say, have women worth, or have they none?

96 Or had they some, but with our Queen is't gone?

97 Nay Masculines, you have thus tax'd us long,

98 But she, though dead, will vindicate our wrong.

99 Let such as say our sex is void of reason

100 Know 'tis a slander now, but once was treason.

101 But happy England, which had such a Queen,

happy, happy, had those days still been,

102 But happiness lies in a higher sphere.

103 Then wonder not, Eliza moves not here.

104 Full fraught with honour, riches, and with days,

105 She set, she set, like Titan in his rays.

106 No more shall rise or set such glorious Sun,

107 Until the heaven's great revolution:

108 If then new things, their old form must retain,

109 Eliza shall rule Albian once again.

Her Epitaph.

Here sleeps T H E Queen, this is the royal bed
O' th' Damask Rose, sprung from the white and red,
Whose sweet perfume fills the all-filling air,
This Rose is withered, once so lovely fair:
On neither tree did grow such Rose before,
The greater was our gain, our loss the more.
Another.

Here lies the pride of Queens, pattern of Kings:
So blaze it fame, here's feathers for thy wings.
Here lies the envy'd, yet unparallel'd Prince,
Whose living virtues speak (though dead long since).
If many worlds, as that fantastic framed,
In every one, be her great glory famed.

Focus Questions:

1. Which of Elizabeth's qualities does Hutchinson most admire?

2. What is Hutchinson arguing in lines 29 ff.?

3. What images of women does Hutchinson chose to apply to Elizabeth?

2-9 Women in the Courts— Seventeenth Century Maryland

Colonial courts were frequently the setting where a woman's behavior was put on trial. Cases often included gossip, slander, witchcraft, and frowned-upon sexual acts. Additionally women were sometimes asked to serve as jurors (specifically in the case of witchcraft or where a body search was required).

Source: Henning, William Waller. Editor. *The Statutes at Large, Being a Collection of All the Laws of Virginia.* Charlottesville: University of Virginia Press, 1969. Reprinted in DuBois and Dumenil, 58-60.

Michael Baisey's Wife (1654)

Richard Manship Sworne saith that the wife of Peter Godson related . . . that Michael Baiseys wifes eldest Son was not the Son of Anthony Rawlins her former husband, but She knw one at Maryland that was the father of him, but Named not the man, and that the Said Michael Baisey's wife was a whore and a Strumpett up and Down the Countrey, and Said that Thomas Ward of Kent told her Soe.

Elizabeth Manship Sworne Saith the Same.

Margaret Herring Sworne Saith that the wife of Peter Godson affirmed that Anthony Rawlins Son was not Son but the Son of another man at Maryland . . .

Whereas Peter Godsons wife hath Slandered the wife of Michael Baisey & Saying She was a whore & a Strumpet up and Down the Countery, It is ordered that the Said Godson's wife Shall be Committed into the Sheriffs hand untill She Shall find Security for the behaviour which the plft [plaintiff] is Satisfied with as he hath declared in Court . . .

Whereas Mrs. Godson was bound in a bond of Good behaviour from the 21st of October till the 5th of December towards the wife of Michael Baisey, and none appearing to renew the Said Bond, It is ordered that she be remitted from Bond of Good behaviour.

Richard Manship's Wife (1654)

Bartho: Herringe aged forty yeares or thereabouts Sworne Saith, That Peter Godson and Richard Manship meeting in your Pettrs plantation, Richard Manship asked the Said Peter Godson whether he would prove his wife a Witch, Peter Godson replyed take notice what I Say, I came to your house where your wife layd two Straws and the woman in a Jesting way Said they Say I am a witch, if I am a witch they Say I have not power to Skip over these two Strawes and bid the Said Peter Godson to Skip over them and about a day after the Said Godson Said he was Lame, there-upon would Maintaine his wife to be a witch

Bartho: Herringe . . .

John Killy aged twenty five yeares or there abouts Sworne Sayth. That at the house of Phillip Hide, Richard Manship Said to Peter Godson you Said you would prove my wife a Witch, Peter Godson answered Gentlemen take Notice what I Say I will prove her a witch beare Witmess you that Stand by.

John Killy

Magaret Herringe aged twenty three or there-abouts Sworne Saith, That Rich: Manship asked Peter Godson if he would prove his wife a witch, and Peter desired them that were present to take Notice what he Said your wife tooke four Strawes and Said in the Name of Jesus Come over these Strawes, and upon this your wife is a witch and I will prove her one.

Whereas Peter Godson and his wife had defamed Richard Manship's wife in Saying She was a witch and Uttered other Slanderous Speeches agst her, which was Composed and Determined by the pltf and defendant before mr Richard Preston, Soe as Peter Godson Should pay Charges of Warrants and Subpeonas in

these Actions which Richard Manship desired may be Manifested in Court that the Said Peter Godson & his wife have acknowledged themselves Sorry for their Speeches and pay Charges.

Judith Catchpole (1656)

At a Generall Provinciall Court Held at

Putuxent September 22th

Present Capt William ffuller, mr John Pott Present

mr Richard Preston: mr Michael Brooke

mr Edward Lloyd

Whereas Judith Catchpole being brought before the Court upon Suspicion of Murdering a Child which She is accused to have brought forth, and denying the fact or that She ever had Child the Court hath ordered that a jury of able women be Impannelled and to give in their Verdict to the best of their judgment whether She the Said Judith hath ever had a Child

Or not . . .

The Names of the Jury of women Impannelled to Search the body of Judith Catchpole . . .

Rose Smith	mrs Cannady
mrs Belcher	mrs Bussey
mrs Chaplin	mrs Brooke
mrs Brooke	Elizabeth Claxton
mrs Battin	Elizabeth Potter
	Dorothy Day

We the Jury of Women before named having according to our Charge and oath Searched the body of Judith Catchpole doe give in our Verdict according to our best judgment that the Said Judith Catchpole hath not had any Child within the time Charged.

Whereas Judith Catchpole Servant to William Dorrington of this Province of Maryland Was appre-hended and brought before this Court upon Suspicion of Murthering a Chile in her Voyage at Sea bound for this Province in the Ship Mary and ffrancis who Set forth of England upon her intended Voyage in or about october Last 1655 and arrived in this Province in or about January following, and her accuser being deceased and no murther appearing upon her Examination denying the fact; was Ordered that her body Should be Searcht by a Jury of able women, which being done the said Jury returning their Verdict to this Court that they found that the Said Judith had not any Child within the time Chargd And also it appearing to this Court by Severall Testimonies that the party accusing was not in Sound Mind, whereby it is Conceived the Said Judith Catchpole is not Iditable, The Court doth therefore order that upon the reasons aforesaid, the She the Said Judith Catchpole be acquitted of that Charge unless further Evidence appeare.

FOCUS QUESTIONS:

1. What was Mrs. Godson's punishment for slandering Mrs. Baisey? How did this differ from the Peter Godson's punishment for slandering Mrs. Manship?
2. What evidence did Peter Godson have for accusing Mrs. Manship of being a witch? Did the witnesses corroborate his story?
3. What do these documents tell you about how privacy was perceived both in everyday life and in colonial courts?

2-10 "The Trappan'd Maiden: or, The Distressed Damsel."

Many colonists came to America as indentured servants, working from three to seven years to pay for their passage. By 1625, forty percent of the population of Virginia (excluding Native Americans) was indentured servants. Prior to the Revolutionary War it is estimated nearly half of the white population of Philadelphia had at one time in their lives been bonded servants. After the Revolutionary War fewer people came as indentured servants and the practice died out by 1800.

Source: John Ashton, *Eighteenth Century Waifs*, London: Hurst and Blackett, Publishers, 1887. pp 117-120.

Five years served I, under Master Guy,
In the land of Virginny-o
Which made me for to know sorrow, grief and woe,
When that I was weary, weary, weary-o.

When my dame says go, then I must do so,
In the land of Virginny-o,

When she sits at meat, then I have none to eat,
When that I was weary, weary, weary-o.

As soon as it is day, to work I must away,
In the land of Virginny-o
Then my dame she knocks, with her tinder box,
When that I was weary, weary, weary-o.

I have played my part, both at plow and cart,
In the land of Virginny-o
Billets from the wood upon my back they load,
When that I was weary, weary, weary-o.

A thousand woes beside, that I do here abide,
In the land of Virginny-o
In misery I spend my time that hath no end,
When that I was weary, weary, weary-o.

FOCUS QUESTIONS:

1. How does the singer view her life as an indentured servant?
2. Why would anyone voluntarily take up such a life?

2-11 The Confession of Margaret Jacobs (1692)

The following confession of Margaret Jacobs, thought it has for its background the Salem Witch Trials, is not one admitting to witchcraft, but recanting an accusation made by Jacobs earlier that year against her grandfather and another man, for which the two latter were hung. Jacobs also wrote a letter from prison to her father, hoping for "joyful and happy meeting in heaven".

Source: George Lincoln Burr, ed., *Narratives of the Witchcraft Cases, 1648–1706*, New York: Charles Scribners Sons, 1914. pp 364-365.

"The humble declaration of Margaret Jacobs unto the honoured court now sitting at Salem, sheweth

"That whereas your poor and humble declarant being closely confined here in Salem jail for the crime of witchcraft, which crime, thanks be to the Lord, I am altogether ignorant of, as will appear at the great day of judgment. May it please the honored court, I was cried out upon by some of the possessed persons, as afflicting of them; whereupon I was brought to my examination, which persons at the sight of me fell down, which did very much startle and affright me. The Lord above knows I knew nothing, in the least measure, how or who afflicted them; they told me, without doubt I did, or else they would not fall down at me; they told me if I would not confess, I should be put down into the dungeon and would be hanged, but if I would confess I should have my life; the which did so affright me, with my own vile wicked heart, to save my life made me make the confession I did, which confession, may it please the honoured court, is altogether false and untrue. The very first night after I had made my confession, I was in such horror of conscience that I could not sleep, for fear the Devil should carry me away for telling such horrid lies. I was, may it please the honored court, sworn to my confession, as I understand since, but then, at that time, was ignorant of it, not knowing what an oath did mean. The Lord, I hope, in whom I trust, out of the abundance of his mercy, will forgive me my false forswearing myself. What I said was altogether false, against my grandfather, and Mr. Burroughs, which I did to save my life and to have my liberty; but the Lord, charging it to my conscience, made me in so much horror, that I could not contain myself before I had denied my confession, which I did, though I saw nothing but death before me, choosing rather death with a quiet conscience, than to live in such horror, which I could not suffer. Whereupon my denying my confession, I was committed to close prison, where I have enjoyed more felicity in spirit a thousand times than I did before in my enlargement.

"And now, may it please your honours, your poor and humble declarant having, in part, given your honours a description of my condition, do leave it to your honours pious and judicious discretion to take pity and compassion on my young and tender years; to act and do with me as the Lord above and your honours shall see good, having no friend but the Lord to plead my cause for me; not being guilty in the least measure of the crime of witchcraft, nor any other sin that deserves death from man; and your poor and humble declarant shall forever pray, as she is bound in duty, for your honours' happiness in this life, and eternal felicity in the world to come. So prays your honours declarant.

"Margaret Jacobs"

Focus Questions:

1. Why did Jacobs perjure herself and condemn her grandfather and Burroughs? Why does she now recant?

2. Why does Jacobs say she has "enjoyed more felicity in spirit" while in prison?

3. What can you learn from this confession of the nature of the period, and the fervor of the persecutions?

EIGHTEENTH CENTURY REVOLUTIONS, 1700–1800

3-1 Slave Women Making Money at the Market

Slaves' monetary value did not always come in the form of labor performed directly for the slave-owner. Sometimes slaves were hired out to work for employers who did not own them, but rather paid a pre-determined fee to the slave-owner; in other situations, slaves were hired out and the employer paid a wage directly to the slave, who in turn paid some portion of these earnings to the owner. Yet another variation (though one that skirted the law in many slave-holding jurisdictions) permitted slaves to sell goods or produce on the open market, on the condition that the slave-owner be paid a portion of the proceeds. This is what is described here, by one observer of commerce in Charleston, South Carolina.

Source: Excerpted in Olwell, Robert. " 'Loose, Idle, and Disorderly:' Slave Women in the Eighteenth-Century Charleston Marketplace." In David Barry Gaspar and Darlene Clark Hine, eds., *More Than Chattel: Black Women and Slavery in the Americas,* Bloomington: Indiana University Press, 1996. p. 101.

Almost every day ... in and near the Lower Market, ... poultry, fruit, eggs, c. are brought thither from the country for sale. Near that market, constantly resort a great number of loose, idle and disorderly negro women, who are seated there from morn till night, and buy and sell on their own accounts, what they please, in order to pay their wages, and get so much more for themselves as they can; for their owners care little, how their slaves get the money, so they are paid.

FOCUS QUESTIONS:

1. Does the author provide any support for the characterization of the market-women as "loose, idle and disorderly"?

2. Of whom is the author more critical, the slave women or the slave-owners?

3-2 Abigail and John Adams on the Rights of Women

Abigail and John Adams had an extraordinary personal, political, and intellectual partnership. In these letters, exchanged during the months leading up to the Declaration of Independence, the two freely exchange views on women's rights, among other topics. In a subsequent letter to John Sullivan, another leading figure in the American Revolution, John puts forward a new line of reasoning.

Abigail Adams to John Adams, Braintree, 31 March 1776

I long to hear that you have declared an independancy-and by the way in the new Code of Laws which I suppose it will be necessary for you to make I desire you would Remember the Ladies, and be more generous and favourable to them than your ancestors. Do not put such umlimited power into the hands of the Husbands. Remember all Men would be tyrants if they could. If perticular care and attention is not paid to the Laidies we are determined to foment a Rebelion, and will not hold ourselves bound by any Laws in which we have no voice, or Representation.

That your Sex are Naturally Tyrannical is a Truth so thoroughly established as to admit of no dispute, but such of you as wish to be happy willingly give up the harsh title of Master for the more tender and endearing one of Friend. Why then, not put it out of the power of the vicious and the Lawless to use us with cruelty and indignity with impunity. Men of Sense in all Ages abhor those customs which treat us only as the vassals of your Sex. Regard us then as Beings placed by providence under your protection and in immitation of the Supreem Being make use of that power only for our happiness.

John Adams to Abigail Adams, Philadelphia, 14 April 1776

As to Declarations of Independency, be patient. Read our Privateering Laws, and our Commercial Laws. What signifies a Word.

As to your extraordinary Code of Laws, I cannot but laugh. We have been told that our Struggle has loosened the bands of Government every where. That Children and Apprentices were disobedient-that schools and Colledges were grown turbulent-that Indians slighted their Guardians and Negroes grew insolent to their Masters. But your Letter was the first Intimation that another Tribe more numerous and powerful than all the rest were grown discontented.- This is rather too coarse a Compliment but you are so saucy, I wont blot it out.

Depend upon it, We know better than to repeal our Masculine systems. Altho they are in full Force, you know they are little more than Theory. We dare not exert our Power in its full Latitude. We are obliged to go fair, and softly, and in Practice you know We are the subjects. We have only the Name of Masters, and rather than give up this, which would completely subject Us to the Despotism of the Peticoat, I hope General Washington, and all our brave Heroes would fight. I am sure every good Politician would plot, as long as he would against Despotism, Empire, Monarchy, Aristocracy, Oligarchy, or Ochlocracy.-A fine Story indeed. I begin to think the Ministry as deep as they are wicked. After stirring up Tories, Landjobbers, Trimmers, Bigots, Canadians, Indians, Negrows, Hanoverians, Hessians, Russians, Irish Roman Catholicks, Scotch Renegadoes, at last they have stimulated the [illegible in original] to demand new Priviledges and threaten to rebell.

John Adams to John Sullivan, Philadelphia, 26 May 1776

It is certain in Theory, that the only moral Foundation of Government is the Consent of the People. But to what an Extent Shall We carry this Principle? Shall We Say, that every Individual of the Community, old and young, male and female, as well as rich and poor, must consent, expressly to every Act of Legislation? No, you will Say. This is impossible. How then does the Right arise in the Majority to govern the Minority, against their Will? Whence arises the

Right of the Men to govern Women, without their Consent? Whence the Right of the old to bind the Young, without theirs.

But let us first Suppose, that the whole Community of every Age, Rank, Sex, and Condition, has a Right to vote. This Community, is assembled-a Motion is made and carried by a Majority of one Voice. The Minority will not agree to this. Whence arises the Right of the Majority to govern, and the Obligation of the Minority to obey? from Necessity, you will Say, because there can be no other Rule, But why exclude Women? You will Say, because their Delicacy renders them unfit for Practice and Experience, in the great Business of Life, and the hardy Enterprizes of War, as well as the arduous Cares of State. Besides, their attention is So much engaged with the necessary Nurture of their Children, that Nature has made them fittest for domestic Cares. And Children have not Judgment or Will of their own. True. But will not these Reasons apply to others? Is it not equally true, that Men in general in every Society, who are wholly destitute of Property, and also too little acquainted with public Affairs to form a Right Judgment, and too dependent upon other Men to have a Will of their own? If this is a Fact, if you give to every Man, who has no Property, a Vote, will you not make a fine encouraging Provision for Corruption by your fundamental Law? Such is the Frailty of the human Heart, that very few Men, who have no Property, have any Judgment of their own. They talk and vote as they are directed by Some Man of Property, who has attached their Minds to his Interest.

Upon my Word, sir, I have long thought an Army, a Piece of Clock Work and to be governed only by Principles and Maxims, as fixed as any in Mechanicks, and by all that I have read in the History of Mankind, and in Authors, who have Speculated upon Society and Government, I am much inclined to think, a Government must manage a Society in the Same manner; and that this is Machinery too.

Harrington has Shewn that Power always follows property. This I believe to be as infallible a Maxim, in Politics, as, that Action and Reaction are equal, as in Mechanicks. Nay I believe We may advance one Step farther and affirm that the Ballance of Power in a Society, accompanies the Ballance of Property in Land. The only possible Way then of preserving the Ballance of Power on the side of equal Liberty and public Virtue, is to make the Acquisition of Land easy to every Member of Society: to make a Division of the Land into Small Quantities, So that the Multitude may be possessed of landed Estates. If the Multitude is possessed of the Ballance of real Estate, the Multitude will have the Ballance of Power, and in that Case the

Multitude will take Care of the Liberty, Virtue, and Interest of the Multitude in all Acts of Government.

I believe these Principles have been felt, if not understood in the Massachusetts Bay, from the Beginning: And therefore I Should think that Wisdom and Policy would dictate in these Times, to be very cautious of making Alterations. Our people have never been very rigid in Scrutinizing into the Qualifications of Voters, and I presume they will not now begin to be so. But I would not advise them to make any alteration in the Laws, at present, respecting the Qualifications of Voters.

Your Idea, that those Laws, which affect the Lives and personal Liberty of all, or which inflict corporal Punishment, affect those, who are not qualified to vote, as well as those who are, is just. But, So they do Women, as well as Men, Children as well as Adults. What Reason Should there be, for excluding a Man of Twenty years, Eleven Months and twenty-seven days old, from a Vote when you admit one, who is twenty one? The Reason is, you must fix Some Period in Life, when the Understanding and Will of Men in general is fit to be trusted by the Public. Will not the Same Reason justify the State in fixing upon Some certain Quantity of Property, as a Qualification.

The Same Reasoning, which will induce you to admit all Men, who have no Property, to vote, with those who have, for those Laws, which affect the Person will prove that you ought to admit Women and Children: for generally Speaking, Women and Children, have as good Judgment, and as independent Minds as those Men who are wholly destitute of Property: these last being to all Intents and Purposes as much dependent upon others, who will please to feed, cloath, and employ them, as Women are upon their Husbands, or Children on their Parents.

As to your Idea, or proportioning the Votes of Men in Money Matters, to the Property they hold, it is utterly impracticable. There is no possible Way of Ascertaining, at any one Time, how much every Man in a Community, is worth; and if there was, So fluctuating is Trade and Property, that this State of it, would change in half an Hour. The Property of the whole Community, is Shifting every Hour, and no Record can be kept of the Changes.

Society can be governed only by general Rules. Government cannot accommodate itself to every particular Case, as it happens, nor to the Circumstances of particular Persons. It must establish general, comprehensive Regulations for Cases and Persons. The only Question is, which general Rule, will accommodate most Cases and most Persons.

Depend upon it, sir, it is dangerous to open So fruitfull a Source of Controversy and Altercation, as would be opened by attempting to alter the Qualifications of Voters. There will be no End of it. New Claims will arise. Women will demand a Vote. Lads from 12 to 21 will think their Rights not enough attended to, and every Man, who has not a Farthing, will demand an equal Voice with any other in all Acts of State. It tends to confound and destroy all Distinctions, and prostrate all Ranks, to one common Levell. I am &c.

FOCUS QUESTIONS:

1. Why does John Adams want to exclude those without property – women and men – from voting?

2. What does Abigail mean when she enjoins John to "Remember the Ladies"?

3. What evidence is there that Abigail influenced John's thinking or actions?

3-3 A Diary: A Woman Alone in Wartime Philadelphia

Elizabeth Sandwith Drinker was a Quaker who lived with her family in Philadelphia. In August 1777, her husband was part of a group of men banished to Virginia because they were accused of assisting the British cause. Drinker stayed behind. The British Army, meanwhile, occupied the city, and sought "quartering" (lodging privileges) with local families; the Drinker home eventually housed British Major General John Crammond, whose initial entreaties are described here.

Source: Drinker, Elizabeth Sandwith. Extracts from the Journal of Elizabeth Drinker, from 1759 to 1807, A.D., Henry Biddle, ed. Philadelphia: J.B. Lippincott Co., 1889. pp. 73-75.

Dec. 15. Last night about 11 o'clock, as we were going to Bed, we saw 2 soldiers in ye alley, standing by ye Fence. We went down stairs again, and into ye yard. We asked Harry aloud if John and Tom were yet in Bed? Harry answered, Yes. Sister ordered him to untie ye Dog and then come in. While we were contriving in this manner down stairs, Jenny saw them from my room window, move off with a large Bundle which she took to be a Bed. After we had been in Bed about an hour we heard a great noise in ye alley. Jenny, Sister and ye children ran to ye window, and saw ye Baker next door running up ye alley in his shirt, with only a little red Jacket on; ye rest of his Family were with him. We did not discover ye cause of ye uproar until this morning, when we found the Baker had been robbed of some of his wife's clothes—which we suppose was ye bundle ye Fellows went off with some time before.

Peggy York called this morning with a letter which she had received from her Husband from London, acknowledging ye kindness he had received from Pigou and Booth, in consequence of a letter from James & Drinker, for which he returns thanks. She had on the highest and most ridiculous Headdress that I have yet seen.

Polly Reynolds, formerly Ritche, with 2 other women called before dinner. She is here to solicit ye General on account of her Husband, who has been a prisoner in ye Jerseys ever since last Christmas.

Henry Drinker Jr. tells us this evening that W. D. Smith has been called before ye General to day.

Friends have had several meetings lately, and have agreed to send orders to sundry merchants in London for a cargo of provisions and coal, as from ye present prospect, ye inhabitants will stand in need of such a supply. Ye officers and soldiers are quartering themselves upon ye Families generally. One with his Family is to be fixt at J. Howells. I am in daily expectation of their calling upon us. They were much frightened last night at Isaac Catheralls by a soldier who came into ye House, drew his Bayonet on Isaac, and behaved very disorderly. Anthony Morris, son of Samuel is said to be dangerously wounded.

Dec. 18. Ezekiel Edwards is returned from Winchester. I have not seen him, but am told that he brings very disagreeable intelligence; that he has heard it hinted that there is a design of sending our dear Friends to Staunton, which would be sorrowful indeed should it so happen, but it may not.

An officer who calls himself Major Crammond, called this afternoon to look for Quarters for some officer of distinction. I plead off; he would have persuaded me that it was a necessary protection at these times, to have one in ye House. He said that I must consider of it, and that he would call in a day or two. I desired to be excused, and after some more talk we parted. He behaved with much politeness, which has not been ye case at many other places. They have been very rude

and impudent at some Houses.

I wish I may come off so; but at the same time fear we must have some one with us, as it appears likely to be a general thing. This has been a trying day to my spirit.

E. Edwards had a number of letters stolen from him, which were for us poor destitutes. I have just finished a letter to my dearest. 'Tis now past 12 o'clock, and Watch has put me in a flutter by his violent barking, as if some one was in ye alley, which I believe was ye case. Hail since night.

Dec. 19. Sister went out to inquire how Polly Pleasants had managed ye matter in respect to taking in officers, *as* they have had their doors marked. They had been to Jos. Galloway; but E. Story seems likely to settle ye matter with ye quarter master General—one Roberson. While sister was out, Major Crammond came to know if I had consulted any of my friends upon ye matter. I told him that my sister was out on that business; that I expected that we, who were at present lone women, would be excused. He said he feared not, for tho' I might put him off, (as it was for himself he applied); yet, as a great number of foreign Troops were to be quartered in this neighborhood, he believed they might be troublesome. We had a good deal of talk about the mal-behavior of British officers, which he, by no means, justified. I told him how I had been frightened by ye officer, that thief-like stole my servant Girl over ye Fence, and of many other particulars of their bad conduct that had come to my knowledge. He said, that yesterday I had told him what sort of a man would suit in my Family; if I was obliged to take any, he was conscious that some of those qualities were his, (which were early hours, and little company); that there were very few of ye officers he could recommend; that Mr Galloway knew him very well; and that he would call again to morrow to know my mind further. So he went off. I am straitened how to act, and yet determined. I may be troubled with others much worse, for this man appears to be much of a Gentleman—but while I can keep clear of them, I intend so to do. They have marked ye doors of Houses against their consent, and some of ye inhabitants have looked out for officers of reputation, (if any such there be), to come into their Families, by way of protection, and to keep off others.

E. Story called this evening; he says he thinks he shall be able to get us, whose Husbands are gone from us, clear of ye military gentlemen. He says they are much chagrined at the difficulty they find in getting quarters, and ye cool reception they have met with, or something to that effect; that several young Noblemen are at this time obliged to sleep at Taverns, on board Ship, or in ye Redoubts, for which I think they may, in great measure, thank themselves; tho', at the same time, it appears to me there was, perhaps too much backwardness shown towards them in ye beginning. We are told this evening that Owen Jones's Family has been very ill-used indeed, by an officer who wanted to quarter himself, with many others, upon them. He drew his sword ; used very abusive language, and had ye Front door split in pieces. Mary Eddy has some with her, who, they say, will not suffer her to use her own Front door, but oblige her and her Family to go up and down the alley. Molly Foulke has been affronted, and

so have many others. We have come off, as yet, wonderfully well. My resolution and fortitude have failed me much of late; my dear Henry's absence, and ye renewed fears on his account, and thoughts of our dear children, and my health but very middling—all together—it seems, at times, hard to bear up against. . .

FOCUS QUESTIONS:

1. Why was Drinker loathe to house Crammond? What advantages might she expect from quartering him, or some other officer?

2. What seems to bother Drinker most about her situation? Does it seem these issues would have been mitigated if she had been a man instead?

3-4 New Jersey Grants Voting Rights to All Property Holders (1776)

The American Revolutionary War was already underway, and the Declaration of Independence was about to be signed, when leaders in New Jersey quickly drafted and ratified a state constitution. The most notable feature of this document is the relative ease of establishing voting rights.

Source: http://www.njstatelib.org/Research_Guides/ Historical_Documents/nj/NJDOC10A.html

The State of New Jersey Constitution of 1776

WHEREAS all the constitutional authority ever possessed by the kings of Great Britain over these colonies, || or their other dominions, was, by compact, derived from the people, and held of them, for the common interest of the whole society; allegiance and protection are, in the nature of things, reciprocal ties, each equally depending upon the other, and liable to be dissolved by the others being refused or withdrawn. And whereas George the Third, king of Great Britain, has refused protection to the good people of these colonies; and, by assenting to sundry acts of the British parliament, attempted to subject them to the absolute dominion of that body; and has also made war upon them, in the most cruel and unnatural manner, for no other cause, than asserting their just rights — all civil authority under him is necesarily at an end, and a dissolution of government in each colony has consequently taken place.

And whereas, in the present deplorable situation of these colonies, exposed to the fury of a cruel and relentless enemy, some form of government is absolutely necessary, not only for the preservation of good order, but also the more effectually to unite the people, and enable them to exert their whole force in their own necessary defence: and as the honorable the continental congress, the supreme council of the American colonies, has advised such of the colonies as have not yet gone into measures, to adopt for themselves, respectively, such government as shall best conduce to their own happiness and safety, and the well-being of America in general: — We, the representatives of the colony of New Jersey, having been elected by all the counties, in the freest manner, and in congress assembled, have, after mature deliberations, agreed upon a set of charter rights and the form of a Constitution, in manner following, viz.

I. That the government of this Province shall be vested in a Governor, Legislative Council, and General Assembly.

II. That the Legislative Council, and General Assembly, shall be chosen, for the first time, on the second Tuesday in August next; the members whereof shall be the same in number and qualifications as are herein after mentioned; and shall be and remain vested with all the powers and authority to be held by any future Legislative Council and Assembly of this Colony, until the second Tuesday in October, which shall be in the year of our Lord one thousand seven hundred and seventy-seven.

III. That on the second Tuesday in October yearly, and every year forever (with the privilege of adjourning from day to day as occasion may require) the counties shall severally choose one person, to be a member of the Legislative Council of this Colony, who shall be, and have been, for one whole year next before the election, an inhabitant and freeholder in the county in which he is chosen, and worth at least one thousand pounds proclamation money, of real and personal estate, within the same county; that, at the same time, each county shall also choose three members of Assembly; provided that no person shall be entitled to a seat in the said Assembly unless he be, and have been, for one whole year next before the election, an inhabitant of the county he is to represent, and worth five hundred pounds proclamation money, in real and personal estate, in the same county: that on the second Tuesday next after the day of election, the Council and Assembly shall separately meet; and that the consent of both Houses shall be necessary to every law; provided, thast seven shall be a quorum of the Council, for doing business, and that no law shall pass, unless there be a majority of all the Representatives of each body personally present, and agreeing thereto. Provided always, that if a majority of the representatives of this Province, in Council and General Assembly convened, shall, at any time or times hereafter, judge it equitable and proper, to add to or diminish the number or proportion of the members of Assembly for any county or counties in this Colony, then, and in such case, the same may, on the principles of more equal representation, be lawfully done; anything in this Charter to the contrary nothwithstanding: so that the whole number of Representatives in Assembly shall not, at any time, be less than thirty-nine.

IV. That all inhabitants of this Colony, of full age, who are worth fifty pounds proclamation money, clear estate in the same, and have resided within the county in which they claim a vote for twelve months immediately preceding the election, shall be entitled to vote for Representatives in Council and Assembly; and also for all other public officers, that shall be elected by the people of the county at large.

...

XXII. That the common law of England, as well as so much of the statute law, as have been heretofore practised in this Colony, shall still remain in force, until they shall be altered by a future law of the Legislature; such parts only excepted, as are repugnant to the rights and privileges contained in this Charter; and that the inestimable right of trial by jury shall remain confirmed as a part of the law of this Colony, without repeal, forever.

...

In PROVINCIAL CONGRESS, New Jersey, Burlington, July 2, 1776.
By order of Congress.
SAMUEL TUCKER, Pres.
William Paterson, Secretary.

FOCUS QUESTIONS:

1. What qualifications does this constitution establish for voting in New Jersey?
2. What conditions might account for the relative liberalism of this constitution?

3-5 Sarah Osborn's Narrative (1837)

While working as a servant to a blacksmith, Sarah met and married Revolutionary War veteran Aaron Osborn. When Aaron re-enlisted in the U.S. Army, Sarah accompanied him, as described here. This document is the record of a deposition filed by Sarah Osborne in 1837, when she was 81 years old, in support of her application for a pension as the widow of a Revolutionary War veteran.

Source: Sarah Osborn, Narrative, 1837, in John Dann, ed., *The Revolution Remembered*, 1980, pp. 241-246, The University of Chicago Press.

That she was married to Aaron Osborn, who was a soldier during the Revolutionary War. That her first aquaintance with said Osborn commenced in Albany,

in the state of New York, during the hard winter of 1780. That deponent then resided at the house of one John Willis, a blacksmith in said city. That said Osborn came down there from Fort Stanwix and went to work at the business of blacksmithing for said Willis and continued working at intervals for a period of perhaps two months. Said Osborn then informed deponent that he had first enlisted at Goshen in Orange County, New York. That he had been in the service for three years, deponent thinks, about one year of that time at Fort Stanwix, and that his time was out. And, under an assurance that he would go to Goshen with her, she married him at the house of said Willis during the time he was there as above mentioned, to wit, in January 1780 ....

That after deponent had married said Osborn, he informed her that he was returned during the war, and that he desired deponent to go with him. Deponent declined until she was informed by Captain Gregg that her husband should be put on the commissary guard, and that she should have the means of conveyance either in a wagon or on horseback. That deponent then in the same winter season in sleighs accompanied her husband and the forces under command of Captain Gregg on the east side of the Hudson river to Fishkill, then crossed the river and went down to West Point ....

Deponent further says that she and her husband remained at West Point till the departure of the army for the South, a term of perhaps one year and a half, but she cannot be positive as to the length of time. While at West Point, deponent lived at Lieutenant Foot's, who kept a boardinghouse. Deponent was employed in washing and sewing for the soldiers. Her said husband was employed about the camp ....

When the army were about to leave West Point and go south, they crossed over the river to Robinson's Farms and remained there for a length of time to induce the belief, as deponent understood, that they were going to take up quarters there, whereas they recrossed the river in the nighttime into the Jerseys and traveled all night in a direct course for Philadelphia. Deponent was part of the time on horseback and part of the time in a wagon. Deponent's said husband was still serving as one of the commissary's guard ....

They continued their march to Philadelphia, deponent on horseback through the streets, and arrived at a place towards the Schuylkill where the British had burnt some houses, where they encamped for the afternoon and night. Being out of bread, deponent was employed in baking the afternoon and evening. Deponent recollects no females but Sergeant Lamberson's and Lieutenant Forman's wives and a colored woman by the name of Letta. The Quaker ladies who came round urged deponent to stay, but her husband said, "No, he could not leave her behind." Accordingly, next day they continued their march from day to day till they arrived at Baltimore, where deponent and her said husband and the forces under command of General Clinton, Captain Gregg, and several other officers, all of whom she does not recollect, embarked on board a vessel and sailed down the Chesapeake. There were several vessels along, and deponent was in the foremost. ... They continued sail until they had got up the St. James River as far as the tide would carry them, about twelve miles from the mouth, and then landed, and the tide being spent, they had a fine time catching sea lobsters, which they ate.

They, however, marched immediately for a place called Williamsburg, as she thinks, deponent alternately on horseback and on foot. There arrived, they remained two days till the army all came in by land and then marched for Yorktown, or Little Yark as it was then called. The York troops were posted at the right, the Connecticut troops next, and the French to the left. In about one day or less than a day, they reached the place of encampment about one mile from Yorktown. Deponent was on foot and the other females above named and her said husband still on the commissary's guard. Deponent's attention was arrested by the appearance of a large plain between them and Yorktown and an entrenchment thrown up. She also saw a number of dead Negroes lying round their encampment, whom she understood the British had driven out of the town and left to starve, or were first starved and then thrown out. Deponent took her stand just back of the American tents, say about a mile from the town, and busied herself washing, mending, and cooking for the soldiers, in which she was assisted by the other females; some men washed their own clothing. She heard the roar of the artillery for a number of days, and the last night the Americans threw up entrenchments, it was a misty, foggy night, rather wet but not rainy. Every soldier threw up for himself, as she understood, and she afterwards saw and went into the entrenchments. Deponent's said husband was there throwing up entrenchments, and deponent cooked and carried in beef, and bread, and coffee (in a gallon pot) to the soldiers in the entrenchment.

On one occasion when deponent was thus employed carrying in provisions, she met General Washington, who asked her if she "was not afraid of the cannonballs?"

She replied, "No, the bullets would not cheat the gallows," that "It would not do for the men to fight and starve too."

They dug entrenchments nearer and nearer to Yorktown every night or two till the last. While digging that, the enemy fired very heavy till about nine 0' clock next morning, then stopped, and the drums from the enemy beat excessively ....

All at once the officers hurrahed and swung their hats, and deponent asked them, "What is the matter now?"

One of them replied, "Are not you soldier enough to know what it means?"

Deponent replied, "No."

They then replied, "The British have surrendered."

Deponent, having provisions ready, carried the same down to the entrenchments that morning, and four of the soldiers whom she was in the habit of cooking for ate their breakfasts.

Deponent stood on one side of the road and the American officers upon the other side when the British officers came out of the town and rode up to the American officers and delivered up [their swords, which the deponent] thinks were returned again, and the British officers rode right on before the army, who marched out beating and playing a melancholy tune, their drums covered with black handkerchiefs and their fifes with black ribbands tied around them, into an old field and there grounded their arms and then returned into town again to await their destiny ....

On going into town, she noticed two dead Negroes lying by the market house.

She had the curiosity to go into a large building that stood nearby, and there she noticed the cupboards smashed to pieces and china dishes and other ware strewed around upon the floor, and among the rest a pewter cover to a hot basin that had a handle on it. She picked it up, supposing it to belong to the British, but the governor came in and claimed it as his, but said he would have the name of giving it away as it was the last one of twelve that he could see, and accordingly presented it to deponent, and she afterwards brought it home with her to Orange County and sold it for old pewter, which she has a hundred times regretted.

FOCUS QUESTIONS:

1. What tasks did Osborne perform, for her husband and for others?
2. Why does she include a description of her brief conversation with George Washington in this record?

3-6 Letters from Eliza Lucas Pinckney

Eliza Lucas was born into a prominent family in Antigua in 1722. She was industrious and astute; while she was still a teenager, she took over the management of several plantations owned by her family near Charleston, South Carolina. Her greatest claim to fame lies in her contributions to the indigo industry: she experimented with techniques to cultivate and harvest the indigo plant (used in the creation of blue dyes for textiles) and developed indigo as a tremendously profitable cash crop for South Carolina. She married Charles Pinckney, and they had two sons who became leaders during the American Revolution.

Source: Elizabeth Deering Hanscom, ed., *The Friendly Craft: A Collection of American Letters*, New York: Macmillan, 1910. pp. 3-6.

DEAR MADAM, — I flatter myself it will be a satisfaction to you to hear I like this part of the world as my lott has fallen here, which I really do. I prefer England to it 'tis true, but think Carolina greatly preferable to the West Indies, and was my Papa here I should be very happy. We have a very good acquaintance from whom we have received much friendship and Civility. Charles Town the principal one in this province is a polite agreeable place, the people live very Gentile and very much in the English taste. The Country is in general fertile and abounds with Venson and with fowl. The Venson is much higher flavoured than in England but 'tis seldom fatt.

My Papa and Mama's great indulgence to mee leaves it to mee to chuse our place of residence either in town or country, but I think it more prudent as well as most agreeable to my Mama and selfe to be in the Country during my father's absence. Wee are 17 mile by land, and 6 by water from Charles Town where wee have about 6 agreeable families around us with whom wee live in great harmony. I have a little library well furnished (for my Papa has left mee most of his books) in which I spend part of my time. My Musick and the Garden which I am very fond of take up the rest that is not imployed in business, of work my father has left mee a pretty good share, and indeed 'twas unavoidable, as my Mama's bad state of health prevents her going thro' any fatigue.

I have the business of 3 plantations to transact, which requires much writing and more business and fatigue of other sorts than you can imagine, but least you should imagine it too burthensome to a girl at my early time of life, give mee leave to assure you I think myself happy that I can be useful to so good a father. By rising very early I find I can go through with much business, but least you should think I Shall be quite moaped with this way of life, I am to inform you there is two worthy ladies in Charles Town, Mrs Pinckney and Mrs Cleland who are partial enough to mee to wish to have mee with them, and insist upon my making their houses my home when in Town, and press mee to relax a little much oftener than 'tis in my power to accept of their obliging intreaties, but I am sometimes with one or the other for three weeks or a monthe at a time, and then enjoy all the pleasures Charles Town affords. But nothing gives mee more than subscribing myself

Dear Madam Your.
most affectionet and·
most obliged humble Servant
Pray remember me in the best manner to my ELIZA
LUCAS worthy friend Mr. Boddicott.
To my good friend Mrs. Boddicott
May ye 2ord [probably 1740]

****

WHY my dear Miss Bartlett, will you so often repeat your desire to know how I trifle away my time in our retirement in my father's absence: could it afford you advantage or pleasure I would not have hesitated, but as you can expect neither from it I would have been excused; however, to show you my readiness in obeying your commands, here it is.

In general then I rise at five o' Clock in the morning, read till seven — then take a walk in the garden or fields, see that the Servants are at their respective business, then to breakfast. The first hour after breakfast is spent in musick, the next is constantly employed in recolecting something I have learned, least for want of practice it should be quite lost, such as french and short hand.

After that, I devote the rest of the time till I dress for dinner, to our little polly, and two black girls who I teach to read, and if I have my papa's approbation (my mama's I have got) I intend for school mistress's for the rest of the Negroe children. Another scheme you see, but to proceed, the first hour after dinner, as the first after breakfast, at musick, the rest of the afternoon in needle work till candle light, and from that time to bed time read or write; 'tis the fashion here to carry our work abroad with us so that having company, without they are great strangers, is no interruption to your affair, but I have particular matters for particular days which is an interruption to mine. Mondays my musick Master is here. Tuesday my friend Mrs. Chardon (about 3 miles distant) and I are constantly engaged to each other, she at our house one Tuesday I at hers the next, and this is one of the happiest days I spend at Wappoo. Thursday the whole day except what the necessary affairs of the family take up, is spent in writing, either on the business of the plantations or on letters to my friends. Every other Friday, if no company, we go a vizeting, so that I go abroad once a week and no oftener.

Now you may form some judgment of what time I can have to work my lappets. I own I never go to them with a quite easy conscience as I know my father has an avertion to my employing my time in that poreing work, but they are begun, and must be finished. I hate to undertake anything and not go thro' with it, but by way of relaxation from the other, I have begun a piece of work of a quicker sort, which requires neither eyes nor genius, at least not very good ones, would you ever guess it to be a shrimp nett ? for so it is.

O ! I had like to forgot the last thing I have done a great while. I have planted a large fig orchard, with design to dry them, and export them. I have reckoned my expence and the prophets to arise from those figgs, but was I to tell you how great an Estate I am to make this way, and how 'tis to be laid out, you would think me far gone in romance. Your good Uncle I know has long thought I have a fertile brain at scheming, I only confirm him in his oppinion; but I own I love the vegitable world extreamely. I think it an innocent and useful amusement, and pray tell him if he laughs much at my projects, I never intend to have any hand in a silver mine, and he will understand as well as you, what I mean !

Our best respects wait on him, and Mrs Pinckney . . .

FOCUS QUESTIONS:

1. What activities occupy Pinckney? How does she present her activities to her correspondents?

3-7 Sentiments of An American Woman (1780)

Esther DeBerdt was born in Britain, and moved to the colonies after marrying Philadelphia businessman Joseph Reed. She became an American patriot, and organized the Philadelphia Ladies Association in the summer of 1780. This organization raised money that was used to provide clothing and supplies to American soldiers in the Revolutionary War.

Source: http://hdl.loc.gov/loc.rbc/rbpe.14600300

ON the commencement of actual war, the Women of America manifested a firm resolution to contribute as much as could depend on them, to the deliverance of their country. Animated by the purest patriotism, they are sensible of sorrow at this day, in not offering more than barren wishes for the success of so glorious a Revolution. They aspire to render themselves more really useful; and this sentiment is universal from the north to the south of the Thirteen United States. Our ambition is kindled by the same of those heroines of antiquity, who have rendered their sex illustrious, and have proved to the universe, that, if the weakness of our Constitution, if opinion and manners did not forbid us to march to glory by the same paths as the Men, we should at least equal, and sometimes surpass them in our love for the public good. I glory in all that which my sex has done great and commendable. I call to mind with enthusiasm and with admiration, all those acts of courage, of constancy and patriotism, which history has transmitted to us: The people favoured by Heaven, preserved from destruction by the virtues, the zeal and the resolution of Deborah, of Judith, of Esther! The fortitude of the mother of the Massachabees, in giving up her sons to die before her eyes: Rome saved from the fury of a victorious enemy by the efforts of Volumnia, and other Roman Ladies: So many famous sieges where the Women have been seen forgeting the weakness of their sex, building new walls, digging trenches with their feeble hands, furnishing arms to their defenders, they themselves darting the missile weapons on the enemy, resigning the ornaments of their apparel, and their fortune, to fill the public treasury, and to hasten the deliverance of their country; burying themselves under its ruins, throwing themselves into the flames rather than submit to the disgrace of humiliation before a proud enemy.

Born for liberty, disdaining to bear the irons of a tyrannic Government, we associate ourselves to the grandeur of those Sovereigns, cherished and revered, who have held with so much splendour the scepter of the greatest States, The Batildas, the Elizabeths, the Maries, the Catharines, who have extended the empire of liberty, and contented to reign by sweetness and justice, have broken the chains of slavery, forged by tryants in the times of ignorance and barbarity. The Spanish Women, do they not make, at this moment, the most patriotic sacrifices, to encrease the means of victory in the hands of their Sovereign. He is a friend to the French Nation. They are our allies. We call to mind, doubly interested, that it was a French Maid who kindled up amongst her fellow-citizens, the flame of patriotism buried under long misfortunes: It was the Maid of Orleans who drove from the kingdom of France the ancestors of those same British, whose odious yoke we have just shaken off; and whom it is necessary that we drive from this Continent.

But I must limit myself to the recollection of this small number of atchievements. Who knows if persons disposed to censure, and sometimes too severely with regard to us, may not disapprove our appearing acquainted even with the actions of which our sex boasts? We are at least certain, that he cannot be a good citizen who will not applaud our efforts for the relief of the armies which defend our lives, our possessions, our liberty? The situation of our soldiery has

been represented to me; the evils inseparable from war, and the firm and generous spirit which has enabled them to support these. But it has been said, that they may apprehend, that, in the course of a long war, the view of their distresses may be lost, and their services be forgottten. Forgotten! never; I can answer in the name of all my sex. Brave Americans, your disinterestedness, your courage, and your constancy will always be dear to America, as long as she shall preserve her virtue.

We know that at a distance from the theatre of war, if we enjoy any tranquility, it is the fruit of your watchings, your labours, your dangers. If I live happy in the midst of my family; if my husband cultivates his field, and reaps his harvest in peace; if, surrounded with my children, I myself nourish the youngest, and press it to my bosom, without being affraid of feeing myself separated from it, by a ferocious enemy; if the house in which we dwell; if our barns, our orchards are safe at the present time from the hands of those incendiaries, it is to you that we owe it. And shall we hesitate to evidence to you our gratitude? Shall we hesitate to wear a cloathing more simple; hair dressed less elegant, while at the price of this small privation, we shall deserve your benedictions. Who, amongst us, will not renounce with the highest pleasure, those vain ornaments, when-she shall consider that the valiant defenders of America will be able to draw some advantage from the money which she may have laid out in these; that they will be better defended from the rigours of the seasons, that after their painful toils, they will receive some extraordinary and unexpected relief; that these presents will perhaps be valued by them at a greater price, when they will have it in their power to say: *This is the offering of the Ladies.* The time is arrived to display the same sentiments which animated us at the beginning of the Revolution, when we renounced the use of teas, however agreeable to our taste, rather than receive them from our persecutors; when we made it appear to them that we placed former necessaries in the rank of superfluities, when our liberty was interested; when our republican and laborious hands spun the flax, prepared the linen intended for the use of our soldiers; when exiles and fugitives we supported with courage all the evils which are the concomitants of war. Let us not lose a moment; let us be engaged to offer the homage of our gratitude at the altar of military valour, and you, our brave deliverers, while mercenary slaves combat to cause you to share with them, the irons with which they are loaded, receive with a free hand our offering, the purest which can be presented to your virtue,

By An AMERICAN WOMAN.

FOCUS QUESTIONS:

1. Why does Reed dwell on the achievements of "heroines of antiquity"? What types of women does she mention?
2. What does Reed see as the best role for women in the American Revolution?
3. Do you see any evidence that Reed would prefer for women to take an even more active role in the American Revolution than that which she explicitly advocates here?

3-8 Revolutionary Broadside (1770)

Economic factors played an important role in the American Revolution. Boycotts of British goods were an important early step in what became the movement for independence.

Source: http://hdl.loc.gov/loc.rbc/rbpe.0370020a

WILLIAM JACKSON,
An *IMPORTER*; at the
BRAZEN HEAD,
North Side of the TOWN-HOUSE,
and Opposite the Town-Pump, in

Corn-hill, BOSTON

It is desired that the SONS and DAUGHTERS of LIBERTY, would not buy any one thing of him, for in so doing they will bring Disgrace upon *themselves*, and their *Posterity*, for *ever* and *ever*, AMEN.

FOCUS QUESTIONS:

1. What does the wording of this broadside suggest about the importance of American women as consumers?
2. What assumptions does the author appear to make about women's political knowledge and convictions?

3-9 Elizabeth Sprigs, An Indentured Servant, Writes Her Father

Indentured servitude, in which a poor English or European person pledged to work for a certain period for an American colonist in exchange for passage across the Atlantic, often resulted in exploitation of the servant. Such was apparently the case for Elizabeth Sprigs of Maryland.

Source: Elizabeth Sprigs, "Letter to Mr. John Sprigs in White Cross Street near Cripple Gate, London, September 22, 1756," in Isabel Calder, ed., *Colonial Captivities, Marches, and Journeys* (New York: Macmillan Company, 1935), 151–52. Reprinted by permission of the Connecticut Chapter of the National Society of Colonial Dames of America.

Maryland, Sept'r 22'd 1756

Honored Father

My being for ever banished from your sight, will I hope pardon the Boldness I now take of troubling you with these, my long silence has been purely owning to my undutifullness to you, and well knowing I had offended in the highest Degree, put a tie to my tongue and pen, for fear I should be extinct from your good Graces and add a further Trouble to you, but too well knowing your care and tenderness for me so long as I retain'd my Duty to you, induced me once again to endeavor if possible, to kindle up that flame again. O Dear Father, believe what I am going to relate the words of truth and sincerity, and Balance my former bad Conduct my sufferings here, and then I am sure you'll pity your Destress Daughter, What we unfortunate English People suffer here is beyond the probability of you in England to Conceive, let it suffice that I one of the unhappy Number, am toiling almost Day and Night, and very often in the Horses drudgery, with only this comfort that you Bitch you do not halfe enough, and then tied up and whipp'd to that Degree that you'd not serve an Animal, scarce any thing but Indian Corn and Salt to eat and that even begrudged nay many Negroes are better used, almost naked no shoes nor stockings to wear, and the comfort after slaving during Masters pleasure, what rest we can get is to rap ourselves up in a Blanket and ly upon the Ground, this is the deplorable Condition your poor Betty endures, and now I beg if you have any Bowels of Compassion left show it by sending me some Relief, Clothing is the principal thing wanting, which if you should condiscend to, may easily send them to me by any of the ships bound to Baltimore Town Patapsco River Maryland, and give me leave to conclude in Duty to you and Uncles and Aunts, and Respect to all Friends

Honored Father
Your undutifull and Disobedient Child
Elizabeth Sprigs

FOCUS QUESTIONS:

1. Why does Sprigs describe herself as "undutifull and Disobedient"?
2. What forms of abuse does Sprig describe here? What is Sprig's reaction to her treatment?

3-10 Thomas Jefferson's Slaves Join the British (1781)

Like most slave-holders, Thomas Jefferson kept good records of the whereabouts and health status of his slaves.

Source: In Major Problems in American Women's History. 2nd edition. Mary Beth Norton and Ruth M. Alexander, editors. Lexington, MA: D.C. Heath and Company, 1996, 82-83.

FOCUS QUESTIONS:

1. What does the record of many slaves joining the British suggest? What is suggested by the fact that some of them returned?

2. Among those who "joined the enemy," what approximately seems to be the proportion of men, women, and children?

DEATHS ETC.

1781.	Hannibal. Patty. Sam. Sally. Nanny Fanny Prince Nancy	} fled to the enemy & died.
Elkhill		
	Flora. (Black Sall's) Quomina (Black Sall's)	} joined enemy & died.
	Black Sall Jame. (Bl. Sall's) Joe. (Sue's.)	} joined enemy, returned & died.
Cumbl^d.	Lucy [erasure] [erasure] Sam.	} joined enemy.
Elk-hill Shadwell.	Jenny [erasure] Harry	
Monticello.	Barnaby. run away. returned & died.	
Elkhill.	York. Isabel. Jack. Hana's child. Phoebe's child	} caught small pox from enemy & died.

[note Judy & Nat of Elkhill, Will & Robin of Shadwell joined the enemy, but came back again & lived. so did Isabel, Hannibal's daughter. aftwds given to A.S. Jefferson.]

Elk-hill.	Branford Sue. Sue's daur.	} caught the camp fever from the negroes who returned: & died
Monticello Elk-hill	Old Jenny Phoebe (Sue's) Nanny (Tom's)	} 1782

3-11 The Rights of Man and Woman in Post-Revolutionary America

This 1998 article in a scholarly journal was written by Rosemarie Zagarri, a history professor at George Mason University. Zagarri analyzes a variety of sources to trace emerging languages and understandings of "women's rights" in the United States between 1792 and 1825.

Source: The Rights of Man and Woman in Post-Revolutionary America Author(s): Rosemarie Zagarri Source: The William and Mary Quarterly, Third Series, Vol. 55, No. 2, (Apr., 1998), pp. 203- 230 Published by: Omohundro Institute of Early American History and Culture Stable URL: http://www.jstor.org/stable/2674382 Accessed: 12/08/2008 16:08

On July 4, 1804, a group of young men in Harrisburg, Pennsylvania, offered a series of toasts to commemorate the nation's Independence. Among their testimonials, they offered one to a cherished ideal: "[To] the rights of men, and the rights of women—. May the former never be infringed, nor the latter curtailed."[1] This apparently simple statement provides a tantalizing clue to the complex relationship between politics and gender in the early national era. In one sense, it points to an important change in women's status. The men acknowledged, even celebrated, an innovative and controversial idea: women along with men should be regarded as the bearers of rights. In the wake of the American Revolution and especially after the publication of Mary Wollstonecraft's *Vindication of the Rights of Woman* (1792), women gained a dignity and an esteem that had hitherto been denied them—though the exact nature of their rights was, as we shall see, a matter still to be determined.

The revelers, however, did something more. They made a pointed distinction between the rights of males and females, a distinction based on sex. The danger to men's rights came from an infringement on their liberties, especially their political liberties, whereas the threat to women's rights came from a curtailment of their privileges, which were nonpolitical in nature. Put simply, men's rights involved liberties that allowed choices, while women's rights consisted of benefits that imposed duties. Rather than an abstract, universal proposition, rights became a gendered variable.

The differentiation of rights on the basis of sex reveals a crucial, but previously overlooked, bifurcation in the evolution of natural rights ideology in the early years of the republic. At the same time Americans were debating the "rights of man," they conducted a parallel discussion about the "rights of woman." The latter debate, however, did not occur within official political institutions, nor was it principally concerned with political rights. To reconstruct this debate, we must broaden our understanding of politics and employ sources not usually considered in the writing of traditional political history. Ladies' magazines, literary periodicals, and prescriptive literature for women provide a glimpse into a world of ideas that had not yet surfaced in the formal political realm.[2]

. . . In the post-Revolutionary era, Americans attempted to reconcile two conflicting principles: the equality of the sexes and the subordination of women to men. In the process, they came to define the rights of women in contrast to the rights of men. Yet they did not attribute different rights to each sex arbitrarily, merely on the basis of whim or prejudice. Instead, they drew on two separate preexisting traditions of natural rights, one inherited from Locke and the other from Scottish Enlightenment. To men, writers applied a Lockean conception of rights that emphasized equality, individual autonomy, and the expansion of personal freedoms. By accentuating the importance of individual liberty, Lockean discourse endowed unfranchised white males with the moral authority to challenge their exclusion from the political process. To women, authors applied a Scottish theory that treated rights as benefits, conferred by God and expressed in the performance of duties to society. The stress on duty and obligation, rather than on liberty and choice, gave women's rights a fundamentally different character from those of men. Women's rights were to be nonpolitical in nature, confined to the traditional feminine role of wife and mother.

---

1 "July 4th Toasts," *Carlisle [Pa.] Gazette,* July 20, 1804. Toasts to the "Rights of Women" were not uncommon in this period. See David Waldstreicher, *In the Midst of Perpetual Fetes: The Making of American Nationalism, 1776-1820* (Chapel Hill, 1997), 166-71, 232-41.

2 For other works that have pioneered the broader exploration of the role of women in politics see Paula Baker, "The Domestication of Politics: Women and the American Political Society, 1780-1920," *American Historical Review,* 89 (1984), 620-47; Jan Lewis, "The Republican Wife: Virtue and Seduction in the Early Republic," *William and Mary Quarterly,* 3d Ser., 64 (1987), 689-721; Ruth H. Bloch, "The Gendered Meanings of Virtue in Revolutionary America," *Signs: Journal of Women in Culture and Society,* 13 (1987), 37-58; and Mary P. Ryan, *Women in Public: Between Banners and Ballots, 1825-1880* (Baltimore, 1990).

While these developments may appear to confirm the feminist interpretation, a close reading of the sources suggests otherwise. Efforts to constrict the meaning of women's rights did not succeed. What the feminist critique ignores is the ability of rights language, evident as early as the 1790s, to undermine the gendered limitations of political theory. Once women had attained the status of rights bearers, no formal theory, whether of Scottish or Lockean origins, could contain the radical power of rights talk. Soon after the Revolution, and long before the emergence of the first women's rights movement, rights discourse itself expanded the range of rights that women could and would claim.

FOCUS QUESTIONS:

1. Summarize the distinction between men's (Lockean) rights and women's (Scottish traditional) rights.

2. Does this distinction seem to apply to other documents you have read in this chapter? If you believe it does, provide examples; if not, explain why this might be the case, and whether it invalidates Zagarri's argument.

3-12 Molly Wallace, Valedictory Oration (1792)

In this fascinating document, Molly Wallace, valedictory speaker at the Young Ladies Academy of Philadelphia, discusses whether women should be allowed to speak in public while, of course, speaking in public. In a time that tended to agree with Samuel Johnson that a woman speaking in public was similar to a trained animal act, Wallace's speech is all the more interesting.

The silent and solemn attention of a respectable audience, has often, at the beginning of discourses intimidated, even veterans, in the art of public elocution. What then must my situation be, when my sex, my youth and inexperience all conspire to make me tremble at the talk which I have undertaken? . . . With some, however, it has been made a question, whether we ought ever to appear in so public a manner. Our natural timidity, the domestic situation to which by nature and custom we seem destined, are, urged as arguments against what I have now undertaken:- Many sarcastical observations have been handed out against female oratory: But to what do they amount? Do they not plainly inform us, that, because we are females, we ought therefore to be deprived of what is perhaps the most effectual means of acquiring a just, natural and graceful delivery? No one will pretend to deny, that we should be taught to read in the best manner. And if to read, why not to speak? . . . But yet it might be asked, what, has a female character to do with declamation? That she should harangue at the head of an Army, in the Senate, or before a popular Assembly, is not pretended, neither is it requested that she ought to be an adept in the stormy and contentious eloquence of the bar, or in the abstract and subtle reasoning of the Senate; -we look not for a female Pitt, Cicero, or Demosthenes. There are more humble and milder scenes than those which I have mentioned, in which a woman may display her elocution. There are numerous topics, on which she may discourse without impropriety, in the discussion of which, she may instruct and please others, and in which she may exercise and improve her own understanding. After all, we do not expect women should become perfect orators. Why then should they be taught to speak in public? This question may possibly be answered by asking several others. Why is a boy diligently and carefully taught the Latin, the Greek, or the Hebrew language, in which he will seldom have occasion, either to write or to converse? Why is he taught to demonstrate the propositions of Euclid, when during his whole life, he will not perhaps make use of one of them? Are we taught to dance merely for the sake of becoming dancers? No, certainly. These things are commonly studied, more on account of the habits, which the learning of them establishes, than on account of any important advantages which the mere knowledge of them can afford. So a young lady, from the exercise of speaking before a properly selected audience, may acquire some valuable habits, which, otherwise she can obtain from no examples, and that no precept can give. But, this exercise can with propriety be performed only before a select audience: a promiscuous and indiscriminate one, for obvious reasons, would be absolutely unsuitable, and should always be carefully avoided. . . .

FOCUS QUESTIONS:

1. Summarize Molly Wallace's defense of her right, and a woman's right, to speak publicly. What caution does she also offer to her audience regarding the propriety of women speaking in public?

CHAPTER 4

FRONTIERS OF TRADE AND EMPIRE, 1750-1860

4-1 Captivity Among the Sioux

"Captivity narratives" – first-person accounts written by women of European descent who were held hostage by Native Americans – formed a popular genre in American literature from the time of the Puritans in 17th-century New England, through the westward expansion of the 19th century. In this example, Fanny Wiggins Kelly describes her experiences. Fanny, her husband, and their adopted daughter Mary were part of a small group of settlers traveling to Idaho in the summer of 1864. Their wagon train was attacked by a band of Sioux; Fanny's husband escaped, and Fanny and Mary were taken hostage. Fanny and her captors spent several weeks in intermittent skirmishes with the U.S. Army before joining a large Sioux encampment. Early in the winter of 1864-65, Fanny was ransomed to a U.S. army fort in the Dakotas, where she was reunited with her husband.

Source: Kelly, Fanny. *Narrative of My Captivity Among the Sioux Indians: With a Brief Account of General Sully's Indian Expedition in 1864, Bearing Upon Events Occurring in My Captivity.* (Chicago: R.R. Donnelley & Sons Co., 1891) 43-59, 79-86.

Soon [after the attack] they had another horse saddled for me, and assisted me to mount him. I looked around for my little Mary. There she stood, a poor helpless lamb, in the midst of blood-thirsty savages. I stretched out my arms for her imploringly. For a moment they hesitated; then, to my unspeakable joy, they yielded, and gave me my child.

They then started on, leading my horse; they also gave me a rope that was fastened around the horse's under jaw. The air was cool, and the sky was bright with the glitter of starlight.

In the darkness of our ride, I conceived a plan for the escape of little Mary. I whispered in her childish ear, "Mary, we are only a few miles from our camp, and the stream we have crossed you can easily wade through. I have dropped letters on the way, you know, to guide our friends in the direction we have taken;

they will guide you back again, and it may be your only chance of escape from destruction. Drop gently down, and lie on the ground for a little while, to avoid being seen; then retrace your steps, and may God in mercy go with you. If I can, I will follow you." The child, whose judgment was remarkable for her age, readily acceded to this plan; her eye brightened and her young heart throbbed as she thought of its success. Watching the opportunity, I dropped her gently, carefully, and unobserved, to the ground, and she lay there, while the Indians pursued their way, unconscious of their loss. To portray my feelings upon this separation would be impossible. The agony I suffered was indescribable. I was firmly convinced that my course was wise – that I had given her the only chance of escape within my power; yet the terrible uncertainty of what her fate might be in the way before her, was almost unbearable. I continued to think of it so deeply that at last I grew desperate, and resolved to follow her at every risk. Accordingly, watching an opportunity, I, too, slipped to the ground under the friendly cover of night, and the horse went on without its rider. My plan was not successful. My flight was soon discovered, and the Indian wheeled around- and rode back in my pursuit. Crouching in the undergrowth I might have escaped in the darkness, were it not for their cunning. Forming in a line of forty or fifty abreast, they actually covered the ground as they rode past me. The horses themselves were thus led to betray me, for, being frightened at my crouching form, they stopped and reared, thus informing them of my hiding place. With great presence of mind I arose the moment I found myself discovered, and relating my story, the invention of an instant, I succeeded partially in allaying their anger. I told them the child had fallen asleep and dropped from the horse; that I had endeavored to call their attention to it, but in vain; and, fearing I would be unable to find her if we rode further, I had jumped down and attempted the search alone. The Indians used great violence toward me, assuring me that if any further attempts were made to escape, my punishment would be accordingly. They then promised to send a party out in search of the child when it became light. Poor little Mary! alone in the wilderness, a little, helpless child; who can portray her terror! With faith to trust, and courage to dare, that little, trembling form through the long hours of the night kept watch.

…I made superhuman efforts to appear cheerful, for my only refuge was in being submissive and practicing conciliation. My fear of them was too powerful to allow me to give way to emotion for one moment. There were sentinels stationed at different places to give the alarm, in case of any one approaching to rescue, and I afterward learned that in such a case I would have been instantly murdered. Next morning I learned, by signs, that Indians had gone out in search of little Mary, scattering themselves over the hills, in squads.

***

[In the following days] Another burden had been added to my almost worn-out frame, the leading of an unruly horse; and my arms were so full of the implements I was forced to carry, that I threw away the pipe of the old chief – a tube nearly three feet long, and given me to take care of. …The chief declared that I should die for having caused the loss of his pipe. An untamed horse was brought, and they told me I would be placed on it as a target for their deadliest arrows, and the animal might then run at will, carrying my body where it would. Helpless, and almost dying with terror at my situation, I sank on a rocky seat in their midst. They were all armed, and anxiously awaited the signal. They had pistols, bows, and spears; and I noticed some stoop, and raise blazing fire-brands to frighten the pawing beast that was to bear me to death. In speechless agony I raised my soul to God! Soon it would stand before his throne, and with all the pleading passion of my sinking soul I prayed for pardon and … for my own salvation, and the forgiveness of my enemies; and remembering a purse of money which was in my pocket, knowing that it would decay with my body in the wilderness, I drew it out, and, with suffused eyes, divided it among them, though my hands were growing powerless and my sight failing. One hundred and twenty dollars in notes I gave them, telling them its value as I did so, when, to my astonishment, a change came over their faces. They laid their weapons on the ground, seemingly pleased, and anxious to understand, requesting me to explain the worth of each note clearly, by holding up my fingers. Eagerly I tried to obey, perceiving the hope their milder manner held out; but my cold hands fell powerless by my side, my tongue refused to utter a sound, and, unconsciously, I sank to the ground [where I] lay silent till

day-break, when the camp was again put in motion, and, at their bidding, I mounted one horse and led another, as I had done on the day previous. …

***

[After a few weeks] The Indians gave me to understand that when we crossed this stream, and a short distance beyond, we would be at their home. Here they paused to dress, so as to make a gay appearance and imposing entrance into the village. Except when in full dress, an Indian's wearing apparel consists only of a buffalo robe, which is also part of a fine toilet. It is very inconveniently disposed about the person, without fastening, and must be held in position with the hands. Here the clothing taken from our train was brought into great demand, and each warrior that had been fortunate enough to possess himself of any article of our dress, now arrayed himself to the best advantage the garments and their limited ideas of civilization permitted; -and, in some instances, when the toilet was considered complete, changes for less attractive articles of display were made with companions who had not been so fortunate as others in the division of the goods, that they might also share in the sport afforded by this derisive display. Their peculiar ideas of tasteful dress rendered them grotesque in appearance. One brawny face appeared under the shade of my hat, smiling with evident satisfaction at the superiority of his decorations over those of his less fortunate companions; another was shaded from the scorching rays of the sun by a tiny parasol, and the brown hand that held it aloft was thinly covered by a silk glove, which was about the only article of clothing, except the invariable breech-cloth, that the warrior wore. … Ottawa, or Silver Horn, the war chief, was arrayed in full costume. He was very old, over seventy-five, partially blind, and a little below the medium height. He was very ferocious and savage looking, and now, when in costume, looked frightful. His face was red, with stripes of black, and around each eye a circlet of bright yellow. His long, black hair was divided into two braids, with a scalp-lock on top of the head. His ears held great brass wire rings, full six inches in diameter, and chains and bead necklaces were suspended from his neck; armlets and bracelets of brass, together with a string of bears' claws, completed his jewelry. He wore also leggings of deer skin, and a shirt of the same material, beautifully ornamented with beads, and fringed with scalp-locks, that he claimed to have taken from his enemies, both red and white. Over his shoulders hung a great, bright-colored quilt, that had been taken from our stores. He wore a crown of eagle feathers on his head…. His horse, a noble-looking animal, was no less gorgeously arrayed. His ears were pierced, like his master's, and his neck was encircled by a wreath of bears' claws, taken from animals that the chief had slain. Some bells and a human scalp hung from his mane, forming together, thus arrayed, a museum of the trophies of the old chief's prowess on the war path, and of skill in the chase.

.... Great crowds of curious Indians came flocking in to stare at me. The women brought their children. Some of them, whose fair complexion astonished me, I afterward learned were the offspring of fort marriages. One fair little boy, who, with his mother, had just returned from Fort Laramie, came close to me. Finding the squaw could speak a few words in English, I addressed her, and was told, in reply to my questions, that she had been the wife of a captain there, but that 'his white wife' arriving from the East, his Indian wife was told to return to her people; she did so, taking her child with her. ...

...The women of the chief's family... seemed kindly disposed toward me, and one of them brought me a dish of meat; many others followed her example, even from the neighboring lodges, and really seemed to pity me, and showed great evidences of compassion, and tried to express their sympathy in signs, because I had been torn from my own people, and compelled to come such a long fatiguing journey, and examined me all over and over again, and all about my dress, hands, and feet particularly. Then, to their great surprise, they discovered my bruised and almost broken limbs that occurred when first taken, also from the fall of the horse the first night of my captivity, and proceeded at once to dress my wounds.

I was just beginning to rejoice in the dawning kindness that seemed to soften their swarthy faces, when a messenger from the war chief arrived, accompanied by a small party of young warriors sent to conduct me to the chief's presence. I did not at first comprehend the summons, and, as every fresh announcement only awakened new fears, I dreaded to comply, yet dared not refuse. Seeing my hesitation, the senior wife allowed a little daughter of the chiefs, whose name was Yellow Bird, to accompany me, and I was then conducted to several feasts, at each of which I was received with kindness, and promised good will and protection. It was here that the chief himself first condescended to speak kindly to me, and this and the companionship of the child Yellow Bird, who seemed to approach me with a trusting grace and freedom unlike the scared shyness of Indian children generally, inspired hope. The chief here told me that henceforth I could call Yellow Bird my own, to take the place of my little girl that had been killed. I did not at once comprehend all of his meaning, still it gave me some hope of security. ...At nightfall we returned to the lodge, which, they told me, I must henceforth regard as home....

FOCUS QUESTIONS:

1. At what points do Kelly's attitudes towards her captors seem to change? What evidence is there of Kelly feeling fear of the Sioux? Does she ever seem to feel admiration, sympathy, gratitude, or curiousity?

2. Kelly requested compensation from the U.S. government for the material losses she experienced in the course of her capture and captivity. What parts of this document might be designed to justify her claims?

3. Why did Kelly encourage Mary to escape? What were the results? What other courses of action were available to Kelly and Mary?

4-2 A Citizen Protests the Rape of Indian Women in California (1862)

This newspaper editorial publicizes the generally under-reported problem of rape. In this case, the writer objects to the rape of Native American women in rural California by soldiers; the writer is particularly disturbed by the apparent participation of an officer in the events described.

Source: *In Major Problems in American Women's History.* 2nd edition. Mary Beth Norton and Ruth M. Alexander, editors. Lexington, MA: D.C. Heath and Company, 1996, 190-191.

Editor Beacon: —-It is well known that there is, or has been, a body of soldiers this county for several weeks past, for the avowed object of defending and protecting the citizens of the county against Indian depredations .... On Friday night a party of these soldiers visited the ranch of Col. Washington, and made themselves annoying to the Indians in the rancheria. This party was small, only three, as reported. Saturday night, the 4th of October, 1862, was made memorable by the visit of a portion of this command, headed, aided and abetted by the commanding officer, Lieut. — -, (or some one assuming his title,) to the farm of Col. Washington, and to the rancheria of peaceful and domesticated Indians resident thereon. Not one of the soldiers, private or Lieutenant, (or pretended Lieutenant, if such he was,) called at the farm house, but rode by and entered the Indian rancheria, with demands for Indian women, for the purpose of prostitution! They were requested leave and ordered off the place. They answered they would do as they pleased, as they had the power. They were then told that it was true they were the strongest, and no force at hand was sufficient to contend with them, and they were left in the Indian rancheria. Most of the young squaws in the rancheria had by this time ran off and concealed themselves, and were beyond the reach and brutal grasp of the ravishers. They, however, were to be satiated, and like brutes dragged the old, decrepit "tar-heads" forth, and as many as three of the soldiers, in rapid succession, had forced intercourse with old squaws. Such was the conduct of the portion of the command of Co. E, on the night of the 4th of October, 1862, who visited the Indian rancheria at the Old Mill Place, about 3 miles from N. L. headquarters. It is but proper, after consulting with those who are acquainted with the outrage, to say that the Lieut. (or pretended Lieut., if such he was,) did not arrive at the scene of action until after the larger portion of his men were on the ground - But it is absolutely certain that he was there - that he put his horse in the stable to hay, and then prowled around and through the Indian rancherias in quest of some squaw. Whether he found a fit subject upon which to practice his virtuous and civilizing purposes, the writer is not informed. He, however, saddled up and left the scene of moral exploit about daylight. In justice to decency, humanity and civilization, these brutes should be punished. It is due to the honor, the reputation, the chivalry of the army of the United States, that the insignia of rank and position should be tom from the person of the Lieutenant (if it was he who was there,) as an officer unworthy its trust and confidence.

FOCUS QUESTIONS:

1. What can you infer from this passage about the organization of Colonel Washington's farm? How do the Native Americans on the farm respond to the soldiers?

2. What aspects of the rapes particularly offend the author of the editorial?

4-3 Occurrences in Hispanic California

María de las Angustias de las Guerra de Ord (1815-1880) was a member of a prominent family of ranchers in early California. Her father commanded the presidio at Santa Barbara. Shortly before her death, she was interviewed for a major oral-history project. Her testimony below details a revolt that took place simultaneously at several southern California missions, when Angustias de las Guerra de Ord was about nine years old.

Source: From testimonial by María de las Angustias de las Guerra de Ord recorded for Hubert Howe Bancroft's 1884-1890 *History of California*, excerpted in *Herencia: The Anthology of Hispanic Literature of the United States*, Nicolas Kanellos, ed. (New York: Oxford University Press, 2002), 95-100.

In 1824, when I was about 9 years old, while Capt. Dn Luis Anto Arguello was acting governor of California, then under the flag of Mexico, there occurred an uprising of the Indians of the Missions of La Purisima, Santa Ines, and Santa Barbara. A soldier came flying from one of those Missions to notify my father, at the time Comandante at Santa Barbara, that the Indians were in revolt and threatening the white families. This was Oil a Saturday between noon and 2:00 p.m. Immediately my father ordered my uncle, Dn Antonio Anastasio Carrillo, with 15 men to aid the Missions and the families. That night my uncle Dn Carlos Antonio Carrillo prepared to leave by the next day with a somewhat larger force. As it was Sunday, Padre Antonio Ripoll, one of the fathers of the Mission, came here to say Mass for us. My father directed that he should say his Mass, without loss of time because when the troop was ready it should march. The padre was very sad and my father asked him what was the matter. He said the Indians did not want to go to Mass. Then my father asked if this was something new. The padre, answered that the Indians were alarmed because troops had been sent to Santa Ines and La Purisima. Then my father begged that he speak the truth-had the Indians risen? Padre Ripoll replied that it was so. My father then arranged that the missionary could not give warning, and that the troops should remain in the presidio and for him to go with them to Santa Barbara [Mission] and attack the Indians. Padre Ripoll got to his feet crying like a woman, and said, "My God! Don't kill my children. I will go to see them first. The' troops need not go." My father did not want him to go, fearing they would attack him. But h~ went. As soon as the Indians saw him they said they were going to kill him. But some of the Indians were opposed and they advised him to return to the presidio, because the others had no intention of sparing him, but were bent on killing as many white people as they could, and then retire to the mountains. This about killing the white people, Padre Ripoll did not tell us but the Indian who accompanied him did.

The associate of Padre Ripoll at the Mission was Padre Anto Jayme, a man of advanced age who walked with difficulty. When the Indians forced Padre Ripoll to return to the presidio, he begged his associate to go with him, but the Indians refused to allow it and gave assurance that they would do no harm to Padre Jayme. When Padre Ripoll arrived at the house my father asked him what result he had had with the Indians, and the answer was, crying, that they would do nothing to Padre Jayme. My father went at once to the Mission with the troops and there saw no Indians except those who were in the corridor who had put Padre Jayme on the parapet and were firing their arrows from behind him. There was at the Mission a Russian called Jose who was a servant there. He was among the Indians shooting a firearm. The troops from here killed some Indians who exposed themselves darting from behind the rocks to shoot their arrows. A few attracted the attention of the troops while the bulk of the Indians went from the Mission toward the mountains. . . By 1 o'clock the Mission was almost abandoned by the Indians, but the troops did not know it then. At that hour they retired to the presidio to get

food, carrying 2 wounded companions. All this while Padre Ripoll was in a room which had a window toward the Mission. He had nothing to drink. My mother sent him a little broth. I went in with the servant and told him "they have killed some Indians." The padre began to cry and would not take even one drop of broth. I ran out overwhelmed for having given to him news that had saddened him so. . . A little later the Indian sacristan of the Mission arrived with the keys of the church and he told the padre that the Indian alcaldes were saying they would take away everything in the Mission because it was thdrs, but of that which was in the church they would take nothing because it was God's; that the revolting Indians had now gone to the Tular. Padre Ripoll loved his neophytes as a devoted mother. His emotions were so great that he became ill, though not seriously so. That same afternoon 2 Indians came bringing Padre Jayme to my father's house. During the whole day in the Mission the Indians did not forget to give him his food. The priests stayed on at our house. This outbreak was on February 27, 1824.

FOCUS QUESTIONS:

1. Does Angustias de las Guerra de Ord seem to admire anyone's conduct here?

2. How might Angustias de las Guerra de Ord's perspective as a young girl influence her observations and memories?

4-4 Sacagawea Interprets for Lewis and Clark (1804)

In November 1804, Meriwether Lewis, William Clark, and the Corps of Discovery arrived at the Hidatsa-Mandan villages near present day Bismarck, North Dakota. There they met and hired Toussaint Charbonneau, a French-Canadian fur trader and Sacagawea ("Canoe Launcher"), one of his two Shoshone "wives." Lewis and Clark believed Sacagawea could be important in trading for horses when the Corps reached the Bitterroot mountains and the Shoshones. While Sacagawea did not speak English, she spoke Shoshone and Hidatsa. Charbonneau spoke Hidatsa and French. It was hoped that when the expedition met the Shoshones, Sacagawea would talk with them, then translate to Hidatsa for Charbonneau, who would translate into French. The Corps' Francois Labiche spoke French and English, and would make the final translation so that Lewis and Clark could understand.

Source: Meriwether Lewis and William Clark, History of the Expedition of Captains Lewis and Clark, 2 Vols. (Chicago: A. C. McClurg & Co., 1924), 1: 406–411.

SATURDAY, August 17. Captain Lewis rose very early and despatched Drewyer and the Indian down the river in quest of the boats. Shields was sent out at the same time to hunt, while M'Neal prepared a breakfast out of the remainder of the meat. Drewyer had been gone about two hours, and the Indians were all anxiously waiting for some news, when an Indian who had straggled a short distance down the river returned with a report that he had seen the white men, who were only a short distance below, and were coming on. The Indians were all transported with joy, and the chief in the warmth of his satisfaction renewed his embrace to Captain Lewis, who was quite as much delighted as the Indians themselves. The report proved most agreeably true. On setting out at seven o'clock, Captain Clark, with Charbonneau and his wife, walked on shore; but they had not gone more than a mile before

Captain Clark saw Sacagawea, who was with her husband one hundred yards ahead, begin to dance and show every mark of the most extravagant joy, turning round him and pointing to several Indians, whom he now saw advancing on horseback, sucking her fingers at the same time to indicate that they were of her native tribe. As they advanced Captain Clark discovered among them Drewyer dressed like an Indian, from whom he learnt the situation of the party. While the boats were performing the circuit he went towards the forks with the Indians, who, as they went along, sang aloud with the greatest appearance of delight. We soon drew near to the camp, and just as we approached it a woman made her way through the crowd towards Sacagawea, and recognising each other, they embraced with the most tender affection. The meeting of these two young women had in it something peculiarly touching, not only in the ardent manner in which their feelings were expressed, but from the real interest of their situation. They had been companions in childhood; in the war with the Minnetarees they had both been taken prisoners in the same battle, they had shared and softened the rigours of their captivity, till one of them had escaped from the Minnetarees, with scarce a hope of ever seeing her friend relieved from the hands of her enemies. While Sacagawea was renewing among the women the friendships of former days, Captain Clark went on, and was received by Captain Lewis and the chief, who, after the first embraces and salutations were over, conducted him to a sort of circular tent or shade of willows. Here he was seated on a white robe, and the chief immediately tied in his hair six small shells resembling pearls, an ornament highly valued by these people, who procured them in the course of trade from the seacoast. The moccasins of the whole party were then taken off, and after much ceremony the smoking began. After this the conference was to be opened, and glad of an opportunity of being able to converse more intelligibly, Sacagawea was sent for; she came into the tent, sat down, and was beginning to interpret, when in the person of Cameahwait she recognised her brother; she instantly jumped up and ran and embraced him, throwing over him her blanket and weeping profusely; the chief was himself moved, though not in the same degree. After some conversation between them she resumed her seat, and attempted to interpret for us, but her new situation seemed to overpower her, and she was frequently interrupted by her tears. After the council was finished, the unfortunate woman learnt that all her family were dead except two brothers, one of whom was absent, and a son of her eldest sister, a small boy, who was immediately adopted by her. The canoes arriving soon after, we formed a camp in a meadow on the left side, a little below the forks, took out our baggage, and by means of our sails and willow poles formed a canopy for our Indian visitors. About four o'clock the chiefs and warriors were collected, and after the customary ceremony of taking off the moccasins and smoking a pipe, we explained to them in a long harangue the purposes of our visit, making themselves one conspicuous object of the good wishes of our government, on whose strength as well as its friendly disposition we expatiated. We told them of their dependence on the will of our government for all future supplies of whatever was necessary either for their comfort or defence; that as we were sent to discover the best route by which merchandise could be conveyed to them, and no trade would be begun before our return, it was mutually advantageous that we should proceed with as little delay as possible; that we were under the necessity of requesting them to furnish us with horses to transport our baggage across the mountains, and a guide to show us the route, but that they should be amply remunerated for their horses, as well as for every other service they should render us. In the meantime our first wish was, that they should immediately collect as many horses as were necessary to transport our baggage to their village, where, at our leisure, we would trade with them for as many horses as they could spare.

The speech made a favourable impression; the chief in reply thanked us for our expressions of friendship towards himself and his nation, and declared their willingness to render us every service. He lamented that it would be so long before they should be supplied with firearms, but that till then they could subsist as they had heretofore done. He concluded by saying that there were not horses here sufficient to transport our goods, but that he would return to the village tomorrow, and bring all his own horses, and encourage his people to come over with theirs. The conference being ended to our satisfaction, we now inquired of Cameahwait what chiefs were among the party, and he pointed out two of them. We then distributed our presents: to Cameahwait we gave a medal of the small size, with the likeness of President Jefferson, and on the reverse a figure of hands clasped with a pipe and tomahawk; to this was added a uniform coat, a shirt, a pair of scarlet leggings, a carrot of tobacco, and some small articles. Each of the other chiefs received a small medal struck during the presidency of General Washington, a shirt, handkerchief, leggings, a knife, and some tobacco. Medals of the same sort were also presented to two young warriors, who though not chiefs were promising youths and very much respected in the tribe. These honorary gifts were followed by presents of paint, moccasins, awls, knives, beads, and looking-glasses. We also gave them all a plentiful meal of Indian corn, of which the hull is taken off by being boiled in lye; and as this was the first they had ever tasted, they were very much pleased with it. They had indeed abundant sources of surprise in all they saw: the appearance of the men, their arms, their clothing, the canoes, the strange looks of the negro, and the sagacity of our dog, all in turn shared their admiration, which was raised to astonishment by a shot from the airgun; this operation was instantly considered as a great medicine, by which they as well as the other Indians mean something emanating directly from the Great Spirit, or produced by his invisible and incomprehensible agency. The display of all these riches had been intermixed with inquiries into the geographical situation of their country, for we had learnt by experience that to keep the savages in good temper their attention should not be wearied with too much business, but that the serious affairs should be enlivened by a mixture of what is new and entertaining. Our hunters brought in very seasonably four deer and an antelope, the last of which we gave to the Indians, who in a very short time devoured it. After the council was over, we consulted as to our future operations. The game does not promise to last here for a number of days, and this circumstance combined with many others to induce our going on as soon as possible. Our Indian information as to the state of the Columbia is of a very alarming kind, and our first object is of course to ascertain the practicability of descending it, of which the Indians discourage our expectations. It was therefore agreed that Captain Clark should set off in the morning with eleven men, furnished, besides their arms, with tools for making canoes; that he should take Charbonneau and his wife to the camp of the Shoshonees, where he was to leave them, in order to hasten the collection of horses; that he was then to lead his men down to the Columbia, and if he found it navigable, and the timber in sufficient quantity, begin to build canoes. As soon as he had decided as to the propriety of proceeding down the Columbia or across the mountains, he was to send back one of the men with information of it to Captain Lewis, who by that time would have brought up the whole party and the rest of the baggage as far as the Shoshonee village.

Preparations were accordingly made this evening for such an arrangement. The sun is excessively hot in the day time, but the nights very cold, and rendered still more unpleasant from the want of any fuel except willow brush. The appearances, too, of game for many days' subsistence are not very favourable.

FOCUS QUESTIONS:

1. The Shoshone were known to have horses that the Corps of Discovery would need to cross the western mountains. What do you think the expedition would have done had they not found a Shoshone band or been able to trade for horses?

2. What was the relationship between Sacagawea and the Shoshone band encountered by the Corps? Do you think this relationship aided in the trading process and the success of the expedition? Why or why not?

4-5 Across the Plains With Catherine Sager Pringle (1844)

As a child, Catherine Sager Pringle emigrated with her family from Ohio to Missouri and soon participated in the long overland journey to Oregon. She preserved her experiences in her diary in 1860. In this excerpt from her first chapter, Pringle relates incidents on the trail and the emotional story of the death of her parents.

Source: The Oregon Trail Web Site http://www.isu.edu/~trin-mich/OO.ar.sager1.html

On the Plains in 1844

My father was one of the restless ones who are not content to remain in one place long at a time. Late in the fall of 1838 we emigrated from Ohio to Missouri. Our first halting place was on Green River, but the next year we took a farm in Platte County. He engaged in farming and blacksmithing, and had a wide reputation for ingenuity. Anything they needed, made or mended, sought his shop. In 1843, Dr. Whitman came to Missouri. The healthful climate induced my mother to favor moving to Oregon. Immigration was the theme all winter, and we decided to start for Oregon. Late in 1843 father sold his property and moved near St. Joseph, and in April, 1844, we started across the plains. The first encampments were a great pleasure to us children. We were five girls and two boys, ranging from the girl baby to be born on the way to the oldest boy, hardly old enough to be any help.

Starting on the Plains

We waited several days at the Missouri River. Many friends came that far to see the emigrants start on their long journey, and there was much sadness at the parting, and a sorrowful company crossed the Missouri that bright spring morning. The motion of the wagon made us all sick, and it was weeks before we got used to the seasick motion. Rain came down and required us to tie down the wagon covers, and so increased our sickness by confining the air we breathed.

Our cattle recrossed in the night and went back to their winter quarters. This caused delay in recovering them and a weary, forced march to rejoin the train. This was divided into companies, and we were in that commanded by William Shaw. Soon after starting Indians raided our camp one night and drove off a number of cattle. They were pursued, but never recovered.

Soon everything went smooth and our train made steady headway. The weather was fine and we enjoyed the journey pleasantly. There were several musical instruments among the emigrants, and these sounded clearly on the evening air when camp was made and merry talk and laughter resounded from almost every camp-fire.

Incidents of Travel

We had one wagon, two steady yoke of old cattle, and several of young and not well-broken ones. Father was no ox driver, and had trouble with these until one day he called on Captain Shaw for assistance. It was furnished by the good captain pelting the refractory steers with stones until they were glad to come to terms.

Reaching the buffalo country, our father would get some one to drive his team and start on the hunt, for he was enthusiastic in his love of such sport. He not only killed the great bison, but often brought home on his shoulder the timid antelope that had fallen at his unerring aim, and that are not often shot by ordinary marksmen. Soon after crossing South Platte the unwieldy oxen ran on a bank and overturned the wagon, greatly injuring our mother. She lay long insensible in the tent put up for the occasion.

August 1st we nooned in a beautiful grove on the north side of the Platte. We had by this time got used to climbing in and out of the wagon when in motion. When performing this feat that afternoon my dress caught on an axle helve and I was thrown under the wagon wheel, which passed over and badly crushed my limb before father could stop the team. He picked me up and saw the extent of the injury when the injured limb hung dangling in the air.

The Father Dying on the Plains

In a broken voice he exclaimed: "My dear child, your leg is broken all to pieces!" The news soon spread along the train and a halt was called. A surgeon was found and the limb set; then we pushed on the same night to Laramie, where we arrived soon after dark. This accident confined me to the wagon the remainder of the long journey.

After Laramie we entered the great American desert, which was hard on the teams. Sickness became common.

Father and the boys were all sick, and we were dependent for a driver on the Dutch doctor who set my leg. He offered his services and was employed, but though an excellent surgeon, he knew little about driving oxen. Some of them often had to rise from their sick beds to wade streams and get the oxen safely across. One day four buffalo ran between our wagon and the one behind. Though feeble, father seized his gun and gave chase to them. This imprudent act prostrated him again, and it soon became apparent that his days were numbered. He was fully conscious of the fact, but could not be reconciled to the thought of leaving his large and helpless family in such precarious circumstances. The evening before his death we crossed Green River and camped on the bank. Looking where I lay helpless, he said: "Poor child! What will become of you?" Captain Shaw found him weeping bitterly. He said his last hour had come, and his heart was filled with anguish for his family. His wife was ill, the children small, and one likely to be a cripple. They had no relatives near, and a long journey lay before them. In piteous tones he begged the Captain to take charge of them and see them through. This he stoutly promised. Father was buried the next day on the banks of Green River. His coffin was made of two troughs dug out of the body of a tree, but next year emigrants found his bleaching bones, as the Indians had disinterred the remains.

We hired a young man to drive, as mother was afraid to trust the doctor, but the kindhearted German would not leave her, and declared his intention to see her safe in the Willamette. At Fort Bridger the stream was full of fish, and we made nets of wagon sheets to catch them. That evening the new driver told mother he would hunt for game if she would let him use the gun. He took it, and we never saw him again. He made for the train in advance, where he had a sweetheart. We found the gun waiting our arrival at Whitman's. Then we got along as best we could with the doctor's help.

Mother planned to get to Whitman's and winter there, but she was rapidly failing under her sorrows. The nights and mornings were very cold, and she took cold from the exposure unavoidably. With camp fever and a sore mouth, she fought bravely against fate for the sake of her children, but she was taken delirious soon after reaching Fort Bridger, and was bed-fast. Travelling in this condition over a road clouded with dust, she suffered intensely. She talked of her husband, addressing him as though present, beseeching him in piteous tones to relieve her sufferings, until at last she became unconscious. Her babe was cared for by the women of the train. Those kind-hearted women would also come in at night and wash the dust from the mother's face and otherwise make her comfortable. We travelled a rough road the day she died, and she moaned fearfully all the time. At night one of the women came in as usual, but she made no reply to questions, so she thought her asleep, and washed her face, then took her hand and discovered the pulse was nearly gone. She lived but a few moments, and her last words were, "Oh, Henry! If you only knew how we have suffered." The tent was set up, the corpse laid out, and next morning we took the last look at our mother's face. The grave was near the road; willow brush was laid in the bottom and covered the body, the earth filled in-then the train moved on.

Her name was cut on a headboard, and that was all that could be done. So in twenty-six days we became orphans. Seven children of us, the oldest fourteen and the youngest a babe. A few days before her death, finding herself in possession of her faculties and fully aware of the coming end, she had taken an affectionate farewell of her children and charged the doctor to take care of us. She made the same request of Captain Shaw. The baby was taken by a woman in the train, and all were literally adopted by the company. No one there but was ready to do us any possible favor. This was especially true of Captain Shaw and his wife. Their kindness will ever be cherished in grateful remembrance by us all. Our parents could not have been more solicitous or careful. When our flour gave out they gave us bread as long as they had any, actually dividing their last loaf. To this day Uncle Billy and Aunt Sally, &c; we call them, regard us with the affection of parents. Blessings on his hoary head!

At Snake River they lay by to make our wagon into a cart, as our team was wearing out. Into this was loaded what was necessary. Some things were sold and some left on the plains. The last of September we arrived at Grande Ronde, where one of my sister's clothes caught fire, and she would have burned to death only that the Gennan doctor, at the cost of burning his hands, saved her. One night the captain heard a child crying, and found my little sister had got out of the wagon and was perishing in the freezing air, for the nights were very cold. We had been out of flour and living on meat alone, so a few were sent in advance to get supplies from Dr. Whitman and return to us. Having so light a load we could travel faster than the other teams, and went on with Captain Shaw and the advance. Through the Blue Mountains cattle were giving out and left lying in the road. We made but a few miles a day. We were in the country of "Dr. Whitman's Indians," as they called themselves. They were returning from buffalo hunting and frequented our camps. They were loud in praise of the missionaries and anxious to assist us. Often they would drive up some beast that had been left behind as given out and return it to its owner.

One day when we were making a fire of wet wood Francis thought to help the matter by holding his powder-horn over a small blaze. Of course the powder-horn exploded, and the wonder was he was left alive. He ran to a creek near by and bathed his hands and face, and came back destitute of winkers and eyebrows, and his face was blackened beyond recognition. Such were the incidents and dangerous and humorous features of the journey.

We reached Umatilla October 15th, and lay by while Captain Shaw went on to Whitman's station to see if the doctor would take care of us, if only until he could become located in the Willamette. We purchased of the Indians the first potatoes we had eaten since we started on our long and sad journey. October 17th we started for our destination, leaving the baby very sick, with doubts of its recovery. Mrs. Shaw took an affectionate leave of us all, and stood looking after us as long as we were in sight. Speaking of it in later years, she said she never saw a more pitiful sight than that cartful of orphans going to find a home among strangers.

We reached the station in the forenoon. For weeks this place had been a subject for our talk by day and formed our dreams at night. We expected to see log houses, occupied by Indians and such people as we had seen about the forts. Instead we saw a large white house surrounded with palisades. A short distance from the doctor's dwelling was another large adobe house, built by Mr. Gray, but now used by immigrants in the winter, and for a granary in the summer. It was situated near the mill pond, and the grist mill was not far from it.

Between the two houses were the blacksmith shop and the corral, enclosed with slabs set up endways. The garden lay between the mill and the house, and a large field was on the opposite side. A good-sized ditch passed in front of the house, connecting with the mill pond, intersecting other ditches all around the farm, for the purpose of irrigating the land.

We drove up and halted near this ditch. Captain Shaw was in the house conversing with Mrs. Whitman. Glancing through the window, he saw us, and turning to her said: "Your children have come; will you go out and see them?" He then came out and told the boys to "Help the girls out and get their bonnets." Alas! it was easy to talk of bonnets, but not to find them! But one or two were finally discovered by the time Mrs. Whitman had come out. Here was a scene for an artist to describe! Foremost stood the little cart, with the tired oxen that had been unyoked lying near it. Sitting in the front end of the cart was John, weeping bitterly; on the opposite side stood Francis, his arms on the wheel and his head resting on his arms, sobbing aloud; on the near side the little girls were huddled together, bareheaded and barefooted, looking at the boys and then at the house, dreading we knew not what. By the oxen stood the good German doctor, with his whip in his hand, regarding the scene with suppressed emotion.

Thus Mrs. Whitman found us. She was a large, well-formed woman, fair complexioned, with beautiful auburn hair, nose rather large, and large gray eyes. She had on a dark calico dress and gingham sunbonnet. We thought as we shyly looked at her that she was the prettiest woman we had ever seen. She spoke kindly to us as she came up, but like frightened things we ran behind the cart, peeping shyly around at her. She then addressed the boys, asking why they wept, adding: "Poor boys. no wonder you weep!" She then began to arrange things as we threw them out, at the same time conversing with an Indian woman sitting on the ground near by.

A little girl about seven years old soon came and stood regarding us with a timid look. This was little Helen Mar Meed, and though a half-breed, she looked very pretty to us in her green dress and white apron and neat sunbonnet.

Having arranged everything in compact form Mrs. Whitman directed the doctor and the boys where to carry them, and told Helen to show the little girls the way to the house. Seeing my lameness, she kindly took me by the hand and my little sister by the other hand, and thus led us in. As we reached the steps, Captain Shaw asked if she had children of her own. Pointing to a grave at the foot of the hill not far off, she said: "All the child I ever had sleeps yonder." She added that it was a great pleasure to her that she could see the grave from the door. The doctor and boys having deposited the things as directed, went over to the mansion. As we entered the house we saw a girl about nine years old washing dishes. Mrs. Whitman spoke cheerfully to her and said: "Well, Mary Ann, how do you think you will

like all these sisters?" Seated in her arm-chair, she placed the youngest on her lap, and calling us round her, asked our names, about our parents, and the baby, often exclaiming as we told our artless story, "Poor children!"

Dr. Whitman came in from the mill and stood in the door, looking as though surprised at the large addition so suddenly made to the family. We were a sight calculated to excite surprise, dirty and sunburned until we looked more like Indians than white children. Added to this, John had cropped our hair so that it hung in uneven locks and added to our uncouth appearance. Seeing her husband standing there, Mrs. Whitman said, with a laugh: "Come in, doctor, and see your children." He sat down and tried to take little Louisa in his arms, but she ran screaming to me, much to the discomfiture of the doctor and amusement of his wife. She then related to him what we had told her in reference to the baby, and expressed her fears lest it should die, saying it was the baby she wanted most of all.

Our mother had asked that we might not be separated, so Captain Shaw now urged the doctor to take charge of us all.

He feared the Board might object, as he was sent as a missionary to the Indians. The captain argued that a missionary's duty was to do good, and we certainly were objects worthy of missionary charity. He was finally persuaded to keep us all until spring. His wife did not readily consent, but he told her he wanted boys as well as the girls. Finding the boys willing to stay, he made a written agreement with Captain Shaw that he would take charge of them. Before Captain Shaw reached the valley, Dr. Whitman overtook him and told him he was pleased with the children and he need give himself no further care concerning them. The baby was brought over in few days. It was very sick, but under Mrs. Whitman's judicious care was soon restored to health.

Our faithful friend, the German doctor, left us at last, safe in the motherly care of Mrs. Whitman. Well had he kept his promise to our dying mother.

FOCUS QUESTIONS:

1. What were some of the more unfortunate accidents witnessed or experienced by Catherine Sager Pringle along the trail? How many of these mishaps might have been anticipated by the immigrants?

2. What do you think Catherine Sager Pringle learned about herself during her trip across the plains in 1844?

DOMESTIC ECONOMIES AND NORTHERN LIVES, 1800–1860

5-1 Beecher Sisters on Housekeeping

Catharine Beecher and Harriet Beecher Stowe were leading thinkers, activists, and writers of the women's rights and abolitionist movements. (See other documents by one or the other of these sisters in this chapter, chapter 6, and chapter 8.) Their guides to housekeeping and home-making were wildly popular in the nineteenth century; they mixed moralizing with practical instruction in a variety of subjects, from hygiene to how to select a stove.

Source: Catharine Beecher and Harriet Beecher Stowe, *The American Woman's Home*. New York: J.B. Ford, 1869.

INTRODUCTION

The authors of this volume, while they sympathize with every honest effort to relieve the disabilities and sufferings of their sex, are confident that the chief cause of these evils is the fact that the honor and duties of the family state are not duly appreciated, that women are not trained for these duties as men are trained for their trades and professions, and that, as the consequence, family labor is poorly done, poorly paid, and regarded as menial and disgraceful.

To be the nurse of young children, a cook, or a housemaid, is regarded as the lowest and last resort of poverty, and one which no woman of culture and position can assume without loss of caste and respectability. . .

I

THE CHRISTIAN FAMILY

It is the aim of this volume to elevate both the honor and the remuneration of all the employments that sustain the many difficult and sacred duties of the family state, and thus to render each department of a woman's true profession as much desired and respected as are the most honored professions of men.

What, then, is the end designed by the family state which Jesus Christ came into this world to secure?

It is to provide for the training of our race to the highest possible intelligence, virtue, and happiness, by means of the self sacrificing labors of the wise and good, and this with chief reference to a future immortal existence.

The distinctive feature of the family is self-sacrificing labor of the stronger and wiser members to raise the weaker and more ignorant to equal advantages. The father undergoes toil and self-denial to provide a home, and then the mother becomes a self-sacrificing laborer to train its inmates. The useless, troublesome infant is served in the humblest offices; while both parents unite in training it to an equality with themselves in every advantage. Soon the older children become helpers to raise the younger to a level with their own. When any are sick, those who are well become self-sacrificing ministers. When the parents are old and useless, the children become their self-sacrificing servants.

Thus the discipline of the family state is one of daily self-devotion of the stronger and wiser to elevate and support the weaker members. Nothing could be more contrary to the first principles than for the older and more capable children to combine to secure to themselves the highest advantages, enforcing the drudgeries on the younger, at the sacrifice of their equal culture.

Jesus Christ came to teach the fatherhood of God and consequent brotherhood of man. He came as the "first-born Son" of God and the Elder Brother of man, to teach by example the self-sacrifice by which the great family of man is to be raised to equality of advantages as children of God. For this end, he "humbled himself" from the highest to the lowest place. He chose for his birthplace the most despised village; for his parents, the lowest in rank; for his trade, to labor with his hands as a carpenter, being "subject to his parents" thirty years. And, what is very significant, his trade was that which prepares the family home, as if he would teach that the great duty of man is labor—to provide and train weak and ignorant creatures. Jesus Christ worked with his hands nearly thirty years, and preached less than three. And he taught that his kingdom is exactly opposite to that of the world, where all are striving for the highest positions. "Whoso will be great shall be your minister, and whoso will be chiefest shall be servant of all."

The family state then, is the aptest earthly illustration of the heavenly kingdom, and in it woman is its chief minister. Her great mission is self-denial, in training its members to self-sacrificing labors for the ignorant and weak: if not her own children, then the neglected children of her Father in heaven. She is to rear all under her care to lay up treasures, not on earth, but in heaven. All the pleasures of life end here; but those who train immortal minds are to reap the fruit of their labor through eternal ages. . .

FOCUS QUESTIONS:

1. Why do Beecher and Stowe devote so much effort to drawing parallels between family structure and Christianity? Do you think they convinced their readers of their point?

2. What benefits do Beecher and Stowe claim a woman will gain through her work in the home?

5-2 Catharine Beecher on Women's Interests

Catharine Beecher thought about, wrote about, and worked for women's rights and female education throughout much of the nineteenth century – she was born in 1800, and died in 1878. (See other documents by her in this chapter, and in chapter 8.)

Source: Catharine Beecher, *A Treatise on Domestic Economy*. Boston: Thomas H. Webb & Co., 1842. pp. 33-34.

It appears, then, that it is in America, alone, that women are raised to an equality with the other sex; and that, both in theory and practice, their interests are regarded as of equal value. They are made subordinate in station, only where a regard to their best interests demands it, while, as if in compensation for this, by custom and courtesy, they are always treated as superiors. Universally, in this Country, through every class of society, precedence is given to woman, in all the comforts, conveniences, and courtesies, of life.

In civil and political affairs, American women take no interest or concern, except so far as they sympathize with their family and personal friends; but in all cases, in which they do feel a concern, their opinions and feelings have a consideration, equal, or even superior, to that of the other sex.

In matters pertaining to the education of their children, in the selection and support of a clergyman, in all benevolent enterprises, and in all questions relating to morals or manners, they have a superior influence. In such concerns, it would be impossible to carry a point, contrary to their judgement and feelings; while an enterprise, sustained by them, will seldom fail of success.

If those who are bewailing themselves over the fancied wrongs and injuries of women in this Nation, could only see things as they are, they would know, that, whatever remnants of a barbarous or aristocratic age may remain in our civil institutions, in reference to the interests of women, it is only because they are ignorant of them, or do not use their influence to have them rectified; for it is very certain that there is nothing reasonable, which American women would unite in asking, that would not readily be bestowed.

The preceding remarks, then, illustrate the position that the democratic institutions of this Country are in reality no other than the principles of Christianity carried into operation, and that they tend to place woman in her true position in society, as having equal rights with the other sex; and that, in fact, they have secured to American women a lofty and fortunate position, which, as yet, has been attained by women of no other nation.

FOCUS QUESTIONS:

1. How does Beecher link women's status in the United States with democracy, and with Christianity?

2. Does Beecher 'blame the victim' for not seeking greater attention to women's "interests"?

3. What does Beecher propose here that women should do to improve their status?

5-3 Reasons for Entering Prostitution (1859)

William Sanger surveyed 2000 prostitutes to ascertain why they turned to that line of work, and published his results in 1859.

Source: In *Major Problems in American Women's History.* 2nd edition. Mary Beth Norton and Ruth M. Alexander, editors. Lexington, MA: D.C. Heath and Company, 1996, 219-220

Question. WHAT WAS THE CAUSE OF YOUR BECOMING A PROSTITUTE?

CAUSES	NUMBERS
Inclination	513
Destitution	525
Seduced and abandoned	258
Drink, and the desire to drink	181
Ill-treatment of parents, relatives, or husbands	164
As an easy life	124
Bad company	84
Persuaded by prostitutes	71
Too idle to work	29
Violated	27
Seduced on board emigrant ships	16
in emigrant boarding houses	8
Total	2000

This question is probably the most important of the series, as the replies lay open to a considerable extent those hidden springs of evil which have hitherto been known only from their results. First in order stands the reply "Inclination," which can only be understood as meaning a voluntary resort to prostitution in order to gratify the sexual passions. Five hundred and thirteen women, more than one fourth of the gross number, give this as their reason. If their representations were borne out by facts, it would make the task of grappling with the vice a most arduous one, and afford very slight grounds to hope for any amelioration; but it is imagined that the circumstances which induced the ruin of most of those who gave the answer will prove that, if a positive inclination to vice was the proximate cause of the fall, it was but the result of other and controlling influences. In itself such an answer would imply an innate depravity, a want of true womanly feeling, which is actually incredible. The force of desire can neither be denied nor disputed, but still in the bosoms of most females that force exists in a slumbering state until aroused by some outside influences. No woman can understand its power until some positive cause of excitement exists. What is sufficient to awaken the dormant passion is a question that admits innumerable answers. Acquaintance with the opposite sex, particularly if extended so far as to become a reciprocal affection, will tend to this; so will the companionship of females who have yielded to its power; and so will the excitement of intoxication. But it must be repeated, and most decidedly, that without these or some other equally stimulating cause, the full force of sexual desire is seldom known to a virtuous woman. In the male sex nature has provided a more susceptible organization than in females, apparently with the beneficent design of repressing those evils which must result from mutual appetite equally felt by both. In other words, man is the *aggressive* animal, so far as sexual desire is involved. Were it otherwise, and the passions in both sexes equal, illegitimacy and prostitution would be far more rife in our midst than at present. . . .

FOCUS QUESTIONS:

1. What assumptions are embedded in the survey questions?

2. What assumptions does Sanger make in his writing?

3. Does Sanger consider any attributes of identity other than gender in analyzing sexual desire?

5-4 A Lowell Mill Girl Settles In (1845-1848)

Young single women were able to earn their livelihood and experience independence working in New England's textile mills. The facilities at Lowell, Massachusetts, were the first, largest, and best-known; the workforce was roughly three-quarters female, and young women were recruited from throughout the region. Lowell was also the site of early attempts at labor organization, as recounted in "A Factory Girl's Lament" (chapter 7). The letters of Mary S. Paul to her father reflect the mix of pride, exhaustion, homesickness, and concern with getting ahead that were typical among "Lowell Mill Girls."

Source: http://library.uml.edu/clh/All/Pau.htm

Saturday Sept. 13th 1845

Dear Father

I received your letter this afternoon by Wm Griffith. You wished me to write if I had seen Mr. Angell. I have neither written to him nor seen him nor has he written to me. I began to write but I could not write what I wanted to. I think if I could see him I could convince him of his error if he would let me talk. I am very glad you sent my shoes. They fit very well indeed they large enough.

I want you to consent to let me go to Lowell if you can. I think it would be much better for me than to stay about here. I could earn more to begin with than I can any where about here. I am in need of clothes which I cannot get if I stay about here and for that reason I want to go to Lowell or some other place. We all think if I could go with some steady girl that I might do well. I want you to think of it and make up your mind. Mercy Jane Griffith is going to start in four or five weeks. Aunt Miller and Aunt Sarah think it would be a good chance for me to go if you would consent-which I want you to do if possible. I want to see you and talk with you about it.

Aunt Sarah gains slowly.

Mary

Woodstock Nov 8 1845

Dear Father

As you wanted me to let you know when I am going to start for Lowell, I improve this opportunity to write you. Next Thursday the 13th of this month is the day set or the Thursday afternoon. I should like to have you come down. If you come bring Henry if you can for I should like to see him before I go. Julius has got the money for me.

Yours Mary

Lowell Nov 20th 1845

Dear Father

An opportunity now presents itself which I improve in writing to you. I started for this place at the time I talked of which was Thursday. I left Whitneys at nine o'clock stopped at Windsor at 12 and staid till 3 and started again. Did not stop again for any length of time till we arrived at Lowell. Went to a boarding house and staid until Monday night. On Saturday after I got here Luthera Griffith went round with me to find a place but we were unsuccessful. On Monday we started again and were more successful, We found a place in a spinning room and the next morning I went to work. I like very well have 50 cts first payment increasing every payment as I get along in work have a first rate overseer and a very good boarding place. I work on the Lawrence Corporation. Mill is No 2 spinning room. I was very sorry that you did not come to see me start. I wanted to see you and Henry but I suppose that you were otherways engaged. I hoped to see Julius but did not much expect to for I sposed he was engaged in other matters. He got six dollars for me which I was very glad of. It cost me $3.25 to come. Stage fare was $3.00 and lodging at Windsor, 25 cts. Had to pay only 25 cts for board for 9 days after I got here before I went into the mill. Had 2.50 left with which I got a bonnet and some other small articles. Tell Harriet Burbank to send me paper. Tell her I shall send her one as soon as possible. You must write as soon as you receive this. Tell Henry I should like to hear from him. If you hear anything from William write for I want to know what he is doing. I shall write to Uncle Millers folks the first opportunity. Aunt Nancy presented me with a new alpacca dress before I came away from there which I was very glad of. I think of staying here a year certain, if not more. I wish that you and Henry would come down here. I think that you might do well. I guess that Henry could get into the mill and I think that Julius might get in too. Tell all friends that I should like to hear from them.

excuse bad writing and mistakes

This from your own daughter

Mary

P.S. Be sure and direct to No. 15 Lawrence Corporation.

Lowell Dec 21st 1845

Dear Father

I received your letter on Thursday the 14th with much pleasure. I am well which is one comfort. My life and health are spared while others are cut off. Last Thursday one girl fell down and broke her neck which caused instant death. She was going in or coming out of the mill and slipped down it being very icy. The same day a man was killed by the [railroad] cars. Another had nearly all of his ribs broken. Another was nearly killed by falling down and having a bale of cotton fall on him. Last Tuesday we were paid. In all I had six dollars and sixty cents paid $4.68 for board. With the rest I got me a pair of rubbers and a pair of .50 cts shoes. Next payment I am to have a dollar a week beside my board. We have not had much snow the deepest being not more than 4 inches. It has been very warm for winter. Perhaps you would like something about our regulations about going in and coming out of the mill. At 5 o'clock in the morning the bell rings for the folks to get up and get breakfast. At half past six it rings for the girls to get up and at seven they are called into the mill. At half past 12 we have dinner are called back again at one and stay till half past seven. I get along very well with my work. I can doff as fast as any girl in our room. I think I shall have frames before long. The usual time allowed for learning is six months but I think I shall have frames before I have been in three as I get along so fast. I think that the factory is the best place for me and if any girl wants employment I advise them to come to Lowell. Tell Harriet that though she does not hear from me she is not forgotten. I have little time to devote to writing that I cannot write all I want to. There are half a dozen letters which I ought to write to day but I have not time. Tell Harriet I send my love to her and all of the girls. Give my love to Mrs. Clement. Tell Henry this will answer for him and you too for this time.

This from

Mary S Paul

Lowell April 12th 1846

Dear Father

I received your letter with much pleasure but was sorry to hear that you had been lame. I had waited for a long time to hear from you but no letter came so last Sunday I thought I would write again which I did and was going to send it to the [post] office Monday but at noon I received a letter from William and so I did not send it at all. Last Friday I received a letter from you. You wanted to know what I am doing. I am at work in a spinning room and tending four sides of warp which is one girls work. The overseer tells me that he never had a girl get along better than I do and that he will do the best he can by me. I stand it well, though they tell me that I am growing very poor. I was paid nine shillings a week last payment and am to have more this one though we have been out considerable for backwater which will take off a good deal. The Agent promises to pay us nearly as much as we should have made but I do not think that he will. The payment was up last night and we are to be paid this week. I have a very good boarding place have enough to eat and that which is good enough. The girls are all kind and obliging. The girls that I room with are all from Vermont and good girls too. Now I will tell you about our rules at the boarding house. We have none in particular except that we have to go to bed about 10. o'clock. At half past 4 in the morning the bell rings for us to get up and at five for us to go into the mill. At seven we are called out to breakfast are allowed half an hour between bells and the same at noon till the first of May when we have three quarters [of an hour] till the first of September. We have dinner at half past 12 and supper at seven. If Julius should go to Boston tell him to come this way and see me. He must come to the Lawrence Counting room and call for me. He can ask some one to show him where the Lawrence is. I hope he will not fail to go. I forgot to tell you that I have not seen a particle of snow for six weeks and it is settled going we have had a very mild winter and but little snow. I saw Ann Hersey last Sunday. I did not know her till she told me who she was. I see the Griffith girls often. I received a letter from a girl in Bridgewater in which she told me that Mrs Angell had heard some way that I could not get work and that she was much pleased and said that I was so bad that no one would have me. I believe I have written all so I will close for I have a letter to write to William this afternoon.

Yours affectionately

Mary S Paul

P.S. Give my love to all that enquire for me and tell them to write me a long long letter. Tell Harriet I shall send her a paper.

Lowell Nov 5th 1848

Dear Father

Doubtless you have been looking for a letter from me all the week past. I would have written but wished to find whether I should be able to stand it-to do the work that I am now doing. I was unable to get my old place in the cloth room on the Suffolk or on any other corporation. I next tried the dressrooms on the Lawrence Cor, but did not succeed in getting a place. I almost concluded to give up and go back to Claremont, but thought I would try once more. So I went to my old overseer on the Tremont Cor. I had no idea that he would want one, but he did, and I went to work last Tuesday warping—the same work I used to do.

It is very hard indeed and sometimes I think I shall not be able to endure it. I never worked so hard in my life but perhaps I shall get used to it. I shall try hard to do so for there is no other work that I can do unless I spin and that I shall not undertake on any account. I presume you have heard before this that the wages are to be reduced on the 20th of this month. It is true and there seems to be a good deal of excitement on the subject but I can not tell what will be the consequence. The companies pretend they are losing immense sums every *day* and therefore they are obliged to lessen the wages, but this seems perfectly absurd to me for they are constantly making *repairs* and it seems to me that this would not be if there were really any danger of their being obliged to *stop* the mills.

It is very difficult for any one to get into the mill on any corporation. All seem to be very full of help. I expect to be paid about two dollars a week but it will be dearly earned .24 I cannot tell how it is but never since I have worked in the mill have I been so very tired as I have for the last week but it may be owing to the long rest I have had for the last six months. I have not told you that I do not board on the Lawrence. The reason of this is because I wish to be nearer the mill and I do not wish to pay the extra $.12 per week

(I should not be obliged to do it if I boarded at 15) and I know that they are not able to give it me. Beside this I am so near I can go and see them as often as I wish. So considering all things I think I have done the best I could. I do not like here very well and am very sure I never shall as well as at Mother Guilds. I can now realize how very kind the whole family have ever been to me. It seems like going home when I go there which is every day. But now I see I have not told you yet where I do board. It is at No. 5 Tremont Corporation. Please enlighten all who wish for information. There is one thing which I forgot to bring with me and which I want very much. That is my rubbers. They hang in the back room at uncle Jerrys.26 If Olive comes down here I presume you can send them by her, but if you should not have the opportunity to send them do not trouble yourself about them. There is another thing I wish to mention-about my fare down here. If you paid it all the way as I understand you did there is something wrong about it. When we stopped at Concord to take the cars, I went to the ticket office to get a ticket which I knew I should be obliged to have. When I called for it I told the man that my fare to Lowell was paid all the way and I wanted a ticket to Lowell. He told me if this was the case the Stagedriver would get the ticket for me and I supposed of course he would. But he did *not*, and when the ticket master called for my ticket in the *cars*, I was obliged to give him a dollar. Sometimes I have thought that the fare might not have been paid beside farther than Concord. If this is the case all is right. But if it is not, then I have paid a dollar too much and gained the character of trying to cheat the company out of my fare, for the man thought I was lying to him. I suppose I want to know how it is and wish it could be settled for I do not like that any one should think me capable of such a thing, even though that person be an utter stranger. But enough of this. The Whigs of Lowell had a great time on the night of the 3rd. They had an immense procession of men on foot bearing *torches* and *banners* got up for the occasion. The houses were illuminated (Whigs houses) and by the way I should think the whole of *Lowell* were Whigs. I went out to see the illuminations and they did truly look splendid. The Merrimack house was illuminated from attic to cellar. Every pane of glass in the house had a half candle to it and there were many others lighted in the same way. One entire block on the Merrimack Cor[poration] with the exception of one tenement which doubtless was occupied by a free soiler who would not illuminate on any account whatever.

(Monday Eve) I have been to work today and think I shall manage to get along with the work. I am not so tired as I was last week. I have not yet found out what wages I shall get but presume they will be about $2.00 per week exclusive of board. I think of nothing further to write excepting I wish you to prevail on Henry to write to me, also tell *Olive* to write and *Eveline* when she comes.

Give my love to uncle Jerry and aunt Betsey and tell little Lois that "Cousin Carra" thanks her very much for the *apple* she sent her. Her health is about the same that it was when she was at Claremont. No one has much hope of her ever being any better.

Write soon. Yours affectionately

Mary S Paul

P.S. Do not forget to direct to No. 5 Tremont Cor and tell all others to do the same.

FOCUS QUESTIONS:

1. What does Paul seem to like best about her situation? What disturbs her most?

2. Based on the evidence here, does Paul seem to be exploited?

3. What steps does Paul take to try to preserve or improve her reputation? What about her social standing, and her position in her family?

5-5 Women's Bonds

Sarah Alden Bradford Ripley was a New England intellectual and educator. She and her husband, Samuel Ripley, were part of a circle that included Transcendentalist writer Ralph Waldo Emerson. They lived in the suburbs of Boston, where they raised seven children and ran a boarding school for boys.

Source: Mrs. Samuel Ripley, from *Women of Our First Century.* Philadelphia: J.B. Lippencott & Co., 1877. pp. 85-86.

"DEAR SOPHIA,—

"Can there be a possible chance that I may never look upon your dear face again? Am I to stand on the declivity of life, while one after another drops from my side of those who have been so long parts of myself? You are the vision of my nights; you appear to me for the first time in the little parlor of the house in South Street, a graceful and bright being of sixteen or seventeen, with a becoming straw hat and a most agreeable smile. I still see the corner of the room where you sat, though I see nothing else connected with the visit. Then the scene changes to your uncle Blake's, where I found you one morning practicing on the guitar before the family had arisen from their beds. After your closer connection with us as a family, our interviews so crowd together in the background of the past that I am kept awake as if solving a mathematical problem to arrange them in their proper time and place as they press in confusion upon the scene. How much we enjoyed those evening rides to Cambridge, to the house you had planned and built, where we forgot, for an hour or two, the school bondage of home! How much you did to soften the pillow of decline and death for the father I loved and respected so much! How can I recall or arrange the happy meeting we have had together as a family in Waltham or Lowell! How much Martha has always enjoyed, and still enjoys, your society! Do you wonder that I should desire to see you now? Still, I should not be willing to see you at the risk of exciting and doing you harm. So I will try to content myself with thinking of you with hope when I can. But sorrow, not hope, is the color of old age.

"Your Sister"

FOCUS QUESTIONS:

1. What traits does Ripley value in Bradford? What is the basis of their bond?

2. What does the history of their relationship as recounted here tell us about women's roles in the mid-nineteenth century?

5-6 Drunks of Many Colors, All Men

There was a significant overlap between women who were involved in the women's rights movement, abolitionism and temperance – activists who sought to reduce or eliminate the consumption of alcohol. Men's drunkenness, and especially lower-class men's drunkenness, was often cited by those in the temperance movement as the cause of financial ruin, destruction of families, and general moral decay.

Source: Shadd, Mary Ann. "Editorials." The Provincial Freeman 1854-1859. Excerpted in Dorothy Sterling, *We are Your Sisters: Black Women in the Nineteenth Century.* New York: W. W. Norton & Company, 1997. pp. 169-170.

INTEMPERANCE-A colored man passed under the windows of this office on Saturday, "full of strange oaths," and very indiscreet expressions, the promptings of the god to whom he had been pouring in his libations. There is a law against furnishing drink to Indians, and we cannot but think that a similar restriction applied to the "sons of Ham" would be a wholesome protection both to themselves and others - Planet.

The Planet gets worse, and worse! Whenever it can put a word in edge-wise which will bear unjustly upon colored men it does so. The colored people are not wild Indians, neither do they drink more whiskey than their white friends hereabouts. Every colored man must be prohibited from drinking because one drank freely. Who patronize the saloons, taverns &c in this place? Indians and colored men only? No! We believe in passing a strict prohibitory law that will not only prevent Indians and colored men from getting drunk, but will stop white men as well and not only the "inferior" classes but a drunken Editor occasionally.

FOCUS QUESTIONS:

1. What is the first writer's point?
2. Why does the second writer take a humorous approach to the subject?

5-7 The Indestructible Skirt

Technology and industry were not infrequently deployed in the service of fashion – a growth market, in the period when the groundwork for modern consumer culture was laid in the United States.

Source: "W.S. & C.H. Thomson's Skirt Manufactory." *Harper's Weekly.* February 19, 1859.

EMPLOYMENT OF WOMEN

Article IV

THOMSON'S CROWN-SKIRT FACTORY.

The accompanying illustrations will introduce our readers to another of the great manufacturing establishments of New York—Thomson's Skirt Factory; an establishment which provides healthy and lucrative employment for one thousand girls, and furnishes an indispensable article of dress to from three thousand to four thousand ladies daily.

The manufacture of hoop skirts has been heretofore described in this journal. We need only add here that the peculiarities of Messrs. Thomson's manufactures appear to be an "eyelet fastening," by which the tapes and hoops of skirts are fastened, and which is said to be indestructible; a watch-spring contrivance, by whose aid a "graceful backward fall" is said to be given to the dress; a "slide" which will not slip; and a "skirt-supporter," which obviates the pressure on the lower part of the trunk, and throws the weight of all the skirts upon the shoulders.

The number of girls employed by the Messrs. Thomson will average, as we said, one thousand. The wages of these girls vary, of course, according to their experience, industry, and skill. Smart girls, we are told, can easily make $4 a week, and a salary as high as $16 is paid at least in one instance. Four dollars a week, it need hardly be remarked, is very fair remuneration for labor which is neither excessive nor unhealthy. Most of the girls who work in this factory have been taken from the ranks of plain sewers, and education to the hoop skirt manufacture. The whole establishment is under the superintendence of a woman, who from the first has exercised control over the employment of hands, the arrangement of work, and the remuneration paid. Even the accountants of the factory are women.

The quantities of raw material consumed in these large establishments are enormous. Of steel-spring wire over 800,000 yards, and of tape 150,000 yards, are used per week, making together a line long enough to reach from New York to Boston. Five hundred labor-saving machines of various kinds are in constant use; many of which produce effects almost magical. One clasp cutting machine, for instance, produces the incredible number of 200 clasps a minute. Nor is this enormous supply excessive; for over 250,000 clasps, slides, and eyelets are swallowed up in hoop skirts daily.

The revilers of the hoop will thus perceive that it is, after all, an institution not wholly useless, inasmuch as in this establishment alone it feeds, clothes, and warms over one thousand females, many of whom have children or aged persons depending on them. We are glad to hear that the profits of the manufacture are

going to produce yet another benefit. The Messrs. Thomson, we understand, contemplate the establishment of a library for their employees, and likewise propose to have a competent lecturer give, in one of the great halls of their establishment, a course of free lectures to the girls and their friends. This is not such a heartless age after all.

FOCUS QUESTIONS:

1. What impresses the author most about the skirt factory?
2. What impresses you the most about the description of the skirt factory? What about the skirts?
3. What limitations would a garment like this place on its wearer?

5-8 Mothers and the Early Habits of Industry (1834)

Mothers were held accountable for the moral and practical development of children. As the United States industrialized and new forms of labor were connected with material success, mothers were expected to adjust their child-rearing techniques.

If, as a distinguished writer has observed, "Man is a bundle of habits," there is perhaps scarcely a subject to which maternal influence should be more unceasingly directed, than the early formation of right habits. And probably there is no one habit more important in a character formed for usefulness, than that of industry and regular application to business. This habit should be commenced at a very early period; long before the little ones can be very profitable from the fruits of their industry. I know it is often alleged that the labour and care of teaching young children various useful employments, is greater than all the benefits which may be expected to result. But this, I believe, is a fact only in regard to a few of their first lessons. I have a friend, who is both a gentleman and a scholar. For the sake of employment, his father required his little son, from the early age of eight years, to copy all his letters. I have often heard this friend ascribe his business talent, which, in regard to despatch, punctuality, and order, is seldom equalled, to his father's unremitting efforts, to keep him, at stated intervals, regularly employed. In the formation of character, I had almost said, habits are every thing. Could the whole amount of knowledge, which a young man has acquired, just entering profes-

sional life, after nine years laborious preparatory study, have been at once imparted to his mind, without any effort on his part, the value to him would be immeasurably less than the slow process by which it was acquired. The mental discipline, the intellectual habits, are worth even more to him than the knowledge gained. But the importance of a habit may perhaps be best ascertained by its practical result. We refer mothers to the annals of great and good men, in all ages of the world, who have been the benefactors of mankind. By attention to their early history, it will be found, that their learning and talents are not merely the effects of genius, as many suppose, but are the precious fruits of which industry and persevering application were the early bud. The Bible furnishes impressive examples on this subject. Adam in a state of innocence, was required to "dress the garden, and to keep it." The glorified beings in heaven rest not day nor night. It is said of the great exemplar of the Christian, that "he went about doing good." We are both instructed and warned by such scripture passages as the following: Ex. xx. 9. Eccl. ix. 10: v. 12. Prov. xxiv. 30-34: xx. 4. Ezekiel x. 49. Rom. xii. 11. 2 Thess. v. 10-12. Rev. vii. 15. When habits of industry and personal effort have been faithfully cherished, it will not be difficult to cultivate those of benevolence and self-denial. Children should be early encouraged and induced to contribute to the various institutions of benevolence in our country; but let it never be done without an effort, and a sacrifice, on their part. They should be made to feel, with David, that "they will not offer to the Lord a sacrifice which costs them nothing." It is a principle which they may easily apprehend, and one that will be of great value in forming their future characters. At a very early age they can be made to understand something of the wants and woes of the heathen world; and when their sympathies are excited, instruct them in what manner they may begin to aid in sending abroad the blessings of salvation. Mothers may encourage their little ones to resolve how much they will endeavour to earn in this way, and for such purposes in a year. Let a little book of accounts be prepared for them, in which all their little earnings shall regularly be entered, and as soon as they are able, let them keep these accounts themselves. In this way, several useful habits may be associated,- children may be thus early taught that money is valuable, rather as enabling them to do good, than as a means of selfish or sensual gratification. The want of suitable regular employment for children, particularly for boys, is an evil extensively felt and deplored, especially by men in professional life, and the inhabitants of large cities and populous villages. Perhaps there is no one class of persons in our country, so highly favored in this particular as farmers; and it is one of the peculiar blessings of their condition, of which I fear they are not sufficiently aware, to be suitably grateful. But in respect to others, a remedy must be supplied, or their children will be ruined. If all other resources fail, it is better to consider a regular portion of each day as "a time to cast away stones, and a time to gather stones together," to be again dispersed for the same object, rather than indulge or connive at habits of idleness. At one of the most respectable colleges in New-England, the President and Professors have had the wisdom and precaution for a number of years, regularly to send their sons, during a considerable portion of each year, among their friends in the country, to labor on farms. The boys themselves are delighted with the plan, and all the judicious commend it, as affording the most healthful, improving, and pleasant employment. And

probably even greater attainments are made in their studies, than if constantly confined in school the whole year. And perhaps not the least advantage which will result, will be found in giving to them an athletic frame, and a sound and vigorous constitution. But in respect to daughters, the evil cannot be so great. The domestic duties of every family furnish sufficient employment to give a habit of industry to our daughters. And with these duties, it is disgraceful for any young lady to be wholly unacquainted; not less disgraceful, certainly, than to be ignorant of her alphabet; if the value of knowledge is to be estimated by its practical utility. Whenever a young lady becomes herself the mistress of a family, no matter how elevated her station may be, "looking well to the ways of her household" is her profession. What would be thought of the physician, or the pastor, who should enter upon his profession, ignorant of the duties it involved, because he was rich enough to employ a substitute? A knowledge of domestic duties in its various branches and operations, are indispensable for females, and mothers are held responsible, that their daughters acquire it, by a systematic and thorough course of training.

Focus Questions:

1. What habits are said to be most useful? How is the encouragement of this habit beneficial to the growth of urban America and the rise of industry and commerce?

2. Why does the author view idleness as a more significant problem for boys than for girls?

3. What professional skills should be learned by boys? How do these skills compare or contrast with the professional skills recommended for girls?

5-9 Female Industry Association, from the New York Herald (1845)

The wide variety of industrial trades in which women worked is demonstrated in this document along with the appalling conditions under which they worked and the terrible wage they received. This early meeting was an effort to band together to improve wages and conditions. The condescending tone of the newspaper demonstrates that difficulty of their efforts.

Seldom or never did the Superior Court of the City Hall contain such an array of beauty under suffering, together with common sense and good order, as it did yesterday, on the occasion of the meeting of the female industrial classes, in their endeavors to remedy the

wrongs and oppressions under which they labor, and, for some time past, have labored. At the hour appointed for the adjourned meeting, four o'clock, about 700 females, generally of the most interesting age and appearance, were assembled; and, after a trifling delay, a young lady stepped forward, and in rather a low, diffident tone, moved that Miss Gray take the Chair, which, having been put and carried in the usual business-like way- Miss Gray (a young woman, neatly dressed, of some 22 or 24 years of age, fair complexion, interesting, thoughtful and intelligent cast of countenance) came forward from the back part of the room. She proceeded to make a few observations on the nature and objects of their movements and intentions, and stated that, finding the class she belonged to were unable to support themselves, honestly and respectably, by their industry, under the present prices they received for their work, had, therefore, come to the determination of endeavoring to obtain something better, by appealing to the public at large, and showing the amount of sufferings under which they at present labored. She then went on to give instances of what wages they were in the habit of receiving in different branches of the business in which she was engaged, and mentioned several employers by name who only paid them from $.10 to $.18 per day; others, who were proficient in the business, after 12 or 14 hours hard labor, could only get about $.25 per day; one employer offered them $.20 per day, and said that if they did not take it, he would obtain girls from Connecticut who would work for less even than what he offered. The only employer who had done them justice was Mr. Beck, of Fourteenth street, who only allowed his girls to be out about two hours, when he complied with their reasonable demands. He was a man who was worthy of the thanks of every girl present, and they wished him health, wealth, and happiness. How was it possible that on such an income they could support themselves decently and honestly, let alone supporting widowed mothers, and some two, three, or four help-less brothers and sisters, which many of them had. Pieces of work for which they last year got seven shillings, this year they could only get three shillings. A female stepped forward . . . and enquired if the association was confined to any one branch of business, or was it open to all who were suffering under like privations and injustice? The Chairwoman observed that it was opened to all who were alike oppressed, and it was only by a firm cooperation they could accomplish what they were laboring for. Another female of equally interesting appearance (Mrs. Storms) then came forward and said that it was necessary the nature and objects of the party should be distinctly understood, particularly by those who were immediately interested; their own position should be fully known. If the supply of labor in the market was greater than the demand, it followed as a matter of course that they could not control the prices; and, therefore, it would be well for those present to look around them and see into what other channels they could turn their industry with advantage. There were many branches of business in which men were employed that they could as well fill. Let them memorialize the merchants in the dry goods department, for instance, and show them this also. That there were hundreds of females in this city who were able to keep the books as well as any man in it. There were various other branches of business in which men were employed for which females alone were suitable and intended. Let these men go to the fields and seek their livelihood as men ought to do, and leave the females their legitimate employment. There were the drapers also, and a number of other branches of trade in which females could be as well if not better and more properly employed. By these means, some thousands would be afforded employment in branches much more valuable to themselves and the community generally. She then proceeded to recommend those present to be moderate in their demands, and not to ask for more than the circumstances of trade would warrant, for if they acted otherwise, it would tend to their more ultimate ruin. Under present circumstances, a very few years broke down their constitutions, and they had no other resource but the alms-house, and what could bring this about sooner than the bread and water diet and rough shelter, which many of them at present were obliged to put up with.

The proceedings of the previous meeting were then read and approved of. A number of delegates from the following trades entered their names to act as a Committee to regulate future proceedings: tailoresses, plain and coarse sewing, shirt makers, book-folders and stitchers, cap makers, straw workers, dress makers, crimpers, fringe and lace makers, &c.

The following preamble and resolutions were agreed to: Whereas, the young women attached to the different trades in the city of New York, having toiled a long time for a remuneration totally inadequate for the maintenance of life, and feeling the truth of the Gospel assertion, that "the laborer is worthy of his hire," have determined to take upon themselves the task of asserting their rights against unjust and mercenary employers. It must be remembered by those to whom we address ourselves, that our object is not extortion; our desire, not to reap advantages which will be denied to our employers. The boon we ask is founded upon right, alone! The high prices demanded by tradesmen for their goods renders them amply able to advance wages to a standard, which, while it obviates the present cause of complaint, will render laborers only the more cheerful at their work, and still more earnest and willing to serve their employers. The scarcity of employment, and the low rates of pay which have so long prevailed, have, undoubtedly driven many virtuous females to courses which might, otherwise, have been avoided. Many of the female operatives of this city have families dependent upon their exertions; aged fathers and mothers-young brothers-helpless sisters, who, but for their exertions, must inevitably starve, or betake themselves to that scarcely less horrible alternative-the poor house! Such a picture is enough to bestir the most inert to active exertion; the love of life is a passion inherent in us all, and we feel persuaded that we need no better excuse for the movement to which the glaring injustice of our employers has driven us! . . .

FOCUS QUESTIONS:

1. What gender inequalities and difficulties are noted in these minutes? What solutions are proposed and discussed?
2. Summarize the resolutions that are finally made.

5-10 The Harbinger, Female Workers of Lowell (1836)

The famous Lowell system of factory management attracted young farm girls to work in the fully mechanized factories of Lowell. The system was paternalistic and included, at first, good wages, clean places to live and close supervision. The response was great but as economic times declined, so did wages and working conditions. This document explores the life of Lowell factory workers during this time.

We have lately visited the cities of Lowell [Mass.] and Manchester [N.H.] and have had an opportunity of examining the factory system more closely than before. We had distrusted the accounts which we had heard from persons engaged in the labor reform now beginning to agitate New England. We could scarcely credit the statements made in relation to the exhausting nature of the labor in the mills, and to the manner in which the young women-the operatives-lived in their boardinghouses, six sleeping in a room, poorly ventilated. We went through many of the mills, talked particularly to a large number of the operatives, and ate at their boardinghouses, on purpose to ascertain by personal inspection the facts of the case. We assure our readers that very little information is possessed, and no correct judgments formed, by the public at large, of our factory system, which is the first germ of the industrial or commercial feudalism that is to spread over our land. . . . In Lowell live between seven and eight thousand young women, who are generally daughters of farmers of the different states of New England. Some of them are members of families that were rich in the generation before. . . . The operatives work thirteen hours a day in the summer time, and from daylight to dark in the winter. At half past four in the morning the factory bell rings, and at five the girls must be in the mills. A clerk, placed as a watch, observes those who are a few minutes behind the time, and effectual means are taken to stimulate to punctuality. This is the morning commencement of the industrial discipline (should we not rather say industrial tyranny?) which is established in these associations of this moral and Christian community. At seven the girls are allowed thirty minutes for breakfast, and at noon thirty minutes more for dinner, except during the first quarter of the year, when the time is extended to forty-five minutes. But within this time they must hurry to their boardinghouses and return to the factory, and that through the hot sun or the rain or the cold. A meal eaten under such circumstances must be quite unfavorable to digestion and health, as any medical man will inform us. After seven o'clock in the evening the factory bell sounds the close of the day's work. Thus thirteen hours per day of close attention and monotonous labor are extracted from the young women in these manufactories. . . . So fatigued-we should say, exhausted and worn out, but we wish to speak of the system in the simplest language-are numbers of girls that they go to bed soon after their evening meal, and endeavor by a comparatively long sleep to resuscitate their weakened frames for the toil of the coming day. When capital has got thirteen hours of labor daily out of a being, it can get nothing more. It would be a poor speculation in an industrial point of view to own the operative; for the trouble and expense of providing for times of sickness and old age would more than counterbalance the difference between the price of wages and the expenses of board and clothing. The far greater number of fortunes accumulated by the North in comparison with the South shows that hireling labor is more profitable for capital than slave labor. Now let us examine the nature of the labor itself, and the conditions under which it is performed. Enter with us into the large rooms, when the looms are at work. The largest that we saw is in the Amoskeag Mills at Manchester. . . . The din and clatter of these five hundred looms, under full operation, struck us on first entering as something frightful and infernal, for it seemed such an atrocious violation of one of the faculties of the human soul, the sense of hearing. After a while we became somewhat used to it, and by speaking quite close to the ear of an operative and quite loud, we could hold a conversation and make the inquiries we wished. The girls attended upon an average three looms; many attended four, but this requires a very active person, and the most unremitting care. However, a great many do it. Attention to two is as much as should be demanded of an operative. This gives us some idea of the application required during the thirteen hours of daily labor. The atmosphere of such a room cannot of course be pure; on the contrary, it is charged with cotton filaments and dust, which, we are told, are very injurious to the lungs. On entering the room, although the day was warm, we remarked that the windows were down. We asked the reason, and a young woman answered very naively, and without seeming to be in the least aware that this privation of fresh air was anything else than perfectly natural, that "when the wind blew, the threads did not work well." After we had been in the room for fifteen or twenty minutes, we found ourselves, as did the persons who accompanied us, in quite a perspiration, produced by a certain moisture which we observed in the air, as well as by the heat. . . . The young women sleep upon an average six in a room, three beds to a room. There is no privacy, no retirement, here. It is almost impossible to read or write alone, as the parlor is full and so many sleep in the same chamber. A young woman remarked to us that if she had a letter to write, she did it on the head of a bandbox, sitting on a trunk, as there was no space for a table. So live and toil the young women of our country in the boardinghouses and manufactories which the rich and influential of our land have built for them.

FOCUS QUESTIONS:

1. Summarize this accounts description of living conditions in Lowell. What is the daily life of a Lowell worker like?

2. Describe the working conditions presented in this account? What hazards and unhealthful conditions are observed?

5-11 A Lowell Mill Girl Tells her Story (1836)

Harriet Hanson Robinson worked in the textile mills of Lowell, Massachusetts from the age of ten in 1834 until 1848. Later, as the wife of a newspaper editor, Robinson wrote an account of her earlier life as female factory worker and a description of the strike of 1836. Deeply involved in the political culture of her time, Robinson explained some of the family dynamics involved, and portrayed women as active participants in their own lives.

Source: Internet Modern History; http://www.fordham.edu/halsall/mod/robinson-lowell.html

In what follows, I shall confine myself to a description of factory life in Lowell, Massachusetts, from 1832 to 1848, since, with that phase of Early Factory Labor in New England, I am the most familiar—because I was a part of it. In 1832, Lowell was little more than a factory village. Five "corporations" were started, and the cotton mills belonging to them were building. Help was in great demand and stories were told all over the country of the new factory place, and the high wages that were offered to all classes of workpeople; stories that reached the ears of mechanics' and farmers' sons and gave new life to lonely and dependent women in distant towns and farmhouses. . . . Troops of young girls came from different parts of New England, and from Canada, and men were employed to collect them at so much a head, and deliver them at the factories. * * * At the time the Lowell cotton mills were started the caste of the factory girl was the lowest among the employ-ments of women. In England and in France, particularly, great injustice had been done to her real character. She was represented as subjected to influences that must destroy her purity and self-respect. In the eyes of her overseer she was but a brute, a slave, to be beaten, pinched and pushed about. It was to overcome this prejudice that such high wages had been offered to women that they might be induced to become mill girls, in spite of the opprobrium that still clung to this degrading occupation. . . . The early mill girls were of different ages. Some were not over ten years old; a few were in middle life, but the majority were between the ages of sixteen and twenty-five. The very young girls were called "doffers." They "doffed," or took off, the full bobbins from the spinning frames, and replaced them with empty ones. These mites worked about fifteen minutes every hour and the rest of the time was their own. When the overseer was kind they were allowed to read, knit, or go outside the mill yard to play. They were paid two dollars a week. The working hours of all the girls extended from five o'clock in the morning until seven in the evening, with one half hour each, for breakfast and dinner. Even the doffers were forced to be on duty nearly fourteen hours a day. This was the greatest hardship in the lives of these children. Several years later a ten hour law was passed, but not until long after some of these little doffers were old enough to appear before the legislative committee on the subject, and plead, by their presence, for a reduction of the hours of labor. Those of the mill girls who had homes generally worked from eight to ten months in the year; the rest of the time was spent with parents or friends. A few taught school during the summer months. Their life in the factory was made pleasant to them. In those days there was no need of advocating the doctrine of the proper relation between employer and employed. Help was too valuable to be ill-treated... * * * The most prevailing incentive to labor was to secure the means of education for some male member of the family. To make a gentleman of a brother or a son, to give him a college education, was the dominant thought in the minds of a great many of the better class of mill girls. I have known more than one to give every cent of her wages, month after month, to her brother, that he might get the education necessary to enter some profession. I have known a mother to work years in this way for her boy. I have known women to educate young men by their earnings, who were not sons or relatives. There are many men now living who were helped to an education by the wages of the early mill girls. It is well to digress here a little, and speak of the influence the possession of money had on the characters of some of these women. We can hardly realize what a change the cotton factory made in the status of the working women. Hitherto woman had always been a money saving rather than a money earning, member of the community. Her labor could command but small return. If she worked out as servant, or "help," her wages were from 50 cents to $1.00 a week; or, if she went from house to house by the day to spin and weave, or do tailoress work, she could get but 75 cents a week and her meals. As teacher, her services were not in demand, and the arts, the professions, and even the trades and industries, were nearly all closed to her. As late as 1840 there were only seven vocations outside the home into which the women of New England had entered. At this time woman had no property rights. A widow could be left without her share of her husband's (or the family) property, an "encumbrance" to his estate. A father could make his will without reference to his daughter's share of the inheritance. He usually left her a home on the farm as long as she remained single. A woman was not supposed to be capable of spending her own, or of using other people's money. In Massachusetts, before 1840, a woman could not, legally, be treasurer of her own sewing society, unless some man were responsible for her. The law took no cognizance of woman as a money spender. She was a ward, an appendage, a relict. Thus it happened that if a woman did not choose to marry, or, when left a widow, to remarry, she had no choice but to enter one of the few employments open to her, or to become a burden on the charity of some relative. * * * One of the first strikes that ever took place in this country was in Lowell in 1836. When it was announced that the wages were to be cut down, great indignation was felt, and it was decided to strike or "turn out" en masse. This was done. The mills were shut down, and the girls went from their several corporations in procession to the grove on Chapel Hill, and listened to incendiary speeches from some early labor reformers. One of the girls stood on a pump and gave vent to the feelings of her companions in a neat speech, declaring that it was their duty to resist all attempts at cutting down the wages. This was the first time a woman had spoken in public in Lowell, and the event caused surprise and consternation among her audience. It is hardly necessary to say that, so far as practical results are concerned, this strike did no good. The corporation would not come to terms. The girls were soon tired of holding out, and they went back to their work at the reduced rate of wages. The ill-success of this early attempt at resistance on the part of the wage element seems to have made a precedent for the issue of many succeeding strikes.

FOCUS QUESTIONS:

1. According to Harriet Hanson Robinson, what was one of the primary reasons why women worked in the mills?

2. Describe the life of a mill girl as depicted by Robinson. What is her assessment of the efficacy of the strike in 1836?

FAMILY BUSINESS: SLAVERY AND PATRIARCHY, 1800–1860

6-1 An Enslaved Wife's Letter to Her Husband (1840)

One of the most appalling aspects of slavery was the separation of families. The law did not recognize any legal status for slave marriages or, in general, family rights. Thus, slave-owners were free to exercise their property rights to buy and sell slaves individually. Many slave families were separated, with members sold to different owners. Slaves used a variety of means, including letters and informal communication networks, to attempt to stay in contact with loved ones. As this letter suggests, they were only sometimes successful.

Source: In *Major Problems in American Women's History.* 2nd edition. Mary Beth Norton and Ruth M. Alexander, editors. Lexington, MA: D.C. Heath and Company, 1996, 144-145

Richmond Va. October 27 1840

Dear Husband —

this is the third letter that I have written to you, and have not received any from you; and dont no the reason that I have not received any from you. I think very hard of it. the trader has been here three times to Look at me. I wish that you would try to see if you can get any one to buy me up there. if you dont come down here this Sunday, perhaps you wont see me anymore. give my love to them all, and tell them all that perhaps I shan't see you any more. give my love to your mother in particular, and to mamy wines, and to aunt betsy, and all the children; tell Jane and Mother they must come down a fortnight before christmas. I wish to see you all, but I expect I nevershall see you all — never no more.

I remain your Dear and affectionate Wife,

Sargry Brown.

FOCUS QUESTIONS:

1. What steps has Sargry Brown taken, and what does she suggest her husband should do, to try to reunite?

2. What are Brown's biggest concerns?

6-2 Escape from Slavery

Fugitive-slave narratives were widely read in the years leading up to the U.S. Civil War. Running a Thousand Miles for Freedom, or The Escape of William and Ellen Craft from Slavery, *published in 1860, was particularly popular. William Craft describes his and his wife's escape from slavery in Georgia to free lives, first in Boston and eventually in England, where they were active in abolitionist circles.*

Laws, social standards, and everyday practice are rarely perfectly aligned in any society. They were often in direct conflict with each other in the slave-holding South. In the first of these excerpts, Craft alludes to the particular dangers slavery holds for women. In the second passage, he outlines plans for escape, and in the third he details some of the humiliations he and his wife faced even after winning their freedom.

Source: Craft, William. *Running a Thousand Miles for Freedom, or The Escape of William and Ellen Craft from Slavery.* London: W. Tweedie, 1860. pp 7-18, 29-31, 104-107

My wife's new mistress was decidedly more humane than the majority of her class. My wife has always given her credit for not exposing her to many of the worst features of slavery. For instance, it is a common practice in the slave States for ladies, when angry with their maids, to send them to the calybuce sugar-house, or to some other place established for the purpose of punishing slaves, and have them severely flogged; and I am sorry it is a fact, that the villains to whom those defenceless creatures are sent, not only flog them as they are ordered, but frequently compel them to submit to the greatest indignity. Oh! if there is any one thing under the wide canopy of heaven, horrible enough to stir a man's soul, and to make his very blood boil, it is the thought of his dear wife, his unprotected sister, or his young and virtuous daughters, struggling to save themselves from falling a prey to such demons!

It always appears strange to me that any one who was not born a slaveholder, and steeped to the very core in the demoralizing atmosphere of the Southern States, can in any way palliate slavery. It is still more surprising to see virtuous ladies looking with patience upon, and remaining indifferent to, the existence of a system that exposes nearly two millions of their own sex in the manner I have mentioned, and that too in a professedly free and Christian country. There is, however, great consolation in knowing that God is just, and will not let the oppressor of the weak, and the spoiler of the virtuous, escape unpunished here and hereafter.

I believe a similar retribution to that which destroyed Sodom is hanging over the slaveholders. My sincere prayer is that they may not provoke God, by persisting in a reckless course of wickedness, to pour out his consuming wrath upon them.

I must now return to our history.

My old master had the reputation of being a very humane and Christian man, but he thought nothing of selling my poor old father, and dear aged mother, at separate times, to different persons, to be dragged off never to behold each other again, till summoned to appear before the great tribunal of heaven. But, oh! what a happy meeting it will be on that great day for those faithful souls. I say a happy meeting, because I never saw persons more devoted to the service of God than they. But how will the case stand with those reckless traffickers in human flesh and blood, who plunged the poisonous dagger of separation into those loving hearts which God had for so many years closely joined together—nay, sealed as it were with his own hands for the eternal courts of heaven? It is not for me to say what will become of those heartless tyrants. I must leave them in the hands of an all-wise and just God, who will, in his own good time, and in his own way, avenge the wrongs of his oppressed people.

My old master also sold a dear brother and a sister, in the same manner as he did my father and mother. The reason he assigned for disposing of my parents, as well as of several other aged slaves, was, that "they were getting old, and would soon become valueless in the market, and therefore he intended to sell off all the old stock, and buy in a young lot." A most disgraceful conclusion for a man to come to, who made such great professions of religion!

This shameful conduct gave me a thorough hatred, not for true Christianity, but for slave-holding piety.

My old master, then, wishing to make the most of the rest of his slaves, apprenticed a brother and myself out to learn trades: he to a blacksmith, and myself to a cabinet-maker. If a slave has a good trade, he will let or sell for more than a person without one, and many slaveholders have their slaves taught trades on this account. But before our time expired, my old master wanted money; so he sold my brother, and then mortgaged my sister, a dear girl about fourteen years of age, and myself, then about sixteen, to one of the banks, to get money to speculate in cotton. This we knew nothing of at the moment; but time rolled on, the money became due, my master was unable to meet his payments; so the bank had us placed upon the auction stand and sold to the highest bidder.

My poor sister was sold first: she was knocked down to a planter who resided at some distance in the country. Then I was called upon the stand. While the auctioneer was crying the bids, I saw the man that had purchased my sister getting her into a cart, to take her to his home. I at once asked a slave friend who was standing near the platform, to run and ask the gentleman if he would please to wait till I was sold, in order that I might have an opportunity of bidding her good-bye. He sent me word back that he had some distance to go and could not wait.

I then turned to the auctioneer, fell upon my knees, and humbly prayed him to let me just step down and bid my last sister farewell. But, instead of granting me this request, he grasped me by the neck, and in a commanding tone of voice, and with a violent oath, exclaimed, "Get up! You can do the wench no good; therefore there is no use in your seeing her."

On rising, I saw the cart in which she sat moving slowly off; and, as she clasped her hands with a grasp that indicated despair, and looked pitifully round towards me, I also saw the large silent tears trickling down her cheeks. She made a farewell bow, and buried her face in her lap. This seemed more than I could bear. It appeared to swell my aching heart to its utmost. But before I could fairly recover, the poor girl was gone;— gone, and I have never had the good fortune to see her from that day to this! Perhaps I should have never heard of her again, had it not been for the untiring efforts of my good old mother, who became free a few years ago by purchase, and, after a great deal of difficulty, found my sister residing with a family in Mississippi. My mother at once wrote to me, informing me of the fact, and requesting me to do something to get her free; and I am happy to say that, partly by lecturing occasionally, and through the sale of an engraving of my wife in the disguise in which she escaped, together with the extreme kindness and generosity of Miss Burdett Coutts, Mr. George Richardson of Plymouth, and a few other friends, I have nearly accomplished this. It would be to me a great and ever-glorious achievement to restore my sister to our dear mother, from whom she was forcibly driven in early life.

I was knocked down to the cashier of the bank to which we were mortgaged, and ordered to return to the cabinet shop where I previously worked.

But the thought of the harsh auctioneer not allowing me to bid my dear sister farewell, sent red-hot indignation darting like lighting through every vein. It quenched my tears, and appeared to set my brain on fire, and made me crave for power to avenge our wrongs! But, alas! we were only slaves, and had no legal rights; consequently we were compelled to smother our wounded feelings, and crouch beneath the iron heel of despotism.

I must now give the account of our escape; but, before doing so, it may be well to quote a few passages from the fundamental laws of slavery; in order to give some idea of the legal as well as the social tyranny from which we fled.

According to the law of Louisiana, "A slave is one who is in the power of a master to whom he belongs. The master may sell him, dispose of his person, his industry, and his labour; he can do nothing, possess nothing, nor acquire anything but what must belong to his master." — *Civil Code, art. 35.*

In South Carolina it is expressed in the following language:—"Slaves shall be deemed, sold, taken, reputed and judged in law to be *chattels personal* in the hands of their owners and possessors, and their executors, administrators, and assigns, *to all intents, constructions, and purposes whatsoever.—2 Brevard's Digest, 229.*

The Constitution of Georgia has the following (Art. 4, sec. 12):—"Any person who shall maliciously dismember or deprive a slave of life, shall suffer such punishment as would be inflicted in case the like offence had been committed on a free white person, and on the like proof, except in case of insurrection of such slave, and unless SUCH DEATH SHOULD HAPPEN BY ACCIDENT IN GIVING SUCH SLAVE MODERATE CORRECTION."—*Prince's Digest, 559.*

I have known slaves to be beaten to death, but as they died under "moderate correction," it was quite lawful; and of course the murderers were not interfered with.

"If any slave, who shall be out of the house or plantation where such slave shall live, or shall be usually employed, or without some white person in company with such slave, shall *refuse to submit* to undergo the examination of *any white* person, (let him be ever so drunk or crazy), it shall be lawful for such white person to pursue, apprehend, and moderately correct such slave; and if such slave shall assault and strike such white person, such slave may be *lawfully killed.*"—*2 Brevard's Digest, 231.*

"Provided always," says the law, "that such striking be not done by the command and in the defence of the person or property of the owner, or other person having the government of such slave; in which case the slave shall be wholly excused."

According to this law, if a slave, by the direction of overseer, strike a white person who is beating said overseer's pig, "the slave shall be wholly excused." But, should the bondman, of his own accord, fight to defend his wife, or should his terrified daughter instinctively raise her hand and strike the wretch who attempts to violate her chastity, he or she shall, saith the model republican law, suffer death.

From having been myself a slave for nearly twenty-three years, I am quite prepared to say, that the practical working of slavery is worse than the odious laws by which it is governed.

At an early age we were taken by the persons who held us as property to Macon, the largest town in the interior of the State of Georgia, at which place we became acquainted with each other for several years before our marriage; in fact, our marriage was postponed for some time simply because one of the unjust and worse than Pagan laws under which we lived compelled all children of slave mothers to follow their condition. That is to say, the father of the slave may be the President of the Republic; but if the mother should be a slave at the infant's birth, the poor child is ever legally doomed to the same cruel fate.

It is a common practice for gentlemen (if I may call them such), moving in the highest circles of society, to be the fathers of children by their slaves, whom they can and do sell with the greatest impunity; and the more pious, beautiful, and virtuous the girls are, the greater the price they bring, and that too for the most infamous purposes.

Any man with money (let him be ever such a rough brute), can buy a beautiful and virtuous girl, and force her to live with him in a criminal connexion; and as the law says a slave shall have no higher appeal than the mere will of the master, she cannot escape, unless it be by flight or death.

In endeavouring to reconcile a girl to her fate, the master sometimes says that he would marry her if it was not unlawful. However, he will always consider her to be his wife, and will treat her as such; and she, on the other hand, may regard him as her lawful husband; and if they have any children, they will be free and well educated.

I am in duty bound to add, that while a great majority of such men care nothing for the happiness of the women with whom they live, nor for the children of whom they are the fathers, there are those to be found, even in that heterogeneous mass of licentious monsters, who are true to their pledges. But as the woman and her children are legally the property of the man, who stands in the anomalous relation to them of husband and father, as well as master, they are liable to be seized and sold for his debts, should he become involved.

There are several cases on record where such persons have been sold and separated for life. I know of some myself, but I have only space to glance at one.

I knew a very humane and wealthy gentleman, that bought a woman, with whom he lived as his wife. They brought up a family of children, among whom were three nearly white, well educated, and beautiful girls.

On the father being suddenly killed it was found that he had not left a will; but, as the family had always heard him say that he had no surviving relatives, they felt that their liberty and property were quite secured to them, and, knowing the insults to which they were exposed, now their protector was no more, they were making preparations to leave for a free State.

But, poor creatures, they were soon sadly undeceived. A villain residing at a distance, hearing of the circumstance, came forward and swore that he was a relative of the deceased; and as this man bore, or assumed, Mr. Slator's name, the case was brought before one of those horrible tribunals, presided over by a second Judge Jeffreys, and calling itself a court of justice, but before whom no coloured person, nor an abolitionist, was ever known to get his full rights.

A verdict was given in favour of the plaintiff, whom the better portion of the community thought had wilfully conspired to cheat the family.

Knowing that slaveholders have the privilege of taking their slaves to any part of the country they think proper, it occurred to me that, as my wife was nearly white, I might get her to disguise herself as an invalid gentleman, and assume to be my master, while I could attend as his slave, and that in this manner we might effect our escape. After I thought of the plan, I suggested it to my wife, but at first she shrank from the idea.

She thought it was almost impossible for her to assume that disguise, and travel a distance of 1,000 miles across the slave States. However, on the other hand, she also thought of her condition. She saw that the laws under which we lived did not recognize her to be a woman, but a mere chattel, to be bought and sold, or otherwise dealt with as her owner might see fit. Therefore the more she contemplated her helpless condition, the more anxious she was to escape from it. So she said, "I think it is almost too much for us to undertake; however, I feel that God is on our side, and with his assistance, notwithstanding all the difficulties, we shall be able to succeed. Therefore, if you will purchase the disguise, I will try to carry out the plan."

But after I concluded to purchase the disguise, I was afraid to go to any one to ask him to sell me the articles. It is unlawful in Georgia for a white man to trade with slaves without the master's consent. But, notwithstanding this, many persons will sell a slave any article that he can get the money to buy. Not that they sympathize with the slave, but merely because his testimony is not admitted in court against a free white person.

Therefore, with little difficulty I went to different parts of the town, at odd times, and purchased things piece by piece, (except the trowsers which she found necessary to make,) and took them home to the house where my wife resided. She being a ladies' maid, and a favourite slave in the family, was allowed a little room to herself; and amongst other pieces of furniture which I had made in my overtime, was a chest of drawers; so when I took the articles home, she locked them up carefully in these drawers. No one about the premises knew that she had anything of the kind. So when we fancied we had everything ready the time was fixed for the flight. But we knew it would not do to start off without first getting our master's consent to be away for a few days. Had we left without this, they would soon have had us back into slavery, and probably we should never have got another fair opportunity of even attempting to escape.

On leaving Boston, it was our intention to reach Halifax at least two or three days before the steamer from Boston touched there, *en route* for Liverpool; but, having been detained so long at Portland and St. John's, we had the misfortune to arrive at Halifax at dark, just two hours after the steamer had gone; consequently we had to wait there a fortnight, for the *Cambria*.

The coach was patched up, and reached Halifax with the luggage, soon after the passengers arrived. The only respectable hotel that was then in the town had suspended business, and was closed; so we went to the inn, opposite the market, where the coach stopped: a most miserable, dirty hole it was.

Knowing that we were still under the influence of the low Yankee prejudice, I sent my wife in with the other passengers, to engage a bed for herself and husband. I stopped outside in the rain till the coach came up. If I had gone in and asked for a bed they would have been quite full. But as they thought my wife was white, she had no difficulty in securing apartments, into which the luggage was afterwards carried. The landlady, observing that I took an interest in the baggage, became somewhat uneasy, and went into my wife's room, and said to her, "Do you know the dark man downstairs?" "Yes, he is my husband." "Oh! I mean the black man—the *nigger*?" "I quite understand you; he is my husband." "My God!" exclaimed the woman as she flounced out and banged to the door. On going upstairs, I heard what had taken place: but, as we were there, and did not mean to leave that night, we did not disturb ourselves. On our ordering tea, the landlady sent word back to say that we must take it in the kitchen, or in our bed-room, as she had no other room for "niggers." We replied that we were not particular, and that they could send it up to our room,—which they did.

After the pro-slavery persons who were staying there heard that we were in, the whole house became agitated, and all sorts of oaths and fearful threats were heaped upon the "d—d niggers, for coming among white folks." Some of them said they would not stop there a minute if there was another house to go to.

The mistress came up the next morning to know how long we wished to stop. We said a fortnight. "Oh! dear me, it is impossible for us to accommodate you, and I think you had better go: you must understand, I have no prejudice myself; I think a good deal of the coloured people, and have always been their friend; but if you stop here we shall lose all our customers, which we can't do no-how." We said we were glad to hear that she had "no prejudice," and was such a staunch friend to the coloured people. We also informed her that we would be sorry for her "customers" to leave on our account; and as it was not our intention to interfere with anyone, it was foolish for them to be frightened away. However, if she would get us a comfortable place, we would be glad to leave. The landlady said she would go out and try. After spending the whole morning in canvassing the town, she came to our room and said, "I have been from one end of the place to the other, but everybody is full." Having a little foretaste of the vulgar prejudice of the town, we did not wonder at this result. However, the landlady gave me the address of some respectable coloured families, whom she thought, "under the circumstances," might be induced to take us. And, as we were not at all comfortable—being compelled to sit, eat and sleep, in the same small room—we were quite willing to change our quarters.

FOCUS QUESTIONS:

1. What is the overall tone of this writing? What is the author trying to accomplish?

2. In the first excerpt, who are the victims? What are the social, moral, and practical consequences of the actions of the "very humane and wealthy gentleman"?

3. In the second passage, what is Ellen Craft's role?

4. Is the landlady presented as a sympathetic character? Why or why not?

6-3 Mourning a Friend

Mourning was taken seriously in the nineteenth century. Both women and men were expected to express grief in a variety of ways at the death of family members and friends. This brief note was published in an African-American newspaper, Freedom's Journal, in 1827. It mixes general reflections on mortality with reminiscences of a deceased friend.

Source: *Freedom's Journal,* Vol. 1, No. 30, December 7, 1827, p. 154.

For The Freedom's Journal, Thoughts on the Death of a Female Friend.

Melancholy and alone I sat, my thoughts deeply occupied on retired greatness, were interrupted only at intervals, with a rattling noise of the windows, which evinced, that the winds, though invisible, are nor void of power.

To think at all, is either to conserve with the transactions of folly, or with the days of idle childhood; either to array in our imagination, the many favours of a good and gracious God, or to remind our memories of the happy friendship, which were wont to exist between us and friends, who, long since, have retired to the calm valley of the dead.

To contemplate, is to converse with our passed lives, and to scan our passed transactions; to behold our crimes with sorrow—to shrink from them, and learn that man is fallible, and we unworthy of our being as rational creatures, or, to simile and say to our consciences, Thou reasonest well! innocence deprives your being my accuser, and all within is peace.

My mind being literally involved in contemplation, hurried from the passed, viewed the present, and in vain would direct its thoughts on ward to the future.

It mussed on departed worth, and on the everlasting retirement of good and virtuous friends. In its summoning to its memory all with whom it once was familiar, that now sleep in *death*, one, more nearly related, whose amiable soul having bequeathed the dross and baubles of a transient world, to the enjoyment of unquickened spirits, stood fore most in the eye of its imagination, and all her amiable qualities gradually recurred to its memory, only, that her loss might he felt the more severely, and her eternal sleep be known to be more happy. She was not one whose disposition pleased, but by intervals—when she spoke, her language was wont to please; to instruct, and engage all who moved in her domestic, and justly coveted society. She spoke, not as she was to have lived for ages, but as one whose probationary was short and uncertain. She was as a crown of jewels set upon her husband's head. Her feet were ever within the precincts of her own dwelling: unlike most of her sex, she never uttered but what were the ornaments of a virtuous mind, that edified and was opposed to slander. Once my friend, she has gone the way of mortals. The debt is paid, Mortality has put on immortality, and Eliza, forgetful of mortals, enjoys happiness in heaven.

G.

Focus Questions:

1. Approximately what fraction of the text reads as formulaic expressions of grief and reflection, and what portion seems specific to the particular deceased friend?

2. What biographical details can you discern in this passage about the deceased? What have you learned about the author?

3. What might be the purpose of publishing reflections such as this?

6-4 'Yaller Gals'

"Yellow" was a slang term for people of mixed African and European ancestry. Because of the so-called "one-drop rule" – the pervasive belief that anyone with even "one drop" of "Negro blood" (usually, in slightly more practical terms, a person with one great-great-grand-parent of African ancestry) is essentially "black" – slaves included people of many hues. The term "yellow" was not complimentary, but the people to whom it was applied often enjoyed privileges that were far out of reach for darker-skinned slaves. In this passage, a slave describes the not-uncommon phenomenon of sexual liaisons – including long-term relationships – between slave-owners and 'yellow girls.'

Source: Sterling, Dorothy. "Two Ex-Slaves Recall Theirs Masters''Yaller Girls.'" *We Are Your Sisters: Black Women in the Nineteenth Century.* New York: W.W. Norton & Company, 1984. 28.

Mr. Mordicia had his yaller gals in one quarter to dere selves and dese gals belongs to de Mordicia men, dere friends an' de overseers. When a baby was born in dat quarter dey'd sen' it over to de black quarter at birth. Some of dese gal babies got grown an' after goin' back to de yaller quarter had chilluns for her own dad or brother. De yaller women was highfalutin'. Dey thought they was better dan black ones.

Once Massa goes to Baton Rouge and brung back a yaller girl dressed in fine style. She was a seamster nigger. He builds her a house 'way from the quarters, and she done fine sewing for the whites. This yaller girl breeds fast and gits a mess of white young-uns. She larnt them fine manners and combs out they hair.

Oncet two of them goes down the hill to the dollhouse, where the Missy's children am playing. They wants to go in the dollhouse and one the Missy's boys say, "That's for white children." They say, "We ain't no niggers, 'cause we got the same daddy you has, and he comes to see us near every day." They is fussing, and Missy is listening out her chamber window. She heard them white niggers say, "We call him daddy when he comes to our house to see our mama."

When Massa come home that evening, his wife hardly say nothing to him, and he asks her what the matter and she tells him, "I'm studying in my mind 'bout them white young-uns of that yaller nigger wench from Baton Rouge." He say, "Now, honey, I fotches that gal just for you, 'cause she a fine seamster." She say, "It look kind of funny they got the same kind of hair and eyes as my children, and they got a nose like yours." She say, "Over in Mississippi I got a home and plenty with my daddy."

Well, she didn't never leave, and Massa bought

her a fine, new span of surrey hosses. But she don't never have no more children. That yaller gal has more white young-uns, but they don't never go down the hill no more to the big house.

1. Summarize what is being described here.
2. Does the speaker pass any judgments? If so, who or what is judged?
3. With whom do the master's loyalties seem to lie?

6-5 Slaves Gather in the Great Market of St. John

This excerpt was written by Methodist missionaries in a letter to their Missionary Society in London. In it, they describe events surrounding a gathering of slaves in the Great Market of St. John, protesting the 1831 banning of Sunday markets—a privilege they had earned in the early eighteenth century.

Source: Excerpted in Gaspar, David Barry. " From 'The Sense of Their Slavery:' Slave Women and Resistance in Antigua, 1632-1763." In *More Than Chattel: Black Women and Slavery in the Americas.* Gaspar, David Barry and Darlene Clark Hine. Editors. Bloomington: University of Indiana Press, 1996, 218-219.

It is said, more than two thirds of these people brought nothing for Sale, but were generally armed with strong bludgeons secured by twine to the wrists. The Sellers were almost to an individual females, the rest men. They asserted that Sunday was their own day, and declared their determination not to resign the right of selling on that day. Their language was frequently violent and menacing, and accompanied by furious gesticulations and brandished cudgels. Matters appeared to assume a very threatening aspect. The appearance of a detachment of the 86th Regiment which was marched to the entrance of the Great Market, and then wheeled off up the New-Street, seemed for a few Minutes to have struck the fatal spark. The Multitude was instantly in Commotion, and very alarming indications of rage and resistance were witnessed throughout. Happily, however, this ebullition did not continue long: two or three parties being persuaded to depart, others slowly followed their example, and about half past six the last company (7 or 8) of obstinate Women retired to the Country.

FOCUS QUESTIONS:

1. Why do you think most of the Sellers in this passage are women? What does this say about gender roles in slave society?
2. What roles do violence, or the threat of violence, play in these events?

6-6 The Trials of a Slave Girl

Harriet Jacobs was born into slavery in Edenton, North Carolina, in 1813. After suffering years of physical and sexual abuse from her owner, Dr. James Norcom ("Dr. Flint"), Jacobs became involved with a white neighbor, Samuel Sawyer, simply so she could stay away from Norcom. Sawyer and Jacobs had two children together, Joseph and Louisa. In 1842, Jacobs escaped to the North where she became active in the antislavery movement. At the urging of several female abolitionists, she wrote Incidents in the Life of a Slave Girl, which was published in Boston in 1861 under the pseudonym, Linda Brent. The book is significant for its description of the sexual abuse of female slaves, avoided by most nineteenth-century critics of the institution.

Source: Jacobs, Harriet Ann, 1813–1897, Incidents in the Life of a Slave Girl: Written by Herself, Electronic Edition. http:docsouth.unc.edu/jacobs/jacobs.html#jac44

DURING the first years of my service in Dr. Flint's family, I was accustomed to share some indulgences with the children of my mistress. Though this seemed to me no more than right, I was grateful for it, and tried to merit the kindness by the faithful discharge of my duties. But I now entered on my fifteenth year—a sad epoch in the life of a slave girl. My master began to whisper foul words in my ear. Young as I was, I could not remain ignorant of their import. I tried to treat them with indifference or contempt. The master's age, my extreme youth, and the fear that his conduct would be reported to my grandmother, made him bear this treatment for many months. He was a crafty man, and resorted to many means to accomplish his purposes.

Sometimes he had stormy, terrific ways, that made his victims tremble; sometimes he assumed a gentleness that he thought must surely subdue. Of the two, I preferred his stormy moods, although they left me trembling. He tried his utmost to corrupt the pure principles my grandmother had instilled. He peopled my young mind with unclean images, such as only a vile monster could think of. I turned from him with disgust and hatred. But he was my master. I was compelled to live under the same roof with him—where I saw a man forty years my senior daily violating the most sacred commandments of nature. He told me I was his property; that I must be subject to his will in all things. My soul revolted against the mean tyranny. But where could I turn for protection? No matter whether the slave girl be as black as ebony or as fair as her mistress. In either case, there is no shadow of law to protect her from insult, from violence, or even from death; all these are inflicted by fiends who bear the shape of men. The mistress, who ought to protect the helpless victim, has no other feelings towards her but those of jealousy and rage. The degradation, the wrongs, the vices, that grow out of slavery, are more than I can describe. They are greater than you would willingly believe. Surely, if you credited one half the truths that are told you concerning the helpless millions suffering in this cruel bondage, you at the north would not help to tighten the yoke. You surely would refuse to do for the master, on your own soil, the mean and cruel work which trained bloodhounds and the lowest class of whites do for him at the south.

Every where the years bring to all enough of sin and sorrow; but in slavery the very dawn of life is darkened by these shadows. Even the little child, who is accustomed to wait on her mistress and her children, will learn, before she is twelve years old, why it is that her mistress hates such and such a one among the slaves. Perhaps the child's own mother is among those hated ones. She listens to violent outbreaks of jealous passion, and cannot help understanding what is the cause. She will become prematurely knowing in evil things. Soon she will learn to tremble when she hears her master's footfall. She will be compelled to realize that she is no longer a child. If God has bestowed beauty upon her, it will prove her greatest curse. That which commands admiration in the white woman only hastens the degradation of the female slave. I know that some are too much brutalized by slavery to feel the humiliation of their position; but many slaves feel it most acutely, and shrink from the memory of it. I cannot tell how much I suffered in the presence of these wrongs, nor how I am still pained by the retrospect. My master met me at every turn, reminding me that I belonged to him, and swearing by heaven and earth that he would compel me to submit to him. If I went out for a breath of fresh air, after a day of unwearied toil, his footsteps dogged me. If I knelt by my mother's grave, his dark shadow fell on me even there. The light heart which nature had given me became heavy with sad forebodings. The other slaves in my master's house noticed the change. Many of them pitied me; but none dared to ask the cause. They had no need to inquire. They knew too well the guilty practices under that roof; and they were aware that to speak of them was an offence that never went unpunished.

I longed for some one to confide in. I would have given the world to have laid my head on my grandmother's faithful bosom, and told her all my troubles. But Dr. Flint swore he would kill me, if I was not as silent as the grave. Then, although my grandmother was all in all to me, I feared her as well as loved her. I had been accustomed to look up to her with a respect bordering upon awe. I was very young, and felt shamefaced about telling her such impure things, especially as I knew her to be very strict on such subjects. Moreover, she was a woman of a high spirit. She was usually very quiet in her demeanor; but if her indignation was once roused, it was not very easily quelled. I had been told that she once chased a white gentleman with a loaded pistol, because he insulted one of her daughters. I dreaded the consequences of a violent outbreak; and both pride and fear kept me silent. But though I did not confide in my grandmother, and even evaded her vigilant watchfulness and inquiry, her presence in the neighborhood was some protection to me. Though she had been a slave, Dr. Flint was afraid of her. He dreaded her scorching rebukes. Moreover, she was known and patronized by many people; and he did not wish to have his villany made public. It was lucky for me that I did not live on a distant plantation, but in a town not so large that the inhabitants were ignorant of each other's affairs. Bad as are the laws and customs in a slaveholding community, the doctor, as a professional man, deemed it prudent to keep up some outward show of decency.

O, what days and nights of fear and sorrow that man caused me! Reader, it is not to awaken sympathy for myself that I am telling you truthfully what I suffered in slavery. I do it to kindle a flame of compassion in your hearts for my sisters who are still in bondage, suffering as I once suffered.

I once saw two beautiful children playing together. One was a fair white child; the other was her slave, and also her sister. When I saw them embracing each other, and heard their joyous laughter, I turned sadly away from the lovely sight. I foresaw the inevitable blight that would fall on the little slave's heart. I knew how soon her laughter would be changed to sighs. The fair child grew up to be a still fairer woman. From childhood to womanhood her pathway was blooming with flowers, and overarched by a sunny sky. Scarcely one day of her life had been clouded when the sun rose on her happy bridal morning.

How had those years dealt with her slave sister, the little playmate of her childhood? She, also, was very beautiful; but the flowers and sunshine of love were not for her. She drank the cup of sin, and shame, and misery, whereof her persecuted race are compelled to drink.

In view of these things, why are ye silent, ye free men and women of the north? Why do your tongues falter in maintenance of the right? Would that I had more ability! But my heart is so full, and my pen is so weak! There are noble men and women who plead for us, striving to help those who cannot help themselves. God bless them! God give them strength and courage to go on! God bless those, every where, who are laboring to advance the cause of humanity! . . .

Dr. Flint contrived a new plan. He seemed to have an idea that my fear of my mistress was his greatest obstacle. In the blandest tones, he told me that he was going to build a small house for me, in a secluded place, four miles away from the town. I shuddered; but I was constrained to listen, while he talked of his intention to give me a home of my own, and to make a lady of me. Hitherto, I had escaped my dreaded fate, by being in the midst of people. My grandmother had already had high words with my master about me. She had told him pretty plainly what she thought of his character, and there was considerable gossip in the neighborhood about our affairs, to which the open-mouthed jealousy of Mrs. Flint contributed not a little. When my master said he was going to build a house for me, and that he could do it with little trouble and expense, I was in hopes something would happen to frustrate his scheme; but I soon heard that the house was actually begun. I vowed before my Maker that I would never enter it. I had rather toil on the plantation from dawn till dark; I had rather live and die in jail, than drag on, from day to day, through such a living death. I was determined that the master, whom I so hated and loathed, who had blighted the prospects of my youth, and made my life a desert, should not, after my long struggle with him, succeed at last in trampling his victim under his feet. I would do any thing, every thing, for the sake of defeating him. What could I do? I thought and thought, till I became desperate, and made a plunge into the abyss.

And now, reader, I come to a period in my unhappy life, which I would gladly forget if I could. The remembrance fills me with sorrow and shame. It pains me to tell you of it; but I have promised to tell you the truth, and I will do it honestly, let it cost me what it may. I will not try to screen myself behind the plea of compulsion from a master; for it was not so. Neither can I plead ignorance or thoughtlessness. For years, my master had done his utmost to pollute my mind with foul images, and to destroy the pure principles inculcated by my grandmother, and the good mistress of my childhood. The influences of slavery had had the same effect on me that they had on other young girls; they had made me prematurely knowing, concerning the evil ways of the world. I know what I did, and I did it with deliberate calculation.

But, O, ye happy women, whose purity has been sheltered from childhood, who have been free to choose the objects of your affection, whose homes are protected by law, do not judge the poor desolate slave girl too severely! If slavery had been abolished, I, also, could have married the man of my choice; I could have had a home shielded by the laws; and I should have been spared the painful task of confessing what I am now about to relate; but all my prospects had been blighted by slavery. I wanted to keep myself pure; and, under the most adverse circumstances, I tried hard to preserve my self-respect; but I was struggling alone in the powerful grasp of the demon Slavery; and the monster proved too strong for me. I felt as if I was forsaken by God and man; as if all my efforts must be frustrated; and I became reckless in my despair.

I have told you that Dr. Flint's persecutions and his wife's jealousy had given rise to some gossip in the neighborhood. Among others, it chanced that a white unmarried gentleman had obtained some knowledge of the circumstances in which I was placed. He knew my grandmother, and often spoke to me in the street. He became interested for me, and asked questions about my master, which I answered in part. He expressed a great deal of sympathy, and a wish to aid me. He constantly sought opportunities to see me, and wrote to me frequently. I was a poor slave girl, only fifteen years old.

So much attention from a superior person was, of course, flattering; for human nature is the same in all. I also felt grateful for his sympathy, and encouraged by his kind words. It seemed to me a great thing to have such a friend. By degrees, a more tender feeling crept into my heart. He was an educated and eloquent gentleman; too eloquent, alas, for the poor slave girl who trusted in him. Of course I saw whither all this was tending. I knew the impassable gulf between us; but to be an object of interest to a man who is not married, and who is not her master, is agreeable to the pride and feelings of a slave, if her miserable situation has left her any pride or sentiment. It seems less degrading to give one's self, than to submit to compulsion. There is something akin to freedom in having a lover who has no control over you, except that which he gains by kindness and attachment. A master may treat you as rudely as he pleases, and you dare not speak; moreover, the wrong does not seem so great with an unmarried man, as with one who has a wife to be made unhappy. There may be sophistry in all this; but the condition of a slave confuses all principles of morality, and, in fact, renders the practice of them impossible.

When I found that my master had actually begun to build the lonely cottage, other feelings mixed with those I have described. Revenge, and calculations of interest, were added to flattered vanity and sincere gratitude for kindness. I knew nothing would enrage Dr. Flint so much as to know that I favored another; and it was something to triumph over my tyrant even in that small way. I thought he would revenge himself by selling me, and I was sure my friend, Mr. Sands, would buy me. He was a man of more generosity and feeling than my master, and I thought my freedom could be easily obtained from him. The crisis of my fate now came so near that I was desperate. I shuttered to think of being the mother of children that should be owned by my old tyrant. I knew that as soon as a new fancy took him, his victims were sold far off to get rid of them; especially if they had children. I had seen several women sold, with his babies at the breast. He never allowed his offspring by slaves to remain long in sight of himself and his wife. Of a man who was not my master I could ask to have my children well supported; and in this case, I felt confident I should obtain the boon. I also felt quite sure that they would be made free. With all these thoughts revolving in my mind, and seeing no other way of escaping the doom I so much dreaded, I made a headlong plunge. Pity me, and pardon me, O virtuous reader! You never knew what it is to be a slave; to be entirely unprotected by law or custom; to have the laws reduce you to the condition of a chattel, entirely subject to the will of another. You never exhausted your ingenuity in avoiding the snares, and eluding the power of a hated tyrant; you never shuddered at the sound of his footsteps, and trembled within hearing of his voice. I know I did wrong. No one can feel it more sensibly than I do. The painful and humil-

iating memory will haunt me to my dying day. Still, in looking back, calmly, on the events of my life, I feel that the slave woman ought not to be judged by the same standard as others.

The months passed on. I had many unhappy hours. I secretly mourned over the sorrow I was bringing on my grandmother, who had so tried to shield me from harm. I knew that I was the greatest comfort of her old age, and that it was a source of pride to her that I had not degraded myself, like most of the slaves. I wanted to confess to her that I was no longer worthy of her love; but I could not utter the dreaded words.

As for Dr. Flint, I had a feeling of satisfaction and triumph in the thought of telling him. From time to time he told me of his intended arrangements, and I was silent. At last, he came and told me the cottage was completed, and ordered me to go to it. I told him I would never enter it. He said, "I have heard enough of such talk as that. You shall go, if you are carried by force; and you shall remain there." I replied, "I will never go there. In a few months I shall be a mother."

He stood and looked at me in dumb amazement, and left the house without a word. I thought I should be happy in my triumph over him. But now that the truth was out, and my relatives would hear of it, I felt wretched. Humble as were their circumstances, they had pride in my good character. Now, how could I look them in the face? My self-respect was gone! I had resolved that I would be virtuous, though I was a slave. I had said, "Let the storm beat! I will brave it till I die." And now, how humiliated I felt!

I went to my grandmother. My lips moved to make confession, but the words stuck in my throat. I sat down in the shade of a tree at her door and began to sew. I think she saw something unusual was the matter with me. The mother of slaves is very watchful. She knows there is no security for her children. After they have entered their teens she lives in daily expectation of trouble. This leads to many questions. If the girl is of a sensitive nature, timidity keeps her from answering truthfully, and this well-meant course has a tendency to drive her from maternal counsels. Presently, in came my mistress, like a mad woman, and accused me concerning her husband. My grandmother, whose suspicions had been previously awakened, believed what she said. She exclaimed, "O Linda! has it come to this? I had rather see you dead than to see you as you now are. You are a disgrace to your dead mother." She tore from my fingers my mother's wedding ring and her silver thimble. "Go away!" she exclaimed, "and never come to my house, again." Her reproaches fell so hot and heavy, that they left me no chance to answer. Bitter tears, such as the eyes never shed but once, were my only answer. I rose from my seat, but fell back again, sobbing. She did not speak to me; but the tears were running down her furrowed cheeks, and they scorched me like fire. She had always been so kind to me! So kind! How I longed to throw myself at her feet, and tell her all the truth! But she had ordered me to go, and never to come there again. After a few minutes, I mustered strength, and started to obey her. With what feelings did I now close that little gate, which I used to open with such an eager hand in my childhood! It closed upon me with a sound I never heard before.

Where could I go? I was afraid to return to my master's. I walked on recklessly, not caring where I went, or what would become of me. When I had gone four or five miles, fatigue compelled me to stop. I sat down on the stump of an old tree. The stars were shining through the boughs above me. How they mocked me, with their bright, calm light! The hours passed by, and as I sat there alone a chilliness and deadly sickness came over me. I sank on the ground. My mind was full of horrid thoughts. I prayed to die; but the prayer was not answered. At last, with great effort I roused myself, and walked some distance further, to the house of a woman who had been a friend of my mother. When I told her why I was there, she spoke soothingly to me; but I could not be comforted. I thought I could bear my

shame if I could only be reconciled to my grandmother. I longed to open my heart to her. I thought if she could know the real state of the case, and all I had been bearing for years, she would perhaps judge me less harshly. My friend advised me to send for her. I did so; but days of agonizing suspense passed before she came. Had she utterly forsaken me? No. She came at last. I knelt before her, and told her the things that had poisoned my life; how long I had been persecuted; that I saw no way of escape; and in an hour of extremity I had become desperate. She listened in silence. I told her I would bear any thing and do any thing, if in time I had hopes of obtaining her forgiveness. I begged of her to pity me, for my dead mother's sake. And she did pity me. She did not say, "I forgive you;" but she looked at me lovingly, with her eyes full of tears. She laid her old hand gently on my head, and murmured, "Poor child! Poor child!"

FOCUS QUESTIONS:

1. Based upon your reading of this excerpt from Harriet Jacobs's narrative, what power and influence did the matriarchs of the slave family have in both the slave community and among white owners? Why do you think this was so?

2. Why do you think the wives and mothers of slave owners did not do more to stop the physical and sexual abuse of female slaves?

6-7 Matilda's Letter to the Editor

Formal education was a scarce, and highly valued, resource for African Americans in the nineteenth century. In many jurisdictions it was illegal to teach slaves how to read or write; free blacks also faced difficulties in gaining literacy. In this letter to the editor, "Matilda" makes a special plea for the desirability of educating African American women.

Source: Freedom's Journal, Vol. I, No. 22, August 10, 1827, p. 86.

Messrs, Editors

Will you allow a female the offer a few remarks upon a subject that you must allow to the all-important. I don't know that in any of your papers, you have said sufficient upon the education of females. I hope you are not to be classed with those, who think that

our mathematical knowledge should be limited to "fathoming the dish-kettle," and that we have acquired enough of history, if we know that our grandfather's father lived and died. "This true the time has been, when to darn a stocking and cook a pudding well," was considered the end and aim of a woman's being. But those were days when ignorance blinded men's eyes. The diffusion of knowledge has destroyed those degrading opinions, and men of the present age allow, that we have minds that are capable and deserving of culture. There are difficulties, and great difficulties in the way of our advancement; but that should only stir us to greater efforts. We possess not the advantage with those of our sex, whose skin are not colored like our own; but we can improve what little we have, and make our one talent produce two-fold. The influence that we have over the male sex demands, that our minds should be instructed and improved with the principle of education and religion in order that this influence should be properly directed. Ignorant ourselves, how can we up expected to form the minds of our youth and conduct them in the paths of knowledge? how can we "teach the young idea, how to shoot," if we have none ourselves? There is a great responsibility resting somewhere and it is time for us to be up and doing. I would address myself to all mothers, and say to them that while it is necessary to possess a knowledge of cookery, and the various mysteries of pudding-making, something more is requisite. It is their bounden duty to store their daughters' minds with useful learning. They should be made to devote their leisure time to reading books, whence they would derive valuable information, which could never be taken from them. I will not longer trespass on your time and patience. I merely throw out these hints, in order that some more able pen will take up the subject.

MATILDA.

FOCUS QUESTIONS:

1. What reasoning does Matilda use in arguing that women should be educated?

2. Why does the author use humor in her argument? Is it effective?

6-8 New England Writer Portrays Slavery (1852)

Although she authored several books on New England, Harriet Beecher Stowe was best known for her portrayal of slavery in Uncle Tom's Cabin. The daughter of the most important Puritan preacher of her day, Stowe had a long concern with humanitarian causes. The death of one of Stowe's children prompted her to become involved with the abolitionist movement. Uncle Tom's Cabin outraged the south and solidified the anti-slavery movement in the north. Some even feel the book was one of the factors that brought on the Civil War. The following section finds Uncle Tom, recently purchased by the cruel Simon Legree, on his way to Legree's plantation.

Source: Harriet Beecher Stowe, *Uncle Tom's Cabin; or, Life among the Lowly* (Boston: J.P. Jewett, 1851).

Trailing wearily behind a rude wagon, and over a ruder road, Tom and his associates faced onward.

In the wagon was seated Simon Legree; and the two women, still fettered together, were stowed away with some baggage in the back part of it, and the whole company were seeking Legree's plantation, which lay a good distance off.

It was a wild, forsaken road, now winding through dreary pine barrens, where the wind whispered mournfully, and now over log causeways, through long cypress swamps, the doleful trees rising out of the slimy, spongy ground, hung with long wreaths of funereal black moss, while ever and anon the loathsome form of the moccasin snake might be seen sliding among broken stumps and shattered branches that lay here and there, rotting in the water.

It is disconsolate enough, this riding, to the stranger, who, with well-filled pocket and well-appointed horse, threads the lonely way on some errand of business; but wilder, drearier, to the man enthralled, whom every weary step bears further from all that man loves and prays for.

So one should have thought, that witnessed the sunken and dejected expression on those dark faces; the wistful, patient weariness with which those sad eyes rested on object after object that passed them in their sad journey.

Simon rode on, however, apparently well pleased, occasionally pulling away at a flask of spirit, which he kept in his pocket.

"I say, *you!*" he said, as he turned back and caught a glance at the dispirited faces behind him! "Strike up a song, boys,—come!"

The men looked at each other, and the *"come"* was repeated, with a smart crack of the whip which the driver carried in his hands. Tom began a Methodist hymn,

"Jerusalem, my happy home,
Name ever dear to me!
When shall my sorrow have an end,
Thy joys when shall—"

"Shut up, you black cuss!" roared Legree; "did ye think I wanted any o' yer infernal old Methodism? I say, tune up, now, something real rowdy,—quick!"

One of the other men struck up one of those unmeaning songs, common among the slaves.

"Mas'r see'd me cotch a coon,
High boys, high!

He laughed to split,—d'ye see the moon,
Ho! ho! ho! boys, ho!
Ho! yo! hi—e! oh!"

The singer appeared to make up the song to his own pleasure, generally hitting on rhyme, without much attempt at reason; and all the party took up the chorus, at intervals,

"Ho! ho! ho! boys, ho!
High—e—oh! high—e—oh!"

It was sung very boisterously, and with a forced attempt at merriment; but no wail of despair, no words of impassioned prayer, could have had such a depth of woe in them as the wild notes of the chorus. As if the poor, dumb heart, threatened,—prisoned,—took refuge in that inarticulate sanctuary of music, and found there a language in which to breathe its prayer to God! There was a prayer in it, which Simon could not hear. He only heard the boys singing noisily, and was well pleased; he was making them "keep up their spirits."

"Well, my little dear," said he, turning, to Emmeline, and laying his hand on her shoulder, "we're almost home!"

When Legree scolded and stormed, Emmeline was terrified; but when he laid his hand on her, and spoke as he now did, she felt as if she had rather he would strike her. The expression of his eyes made her soul sick, and her flesh creep. Involuntarily she clung closer to the mulatto woman by her side, as if she were her mother.

"You didn't ever wear ear-rings," he said, taking hold of her small ear with his coarse fingers.

"No, Mas'r!" said Emmeline, trembling and looking down.

"Well, I'll give you a pair, when we get home, if you're a good girl. You needn't be so frightened; I don't mean to make you work very hard. You'll have fine times with me, and live like a lady,—only be a good girl."

Legree had been drinking to that degree that he was inclining to be very gracious; and it was about this time that the enclosures of the plantation rose to view. The estate had formerly belonged to a gentleman of opulence and taste, who had bestowed some considerable attention to the adornment of his grounds. Having died insolvent, it had been purchased, at a bar-gain, by Legree, who used it, as he did everything else, merely as an implement for money-making. The place had the ragged, forlorn appearance, which is always produced by the evidence that the care of the former owner has been left to go to utter decay.

What was once a smooth-shaven lawn before the house, dotted here and there with ornamental shrubs, was now covered with frowsy tangled grass, with horse-posts set up, here and there, in it, where the turf was stamped away, and the ground littered with broken pails, cobs of corn, and other slovenly remains. Here and there, a mildewed jessamine or honeysuckle hung raggedly from some ornamental support, which had been pushed to one side by being used as a horse-post. What once was a large garden was now all grown over with weeds, through which, here and there, some solitary exotic reared its forsaken head. What had been a conservatory had now no window-sashes, and on the mouldering shelves stood some dry, forsaken flower-pots, with sticks in them, whose dried leaves showed they had once been plants.

The wagon rolled up a weedy gravel walk, under a noble avenue of China trees, whose graceful forms and ever-springing foliage seemed to be the only things there that neglect could not daunt or alter,—like noble spirits, so deeply rooted in goodness, as to flourish and grow stronger amid discouragement and decay.

The house had been large and handsome. It was built in a manner common at the South; a wide verandah of two stories running round every part of the house, into which every outer door opened, the lower tier being supported by brick pillars.

But the place looked desolate and uncomfortable; some windows stopped up with boards, some with shattered panes, and shutters hanging by a single hinge,—all telling of coarse neglect and discomfort.

Bits, of board, straw, old decayed barrels and boxes, garnished the ground in all directions; and three or four ferocious-looking dogs, roused by the sound of the wagon-wheels, came tearing out, and were with difficulty restrained from laying hold of Tom and his companions, by the effort of the ragged servants who came after them.

"Ye see what ye'd get!" said Legree, caressing the dogs with grim satisfaction, and turning to Tom and his companions. "Ye see what ye'd get, if ye try to run off. These yer dogs has been raised to track niggers; and they'd jest as soon chaw one on ye up as eat their supper. So, mind yerself! How now, Sambo!" he said, to a ragged fellow, without any brim to his hat, who was officious in his attentions. "How have things been going?"

"Fust rate, Mas'r."

"Quimbo," said Legree to another, who was making demonstrations to attract his attention, "ye minded what I telled ye?"

"Guess I did, didn't I?"

These two colored men were the two principal hands on the plantation. Legree had trained them in savageness and brutality as systematically as he had his bulldogs; and, by long practice in hardness and cruelty, brought their whole nature to about the same range of capacities. It is a common remark, and one that is thought to militate strongly against the character of the race, that the Negro overseer is always more tyrannical and cruel than the white one. This is simply saying that the Negro mind has been more crushed and debased than the white. It is no more true of this race than of every oppressed race, the world over. The slave is always a tyrant, if he can get a chance to be one.

Legree, like some potentates we read of in history, governed his plantation by a sort of resolution of forces. Sambo and Quimbo cordially hated each other; the plantation hands, one and all, cordially hated them; and, by playing off one against another, he was pretty sure, through one or the other of the three parties, to get informed of whatever was on foot in the place.

Nobody can live entirely without social intercourse; and Legree encouraged his two black satellites to a kind of coarse familiarity with him,—a familiarity, however, at any moment liable to get one or the other of them into trouble; for, on the slightest provocation, one of them always stood ready, at a nod, to be a minister of his vengeance on the other.

As they stood there now by Legree, they seemed an apt illustration of the fact that brutal men are lower even than animals. Their coarse, dark, heavy features; their great eyes, rolling enviously on each other; their barbarous, guttural, half-brute intonation; their dilapidated garments fluttering in the wind,—were all in admirable keeping with the vile and unwholesome character of everything about the place.

"Here, you Sambo," said Legree, "take these yer boys down to the quarters; and here's a gal I've got for *you*," said he, as he separated the mulatto woman from Emmeline, and pushed her towards him;—"I promised

to bring you one, you know."

The woman gave a sudden start, and, drawing back, said, suddenly,

"O, Mas'r! I left my old man in New Orleans."

"What of that, you——;won't you want one here? None o' your words,—go long!" said Legree, raising his whip.

"Come, mistress," he said to Emmeline, "you go in here with me."

A dark, wild face was seen, for a moment, to glance at the window of the house; and, as Legree opened the door, a female voice said something, in a quick, imperative tone. Tom, who was looking, with anxious interest, after Emmeline, as she went in, noticed this, and heard Legree answer angrily, "You may hold your tongue! I'll do as I please, for all you!"

Tom heard no more; for he was soon following Sambo to the quarters. The quarters was a little sort of street of rude shanties, in a row, in a part of the plantation, far off from the house. They had a forlorn, brutal, forsaken air. Tom's heart sank when he saw them. He had been comforting himself with the thought of a cottage, rude, indeed, but one which he might make neat and quiet, and where he might have a shelf for his Bible, and a place to be alone out of his laboring hours. He looked into several; they were mere rude shells, destitute of any species of furniture, except a heap of straw, foul with dirt, spread confusedly over the floor, which was merely the bare ground, trodden hard by the tramping of innumerable feet.

"Which of these will be mine?" said he, to Sambo, submissively.

"Dunno; ken turn in here, I spose," said Sambo; "spects thar's room for another thar; thar's a pretty smart heap o' niggers to each on 'em, now; sure, I dunno what I's to do with more."

FOCUS QUESTIONS:

1. If Uncle Tom's Cabin was indeed one of the factors in starting the Civil War, what does this say about the role of fiction in history? Is it worthy of consideration by historians? Why would this book have inflamed the south? Why would it have been so widely read in the north?

2. How does Stowe's portrayal of slave life compare with actual accounts you have read elsewhere?

6-9 An Enslaved Wife's Letter to Her Husband (1852)

As we saw in the earlier "Enslaved Wife's Letter to Her Husband, 1840," the breakup of families was a cruel but common consequence of slavery. In this case, it seems that Marie has already been separated not only from her husband, but also from a child, Albert.

Source: In *Major Problems in American Women's History.* 2nd edition. Mary Beth Norton and Ruth M. Alexander, editors. Lexington, MA: D.C. Heath and Company, 1996, 144.

Charlottesville [Virginia], Oct. 8, 1852

Dear Husband

I write you a letter to let you know of my distress. My master has sold Albert to a trader on Monday court day and myself and other child is for sale also and I want you to let [me] hear from you very soon before next cort if you can. I don't know when I don't want you to wait till Christmas.

I want you to tell Dr. Hamilton your master if either will buy me they can attend to it know and then I can go afterwards.

I don't want a trader to get me. They asked me if I had got any person to buy me and I told them no. They told me to the court house too they never put me up. A man buy the name of brady bought albert and is gone I don't know whare. They say he lives in Scottsville. My things is in several places some is in stanton and if I would be sold I don't know what will become of them. I don't expect to meet with the luck to get that way till I am quite heartsick.

nothing more I am and ever will be your kind wife

Marie Perkins

FOCUS QUESTIONS:

1. What steps has Marie Perkins taken, and what does she suggest her husband should do, to try to reunite her family?
2. What is the significance of Christmas?

6-10 Rose Williams's Forced Marriage in Texas

Part of a female slave's economic value lay in her reproductive potential, since the owner of a mother automatically gained ownership of the mother's baby. It was not unusual for slaveowners to attempt to "breed" slaves in ways that would maximize their economic gain – though the moral and practical risks of such attempts are obvious.

This passage is excerpted from an oral history provided by Rose Williams, who begins her account: "What I say am the facts. If I's one day old, I's way over ninety, and I's born in Bell County, right here in Texas, …"

Souce: In *Major Problems in American Women's History.* 2nd edition. Mary Beth Norton and Ruth M. Alexander, editors. Lexington, MA: D.C. Heath and Company, 1996, 142-143.

I has the correct memorandum of when the war start. Massa Black sold we-uns right then. Mammy and Pappy powerful glad to git sold, and they and I is put on the block with 'bout ten other niggers. When we-uns gits to the trading block, there lots of white folks there what come to look us over. One man shows the interest in Pappy. Him named Hawkins. He talk to Pappy, and Pappy talk to him and say, "Them my woman and childs. Please buy all of us and have mercy on we-uns." Massa Hawkins say, "That gal am a likely-looking nigger; she am portly and strong. But three am more than I wants, I guesses."

The sale start, and 'fore long Pappy am put on the block. Massa Hawkins wins the bid for Pappy, and when Mammy am put on the block, he wins the bid for her. Then there am three or four other niggers sold before my time comes. Then Massa Black calls me to the block, and the auction man say, "What am I offer for this portly, strong young wench. She's never been 'bused and will make the good breeder."

I wants to hear Massa Hawkins bid, but him say nothing. Two other men am bidding 'gainst each other, and I sure has the worriment. There am tears coming down my cheeks' cause I's being sold to some man that would make separation from my mammy. One man bids $500, and the auction man ask, "Do I hear more? She am gwine at $500." Then someone say, "$525," and the auction man say, "She am sold for $525 to Massa Hawkins." Am I glad and 'cited! Why, I's quivering all over.

Massa. Hawkins takes we-uns to his place, and it

am a nice plantation. Lots better than Massa Black's. There is 'bout fifty niggers what is growed and lots of children. The first thing Massa do when we-uns gits home am give we-uns rations and a cabin. You must believe this nigger when I says them rations a feast for us. There plenty meat and tea and coffee and white flour. I's never tasted white flour and coffee, and Mammy fix some biscuits and coffee. Well, the biscuits was yum, yum, yum to me, but the coffee I doesn't like.

The quarters am pretty good. There am twelve cabins all made from logs and a table and some benches and bunks for sleeping and a fireplace for cooking and the heat. There am no floor, just the ground.

Massa Hawkins am good to he niggers and not force 'em work too hard. There am as much difference 'tween him and Old Massa Black in the way of treatment as 'twixt the Lord and the devil. Massa Hawkins 'lows he niggers have reasonable par-ties and go fishing, but we-uns am never tooken to church and has no books forlaming. There am no education for the niggers.

There am one thing Massa Hawkins does to me what I can't shunt from my mind. I knows he don't do it for meanness, but I always holds it 'gainst him. What he done am force me to live with that nigger, Rufus, 'gainst my wants.

After I been at he place 'bout a year, the massa come to me and say, "You gwine live with Rufus in that cabin over yonder. Go fix it for living." I's 'bout sixteen year old and has no laming, and I's just ignomus child. I's thought that him mean for me to tend the cabin for Rufus and some other niggers. Well, that am start the pestigation for me.

I's took charge of the cabin after work am done and fixes supper. Now, I don't like that Rufus, 'cause he a bully. He am big and 'cause he so, he think everybody do what him say. We-uns has supper, then I goes here and there talking, till I's ready for sleep, and then I gits in the bunk. After I's in, that nigger come crawl in the bunk with me 'fore I knows it. I says, "What you means, you fool nigger?" He say for me to hush the mouth. "This am my bunk, too," he say.

"You's teched in the head. Git out," I's told him, and I puts the feet 'gainst him and give him a shove, and out he go on the floor 'fore he know what I's doing. That nigger jump up and he mad. He look like the wild bear. He starts for the bunk, and I jumps quick for the poker. It am 'bout three feet long, and when he comes at me I lets him have it over the head. Did that nigger stop in he tracks? I's say he did. He looks at me

steady for a minute, and you could tell he thinking hard. Then he go and set on the bench and say, "Just wait. You thinks it am smart, but you am foolish in the head. They's gwine larn you something."

"Hush your big mouth and stay 'way from this nigger, that all I wants," I say, and just sets and hold that poker in the hand. He just sets, looking like the bull. There we-uns sets and sets for 'bout an hour, and then he go out, and I bars the door.

The next day I goes to the missy and tells her what Rufus wants, and Missy say that am the massa's wishes. She say, "You am the portly gal, and Rufus am the portly man. The massa wants you-uns for to bring forth portly children."

I's thinking 'bout what the missy say, but say to myself, "I's not gwine live with that Rufus." That night when him come in the cabin, I grabs the poker and sits on the bench and says, "Git 'way from me, nigger, 'fore I bust your brains out and stomp on them." He say nothing and git out.

The next day the massa call me and tell me, "Woman, I's pay big money for you, and I's done that for the cause I wants you to raise me childrens. I's put you to live with Rufus for that purpose. Now, if you doesn't want whipping at the stake, u do what I wants."

I thinks 'bout Massa buying me offen the block and saving me from being separated from my folks and 'bout being whipped at the stake. There it am. What am I s to do? So I 'cides to do as the massa wish, and so I yields. . . .

I never marries, 'cause one 'sperience am 'nough for this nigger. After what I des for the massa, I's never wants no truck with any man. The Lord forgive this bred woman, but he have to 'scuse me and look for some others for to 'plenish the earth.

FOCUS QUESTIONS:

1. How would you characterize Williams' feelings about the events she narrates?

2. What impression do you get of Massa Hawkins?

3. Why does Williams "yield"? What are the results?

RELIGION AND REFORM, 1800–1860

7-1 Resolutions of the Anti-Slavery Convention of American Women

Angelina Grimke and her sister Sarah were prominent abolitionists. Angelina was born in Charleston, South Carolina, in 1805. Her father was a judge, and a slaveholder. The sisters rejected slavery and moved north, where they wrote and spoke publicly against slavery. (See also the document in this chapter, "Southern Belle Denounces Slavery.") Angelina and Sarah laid much of the groundwork for later leaders of the women's rights movement. The sisters operated a boarding school, where students included children of women's rights pioneer Elizabeth Cady Stanton (see Stanton's 1860 speech to the American Anti-Slavery Society in this chapter).

Source: *An Appeal to the Women of the Nominally Free States Issued by an Anti-Slavery Convention of American Women,* Boston: Isaac Knapp, 1838: 3-8, 11, 13-14, 20-21, 23-24.

BELOVED SISTERS:

The wrongs of outraged millions, and the foreshadows of coming judgments, constrain us, under a solemn sense of responsibility to press upon your consideration the subject of American Slavery. The women of the North have high and holy duties to perform in the work of emancipation — duties to themselves, to the suffering slave, to the slaveholder, to the church, to their country, and to the world at large, and, above all to their God. Duties, which if not performed now, may never be performed at all.

Multitudes will doubtless deem such an address ill-timed and ill directed. Many regard the excitement produced by the agitation of this subject as an evidence of the impolicy of free discussion, and a sufficient excuse for their own inactivity. Others so undervalue the rights and responsibilities of woman as to scoff and gainsay whenever she goes forth to duties beyond the parlor and the nursery . . .

Every citizen should feel an intense interest in the political concerns of the country, because the honor, happiness, and well being of every class, are bound up in its politics, government and laws. Are we aliens because we are women? Are we bereft of citizenship because we are the *mothers, wives,* and *daughters* of a mighty, people? Have *women* no country-no interest stakes in public weal-no liabilities in common peril-no partnership in a nation's guilt and shame? Has *woman* no home nor household altars, nor endearing ties of kindred, nor sway with man, nor power at a mercy seat, nor voice to cheer, nor hand to raise the drooping, and to bind the broken?

But before we can appreciate the bearings of this subject, and our duties with regard to it, we must first know what slavery is; and then trace out its manifold and monstrous relations. We can thus discover whether women have any duties to discharge its abolition. We will then attempt to show WHY Northern women should labor for its overthrow, and lastly HOW they can aid in this work of faith, and labor of love.

What then is Slavery? It is that crime, which casts man down from that exaltation where God has placed him, "a little lower than the angels," and sinks him to a level with the beasts of the field. This intelligent and immortal being is confounded with the brutes that perish; he whose spirit was formed to rise in aspirations of gratitude and praise whilst here, and to spend an eternity with God in heaven, is herded with the beasts, whose spirits go downward with their bodies of clay, to the dust of which they were made. Slavery is that crime by which man is robbed of his inalienable right to liberty, and the pursuit of happiness, the diadem of glory, and honor, with which he was crowned, and that sceptre of dominion which was placed in his hand when he was ushered upon the theatre of creation, and was divinely commissioned to "have dominion over the fish of the sea, and over the fowls of the air, and over the cattle, and over all the earth, and every creeping thing that creepeth upon the earth."

****

This is a very imperfect outline of the political bearings of this great question; and it is gravely urged that as it is a *political subject, women* have no concernment with it, this doctrine of the North is a sycophantic response to the declaration of a Southern representative, that women have no right to send up petitions to Congress. We know, dear sisters, that the open and the secret enemies of freedom in our country have dreaded our influence, and therefore have reprobated our interference, and in order to blind us to our responsibilities, have thrown dust into our eyes, well knowing that if the organ of vision is only clear, the whole body, the moving and acting faculties will become full of light, and will soon be thrown into powerful action. Some, who pretend to be very jealous for the honor of our sex, and are very anxious that *we* should scrupulously maintain the dignity and delicacy of female propriety, continually urge this objection to female effort We grant that it is a political, as well as a moral subject: does this exonerate women from their duties as subjects of the government, as members of the great human family? Have women never wisely and laudably exercised political responsibilities?

****

. . . And, dear sisters, in a country where women are degraded and brutalized, and where their exposed persons bleed under the lash—where they are sold in the shambles of "negro brokers"—robbed of their hard earnings-torn from their husbands, and forcibly plundered of their virtue and their offspring; surely, in such a country, it is very natural that *women* should wish to know "the reason *why*"— especially when these outrages of blood and nameless horror are practised in violation of the principles of our national Bill of Rights and the Preamble of our Constitution. We do not, then, and cannot concede the position, that because this is a *political subject* women ought to fold their hands in idleness, and close their eyes and ears to the "horrible things" that are practised in our land. The denial of our duty to act, is a bold denial of our right to act, and if we have no right to act, then may *we* well be termed "the white slaves of the North"-for, like our brethren in bonds, we must seal our lips in silence and despair.

****

Out of the millions of slaves who have been stolen from Africa, a very great number must have been women, who were torn from the arms of their fathers and husbands, brothers, and children, and subjected to all the horrors of the middle passage and the still greater sufferings of slavery in a foreign land.' ... The great mass of female slaves in the southern states are the descendants of these hapless strangers: 1,000,000 of them now wear the iron yoke of slavery in this land of boasted liberty and law. They are our country-women-they *are our sisters*, and to us, as women, they have a right to look for sympathy with their sorrows, and effort and prayer for their rescue. Upon those of us especially, who have named the name of Christ, they have peculiar claims, and claims which *we must answer or we shall incur a heavy load of guilt.*

Multitudes of the Southern women hold men, women and children as *property*. They are pampered in luxury, and nursed in the school of tyranny. . . Such facts ought to be known, that the women of the North may understand *their* duties, and be incited to perform them . . .

And now, dear sisters, let us not forget that *Northern* women are participators in the crime of Slavery-too many of us have surrendered our hearts and hands to the wealthy planters of the South, and gone down with them to live on the unrequited toil of the Slave. Too many of us have ourselves become slaveholders, our hearts have been hardened under the searing influence of the system, and we too, have learned to be tyrants in the school of despots . . .

. . . But let it be so no longer. Let us henceforward resolve, that the women of the free states never again will barter their principles for the blood bought luxuries of the South — never again will regard with complacency, much less with the tender sentiments of love, any man "who buildeth his house by unrighteousness and his chambers by wrong, that useth his neighbor's service *without* wages, and giveth him not for his work." . . .

FOCUS QUESTIONS:

1. Angelina and Sarah Grimke's participation in public life and politics was highly controversial. Does anything in this text serve to either challenge or ameliorate the concerns of those who disapprove of women's roles in the public sphere?

2. How does Grimke link women's roles and status with opposition to slavery?

7-2 Cherokee Women, Beware

This brief notice appeared in an issue of the Cherokee Phoenix, a newspaper published by the Cherokee Nation between 1828 and 1834.

Source: *Cherokee Phoenix*, July 16, 1831.

CHEROKEE WOMEN BEWARE

It is said the Georgia Guard have received orders, from the Governor we suppose, to inflict corporeal punishment on such females as shall hereafter be guilty of insulting them. We presume they are to be the judges of what constitutes *insult*. We will simply give our opinion upon this subject. According to our understanding of insult, we think, first it is very undignified for a female to exercise it under any circumstances; and second, it is equally indignified for any gentleman to inflict a corporeal punishment on a female who may be guilty of such a crime.

FOCUS QUESTIONS:

1. What is the tone of this notice? Why did the authors choose this tone?
2. What does this notice suggest about the quality of gender relations among the Cherokee in this period?

7-3 Constitution of the Colored Female Religious and Moral Society of Salem

The Colored Female Religious and Moral Society of Salem, Massachusetts, founded in 1818, was one of the many women's self-help groups established in this period.

Souce: Source: Skinner, Ellen *Women and the National Experience: Primary Sources in American History*, 2nd edition. New York: Longman, 2003

Article I.—At the weekly meeting of the Society, when the appointed hour arrives, and a number are convened, the exercises shall begin by reading in some profitable book, till all have come in who are expected.

Art. II—A prayer shall then be made by one of the members, and after that, a chapter in the Bible shall be read, and religious conversation be attended to, as time will allow.

Art. III—Four quarterly days in the year, in January, in April, July and October, beginning on the first day of every January, to be observed as day of solemn fasting and prayer.

Art. IV—We promise not to ridicule or divulge the supposed or apparent infirmities of any fellow member; but to keep secret all things relating to the Society, the discovery of which might tend to do hurt to the Society or any individual.

Art. V—We resolve to be charitably watchful over each other; to advise, caution and admonish where we may judge there is occasion, and that it may be useful; and we promise not to resent, but kindly and thankfully receive such friendly advice or reproof from any one of our members.

Art. VI—Any female can become a member of this Society by conforming to the Constitution, and paying in fifty two cents per year.

Art. VII—This Society is formed for the benefit of the sick and destitute of those members belonging to the Society.

Art. VIII—If any member commit any scandalous sin, or walk unruly, and after proper reproof continue manifestly impenitent, she shall be excluded from us, until she give evidence of her repentance.

Art. IX—When any person shall manifest to any one of us a desire to join the Society, it shall be mentioned in one of our meetings that all may have opportunity, who desire it, to satisfy themselves respecting the character and conversation of the person offering to join; and if at the meeting on the next week, there be no objection to her being admitted, she may apply to the head of the Society, who will read our Articles to her, and if she is willing and does sign them, she shall be considered as a member of the Society, regularly admitted.

Art. X—As to any other matters which we shall hereafter find conducive to the benefit and good regulation of our Society, we engage to leave to the discretion and decision of a major part of us, to whose determination we promise quietly to agree and submit.

President—Mrs. Clarissa C. Lawrence
Vice-President—Mrs. Eleanor Jones
Treasurer—Miss Betsey Blanchard
Secretary—Mrs. Sally Coleman
Visiting Committee—Mrs. Mercy Norris
　　　　　　　　　　Mrs. Nancy Randolph

1. What is the purpose of this society?

2. What mechanisms do the members propose to allow new members to enter, and to ensure that the members are working towards common goals?

7-4 The Factory Girl's Lament

The Lowell "factory girls" — female workers in the textile mills of Lowell, Massachusetts — went on strike repeatedly in the 1830s. Strikes were staged to protest reduced wages, or to protect established workplace conditions. Wage-earning women sought independence and autonomy though their labor. Strikers' public demonstrations and marches featured songs such as this one.

Source: In Alice Kessler-Harris. *Out to Work: A History of Wage-Earning Women in the United States.* New York: Oxford University Press, 1982, 41.

Oh isn't it a pity that such a pretty girl as I
Should be sent to the factory to pine away and die.

Oh! I cannot be a slave
I will not be a slave
For I'm so fond of liberty
That I can not be a slave.

FOCUS QUESTIONS:

1. Abolitionists were prominent in Massachusetts during this period; a female antislavery society was founded in Lowell in 1833. What overlap is there between the language and imagery of this song, and that used by abolitionists?

2. What actions are proposed or implied by this song?

7-5 An Address to the Daughters of New England

This article appeared in the "Ladies Department" of The Liberator, a prominent weekly newspaper founded by abolitionist William Lloyd Garrison in Boston in 1831. The editors of The Liberator introduced this piece: "The writer of the following Appeal is a young lady only 13 years old, residing in North Providence. In intelligence and philanthropy, she is in advance of a large number of her sex."

Source: *The Liberator,* March 3, 1832

AN ADDRESS TO THE DAUGHTERS OF NEW-ENGLAND.

Awake, ye multitude, that have slumbered so long! Awake! in behalf of the injured children of Africa. And think not because ye are women, that ye can take no part in the glorious cause of emancipation. You have influence—exert it. Arm your fathers and brothers with the patriotic feelings of liberty and equal rights. Although the inhabitants of New-England are an exception in the vast multitude denominated slaveholders, shut not your hearts against the cries of the oppressed, which go up from the sister states. Woman's voice, though weak, may be heard; for it is hers, in a peculiar manner, to plead the cause of suffering innocence. And let not posterity have cause to say that you remained inactive, while two millions of your fellow mortals were oppressed with the yoke of bondage. Your land is the boasted land of liberty! But how much like vain mockery must this name appear to other nations! and what a discord does it make with those tones of oppressed, which rise in condemnation from the centre of the nation! Had that Congress which declared the independence and freedom of these United States, allowed it to have its influence over all, as it should have done, it would have presented a brighter era in the chronicles of liberty than has been presented to the world, or probably ever will be. Your land is the one that makes the greatest pretensions to freedom, and yet holds slaves in as much degradation as any spot on earth. In many cases, it is not only the body is enslaved, but the mind is also held in chains; to be riven only by death when it shall leave its frail tenement of suffering, and soar to those regions where it is destined to rove in freedom. Let not the ignorance of the blacks plead as an excuse for continuing them in servitude; for is not their being so, entirely the fault of the whites? Was not Egypt the birth-place of the arts and sciences? and did she not long remain the proud mistress of knowledge, and long wield the scepter of literature? And now that Egypt has fallen, and nought remains of her glory but what is recorded in the pages of history, or what meets the eye of the traveler, in his wanderings amid the wreck of grandeur which he finds everywhere in this once flourishing country; let us not forget that it is a country in Africa, that degraded Africa, whose sons and daughters are bought and sold and enslaved! And the soil of Africa covers the remains of many a noble patriarch, whose heart may have glowed with the generous feelings of freedom, and the archives of whose nation hold up as possessing intellects equal, if not superior to many who now flourish in our own country, as the supporters of slavery. Daughters of Columbia! ye that live in the far-famed land of Liberty! ye that have so often heard it extolled as the seat of independence and freedom! arise, throw off the veil which now obscures

your reasons, and let your names be enrolled as the defenders of liberty. A.F. M

FOCUS QUESTIONS:

1. What special roles or responsibilities does the author propose for women in opposing slavery?

2. What does the author do to put American slavery into an international context? Does this seem to be an effective form of argument?

3. Does the claim that this was written by a 13-year-old girl influence the way you read the article?

7-6 The Shakers

Shakers were members of a Protestant denomination that was established in England by Jane and James Wardley in the mid-eighteenth century. Anne Lee was the leader of the Shaker community in the American colonies, and led the settlement of Niskayuna, New York. All Shakers were expected to practice celibacy; the community grew through conversion and the adoption of orphans. American Shakers were also expected to follow the doctrine that Anne Lee was a female embodiment of the divine.

Source: *North American Review* 16 (January 1823): 81, 93-95.

Anne Lee was born in 1736 at Manchester, in England. Her father was a blacksmith by trade, and Anne was brought up in his house, in that eligible part of the city, called *Toad lane.* She was herself educated to the trade of cutter of hatters' fur; and had five brothers and two sisters. She was married in early life to Abraham Standley, a blacksmith, and had four children, all of whom died in infancy. At the age of twenty-two, she became a member of Wardley's society, then in its infancy, and having been, as far as we can collect out of the technical jargon of the work before us, remarkably docile, as a disciple of the leaders; and being, it would seem, of a susceptible nature, adapted to violent religious excitement; and perceiving perhaps the advantage to be attained on the principles of the sect, which conceded to the one sex an equality in all the prerogatives usually arrogated to themselves by the other, Anne became at last the acknowledge leader of this vulgar fanaticism, and in 1770 bore her first testimony. This testimony appears to have been the injunction of celibacy, as the perfection of human nature, and

the holding forth of herself as a divine person. She was from the time received as the spiritual parent of the faithful, honored with the title of Anne the Mother, and styled by herself *Anne the Word!*

The most interesting aspect, under which this institution presents itself, is that of a new form of *monachism.* To enjoin celibacy on about two hundred and fifty men, and as many women, gathered into four or five families, each consisting equally of either sex, and without any aid from the laws of the land or the public sentiment toward enforcing the rules of the institution, is, to say the least, a bold experiment in anthropology. If public scandal say true, it has not proved altogether a successful one. Several persons have, from time to time, seceded from the various communities of Shakers, and some of these have published accounts, unfavorable to the purity of these establishments. * We must own, however, that such accounts are not entitled to implicit faith, and the common principles of human nature, as well as charity, would lead us to think that it would be impossible to hold these societies together, were any of their leaders as insincere and corrupt, as some are represented to be. Considering that they have no legal power in their hands, and that society does not second their discipline, nothing short of extreme purity in those, who administer it, would prevent its rapid degeneracy and extinction.

When we look into the history of monastic institutions, we find them originating in as voluntary and self devoted a spirit, as that which enlisted the first converts to Shakerism; but we also find that these institutions were *kept up*, by means very different from those, by which their first establishment was effected; means which our Shakers can never command. Separate houses were erected for monks and nuns: the genius of Shakerism requires that the brethren and sisters in the faith be gathered together in the same families. Large bequests in lands and goods were made by the state and individuals on the most inalienable tenures to the religious houses; our governments will certainly give the Shakers nothing, nor incorporate them with powers to receive more than very frugal legacies. The whole power of government, ecclesiastical and civil, was exerted to enforce on those once devoted, the observance of the monastic vow; and to be built up alive into a stone wall was the mildest punishment for violating it. We presume that if any suspicion should get abroad, among the neighbors of a Shaker settlement, that any such means were put in practice against an apostate Shaker or Shakeress, two hours would not elapse without subjecting their abodes to a more violent shaking, on the part of the mob, than any thing ever witnessed at Neskayuna or in Toad lane. Or if this were not done, it is more than probable the grand jury would begin to stir in the business: and it would take more than the ingenuity of our authors to spiritualize the letter of the old common law. In fact, since the mode of settling things by judge and jury has gotten into vogue, monastic institutions have declined in the world; and certainly of all countries, ours is the last where they could be expected to revive.

It may be asked then what holds these families together, in defiance of the law of nature, unaided by the law of the land. To this a partial answer is obvious. Religious enthusiasm was certainly the first principle of the growth of the Shakers. It was accident probably, which gave their establishments an agricultural form in this country. Some substantial farmer became a Shaker, and threw his acres into the common stock. Indigent brethren came and settled with him, and thus the nucleus of a community was formed. If well administered, it is plain that the increase of such an establishment will be rapid. The surplus gains invested in new lands will increase the temptation to converts to share the abundance, and in short the thing grows because it is: as a snow ball, ready in itself to melt, gathers as it is moved. Moreover, we do not set it all down to mere direct interest. Their community doubtless finds recruits from the wide spread *caste* of the friendless and deserted. Many poor isolated beings exist scattered about, even in this happy land; – surrounded by prosperous families but amalgamated with none, and lonely in the crowd. Single females without friends and protectors, orphan children without relations, pilgrims in the world struck with melancholy by the way, widows, and fathers who have lost children, all those who in one way or the other seem left out of the game or the battle of life, furnish recruits to the Shakers. The families of their neighbors cannot take them all in, and after human pity has been strained to the last degree of cousinship, there will still remain many forlorn individuals in the world. Can it be wondered that such persons are desirous of entering a community, which not only elevates them at once to competence, but divides with them share of the corporate identity; and gives them a little consequence in the eyes of their fellows; and puts their rights, happiness and feelings, under the protection of a numerous society? We have been told that in the late war, the widows and children of some of those, who had enlisted in our army, and were slain on the frontiers, repaired to these asylums. One could forgive some absurdity in religious rites to a people, who stood ready to open their gates to the families thus left desolate. Some blacks may also be seen on their benches, specimens of a branch of that race rapidly disappearing among us.

FOCUS QUESTIONS:

1. How does the author explain the success of Shaker communities?

2. What does the author present as the principal difficulties of Shaker life?

3. What does Anne Lee's leadership of a religious community suggest about women's roles in eighteenth-century America?

7-7 Elizabeth Cady Stanton Speaks to the American Anti-Slavery Society (1860)

Elizabeth Cady Stanton was a leader of the nineteenth-century women's rights movement. Together with Susan B. Anthony, Lucretia Mott, and others, she was a lead organizer of the Women's Rights Convention held at Seneca Falls, New York, in 1848. (See "Declaration of Rights and Sentiments," chapter 8.) Stanton was also active in abolitionist causes.

NOTE: Although some of her wording is offensive to us now, it was widespread at the time. It is important to remember that her ideas were considered radically enlightened in her time.

Source: Reprinted from Ellen DuBois, *Elizabeth Cady Stanton, Susan B. Anthony, Correspondence, Writings, Speeches.* New York, Schocken Books, Inc. 1981: 78 – 85.

This is generally known as the platform of one idea – that is negro slavery. In a certain sense this may be true, but the most casual observation of this whole anti-slavery movement, of your lives, conventions, public speeches and journals, show this one idea to be a great humanitarian one. The motto of your leading organ, "The world is my country and all mankind my countrymen," proclaims the magnitude and universality of this one idea, which takes in the whole human family, irrespective of nation, color, caste, or sex, with all their interests, temporal and spiritual – a question of religion, philanthropy, political economy, commerce, education and social life on which depends the very existence of this republic, of the state, of the family, the sacredness of the lives and property of Northern freemen, the holiness of the marriage relation, and perpetuity of the Christian religion. Such are the various phases of the question you are wont to debate in your conventions. They all grow out of and legitimately belong to that so-called petty, insignificant, annoying subject, which thrusts upon its head everywhere in Church and State –"the eternal nigger." But in settling the question of the negro's rights, we find out the exact limits of our own, for rights never clash or interfere; and where no individual in a community is denied his rights, the mass are the more perfectly protected in theirs; for whenever any class is subject to fraud or injustice, it shows that the spirit of tyranny is at work, and no one can tell where or how or when the infection will spread. . . .

It was thought a small matter to kidnap a black man in Africa, and set him to work in the rice swamps of Georgia; but when we look at the panorama of horrors that followed that event, at all the statute laws that were enacted to make that act legal, at the perversion of man's moral sense and innate love of justice in being compelled to defend such laws; when we consider the long, hard tussle we have witnessed here for near a century between the spirit of Liberty and Slavery, we may, in some measure, appreciate the magnitude of the wrong done to that one, lone, friendless negro, who, under the cover of darkness and the star-spangled banner, was stolen from his African hut and lodged in the hold of the American slaver. That one act has, in its consequences, convulsed this Union. It has corrupted our churches, our politics, our press; laid violent hands on Northern freemen at their own firesides; it has gagged our statesmen, and stricken our Northern Senators dumb in their seats; yes, beneath the flag of freedom, Liberty has crouched in fear.

That grand declaration of rights made by WILLIAM LLOYD GARRISON, while yet a printer's boy, was on a higher plane than that of '76. His was uttered with the Christian's view of the dignity of man, the value of the immortal being; the other but from the self-respect of one proud race. But, in spite of noble words, deeds of thirty years of protest, prayers, and preaching, slavery still lives, the negro toils on in his weary bondage, his chains have not yet melted in the intense heat of the sun of righteousness; but in the discussion of this question, in grappling with its foes, how many of us have worked out our salvation; what mountains of superstition have been rolled off the human soul! I have always regarded Garrison as the great missionary of the gospel of Jesus to this guilty nation, for he has waged an uncompromising warfare with the deadly sins of both Church and State. . . .

. . . The mission of this Radical Anti-Slavery Movement is not to the African slave alone, but to the slaves of custom, creed and sex, as well. . . .

Eloquently and earnestly as noble men have denounced slavery on this platform, they have been able to take only an objective view. They can describe the general features of that infernal system – the horrors of the African slave trade, the agonizing sufferings of the middle-passage, and auction-block, the slave-pen and coffle, the diabolism of the internal traffic, the cruel severing of family ties, the hopeless degradation of woman; all that is outward they can see; but a privileged class can never conceive the feelings of those who are born to contempt, to inferiority, to degradation. Herein is woman more fully identified with the slave than man can possibly be, for she can take the subjective view. She early learns the misfortune of being born an heir to the crown of thorns, to martyrdom, to womanhood. For a while the man is born to do whatever he can, for the woman and the negro there is no such privilege. There is a Procrustean bedstead ever ready for them, body and soul, and all mankind stand on the alert to restrain their impulses, check their aspirations, fetter their limbs, lest, in their freedom and strength, in their full development, they should take an even platform with proud man himself. To you, white man, the world throws wide her gates; the way is clear to wealth, to fame, to glory, to renown; the high place of independence and honor and trust are yours; all your efforts are praised and encouraged; all your successes are welcomed with loud hurrahs and cheers; but the black man and the woman are born to shame. The badge of degradation is the skin and sex – the "scarlet letter" so sadly worn upon the breast. Children, even, can define the sphere of the black man, and the most ignorant Irishman hiss him into it, while striplings, mere swaddlings of law and divinity, can talk quite glibly of woman's sphere, and pedant priests at the alter discourse most lovingly of her holy mission to cook his meat, and bear him children, and minister to his sickly lust.

In conversation with a reverend gentleman, not long ago, I chanced to speak of the injustice done to woman. Ah! said he, so far from complaining, your heart should go out in thankfulness that you are an American woman, for in no country in the world does woman hold so high a position as here. Why, sir, said I, you must be very ignorant, or very false. Is my political position as high as that of Victoria, Queen of the mightiest nation on the globe? Are not nearly two millions of native-born American woman, at this very hour, doomed to the foulest slavery that angels ever wept to witness? Are they not doubly damned as immortal beasts of burden in the field, and sad mothers of a most accursed race? Are not they raised for the express purpose of lust? Are they not chained and driven in the slave-coffle at the crack of the whip of an unfeeling driver? Are they not sold on the auction-block? Are they not exposed naked to the course jests and voluptuous eyes of brutal men? Are they not trained up in ignorance of all laws, both human and divine, and denied the right to read the Bible? For them there is no Sabbath, no Jesus, no Heaven, no hope, no holy mission of wife and mother, no privacy of home, nothing sacred to look for, but an eternal sleep in dust and the grave. And these are the daughters and sisters of the first men in the Southern states: think of fathers and brothers selling their own flesh on the auction block, exposing beautiful women of refinement and education in a New Orleans market, and selling them, body and soul, to the highest bidder! And this is the condition of woman in republican, Christian America, and you dare not look me in the face, and tell me that, for blessings such as these, my heart should go out in thankfulness! No, proud priest, you may cover your soul in holy robes, and hide your manhood in a pulpit, and, like the Pharisee of old, turn your face away from the sufferings of your race; but I am a Christian – a follower of Jesus – and "whatever is done unto one of the least of these my sisters is done also unto me." Though, in person of the poor trembling slave mother, you have bound me with heavy burdens most grievous to bear, though you have dome all you could to quench the spark of immortality, which, from the throne of God, brought me into being . . . yet can I still speak to him. . . . I have asked the ever lasting hills, that in their upward yearnings seem to touch the heavens if I, an immortal being, though clothed in womanhood, was made for the vile purposes to which proud Southern man has doomed me, and in solemn chorus they all chanted, NO! I have turned my eyes within, I have asked this bleeding heart, so full of love to God and man, so generous and self-sacrificing, ever longing for the pure, the holy, the divine, if this graceful form, this soft and tender flesh was made to crawl and shiver in the cold, foul embrace of Southern tyrants; and in stifled sobs, it answered, NO! Think you, oh Christian priests, meekly I will take your insults, taunts and sneers? To you my gratitude is due for all the peculiar blessings of slavery, for you have had the morals of this nation in your keeping. Behold the depths into which you have plunged me – the bottomless pit of human misery! But perchance your head grows dizzy to look down so far, and your heart faint to see what torture I can bear! It is enough.

But . . . I rejoice that it has been given to woman to drink the very dregs of human wretchedness and woe. For now, by an eternal law of matter and of mind, when the reaction comes, upward and upward, and still upward, she shall rise. Behold how far above your priestly robes, your bloody alters, your foul incense, your steepled synagogues she shall stand secure on holy mounts, mid clouds of dazzling radiance, to which, in your gross vision, you shall not dare even to lift your eyes! (Applause.)

Focus Questions:

1. How does Stanton link women's oppression and slavery? Do you think her argument is effective?

2. In what way does Stanton claim slavery harms non-slave women?

3. What groups might be considered "slaves of custom, creed, and sex"?

7-8 A Warning to Mothers from the Female Moral Reform Society

The Female Moral Reform Society was a national organization that provided many nineteenth-century women with access to the public sphere. The Society's opposition to masturbation was hardly unique; physicians, clergy, and many others blamed a variety of physical and social ills on sexual self-stimulation, and many contraptions that reportedly prevented masturbation were patented in the nineteenth century.

Source: In *Major Problems in American Women's History.* 2nd edition. Mary Beth Norton and Ruth M. Alexander, editors. Lexington, MA: D.C. Heath and Company, 1996, 218-219

BELOVED SISTERS.

Will you permit an associated band, most of whom share responsibilities similar to your own, and know with yourselves the deep yearnings of maternal love, to call your attention, for a few moments, to a forbidding, but most important subject. Be assured that nothing but the fixed conviction that it is a subject affecting the temporal and eternal well-being of the young immortals committed to your care, would induce us to commend it to your consideration through the Press. We refer to a species of licentiousness from which neither age nor sex is exempt; a vice that has done its work of ruin, physical, mental, and moral, when no eye but that of Omniscience could behold it, a vice that has been practised in ten thousand instances, without a correct knowledge of its consequences, or its guilt, until it has paved the way for the most revolting excesses in 'crime. .

Recently it has pleased, our Heavenly Father to bring before our minds a flood of light, by which we have been solemnly convinced, that in nine cases out of ten, "solitary vice" [masturbation] is the first cause of social licentiousness, and the foundation and hidden source of the present corrupt state of society. . . .

The dangers to which all classes of the rising generation are exposed, are great beyond expression, they are dangers, too, that may stain the soul with guilt, and yet elude the vigilance of the most watchful parent, unless obviated *from the cradle*, by proper training and correct instruction. . . .

"A pupil in a select school, a child but ten years of age, confessed to her teacher, that she had been guilty of the sin alluded to for years, although she had never been taught it, and knew not that any one living practised it but herself. Her mind was fast sinking, she was wholly unable to reckon even small sums. This child had been religiously educated, but she was reared where the table was made a snare. Rich and high seasoned food, and abundance of dainties were given her, bathing was neglected, and a precocious development of the passions, and their consequent indulgence, was, in this case, the result." "A child, under 12 years of age, whose morals in every respect had been care-fully guarded, and who had never, except in one instance, been exposed, to the influence of an evil associate; on being questioned by her mother, confessed with tears that the sin had been taught her by the suspected individual." "A son of a highly respectable physician, under three years of age, with no teacher but depraved instinct, had become so addicted to this pernicious habit, that the mother was obliged to provide a close night dress, and watch his waking hours with unceasing care.". . ."A theological student, of superior mind and high attainments, deservedly beloved by numerous friends, and eminently fitted to be the centre of attraction in the highest circles of refinement, became a subject of this debasing vice. Presently his health failed, and abused reason deserted his throne. He was carried from the seminary to his friends, a maniac, and after lingering a few days, was ushered into the presence of his Judge." A physician, who has long had an extensive practice in this city, confidently affirms that most of the young men in feeble health, who go south, to escape or re-cover from consumption, are the victims of this body and soule destroying sin. . . .

FOCUS QUESTIONS:

1. Putting aside the absurd claims in this text, is there any way that masturbation could pose a threat to the social order or to individual morality?

2. Why would mothers be charged with responsibility for preventing masturbation?

7-9 A Call for Women to Become Abolitionists

Women helped organize the American Anti-Slavery Society, held fundraising antislavery bazaars, circulated antislavery petitions, and otherwise promoted the abolitionist cause. This essay is one of the earliest appeals to women. It also shows that women's participation in the movement was sometimes opposed even by women themselves. This excerpt is a response to a woman who objected to other women publicly advocating emancipation.

Source: Elizabeth Margaret Chandler, *The Poetical Works of Elizabeth Margaret Chandler* (Philadelphia, 1836), 21-23.

We have been so long accustomed to consider the duty of the female sex, with regard to slavery, as entirely plain, that we had almost imagined it must be equally so to any unprejudiced thinker upon the subject. Not that we expected to find no difference of feeling, or contrariety of sentiment; apathy and prejudices we were prepared for; but we certainly had not thought that the interference of woman in behalf of suffering humanity, could be seriously objected to, as improper, and at variance with right principles. Yet this we are sorry to find is the light in which it is regarded by one of our own sex—a lady, whose talents and character we respect very highly, and whose approbation of the course we are pursuing, we should be proud to have obtained. But as this is withheld, and it is probable she may not be singular in her opinions, we have taken the liberty of quoting some of her sentiments, and appending to them a statement of our own ideas on the same subject

"Should you inquire why I do not devote myself more sedulously to promote the cause of emancipation?—I would tell you, that I think it is a work which requires the energies of men."

And so it does; but it requires also the influence of woman. She was given to man 'to be a helpmeet [helpmate] for him;' and it is therefore her duty, whenever she can do so, to lend him her aid in every great work of philanthropy. In this her cooperation may be of essential service, without leading her one step beyond her own proper sphere....

"It is a subject so connected with those of government, of law and politics, that I should fear the direct or even apparent interference of my own sex, would be a departure from that propriety of character which nature, as well as society, imposes on woman."

It is true that it is a question of government and politics, but it also rests upon the broader basis of humanity and justice; and it is on this ground only, that we advocate the interference of women. We have not the least desire to see our own sex transformed into a race of politicians; but we do not think that in this case such consequences are in the least to be apprehended. To plead for the miserable, to endeavor to alleviate the bitterness of their destiny, and to soften the stern bosoms of their oppressors into gentleness and mercy, can never be unfeminine or unbefitting the delicacy of woman! She does not advocate Emancipation because slavery is at variance with the political interests of the state, but because it is an outrage against humanity and morality and religion; because it is criminal, and because her own supineness makes her a sharer in the crime; and because a great number of her own sex are among its victims. It is therefore, that she should steadily and conscientiously rank among the number of its opponents, and refuse to be benefited by its advantages. She does not by this become a partisan of any system of policy—she seeks only to shield from outrage all that is most holy in her religion! She does not seek to direct, or share with men, the government of the state; but she entreats them to lift the iron foot of despotism from the neck of her sisterhood; and this we consider not only quite within the sphere of her privileges, but also of her positive duties.

FOCUS QUESTIONS:

1. Does the author call on women to take greater responsibility in government?

2. What are the practical results for women's rights in her call for women's involvement in the abolitionist movement?

7-10 Southern Belle Denounces Slavery

Angelina Grimke was the daughter of a southern aristocrat and herself a staunch abolitionist. Angelina and her sister, Sarah, moved to Philadelphia, converted to the Quaker religion and became active in the abolition movement. Angelina became dissatisfied with the pacifism of the Quakers and wrote "An Appeal to the Christian Women of the South," which was banned in the South and prompted a call for her arrest in South Carolina. Grimke's position was extremely radical for a southern woman in her day. Grimke's speech, "Bearing Witness Against Slavery," reprinted here, was delivered at the 1838 National Anti-Slavery Convention in Philadelphia. The convention was greeted by an angry mob who waited outside, jeering and throwing rocks for three days, the mob finally storming the building and setting fire to it on the third day.

Source: Carolina Herron, ed., *Selected Works of Angelina Weld Grimke* (New York: Oxford University Press, 1991).

Do you ask, "What has the North to do with slavery?" Hear it, hear it! Those voices without tell us that the spirit of slavery is *here*, and has been roused to wrath by our Conventions; for surely liberty would not foam and tear herself with rage, because her friends are multiplied daily, and meetings are held in quick succession to set forth her virtues and extend her peaceful kingdom. This opposition shows that slavery has done its deadliest work in the hearts of our citizens. Do you ask, then, "What has the North to do?" I answer, cast out first the spirit of slavery from your own hearts, and then lend your aid to convert the South. Each one present has a work to do, be his or her situation what it may, however limited their means or insignificant their supposed influence. The great men of this country will not do this work; the Church will never do it. A desire to please the world, to keep the favor of all parties and of all conditions, makes them dumb on this and every other unpopular subject.

As a Southerner, I feel that it is my duty to stand up here to-night and bear testimony against slavery. I have seen it! I have seen it! I know it has horrors that can never be described. I was brought up under its wing. I witnessed for many years its demoralizing influences and its destructiveness to human happiness. I have never seen a happy slave. I have seen him dance in his chains, it is true, but he was not happy. There is a wide difference between happiness and mirth. Man can not enjoy happiness while his manhood is destroyed. Slaves, however, may be, and sometimes are mirthful. When hope is extinguished, they say, "Let us eat and drink, for to-morrow we die." [Here stones were thrown at the windows—a great noise without and commotion within.]

What is a mob? What would the breaking of every window be? What would the leveling of this hall be? Any evidence that we are wrong, or that slavery is a good and wholesome institution? What if the mob should now burst in upon us, break up our meeting, and commit violence upon our persons, would that be anything compared with what the slaves endure? No, no; and we do not remember them, "as bound with them," if we shrink in the time of peril, or feel unwilling to sacrifice ourselves, if need be, for their sake. [Great noise.] I thank the Lord that there is yet life enough left to feel the truth, even though it rages at it; that conscience is not so completely seared as to be unmoved by the truth of the living God. [Another outbreak of the mob and confusion in the house.]

How wonderfully constituted is the human mind! How it resists, as long as it can, all efforts to reclaim it from error! I feel that all this disturbance is but an evidence that our efforts are the best that could have been adopted, or else the friends of slavery would not care for what we say and do. The South know what we do. I am thankful that they are reached by our efforts. Many times have I wept in the land of my birth over the system of slavery. I knew of none who sympathized in my feelings; I was unaware that any efforts were made to deliver the oppressed; no voice in the wilderness was heard calling on the people to repent and do works meet for repentance, and my heart sickened within me. Oh, how should I have rejoiced to know that such efforts as these were being made. I only wonder that I had such feelings. But in the midst of temptation I was preserved, and my sympathy grew warmer, and my hatred of slavery more inveterate, until at last I have exiled myself from my native land, because I could no longer endure to hear the wailing of the slave.

I fled to the land of Penn; for here, thought I, sympathy for the slave will surely be found. But I found it not. The people were kind and hospitable, but the slave had no place in their thoughts. I therefore shut up my grief in my own heart. I remembered that I was a Carolinian, from a State which framed this iniquity by law. Every Southern breeze wafted to me the discordant tones of weeping and wailing, shrieks and groans, mingled with prayers and blasphemous curses. My heart sank within me at the abominations in the midst of which I had been born and educated. What will it avail, cried I, in bitterness of spirit, to expose to the gaze of strangers the horrors and pollutions of slavery, when there is no ear to hear nor heart to feel and pray for the slave? But how different do I feel now! Animated with hope, nay, with an assurance of the triumph of liberty and good-will to man, I will lift up my voice like a trumpet, and show this people what they can do to influence the Southern mind and overthrow slavery. [Shouting, and stones against the windows.]

We often hear the question asked, "What shall we do?" Here is an opportunity. Every man and every woman present may do something, by showing that we fear not a mob, and in the midst of revilings and threatenings, pleading the cause of those who are ready to perish. Let me urge every one to buy the books written on this subject; read them, and lend them to your neighbors. Give your money no longer for things which pander to pride and lust, but aid in scattering "the living coals of truth upon the naked heart of the nation"; in circulating appeals to the sympathies of Christians in behalf of the outraged slave.

But it is said by some, our "books and papers do not speak the truth"; why, then, do they not contradict what we say? They can not. Moreover, the South has entreated, nay, commanded us, to be silent; and what greater evidence of the truth of our publications could be desired?

Women of Philadelphia! allow me as a Southern woman, with much attachment to the land of my birth, to entreat you to come up to this work. Especially, let me urge you to petition. Men may settle this and other questions at the ballot-box, but you have no such right. It is only through petitions that you can reach the Legislature. It is, therefore, peculiarly your duty to petition. Do you say, "It does no good!" The South already turns pale at the number sent. They have read the reports of the proceedings of Congress, and there have seen that among other petitions were very many from

the women of the North on the subject of slavery. Men who hold the rod over slaves rule in the councils of the nation; and they deny our right to petition and remonstrate against abuses of our sex and our kind. We have these rights, however, from our God. Only let us exercise them, and, though often turned away unanswered, let us remember the influence of importunity upon the unjust judge, and act accordingly. The fact that the South looks jealously upon our measures shows that they are effectual. There is, therefore, no cause for doubting or despair.

It was remarked in England that women did much to abolish slavery in her colonies. Nor are they now idle. Numerous petitions from them have recently been presented to the Queen to abolish apprenticeship, with its cruelties, nearly equal to those of the system whose place it supplies. One petition, two miles and a quarter long, has been presented. And do you think these labors will be in vain? Let the history of the past answer. When the women of these States send up to Congress such a petition our legislators will arise, as did those of England, and say: "When all the maids and matrons of the land are knocking at our doors we must legislate." Let the zeal and love, the faith and works of our English sisters quicken ours; that while the slaves continue to suffer, and when they shout for deliverance, we may feel the satisfaction of "having done what we could."

FOCUS QUESTIONS:

1. What can you discern about the role of women within the abolitionist movement from Grimke's speech? What specific things are the women doing?

2. What do you think about Grimke's courage? How is it demonstrated within this speech? Why do you think more Southern women did not join her?

POLITICS AND POWER:
THE MOVEMENT FOR WOMAN'S RIGHTS, 1800–1860

8-1 New York Married Women's Property Act

Gaining the legal right to hold property independently of a father or husband was a significant victory for women. New York was the first state to grant women property rights, as spelled out in this 1848 law.

Source: http://memory.loc.gov/ammem/awhhtml/awlaw3/ property_law.html

AN ACT for the effectual protection of the property of married women.

Passed April 7, 1848.

The People of the State of New York, represented in Senate and Assembly do enact as follows:

Sec. 1. The real and personal property of any female who may hereafter marry, and which she shall own at the time of marriage, and the rents issues and profits thereof shall not be subject to the disposal of her husband, nor be liable for his debts, and shall continue her sole and separate property, as if she were a single female.

Sec. 2 The real and personal property, and the rents issues and profits thereof of any female now married shall not be subject to the disposal of her husband; but shall be her sole and separate property as if she were a single female except so far as the same may be liable for the debts of her husband heretofore contracted.

Sec. 3. It shall be lawful for any married female to receive, by gift, grant devise or bequest, from any person other than her husband and hold to her sole and separate use, as if she were a single female, real and personal property, and the rents, issues and profits thereof, and the same shall not be subject to the disposal of her husband, nor be liable for his debts.

Sec. 4. All contracts made between persons in contemplation of marriage shall remain in full force after such marriage takes place.

FOCUS QUESTIONS

1. What are some of the practical effects for a married woman of being able to hold property "as if she were a single female"?

2. Why does the law specifically refer to women's potential liability for her husband's debts?

8-2 From A History of Women in Trade Unions

Trade unions were dominated by men. From the 1830s throughout the rest of the nineteenth century and beyond, the trade union leadership and press put forward the argument that, because women were generally paid less than men, their presence in the workforce depressed wages for men. This U.S. government report from the early twentieth century encapsulates the view.

Source: John Andrews and W.D.P. Bliss, *A History of Women in Trade Unions. Volume 10 of Report on the Conditions of Woman and Child Earners in the United States,* U.S. Department of Labor, 1911.

One thing . . . must be apparent to every reflecting female, that all her exertions are scarce sufficient to keep her alive; that the price of her labor each year is reduced, and that she in a measure stands in the way of the male when attempting to raise his prices or equalize his labor, and that her efforts to sustain herself and family are actually the same as tying a stone around the neck of her natural protector, Man, and destroying him with the weight she has brought to his assistance. This is the true and natural consequence of female labor when carried beyond the family.

FOCUS QUESTIONS

1. If we accept as legitimate men's concerns about their wage levels in a mixed-gender work environment, what alternative response to women's lower wages might have preserved men's earnings?

2. What assumptions do the writers make about women's roles in the workplace and in the family? What assumptions do they make about women's reasons for working?

8-3 Catharine Beecher's Essay on the Education of Female Teachers

Catharine Beecher was an influential advocate of early education for girls. Catharine, born in 1800, was the eldest of thirteen children; her siblings included the famous abolitionist Harriet Beecher Stowe (author of Uncle Tom's Cabin, published in 1852) and the renowned clergyman Henry Ward Beecher.

Source: Catharine Beecher, *An Essay on the Education of Female Teachers*, J.B. Ford and Company, 1874: 27-33.

CHAPTER IV

HARTFORD SEMINARY

The preceding particulars of personal and family history will indicate that much which is often ascribed to remarkable native talents, is result of appropriate culture. And in the following narrative of what has been accomplished by my co-laborers and myself the last fifty years, it will be seen that it was achieved chiefly by good, common sense, persevering energy and high religious principle, and not by remarkable genius, or by the aid of that literary and scientific training sough in our colleges and regarded as a marked privilege of which women have been unjustly deprived.

When nearly twenty I began preparation to teach, by taking lessons on the piano and in this, as in my domestic training, I was favored by a very thorough and accurate teacher had no special taste or talent in that direction as was manifest from the fact that when I was eleven years old, a lady parishioner gave me lessons for two years, and having no piano, I did not feel interest enough to accept her invitation or that of another friend to use their instruments.

My success in this case was chiefly owing to the quickening of my faculties by *interest* in gaining a *practical* result, that of making myself independent, and aiding to support my family. For though I had forgot-

ten both notes and keys, under the training of a friend warmly interested in my success, in a year and a half I was recommended to teach in a school, in New London and play the organ in an Episcopal church. I also taught drawing and painting—having been further qualified by a lady who bad taken lessons of the best masters in New York. But at that period very humble performances in these accomplishments gave satisfaction.

When, at twenty-two, I commenced preparation to teach "the higher branches" in which I had had no knowledge also was favored by most thorough instruction from a friend in the family where I spent the winter. Then it was that I first took in hand the mystical performances in Daboll's Arithmetic, and as my domestic training had formed a habit of enquiring why any practical operation was to be performed, I began to annoy my teacher with demanding *why* the figures were to be put thus, and so, and *why* a given, answer was gained. And so when I lad pupils in this branch taught as no book then in use did, and finally made an arithmetic first issued in manuscript by my teachers, and then published. Of this book Prof. Olmstead, of Vale College, wrote to me thus:

"Your Arithmetic I have put into the hands of my children, giving it a decided preference over those in common use. Reflecting how I might best serve you, it has occurred to me that when your revised edition is out, I may write a notice of it, more or less extended, for the *Christian Spectator*, which could be used by your publisher."

This fact is the more striking, because of all studies I ever attempted this was both ';he most difficult and most uninteresting; so that my success was wholly owing to the interest excited by its practical usefulness in my profession. That same wincer, beside completing Daboll, I went through Day's Algebra, a few exercises in Geometry, a work on Logic, and two small works prepared for schools, on Chemistry and Natural Philosophy.

Then, associated with my next sister, I commenced

a school for young ladies in Hartford, Conn. We began in the upper chamber of a store with seven young ladies, receiving none under twelve; and my younger sister (now Mrs. H. B. Stowe) joined us as a pupil when she had attained that age.

Soon the increase of pupils removed us to a larger chamber, and thence to the basement of a church, where nearly one hundred young ladies had only one room, no globe or large maps, and, most of the time, no black-board, and only two teachers. At this time I had heard that Mrs. Willard and one or two others were teaching the higher branches, but I knew nothing of their methods. All the improvements I made were the result of the practical training of domestic life, in which the constant aim had been to find the *best* way of doing anything and everything; together with he very thorough manner in which, at mature age, I was taught.

At the end of four laborious years, I drew the plan of the present seminary, except the part containing the Calisthenic hall,—Mr. Daniel Wadsworth aiding in preparing the front elevation. This I submitted to some of the leading gentlemen of Hartford, and asked to have such a building erected by subscription. Many of them were surprised and almost dismayed at the "visionary and impracticable suggestion, and when it became current that I wanted a study hall to hold one hundred and fifty pupils, a lecture room, and six recitation rooms, the absurdity of it was apparent to most of the city fathers, and, with some, excited ridicule. But the more intelligent and influential women came to my aid, and soon all I ought was granted. This was my first experience of the moral power and good judgment of American women, which has been my chief reliance ever since.

FOCUS QUESTIONS

1. How did Beecher determine which subjects to teach to girls? What teaching methods did she emphasize in training teachers?

2. To what does Beecher ascribe her success? What is the importance of family and social networks?

3. Is she optimistic about the future for women's education?

8-4 Declaration of Sentiments and Resolutions, Seneca Falls

Organized by Lucretia Mott and Elizabeth Cady Stanton, the 1848 Seneca Falls Convention in New York was the first national women's rights convention in the United States. This document, obviously modeled on the Declaration of Independence, listed the ways in which women had been denied the basic rights inherent in the American idea. It was drafted by Stanton, and approved with minor alterations by the convention. Though 40 men attended (including Fredrick Douglass) the convention blamed men for the unjust treatment of women and stated that women must earn independence for themselves. The meeting become the first of many and provided impetus for the burgeoning women' movement.

Source: E. C. Stanton, S. B. Anthony, and Matilda Joslyn Gage, eds., *History of Woman Suffrage*, vol. 1 (Rochester, NY: Charles Mann, 1881), pp. 70–72.

We hold these truths to be self-evident: that all men and women are created equal; that they are endowed by their Creator with certain inalienable rights; that among these are life, liberty, and the pursuit of happiness; that to secure these rights governments are instituted, deriving their just powers from the consent of the governed. . . . But when a long train of abuses and usurpations, pursuing invariably the same object evinces a design to reduce them under absolute despotism, it is their duty to throw off such government, and to provide new guards for their future security. Such has been the patient sufferance of the women under this government, and such is now the necessity which constrains them to demand the equal station to which they are entitled. The history of mankind is a history of repeated injuries and usurpations on the part of man toward woman, having in direct object the establishment of an absolute tyranny over her. To prove this, let facts be submitted to a candid world. He has never permitted her to exercise her inalienable right to the elective franchise. He has compelled her to submit to laws, in the formation of which she had no voice. He has withheld from her rights which are given to the most ignorant and degraded men—both natives and foreigners. Having deprived her of this first right of a citizen, the elective franchise, thereby leaving her without representation in the halls of legislation, he has oppressed her on all sides. He has made her, if married, in the eye of the law, civilly dead. He has taken from her all right in property, even to the wages she earns. He has made her, morally, an irresponsible being, as she can commit many crimes with impunity, provided they be done in the presence of her husband. In the covenant of marriage, she is compelled to promise obedience to her husband, he becoming, to all intents and purposes, her master—the law giving him power to deprive her of her liberty, and to administer chastisement. He has so framed the laws of divorce, as to what shall be the proper causes, and in case of separation, to whom the guardianship of the children shall be given, as to be wholly regardless of the happiness of women—the law, in all cases, going upon a false supposition of the supremacy of man, and giving all power into his hands.

After depriving her of all rights as a married woman, if single, and the owner of property, he has taxed her to support a government which recognizes her only when her property can be made profitable to it. He has monopolized nearly all the profitable employments, and from those she is permitted to follow, she receives but a scanty remuneration. He closes against her all the avenues to wealth and distinction which he considers most honorable to himself. As a teacher of theology, medicine, or law, she is not known. He has denied her the facilities for obtaining a thorough education, all colleges being closed against her. He allows her in Church, as well as State, but a subordinate position, claiming Apostolic authority for her exclusion from the ministry, and, with some exceptions, from any public participation in the affairs of the Church. He has created a false public sentiment by giving to the world a different code of morals for men and women, by which moral delinquencies which exclude women from society, are not only tolerated, but deemed of little account in man. He has usurped the prerogative of Jehovah himself, claiming it as his right to assign for her a sphere of action, when that belongs to her conscience and to her God. He has endeavored, in every way that he could, to destroy her confidence in her own powers, to lessen her self-respect, and to make her willing to lead a dependent and abject life. Now, in view of this entire disfranchisement of one-half the people of this country, their social and religious degradation—in view of the unjust laws above mentioned, and because women do feel themselves aggrieved, oppressed, and fraudulently deprived of their most sacred rights, we insist that they have immediate admission to all the rights and privileges which belong to them as citizens of the United States. In entering upon the great work before us, we anticipate no small amount of misconception, misrepresentation, and ridicule; but we shall use every instrumentality within our power to effect our object. We shall employ agents, circulate tracts, petition the State and National legislatures, and endeavor to enlist the pulpit and the press in our behalf. We hope this Convention will be followed by a series of Conventions embracing every part of the country. The following resolutions were adopted:

Resolved, That such laws as conflict, in any way, with the true and substantial happiness of woman, are contrary to the great precept of nature and of no validity, for this is "superior in obligation to any other."

Resolved, That all laws which prevent woman from occupying such a station in society as her conscience shall dictate, or which place her in a position inferior to that of man, are contrary to the great precept of nature, and therefore of no force or authority.

Resolved, That woman is man's equal—was intended to be so by the Creator, and the highest good of the race demands that she should be recognized as such.

Resolved, That the women of this country ought to be enlightened in regard to the laws under which they live, that they may no longer publish their degradation by declaring themselves satisfied with their present position, nor their ignorance, by asserting that they have all the rights they want.

Resolved, That inasmuch as man, while claiming for himself intellectual superiority, does accord to woman moral superiority, it is pre-eminently his duty to encourage her to speak and teach, as she has an opportunity, in all religious assemblies.

Resolved, That the same amount of virtue, delicacy, and refinement of behavior that is required of woman in the social state, should also be required of man, and the same transgressions should be visited with equal severity on both man and woman.

Resolved, That the objection of indelicacy and impropriety, which is so often brought against woman when she addresses a public audience, comes with a very ill-grace from those who encourage, by their attendance, her appearance on the stage, in the concert, or in feats of the circus.

Resolved, That woman has too long rested satisfied in the circumscribed limits which corrupt customs and a perverted application of the Scriptures have marked out for her, and that it is time she should move in the enlarged sphere which her great Creator has assigned her.

Resolved, That it is the duty of the women of this country to secure to themselves their sacred right to the elective franchise.

Resolved, That the equality of human rights results necessarily from the fact of the identity of the race in capabilities and responsibilities.

Resolved, therefore, That, being invested by the Creator with the same capabilities, and the same consciousness of responsibility for their exercise, it is demonstrably the right and duty of woman, equally with man, to promote every righteous cause by every righteous means; and especially in regard to the great subjects of morals and religion, it is self evidently her right to participate with her brother in teaching them, both in private and in public, by writing and by speaking, by any instrumentalities proper to be used, and in any assemblies proper to be held; and this being a self-evident truth growing out of the divinely implanted principles of human nature, any custom or authority adverse to it, whether modern or wearing the hoary sanction of antiquity, is to be regarded as a self-evident

falsehood, and at war with mankind.

Resolved, That the speedy success of our cause depends upon the zealous and untiring efforts of both men and women, for the overthrow of the monopoly of the pulpit, and for the securing to woman an equal participation with men in the various trades, professions, and commerce.

FOCUS QUESTIONS:

1. In the "Resolutions" at the end of the document, how does Stanton attempt to persuade men to agree to equal rights for women?
2. Even though the women's rights movement followed closely on the heels of abolitionism, slaves gained emancipation more than fifty years before women won the right to vote in national elections. Why do you think this was the case?

8-5 Letters on the Equality of the Sexes

Sarah Grimke and her sister Angelina were abolitionist activists and early leaders of the women's rights movement. (See documents by Angelina Grimke in chapter seven, "Resolutions of the Anti-Slavery Convention of American Women" and "Southern Belle Denounces Slavery.") This text is excerpted from a volume of letters that Sarah Grimke addressed to the president of the Boston Anti-Slavery Society, Mary S. Parker.

Source: Sarah Grimke, *Letters on the Equality of the Sexes, and the Condition of Woman* (Boston: Isaac Knapp, 1838), p. 16.

The Lord Jesus defines the duties of his followers in his Sermon on the Mount. He lays down grand principles by which they should be governed, without any reference to sex or condition : — 'Ye are the light of the world. A city that is set on a hill cannot be hid. Neither

do men light a candle and put it under a bushel, but on a candlestick, and it giveth light unto all that are in the house. Let your light so shine before men, that they may see your good works, and glorify your Father which is in Heaven.' I follow him through all his precepts, and find him giving the same directions to women as to men, never even referring to the distinction now so strenuously insisted upon between masculine and feminine virtues : this is one of the antichristian 'traditions of men' which are taught instead of the 'commandments of God.' Men and women were CREATED EQUAL; they are both moral and accountable beings, and whatever is right for man to do, is right for woman.

FOCUS QUESTIONS:

1. Why were religious arguments such as this one important to nineteenth-century activists?
2. Can you think of any logical refutation to Grimke's line of reasoning?

8-6 Course of Instruction, Mount Holyoke Female Seminary

Mount Holyoke Female Seminary – the precursor to today's Mount Holyoke College, in South Hadley, Massachusetts – was the first American institution of higher education for women. It was founded by Mary Lyon, and opened in 1837. Lyon's goal was to offer an education equal to what was offered at men's colleges at the time, and to keep expenses low so that a high-quality education would be available to a relatively diverse pool of women.

Source: Mary Lyon, *Third Annual Catalogue of the Officers and Members of the Mount Holyoke Female Seminary* (South Hadley, MA: 1839-1840), "Appendix: Course of Instruction," pp. 8-12.

APPENDIX.

COURSE OF INSTRUCTION.

There is a regular English course of study, occupying three years. Some devote a part of their, time to Latin, and continue more than one year in the same class. This is very desirable for all who expect to complete the regular course. It is contemplated that the course of study will embrace four years to give a regular time to Latin. It is hoped that the improvement of the pupils, ad the expectation of friends will soon justify such an addition.

STUDIES OF THE JUNIOR CLASS.

Ancient Geography. Ancient and Modern History:—Text books, Worchester's Elements Goldsmith's Greece, Rome, and England, and Grim Shaw's France. Day's Algebra begun. Sullivan's Political Class Book. Lee's Physiology. Outline of Botany. Outline of Natural Philosophy. Smellie's Philosophy of Natural History. English Grammar:—Murray's Grammar and Exercises, Pope's Essay on Man.

STUDIES OF THE MIDDLE CLASS.

Day's Algebra finished. Play fair's Euclid (old edition) begun. Abercrombie on the Intellectual Powers. Marsh's Ecclesiastical history. Beck's Botany begun. Beck's Chemistry. Wilkins's Astronomy. Newman's Rhetoric. Geology. Alexander's Evidences of Christianity. English Grammar continued: —Young's Night Thoughts

STUDIES OF THE SENIOR CLASS.

Playfair's Euclid finished. Olmsted's Natural Philosophy. Beek's Botany continued. Paley's Natural Theology. Whately's Logic. Wharcly's Rhetoric. Intellectual Philosophy. Wayland's Moral Philosophy. Wayland's Moral Philosophy. Wayland's Political Economy. Buther's Analogy. Million's Paradise Lost.

Particular attention is given to composition, reading, and calisthenics through the whole course. The Bible lesson is recited on the Sabbath and reviewed during the week. Regular instruction is given in vocal music, and in linear and prospective drawing. Those who have attended to instrumental music, can have the use of a piano a few hours in a week.

As books and stationery can he had at the Seminary on very low terms, young ladies need not purchase them elsewhere. They are requested, however, to bring with them any of the preceding list of text books, which they may own—also a Bible, an English Dictionary, and if they own them, a Concordance, a Commentary on the Bible, Village Ilymns, Walts' Psalms and Hymns, Parker's Progressive Exercises in Reading, books containing selections in poetry and prose for improvement in Reading, a Modern Atlas, an Ancient Atlas, Burritt's Celestial Atlas, and standard poetical works.

TERMS FOR ADMISSION.

The studies requisite for admission use an acquaintance with the general principles of English Grammar, a good knowledge of Modern Geography, Goodrich's History of the United Slates, Walls on the Mind, Colburn's First Lessons, and the whole of Adams's New Arithmetic.

None are received under sixteen years of age. Except in extraordinary cases no candidate will be accepted expecting to enter after the year commences, or to leave till its close.

EXAMINATIONS AND CLASSIFICATION.

Examinations for admission to the regular classes take place at the beginning of the year. Every candidate for admission to the Junior class is examined on the preparatory studies. Every candidate for an advanced standing is examined on the regular studies with which she ii acquainted. Those who continue members of the Seminary are regularly examined at the commencement of each year, before they are admitted to the next higher class. None can be admitted to the

Junior class without passing a good examination on all the preparatory studies, whatever may be their attainments in other branches. But individuals may be admitted to the Middle and Senior classes by passing a good examination on all the preparatory studies, and in as many branches of the regular course as shall be equivalent to a full preparation. It is however very desirable that all candidates for admission to the Middle class should be acquainted with all the Junior studies, and it is much more important, that candidates for admission to the Senior class should have a good knowledge of both the Junior and Middle studies. For the present, the members of the Junior and Middle classes will to some extent recite promiscuously together, as their preparation and necessities may require. But the Senior class, in recitations, are to be kept distinct from the other members of the Seminary, and to pursue a regular course a class.

VACATIONS.

There are three vacations in a year—the first of one week in February—the second of two weeks in May—the third of nine weeks at the close of the year. The plan of including most of the time for vacations in one, is an accommodation to many who are too far from home to return during the year. It gives the pupils the time for relaxation, which is most needed for that object, and which is least valuable for study, and at a pleasant season of the year for journeying.

It is important that all the young ladies come expecting to continue through the year without being absent at all, except during vacations, and during a recess of two days connected with thanksgiving. No one can leave at the commencement of a vacation till her last recitation is finished, and every one should return in season to prepare as well as recite her first lesson.

STUDY HOURS AND RECREATION.

Both parts of every day arc devoted to study except Saturday. The regular study hours commence at halt past seven in the morning, at half past one in the afternoon, and at seven or eight in the evening according to the season of the year. The regular hours for daily recreation embrace the time from half past eleven to hell past one, and from four to seven in winter, and from five to eight in summer.

Young ladies do not study during the regular hours for recreation. Their health and improvement are more promoted by giving up these hours cheerfully, to relaxation exercise and social intercourse. It is also important that their study hours be uninterrupted. All the calls and visits they make during term time should be confined to Saturday and the regular recreation hours. Without a very high standard of punctuality, it is impossible to maintain a high standard for study and correct scholarship. The loss of a single lesson, or of the study hours of one evening, may be felt for many weeks. One imperfect lesson often discourages a pupil, and produces a succession of similar lessons; one absence prepares the way for another, and a deficiency of promptuess in one, will have its influence on others. Perfect punctuality without interruption through the whole year is, therefore, the standard presented to every pupil on entering the Seminary.

EXPENSES.

Board and tuition, exclusive of fuel and lights, will be $60 a year—$30 to be paid on entrance, and $30 the First of February. No deduction will be made for a short absence. In case of a protracted absence, the charge will be made by the week, and not by the year, but it will be higher in proportion, at the rate of $80 a year.

FAMILY ACCOMMODATIONS.

All the teachers and pupils board in the establishment. None are received to board elsewhere. The family and school are so organized, that they form constituent parts of the same whole; each advancing the interests of the ether, and both uniting to promote the improvement, comfort fort, and happiness of the household. Every thing relative to the improvement and division of time, to giving and receiving instruction, and to social intercourse, partakes, more of the simplicity of the family circle1 than of the common restrictive rules of the school system.

MORAL AND RELIGIOUS INFLUENCE.

This Institution has been given to the public as the result of benevolent efforts. That it would be decidedly religious in its influence has been the expectation of its friends. The location of the Seminary, and all the surrounding circumstances are favorable to such an influence. A very large proportion of the pupils are professors of religion.

DOMESTIC DEPARTMENTS.

All the members of the school aid to some extent in the domestic labor of the family. The portion of time thus occupied, is so small that it does not retard their progress in study, but rather facilitates it by its invigorating influence. The division of labor is very systematic; giving to each young lady not much change or variety in a year, and enabling her to perform her past in a proper manner without solicitude. In ordinary cases, to each one is assigned that in which she has been well trained at home. No one will expect to receive instruction in any thing, with which she is entirely unacquainted. It is in part of the design of this Seminary to teach young ladies domestic work. This branch of education is exceedingly important, but a literary institution is not the place to gain it. Home k the proper place for the daughters of our country to be laught on this subject; and the mother is the appropriate teacher. Some may inquire, "What then can ho the design of this arrangement?" It may be replied, that the family work must be performed—that it is difficult to find hired domestics, and to retain them any considerable time when they are found—and that young ladies engaged in study suffer much in their vigor and intellectual energy, and in their future health for the want or exercise. The construction of the building and the

family arrangements are such, as render it convenient and suitable for the members of the school to take exercise in the domestic department, thus receiving a benefit themselves, and conferring a benefit on others.

This feature of the Institution will not relieve mothers from the responsibility of giving their daughters a thorough domestic education; but it will rather throw before those who are seeking for them the privileges of this Seminary, additional motives to be faithful in this important duty.

FOCUS QUESTION:

1. What subjects are emphasized? What would an education along these lines seem to qualify a graduate to do?

2. What evidence do you see of efforts to keep costs down? What advantages and disadvantages are there to the way student activities and housing are structured?

8-7 From "Discourse on Woman," by Lucretia Mott

Lucretia Coffin Mott was an activist for women's rights, abolition, and other causes. Her political views were influenced by her upbringing as a Quaker. Mott helped Elizabeth Cady Stanton organize the Seneca Falls Convention on Women's Rights, though she disagreed with Stanton and others who sought to reform divorce laws to treat women more favorably; Mott opposed divorce on principle.

Source: Hallowell, Anna Davis. *James and Lucretia Mott: Life and Letters*, Boston: Houghton, Mifflin and Company, 1884. pp. 500-506.

Walker, of Cincinnati, in his Introduction to American Law, says: "With regard to political rights, females form a positive exception to the general doctrine of equality. They have no part or lot in the formation or administration of government. They cannot vote or hold office. We require them to contribute their share in the way of taxes, to the support of government, but allow them no voice in its direction. We hold them amenable to the laws when made, but allow them no share in making them. This language, applied to males, would be the exact definition of political slavery; applied to females, custom does not teach us so to regard it." Woman, however, is beginning so to regard it.

"The law of husband and wife, as you gather it from the books, is a disgrace to any civilized nation. The theory of the law degrades the wife almost to the level of slaves. When a woman marries, we call her condition coverture, and speak of her as a femme covert . The old writers call the husband baron, and sometimes, in plain English, lord… The merging of her name in that of her husband is emblematic of the fate of all her legal rights. The torch of Hymen serves but to light the pile, on which these rights are offered up. The legal theory is, that marriage makes the husband and wife one person, and that person is the husband . On this subject, reform is loudly called for. There is no foundation in reason or expediency, for the absolute and slavish subjection of the wife to the husband, which forms the foundation of the present legal relations. Were woman, in point of fact, the abject thing which the law, in theory, considers her to be when married, she would not be worthy the companionship of man."

I would ask if such a code of laws does not require change? If such a condition of the wife in society does not claim redress? On no good ground can reform be delayed. Blackstone says, "The very being and legal existence of woman is suspended during marriage,—incorporated or consolidated into that of her husband, under whose protection and cover she performs every thing." Hurlbut, in his Essays upon Human Rights, says: "The laws touching the rights of woman are at variance with the laws of the Creator. Rights are human rights, and pertain to human beings, without distinction of sex. Laws should not be made for man or for woman, but for mankind. Man was not born to command, nor woman to obey…The law of France, Spain, and Holland, and one of our own States, Louisiana, recognizes the wife's right to property, more than the common law of England…The laws depriving woman of the right of property is handed down to us from dark and feudal times, and not consistent with the wiser, better, purer spirit of the age. The wife is a mere pensioner on the bounty of her husband. Her lost rights are appropriated to himself. But justice and benevolence are abroad in our land, awakening the spirit of inquiry and innovation; and the Gothic fabric of the British law will fall before it, save where it is based upon the foundation of truth and justice."

May these statements lead you to reflect upon this subject, that you may know what woman's condition is in society—what her restrictions are, and seek to remove them. In how many cases in our country, the husband and wife begin life together, and by equal industry and united effort accumulate to themselves a comfortable home. In the event of the death of the wife, the household remains undisturbed, his farm or his workshop is not broken up, or in any way molested. But when the husband dies, he either gives his wife a portion of their joint accumulation, or the law apportions to her a share; the homestead is broken up, and she is dispossessed of that which she earned equally with him; for what she lacked in physical strength, she made up in constancy of labor and toil, day and evening. The sons then coming into possession of the property, as has been the custom until of latter time, speak of having to keep their mother, when she in reality is aiding to keep them. Where is the justice of this state of things? The change in the law of this State and of New York, in relation to the property of the wife, go to a limited extend, toward the redress of these wrongs; but they are far more extensive, and involve much more, than I have time this evening to point out.

On no good ground can the legal existence of the wife be suspended during marriage, and her property surrendered to her husband. In the intelligent ranks of society, the wife may not in point of fact, be so degraded as the law would degrade her; because public sentiment is above the law. Still, while the law stands, she is liable to the disabilities which it imposes. Among the ignorant classes of society, woman is made to bear heavy burdens, and is degraded almost to the level of the slave.

There are many instances now in our city, where the wife suffers much from the power of the husband to claim all that she can earn with her own hands. In my intercourse with the poorer class of people, I have known cases of extreme cruelty, from the hard earnings of the wife being thus robbed by the husband, and no redress at law.

An article in one of the daily papers lately, presented the condition of needle women in England. There might be a presentation of this class in our own country, which would make the heart bleed. Public attention should be turned to this subject, in order that avenues of more profitable employment may be opened to women. There are many kinds of business which women, equally with men, may follow with respectability and success. Their talents and energies should be called forth, and their powers brought into the highest exercise. The efforts of women in France are sometimes pointed to in ridicule and sarcasm, but depend upon it, the opening of profitable employment to women in that country, is doing much for the enfranchisement of the sex. In England also, it is not an uncommon thing for a wife to take up the business of her deceased husband and carry it on with success.

Our respected British Consul stated to me a circumstance which occurred some years ago, of an editor of a political paper having died in England; it was proposed to his wife, an able writer, to take the editorial chair. She accepted. The patronage of the paper was greatly increased, and she a short time since retired from her labors with a handsome fortune. In that country however, the opportunities are by no means general for Woman's elevation.

In visiting the public school in London, a few years since, I noticed that the boys were employed in linear drawing, and instructed upon the black board, in the higher branches of arithmetic and mathematics; while the girls, after a short exercise in the mere elements of arithmetic, were seated, during the bright hours of the morning, stitching wristbands . I asked, Why there should be this difference made; why they too should not have the black board? The answer was, that they would not probably fill any station in society requiring such knowledge.

But the demand for a more extended education will not cease, until girls and boys have equal instruction, in all the departments of useful knowledge. We have as yet no high school for girls in this state. The normal school may be a preparation for such an establishment. In the late convention for general education, it was cheering to hear the testimony borne to woman's capabilities for head teachers of the public schools. A resolution there offered for equal salaries to male and female teachers, when equally qualified, as practised in Louisiana, I regret to say was checked in its passage, by Bishop Potter; by him who has done so much for the encouragement of education, and who gave his countenance and influence to that convention. Still the fact of such a resolution being offered, augurs a time coming for woman, which she may well hail. At the last examination of the public schools in this city, one of the alumni delivered an address on Woman, not as is too common, in eulogistic strains, but directing the attention to the injustice done to woman in her position in society, in a variety of ways. The unequal wages she receives for her constant toil, c., presenting facts calculated to arouse attention to the subject.

Women's property has been taxed, equally with that of men's, to sustain colleges endowed by the states; but they have not been permitted to enter those high seminaries of learning. Within a few years, however, some colleges have been instituted, where young women are admitted, nearly upon equal terms with young men; and numbers are availing themselves of their long denied rights. This is among the signs of the times, indicative of an advance for women. The book of knowledge is not opened to her in vain. Already is she aiming to occupy important posts of honor and profit in our country. We have three female editors in our state—some in other states of the Union. Numbers are entering the medical profession—one received a diploma last year; others are preparing for a like result.

Let woman then go on—not asking as favor, but claiming as right, the removal of all the hindrances to her elevation in the scale of being—let her receive encouragement for the proper cultivation of all her powers, so that she may enter profitably into the active business of life; employing her own hands, in ministering to her necessities, strengthening her physical being by proper exercise, and observance of the laws of health. Let her not be ambitious to display a fair hand, and to promenade the fashionable streets of our city, but rather, coveting earnestly the best gifts, let her strive to occupy such walks in society, as will befit her true dignity in all the relations of life. No fear that she will then transcend the proper limits of female delicacy. True modesty will be as fully preserved, in acting out those important vocations to which she may be called, as in the nursery or at the fireside, ministering to man's self-indulgence.

Then in the marriage union, the independence of the husband and wife will be equal, their dependence mutual, and their obligations reciprocal.

In conclusion, let me say, "Credit not the old fashioned absurdity, that woman's is a secondary lot, ministering to the necessities of her lord and master! It is a higher destiny I would award you. If your immortality is as complete, and your gift of mind as capable as ours, of increase and elevation, I would put no wisdom of mine against God's evident allotment. I would charge you to water the undying bud, and give it healthy culture, and open its beauty to the sun—and then you may hope, that when your life is bound up with another, you will go on equally, and in a fellowship that shall pervade every earthly interest."

FOCUS QUESTIONS:

1. How does Mott link women's rights within marriage to general political and economic rights?
2. Is Mott's comparison of women to slaves convincing?

8-8 Emma Willard Proposes a Female Seminary in Greece

Emma Willard established a number of schools for girls in the early 1800s in the various places she lived, including Middlebury, Vermont, and Troy, New York. In the mid-nineteenth century she traveled extensively in Europe, where she continued her advocacy on behalf of women's education.

Source: Willard, Emma. "Female Education: Or, a Series of Addresses In Favor Of Establishing At Athens, In Greece, A Female Seminary Especially Designed to Instruct Female Teachers." Troy: 1833. pp. 9-10, 12.

In further considering the subject of benefiting the Greeks, all will acknowledge that if we would impart to them the blessings of education, we must begin with those in the nation who are now young. The half of these are females. There are many reasons for considering their education at least of equal importance with that of the other sex. But I wish not to exhaust the subject of female education, for I know that there are those among us of the other sex, more capable than myself to do it justice, who are convinced of its importance; and I see in this circumstance the most consoling hopes of the future accomplishment of what has long been the leading motive of my life. Justice will yet be done. Woman will have her rights. I see it in the course of events. Though it may not come till I am in my grave—yet come it will; for men of the highest and most cultivated intellect, of the purest and most pious hearts, now perceive its necessity to the well being of the world, where it is their glory to be workers together with God, to produce a moral revolution.

When these take up our cause in earnest, they will with ease effect what we desire; and they will find their reward even while performing the noble work. It is theirs in the order of nature to protect our public rights; ours, to show our gratitude by gladdening with smiles and heart-felt kindness, their domestic and social existence.

But what if men neglect our rights? The history of the present time answers the question, and some of our greatest evils may be traced to this source. What but the neglect of our moral and intellectual education, is the cause that the tender being whom God made capable of being morally the best, becomes in so many horrid instances morally the worst of our race.

In speaking of the faults of my own sex, I would not by any means exculpate them, or lay all the blame upon the other. But when men in their legislative capacity, forget our rights—when in expending millions for the education of male youth, they bestow not a thought on us—when in some cases, as might be shown, they make laws oppressive to us, it is not strange that some among us of impetuous spirits, madly seek to break the social order, and dissolve that golden link which God himself has instituted, and in which woman, in obedience to her nature, and the express commands of God, acknowledges man as her head. Men of disordered minds, or ambitious views, have encouraged the phrenzy. Hence the ravings of Mary Wolstoncraft, of Frances Wright and Robert Owen; and hence the frantic sect which are now denouncing marriage, and disturbing Paris, under the name of St. Simoniens. But there are women who can feel for their sex, as patriots feel for their country. If such an one steps forward in defence of their rights, she must indeed have the spirit of a martyr. While she resists the impulse of her own sensitive and shrinking nature, she must encounter from the men, the imputation of having cast off that feminine sensitiveness which is what most recommends her to them. Thus situated, most women of the finest minds, muse in pensive silence on the injustice they cannot but feel; and often, when such women are found moody, and are thought capricious, it is this which is the cause of their ill humour and dejection; and hence the delight they feel when men step forward to advocate their cause.

Again I say, it is because our men perceive this, that I have hopes for the future. When I assert that it is hard for a woman to step forward in public vindication of the rights of her sex, my assertion will have some weight, because in this case it is *testimony*. Men see this, and their generous minds will be moved, themselves, to undertake the work of kindness and of justice, graceful in them and grateful to us.

Societies of women, too, will doubtless hereafter be formed to aid in its accomplishment; and what is the society now proposed but a society for this noble purpose?

That the system of female education commenced among us, is incomparably better than the systems of public education for our sex in the old states of Europe, I could say much to prove. I could bring forward the testimony of some of the most distinguished women of France, expressed in letters which I have had the honor to receive from them. I could adduce conversations with some of those of Great Britain; but time would fail, and the subject will be treated in the book which I have given to aid the project now before us. Besides, I doubt not you are already convinced of the fact. We would that we could impart to those nations, sounder views on this subject, and better systems. But they would not receive them from us. Grown old in their ways, and regarding us as young, they would turn with supercilious contempt from any efforts of ours to improve them. Not so with Greece; she looks to us and solicits us to teach her. Should we impart to her the elements of moral vigor, she will increase in strength as in years, and when at length their vices shall have sunk them to the grave of nations,—when society shall with them, as now with the Greeks, be dissolved to its original elements, then Greece may impart to them what she now receives from us. But, if we are to undertake this work, the present is the time. A little money, as Mr. Richard can inform us, will now do much; and small means may now effect what could not be done at all, should we wait till female schools on the old European plan are established. The schools which first take root, will grow with the growth of the nation; and as we confidently hope, they will ere long be supported by the Greeks, if we defray their first expenses.

FOCUS QUESTIONS:

1. Why would there be symbolic value for an American women's rights activist in establishing a school for women in Greece?

2. How does Willard differentiate the rights and responsibilities of women, and of men?

8-9 The Oberlin Experiment

The Oberlin Collegiate Institute (today's Oberlin College) was founded in 1833, and has had liberal admissions policies throughout its history: it admitted African-American students starting in 1835, and educated women and men in the same classes starting in 1837. The author of this article served as a legislator and governor in Ohio and Michigan in the early to mid-1800s.

Souce: William Woodbridge, *Annals of American Education,* 1838.

OBERLIN COLLEGIATE INSTITUTE.

We have received a Catalogue of the Trustees, Officers, and Students of the Oberlin Collegiate Institute, for 1838, of which an account has been given, from time to time, in this journal. We perceive that the whole number of names on the Catalogue, is 391. Of these, 265 are males, and 126 are females. Of the males, 97 belong to the preparatory department, 44 to the logical school, 9 are attending a shorter course of study, 2 are irregular students, and 113 are attending the collegiate course. Of the females, 21 belong to the preparatory department, and 105 to the collegiate school.

There are many things in regard to this Institution to render it interesting to every friend of education. Its moral tone and standing—its broad temperance principles—its banner of freedom—the large benevolence it inculcates and encourages, and the habits of industry, in both sexes, which it enjoins and secures, give it a prominence in the view of the Christian philanthropist, which few literary or religious institutions can claim.

But its most interesting feature—to us,—is the uniting of the sexes in a course of liberal study, and the unexpected results which have followed. Many good men among us, when they heard that males and females were to recite together, sit at the table together, &c., constituting one large family, and living together in some measure on the principles of a well-ordered Christian household,—did not fail to predict a failure. Yet the Institution has flourished, and the experiment is unequivocally successful. We consider it now fully established, that the sexes may be educated together.

This discovery is one of the most important ever made. The benefits which are likely to flow from it are immense. Woman is to be free. The hour of her emancipation is at hand. Daughters of America, rejoice!

FOCUS QUESTIONS:

1. Why does the author assume that these developments are cause for women to rejoice? Does the author see any impact on men?

2. Beyond coeducation, what attributes of Oberlin does Woodbridge praise? What does this suggest about his values?

8-10 Elizabeth McClintock and Elizabeth Cady Stanton Challenge Mr. Sulley's Comments on the Seneca Falls Women's Rights Convention (1848)

In this 1848 letter to the editors of The National Reformer, Elizabeth McClintock and Elizabeth Cady Stanton refuted a recently published commentary by "Mr. Sulley" on the 1848 Seneca Falls Women's Rights Convention. McClintock had been a speaker at the convention, and Stanton was the main organizer of the event (see her other documents in this volume, including the "Declaration of Sentiments and Resolutions, Seneca Falls" in this chapter).

Source: McClintock, E.W. and Stanton, E.W. "Letter to the Editor." National Reformer. September 21, 1848. Reprinted in Major Problems in American Women's History, Norton and Alexander, 3rd Edition, 104-105.

For the National Reformer.

Woman's Rights.

Messrs. Editors:—As you announce Mr. Sulley, (the author of the article headed "Woman's Rights Convention," published in your paper of last week) as a man who seeks to know the truth, and one who will do justice to any subject he examines, and as he declares himself to be a great lover of his race, and one who has thought deeply on the subject of human improvement, I humbly ask *him* what are these other means to which he refers, by which the present social, civil and religious condition of woman can be improved. It is evident, aside from his own assertion, that Mr. Sulley has thought much on this subject, for he says, "I am not one of those who think that no improvement can be made in the condition of woman, even in this favored land." He is interested, too, in our movement, and has been kind enough to tell us what means will not effect what we desire. He says those recommended and presented by the convention will not do. He thinks legislative action cannot alter the laws of nature. Does Mr. Sulley assume that our present degradaetion is in accordance with the laws of God? Mr. Sulley having been announced as a lover of truth, we rejoiced in the belief that at length we had found one opponent who would meet us in fair argument, one who though not agreeing with us fully in our measures, was yet sufficiently interested in this subject to give us some plan by which the elevation of woman might be effected. But alas! we have the same old story over again—ridicule, ridicule, ridicule. We have hints of great arguments that could be produced—profound philosophy, fully convincing and satisfactory to all thinking minds, but he gives us nothing tangible, not even the end of the tail of any of these truths, by which could we get a fair hold, we might draw out all the rest. Mr. Sulley thinks our convention was a mere pompous outward show; because, forsooth, we could not give on the spot, a panacea for all the ills of life—because we could not answer Mr. Sulley's silly questions in a manner to satisfy him, though the audience thought him fully answered. We did not assemble to discuss the details of social life—we did not propose to petition the legislature to make our husbands just, generous and courteous; no, we assembled to protest against an unjust form of government, existing without the consent of the governed; to declare our right to be free as man is free: to claim our right to the elective franchise, our right to be repre-

sented in a government which we are taxed to support; to have such laws as give to man the right to chastise and imprison his wife, to take the wages which she earns—the property which she inherits, and in case of separation the children of her love; laws which make her the more dependant on his bounty: it was to protect against such disgraceful laws, and to have them, if possible, forever erased from our statute books, as a shame and reproach to a republican, christian people in the enlightened nineteenth century. We did not meet to decide home questions—to say who should be the ruling spirit, the presiding genius of every household—who should be the umpire to settle the many differences in domestic life. . . .Mr. S. expressed a wish to quote the Bible on this subject, but found it would have no authority with us. We affirm that we believe in the Bible. We consider that Book to be the great charter of human rights, and we are willing, yes, desirous to go into the Bible argument on this subject, for its spirit is wholly with the side of Freedom.. . .

E. W. MCCLINTOCK, E. C. STANTON.

FOCUS QUESTIONS:

1. How do McClintock and Stanton summarize the goals of the Seneca Falls Women's Rights Convention?

2. Why do the authors refer to the Bible near the end of their letter?

8-11 Sojourner Truth's Address, as Recalled by Frances D. Gage

Frances D. Gage, a pioneer in the Women's Rights Movement during the early nineteenth century, recorded her impressions of Sojourner Truth's speech at the Woman's Rights Convention in Akron, Ohio in 1851. Gage wrote this reminiscence some twelve years after the fact, and tried to capture Truth's speech as she remembered it, complete with what Gage perceived to be Truth's manner of speech and actions before the audience.

Source: E. C. Stanton, S. B. Anthony, and Matilda Joslyn Gage, eds., History of Woman Suffrage, vol. 1 (Rochester, NY: Charles Mann, 1881), pp. 115–117.

Reminiscences by Frances D. Gage

The leaders of the movement trembled upon seeing a tall, gaunt black woman in a gray dress and white turban, surmounted with an uncouth sun-bonnet, march deliberately into the church, walk with the air of a queen up the aisle, and take her seat upon the pulpit steps. A buzz of disapprobation was heard all over the house and there fell on the listening ear, "An abolition affair!" "Woman's rights and niggers!" "I told you so! "Go it, darkey!". . .When, slowly from her seat in the corner rose Sojourner Truth, who, till now, had scarcely lifted her head. "Don't let her speak!" gasped half a dozen in my ear. She moved slowly and solemnly to the front, laid her old bonnet at her feet, and turned her great speaking eyes to me.

There was a hissing sound of disapprobation above and below. I rose and announced "Sojourner Truth," and begged the audience to keep silence for a few moments. . ..

"Wall, chilern, whar dar is so much racket dar must be somethin' out o' kilter. I tink dat 'twixt de niggers of de Souf and de womin at de Norf, all talkin' 'bout rights, de white men will be in a fix pretty soon.

But what's all dis here talkin' 'bout?

"Dat man ober dar say dat womin needs to be helped into carriages, and lifted ober ditches, and to hab de best place everywhar. Nobody eber helps me into carriages, or ober mud-puddles, or gibs me any best place!" . . ."And a'n't I a woman? Look at me! Look at my arm! (and she bared her right arm to the shoulder, showing her tremendous muscular power)."I have ploughed, and planted, and gathered into barns, and no man could head me! And a'n't I a woman? I could work as much and eat as much as a manÑwhen I could get itÑand bear de lash as well! And a'n't I a woman? I have borne thirteen chilern, and seen 'em mos' all sold off to slavery, and when I cried out with my mother's grief, none but Jesus heard me! And a'n't I a woman?

"Den dey talks 'bout dis ting in de head; what dis dey call it?" ("Intellect," whispered some one near.) "Dat's it, honey. What's dat got to do wid womin's rights or nigger's rights? If my cup won't hold but a pint, and yourn holds a quart, wouldn't ye be mean not to let me have my little half-measure full?" And she pointed her significant finger, and sent a keen glance at the minister who had made the argument. The cheering was long and loud.

"Den dat little man in black dar, he say women can't have as much rights as men, 'cause Christ wan't a woman! Whar did your Christ come from?" Rolling thunder couldn't have stilled that crowd, as did those deep, wonderful tones, as she stood there with out-stretched arms and eyes of fire. Raising her voice still louder, she repeated, "Whar did your Christ come from? From God and a woman! Man had nothin' to do wid Him." Oh, what a rebuke that was to that little man.

Turning again to another objector, she took up the defense of Mother Eve. I can not follow her through it all. It was pointed, and witty, and solemn; eliciting at almost every sentence deafening applause; and she ended by asserting: "If de fust woman God ever made was strong enough to turn de world upside down all alone, dese women togedder (and she glanced her eye over the platform) ought to be able to turn it back, and get it right side up again! And now dey is asking to do it, de men better let 'em." Long-continued cheering greeted this. "'Bleeged to ye for hearin' on me, and now ole Sojourner han't got nothin' more to say."

Amid roars of applause, she returned to her corner, leaving more than one of us with streaming eyes, and hearts beating with gratitude. She had taken us up in her arms and carried us safely over the slough of difficulty turning the whole tide in our favor. I have never in my life seen anything like the magical influence that subdued the mobbish spirit of the day, and turned the sneers and jeers of an excited crowd into notes of respect and admiration. Hundreds rushed up to shake hands with her, and congratulate the glorious old mother, and bid her God-speed on her mission of "testifyin' agin concerning the wickedness of this 'ere people."

FOCUS QUESTIONS:

1. Describe Gage's impression of the audience's different responses to Sojourner Truth's manner and message. What does Gage's impression seem to be?

2. Summarize Sojourner Truth's message to the Woman's Rights Convention. How is this message similar to and different from the message the reader and the crowd might expect from her?

THE CIVIL WAR, 1861–1865

9-1 Mary Boykin Chesnut, A Confederate Lady's Diary (1861)

Born into the political and social elite of southern society, Chesnut was the daughter of a Senator and Governor of South Carolina. She married James Chesnut, one of the largest land owners in the state and soon to be Senator. After secession, he became a confederate congressman and later aide to Jefferson Davis. Mary Chesnut's house became a salon for leading members of Confederate society. During the war, Chesnut kept a diary that became famous for its portrayal of the Confederacy. This selection reveals the ambivalence that many in the South had towards slavery.

I wonder if it be a sin to think slavery a curse to any land. Sumner said not one word of this hated institution which is not true. Men & women are punished when their masters & mistresses are brutes & not when they do wrong-& then we live surrounded by prostitutes. An abandoned woman is sent out of any decent house elsewhere. Who thinks any worse of a Negro or Mulatto woman for being a thing we can't name. God forgive *us*, but ours is a *monstrous* system & wrong & iniquity. Perhaps the rest of the world is as bad. This is *only* what I see: like the patriarchs of old, our men live all in one house with their wives & their concubines, & the Mulattos one sees in every family exactly resemble the white children-& every lady tells you who is the father of all the Mulatto children in everybody's household, but those in her own, she seems to think drop from the clouds or pretends so to think-. Good women we have, *but* they talk of *nastiness tho* they never do wrong; they talk day & night of

-. My disgust sometimes is boiling over-but they are, I believe, in conduct the purest women God ever made. Thank God for my countrywomen-alas for the men! No worse than men everywhere, but the lower their mistresses, the more degraded they must be.

My mother-in-law told me when I was first married not to send my female servants in the street on errands. They were there tempted, led astray-& then she said placidly, "So they told *me* when I came here-& I was very particular, *but you see with what* result." Mr. Harris said it was so patriarchal. So it is-flocks & herds & slaves-& wife Leah does not suffice. Rachel must be *added*, if not *married* & all the time they seem to think themselves patterns-models of husbands & fathers.

Mrs. Davis told me "everybody described my husband's father as an odd character, a Millionaire who did nothing for his son whatever, left him to struggle with poverty," &c. I replied, "Mr. Chesnut Senior thinks himself the best of fathers-& his son thinks likewise. I have nothing to say-but it is true, he has no money but what he makes as a lawyer," &c. Again I say, my countrywomen are as pure as angels-tho surrounded by another race who are-the social evil!

FOCUS QUESTIONS:

1. What are Chesnut's sentiments and chief concerns in this account? In what ways does this diary entry reveal a "pre-war" sense of awareness? In other words, identify the events and thoughts that make up this entry? How might these concerns change in the coming months?

9-2 A Union Spy Makes Her Way Behind Confederate Lines

About 400 women are known to have disguised themselves as men in order to enlist in either the Union or Confederate Armies in the course of the U.S. Civil War; there were almost certainly more women whose identities were never revealed. Sarah Emma Edmonds, under the alias "Frank Thompson," enlisted as a male nurse in the Union Army in 1861. She later served as a spy, adopting various disguises to infiltrate Confederate camps. In this passage, "Frank Thompson" transforms into a black manservant/spy.

NOTE: Phrenology was a nineteenth-century pseudo-science, based on the idea that measurements of different parts of a person's skull could reveal personality traits and abilities. "Contraband" was slang used early in the Civil War to describe escaped slaves who had achieved functional, if not technical, freedom.

Source: *Nurse and spy in the Union army: comprising the adventures and experiences of a woman in hospitals, camps and battle-fields.* Edmonds, S. Emma E. Hartford, Philadelphia: W. S. Williams & co., Jones bros. & co, 1865. pp. 104-109.

I was becoming dissatisfied with my situation as nurse, and was determined to leave the hospital.... Chaplain B. told me that he knew of a situation he could get for me if I had sufficient moral courage to undertake its duties; and, said he, "it is a situation of great danger and of vast responsibility." That morning a detachment of the Thirty-seventh New York had been sent out as scouts, and had returned bringing in several prisoners, who stated that one of the Federal spies had been captured at Richmond and was to be executed. This information proved to be correct, and we lost a valuable soldier from the secret service of the United States. Now it was necessary for that vacancy to be supplied, and, as the Chaplain had said with reference to it, it was a situation of great danger and vast responsibility, and this was the one which Mr. B. could procure for me. But was I capable of filling it with honor to myself and advantage to the Federal Government? This was an important question for me to consider ere I proceeded further. I did consider it thoroughly, and made up my mind to accept it with all its fearful responsibilities. The subject of life and death was not weighed in the balance; I left that in the hands of my Creator, feeling assured that I was just as safe in passing the picket lines of the enemy, if it was God's will that I should go there, as I would be in the Federal camp. And if not, then His will be done: Then welcome death, the end of fears. My name was sent in to headquarters, and I was soon summoned to appear there myself. Mr. and Mrs. B. accompanied me. We were ushered into the presence of Generals Mc., M. and H., where I was questioned and cross-questioned with regard to my views of the rebellion and my motive in wishing to engage in so perilous an undertaking. My views were freely given, my object briefly stated, and I had passed trial number one. Next I was examined with regard to my knowledge of the use of firearms, and in that department I sustained my character in a manner worthy of a veteran. Then I was again cross-questioned, but this time by a new committee of military stars. Next came a phrenological examination, and finding that my organs of secretiveness, combativeness, etc., were largely developed, the oath of allegiance was administered, and I was dismissed with a few complimentary remarks which made the good Mr. B. feel quite proud of his protege. This was the third time that I had taken the oath of allegiance to the United States, and I began to think, as many of our soldiers do, that profanity had become a military necessity. I had three days in which to prepare for my debut into rebeldom, and I commenced at once to remodel, transform and metamorphose for the occasion. Early next morning I started for Fortress Monroe, where I procured a number of articles indispensably necessary to a complete disguise. In the first place I purchased a suit of contraband clothing, real plantation style, and then I went to a barber and had my hair sheared close to my head. Next came the coloring process — head, face, neck, hands and arms were colored black as any African, and then, to complete my contraband costume, I required a wig of real negro wool. But how or where was it to be found? There was no such thing at the Fortress, and none short of Washington. Happily I found the mail-boat was about to start, and hastened on board, and finding a Postmaster with whom I was acquainted, I stepped forward to speak to him, forgetting my contraband appearance, and was saluted with "Well, Massa Cuff — what will you have?" Said I: "Massa send me to you wid dis yere money for you to fotch him a darkie wig from Washington." "What the does he want of a darkie wig?" asked the Postmaster. "No matter, dat's my orders; guess it's for some'noiterin' business." "Oh, for reconnoitering you mean; all right old fellow, I will bring it, tell him." I remained at Fortress Monroe until the Postmaster returned with the article which was to complete my disguise, and then returned to camp near Yorktown. On my return, I found myself without friends — a striking illustration of the frailty of human friendship — I had been forgotten in those three short days. I went to Mrs. B.'s tent and inquired if she wanted to hire a boy to take care of her horse. She was very civil to me, asked if I came from Fortress Monroe, and whether I could cook. She did not want to hire me, but she thought she could find some one who did require a boy. Off she went to Dr. E. and told him that there was a smart little contraband there who was in search of work. Dr. E. came along, looking as important as two year old doctors generally do. "Well, my boy, how much work can you do in a day?" "Oh, I reckon I kin work right smart; kin do heaps o' work. Will you hire me, Massa?" "Don't know but I may; can you cook?" "Yes, Massa, kin cook anything I ebber seen." "How much do you think you can earn a month?" "Guess I kin earn ten dollars easy nuff." Turning to Mrs. B. he said in an undertone: "That darkie understands his business." "Yes indeed, I would hire him by all means, Doctor," said Mrs. B. "Well, if you wish, you can stay with me a month, and by that time I will be a better judge how much you can earn." So saying Dr. E. proceeded to give a synopsis of a contraband's duty toward a master of whom he expected ten dollars per month, especially emphasising the last clause. Then I was introduced to the culinary department, which comprised flour, pork, beans, a small portable stove, a spider, and a medicine chest. It was now supper time, and I was supposed to understand my business sufficiently to prepare supper without asking any questions whatever, and also to display some of my boasted talents by making warm biscuit for

supper. But how was I to make biscuit with my colored hands? and how dare I wash them for fear the color would wash off? All this trouble was soon put to an end, however, by Jack's making his appearance while I was stirring up the biscuit with a stick, and in his bustling, officious, negro style, he said; "See here nig — you don't know nuffin bout makin bisket. Jis let me show you once, and dat ar will save you heaps o' trouble wid Massa doct'r for time to come." I very willingly accepted of this proffered assistance, for I had all the necessary ingredients in the dish, with pork fat for shortening, and soda and cream-tartar, which I found in the medicine chest, ready for kneading and rolling out. After washing his hands and rolling up his sleeves, Jack went to work with a flourish and a grin of satisfaction at being "boss" over the new cook. Tea made, biscuit baked, and the medicine chest set off with tin cups, plates, etc., supper was announced. Dr. E. was much pleased with the general appearance of things, and was evidently beginning to think that he had found rather an intelligent contraband for a cook. ...

Focus Questions:

1. What impression do you get of Edmonds as a person? What does Edmonds present as her motivations for her service?

2. Why would hundreds of women disguise themselves as men to join armies on either side of the Civil War?

9-3 The Journal of a Confederate Nurse

Women served as nurses on both the Confederate and Union sides of the Civil War. Kate Cumming was unusual in that she kept a detailed journal of her experiences, which she published in 1866.

Source: Harwell, Richard Barksdale, ed. *Kate: the Journal of a Confederate Nurse: The Journal of a Confederate Nurse by Kate Cumming.* Baton Rouge: Louisiana State University Press, 1959. pp. 65-66, 307.

There is a good deal of trouble about the ladies in some of the hospitals of this department. Our friends here have advised us to go home, as they say it is not considered respectable to go into one. I must confess, from all I had heard and seen, for awhile I wavered about- the propriety of it; but when I remembered the suffering I had witnessed, and the relief I had given,

my mind was made up to go into one if allowed to do so. Mrs. Williamson and Mrs. May have come to the same conclusion on the subject as myself. God has said," Who can harm you if you be followers of that which is good? " I thought of this, and believed it, and gained strength from it. Christians should not mind what the world says, so that they are conscious of striving to do their duty to their God.

It seems strange that the aristocratic women of Great Britain have done with honor what is a disgrace for their sisters on this side of the Atlantic to do. This is not the first time I have heard these remarks. Not respectable! And who has made it so? If the Christian, high-toned, and educated women of our land shirk their duty, why others have to do it for them. It is useless to say the surgeons will not allow us; we have our rights, and if asserted properly will get them. This is our right, and ours alone.

In a book called the "Sunny South," written by the lamented Rev. J. H. Ingraham, are the following words

"Soldiers fight the battles of our country, and the least we can do is to cherish them in their helplessness, and bind up their wounds, and all *true* women will do it, who love their country." Who among us does not echo his sentiments? Women of the South, let us remember that our fathers, husbands, brothers, and sons are giving up all that mortals can for us; that they are exposed hourly to the deadly missiles of the enemy; the fatigues of hard marching, through burning suns, frost, and sleet; pressed by hunger and thirst; subject to diseases of all kinds from exposure; and last, though by no means least, the evil influences that are common in a large army. Are we aware of all this, and unwilling to nurse these brave heroes who are sacrificing so much for us? What, in the name of common sense, are we to do? Sit calmly down, knowing that there is many a parched lip which would bless us for a drop of water, and many a wound to be bound up? These things are not to be done, because it is not considered respectable! Heaven help the future of our country, for nothing but God's special aid can save any country where such doctrines are inculcated.

Women of the South, let us remember we have a foe as relentless as Tamerlane or Atilla, who, if we are to believe his own threats, has resolved to lay our towns in ashes, lay waste our fields, and make our fair land a blackened mass of ruins if we will not submit to his domination; and, unless every man and woman in the South do their duty, he will succeed, even though we had a president gifted with the wisdom of Solomon, and generals endowed with the genius of Frederick or Napoleon. I know there are hundreds of our women who look on this subject in the proper light, having household duties to attend to, which they can not leave; but have we not thousands who, at this moment, do not know what to do to pass the time that is hanging heavily on their hands? I mean the young: the old are not able for the work. If it will hurt a young girl to do what, in all ages, has been the special duty of woman—to relieve the suffering—it is high time the youth of our land were kept from the camp and field. If one is a disgrace, so is the other.

The negroes are free: and the poor creatures are acting like children out on a frolic. The main portion of the women do little else than walk the streets, dressed in all kinds of gaudy attire. All are doing their own work, as a negro can not be hired at any price. But they have behaved much beter than we had any right to expect, as they have been put up to all kinds of mischief by the enemy. Many of them seem to despise the Federals, and it is not much wonder, as they treat them so badly.

A lady told me that they robbed a poor old woman, that she had left in her house in the country of every thing that she had. They have treated all who fell into their hands in the same way.

As a rule the Federal soldiers have behaved very well to the citizens; they are any thing but exultant—and they need not be, when they consider that they succeeded by overwhelming numbers alone. They found that they could gain nothing by fighting themselves, so they hired foreigners, and at last had to take the *darky*; and Sambo boasts that the *rebels* could not be conquered until he took the field. Many think if we had put negroes into the army at the start, that we should have had another tale to tell to-day; and I am confident that if we had freed the negro, we would have had the aid of foreign powers. I believe now that Great Britain was consistent in her hatred to slavery. And she dreaded bringing war upon her people, as she knew more about its horrors than we did. In this I can not blame her. We all know that the majority of her people sympathized with us, and did much to render us aid. To be sure the northerners got men and ammunition from her, but then they had money, which is a lever even with Britons. But all is gone now, and we must try and " let the dead past bury its dead!"

This year has developed the fate of the South. Time has revealed the utter loss of all our hopes. A change must pass over every political and social idea, custom, and relation. The consummation makes the year just passed ever memorable in our annals. In it gathers all the interest of the bloody tragedy; from it begins a new era, midst poverty, tears, and sad memories of the past. O, may we learn the lesson that all of this is designed to teach; that all things sublunary are transient and fleeting, and lift our souls to that which is alone ever-during and immutable—God and eternity! And forgetting the past, save in the lessons which it teaches, let us . . . redeem the time, live humbly, and trust God for future good. . . .

FOCUS QUESTIONS:

1. What is suggested by the phrase "*true* women"?

2. Why does Cumming refer repeatedly to Great Britain?

3. What seems to be her attitude regarding slavery and former slaves? What about free blacks?

4. What does Cumming see as the fundamental rights and responsibilities of Southern women? Of women more generally?

9-4 Clara Barton, Medical Life at the Battlefield (1862)

Born in Massachusetts, Clare Barton was a teacher and clerk in the U.S. Patent Office. Upon the arrival of the Civil War, she organized a network, separate from the government, to get food, supplies and nursing aid to the soldiers. She served as a nurse on several battlefields including Fredricksburg and Antietam. After the war, Barton went to Europe for a time where she became involved in the International Red Cross. Upon her return she worked for the establishment of the American Red Cross. Though she had much government opposition to her efforts, in 1882 the Senate ratified the Geneva Convention and the American Red Cross was born. At the age of 77 Barton again served conflict during the Spanish-American war. These letters reveal the horrific nature of the Civil War battlefield.

I was strong and thought I might go to the rescue of the men who fell. . . . What could I do but go with them, or work for them and my country? The patriot blood of my father was warm in my veins. The country which he had fought for, I might at least work for. . . .

But I struggled long and hard with my sense of propriety-with the appalling fact that I was only a woman whispering in one ear, and thundering in the other the groans of suffering men dying like dogs-unfed and unsheltered, for the life of every institution which had protected and educated me!

I said that I struggled with my sense of propriety and I say it with humiliation and shame. I am ashamed that I thought of such a thing.

When our armies fought on Cedar Mountain, I broke the shackles and went to the field. . . .

Five days and nights with three hours sleep-a narrow escape from capture-and some days of getting the wounded into hospitals at Washington, brought Saturday, August 30. And if you chance to feel, that the positions I occupied were rough and unseemly for a *woman-I* can only reply that they were rough and unseemly for *men*. But under all, lay the life of the nation. I had inherited the rich blessing of health and strength of constitution-such as are seldom given to woman-and I felt that some return was due from me and that I ought to be there. . . .

. . . . Our coaches were not elegant or commodious; they had no seats, no platforms, no steps, a slide door on the side the only entrance, and this higher than my head. For my man attaining my elevated position, I must beg of you to draw on your imaginations and spare me the labor of reproducing the boxes, boards, and rails, which in those days, seemed to help me up and down the world. We did not criticize the unsightly helpers and were thankful that the stiff springs did not quite jostle us out. This need not be limited to this particular trip or train, but will for all that I have known in Army life. This is the kind of conveyance which your tons of generous gifts have reached the field with the freights. These trains through day and night, sunshine and heat and cold, have thundered over heights, across plains, the ravines, and over hastily built army bridges 90 feet across the stream beneath.

At 10 o'clock Sunday (August 31) our train drew up at Fairfax Station. The ground, for acres, was a thinly wooded slope-and among the trees on the leaves and grass, were laid the wounded who pouring in by scores of wagonloads, as picked up on the field the flag of truce. All day they came and the whole hillside was red. Bales of hay were broken open and scattered over the ground littering of cattle, and the sore, famishing men were laid upon it.

And when the night shut in, in the mist and darkness about us, we knew that standing apart from the world of anxious hearts, throbbing over the whole country, we were a little band of almost empty handed workers literally by our selves in the wild woods of Virginia, with 3,000 suffering men crowded upon the few acres within our reach.

After gathering up every available implement or convenience for our work, our domestic inventory stood 2 water buckets, 5 tin cups, 1 camp kettle, 1 stew pan, 2 lanterns, 4 bread knives, 3 plates, and a 2-quart tin dish, and 3,000 guest to serve.

You will perceive by this, that I had not yet learned to equip myself, for I was no Pallas, ready armed, but grew into my work by hard thinking and sad experience. It may serve to relieve your apprehension for the future of my labors if I assure you that I was never caught so again.

But the most fearful scene was reserved for the night. I have said that the ground was littered with dry hay and that we had only two lanterns, but there were plenty of candles. The wounded were laid so close that it was impossible to move about in the dark. The slightest misstep brought a torrent of groans from some poor mangled fellow in your path.

Consequently here were seen persons of all grades

from the careful man of God who walked with a prayer upon his lips to the careless driver hunting for his lost whip,-each wandering about among this hay with an open flaming candle in his hands.

The slightest accident, the mere dropping of a light could have enveloped in flames this whole mass of helpless men.

How we watched and pleaded and cautioned as we worked and wept that night! How we put socks and slippers upon their cold feet, wrapped your blankets and quilts about them, and when we no longer these to give, how we covered them in the hay and left them to their rest! . .

The slight, naked chest of a fair-haired lad caught my eye, dropping down beside him, I bent low to draw the remnant of his blouse about him, when with a quick cry he threw his left arm across my neck and, burying his face in the folds of my dress, wept like a child at his mother's knee. I took his head in my hands and held it until great burst of grief passed away. "And do you know me?" he asked at length, "I am Charley Hamilton, we used to carry your satchel home from school!" My faithful pupil, poor Charley. That mangled

right hand would never carry a satchel again.

About three o'clock in the morning I observed a surgeon with a little flickering candle in hand approaching me with cautious step up in the wood. "Lady," he said as he drew near, "will you go with me? Out on the hills is a poor distressed lad, mortally wounded, and dying. His piteous cries for his sister have touched all our hearts none of us can relieve him but rather seem to distress him by presence."

By this time I was following him back over the bloody track, with great beseeching eyes of anguish on every side looking up into our faces, saying so plainly, "Don't step on us."

FOCUS QUESTIONS:

1. What does Barton's account reveal about the difficulties and obstacles facing army nurses and medical personnel during the war?

2. Given the description presented by Barton, what conclusions can be made regarding the conditions of battle for the soldiers. How effective was the care given to the injured?

9-5 A Nurse Suppresses Emotion

Both sides suffered thousands of casualties in the Battle of Seven Pines on May 31 and June 1, 1862, part of the Virginia Peninsula campaign. Amy Morris Bradley tended to the wounded on board the ship Knickerbocker.

Source: Bradley, Amy Morris."Experiences Nursing Wounded Soldiers After the Battle of Seven Pines."In Giesberg, Judith Ann. *Civil War Sisterhood: The U.S. Sanitary Commission and Women's Politics in Transition.* Boston: Northeastern University Press, 2000, p. 127.

I shall never forget my feelings as one by one those mutilated forms were brought in on stretchers

and carefully placed on those comfortable cots! What, said I, must I see human beings thus mangled? O, My God why is it? Why is it? For nearly an hour I could not get control of my feelings! But when the surgeon said, Miss Bradley, you must not do so, but prepare to assist these poor fellows. I realized that tears must be choked back and the heart only know its own suffering! Action is the watchword of the hour!

FOCUS QUESTIONS:

1. In addition to the direct hindrance of her work, how might Bradley's expression of emotions be perceived as harmful?

2. Do you think the surgeon would have treated a male nurse the same way he treated Bradley?

9-6 A Plantation Mistress Observes the Eve of the Civil War

Kezia Brevard was a childless widow. She administered her own plantation in rural South Carolina, and kept a journal of her thoughts in the period leading up the outbreak of the Civil War.

Source: John H. Moore, ed. *A Plantation Mistress on the Eve of the Civil War: The Diary of Keziah Goodwyn Hopkins Brevard, 1860-1861.* Columbia: University of South Carolina Press, 1996. pp. 54, 64-65, 110-111.

November 1860

28 Wednesday

Still quite wet & cloudy—all hands in the new ground. I have done very little this day—last night I suffered very much with my arm—tried to spare it to day from too much use of the leaders or mussels. Why is it at times I feel safe as if no dangers were in the distance?— I wish I could feel as free from fear at all times as I do tonight—it is dreadful to dwell on insurrections—many an hour have I laid awake in my life thinking of our danger— Oh God be pleased to prepare me for death & let me die the death of a true christian-seeing & believing as they do. Help us all through this dark vale— O remember my Dear Sister— Oh my God pity such a sufferer—sheds in thy hands, O be merciful—unworthy *as we all are*— help us all from these low grounds & give us bright hopes of Heavenly blessings—draw all reluctant hearts—pass not by my dear brother who has so many excellent traits of character, yet has not found an interest in Christ, our blessed intercessor— Oh Lord—remember all my dear relatives & friends & my servants—comfort them— May the latter know that the same God rules all &will be with all who try to obey his commands.

December 1860

Saturday 29 of Dec./60

This morning very cold & cloudy—a few drops of sleet before 10 A.M.; now it is 5 mi[nutes] of 11A.M. &the sun has shewn a dim light, gone again. Oh God save our dear City Charleston—let not a head be bruised by the Northern people—thou canst save us, Oh save us!!! This Old year truely goes out full of trouble. Let better signs soon gleam on us & Oh that 61 could bring peace & love to thy people. It is now bed time & raining briskly— I gave out COFFEE & Bread to be made for my evening meal—when I made a cup & tasted it, it was such stuff I sent word to Rosanna she certainly had spilt the coffee before it got to the pot— what she had sent me was not coffee—'twas such dreadful tasted stuff I sent the cup of coffee to R—— to taste of—she came to me & said something was the matter with it, she did not know what. R—— went again to the kitchen & returned saying some one had ground *salt in the mill—they* threw the coffee away, not one of them could drink it—some of them said it tasted like Alum—some of them said it tasted like terrible stuff— I felt sick a few seconds since—it seems to be all over now—this is the second time—can it be possi-

ble it was an attempt to poison—somehow I can't think so. So friends if I should be suddenly taken off after a meal—remember the coffee— I would not have any one injured innocently on mere suspicion— I rather suppose some of my lazy negroes ground salt in it for bread. Now Lord let my last & constant prayer be for my Country— Oh save Charleston & all her dear people. What a night this would be for all in trouble.

April 1861

Thursday 4th

This morning damp, cold, cloudy, the sun tries to shine. I feel very sad to day. The news in the papers from Charlotte, No. Ca——, bears me down—down— Col. Myers had out houses burned— Mr. Elms & some other persons—we know not what moment we may be hacked to death in the most cruel manner by our slaves— Oh God devise a way for us to get rid of them quietly & let us all be better christians— Oh God save us—save us—poor worms of the dust we are— I don't know how I feel—feel as if there was nothing on earth to cheer me— Oh my God help me up—help all thy desponding children. I think a desperate state of things exist at the South—our negroes are far more knowing than many will acknowledge— I had a little negro girl about the house to say to me the other day—'twas a sin for big ones like them to say sir to Mass Thomas & Mass Whitfield & little ones like them (T. & W.—a babe & a little boy)—now if black children have this talk what are we to expect from grown negroes—this same little girl has told me I did not know how my negroes hated white folks & how they talked about *me*. Perhaps I trust too much in man—no, I have *no faith* in *man* who will not fall on his knees & plead for aid from above—we can do nothing of ourselves. I have just closed a letter to my Sister Mrs. P. J. Brevard of North Carolina. Vir., K., T., & N. C. still cling to the Old U. S. of America.

Focus Questions:

1. How would you characterize Brevard's relationship with her slaves?

2. In what ways might Brevard's attitude toward her slaves, or theirs toward her, differ if she were a man?

9-7 Charlotte Forten, Life on the Sea Islands (1864)

In 1862, after Union troops captured Port Royal off the coast of South Carolina, the surrounding Sea Islands became the site of the first major attempts to aid freed people. Charlotte Forten was part of a wealthy free black family in Philadelphia. She was one of many northern teachers who volunteered to help educate ex-slaves and demonstrate that African Americans were capable of self-improvement. The following selection, published in 1864, was compiled from letters she wrote to her friend, the poet John Greenleaf Whittier.

Source: *Atlantic Monthly* (1864).

The Sunday after our arrival we attended service at the Baptist Church. The people came in slowly; for they have no way of knowing the hour, except by the sun. By eleven they had all assembled, and the church was well filled. They were neatly dressed in their Sunday attire, the women mostly wearing clean, dark frocks, with white aprons and bright-colored head-hand-kerchiefs. Some had attained to the dignity of straw hats with gay feathers, but these were not nearly as becoming nor as picturesque as the handkerchiefs. The day was warm, and the windows were thrown open as if it were summer, although it was the second day of November. It was very pleasant to listen to the beautiful hymns, and look from the crowd of dark, earnest faces within, upon the grove of noble oaks without. The people sang, "Roll, Jordan, roll," the grandest of all their hymns. There is a great, rolling wave of sound through it all....

Harry, the foreman on the plantation, a man of a good deal of natural intelligence, was most desirous of learning to read. He came in at night to be taught, and learned very rapidly. I never saw any one more determined to learn. We enjoyed hearing him talk about the "gun-shoot,"—so the people call the capture of Bay Point and Hilton Head. They never weary of telling you "how Massa run when he hear de fust gun."

"Why did n't you go with him, Harry?" I asked. "Oh, Miss, 't was n't 'cause Massa did n't try to 'suade me. He tell we dat de Yankees would shoot we, or would sell we to Cuba, an' do all de wust tings to we, when dey come, 'Berry well, Sar,' says I. 'If I go wid you, I be good as dead. If I stay here, I can't be no wust; so if I got to dead, I might's well dead here as anywhere. So I'll stay here an' wait for de "dam Yankees." 'Lor',

Miss, I knowed he was n't tellin' de truth all de time."

"But why did n't you believe him, Harry?"

"Dunno, Miss; somehow we hear de Yankees was our friends, an' dat we'd be free when dey come, an' 'pears like we believe *dat*."

I found this to be true of nearly all the people I talked with, and thought it strange they should have had so much faith in the Northerners. Truly, for years past, they had but little cause to think them very friendly. Cupid told us that his master was so daring as to come back, after he had fled from the island, at the risk of being taken prisoner by our soldiers; and that he ordered the people to get all the furniture together and take it to a plantation on the opposite side of the creek, and to stay on that side themselves. "So," said Cupid, "dey could jus' sweep us all up in a heap, an' put us in de boat. An' he told me to take Patience—dat's my wife—an' de chil'en down to a certain pint, an' den I could come back, if I choose. Jus' as if I was gwine to be sich a goat!" added he, with a look and gesture of ineffable contempt. He and the rest of the people, instead of obeying their master, left the place and hid themselves in the woods; and when he came to look for them, not one of all his "faithful servants" was to be found. A few, principally house-servants, had previously been carried away.

In the evenings, the children frequently came in to sing and shout for us. These "shouts" are very strange,—in truth, almost indescribable. It is necessary to hear and see in order to have any clear idea of them. The children form a ring, and move around in a kind of shuffling dance, singing all the time. Four or five stand apart, and sing very energetically clapping their hands, stamping their feet, and rocking their bodies to and fro. These are the musicians, to whose performance the shouters keep perfect time. The grown people on this plantation did not shout, but they do on some of the other plantations. It is very comical to see little children, not more than three or four years old, entering into the performance with all their might. But the shouting of the grown people is rather solemn and impressive otherwise. We cannot determine whether it has a religious character or not. Some of the people tell us that it has, others that it has not. But as the shouts of the grown people are always in connection with their religious meetings, it is probable that they are the barbarous expression of religion, handed down to them from their African ancestors, and destined to pass away under the influence of Christian teachings. The people on this island have no songs. They sing only hymns, and most of these are sad. Prince, a large black boy from a neighboring plantation, was the principal shouter among the children. It seemed impossible for him to keep still for a moment. His performances were most amusing specimens of Ethiopian gymnastics. Amaretta the younger, a cunning, kittenish little creature of only six years old, had a remarkably sweet voice. Her favorite hymn, which we used to hear her singing to herself as she walked through the yard, is one of the oddest we have heard:—

"What makes ole Satan follow me so?

Satan got nuttin"t all fur to do wid me.

CHORUS

"Tiddy Rosa, hold your light!

Bradder Tony, hold your light!

All de member, hold bright light

On Canaan's shore!"

This is one of the most spirited shouting-tunes. "Tiddy" is their word for sister.

A very queer-looking old man came into the store one day. He was dressed in a complete suit of brilliant Brussels carpeting. Probably it had been taken from his master's house after the "gun-shoot"; but he looked so very dignified that we did not like to question him about it. The people called him Doctor Crofts,—which was, I believe, his master's name, his own being Scipio. He was very jubilant over the new state of things, and said to Mr. H.,—"Don't hab me feelins hurt now. Used to hab me feelins hurt all de time. But don't hab 'em hurt now no more." Poor old soul! We rejoiced with him that he and his brethren no longer have their "feelins" hurt, as in the old time.

FOCUS QUESTIONS:

1. How would you describe Forten's attitudes toward the freed people of the Sea Islands? What differences seem apparent between their world and the one she comes from?

2. How does Forten compare the Sea Island religious practices to those that she is used to? Why were they so different?

3. What feelings do the Sea Islanders express toward education and freedom?

9-8 Harriet Jacobs Describes "Contraband" Conditions to Readers of the *Liberator.*

Former slave Harriet Jacobs gained renown for her 1861 autobiography, Incidents in the Life of a Slave Girl. She wrote under the pseudonym Linda Brent; her book was controversial for its vivid description of the sexual abuse of slave women. She spent much of 1862 in Washington, D.C., using her contacts in abolitionist circles to spread information about, and raise funds for, the thousands of "contraband" – thousands of ex-slaves who fled the Confederacy early in the Civil War – who poured into the Union-held capital.

Source: Sterling, Dorothy. *We are Your Sisters: Black Women in the Nineteenth Century.* New York: W. W. Norton & Company, 1997. pp. 245-247.

Dear Mr. Garrison:

[Washington, D.C., August 1862]

I went to Duff Green's Row, Government headquarters for the contrabands here. I found men, women and children all huddled together without any distinction or regard to age or sex. Some of them were in the most pitiable condition. Many were sick with measles, diptheria, scarlet and typhoid fever. Some had a few filthy rags to lie on, others had nothing but the bare floor for a couch. They were coming in at all times, often through the night and the Superintendent had enough to occupy his time in taking the names of those who came in and those who were sent out. His office was thronged through the day by persons who came to hire the poor creatures. Single women hire at four dollars a month, a woman with one child two and a half or three dollars a month. Men's wages are ten dollars per month. Many of them, accustomed as they have been to field labor, and to living almost entirely out of doors, suffer much from the confinement in this crowded building. The little children pine like prison birds for their native element. It is almost impossible to keep the building in a healthy condition. Each day brings the fresh additions of the hungry, naked and sick.

Hoping to help a little in the good work I wrote to a lady in New York, a true and tried friend of the slave, to ask for such articles as would make comfortable the sick and dying in the hospital. On the Saturday following an immense box was received from New York. Before the sun went down, I had the satisfaction of seeing every man, woman and child with clean garments, lying in a clean bed. What a contrast! They seemed different beings.

Alexandria is strongly Secesh; the inhabitants are kept quiet only at the point of Northern bayonets. In this place, the contrabands are distributed more over the city. The old schoolhouse is the Government headquarters for the women. This I thought the most wretched of all. In this house are scores of women and children with nothing to do, and nothing to do with. Their husbands are at work for the Government. Here they have food and shelter, but they cannot get work.

Let me tell you of another place—Arlington Heights, General Lee's beautiful residence, which has been so faithfully guarded by our Northern army. The men are employed and most of the women. Here they have plenty of exercise in the open air and seem very happy. Many of the regiments are stationed here. It is a delightful place for both the soldiers and the contraband.

My first visit for Alexandria was on a Saturday. To the very old people I gave some clothing. Begging me to come back, they promised to do all they could to help themselves. One old woman said, "Honey, tink when all get still I can go and fine de old place. Tink de Union 'stroy it? You can't get nothing on dis place. Down on de ole place you can raise ebery ting. I ain't seen bacca since I bin here. Neber git aliv in here, where de peoples eben buy pasley." This poor old woman thought it was nice to live where tobacco grew, but it was dreadful to be compelled to buy a bunch of parsley. Some of them have been so degraded by slavery that they do not know the usages of civilized life; they know little else than the handle of the hoe, the plough, the cotton-pod and the overseer's lash. Have patience with them. You have helped to make them what they are; teach them civilization. You owe it to them and you will find them as apt to learn as any other people that come to you stupid from oppression.

Linda*

_____

*Because Jacobs had used the pseudonym, Linda Brent, when her book was published, abolitionists referred to her as Linda or Linda Jacobs.

FOCUS QUESTIONS:

1. What does Jacobs describe as the contrabands' most pressing needs?

2. How do you think this description would differ if it had been written by a man? By someone who had never been a slave?

9-9 Harriet Jacobs Assists a Freedmen's School in Alexandria, Virginia.

Harriet Jacobs and her daughter, Louisa, assisted in the establishment of a school for former slaves in Alexandria, Virginia, in 1864. Here, Jacobs reports on the school's founding in a letter to Hannah Stevenson, leader of the teacher's committee of the New England Freedmen's Aid Society.

NOTE: In this context, "missionaries" refers to teachers who hoped to bring enlightenment to ex-slaves.

Source: Sterling, Dorothy. *We are Your Sisters: Black Women in the Nineteenth Century.* New York: W. W. Norton & Company, 1997. pp. 247-248.

Dear Miss Stevenson:

Alexandria, [Virginia,] March 1 [1864]

I found the school house not finished for the want of funds. I also found many missionary applicants waiting to take charge of the school. I thought it best to wait and see what was the disposition of the Freedmen to whom the Building belonged. The week before the school room was finished I called on one of the colored Trustees, stated the object of bringing the young ladies to Alexandria. He said he would be proud to have the ladies teach in their school, but the white people had made all the arrangements without consulting them. The next morning I was invited to meet with the Trustees at their evening meeting. I extended the invitation to the parties that were contending for the school. I wanted the colored men to learn the time had come when it was their privilege to have something to say. A very few words decided the matter. Miss Jacobs was to have charge of the school with, Miss Lawton her assistant. One gentleman arose to lay his prior claim before the people. A black man arose and said — the gentleman is out of order. This meeting was called in honor of Miss Jacobs and the ladies. After this discussion the poor people were tormented. First one then another would offer to take the school telling them they could not claim the Building unless a white man controlled the school. I went with the trustees to the proper authorities, had their lease for the ground on which the building was erected secured to them for five years. I do not object to white teachers but I think it has a good effect upon these people to convince them their own race can do something for their elevation. It inspires them with confidence to help each other.

After the school room was finished there was a debt of one hundred and eighty dollars to be paid. I wrote to some of my friends in Mass. to beg for some of the articles that might be left over at their fairs. Louisa wrote to a friend in New York. Through their kindness we opened a fair with a handsome fancy table, cleared one hundred and fifty dollars, paid on the school house one hundred and thirty dollars, leav-

ing a surplus in my hands. All day we have three classes at the same time reciting in this room. It makes such confusion. I am anxious to add a small room for recitations. It will cost two hundred dollars. If [you are] willing for the money [you sent] to be used for this purpose, I can raise one hundred and we shall be at work in a few days.

Believe me Grateful

H. Jacobs

FOCUS QUESTIONS:

1. Why does Jacobs emphasize the need for the freedmen to control the school?
2. Why is Jacobs such a successful fundraiser?

9-10 Lincoln's Assassination, As Witnessed by Elizabeth Keckley

Elizabeth Keckley, a seamstress and former slave who had purchased her freedom, designed and made clothes for Mary Todd Lincoln. She became the first lady's friend and confidante, particularly after Lincolns' beloved son Willie died in the White House in 1862, at age eleven. Keckley's own son, George, had been killed while fighting in the Union Army.

Source: Keckley, Elizabeth. Behind the Scenes, or, Thirty years a Slave, and Four Years in the White House. New York: G. W. Carleton & Co., Publishers, 1868.

During my residence in the Capital I made my home with Mr. and Mrs. Walker Lewis, people of my own race, and friends in the truest sense of the word.

The days passed without any incident of particular note disturbing the current of life. On Friday morning, April 14th [1856] —alas! what American does not remember the day—I saw Mrs. Lincoln but for a moment. She told me that she was to attend the theatre that night with the President, but I was not summoned to assist her in making her toilette....

At 11 o'clock at night I was awakened by an old friend and neighbor, Miss M. Brown, with the startling intelligence that the entire Cabinet had been assassinated, and Mr. Lincoln shot, but not mortally wounded. When I heard the words I felt as if the blood had been frozen in my veins, and that my lungs must collapse for the want of air. Mr. Lincoln shot! the Cabinet

assassinated! What could it mean? The streets were alive with wondering, awe-stricken people. Rumors flew thick and fast, and the wildest reports came with every new arrival. The words were repeated with blanched cheeks and quivering lips. I waked Mr. and Mrs. Lewis, and told them that the President was shot, and that I must go to the White House. I could not remain in a state of uncertainty. I felt that the house would not hold me. They tried to quiet me, but gentle words could not calm the wild tempest. They quickly dressed themselves, and we sallied out into the street to drift with the excited throng. We walked rapidly towards the White House, and on our way passed the residence of Secretary Seward, which was surrounded by armed soldiers, keeping back all intruders with the point of the bayonet. We hurried on, and as we approached the White House, saw that it too was surrounded with soldiers Every entrance was strongly guarded, and no one was permitted to pass. The guard at the gate told us that Mr. Lincoln had not been brought home, but refused to give any other information. More excited than ever, we wandered down the street. Grief and anxiety were making me weak, and as we joined the outskirts of a large crowd, I began to feel as meek and humble as a penitent child. A gray-haired old man was passing. I caught a glimpse of his face, and it seemed so full of kindness and sorrow that I gently touched his arm, and imploringly asked:

"Will you please, sir, to tell me whether Mr. Lincoln is dead or not?"

"Not dead," he replied, "but dying. God help us!" and with a heavy step he passed on.

"Not dead, but dying! then indeed God help us!"

We learned that the President was mortally wounded—that he had been shot down in his box at the theatre, and that he was not expected to live till morning; when we returned home with heavy hearts. I could not sleep. I wanted to go to Mrs. Lincoln, as I pictured her wild with grief; but then I did not know where to find her, and I must wait till morning. Never did the hours drag so slowly. Every moment seemed an age, and I could do nothing but walk about and hold my arms in mental agony.

Morning came at last, and a sad morning was it. The flags that floated so gayly yesterday now were draped in black, and hung in silent folds at half-mast. The President was dead, and a nation was mourning for him. Every house was draped in black, and every face wore a solemn look. People spoke in subdued tones, and glided whisperingly, wonderingly, silently about the streets.

About eleven o'clock on Saturday morning a carriage drove up to the door, and a messenger asked for "Elizabeth Keckley."

"Who wants her?" I asked.

"I come from Mrs. Lincoln. If you are Mrs. Keckley, come with me immediately to the White House."

I hastily put on my shawl and bonnet, and was driven at a rapid rate to the White House. Everything about the building was sad and solemn. I was quickly shown to Mrs. Lincoln's room, and on entering, saw Mrs. L. tossing uneasily about upon a bed. The room was darkened, and the only person in it besides the widow of the President was Mrs. Secretary Welles, who had spent the night with her. Bowing to Mrs. Welles, I went to the bedside.

"Why did you not come to me last night, Elizabeth — I sent for you?" Mrs. Lincoln asked in a low whisper.

"I did try to come to you, but I could not find you," I answered, as I laid my hand upon her hot brow.

I afterwards learned, that when she had partially recovered from the first shock of the terrible tragedy in the theatre, Mrs. Welles asked:

"Is there no one, Mrs. Lincoln that you desire to have with you in this terrible affliction?"

"Yes, send for Elizabeth Keckley. I want her just as soon as she can be brought here."

Three messengers, it appears, were successively despatched for me, but all of them mistook the number and failed to find me.

Shortly after entering the room on Saturday morning, Mrs. Welles excused herself, as she said she must go to her own family, and I was left alone with Mrs. Lincoln.

She was nearly exhausted with grief, and when she became a little quiet, I asked and received permission to go into the Guests' Room, where the body of the President lay in state. When I crossed the threshold of the room, I could not help recalling the day on which I had seen little Willie lying in his coffin where the body of his father now lay. I remembered how the President had wept over the pale beautiful face of his gifted boy, and now the President himself was dead. The last time I saw him he spoke kindly to me, but alas! the lips would never move again. The light had faded from his eyes, and when the light went out the soul went with it. What a noble soul was his—noble in all the noble attributes of God! Never did I enter the solemn chamber of death with such palpitating heart and trembling footsteps as I entered it that day. No common mortal had died. The Moses of my people had fallen in the hour of his triumph. Fame had woven her choicest chaplet for his brow. Though the brow was cold and pale in death, the chaplet should not fade, for God had studded it with the glory of the eternal stars.

When I entered the room, the members of the Cabinet and many distinguished officers of the army were grouped around the body of their fallen chief. They made room for me, and, approaching the body, I lifted the white cloth from the white face of the man that I had worshipped as an idol—looked upon as a demi-god. Not-withstanding the violence of the death of the President, there was something beautiful as well as grandly solemn in the expression of the placid face. There lurked the sweetness and gentleness of childhood, and the stately grandeur of godlike intellect. I gazed long at the face, and turned away with tears in my eyes and a choking sensation in my throat. Ah! never was man so widely mourned before. The whole world bowed their heads in grief when Abraham Lincoln died.

Returning to Mrs. Lincoln's room, I found her in a new paroxysm of grief. Robert was bending over his mother with tender affection, and little Tad was crouched at the foot of the bed with a world of agony in his young face. I shall never forget the scene—the wails of a broken heart, the unearthly shrieks, the terrible convulsions, the wild, tempestuous outbursts of grief from the soul. I bathed Mrs. Lincoln's head with cold water, and soothed the terrible tornado as best I could. Tad's grief at his father's death was as great as the grief of his mother, but her terrible outbursts awed the boy into silence. Sometimes he would throw his arms around her neck, and exclaim, between his broken sobs, "Don't cry so, Mamma! don't cry, or you will make me cry, too! You will break my heart."

Mrs. Lincoln could not bear to hear Tad cry, and when he would plead to her not to break his heart, she would calm herself with a great effort, and clasp her child in her arms.

FOCUS QUESTIONS:

1. What is the basis for the bond between Keckley and Lincoln?

2. How might this story have played out differently if Keckley had been white?

9-11 Women Workers After the War

The Civil War created many opportunities for women's work, particularly in the federal government. This excerpt from a study of women's roles during and after the war shows the variety of fields women entered.

Source: Massey, Mary Elizabeth. *Bonnet Brigades.* New York: Alfred Knopf, 1866, pp. 340-343.

Much of woman's postwar progress may be ascribed to her increased employment opportunities, and to continued business and industrial expansion. How much more acute would have been the suffering of war widows, orphans, and impoverished Southerners if only the jobs available in 1861 had been open to them or if they had encountered as widespread opposition as their predecessors! Many conservatives still did not approve of women working outside the home; but while most women worked because of financial need, the ambitious had greater incentive to excel for their chances for advancement and recognition were more numerous. They no longer had to spend a lifetime dependent on others. They could strike out on their own and go to new communities with less risk of criticism than before, and those who did so were generally more realistic, broad-minded, and receptive to new ideas than their sheltered sisters. The economic emancipation of women was the most important single factor in her social, intellectual, and political advancement, and the war did more in four years to change her economic status than had been accomplished in any preceding generation.

When hundreds of jobs in government offices were opened to women during the war, no one could have predicted how significant this would be. By 1875 the number in Washington had doubled. Federal, state, and local agencies, business firms and institutions were employing women clerks, bookkeepers, stenographers, and receptionists. Foreign travelers were intrigued by the "government girls," and none more than the English feminist, Emily Faithfull, who made three visits to the United States during the seventies and early eighties. She marveled that the Civil War "alone procured women admission to the Civil Service," avocation which she found among the most interesting in the nation. She was delighted to hear President Grant, Secretary of the Treasury George Boutweli, Francis Spinner, and other officials praise their work, and she thought American women extremely fortunate to have these opportunities. Competition for jobs was keen because wages were higher and workdays shorter than inmost lines of work, and it was exciting to live in the nation's capital. A Kentuckian employed in the Post Office Department loved her work but hit upon the greatest drawback of these positions when she wrote, "the trouble is . . . you never know how long you can count on them." There was a certain insecurity in that the employee usually depended upon her benefactor's re-election, but she was usually in no greater jeopardy than a man unless the entire female office force was dismissed to make room for men. Rumors that this might happen were constantly circulated but usually proved false, and with the passage of the first effective Civil Service Acts in the eighties the danger was minimized.

The regular overturn of Federal employees made astute politicians of women long before they had the ballot. After every election, officials were deluged with applications from the "female side of the party," as Thomas Donaldson referred to those who "wanted a slice of the loaf." The personal papers of politicians reveal the increasing pressure put on them by women wanting jobs, many of whom were careful to stress their war services or mention that they were the widows or orphans of soldiers. None was more persistent than Dr. Mary Walker, who pestered scores of Republican Congressmen for an appointment, never letting them forget that she had done her bit in the war. Nor did their demise necessarily silence her, for several years after Senator Logan's death she reminded his widow of promises he had made and pleaded with Mrs. Logan "to listen to a recital of the same."

On April 15, 1883, the New York *Tribune* reported that "a book could be filled with the pathetic histories of the women in the Civil Service," yet their stories would have been even more "pathetic" had it not been for these jobs which enabled war widows and others from all parts of the nation to be self-supporting. Josephine Griffing, Julia Wheelock, and others active in the war had positions in Washington, and Annie Etheridge held one in Detroit until she married. Many once ardent Confederates were working in Washington offices not long after the war, including Mrs. George Pickett, who was left penniless when the general died in 1875 and was only too happy to be added to the Federal payroll. Dozens of Southern Unionists were rewarded with appointments during reconstruction, some retaining them into the twentieth century.

If the *Tribune* reporter had searched every office he could not have found a more pathetic story than that of Mrs. Emma Richardson Moses in the Treasury Department. Described as a person "of education, refinement and . . . all that goes to make a true lady," Mrs. Moses was the daughter of an eminent South Carolina jurist who died in the sixties after having been financially ruined by the war. When she married Franklin Moses shortly before the conflict he gave promise of a brilliant future, but after serving as a Confederate officer he cast his lot with the radicals in 1867, was elected carpetbag governor in 1872, became involved in a number of fraudulent schemes and personal scandals, sank deeper and deeper in debt, turned on his friends, and was later arrested several times in the North for petty crimes. Mrs. Moses obtained a divorce in the late seventies, and needing work, accepted a position in Washington. She was lonely and hesitated to force her company on others who she feared held her "responsible for some of the Governor's misdoings." There were hundreds of women who found in government work a chance to "lose" themselves in Washington and earn a living away from tragic memories.

As the government workers proved efficient, their supporters increased. Robert Porter's report on the 1,100 women employed in the Census. Bureau in 1890 is typical of that of many other supervisors. More than half, he said, had scored higher than 85 per cent on the mathematics examination, a field considered by some beyond woman's comprehension, and they computed and "worked the tabulating machines" faster and more accurately than did the men. The women had a "more exact touch, were more expeditious in handling schedules, were more at home in adjusting delicate mechanisms and more anxious to make good records" than their male colleagues. In both business and industry they were often more adept at handling machines, including typewriters and looms, and by the nineties were surpassing men in many lines of work. Women employees increased in offices elsewhere in the nation, and many Southern postmistresses received their appointments because of conditions arising from the war. President Grant made more than 200 such appointments, including Elizabeth Van Lew and Mrs. Armistead Long, wife of a one-armed former Confederate colonel, whom he appointed postmistress in Charlottesville, Virginia. Many women were given similar positions because, as a journalist noted, they could subscribe to the oath that they had not borne arms against the United States Government, which relatively few men in the South could do. That there were no more postmistresses in the United States in 1870 than ten years earlier may be explained by the fact that not half the prewar Southern post offices had been reopened and Union veterans were often appointed postmaster in other areas.

FOCUS QUESTIONS:

1. What are the main types of work described?
2. Does the text make it seem likely that these gains in women's employment will be permanent?

IN THE AGE OF SLAVE EMANCIPATION, 1865–1877

10-1 A Woman's Life-Work

Laura Smith Haviland (1808-1898), wrote her memoirs after a long and eventful life. She joined the Logan Female Anti-Slavery Society, Michigan's first anti-slavery association. Haviland and her husband had a very active stop on the Underground Railroad. She worked through the Civil War, and the following excerpt describes reunions of families of freed slaves and the remarriage" of former slaves during the war.

Source: Laura S. Haviland, *A Woman's Life-Work: labors and experiences of Laura S. Haviland*, Cincinnati: Walden and Stowe, 1882.

I hastened back to Camp Bethel. to witness the marriage of twenty couples that Colonel Eaton, who was a chaplain among them, was to marry with one ceremony. Many of the men were of the newly-enlisted soldiers, and the officers thought they had better be legally married, although many of them had been married a number of years, but only according to slave law, which recognized no legal marriage among slaves. At the appointed hour the twenty couples stood in a row, each couple with right hands clasped; and among them one young couple, that being their first marriage. All gave affirmative answers at the same time; first the men, then the women. After the ceremony Chaplain Eaton offered an earnest prayer, all kneeling. Then he shook hands with them to signify his congratulations, and I followed him in like manner. It was a novel scene, and yet solemn.

FOCUS QUESTIONS:

1. Why were these freedmen and freedwomen married, though the author says that they were already married?

10-2 Contracts Undertaken by Freedwomen (1866, 1867)

The following contract for work was one of many made under the supervision of the Freedmen's Bureau. Such annual contracts set the relationship of employer and servant on a contractual footing. This second contract was also made through the Freedmen's Bureau, but the employment in question was field work.

Source: Contracts undertaken by freedwomen, *We Are Your Sisters: Black Women in the Nineteenth Century*, Dorothy Sterling, ed., New York: W. W. Norton, 1984, 326-328.

Georgia Brooks County

Contract Between James Alvis and Dianna Freedwoman.

Said Dianna agrees to work for said Alvis for the year 1866 till the day of December at any kind of labor Said Alvis direct and to serve him faithfully and constantly.

Should such labors be faithfully performed Said Alvis on his part agrees to furnish quarters and food for said Dianna and her two youngest children, he further agrees to furnish her with Cards Spinning wheel and Cotton to Spin for herself as much as she shall Spin at night after having performed her said Service for said Alvis, and further said Alvis agrees to pay Said Dianna twenty five Dollars in cash at the expiration of said Service.

Said Dianna is to be respectful to said Alvis & family always submissive to their orders and Should she be impudent or idle or neglectful of her duties she is subject to be discharged and forfeit, as shall be just and right between parties Signed in presence of William Alvis James Alvis A. Buckner

Dianna

X

her mark

State of South Carolina

Anderson District

This agreement entered into between I. A. Gray of the one partand Emmie (a freedwoman) of the other part.

Witnesseth that the said Emmie does hereby agree to work for the said Gray for the time of twelve months from the first day of January1867. She agrees to do the cooking washing and all other necessary work about the house. She is to obey all lawful & reasonable commands issued to her by said Gray or his agent, and to be kind & respectful to the same. She is not to leave the premises of said Gray without permission. She is to receive no company or visits of any kind without the permission of said Gray or his agent. For all time lossed by her from sickness or otherwise twenty-five cents per day shall be deducted from her wages. For every day lossed without permission she is to forfeit one dollar and if more than two days be lossed without permission she can be dismissed from the plantation by said Gray with a forfeit of her entire interest in the crop.

In consideration of the foregoing service duly performed I. A. Gray agrees to turn over to the said Emmie one half of the corn & cotton cultivated by herself during the term above mentioned. Said Gray agrees to furnish & feed the necessary horses and farming implements for cultivating said crop. The above mentioned Emmie agrees to board& clothe herself. If she is sick during the year she is to procure if necessary a physician & medacine at her own expense. It is further

agreed by & between the party above mentioned that for all supplys of provision clothing or monies advanced & supplyed by said Gray to said Emmie he the said Gray shall have and hold a lien upon her entire portion of the crop until they have been paid for. It is further agreed that should the said Gray fail to perform his part of this agreement the said Emmie shall have & hold [a] lien upon the entire crop cultivated by herself during the term above mentioned to the full value of what may be due her and until the same is paid over to her.

Witness our hands the 22nd day of February 1867

Signed in presence of

I.A. Gray

W. J. Simpson

D. Sadler

Emmie Gray

X

her mark

FOCUS QUESTIONS:

1. In the contract undertaken by Dianna Freedwoman, what benefits does she get from the arrangements? Does Emmie Gray's contract provide similar benefits?

2. Compare the duties and responsibilities of each party in both contracts. Are they comparable? How can you account for any differences?

3. Considering the heavy responsibilities of the two women in these contracts, can their position be said to have improved when they were freed?

10-3 Dialogue on Woman's Rights

Frances Ellen Watkins Harper (1825-1911) was an African American activist, working for both emancipation and for women's rights. She published novels and poetry. The following was published in the New York Freeman in 1885. It addresses the issue of freedom in terms both of slavery and of women's right to vote.

Source: Harper, Frances Ellen. "Dialogue on Woman's Rights." *New York Freeman* November 28, 1885. *We Are Your Sisters: Black Women in the 19th Century*, Dorothy Sterling, ed., NewYork: W. W. Norton, 1984, 416-417

JACOB

I don't believe a single bit

In those new-fangled ways

Of women running to the polls

And voting nowadays.

Now there's my Betsy, just as good

As any wife need be

Who sits and tells me day by day

That women are not free;

And then I smile and say to her,

"You surely make me laff;

This talk about your rights and wrongs

Is nothing else but chaff."

JOHN

Now, Jacob, I don't think like you;
I think that Betsy Ann
Has just as good a right to vote
As you or any man

JACOB

Now, John, do you believe for true
In women running round,
And when you come to look for them
They are not to be found?
Pray, who would stay at home to nurse,
To cook, to wash and sew,
While women marched unto the polls?
That's what I want to know.

JOHN

Who stays at home when Betsy Ann
Goes out day after day
To wash and iron, cook and sew,
Because she gets her pay?
I'm sure she wouldn't take quite so long
To vote and go her way,
As when she leaves her little ones
And works out day by day

JACOB

Well, I declare, that is the truth!
To vote, it don't take long;
But, then, I kind of think somehow
That women's voting's wrong

JOHN

The masters thought before the war
That slavery was right;
But we who felt the heavy yoke
Didn't see it in that light.
Some thought that it would never do
For us in Southern lands,
To change the fetters on our wrists
For the ballot in our hands.
Now if you don't believe 'twas right
To crowd us from the track
How can you push your wife aside
And try to hold her back?

JACOB

Well, wrong is wrong and right is right,
For woman as for man
I almost think that I will go
And vote with Betsy Ann.

JOHN

I hope you will and show the world
You can be brave and strong
A noble man, who scorns to do
The feeblest woman wrong.

FOCUS QUESTIONS:

1. What arguments are given by the two men in the dialogue for and against women's suffrage?
2. Harper chose to put her words in the mouths of two men. Suggest some reasons for her choice.

10-4 From Della Irving Hayden, *Autobiography* (1917)

Della Irving Hayden (1854-1924) wrote her Autobiography in 1917. In the excerpt below, she writes of her experiences at Hampton Institute, where she went to become a teacher in 1872. Hampton Normal and Agricultural Institute began its formal life in 1870. Booker T. Washington became a student there at about the same time as Hayden.

Source: Hayden, Della Irving. *Autobiography.* 1917, from *We Are Your Sisters: Black Women in the 19th Century*, Dorothy Sterling, ed., New York: W. W. Norton, 1984, 378-380.

When we went in to supper, they had a big yellow bowl with sassafras tea, what we called 'greasy bread', and a little molasses. There were three or four new students and one old student. When we were seated he began to eat. We were waiting, and he said, "Why don't you eat?" We said we were waiting for them to put supper on the table. He told us this was all we would get. We had sassafras tea and cornbread and syrup for supper all those two years. That first night I slept on the floor with seven other girls. We were all new and there was such a rush of girls they had no other place to put us. We didn't know anything about bells, and the next morning when we woke up, every-body had had breakfast and gone over to Academic. We got up and dressed. I had a little piece of cheese and some crackers in my trunk and I ate them.

Then they gave me a room in the barracks with three other girls. They gave us ticks and we carried them to the barn and filled them with straw. We took two pillows and filled them too. We had regular wooden bedsteads. When it rained, it always leaked. I had an old waterproof of my mother's and many a time I put that waterproof on my bed, with a tin basin, too, to catch the water. I could not turn over for fear of upsetting the basin full of water. The boys all slept outdoors in tents. They had a little stove in each tent. There was no heat in the room except what my lamp gave. Miss Mackie [the Lady Principal] made me bathe every morning in cold water, and I have often broken the ice in my pitcher.

[Before completing her education at Hampton, which she did complete in 1877, she worked as a teacher to make money]

I rented a little room 15 by 20 feet, bought two dozen chairs, got a blackboard, stove, table and broom.

I had twenty-one students the first month. We had five acres of land donated to us by Mrs. Marriage Allen of London, England. I taught school in the week and went on Sundays and begged money at the churches, so we were finally able to put up a building with four classrooms that cost about $1,000. The first year I was alone, but now I have three teachers besides myself. In addition to this building we have a dormitory for the girls, with 22 rooms, costing $6,000. We borrowed the money for ten years, and we still owe $3,800 of it. Eight hundred fifty students have attended this school and 40 have graduated. Some are teaching, others are in business, and several have gone to other schools.

FOCUS QUESTIONS:

1. What aspects of life at Hampton were most novel for Harper?

2. What was the role of the community in providing the necessities of schooling?

10-5 France Rollins, Diary (1868)

Frances Anne Rollin (1847-1902) was noted both as one of five African American sisters prominent in late nineteenth-century Charleston, and as an activist for women's suffrage. The following excerpts are from her diary.

Source: Rollins, Frances. "Diary." August 2-October 19, 1868. Reprinted in Sterling, 366-369

Aug. 2 [1868] Reached Columbia about six o'clock. Mr. Whipper met me at the depot with his buggie and took me to my boarding place where an elegant and spacious room awaited me. Charlotte came to see me in the morning but Kate did not. Went to Church in the morning. The Gov. and all the members [of the legislature] were there. Quite an excitement created on account of the disappearance of Joe Howard after the riot of the Ku Klux last night.

Aug. 3 Went to the Committee Room this morning, copied a few bills and left early. Joe Howard heard from at Kingsville. The young man Dallas Smith who was shot and Joe's disappearance made capital of by the rebels. This afternoon on his arrival he was arrested but Mr, Whipper got out a writ of Habeas Corpus and got him out. Joe seemed terribly frightened about it. Kate came to see me this morning.

Aug. 4 At the Committee Room. Joe Howard came

in and spoke. Appeared much frightened. I advised him to get Mr. Whipper to go with him to the examination before the coroner. In the afternoon went back, wrote several letters for Mr. Whipper. He accompanied me home.

Aug. 5 At the Committee Room. Mr. William Johnson called thereto see me on business, walked home with me. When there he raved about Mr. Whipper sending for me to clerk for him. He told me he felt like cutting his throat when he learned I was to come home under Mr. Whipper's auspices.

Aug. 8 Went to Committee Room in afternoon. Went out to dine with Mr. Whipper, to the races but did not go in for the reason no ladies were there.

Aug. 13 This morning at the Committee Room. Quite a time about the Civil Rights Bill.

Aug. 14 I wrote an answer to Mr. Whipper's letter asking a delay of the *decision* (matrimonial). Mr. W. was at the office when I got there also one of the Committee. I waited my chances and placed it between the leaves of a book which he was reading. I saw him take it out.

Aug. 18 To be, or not to be. Wrote all day and the Justice of the Peace Bill in the afternoon. In evening W. came and spoke over the affair. I felt he did not want a *No*. I said *yes*. He kissed me good night.

Aug. 19 Feeling the most curious this morning. Wondering how W. felt. Received a. letter from him. I wonder how he will meet me this evening. Went shopping. W. came while at supper, He froze me up completely. Spent a most curious time which baffles all of my philosophy. What was it? Was the [ghost] of his departed wife present, unseen, unwilling to give up her claim or what? Both of us were unlike our real selves.

Aug. 20 Woke early wondering whether to throw up the sponge or accept a loveless life. Felt as though W. could not love anyone. A letter came from him today which restored and invigorated me. A real love letter.

Aug. 29 Left this morning for Charleston. Things home disheartened me. Ma looked much the same. Carried my book home for Pa. Told Loady [Louisa] about my intended marriage.

Aug. 31 Sent letter to W. today. Went shopping for myself and the children. Loady took the nightgown, chemises and promises to make the dress. Miss Sophia will make the drawers and the reception dress.

Sept. 2 Started for Columbia for my darling.

Sept. 14 Left Columbia for Charleston. Met Pa on returning home. From dusk till nearly midnight the contest lasted between Pa and I. Pa consented at last not to interfere and allow the marriage to come off on Thursday morning. He thought it was too soon, etc.

Sept. 16 Busy as a bee. Could not stop to think how I felt. I was at Miss Sophia Morris to try on the dress. I have not felt yet as though I am to be married tomorrow. W. came in the afternoon to bring the ring to try.

Sept. 17 Up by times this morning getting ready.

Married by Mr. Adams. *Very nervous.* Left for Columbia. Elliott and Lee at the depot. A.O. Jones, Lottie & Katie Ella Tolland at the house. Quite an ovation. In the evening a grand reception. All the State officers nearly ditto for the members of both Houses, a few outsiders.

Sept. 18 Today I am beginning to realize the affairs of the past few days but am happy to have them behind me. W. seems very happy too. May God enable us to continue it. Visitors. In the afternoon Mrs. Cardozo and Mrs. Henry Cardozo, Mr. and Mrs. Ransier, Bob De-large. Bob and W. not speaking. W. E. Johnson come up and congratulated Willie.

Sept. 20 Did not go to Church. Read Enoch Arden for W. and Smalls. In afternoon lots of company. Also John Langston, Purvis and Randolph took tea with us. Mr. Cardozo came to invite W. and I to dinner with him on Monday.

Sept. 21 Clear and bright. Felt put out just a little because W. did not come home in time to dress to go to the dinner. Had a pleasant time at Mr. Cardozo's— Randolph, Haynes, Mr. and Mrs. Adams. John Langston spoke that evening and paid quite a tribute to Willie. Took the girls home.

FOCUS QUESTIONS:

1. This entry was written shortly after the Civil War ended. What opportunities were available to Rollin? What limitations might you infer by reading between the lines?

2. What are the strengths and weaknesses of diaries as primary sources? Consider what other records might be available from the period, particularly for minorities and women.

10-6 Letter from Lucy Skipworth to John Hartwell Cooke (1865)

An extensive correspondence exists between Lucy Skipworth and her master, John Coocke, in the latter's absence from the plantation where she was a slave. This is the last known letter in the correspondence.

Source: Letter from Lucy Skipworth to John Hartwell Cooke. Hopewell, Alabama, December 7, 1865. *We Are Your Sisters: Black Women in the 19ᵗʰ Century*, Dorothy Sterling, ed., New York: W. W. Norton, 1984, 310-311

My dear Master:

Hopewell, [Alabama,] December 7, 1865

I Received your letter a few days ago. I was truly glad to see that you were still alive & not yet gone the way of all the Earth. I was sorry that I had to part from Armistead but I have lived a life of trouble with him, & a white man has ever had to Judge between us, & now to be turned loose from under a master, I know that I could not live with him in no peace, therefore I left him. If you have any hard feelings against me on the subject, I hope that you will forgive me for Jesus sake.

I Have a great desire to come to Va to see you & my relations there & I hope that I maybe able some day to do so. I have looked over my mind in regard to going to Liberia but I cannot get my consent to go there, but I thank you for your advice. None of our people are willing to go. I am still carrying on my School on the plantation & the Children are learning very fast. I have been thinking of putting up a large School next year as I can do more at that than I can at any thing elce, & I can get more children than I can teach.

I am glad that one of your Grandsons is comeing out this winter. We are looking for him every day. Our Turnip patch failed this year. Our Crop of Potatoes were very small also. Some of every bodys blackpeople in this Neighbourhood have left their homes but us. We are all here so far but I cannot tell how it will be another year.

I will now bring my letter to a Close hopeing soon to hear from you again. I am as ever your Servant

Lucy Skipwith

FOCUS QUESTIONS:

1. How would you characterize the relationship between Skipworth and Cocke?
2. Written just months after the conclusion of the Civil War, does this letter reflect what one would expect of such a momentous period?
3. What are Skipworth's duties on the plantation, and can be inferred about her status?

10-7 Fanny Smart to Adam Smart (1866)

The following letter was written by Fanny Smart to her husband Adam Smart. In it she alludes to an annual contract she has made, presumably under the auspices of the Freedmen's Bureau.

Source: Smart, Fanny to Adam Smart. Woodville, Mississippi, February 13, 1866. Reprinted in Sterling, *We Are Your Sisters: Black Women in the 19th Century*, Dorothy Sterling, ed., New York: W. W. Norton, 1984, 316-317

To Adam Smart

Dear Husband:

Woodville, Mississippi, February 13, 1866

I received your letter yesterday. I heard that you was dead. I was glad to hear from you. I now think very strange, that you never wrote to me before. You could not think much of your children, as for me, I dont expect you to think much of as I have been confined,

just got up, have a fine daughter four weeks old, and a little brighter, than you would like to see. You wish to know what arrangements I have made .I expect to stay here this year. I have made a contract to that effect. I am doing very well. My children I have all with me, they are all well, and well taken care off, the same as ever, if one get sick, they are well nursed. I now have eight children, all dependent on me for a support, ondly one, large enough to work for herself, the rest I could not hire for their victuals & cloths. I think you might have sent the children something, or some money. foe can walk and talk. Mat is a great big boy, bad as ever. My baby I call her Cassinda. The children all send howda to you they all want to see you.

From your wife Fanny Smart

FOCUS QUESTIONS:

1. What is Fanny Smart's situation in the year following the end of the Civil War?
2. What might Fanny Smart's options be? What factors might influence her choice?

10-8 Lucy Stone, Speech in Favor of the Fifteenth Amendment (1869)

Lucy Stone was one of many women activists who worked for both abolition and women's rights. Following the Civil War, when the Fourteenth and Fifteenth Amendments were proposed, granting full citizen rights to black men, a rift in the women's movement developed. Lucy Stone split with Susan B. Anthony and Elizabeth Cady Stanton over this issue, with the latter two opposing the amendments as prejudicial to women's rights; Stone supported the amendments.

Source: Stone, Lucy. "Speech in Favor of the Fifteenth Amendment." *History of Women Suffrage*, edited by Elizabeth Cady Stanton, Susan B. Anthony and Matilda Joslyn Gage, New York: Fowler and Wells, Volume 2, 383-384

MRS. LUCY STONE :—Mrs. Stanton will, of course, advocate the precedence for her sex, and Mr. Douglass will strive for the first position for his, and both are perhaps right. If it be true that the government derives its authority from the consent of the governed, we are safe in trusting that principle to the uttermost. If one has a right to say that you can not read and therefore cannot vote, then it may be said that you are a woman and therefore can not vote. We are lost if we turn away from the middle principle and argue for one class. I was once a teacher among fugitive slaves. There was one old man, and every tooth was gone, his hair was white, and his face was full of wrinkles, yet, day after day and hour after hour, he came up to the school-house and tried with patience to learn to read, and by-and-by, when he had spelled out the first few verses of the first chapter of the Gospel of St. John, he said to me, " Now, I want to learn to write." I tried to make him satisfied with what he had acquired, but the old man said, " Mrs. Stone, somewhere in the wide world I have a son ; I have not heard from him in twenty years ; if I should hear from him, I want to write to him, so take hold of my hand and teach me." I did, but before he had proceeded in many lessons, the angels came and gathered him up and bore him to his Father. Let no man speak of an educated suffrage. The gentleman who addressed you claimed that the negroes had the first right to the suffrage, and drew a picture which only his great word-power can do. He again in Massachusetts, when it had cast a majority in favor of Grant and negro suffrage, stood upon the platform and said that woman had better wait for the negro; that is, that both could not be carried, and that the negro had better be the one. But I freely forgave him because he felt as he spoke. But woman suffrage is more imperative than his own ; and I want to remind the audience that when he says what the Ku-Kluxes did all over the South, the Ku-Kluxes here in the North in the shape of men, take away the children from the mother, and separate them as completely as if done on the block of the auctioneer. Over in New Jersey they have a law which says that *any* father—he might be the most brutal man that ever existed—any father, it says, whether he be under age or not, may by his last will and testament dispose of the custody of his child, born or to be born, and that such disposition shall be good against all per-sons, and that the mother may not recover her child; and that law modified in form exists over every State in the Union except in Kansas. Woman has an ocean of wrongs too deep for any plummet, and the negro, too, has an ocean of wrongs that can not be fathomed. There are two great oceans; in the one is the black man, and in the other is the woman. But I thank God for that XV. Amendment, and hope that it will be adopted in every State. I will be thankful in my soul if *any* body can get out of the terrible pit. But I believe that the safety of the government would be more promoted by the admission of woman as an element of restoration and harmony than the negro. I believe that the influence of woman will save the country before every other power. (Applause.) I see the signs of the times pointing to this con-summation, and I believe that in some parts of the country women will vote for the President of these United States in 1872. (Applause.)

Focus Questions:

1. What does Stone mean by her image of "two great oceans"?

2. How does Stone compare the sufferings of women and blacks? Does she set them on an equal footing?

10-9 Washerwomen of Jackson to Mayor Barrows (1866)

The following appeared in a Jackson Mississippi newspaper, as a sort of legal notice.

Source: *"Washerwomen of Jackson to Mayor Barrows." The Daily Clarion [Jackson, Mississippi]. June 20, 1866, from We Are Your Sisters: Black Women in the 19th Century,* Dorothy Sterling, ed., New York: W. W. Norton, 1984.

Mayor Barrows

Dear Sir:

Jackson, Mississippi, June 20, 1866

At a meeting of the colored Washerwomen of this city, on the evening of the 18th of June, the subject of raising the wages was considered, and the following preamble and resolution were unanimously adopted:

Whereas, under the influence of the present high prices of all the necessaries of life, and the attendant high rates of rent, we, the washer-women of the city of Jackson, State of Mississippi, thinking it impossible to live uprightly and honestly in laboring for the present daily and monthly recompense, and hoping to meet with the support of all good citizens, join in adopting unanimously the following resolution:

Be it resolved by the washerwomen of this city and county, That on and after the foregoing date, we join in charging a uniform rate for our labor, and any one belonging to the class of washerwomen, violating this, shall be liable to a fine regulated by the class. We do not wish in the least to charge exorbitant prices, but desire to be able to live comfortably if possible from the fruits of our labor. We present the matter to your Honor, and hope you will not reject it. The prices charged are:

$1.50 per day for washing

$15.00 per month for family washing

$10.00 per month for single individuals

We ask you to consider the matter in our behalf, and should you deem it just and right, your sanction of the movement will be gratefully received.

Yours, very truly,

THE WASHERWOMEN OF JACKSON

FOCUS QUESTIONS:

1. Like many other trades groups, the washerwomen of Jackson sought to regulate their industry. What power did they have to do so?
2. What arguments do these women use to persuade the mayor that they should be paid more?

10-10 The Memorial of Victoria C. Woodhull (1870)

Victoria Woodhull's career is hard to encapsulate in a few words, given her work as newspaper editor and activist, and considering her bid for the presidency. The broadside reproduced below announces her claim that the Fourteenth and Fifteenth Amendments applied to women. Although her challenge was unsuccessful, and its influence on the suffrage movement is debatable, but the Memorial marks an era during which women tested the extent of their rights

The Memorial Of Victoria C. Woodhull

To the Honorable the Senate and House of Representatives of the United States in Congress assembled, respectfully showeth:

That she was born in the State of Ohio, and is above the age of twenty-one years; that she has resided in the State of New York during the past three years; that she is still a resident thereof, and that she is a citizen of the United States, as declared by the XIV Article of Amendments to the Constitution of the United States:

That since the adoption of the XV Article of Amendment to the Constitutions, neither the State of New York nor any other State, nor any Territory, has passed any law to abridge the right of any citizen of the United States to vote, as established by said article, neither on account of sex or otherwise:

That, nevertheless, the right to vote is denied to women citizen of the United States by the operation of Election Laws in the several States and Territories, which laws were enacted prior to the adoption of the said XV Article, and which are inconsistent with the Constitution as amended, and, therefore, are void and of no effect; but which being still enforced by the said States and Territories, render the Constitution inoperative as regards the right of women citizens to vote:

And whereas, Article VI, Section 2, declares "That this Constitution, and the laws of the United States which shall be made in pursuance thereof, and all treaties made or which shall be made under the authority of the United States, shall be the supreme law of the land; and all judges in every State shall be bound thereby, anything in the Constitution and Laws of any State to the contrary notwithstanding.

And whereas, no distinction between citizens is made in the Constitution of the United States on account of sex, but the XIV Article of Amendments to it provides that"no State shall make or enforce any law which shall abridge the privileges and immunities of citizens of the United States.""nor deny to any person within its jurisdiction the equal protection of the laws:"

And whereas, Congress has power to make laws which shall be necessary and proper for carrying into execution all powers vested by the Constitution in the Government of the United States; and to make or alter all regulations in relation to holding election for Senators and Representatives, and especially to enforce, by appropriate legislation, the provisions of the said XIV Article:

And whereas, the continuance of the enforcement

of said local election laws, denying and abridging the Right of Citizens to Vote on account of sex, is a grievance to your memorialist and to various other persons, citizens of the United States, being women,—

Therefore your memorialist would respectfully petition your Honorable Bodies to make such laws as in the wisdom of Congress shall be necessary and proper for carrying into execution the right vested by the Constitution in the citizens of the United States to vote, without regard to sex.

And your memorialist will ever pray.

VICTORIA C. WOODHULL.

Dated New York City, December 19, 1870.

FOCUS QUESTIONS:

1. On what does Woodhull base her claim that the Fourteenth and Fifteenth Amendments extended the suffrage to women?

2. Why does Woodhull invoke the "necessary and proper clause" concerning Congress?

10-11 Victoria Woodhull, Nomination for President of the U.S. (1872)

Victoria Woodhull ran for U.S. president, just two years after her challenge that pushed the limits of the Fourteenth and Fifteenth Amendments. She was selected as the Equal Rights Party's candidate. In the following she accepts her nomination, and lays out the platform of her party.

Source: *Woodhull & Claflin's Weekly.* June 29, 1871, in *Other Powers: The Age of Suffrage, Spiritualism and the Scandalous Victoria Woodhull*, Barbara Goldsmith, 212-213

VICTORIA WOODHULL

Letter Accepting the Presidential Nomination of the Equal Rights Party, 1872

NEW YORK, JUNE 5, 1872 .

Hon. J. D. Reymert, President of the Nominating Convention of the Equal Rights Party, and Associates:

GENTLEMEN AND Ladies: Your communication

received this day, conveying the formal statement to me of the simple fact that the Equal Rights Party, recently represented in convention in this city, has nominated me as the chief standard-bearer of the party in the coming conflict, recalls the vivid sensations of gratitude, renewed responsibility and profound humility with which I was overwhelmed on that memorable evening when the spontaneous acclaim of a great, enthusiastic and admirable assembly of male and female citizens, gave me the same in-formation without waiting for the formalities of announcement. You speak almost as if this simple fact were one of the ordinary events of politics. But to my apprehension it is far more than that. It is not even a common-place historical event. The joint assemblage of all the reformers, of all schools, for the first time in the history of the great transition which human society is undergoing, blended and fused into the same spirit, coming to agree to stand upon the same platform of ideas and measures, and nominating by an outburst of inspiration a woman known to be representative of the most advanced and unmitigated radicalism, and because she was so known; and a negro, one of the boldest of the champions and defenders of human rights, a representative man and a representative woman of the two oppressed and repressed classes, for the two highest offices in the gift of a great people—such an occurrence rises in my mind into the sublimity and pregnant significance of the grander class of the events of history. . . .

In a word, it is the appropriate inauguration of the EQUAL RIGHTS PARTY; which, in its larger aspect, contemplates not American politics merely, or alone; but the establishment of justice throughout the world. It is also the subordination of party strife, among reformers themselves, to the unity of a common cause. . . .

****

The Equal Rights party also recognizes the destiny of nations, and affirms its purpose to be, to work in consonance therewith. It accepts the prophecy of all ages, that the time shall come when, instead of a multitude of constantly opposing nations, the whole world shall be united under a single paternal government, whose citizens shall become a common brotherhood owning a common origin and inheriting a common destiny. I return, in conclusion, to what I have said of the transitional nature of the impending political revolution. When this conflict shall be concluded, either with or without actual bloodshed; when the spirit of

conceding justice shall have been secured, either by convincement or force; the call will be made on all sides for constructive science and wisdom. Sociology is the rising science of the day. The writings and living thoughts of the great students of social phenomena of all ages, in the strictly scientific point of view, will become the common property of the whole people. In the mean time let us do well the preliminary work. Let there be, first, a *whole people*; let there be freedom; let there be the universal desire for the reign of justice; then there will be a fitting preparation for the final grand organization of all human affairs. Finally, I gratefully accept the nomination made of me, and pledge myself to every honorable means to secure, at the earliest possible day, the triumph of the principles enunciated in the platform, which being those of justice, and for the welfare of humanity; I know they must shortly succeed. Your obedient servant,

VICTORIA C. WOODHULL.

FOCUS QUESTIONS:

1. Why does Woodhull feel the time is ripe for her election?

10-12 Susan B. Anthony, Speech after Being Convicted of Voting in the 1873 Presidential Election

In 1872, Susan B. Anthony was one of over 150 women who attempted to vote in the 1872 presidential election. The following speech comes in response to her indictment for her action.

Source: http://www.pbs.org/stantonanthony/resources/index.html

Friends and Fellow-citizens: I stand before you tonight, under indictment for the alleged crime of having voted at the last Presidential election, without having a lawful right to vote. It shall be my work this evening to prove to you that in thus voting, I not only committed no crime, but, instead, simply exercised my citizen's right, guaranteed to me and all United States citizens by the National Constitution, beyond the power of any State to deny.

Our democratic-republican government is based on the idea of the natural right of every individual

member thereof to a voice and a vote in making and executing the laws. We assert the province of government to be to secure the people in the enjoyment of their unalienable rights. We throw to the winds the old dogma that governments can give rights. Before governments were organized, no one denies that each individual possessed the right to protect his own life, liberty and property. And when 100 or 1,000,000 people enter into a free government, they do not barter away their natural rights; they simply pledge themselves to protect each other in the enjoyment of them, through prescribed judicial and legislative tribunals. They agree to abandon the methods of brute force in the adjustment of their differences, and adopt those of civilization.

Nor can you find a word in any of the grand documents left us by the fathers that assumes for government the power to create or to confer rights. The Declaration of Independence, the United States Constitution, the constitutions of the several states and the organic laws of the territories, all alike propose to protect the people in the exercise of their God-given rights. Not one of them pretends to bestow rights.

"All men are created equal, and endowed by their Creator with certain unalienable rights. Among these are life, liberty and the pursuit of happiness. That to secure these, governments are instituted among men, deriving their just powers from the consent of the governed."

Here is no shadow of government authority over rights, nor exclusion of any from their full and equal enjoyment. Here is pronounced the right of all men, and "consequently," as the Quaker preacher said, "of all women," to a voice in the government. And here, in this very first paragraph of the declaration, is the assertion of the natural right of all to the ballot; for, how can "the consent of the governed" be given, if the right to vote be denied. Again:

"That whenever any form of government becomes destructive of these ends, it is the right of the people to alter or abolish it, ad to institute a new government, laying its foundations on such principles, and organizing its powers in such forms as to them shall seem most likely to effect their safety and happiness."

Surely, the right of the whole people to vote is here clearly implied. For however destructive in their happiness this government might become, a disfranchised class could neither alter nor abolish it, nor institute a new one, except by the old brute force method of insurrection and rebellion. One-half of the people of this nation to-day are utterly powerless to blot from the statute books an unjust law, or to write there a new and a just one. The women, dissatisfied as they are with this form of government, that enforces taxation without representation,-that compels them to obey laws to which they have never given their consent,-that imprisons and hangs them without a trial by a jury of their peers, that robs them, in marriage, of the custody of their own persons, wages and children,-are this half of the people left wholly at the mercy of the other half, in direct violation of the spirit and letter of the declarations of the framers of this government, every one of which was based on the immutable principle of equal rights to all. By those declarations, kings, priests, popes, aristocrats, were all alike dethroned, and placed on a common level politically, with the lowliest born subject or serf. By them, too, me, as such, were deprived of their divine right to rule, and placed on a political level with women. By the practice of those declarations all class and caste distinction will be abolished; and slave, serf, plebeian, wife, woman, all alike, bound from their subject position to the proud platform of equality.

The preamble of the federal constitution says:

"We, the people of the United States, in order to form a more perfect union, establish justice, insure domestic tranquility, provide for the common defense, promote the general welfare and secure the blessings of liberty to ourselves and our posterity, do ordain and established this constitution for the United States of America."

It was we, the people, not we, the white male citizens, nor yet we, the male citizens; but we, the whole people, who formed this Union. And we formed it, not to give the blessings or liberty, but to secure them; not to the half of ourselves and the half of our posterity, but to the whole people-women as well as men. And it is downright mockery to talk to women of their enjoyment of the blessings of liberty while they are denied the use of the only means of securing them provided by this democratic-republican government-the ballot.

The early journals of Congress show that when the committee reported to that body the original articles of confederation, the very first article which became the subject of discussion was that respecting equality of suffrage. Article 4th said:

"The better to secure and perpetuate mutual friendship and intercourse between the people of the different States of this Union, the free inhabitants of each of the States, (paupers, vagabonds and fugitives from justice excepted,) shall be entitled to all the privileges and immunities of the free citizens of the several States."

Thus, at the very beginning, did the fathers see the necessity of the universal application of the great principle of equal rights to all-in order to produce the desired result-a harmonious union and a homogeneous people.

Luther Martin, attorney-general of Maryland, in his report to the Legislature of that State of the convention that framed the United States Constitution, said:

"Those who advocated the equality of suffrage took the matter up on the original principles of government: that the reason why each individual man in forming a State government should have an equal vote, is because each individual, before he enters into government, is equally free and equally independent."

James Madison said;

"Under every view of the subject, it seems indispensable that the mass of the citizens should not be without a voice in making the laws which they are to obey, and in choosing the magistrate who are to administer them." Also, "Let it be remembered, finally, that it has ever been the pride and the boast of America that the rights for which she contended were the rights of human nature."

And these assertions of the framers of the United States Constitution of the equal and natural rights of all the people to a voice in the government, have been affirmed and reaffirmed by the leading statesmen of the nation, throughout the entire history of our government.

Thaddeus Stevens, of Pennsylvania, said in 1866:

"I have made up my mind that elective franchise is one of the inalienable rights meant to be secured by the declaration of independence."

B. Gratz Brown, of Missouri, in the three day's discussion in the United States Senate in 1866, on Senator Cowan's motion to strike "male" from the District of Columbia suffrage bill, said:

"Mr. President, I say here on the floor of the American Senate, I stand for universal suffrage; and as a matter of fundamental principle, do not recognize the right of society to limit on any ground of race or sex. I will go farther and say, that I recognize the right of franchise as being intrinsically a natural right. I do not believe that society is authorized to impose any limitation upon it that do not spring out of the necessities of the social state itself. Sir, I have been shocked, in the course of this debate, to hear Senators declare this right only a conventional and political arrangement, a privilege yielded to you and me and others; not a right in any sense, only a concession! Mr. President, I do not hold my liberties by any such tenure. On the contrary, I believe that whenever you establish that doctrine, whenever you crystalize that idea in the public mind of this country, you ring the death-knell of American liberties."

Charles Summer, in his brave protests against the fourteenth and fifteenth amendments, insisted that, so soon as by the thirteenth amendment the slaves became free men, the original powers of the United States Constitution guaranteed to them equal rights-the right to vote and to be voted for. In closing one of his great speeches he said;

"I do not hesitate to say that when the slaves of our country became citizens they took their place in the body politic as a component part of the people, entitled to equal rights, and under the protection of these two guardian principles: First-That all just government stand on the consent of the governed; and second, that taxation without representation is tyranny; and these rights it is the duty of Congress to guarantee as essential to the ideal of a Republic."

The preamble of the Constitution of the State of New York declares the same purpose. It says:

"We, the people of the State of New York, grateful to Almighty God for our freedom, in order to secure its blessings, do establish this Constitution."

Here is not the slightest intimation either of receiving freedom from the United States Constitution, or of the State conferring the blessings of liberty upon the people; and the same is true of every one of the thirty-six State Constitutions. Each and all, alike declare rights God-given, and that to secure the people in the enjoyment of their inalienable rights, is their one and only object in ordaining and establishing government. And all of the State Constitutions are equally emphatic in their recognition of the ballot as the means of securing the people in the enjoyment of these rights.

Article 1 of the New York State Constitution says:

"No member of this State shall be disfranchised or deprived of the rights or privileges secured to any citizen thereof, unless by the law of the land, or the judgement of his peers."

And so carefully guarded is the citizen's right to vote, that the Constitution makes special mention of all who may be excluded. It says:

"Laws may be passed excluding from the right of suffrage all persons who have been or may be convicted of bribery, larceny or any infamous crime."

In naming the various employments that shall not affect the residence of voters-the 3d section of article 2d says "that being kept at any alms house, or other asylum, at public expense, nor being confined at any public prison, shall deprive a person of his residence," and hence his vote. Thus is the right of voting most sacredly hedged about. The only seeming permission in the New York State Constitution for the disfranchisement of women is in section 1st of article 2d, which says:

"Every male citizen of the age of twenty-one years, c., shall be entitled to vote."

But I submit that in view of the explicit assertions of the equal right of the whole people, both in the preamble and previous article of the constitution, this omission of the adjective "female" in the second, should not be construed into a denial; but, instead, counted as of no effect. Mark the direct prohibition: "No member of this State shall be disfranchised, unless by the law of the land, or the judgment of his peers." "The law of the land," is the United States Constitution: and there is no provision in that document that can be fairly construed into a permission to the States to deprive any class of their citizens of their right to vote. Hence New York can get no power from that source to disfranchise one entire half of her members. Nor has "the judgment of their peers" been pronounced against women exercising their right to vote; no disfranchised person is allowed to be judge or juror- and none but disfranchised persons can be women's peers; nor has the legislature passed laws excluding them on account of idiocy of lunacy; nor yet the courts convicted them of bribery, larceny, or any infamous crime. Clearly, then, there is no constitutional ground for the exclusion of women from the ballot-box in the State of New York, No barriers whatever stand to-day between women and the exercise of their right to vote save those of precedent and prejudice.

The clauses of the United States Constitution, cited by our opponents as giving power to the States to disfranchise any classes of citizens they shall please, are contained in sections 2d and 4th of article 1st. The second says:

"The House of Representatives shall be composed of members chosen every second year by the people of the several States; and the electors in each State shall have the qualifications requisite for electors of the most numerous branch of the State Legislature."

This cannot be construed into a concession to the States of the power to destroy the right to become an elector, but simply to prescribe what shall be the qualification, such as competency of intellect, maturity of age, length of residence, that shall be deemed necessary to enable them to make an intelligent choice of candidates. If, as our opponents assert, the last clause of this section makes it the duty of the United States to protect citizens in the several States against higher or different qualifications for electors for representatives in Congress, than for members of Assembly, them must the first clause make it equally imperative for the national government to interfere with the States, and forbid them from arbitrarily cutting off the right of one-half of the people to become electors altogether. Section 4th says:

"The time, places and manner of holding elections for Senators and Representatives shall be prescribed in each State by the Legislative thereof; but Congress may at any time, by law, make or alter such regulations, except as to the places by choosing Senators."

Here is conceded the power only to prescribed times, places and manner of holding the elections; and even with these Congress may interfere, with all excepting the mere place of choosing Senators. Thus

you see, there is not the slightest permission in either section for the States to discriminate against the right of any class of citizens to vote. Surely, to regulate cannot be to annihilate! nor to qualify to wholly deprive. And to this principle every true Democrat and Republican said amen, when applied to black men by Senator Sumner in his great speeches for EQUAL RIGHTS TO ALL from 1865 to 1869; and when, in 1871, I asked that Senator to declare the power of the United States Constitution to protect women in their right to vote-as he had done for black men-he handed me a copy of all his speeches during that reconstruction period, and said:

"Miss Anthony, put sex where I have race or color, and you have here the best and strongest argument I can make for woman. There is not a doubt but women have the constitutional right to vote, and I will never vote for a sixteenth amendment to guarantee it to them. I voted for both the fourteenth and fifteenth under protest; would never have done it but for the pressing emergency of that hour; would have insisted that the power of the original Constitution to protect all citizens in the equal enjoyment of their rights should have been vindicated through the courts. But the newly made freedmen had neither the intelligence, wealth nor time to wait that slow process. Women possess all these in an eminent degree, and I insist that they shall appeal to the courts, and through them establish the power of our American magna charta, to protect every citizen of the Republic. But, friends, when in accordance with Senator Sumner's counsel, I went to the ballot-box, last November, and exercised my citizen's right to vote, the courts did not wait for me to appeal to them-they appealed to me, and indicted me on the charge of having voted illegally.

Senator Sumner, putting sex where he did color, said:

"Qualifications cannot be in their nature permanent or insurmountable. Sex cannot be a qualification any more than size, race, color, or previous condition of servitude. A permanent or insurmountable qualification is equivalent to a de-privation of the suffrage. In other words, it is the tyranny of taxation without representation, against which our revolutionary mothers, as well as fathers, rebelled."

For any State to make sex a qualification that must ever result in the disfranchisement of one entire half of the people, is to pass a bill of attainder, or an ex post facto law, and is therefore a violation of the supreme law of the land. By it, the blessings of liberty are forever withheld from women and their female posterity. To them, this government has no just powers derived from the consent of the governed. To them this government is not a democracy. It is not a republic. It is an odious aristocracy; a hateful obligarchy of sex. The most hateful aristocracy ever established on the face of the globe. An obligarchy of wealth, where the rich govern the poor; an obligarchy of learning, where the educated govern the ignorant; or even an obligarchy of race, where the Saxon rules the African, might be endured; but this obligarchy of sex, which makes father, brothers, husband, sons, the obligarchs over the mother and sisters, the wife and daughters of every household; which ordains all men sovereigns, all women subjects, carries dissension, discord and rebellion into every home of the nation. And this most odious aristocracy exists, too, in the face of Section 4, of Article 4, which says:

"The United States shall guarantee to every State in the Union a republican form of government."

What, I ask you, is the distinctive difference between the inhabitants of a monarchical and those of a republican form of government, save that in the monarchical the people are subjects, helpless, powerless, bound to obey laws made by superiors-while in the republican, the people are citizens, individual sovereigns, all clothed with equal power, to make and unmake both their laws and law makers, and the moment you deprive a person of his right to a voice in the government, you degrade him from the status of a citizen of the republic, to that of a subject, and it matters very little to him whether his monarch be an individual tyrant, as is the Czar of Russia, or a 15,000,000 headed monster, as here in the United States; he is a powerless subject, serf or slave; not a free and independent citizen in any sense.

But is urged, the use of the masculine pronouns he, his and him, in all the constitutions and laws, is proof that only men were meant to be included in their provisions. If you insist on this version of the letter of the law, we shall insist that you be consistent, and accept the other horn of the dilemma, which would compel you to exempt women from taxation for the support of the government, and from penalties for the violation of laws.

A year and a half ago I was at Walla, Walla, Washington Territory. I saw there a theatrical company, called the "Pixley Sisters," playing before crowded houses, every night of the whole week of the territorial fair. The eldest of those three fatherless girls was scarce eighteen. Yet every night a United States officer stretched out his long fingers, and clutched six dollars of the proceeds of the exhibition of those orphan girls, who, but a few years before, were half starvelings in the

streets of Olympia, the capital of the far-off northwest territory. So the poor widow, who keeps a boarding house, manufacturers shirts, or sells apples and peanuts on the street corners of our cities, is compelled to pay taxes from her scanty pittance. I would that the women of this republic, at once, resolve, never again to submit of taxation, until their right to vote be recognized. {Begin handwritten} amen {End handwritten}

Miss Sarah E. Wall, of Worcester, Mass., twenty years ago, took this position. For several years, the officers of the law distrained her property, and sold it to meet the necessary amount; still she persisted, and would not yield an iota, though every foot of her lands should be struck off under the hammer. And now, for several years, the assessor has left her name off the tax list, and the collector passed her by without a call.

Mrs. J. S. Weeden, of Viroqua, Wis., for the past six years, has refused to pay her taxes, though the annual assessment is $75.

Mrs. Ellen Van Valkenburg, of Santa Cruz, Cal., who sued the County Clerk for refusing to register her name, declares she will never pay another dollar of tax until allowed to vote; and all over the country, women property holders are waking up to the injustice of taxation without representation, and ere long will refuse, en masse, to submit to the imposition.

There is no she, or her, or hers, in the tax laws.

The statute of New York reads:

"Every person shall be assessed in the town or ward where he resides when the assessment is made, or the lands owned by him c." "Every collector shall call at least once on the person taxed, or at his usual place of residence, and shall demand payment of the taxes charged on him. If any one shall refues to pay the tax imposed on him, the collector shall levy the same by distress and sale of his property"

The same is true of all the criminal laws:

"No person shall be compelled to be a witness against himself, c."

The same with the law of May 31st, 1870, the 19th section of which I am charged with having violated; not only are all the pronouns in it masculine, but everybody knows that that particular section was intended expressly to hinder the rebels from voting. It reads "If any person shall knowingly vote without his having a lawful right," c. Precisely so with all the papers served on me-the U.S. Marshal's warrant, the bail-bond, the petition for habeas corpus, the bill of indictment-not one of them had a feminine pronoun printed in it; but, to make them applicable to me, the Clerk of the Court made a little carat at the left of "he" and placed an "s" over it, thus making she out of he. Then the letters "is" were scratched out, the little carat under and "er" over, to make her out of his, and I insist if government officials may thus manipulate the pronouns to tax, fine, imprison and hang women, women may take the same liberty with them to secure to themselves their right to a voice in the government.

So long as any classes of men were denied their right to vote, the government made a show of consistency, by exempting them from taxation. When a property qualification of $250 was required of black men in New York, they were not compelled to pay taxes, so long as they were content to report themselves worth less than that sum; but the moment the black man died, and his property fell to his widow or daughter, the black woman's name would be put on the assessor's list, and she be compelled to pay taxes on the same property exempted to her husband. The same is true of ministers in New York. So long as the minister lives, he is exempted from taxation on $1,500 of property, but the moment the breath goes out of his body, his widow's name will go down on the assessor's list, and she will have to pay taxes on the $1,500. So much for the special legislation in favor of women.

In all the penalties and burdens of the government, (except the military,) women are reckoned as citizens, equally with men. Also, in all privileges and immunities, save those of the jury box and ballot box, the two fundamental privileges on which rest all the others. The United States government not only taxes, fines, imprisons and hangs women, but it allows them to pre-empt lands, register ships, and take out passport and naturalization papers. Not only does the law permit single women and widows to the right of naturalization, but Section 2 says: "A married woman may be naturalized without the concurrence of her husband." (I wonder the fathers were not afraid of creating discord in the families of foreigners); and again: "When an alien, having complied with the law, and declared his intention to become a citizen, dies before he is actually naturalized, his widow and children shall be considered citizens, entitled to all rights and privileges as such, on taking the required oath." If a foreign born woman by becoming a naturalized citizen, is entitled to all the rights and privileges of citizenship, is not a native born woman, by her national citizenship, possessed of equal rights and privileges?

The question of the masculine pronouns, yes and nouns, too, has been settled by the United States Supreme Court, in the Case of Silver versus Ladd, December, 1868, in a decision as to whether a woman was entitled to lands, under the Oregon donation law of 1850. Elizabeth Cruthers, a widow, settled upon a claim, received patents. She died, and her son was heir. He died. Then Messrs. Ladd Nott took possession, under the general pre-emption law, December, 1861. The administrator, E. P. Silver, applied for a writ of ejectment at the land office in Oregon City. Both the Register and Receiver decided that an unmarried woman could not hold land under that law. The Commissioner of the General Land Office, at Washington, and the Secretary of the Interior, also gave adverse opinions. Here patents were issued to Ladd Nott, and duly recorded. Then a suit was brought to set aside Ladd's patent, and it was carried through all the State Courts and the Supreme Court of Oregon, each, in turn, giving adverse decisions. At last, in the United States Supreme Court, Associate Justice Miller reversed the decisions of all the lower tribunals, and ordered the land back to the heirs of Mrs. Cruthers. The Court said:

"In construing a benevolent statute of the government, made for the benefit of its own citizens, inviting and encouraging them to settle on its distant public lands, the words a single man, and unmarried man may, especially if aided by the context and other parts of the statute, be taken in a generic sense. Held, accordingly, that the Fourth Section of the Act of Congress, of September 27th, 1850, granting by way of donation, lands in Oregon Territory, to every white settler or occupant, American half-breed Indians included, embraced within the term single man an unmarried woman."

And the attorney, who carried this question to its final success, is now the United States senator elect from Oregon, Hon. J. H. Mitchell, in whom the cause of equal rights to women has an added power on the floor of the United States Senate.

Though the words persons, people, inhabitants, electors, citizens, are all used indiscriminately in the national and state constitutions, there was always a conflict of opinion, prior to the war, as to whether they were synonymous terms, as for instance:

"No person shall be a representative who shall not have been seven years a citizen, and who shall not, when elected, be an inhabitant of that state in which he is chosen. No person shall be a senator who shall not have been a citizen of the United States, and an inhabitant of that state in which he is chosen."

But, whatever there was for a doubt, under the old regime, the adoption of the fourteenth amendment settled that question forever, in its first sentence: "All persons born or naturalized in the United States and subject to the jurisdiction thereof, are citizens of the United States and of the state wherein they reside."

And the second settles the equal status of all persons-all citizens:

"No states shall make or enforce any law which shall abridge the privileges or immunities of citizens; nor shall any state deprive any person of life, liberty or property, without due process of law, nor deny to any person within its jurisdiction the equal protection of the laws."

The only question left to be settled, now, is: Are women persons? And I hardly believe any of our opponents will have the hardihood to say they are not. Being persons, then, women are citizens, and no state has a right to make any new law, or to enforce any old law, that shall abridge their privileges or immunities. Hence, every discrimination against women in the constitutions and laws of the several states, is to-day null and void, precisely as is every one against negroes.

Is the right to vote one of the privileges or immunities of citizens? I think the disfranchised ex-rebels, and the ex-state prisoners will agree with me, that it is not only one of the them, but the one without which all the others are nothing. Seek the first kingdom of the ballot, and all things else shall be given thee, is the political injunction.

Webster, Worcester and Bouvier all define citizen to be a person, in the United States, entitled to vote and hold office.

Prior to the adoption of the thirteenth amendment, by which slavery was forever abolished, and black men transformed from property to persons, the judicial opinions of the country had always been in harmony with these definitions. To be a person was to be a citizen, and to be a citizen was to be a voter.

Associate Justice Washington, in defining the privileges and immunities of the citizen, more than fifty years ago, said: "they included all such privileges as were fundamental in their nature. And among them is the right to exercise the elective franchise, and to hold office."

Even the "Dred Scott" decision, pronounced by the abolitionists and republicans infamous, because it virtually declared "black men had no rights white men were bound to respect," gave this true and logical conclusion, that to be one of the people was to be a citizen and a voter.

Chief Judge Daniels said:

"There is not, it is believed, to be found in the theories of writers on government, or in any actual experiment heretofore tried, an exposition of the term citizen, which has not been considered as conferring the actual possession and enjoyment of the perfect right of acquisition and enjoyment of an entire equality of privileges, civil and political."

Associate Justice Taney said:

"The words people of the United States, and citizens, are synonymous terms, and mean the same thing. They both describe the political body, who, according to our republican institutions, form the sovereignty, and who hold the power and conduct the government, through their representatives. They are what we familiarly call the sovereign people, and every citizen is one of this people, and a constituent member of this sovereignty."

Thus does Judge Taney's decision, which was such a terrible ban to the black man, while he was a slave, now, that he is a person, no longer property, pronounce him a citizen possessed of an entire equality of privileges, civil and political. And not only the black man, but the black woman, and all women as well.

And it was not until after the abolition of slavery, by which the negroes became free men, hence citizens, that the United States Attorney, General Bates, rendered a contrary opinion. He said:

"The constitution uses the word citizen only to express the political quality, (not equality mark,) of the individual in his relation to the nation; to declare that he is a member of the body politic, and bound to it by the reciprocal obligations of allegiance on the one side, and protection on the other. The phrase, a citizen of the United States, without addition or qualification, means neither more nor less than a member of the nation."

Then, to be a citizen of this republic, is no more than to be a subject of an empire. You and I, and all true and patriotic citizens must repudiate this base conclusion. We all know that American citizenship, without addition or qualification, means the possession of equal rights, civil and political. We all know that the crowing glory of every citizen of the United States is, that he can either give or withhold his vote from every law and every legislator under the government.

Did "I am Roman citizen," mean nothing more than that I am a "member" of the body politic of the republic of Rome, bound to it by the reciprocal obligations of allegiance on the one side, and protection on the other? Ridiculously absurd question, you say. When you, young man, shall travel abroad, among the monarchies of the old world, and there proudly boast yourself an "American citizen," will you thereby declare yourself neither more nor less than a "member" of the American nation?

And this opinion of Attorney General Bates, that a black citizen was not a voter, made merely to suit the political exigency of the republican party, in that transition hour between emancipation and enfranchisement, was no less in-famous, in spirit or purpose, than was the decision of Judge Taney, that a black man was not one of the people, rendered in the interest and the behest of the old democratic party, in its darkest hour of subjection to the slave power. Nevertheless, all of the adverse arguments, adverse congressional reports and judicial opinions, thus far, have been based on this purely partisan, time-serving opinion of General Bates, that the normal condition of the citizen of the United States is that of disfranchisement. That only such classes of citizens as have had special legislative guarantee have a legal right to vote.

And if this decision of Attorney General Bates was infamous, as against black men, but yesterday plantation slaves, what shall we pronounce upon Judge Bingham, in the house of Representatives, and Carpenter, in the Senate of the United States, for citing it against the women of the entire nation, vast numbers of whom are the peers of those honorable gentlemen, themselves, in moral!! intellect, culture, wealth, family-paying taxes on large estates, and contributing equally with them and their sex, in every direction, to the growth, prosperity and well-being of the republic? And what shall be said of the judicial opinions of Judges Carter, Jameson, McKay and Sharswood, all based upon this aristocratic, monarchial idea, of the right of one class to govern another?

I am proud to mention the names of the two United States Judges who have given opinions honorable to our republican idea, and honorable to themselves-Judge Howe, of Wyoming Territory, and Judge Underwood, of Virginia.

The former gave it as his opinion a year ago, when the Legislature seemed likely to revoke the law enfranchising the women of that territory, that, in case they succeeded, the women would still possess the right to vote under the fourteenth amendment.

Judge Underwood, of Virginia, in nothing the recent decision of Judge Carter, of the Supreme Court of the District of Columbia to women the right to vote, under the fourteenth and fifteenth amendment, says;

"If the people of the United States, by amendment of their constitution, could expunge, without any explanatory or assisting legislation, an adjective of five letters from all state and local constitutions, and thereby raise millions of our most ignorant fellow-citizens to all of the rights and privileges of electors, why should not the same people, by the same amendment, expunge an adjective of four letters from the same state and local constitutions, and thereby raise other millions of more educated and better informed citizens to equal rights and privileges, without explanatory or assisting legislation?"

If the fourteenth amendment does not secure to all citizens the right to vote, for what purpose was the grand old charter of the fathers lumbered with its unwieldy proportions? The republican party, and Judges Howard and Bingham, who drafted the document, pretended it was to do something for black men; and if that something was not to secure them in their right to vote and hold office, what could it have been? For, by the thirteenth amendment, black men had become people, and hence were entitled to all the privileges and immunities of the government, precisely as were the women of the country, and foreign men not naturalized. According to Associate Justice Washington, they already had the

"Protection of the government, the enjoyment of life and liberty, with the right to acquire and possess property of every kind, and to pursue and obtain happiness and safety, subject to such restraints as the government may justly prescribe for the general welfare of the whole; the right of a citizen of one state to pass through or to reside in any other state for the purpose of trade, agriculture, professional pursuit, or otherwise; to claim the benefit of the writ of habeas corpus, to institute and maintain actions of any kind in the courts of the state; to take, hold, and dispose of property, either real or personal, and an exemption from higher taxes or impositions than are paid by the other citizens of the state."

Thus, you see, those newly freed men were in possession of every possible right, privilege and immunity of the government, except that of suffrage, and hence, needed no constitutional amendment for any other purpose. What right, I ask you, has the Irishman the day after he receives his naturalization papers that he did not possess the day before, save the right to vote and hold office? And the Chinamen, now crowding our Pacific coast, are in precisely the same position. What privilege or immunity has California or Oregon the constitutional right to deny them, save that of the ballot? Clearly, then if the fourteenth amendment was not to secure to black men their right to vote, it did nothing for them, since they possessed everything else before. But, if it was meant to be a prohibition of the states, to deny or abridge their right to vote-which I fully believe-then it did the same for all persons, white women included, born or naturalized in the United States; for the amendment does not say all male persons of African descent, but all persons are citizens.

The second section is simply a threat to punish the states, by reducing their representation on the floor of Congress, should they disfranchise any of their male citizens, on account of color, and does not allow of the inference that the states may disfranchise from any, or all other causes, nor in any wise weaken or invalidate the universal guarantee of the first section. What rule of law or logic would allow the conclusion, that the prohibition of a crime to one person, on severe pains and penalties, was a sanction of that crime to any and all other persons save that one?

But, however much the doctors of the law may disagree, as to whether people and citizens, in the original constitution, were once and the same, or whether the privileges and immunities in the fourteenth amendment include the right of suffrage, the question of the citizen's right to vote is settled forever by the fifteenth amendment. "The citizen's right to vote shall not be denied by the United States, nor any state thereof; on account of race, color, or previous condition of servitude." How can the state deny or abridge the right of the citizen, if the citizen does not possess it? There is no escape from the conclusion, that to vote is the citizen's right, and the specifications of race, color, or previous condition of servitude can, in no way, impair the force of the emphatic assertion, that the citizen's right to vote shall not be denied or abridged.

The political strategy of the second section of the fourteenth amendment, failing to coerce the rebel states into enfranchising their negroes, and the necessities of the republican party demanding their votes throughout the South, to ensure the re-election of Grant in 1872, that party was compelled to place this positive prohibition of the fifteenth amendment upon the United States and all the states thereof.

If we once establish he false principle, that United States citizenship does not carry with it the right to vote in every state in this Union, there is no end to the petty freaks and cunning devices, that will be resorted to, to exclude one and another class of citizens from the right of suffrage.

It will not always be men combining to disfranchise all women; native born men combining to abridge the rights of all naturalized citizens, as in Rhode Island. It will not always be the rich and educated who may combine to cut off the poor and ignorant; but we may live to see the poor, hardworking, uncultivated day laborers, foreign and native born, learning the power of the ballot and their vast majority of numbers, combine and amend state constitutions so as to disfranchise the Vanderbilts and A. T Stewarts, the Conklings and Fentons. It is poor rule that won't work more ways than one. Establish this precedent, admit the right to deny suffrage to the states, and there is no power to foresee the confusion, discord and disruption that may await us. There is, and can be, but one safe principle of government-equal rights to all. And any and every discrimination against any class, whether on account of color, race, nativity, sex, property, culture, can but imbitter and disaffect that class, and thereby endanger the safety of the whole people.

Clearly, then, the national government must not only define the rights of citizens, but it must stretch out its powerful hand and protect them in every state in this Union.

But if you will insist that the fifteenth amendment's emphatic interdiction against robbing United States citizens of their right to vote, "on account of race, color, or previous condition of servitude," is a recognition of the right, either of the United States, or any state, to rob citizens of that right, for any or all other reason, I will prove to you that the class of citizens for which I now plead, and to which I belong, may be, and sure, by all the principles of our government, and many of the laws of the states, included under the term "previous condition of servitude."

First.-The married women and their legal status. What is servitude? "The condition of a slave." What is a slave? "A person who is robbed of the proceeds of his labor; a person who is subject to the will of another."

By the law of Georgia, South Carolina, and all the states of the South, the negro had no right to the custody and control of his person. He belonged to his master. If he was disobedient, the master had the right to use correction. If the negro didn't like the correction, and attempted to run away, the master had a right to use coercion to bring him back.

By the law of every state in this Union to-day, North as well as South, the married woman has no right to the custody and control of her person. The wife belongs to her husband; and if the refuses obedience to his will, he may use moderate correction, and if she doesn't like his moderate correction, and attempts to leave his "bed and board," the husband may use moderate coercion to bring her back. The little word "moderate," you see, is the saving clause for the wife, and would doubtless be overstepped should offended husband administer his correction with the "cat-o'-nine-tails," or accomplish his coercion with blood-hounds.

Again, the slave had no right to the earnings of his hands, they belonged to his master; no right to the custody of his children, they belonged to his master; no right to sue or be sued, or testify in the courts. If he committed a crime, it was the master who must sue or be sued.

In many of the states there has been special legislation, giving to married women the right to property inherited, or received by bequest, or earned by the pursuit of any avocation outside of the home; also, giving her the right to sue and be sued in matters pertaining to such separate property; but not a single state of this Union has eve secured the wife in the enjoyment of her right to the joint ownership of the joint earnings of the marriage copartnership. And since, in the nature of things, the vast majority of married women never earn a dollar, by work outside of their families, nor inherit a dollar from their fathers, it follows that from the day of their marriage to the day of the death of their husbands, not one of them ever has a dollar, except it shall please her husband to let her have it.

In some of the states, also, there have been laws passed giving to the mother a joint right with the father in the guardianship of the children. But twenty years ago, when our woman's rights movement commenced, by the laws of the State of New York, and all the states, the father had the sole custody and control of the children. No matter if he were a brutal, drunken libertine, he had the legal right, without the mother's consent, to apprentice her sons to rumsellers, or her daughters to brothel keepers. He could even will away an unborn child, to some other person than the mother. And in many of the states the law still prevails, and the mothers are still utterly powerless under the common law.

I doubt if there is, to-day, a State in this Union where a married woman can sue or be sued for slander of character, and until quite recently there was not one in which she could sue or be sued for injury of person. However damaging to the wife's reputation any slander may be, she is wholly powerless to institute legal proceedings against her accuser, unless her husband shall join with her; and how often have we hard of the husband conspiring with some outside barbarian to blast the good name of his wife? A married woman cannot testify in courts in cases of joint interest with her husband. A good farmer's wife near Earlville, Ill., who had all the rights she wanted, went to a dentist of the village and had a full set of false teeth, both upper

and under. The dentist pronounced them an admirable fit, and the wife declared they gave her fits to wear them; that she could neither chew nor talk with them in her mouth. The dentist sued the husband; his counsel brought the wife as witness; the judge ruled her off the stand; saying "a married woman cannot be a witness in matters of joint interest between herself and her husband." Think of it, ye good wives, the false teeth in your mouths are joint interest with your husbands, about which you are legally incompetent to speak!! If in our frequent and shocking railroad accidents a married woman is injured in her person, in nearly all of the States, it is her husband who must sue the company, and it is to her husband that the damages, if there are any, will be awarded. In Ashfield, Mass., supposed to be the most advanced of any State in the Union in all things, humanitarian as well as intellectual, a married woman was severely injured by a defective sidewalk. Her husband sued the corporation and recovered $13,000 damages. And those $13,000 belong to him bona fide; and whenever that unfortunate wife wishes a dollar of it to supply her needs she must ask her husband for it; and if the man be of a narrow, selfish, nighardly nature, she will have to hear him say, every time, "What have you done, my dear, with the twenty-five cents I gave you yesterday?" Isn't such a position, ask you, humiliating enough to be called "servitude?" That husband, as would any other husband, in nearly every State of this Union, sued and obtained damages for the loss of the services of his wife, precisely as the master, under the old slave regime, would have done, had his slave been thus injured, and precisely as he himself would have done had it been his ox, cow or horse instead of his wife.

There is an old saying that "a rose by any other name would smell as sweet," and I submit it the deprivation by law of the ownership of one's own person, wages, property, children, the denial of the right as an individual, to sue and be sued, and to testify in the courts, is not a condition of servitude most bitter and absolute, though under the sacred name of marriage?

Does any lawyer doubt my statement of the legal status of married women? I will remind him of the fact that the old common law of England prevails in every State in this Union, except where the Legislature has enacted special laws annulling it. And I am ashamed that not one State has yet blotted from its statue books the old common law of marriage, by which blackstone, summed up in the fewest words possible, is made to say, "husband and wife are one, and that one is the husband."

Thus may all married women, wives and widows,

by the laws of the several States, be technically included in the fifteenth amendment's specification of "condition of servitude," present or previous. And not only married women, but I will also prove to you that by all the great fundamental principles of our free government, the entire womanhood of the nation is in a "condition of servitude" as surely as were our revolutionary fathers, when they rebelled against old King George. Women are taxed without representation, governed without their consent, tried, convicted and punished without a jury of their peers. And is all this tyranny any less humiliating and degrading to women under our democratic-republican government to-day than it was to men under their aristocratic, monarchical government one hundred years ago? There is not an utterance of old John Adams, John Hancock or Patrick Henry, but finds a living response in the soul of every intelligent, patriotic woman of the nation. Bring to me a common-sense woman property holder, and I will show you one whose soul is fired with all the indignation of 1776 every time the tax-gatherer presents himself at her door. You will not find one such but feels her condition of servitude as galling as did James Otis when he said:

"The very act of taxing exercised over those who are not represented appears to me to be depriving them of one of their most essential rights, and if continued, seems to be in effect an entire disfranchisement of every civil right. For, what one civil right is worth a rush after a man's property is subject to be taken from him at pleasure without his consent? If a man is not his own assessor in person, or by deputy, his liberty is gone, or he is wholly at the mercy of others."

What was the three-penny tax on tea, or the paltry tax on paper and sugar to which our revolutionary fathers were subjected, when compared with the taxation of the women of this Republic? The orphaned Pixley sisters, six dollars a day, and even the women, who are proclaiming the tyranny of our taxation without representation, from city to city throughout the country, are often compelled to pay a tax for the poor privilege of defending our rights. And again, to show that disfranchisement was precisely the slavery of which the fathers complained, allow me to cite to you old Ben. Franklin, who in those olden times was admitted to be good authority, not merely in domestic economy, but in political as well; he said:

"Every man of the commonalty, except infants, insane persons and criminals, is, of common right and the law of God, a freeman and entitled to the free enjoyment of liberty.

That liberty or freedom consists in having an actu-

al share in the appointment of those who are to frame the laws, and who are to be the guardians of every man's life, property and peace. For the all of one man is as dear to him as the all of another; and the poor man has an equal right, but more need to have representatives in the Legislature that the rich one. That they who have no voice or vote in the electing of representatives, do not enjoy liberty, but are absolutely enslaved to those who have votes and their representatives; for to be enslaved is to have governors whom other men have set over us, and to be subject to laws made by the representatives of others, without having had representatives of our own to give consent in our behalf."

Suppose I read it with the feminine gender:

"That women who have no voice nor vote in the electing of representatives, do not enjoy liberty, but are absolutely enslaved to men who have votes and their representatives; for to be enslaved is to have governors whom men have set over us, and to be subject to the laws made by the representatives of men, without having representatives of our own to give consent in our behalf."

And yet one more authority; that of Thomas Paine, than whom not one of the Revolutionary patriots more ably vindicated the principles upon which our government is founded:

"The right of voting for representatives is the primary right by which other rights are protected. To take away this right is to reduce man to a state of slavery; for slavery consists in being subject to the will of another; and he that has not a vote in the election of representatives is in this case. The proposal, therefore, to disfranchise any class of men is as criminal as the proposal to take away property."

Is anything further needed to prove woman's condition of servitude sufficiently orthodox to entitle her to the guaranties of the fifteenth amendment?

Is there a man who will not agree with me, that to talk of freedom without the ballot, is mockery-is slavery-to the women of this Republic, precisely as New England's orator Wendell Phillips, at the close of the late war, declared it to be to the newly emancipated black men?

I admit that prior to the rebellion, by common consent, the right to enslave, as well as to disfranchise both native and foreign born citizens, was conceded to the States. But the one grand principle, settled by the war and the reconstruction legislation, is the supremacy of national power to protect the citizens of the

United States in their right to freedom and the elective franchise, against any and every interference on the part of the several States. And again and again, have the American people asserted the triumph of this principle, by their overwhelming majorities for Lincoln and Grant.

The one issue of the last two Presidential elections was, whether the fourteenth and fifteenth amendments should be considered the irrevocable will of the people; and the decision was, they shall be-and that it is only the right, but the duty of the National Government to protect all United States citizens in the full enjoyment and free exercise of all their privileges and immunities against any attempt of any State to deny or abridge.

And in this conclusion Republican and Democrats alike agree.

Senator Frelinghuysen said:

"The heresy of State rights has been completely buried in these amendments, that as amended, the Constitution confers not only national but State citizenship upon all persons born or naturalized within our limits."

The Call for the national Republican convention said:

"Equal suffrage has been engrafted on the national Constitution; the privileges and immunities of American citizenship have become a part of the organic law."

The national Republican platform said:

"Complete liberty and exact equality in the enjoyment of all civil, political and public rights, should be established and maintained throughout the Union by efficient and appropriate State and federal legislation."

If that means anything, it is that Congress should pass a law to require the States to protect women in their equal political rights, and that the States should enact laws making it the duty of inspectors of elections to receive women's votes on precisely the same conditions they do those of men.

Judge Stanley Mathews-a substantial Ohio democrat-in his preliminary speech at the Cincinnati convention, said most emphatically:

"The constitutional amendments have established the political equality of all citizens before the law."

President Grant, in his message to Congress March 30th, 1870, on the adoption of the fifteenth amendment, said:

"A measure which makes at once four millions of people voters, is indeed a measure of greater importance than any act of the kind from the foundation of the Government to the present time."

How could four millions negroes be made voter if two millions were not included?

The California State Republican convention said:

"Among the many practical and substantial triumphs of the principles achieved by the Republican party during the past twelve years, it enumerated with pride and pleasure, the prohibiting of any State from abridging the privileges of any citizen of the Republic, the declaring the civil and political equality of every citizen, and the establishing all these principles in the federal constitution by amendments thereto, as the permanent law."

Benjamin F. Butler, in a recent letter to me, said:

"I do not believe anybody in Congress doubts that the Constitution authorizes the right of women to vote, precisely as if authorizes trial by jury and many other like rights guaranteed to citizens."

And again, General Butler said:

"It is not laws we want; there are plenty of laws-good enough, too. Administrative ability to enforce law is the great want of the age, in this country especially. Everybody talks of law, law. If everybody would insist on the enforcement of law, the government would stand on a firmer basis, and question would settle themselves."

And it is upon this just interpretation of the United States Constitution that our National Woman Suffrage Association which celebrates the twenty-fifth anniversary of the woman's rights movement in New York on the 6th of May next, has based all its arguments and action the past five years.

We no longer petition Legislature or Congress to give us the right to vote. We appeal to the women everywhere to exercise their too long neglected "citizen's right to vote." We appeal to the inspectors of election everywhere to receive the votes of all United States citizens as it is their duty to do. We appeal to United States commissioners and marshals to arrest the inspectors who reject the names and votes of United States citizens, as it is their duty to do, and leave those alone who, like our eighth ward inspectors, perform their duties faithfully and well.

We ask the juries to fail to return verdicts of "guilty" against honest, law-abiding, tax-paying United States citizens for offering their votes at our elections. Or against intelligent, worthy young men, inspectors of elections, for receiving and counting such citizens votes.

We ask the judges to render true and unprejudiced opinions of the law, and wherever there is room for a doubt to give its benefit on the side of liberty and equal rights to women, remembering that "the true rule of interpretation under our national constitution, especially since its amendments, is that anything for human rights is constitutional, everything against human right unconstitutional."

And it is on this line that we propose to fight our battle for the ballot-all peaceably, but nevertheless persistently through to complete triumph, when all United States citizens shall be recognized as equals before the law.

FOCUS QUESTIONS:

1. Upon what legal grounds does Anthony base her right to vote?
2. Why does Anthony state that she has resorted to extra-legal means to achieve her ends?

10-13 Complaints to the Freedmen's Bureau

The Freedmen's Bureau operated for a short time, from 1865 to 1872. The following complaints were brought to the Bureau. The Bureau's agents struggled to enforce the contracts they had helped to write, and to give some justice to freedmen and freedwomen, but clearly they had obstacles to overcome

Source: Complaints to the Freedmen's Bureau, *We Are Your Sisters: Black Women in the 19th Century*, Dorothy Sterling, ed., New York: W. W. Norton, 1984, 332-333

Monks Corner, South Carolina, September 8, 1867

Elizabeth Bash, Cold complains that she worked last year on the plantation of Brantley Pettigrew, white, about 10 miles from Florence, that she left there last January, and did not get anything but her Share of Potatoes. She says she is entitled to a Share of Cotton, Corn, Peas, Rye and Blades. Laborers were to get one-third of the crop.

Baton Rouge, Louisiana, March 25, 1868

Rachel Caruth, freedwoman Presents an agreement between Mrs. E.J. Penny and herself that Rachel agrees to wash, iron, and milk for Mrs. Penny for one year, and Mrs. Penny agrees to give Rachel ($600/100) Six dollars a month payable at the end of the year. In the month of December about one week before Christmas, Mr. and Mrs. Penny turned her off without any kind of settlement, and also ordered her (Rachel) to move from the place immediately. Rachel asked for the wages due her and both Mr. and Mrs. Penny told her (Rachel) to go off that they have not got any money. Rachel states that while in the employ of Mrs. Penny, she received one dress and two under-skirts.

Athens, Georgia, April 15, 1868

Manervia Anderson States that Harvey Wood (White) of Athens Ga. owes her $1 for washing done by her for him and that he (Wood) Say she dont intend to pay me. I asked him this morning for it and he said I acted damned smart. I said Well I want my money. My child is sick. I asked him why he would not pay me. He said I was too damned saucy for him.

Murray County, Georgia, February 8, 1868

The Freedwoman had made a verbal contract to work for Thomas by the day in the absence of her husband who was at work on the R.R. On the last of January 1868 Thomas ordered her to the field very early in the morning before she had had time to properly take care of her child. She refused to go at that time and he cursed and abused her when she told him she was as free as he. On this he kicked her in the head and knocked her down seriously injuring her.

Baton Rouge, Louisiana, June 26, 1866

Rhody Ann Hope Col; Samuel Davison, Beat her with fist and with the trase of an artillery harness. Alledged cause: Daughter of freedwoman was not there at dinner time to keep the flies off the table.

Aberdeen, Mississippi, August 30, 1867

Angiline Hollins Col'd gst James Lea. Complaints are made that you abused her very severely because she would not let her child go to the field to work before breakfast

FOCUS QUESTIONS:

1. Reading these documents, what or who do you find has most changed from the days of slavery? What or who has changed the least?
2. What can you infer protected these women? How well did these protections work?

THE TRANS-MISSISSIPPI WEST, 1860–1900

11-1 Diary of Lucia Eugenia Lamb Everett (1862)

Lucia Lamb Everett (1840-1918) was born in Elk Grove, Illinois, and trained as a teacher. In 1862, she married, and the couple set off for Virginia City, Nevada. The journey took three months. The excerpts below record the first part of their journey.

Source: http://patriot.lib.byu.edu/cdm4/document.php? CISOROOT=/Diaries&CISOPTR=7641

Lucia Eugenia Lamb Everett diary, 1862 May 18-1862 Sept.

Everett, Lucia Eugenia Lamb, 1840-1918

Presented by Miss Harriet Evalyn Everett. 211 N. Church St. Grass Valley, Calif.

Have given with these volumes pictures of both father and mother, taken respectively in 1859 & 1862

Journal Kept by L.E.L. Everett while crossing the Plains, for a friend, Commencing, May 13th, and, Ending Sep 27th, 1862

Very perfect liknesses taken about fiteen years later. Harriet Evaly Everett.

1862

May 1862

May 13, 1862

May, Tuesday 13th, 1862 Chicago Ill The weather today has been varied, and changible, sunshine and showers have continually been interrupting each other. It would be useless for one to attempt to describe <u>egactly what</u> my feelings, have been today;

but I am afraid if the countenance, tells a truthful tale they <u>too</u>, have been varied, for a <u>close</u> observer, migh see that smiles, and tears, were occasionally exchanging places. Six oclock finds, one at the Hatch House, in Chicago, as it was highly reccomended by a friend it appears like a second class Hotel poor accommodations at best. Well I have this day left <u>home</u> . My fathers house can no longer, be called <u>my home</u>, for I have today given my heart and hand to J. A. Everett and been united in the holy bonds of matrimony by Rev. C. Lamb. There was present Bro Hewes wife and daughter Mr. Mrs. & Miss, Clough, also our mutual friend, Eva. (Allen) All, passed off well, so <u>they said</u> Then came the parting, with near, and dear, <u>friends</u> but I will not speak of that for none can tell our feelings. Father, Hatt, and Eva went with us to D[—]ton where after bidding them adieu we stepped on board the cars bound for this place. We left [-] gloomey tavern at 9.45 this evening for Fulton, arriving at the depot, we met there two ladies & a gentleman (friends of J.A) that had come down to see their brother off that is going with us, and also to get a sight at the bride and bridegroom.

May 14, 1862

Wednesday 14th After a tedious ride all night we arrived safe at F__ 6.A.M. put up at the Dermont House where I now am sitting by the window, that Looks out upon the Great Father of waters, which is calm and beautiful, to gaze upon But here I am <u>now</u>, (after a few minutes walks on board a ferry boat, which is plowing its way through the dark muddy waters of the same.

This <u>great river</u> is what I love, it seams truly beautiful to put to one, one so little accustomed, to look upon any thing of the kind But here before we have time to think what to write, pencil, and paper, must be put away for we are at Lyons the landing place on the

Iowa side This is a beau- tiful little place built on the side hill, surrounded with forst trees of every description which grow in abundance. Called on Lizzie Jones, staid to dinner, had a very plesant time they seem to be enjoying life finely. Left Fulton at 4.P.M, for Clinton a short ride of 1/2 miles down the river put up for the night at the Iowa Central House, which is worthy of all praise. Saw a beautiful steamer called The Hawk_Erie State, pass down the river bound for Carrinth, had on board the third Minnesota Beg[-] all hale and hearty, men well armed and equipped and seemingly in the best of spirits.

May 15, 1862

Thursday 15 Left Clinton 8.o.clock A.M. Went on as far as Wheatland Station where the train was waiting our arrival. Here the boys all come on board the cars, and would have taken us by force <u>I suspect,</u> if we had not consented to join the train. It seemed rather hard to take a transfer, from an easy rocking car, to a jolting lumber wagon, so <u>unexpectedly.</u> But I think it will all prove, for the best. We stopped for dinner by the side of the road on the prairie: Spread the eatibles, on the grass, all seemed to take hold and help themselves, as though they relished what was set before them, as well, or better, than if it had been spread in a marble table. cover- ed with the most costly settings. But not so with me our manner of traveling, and everything about me so new, and my thoughts now and then turning toward the home I had left, <u>all combigned</u> , left me without the <u>least</u> appetite, my dinner was untouched. It being a fine day, I enjoyed our afternoon ride very much. The boys selected a beautiful camping ground for this night, on the banks of one of the prettiest little streams I most ever saw.

May 16, 1862

Friday 16th Arose early this morning feeling quite refreshed after enjoying an excellant nights rest. Breakfast over I took a short stroll in the grove, passing near a house, I called for a glass of water. The people seemed kind, and accom odating, but bordering on halfsivalization somewhat <u>I</u> thought, as filthy, as ever one might wish to see. When all was in readiness, we again sat out on our journey.

J.A. and I going on before, as we preferred walking a mile or so. We have today passed over some as pretty country, as I have seen in the State. Arrived about noon at the Cedar River. which is one of the prettiest streams Iowa can boast of. Crossed at the Gaskill Ferry, paying 25, cts a team. Leaving the river, we traveled on to within a mile and a half, of Iowa City, where we halted for the night.

Just across the river is a high hill, with houses scattered here & there along its side, some planted almost at its very top, which could be seen from our camp, just peering over the tops of the highest trees.

May 17, 1862

Saturday 17th Another beautiful day, has dawned upon us, & I would record my sincere thanks to Almighty God for his kind protection that has been about us, thus,– far on our journey, and not only while on our journey, but during all our lives he has cared for, and watched over us. Breakfast being over J.A. and Ed went down to the City to get the horses shod. They had not been gone many minutes, when it commenced raining hard, and continued to rain, at intervals, all day, therefore we did not leave our Camp, (which we called McClellan, today. Between the showers J A and I took a nice walk in the grove, a short distance from Camp which I enjoyed very much. Unless there is a decided change in the weather, this will be the most dis- agree- able night that we have had yet, to <u>camp</u>, being <u>cold</u>, <u>rainey</u>, and windy.

May 18, 1862

Sunday 18th Another Sabbath has commenced, the sun shines out clear and bright but it is cold. Here I am standing beside a lovely little waterfall; how sweet it looks. Many times I have wished I could see just such a little stream, as this when my mother would be describing to me, the brooks and waterfalls, she used to love so well, when young, found amoung the rocks, and hills, of Old New England. Methinks she would feel almost like a child again, could she but hear its musical voice, once more. Lovely little brook, farewell, our acquaintance has been short but plesant. Perhaps never again shall I stand by thy side and listen to thy murmuring voice. Little did I think last Sabbath, that today I should stand where I now do The boys enjoyed quite a laugh this morning, but it was at poor John's expence One of them went out last evening, and bought several dozen of eggs; brought them in late, and put them down in the corner, of the tent. John came along, not minding that they were there, very uncerimoniously seated him self, much to the surprise of us all, and none the less to himself, in the dish of eggs. He thought it a pretty good joke, but would have enjoyed the laugh better, if he had been like the rest, merely a looker on, instead of an interested party. After breakfast J.A. and I went down to the City, intending to go to church, but finding it early church time, we walked around town a little, but did not find much to interest us. it is a desolate looking place to me. and the people are all of the Iowa stamp. By the time we had again arrived at church, it had begun to rain, and thinking we might possibly, get a hard shower, we thought best not to stop, but returned immediately to camp; where we found all sitting around with books, and papers, trying to enjoy themselves as best they could. We read, sang, & walked, in the grove, until suppertime. After supper a young man came in from a neighboring house, with his flute, and play ed quite a number of tunes for us, and we on turn sang some from the Sabbath School Bell for him. Retired for the night about half past ten.

May 19, 1862

Monday 19th It has been a cold & disagreeable day, so that we are not comfortable, even wraped, in shawls, and blankets. We left camp at eight this morn ing stopped at Iowa City for a half hour. Leaving here we cross the Iowa River, made 12 miles through some of the finest farming country I have ever seen Here we halted for dinner. The roads are very bad, it is impossible to travel a great distance in a day. J.A. and I took a short walk in the Grove. After dinner we traveled on a few miles to Marengo which we put up for the night opposite the Rural Inn, on nearing the "City" we met a gentleman & lady riding out in a very neat little buggy drawn by a yoke of Oxen As this was the first sight of the kind I ever saw I concluded it must be a new style peculiar to Iowa only.

May 20, 1862

Tuesday 20th

Sat out on our journey this morning at an early hour, all in the best of spirits. Passed through Maren go, which is a little one horse town, not fenced in. Leaving here we travel ed on, crossing the Iowa R. and three small creeks in one of these which had quite steep banks, our waggon box struck against the tongues, breaking both braces. but with some difficulty, they tied it up, so that we went till night. We have this morn- ing passed through some splendid timber and camped for dinner on as beautiful rolling grass

land as I ever saw. After Lunch J.A. & Ed sat out on horseback to call on their cousins, which lived about a mile & a half across the prairie from where we were but they had not gone half the distance, before they came to a ^narrow creek, but with such steep banks; that they were unable to cross, and were obliged to return without seeing them. It has been a cold unpleasant day for the 20th of May much more befit- ting Oct or November We found the roads today much better than we expect- ed to, made about 25 miles and camped in a beautiful grove. It is now raining hard and looks as though it might continue to all night. Matt sits up in one corner near the oven, tending the cooking arangements, she puts on the <u>airs</u> of a queen. The rest are laying round loose, in every direction, or covering the tent floor completely.

May 21, 1862

Wednesday 21st Still raining hard this morning. Looks rather gloomy for travelers, but the most of the boys are cheerful & even in good spirits; considering the weather. J.A. I think feels rather, blue judging from his Looks At half past seven, sat out on our road, and still raining. Albert & Frank have gone on ahead about one mile to Brooklyn to get the broken wagon tongue repaired. This village like the rest of Iowa is thinly inhabited. houses few and far between. The roads were very bad, and wheeling hard, from this place to our camping ground at noon, which were on the broad prairie, exactly opposite the Green Mountain House. 2 oclock and we are again on our way, traveling through mud, & water, thick, & thin. Passed through Grinnelle this afternoon, which is a small wooden town, and I judge very unhealthy as they told us 12 persons died there today, with Yellow fever. A half hours ride brought us to the banks of Squaw Creek where we stopped for the night, making a distance of 23 miles today. Here we found four Garmons, who were emi- grants like ourselves, only they were bound for Oregon.Mary, Matt & I took a walk, across the creek, to a house, and bought some butter, milk, &c, also visited avery neat little <u>school</u> house nearby. There is not many States that can boast of better <u>common school houses</u>, than Iowa

May 22, 1862

Thursday 22nd After partaking of a hearty break- fast, we again sat out on our way. Passing <u>first</u>, through a wide expance of prairie, entirely uncultivated, then gradually striking into a more settled part of the country Here we discovered seemingly more enterprise among the people, but oweing to the extreme dullness of the times, low price of all kinds of produce, they can make but little improvements; if they would, I have seen but few places in Iowa, that I could possibly, be conten ted to live in, they were along the border of the state on the Mississippi River. Noon—We now find ourselves seated on the banks of another beautiful creek, for which Iowa, is famous I have not enjoyed a dinner as well since I found a very agreeable young married couple, a sister mother and two brothers. Calling at the next tent we found that they were from Belvidere. There was several men but one female, she was dressed in true bloomer style. Appeared to be very well educated, but put on too many airs for this trip. After returning we all had a good old fashioned sing, in the tent.

June 2, 1862

Monday June 2nd Left camp Tuttle at 7 oclock this morning and passed over some fine looking prairie with here and there a cultivated farm and one log school house. We drove some 15 miles to a creek called Jordan there we stopped for dinner. I picked the first rose for this summer on its banks. After leaving the Jordan where perhaps thousands have camped before; we pressed on toward the West Nishnebotona some five miles distant, where we stopped and watered. There had been to all appearances quite a village there someday but it was entirely deserted now and the houses were all falling to pieces. An old mill too, stood upon it's banks but from it's looks it had long since been left idle; When night again overtook us we were camped on the banks of a fine little creek called Mud Creek, and from its clear waters I have done my first washing since leaving home.

June 3, 1862

Tuesday June 3rd 1862 It is now 12 oclock and we are resting for dinner in a fine little valley of a few rods wide; hill's rising on either side very prettily J.A. says it's looks a little like our home in Nevada. The valley here resembles a /great garden, being in many places covered with the greatest variety of flowers. I have just gathered a beautiful boquet some of which I must press and send home to L.E.L. as we have some of the kind there. We are now within 7 miles of Council Bluff and in sight of Omaha. I started on before the teams walked about a mile when J.A. overtook me, we found Mary, & Matt, sitting on the top of one of the very

highest hills. An hour and a half brought us to the City of Council Bluffs. we stopped just in the edge of town. As soon as possible J.A. went up to the P. Office. where he found several letters one of which was for me from Hatt. this did one as much good almost as a visit home would. In the evening all took a walk about town. It is a very clean thrifty looking place. some very handsome residences on the side hill mostly of brick and wood not an old building did I see. Today I am 22 years old it hardly seems possible and yet it is so; I little thought one year ago today that I should spend my next birthday in this place and under the same circumstances that I do. but this only teaches us, how little we can tell what will take place a day or two hence.

June 4, 1862

Wednesday 4th of June We are still in camp. As J.A. had to get some blacksmithing done, and also to finish buying his supplies, for the journey. He has today sold his black horse Douglass, for $100. He felt sorry to part with him but thought it best as he probab- ly would not stand the trip very well. Several of us took a walk down town, this evening and were weighed. J.A. weighes 138 lbs and I 122. Mary & Matt presented me, with a collar, and apron, today

June 5, 1862

Thursday 6th We have all been very busy today making the necessary arrangements for our journey for today we take leave of civilization. I shall feel sorry to leave camp Council as I have become very much attached to it. At 6 oclock & ten minutes we were on our way. There was a feeling of sadness, and regret, stole over me, I never felt on leaving a camp before It seemed to me as we neared the Missourie's shore that in crossing its dark waters, we severed the last links that bound us to home, friends, and country. I could not reallize until I stepped on board the boat Lizzie Balliss, the great distance that intervened between myself, and my old home, and friends, and that that distance was hourly growing longer. But as I gazed upon the dark murkey waters of the M. I fully reallized that it would be years if ever I should behold again those dear, furmilliur faces I had left behind. Although tears will come to my eyes, yet I do not in the least regret the step I have taken for I trust in one that has ever watched over my well being. While passing through Omaha we saw three Indians dressed in their native costume. I have seen them before but not such hard looking beings as these. It will be but a short time now, before they, will be the only inhabitant of the country through which we are passing. we are tented now on Morrises Ranch one mile from O__a we arrived here at 7 and it was after nine before we finished supper. I retire for the night with feelings of sadness mixed with a little ire. Sad on account of leaving my native land so far behind and anger that some foolish person should seek to injure me without the least cause.

June 6, 1862

Friday 6th June, Left the Ranche at 8 oclock taking a westerly direction north of the Platte

FOCUS QUESTIONS:

1. What were the dangers and hardships faced by Everett?
2. What did the journey west mean to Everett?

11-2 A Woman's Story of Pioneer Illinois

Christina Holmes Tillson wrote her memoirs for her daughter, and they were published in 1873. Tillson recounts her journey from Massachusetts to Illinois, and her life in her new home. The two excerpts below describe the beginning of her trip with her husband, and her isolate life.

Source: *A Woman's Story of Pioneer Illinois*, Christina Holmes Tillson, edited by Milo Milton Quaife, Chicago, R. R. Donnelley and Sons, 1919.

OUR JOURNEY

In 1822 it was still a great event to undertake a journey to Illinois, and many were the direful remarks and conclusions about my going. Your grandmother dreaded my starting without any lady companion, and was much relieved to find that a Mrs. Cushman, a widow lady, whose husband had been a lawyer in Halifax, and who had but one child — a son, settled near Cincinnati — was waiting an opportunity to go and end her days with her beloved Joshua, and that your father had offered her a seat in our carriage, which offer had been accepted. Your uncle Robert was also to go. The carriage had been built at Bedford, Massachusetts, under your father's directions, expressly for the journey. Your Great-grandmother Briggs had seen the carriage pass her house, and in telling how she felt at parting with her eldest granddaughter, and the sadness it had given her to see the carriage that was to take me away, was not aware that she said "hearse" instead of carriage. It amused those who heard it, but they had too much reverence for her feelings to tell her of the mistake.

How hard it is to shake off the sadness of our young days. Partings, the breaking up of families and home attachments, have always been to me particularly painful, and the sad forebodings I was constantly hearing at that time of the fearful journey, and the dismal backwoods life which awaited me were not calculated to dispel the clouds that would sometimes come over me. I did not know then, as I realize now, that I was more ready to be influenced by fears than by hopes. My timidity through life has been my infirmity, want of self-confidence and a shrinking from notoriety marked my early life; and it is only from a sense of duty to myself and children that I have, in a measure, overcome the folly that has kept me back from many good performances.

I did not intend to enter into an investigation of my own particular temper and disposition, but found myself — before I was aware of it — doling out my shortcomings. It has been my misfortune to dwell on my own weakness.

We left my father's house at Kingston, October 6, 1822. Our carriage being somewhat such a vehicle as we would now call a two seated buggy, at that time the name buggy was not known. The seats were so made that a trunk could be fitted under each one of them, and there was room in front for a bonnet trunk that held my leghorn bonnet, and a portmanteau containing the gentlemen's change of clothing. Mrs. Cushman's trunk rode behind, and with a little bamboo basket containing my night clothes, brushes, &c., and a lunch basket, we found ourselves pretty closely packed.

We were to travel at about the rate of one hundred miles in three days, and St. Paul-like, commenced our journey coast-wise. We passed through Providence, stopping to dine with Seth Allen, who had formerly been a neighbor of your Grandfather Tillson's. I speak of this because theirs were the last faces I saw of those

I had known before, and not until four years after, when your Uncle Charles arrived in Illinois, did I see any face that I had before looked upon after leaving the Allens' on my second day from home. Our course carried us along the southern, the shore line of Connecticut, passing through New Haven. We arrived at New York in eight days. It being my first visit, I was much disappointed to find the city almost depopulated by the yellow fever. We knew before starting that the fever was prevailing to some extent; but as intelligence did not then, as now, go with lightning speed, and we had been so long on the way, the extent of the sickness was not known to us. We rode into New York in the morning, but it had a very desolate appearance. The inhabitants had closed their places of business, and the merchants had removed their goods out of what was then termed the city. The place where Union Square now is, was country, and those who were willing to risk the chances of yellow fever so near them had erected shanties and were displaying their goods. There was a large brick building where an Irishman kept a decent tavern. They were holding a political caucus the night we stopped there.

At Philadelphia we stayed a day, putting up at a Quaker boarding house. We went out and bought a white merino shawl and some winter trimmings for my large leghorn bonnet. We did not then change as often as now, having a winter, spring, summer, and fall bonnet. Those who had a nice leghorn, as was mine, changed the trimmings with the season. Those who could afford it wore ostrich feathers in the winter, while in the summer flowers were substituted. Feathers at that time were thought to be in bad taste for summer wear. I enjoyed my day in Philadelphia; also my whole journey through New Jersey and Pennsylvania. The country was very different from anything I had seen. Having been brought up on the sandy soil of the old Colony, among the pine woods, where every farmer is a poor man, and those who have farms and are rich have made themselves so by manufacture or commerce, it seemed strange to see the big Dutch barns, which in the distance we continually mistook for churches. The inhabitants also interested me. We stopped every night, and between Philadelphia and Lancaster found ourselves in houses where they could not speak a word of English, and our pantomime performances were sometimes very amusing. I can now recall some things which occurred while your father and I were trying to come to some understanding with

the host and hostess. I can now see your Uncle Robert in his mulberry suit, both arms hanging straight from his shoulders, not speaking or moving himself, but good-naturedly watching the movements of the rest.

Arrived at Wheeling we stopped for breakfast, and then in a ferry boat crossed the Ohio, where I was somewhat disappointed. The river was very low at that time, and its narrow stream between two sandy shores I looked on with other eyes and other emotions than I had in store for the "beautiful Ohio." From Wheeling we went across the country to Williamsburgh, a town twenty miles from Cincinnati, where we were to leave Mrs. Cushman with her son. I should like to describe Mrs. Cushman, but now feel like plodding my way through Ohio. After crossing the Ohio River, a new scene opened to me, and my initiation to a new country began. From Cumberland, Pennsylvania, to Wheeling, we had traveled on the National Road, but it extended no farther, and after that we were left to make our way as best we could over such roads as Ohio at that time could offer. When we were wading through swampy, boggy bottom lands we hailed a corduroy with joy, not that corduroys were our particular fancy, but anything for a variety; and when the jostling, jolting, up and down process became unbearable, a change to a mud hole was quite soothing. We were not all the time, however, in so sad an extremity. We sometimes for hours would ride through high and dry woodlands where there had been roads surveyed and the under-growth cleared out the width of a carriage road, and every few rods we would find what they termed a blaze, which was a tree with the bark hacked off, and these served as guide boards.

[After completing their first dwelling, the Tillson's servant decided to return to St. Louis]

January, 1872

Having brought my reminiscences to the close of the four-and-a-half years of Illinois, I will, before beginning on another year, give a parting retrospect isolation while at our log cabin at the farm. In the four years I had left home once, to go to Vandalia, where I spent nearly a week, taking with me Charley, who was six weeks old. We also took Mr. Black, who had been sick and with us for the four previouss months, but had so far recovered as to be able to enter the auditors office as clerk for Colonel Berry. About a year afterwards I went to Greenville and spent two days with the Blanchards'. The third year of my backwoods life I went to St. Louis, stopping at Collinsville and spending the Sabbath at Deacon Collins'.

That Sunday was communion day, and I there met Mrs. Breath, who with her son Edward for a driver had come down from the Marine settlement in a wagon, drawn by two stout oxen. Ed, the teamster, was afterwards the beloved missionary to Persia, and Mrs. Breath did not feel her dignity lowered or any apology necessary on account of her rude turnout, but simply remarked that they had lost their horses. I also met with Mrs. B—, from St. Louis, who was a visitor there. I saw her in St. Louis when I made my first visit, and when I had all my nice wedding wardrobe, and was complimented on my good taste in dressing. "Like begets like," and I was not aware that two and a half years with such coarse surroundings had told so heavily on my personal appearance. Mrs. B. somewhat officiously tried to convince me of the fact, saying I dressed old enough for a lady of old Mrs. Collins' age. I had had an attack of intermittent fever the autumn previous and lost my hair, so that I had been under the necessity of wearing a cap, and as there had been no style to follow I made rather an outlandish appearance; I had taken one of my best collars, put on a muslin crown, and trimmed it with lace, a thing that in comparison with the checkered cotton handerkerchiefs worn on the heads of our native women was quite a triumph, but when I showed my head to the St. Louis aristocracy I felt decidedly night-cappy. Arriving at St. Louis the Paddocks gave me hints and lectures on the same subject; was there three or four days and brushed up a little. Started for Edwardsville; on our way homeward spent two days at Major Hopkins'. The last night I spent there Charley was taken sick, and in the morning the whole family remonstrated about our leaving with so sick a child.

The flies, which at that season swarmed on the prairie, made it dangerous to attempt crossing in the daytime, as they would attack horses in such a way as to make them perfectly frantic and unmanageable. This was another reason urged why it would be unsafe for us to start, but your father had a business engagement to meet and his mind was made up; so taking a bottle of something to allay Charley's thirst, for he had a high fever, and taking him on my lap, we started on our ride of forty miles. There was a strong wind that day which was fortunate for us as the flies could not settle on the horses as in a calm, and by a most furious driving, which your father well understood, we were enabled to reach home before night.

These three visits were all that I made out of our own neighborhood for the first four-and-a-half years. Twice in that time I spent a day at "Parson Townsend's," seven miles from us. I spent one day at Colonel Seward's, one at Butler Seward's, and occasionally would ride up to "Father Townsend's" and spend a day or part of a day. Among the western neighbors, I dined twice at Esquire Kilpatrick's, in the cabin without a floor; once at Jesse Buzan's, once at Commodore Yoakum's, which, with the exception of one wedding, and one "infare," covered all my absences from the old home.

FOCUS QUESTIONS:

1. What sort of social life was available to Tillson?
2. What role or roles did Tillson play in her community?

11-3 To and Fro in California

Emma H. Adams, unlike Christina Tillson and Lucia Everett, went to the west as a visitor, and a writer. She wrote a series of letters that were published in the Cleveland Leader and Herald and other journals. She travelled by train, travelling throughout the Southwest. The following letter focuses on the lives of women in California in 1884.

Source: Emma H. Adam, *To and Fro in California: With Sketches in Arizona and New Mexico*, Cincinnati, W.M.B.C. Press, 1887.

Women As Cultivators of the Soil

One day in June last the writer was one of a dozen passengers in the "morning stage" from Los Angeles to Pasadena. The vehicle was not one of those oval-shaped, springy, swaying coaches which, as I fancied in my childhood, insure the very perfection of carriage riding, and which the traveler of the present day may test, should he ever erase the rugged Siskiyou Mountains in one of the coaches of the Oregon and California stage-line, but was a long, four-seated conveyance, with high, square top and open side. From it we could obtain a fine view of the picturesque country for miles around.

The passengers were all in their seats only one-half hour after the time, and presently the four-in-hand dashed off from the cigar-store in Temple Block, claiming to be the, head-quarters f the stage company. The little seven-by-nine room is by no means a pleasant waiting point for ladies, and I being usually ahead of time when setting out on such a jaunt, had the pleasure of seeing no end of money set fire to, in little slender rolls of tobacco, during the hour I watched for the stage.

The morning was cloudy. The atmosphere as laden with chilling moisture, which the breeze drove sharply into our faces. Anywhere in the East, under such circumstances an all-day rain might confidently have been predicted; but in Southern California It "never rains when it does," so we were not disappointed to see the mist drift away long before noon. Then down came the genial sunlight, making the earth and ourselves rejoice.

Our road twice crossed the Arroyo Secco, a chatty stream flowing from the Sierra Madre. All around, the country was covered with wrinkles, like, an aged face furrowed by years of care. Now we sped across a pretty valley, decked with venerable live-oaks, ever green; and singularly effective in the landscape, but some of them painfully distorted in shape. Now we were borne up a long hill, from whose top we had a view of scene quite worthy the brush which put the Yo-Semite on canvas.

Upon the seat beside me sat an intelligent lady from e town in Iowa. She had been on a visit to Elsinore, a new colony springing up, with fair prospects, not far from Riverside. Her husband, as I soon learned, was one of its projectors, and, as was entirely proper, she appeared to be much interested in the sale of Elsinore lots. She quietly advised a young man, forming the third party on our seat, and evidently just catching the real-estate fever, to "see Elsinore before investing elsewhere in Southern California." That was kind of her. The new town occupies a location as charming as is its name, on the border of Elsinore Lake, where it would be delightful to dwell. The place has advantages all it own, and might exactly meet the wants and means of this stranger. If so, two men had been helped.

It is very noticeable how quickly bright-minded women from other parts of the country become interested, and then engaged, in real-estate transaction this coast. It is worthy of remark, too, what ability they display in the business, and what success they achieve. Some one has said that as large a proportion of women as men, their fortunes by this sort of trade. They ate quick to discern the favorable or unfavorable points in a piece of property, and seem to know when they have received a good offer from a purchaser.

A friend recently informed me that of a certain large tract of land near the city, which was put on the market lately in small lots, nearly one-half the buyers were women; and also, that it is not a rare thing for numbers of feminine speculators to attend the auction sales of land frequently taking place, and to bid quietly but intelligently for the property.

Of the sixty-five or more women employed as teachers in the public Schools of Los Angeles, there is scarcely one who is not the owner of land somewhere in the State. Numbers of women on the coast—in California, in Oregon—personally superintend considerable farms, the titles to which are in their own name. They themselves make the sales of the crops. In some instances they have brought their land up to a high figure by putting it under fine cultivation. Of the five women who happen to be at this moment in the house where I write, all possess land in or near the city.

Much has been said about an educated and sensible young woman who, with her invalid father, resides in one of the colonies not very distant from Los Angeles. She is the owner of a raisin vineyard of ten or more acres, every vine in which was placed by her own hands. The vineyard is now in full bearing. Every year she superintends the picking, curing, and packing of her prop, and makes her own terms with the dealers. I think she is the possessor also of ten acre of orange trees, in thrifty condition. The story goes that when the little cottage in which they live was in process of erection, the roof being unfinished, a severe storm threatened. This made it necessary for the father—his own carpenter, I presume—to have aid in the shingling. None being obtainable in the small town, the indomitable girl climbed to the roof;. and laid shingles until the work was complete, acquitting herself as at carpentry as she does at raisin-making.

I am now obliged to add that, no sooner had this brave, energetic, girl acquired her pretty home, and become well advanced toward competency, than there chanced that way a Methodist minister, who, admiring her noble qualities, invited her to become his wife. And she, pleased with the idea, accepted the invitation, and is about to be married.

In the same village live two sisters, young women from Wisconsin, who, with a widowed mother, came to the place but a few years ago. With their slender means they purchased a few acres of land near, and soon had growing upon it a raisin vineyard and an orange grove, much of the labor of planting them being performed with their own hands. While their vines and trees were growing, one of them, girl rarely endowed, applied for the position of postmaster in the community, and received the appointment, "her application being indorsed by nearly every voter in the town."

About this time the Southern Pacific Railway, learning that she was an accomplished telegrapher, give her important employment in that occupation, her sister becoming her efficient deputy in the post-office. These young women are the daughters of a Congregational clergyman who died some years ago, and are, of course, cultured, Christian girls. Their womanly ways, promptness, and conscientious discharge of duty as daughters, in the Church, in society, in business, have won them the good will and respect of all parties. As a result of economy and judicious investments in real estate, their combined fortune now, at the close of about five years, amounts to some sixteen thousand dollars.

We are now ell on the way to Pasadena. Suddenly the four-in-hand wheel into a flower-bordered drive way on our right. Then comes to view a trim little cottage crowning one of the "wrinkles". Now out of the front door-way bound two or three young children, shouting "Mamma!" After then comes a babe in somebody's arms. The place was the home, these were the children, of the lady from Elsinore. Ourselves happy over the welcome the received, we bade her adieu, turned back to the main road, and began climbing Hermosa Vista, Hill, one of the sightliest eminences in all this picturesque region, and, as has been said in a previous chapter, the seat of a college for young men.

The summit grained, a short time brought as into Orange Grove Avenue, the finest street in Pasadena. Throughout its entire length vineyards, orange groves, inviting grounds, and comfortable abodes grace both sides. Speeding on a couple of miles, we at past turned into the broad, arched gateway at Carmelita, the beautiful home of Dr. Esta S. Carr and his family. Here the stage left the writer for a twenty-four hours sojourn. As we wound through the drive-way to the house, we noticed among the great variety of choice trees in the grounds, cedars from Lebanon, India, Norway, Oregon, and the Norfolk Islands; also, the maple, butternut, mulberry, palm, bamboos, several species of eucalypti—natives of Australia—and the sturdy sequoia, of Calaveras stock, with other home and foreign trees.

Carmelita is intended to suggest not only the name of its proprietor, but also Mount Carmel, in Syria. Naturally it calls up the days of Elijah, and the scenes of the august, miracle which took place on that summit, with its attendant human slaughter. The cottage, framed in with flowers and vines, occupies the crown of a long descent toward the east. In the foreground, on that side, stands an apricot orchard in splendid condition. Beyond that, a part of the lovely village comes into the picture. Farther away, stretches the rich San Gabriel Valley. On the left, three miles distant, rise the stately Sierra Madre Mountains. Thus are brought into the beautiful panorama the extremes of scenery. Walking about the perfect grounds to-day noting the scope of the improvements on every hand, it is difficult to persuade one's self that seven years have …. to produce fruit and forest trees of such magnitude; and still more difficult to believe the whole in the … of one little woman's effort. . .

. . . This led to the purchase of the forty acres now constituting Carmelita. They were then a mere barren waste. Nat a furrow had ever been turned upon them. Soon after they were acquired Mrs. Carr left her home in Sacramento, came to Pasadena, set men to breaking up the soil on this place, built a temporary habitation for her family, laid out these now beautiful grounds and from that time, with great energy, carried forward her improvements. At that time Mrs. Carr was :the Assistant State Superintendent of the Public Schools of California. For years he had been associated with her husband in educational work.

On many occasions during this period had women of culture and ability sought her advice, with reference to earning a livelihood for themselves. In reply she had often urged the obtaining a support from the soil, in some one of the many pleasant departments of horticulture possible in California. Most, if not all of them, had lacked the conrage to make the attempt. In the development of her forty acres, therefore, she determined to furnish them a practical illustration of the views. she had advocated. And, to-day, Carmelita, with its many different lines of production, is her noble, self-denying answer to a multitude of women desirous of learning how they may support themselves, and provide something for the future.

Mrs. Carr has endeavored to exemplify what a woman may accomplish on a few acres of land in one, two, three, and four years with munch or with little capital. The particulars of her effort are as interesting as useful, but must be excluded from this volume. Suffice it to say that Carmelita is, in many of its departments, a splendid object-lesson for women having families of children to support. It is a favorite project in the mind of Mrs. Carr to some day convert Carmelita into a State school of horticulture for women. May she live to do it!

Of Pasadena itself all the world has heard; how attractive it is; how delightfully situated, at the head of the fair San Gabriel Valley; and how, in the space of a few swift years, it sprang from a desert state into square miles vineyards and orchards of all kinds. It is the gem of Southern California towns, and will long remain such. Tourists can find no lovelier place to winter in. But the man of limited means, seeking a home there for his family, would be shut, out by the high price of land.

11-4 Mrs. Guadalupe Gallegos

Guadalupe Lupita Gallegos narrated the story of her life history to a WPA worker, in as part of the Folklore Project.

Source: The Biography of Guadalupe Lupita Gallegos, http://memory.loc.gov/ammem/wpaintro/nmcat.html

"I was born in Las Vegas, New Mexico on December 12, [1855?]. I was baptized by Father Pinal, a French Priest.

"My parents, Severo Baca and Maria Ignacia, were wealthy, owning several farms, many cattle and sheep, and much money and jewelry. My great grandfather, Santiago Ulibarri, had several children but I was his only great grand-daughter and so I was his pet. Mr. Ulibarri was tall, blond, and green-eyed, and very wealthy."

"His home was Spanish with all the windows opening on the placita, a large yard in the middle. This house was very dark and gloomy and was open to no one except a few Spanish friends. When one entered one of tho'se old Spanish houses it seemed as if one were entering a tomb, so cold and uninviting were they. Several families would live in these houses; the owner's children, their husbands and wives, and their children.

"We lived there shut away from the rest of the world. Mr. Ulibarri was the head of his household and he knew it. He was virtually the dictator of his family. The women were never allowed on the streets witho'ut someone trustworthy to escort them. We obeyed Mr. Ulibarri in everything. Only that which he dictated was done. {Begin handwritten}C 18 -N. Mex.{End handwritten}

FOCUS QUESTIONS:

1. Compare the journey of Adams to those of Everett and Tillson. Why does life in the West appear to have changed so much in less than a decade?

2. Compare also the nature of the writings of these three women (Everett, Tillson and Adams). How does the nature of their writing differ? Consider the time of writing, purpose in writing, and audience.

3. What were the opportunities for women in California? How do the lives of women in California differ from the lives presented in the writings of Tillson and Everett?

"Since it was considered such a disgrace for a lady of the upper class to be seen on the street unescorted, we spent most of our time sewing, and playing the piano. We never dreamed of soiling our hands in the kitchen cooking or cleaning.

"In front of Mr. Ulibarri we were always very dignified and well-behaved, but when he was not present we were often silly, as most girls are. I was the only one of the girls who was permitted to go with Mr. Ulibarri very often. He would have his chocolate in bed about eleven o'clock, arise later and have his regular breakfast.

When the Civil War broke out Lupita was sick with fever and her father wanted to take her south, but her mother refused, because the sympathies of the New Mexicans were with the North.

In her home Lupita was a regular princess. She was the only child and had [everything?] she desired. At noon the servants would come to dress her. Then she would come downstairs, roam thro'ugh the yard, or play with her toys, or go visiting with her parents.

She had an old tutor who taught her to read, write, and to work out problems in arithmetic. When she was ten years old she attended the Loretto Academy in Santa Fe. She had been there only seven months when a fever epidemic broke out, and her parents sent for her at once. She was taught to embroider, to play the piano, and only such things that would make a lady of her.

Lupita's mother, Maria Ignacia, was just a little girl when General Kearny came to Las Vegas to take possession of the territory. Maria Ignacia's father got up unusually early and went for a walk. Where the Normal University now stands he saw a many cannons all pointing toward the town. Immediately he rushed to town to spread the news. The town was in an uproar. Everyone, it seemed was screaming and crying. None wanted to become Americans; all wanted to remain under the Mexican flag.

Maria Ignacia's father refused at first to become an American. He left everything he owned and went to Mexico. All his land confiscated, his stock was killed to feed the troops, and only his house remained to him.

The family which Mr. Ulibarri had been the head of for so many happy years moved to San Migual. After a year Illario Gonzales, head of the family, came back to Las Vegas. He made friends with Kearny, regained some of his possessions and moved into his house where some of the troops had been lodged. [Gonzales?] sent to San Miguel for his family and when they arrived General Kearny, his wife and their six year old daughter moved in with them. The little girl was pretty, having fair hair and blue eyes. General Kearny's men were fed on the cows, sheep, and other stock belonging to Illario Gonzales.

Note:—Mrs. **Gallegos** has been too ill lately to talk very long at a time. Consequently, I have asked her granddaughter, Mary Elba C. De Baca, to get the remainder of the story of her life a little bit at a time and, in turn, tell it to me.

After living in Manuelitas where they had the store Grandmother and her husband moved to Los Alamos where they lived on a farm owned by her mother. After living there for about three months Grandfather came home one day looking very pleased with himself, "Guess what," he said, "I've bought [a?] saw mill at Manuelitas about five miles from where we lived before." And so Grandmother packed up and they moved back to Manuelitas.

Grandfather became resteless before long and went away. Grandmother was left alone with two Indian companions, Maria and Sabina. She says that they were forced to work very hard. They arose at four thirty every morning and prepared breakfast for the peons who worked at the saw mill and spent the rest if the day doing housework and other duties. She remembers and anold man, Juan Antonio, who was an idiot. He would sit{*End handwritten*} on her doorstep from early morning until late at night. This old man had a brother who was a very popular person and a smart politician and Juan Antonio would follow him everywhere on the days that he was not sitting on her [doorstep?]. {*Begin handwritten*}C 18 - N. Mex.{*End handwritten*}

Grandmother remembers also that the penitentes would pass by her house on their way to the morada, singing, singing all the way. There was no other road and she used to see them punish themselves as they passed by her house. At night she got a horrible [creepy?] feeling as they sang their sad melancholy songs.

At the end of three years Grandfather returned home from his roaming and they moved to San Ilario where they bought a large store. Grandfather went to Kansas and bought two tho'usand dollars worth of fine stock. Fine stuff that the poor laboring people of the community couldn't afford to buy. As a result the store was not very successful.

They lived at San Ilario for four years. Four years was a long time for Grandfather to live in any one place and his restless nature got the better of him. He wrote to Grandmother from [Carrizito?] to tell her that he had found a beautiful place he wanted to buy. He told her to pack everything and come. She did and there they lived in a little shack until their home was built. Carrizito was a beautiful place but the nearest neighbors lived six miles away. During the day Grandmother was left along with a little girl, the daughter of a neighbor. At night the owls would hoot and the little girl would say, "tho'se are witches."

Before long her husband tired of the new home and decided to move to El Pajarito. Here they built a lovely two story home. For three years she lived there while her husband continued to travel. She disliked El Pajarito very much. It was a hot desert land with not a single tree. Maria and Sabina joined her here and two days before Christmas she received a letter from her husband telling her to come to Las Vegas. He had bought a home there. On Christmas day they arrived at Las Vegas. Grandfather had bought a house on Grand Avenue and there they lived for three years. Again he was struck with the wanderlust and so they moved to Los Alamos to her father's place. They lived there for awhile and then they moved to San Ilario.

FOCUS QUESTIONS:

1. How did Gallegos' life change from her childhood home to her life with her husband?

2. What opportunities did Gallegos have? What restrictions did she live under?

3. What relationship exists between Gallegos and her husband?

11-5 Rosalie Cunningham to Governor John D. St. John (1870)

The following letter was written by Roseline Cunningham, who hoped to ease her move to Kansas by appealing to the governor of the state. Note the date of her letter, which comes just two years after federal troops were withdrawn from the South, ending Reconstruction. The parties mentioned by Cunningham had in this period roughly the opposite platforms compared to the modern Republicans and Democrats.

Source: Cunningham, Roseline. To Governor John D. St. John. Clay County, Mississippi. June 18, 1870. *We Are Your Sisters: Black Women in the 19th Century*, Dorothy Sterling, ed., New York: W. W. Norton, 1984, 373-374

Governor John D. St. John

Respected sir:

Clay County, Mississippi,

June 18, 1879

I write a few lines to you for information about our emigrating to your state next fall. We are hard working people but can not reap the benefit of our labor. I went to the State of Ohio in 1877 [and] found there is better living in a grain fruits and stock growing state than in a cotton growing one. Rev. Ephraim Strong my brother served in united states army three years during the war of 1861 and was honorable discharged at its close desired me to write to you for information. We wants to know if we can get any assistance from the government or any society to emigrate to Kansas. We have seen some papers from there and feel if we could get there we could make a better support. I have been teaching public schools in the districts ever since they began in Miss. in 18 7 1. When the republican laws rule the state I made right good support at it but since the democratic power has got in we can scarcely board and clothes ourselves. All the people in district I taught are wanting to emigrate to Kansas this fall if they can get assistance from any quarter. If I can get information from you that I can get in any business or a support and get assistance to get there my brother father and husband and I am coming. [A] great many desired me to Write to Kansas for information. I see in the Mo. Republican that you have a freedmen aid society thinking perhaps we could get assistance from it. Please answer our letter and let us know if you can aid us. By doing so you will [aid us] and a great many more and we will be grateful in our hearts. Your humble obedient and grateful

Servant

Roseline Cunningham

FOCUS QUESTIONS:

1. What triggered Cunningham's decision to emigrate?
2. In appealing to Governor St. John, what does Cunningham feel most qualifies her for his help?
3. For whom is Cunningham writing?

11-6 Polygamy in the Downfall of Nations (1904)

This is a newspaper cutting, preserved in a scrapbook collection in the Library of Congress. She was an active member of the Geneva (New York) Political Equality Club and published scientific works. The appeal reproduced below was read to the Club in 1904.

Source: Hemiup, Maria Remington. "Polygamy in the Downfall of Nations." 1904, http://hdl.loc.gov/loc.rbc/rbcmil.scrp1017401

Polygamy in the Downfall of Nations.

AN APPEAL TO CONGRESS, THE SENATE AND House of REPRESENTATIVES.

Gentlemen:—Your attention is earnestly called to the consideration of one of the most important questions ever submitted to a body of men.

A sect known as Mormons; a body antagonistic to the constitution of the United States, ask you to seat their representative in the Senate.

Can a greater insult be offered to free American womanhood? This entering wedge of Mormonism would disrupt a perfect union, thwart justice, uproot domestic tranquility, destroy every opportunity to promote general welfare or to secure liberty for ourselves or posterity.

A Mormon in the Senate is a step toward setting aside the constitution of the United States.

The progress of Mormonism in this country has come from man denying to woman her share of the protection guaranteed in the constitution.

Without free womanhood free manhood is doomed! This fact is thrillingly illustrated In woman's position all along the line of history in the rise and fall of nations. It is fitting, at this time to consider the position woman occupied in Egypt during its early history, when plurality of wives was unknown and Egypt's manhood had attained such nobleness, such renown. Woman had a voice in the government and in the home she was not last but first.

This was not a triumph of woman over man. It was not an ascendancy of woman over man. It was a noble manhood's gallantry and courtesy to woman.

Sulla, desirous of an alliance with Pompey the Great made him divorce his first wife that he might marry Amelia the step-daughter of Sulla, though he had to take her by force from her husband by whom she was pregnant. Amelia survived by a short time, dying in the house of Pompey the Great. Was it strange that woman in this position brought forth fiends of both sexes?

It was under this state of political corruption, and crushed womanhood that the cruel Nero was born: also the women of his court.

The blotting out of God's ordained freedom for women was echoed back in agony and groans. The smoke of martyrs rose up in testimony against man's treachery to women, from thence man's inhumanity to man.

The Power above is never slow to regulate the true balance. Not only in Greece and Rome do we see this; but in the rise and fall of every great nation we witness the same. When a nation sinks into polygamy it is irretrievably lost. Mahommet, at first, was very modest in his demands when compared with American Mormons. He was the servant of a wealthy widow whom he married. Mahommet said his wife was the first to believe in him as a prophet. When he was poor she made him rich. This was his excuse for not putting her away for his younger wives. It was with her consent he entered into polygamous marriages that he might produce his kind. If this woman could have seen the result of the slavery she was entailing on women yet unborn she would have paused ere yielding her influence and wealth to the false prophet.

The recent indignaties of the Sultan of Morocco are illustrative of the religion of polygamy.

MARIA REMINGTON HEMIUP.

Geneva, N.Y.

FOCUS QUESTIONS:

1. What does Hemiup see as the chief threat from allowing a Mormon to become a U.S. senator?

2. What are the social benefits of monogamy, according to Hemiup?

11-7 Zitkala-Sa Travels to the Land of the Big Red Apples (1884)

Zitkala-Sa had a varied career as a writer, teacher and activist. She was raised in the traditional lifestyle of the Sioux, but was educated at a Quaker mission school. She lived her life between two worlds, seemingly at home in neither. The following excerpt describes her experiences at school.

Source: Zitkala-Sa, *School Days of an Indian Girl*, Originally published in *The Atlantic Monthly*,Vol. 85, Issue 508, February, 1900,

THE CUTTING OF MY LONG HAIR.

The first day in the land of apples was a bitter-cold one; for the snow still covered the ground, and the trees were bare. A large bell rang for breakfast, its loud metallic voice crashing through the belfry overhead and into our sensitive ears. The annoying clatter of shoes on bare floors gave us no peace. The constant clash of harsh noises, with an undercurrent of many voices murmuring an unknown tongue, made a bedlam within which I was securely tied. And though my spirit tore itself in struggling for its lost freedom, all was useless.

A paleface woman, with white hair, came up after us. We were placed in a line of girls who were marching into the dining room. These were Indian girls, in stiff shoes and closely clinging dresses. The small girls wore sleeved aprons and shingled hair. As I walked noiselessly in my soft moccasins, I felt like sinking to the floor, for my blanket had been stripped from my shoulders. I looked hard at the Indian girls, who seemed not to care that they were even more immodestly dressed than I, in their tightly fitting clothes. While we marched in, the boys entered at an opposite door. I watched for the three young braves who came in our party. I spied them in the rear ranks, looking as uncomfortable as I felt.

A small bell was tapped, and each of the pupils drew a chair from under the table. Supposing this act meant they were to be seated, I pulled out mine and at once slipped into it from one side.

But when I turned my head, I saw that I was the only one seated, and all the rest at our table remained standing. Just as I began to rise, looking shyly around to see how chairs were to be used, a second bell was sounded. All were seated at last, and I had to crawl back into my chair again. I heard a mans voice at one end of the hail, and I looked around to see him. But all the others hung their heads over their plates. As I glanced at the long chain of tables, I caught the eyes of a pale-face woman upon me. Immediately I dropped my eyes, wondering why I was so keenly watched by the strange woman. The man ceased his mutterings, and then a third bell was tapped. Every one picked up his knife and fork and began eating. I began crying instead, for by this time I was afraid to venture anything more.

But this eating by formula was not the hardest trial in that first day. Late in the morning, my friend Judwin gave me a terrible warning. Judwin knew a few words of English; and she had overheard the paleface woman talk about cutting our long, heavy hair. Our mothers had taught us that only unskilled warriors who were captured had their hair shingled by the enemy. Among our people, short hair was worn by mourners, and shingled hair by cowards!

We discussed our fate some moments, and when Judwin said, We have to submit, because they are strong, I rebelled.

No, I will not submit! I will struggle first! I answered.

I watched my chance, and when no one noticed I disappeared. I crept up the stairs as quietly as I could in my squeaking shoes, my moccasins had been exchanged for shoes. Along the hall I passed, without knowing whither I was going. Turning aside to an open door, I found a large room with three white beds in it. The windows were covered with dark green curtains, which made the room very dim. Thankful that no one was there, I directed my steps toward the corner farthest from the door. On my hands and knees I crawled under the bed, and cuddled myself in the dark corner.

From my hiding place I peered out, shuddering with fear whenever I heard footsteps near by. Though in the hall loud voices were calling my name, and I knew that even Jud6win was searching for me, I did not open my mouth to answer. Then the steps were quickened and the voices became excited. The sounds came nearer and nearer. Women and girls entered the room. I held my breath, and watched them open closet doors and peep behind large trunks. Some one threw up the curtains, and the room was filled with sudden light. What caused them to stoop and look under the bed I do not know. I remember being dragged out, though I resisted by kicking and scratching wildly. In spite of myself, I was carried downstairs and tied fast in a chair.

I cried aloud, shaking my head all the while until I felt the cold blades of the scissors against my neck, and heard them gnaw off one of my thick braids. Then I lost my spirit. Since the day I was taken from my mother I had suffered extreme indignities. People had stared at me. I had been tossed about in the air like a wooden puppet. And now my long hair was shingled like a cowards! In my anguish I moaned for my mother, but no one came to comfort me. Not a soul reasoned quietly with me, as my own mother used to do; for now I was only one of many little animals driven by a herder.

****

INCURRING MY MOTHERS DISPLEASURE.

In the second journey to the East I had not come without some precautions. I had a secret interview with one of our best medicine men, and when I left his wigwam I carried securely in my sleeve a tiny bunch of magic roots. This j~os-session assured me of friends wherever I should go. So absolutely did I believe in its charms that I wore it through all the school routine for more than a year. Then, before I lost my faith in the dead roots, I lost the little buckskin bag containing all my good luck.

At the close of this second term of three years I was the proud owner of my first diploma. The following autumn I ventured upon a college career against my mothers will.

I had written for her approval, but in her reply I found no encouragement. She called my notice to her neighbors children, who had completed their education in three years. They had returned to their homes, and were then talking English with the frontier settlers. Her few words hinted that I had better give up my slow attempt to learn the white mans ways, and be content to roam over the prairies and find my living upon wild roots. I silenced her by deliberate disobedience-

Thus, homeless and heavy-hearted, I began anew my life among strangers. As I hid myself in my little room in the college dormitory, away from the scornful and yet curious eyes of the students, I pined for sympathy. Often I wept in secret, wishing I had gone West, to be nourished by my mothers love, instead of remaining among a cold race whose hearts were frozen hard with prejudice.

During the fall and winter seasons I scarcely had a real friend, though by that time several of my classmates were courteous to me at a safe distance.

My mother had not yet forgiven my rudeness to her, and I had no moment for letter-writing. By daylight and lamplight, I spun with reeds and thistles, until my hands were tired from their weaving, the magic design which promised me the white mans respect.

At length, in the spring term, I entered an oratorical contest among the various classes. As the day of competition approached, it did not seem possible that the event was so near at hand, but it came. In the chapel the classes assembled together, with their invited guests. The high platform was carpeted, and gayly festooned with college colors. A bright white light illumined the room, and outlined clearly the great polished beams that arched the domed ceiling. The assembled crowds filled the air with pulsating murmurs. When the hour for speaking arrived all were hushed. But on the wall the old clock which pointed out the trying moment ticked calmly on.

One after another I saw and heard the orators. Still, I could not realize that they longed for the favorable decision of the judges as much as I did. Each contestant received a loud burst of applause, and some were cheered heartily. Too soon my turn came, and I paused a moment behind the curtains for a deep breath. After my concluding words, I heard the same applause that the others had called out.

Upon my retreating steps, I was astounded to receive from my fellow students a large bouquet of roses tied with flowing ribbons. With the lovely flowers I fled from the stage. This friendly token was a rebuke to me for the hard feelings I had borne them.

Later, the decision of the judges awarded me the first place. Then there was a mad uproar in the hall, where my classmates sang and shouted my name at the top of their lungs; and the disappointed students howled and brayed in fearfully dissonant tin trumpets. In this excitement, happy students rushed forward to offer their congratulations. And I could not conceal a smile when they wished to escort me in a procession to the students parlor, where all were going to calm themselves. Thanking them for the kind spirit which prompted them to make such a proposition, I walked alone with the night to my own little room.

A few weeks afterward, I appeared as the college representative in another contest. This time the competition was among orators from different colleges in our state. It was held at the state capital, in one of the largest opera houses.

Here again was a strong prejudice against my people. In the evening, as the great audience filled the house, the student bodies began warring among themselves. Fortunately, I was spared witnessing any of the noisy wrangling before the contest began. The slurs against the Indian that stained the lips of our opponents were already burning like a dry fever within my breast.

But after the orations were delivered a deeper burn awaited me. There, before that vast ocean of eyes, some cob lege rowdies threw out a large white flag, with a drawing of a most forlorn Indian girl on it. Under this they had printed in bold black letters words that ridiculed the college which was represented by a squaw. Such worse than barbarian rudeness embittered me. While we waited for the verdict of the judges, I gleamed fiercely upon the throngs of palefaces. My teeth were hard set, as I saw the white flag still floating insolently in the air.

Then anxiously we watched the man carry toward the stage the envelope containing the final decision.

There were two prizes given, that night, and one of them was mine!

The evil spirit laughed within me when the white flag dropped out of sight, and the hands which furled it hung limp in defeat.

Leaving the crowd as quickly as possible, I was soon in my room. The rest of the night I sat in an arm-chair and gazed into the crackling fire. I laughed no more in triumph when thus alone. The little taste of victory did not satisfy a hunger in my heart. In my mind I saw my mother far away on the Western plains, and she was holding a charge against me.

Zitkala-Sa.

FOCUS QUESTIONS:

1. What did the cutting of her hair signify to Zitkala-Sa?

2. What two paths seem open to Zitkala-Sa, and what benefits does she expect from each?

3. What are some of the aspects of her life at school that are most difficult for the author?

NEW WOMEN

12-1 The New Womanhood

Winnifred Harper Cooley (1874-1967) wrote The New Womanhood in 1904. In it she examined new opportunities for women, the role of education, and argued for women's suffrage. In the following excerpt from her introduction, she emphasizes the importance of education, and the love of liberty which she feels characterizes the New Woman.

Source: Winnifred Harper Cooley, *The New Womanhood*, New York, Broadway Publishing Company, 1904.

THE EVOLUTION OF THE NEW WOMAN.

There is this fundamental difference between the development of man, and that of woman: he has developed through encouragement; she in spite of discouragement. All the forces of nature and society have tended to hurry him along the road of progress—all the powers have been invoked to keep her back! No one in the world ever ate tempted to define for man his place in the economy of the universe; the stronger half of humanity always has assigned a sphere to woman, and held her, by force of law, public opinion and social control, in this place. Scientifically, man has seen that unless he struggled and proved his right to live, he would be weeded out as "least fit" in the survival of the fittest. Woman, on the other hand, has bad the emphasis put upon *negation*, has been obliged to remain passive until chosen as a wife. Those who objected to the ruling order were not selected, and, therefore, left no descendants; thus, the premium being put upon passivity, and only those being wedded who evinced docility, the race perpetuated itself in negative, docile women.

This being the case, how did any woman ever create a new ideal, and dare to maintain the right to live the life of an individual, to be educated, to be economically independent, and to remain, if she desired, unwed? There was, fortunately, this saving race: an opportunity to inherit from the father as well as from the mother, and thus, bold, untrammeled spirits and brilliant minds sometimes found themselves in the bodies of girls; and so the new women have been evolved, and have left their imprint upon history.

Girls ever have been commanded to *be*; boys to *do*. To the boy we say, "What are you going to *do*, my little man; what great thing will you accomplish?" To the maid, "*Be* quiet, *be* good, be docile!" Some one has said that woman has been expected to keep pace with man, *with her children clinging to her garments!* This is one of those partial truths which allure us by their poesy. She has not been expected or permitted to keep pace with man, ah though in some instances she has aspired to. In the days when she did the spinning and Weaving, the cooking, the washing and ironing; when she bore and reared fifteen and eighteen children, she could not and did not keep pace with man, in civil and intellectual pursuits. But throughout the ages individual women have aspired to be something besides wives and mothers, a men universally are something besides husbands and fathers. These Beacon Lights of woman's history have faintly illumined 'the sea of darkness and defied the harem, unjust laws and every form of domestic tyranny.

The term "new woman" is luminous with meaning; yet it is a paradox; for the advanced woman, the woman who does things, who strives not only to be, but to act, is not *new*, but more numerous than ever before. She has appeared at intervals throughout all time, in the guise of an inspired warrior, a brilliant orator, or organizer, a Greek poetess, a scholar, or a queen.

The new woman is only the old woman with new opportunities! Women of the past were so limited by physical burdens and suppressed by public opinion that the wonder is there are so many beacon lights.

Some men have with delightful inconsistency, at one and the same time, assigned woman to her sphere of domestic drudgery and pointed in derision to the sad scarcity of women in the ranks of genius. "Where are your world-poets, artists, architects, musicians?" they demand. To a man who once asked the Rev. Anna Shaw what work of value women ever had produced, she retorted:

"Women have spent all their time for ages in *making men*; you may judge of the value of the production!"

Opportunity has much to do with the producing of geniuses. The few noted women recorded by history are not prodigies, or accidents, but those peculiarly situated so that they *could* act. We are not to suppose Joan of Arc the only maiden in whose breast the fire of patriotism slumbered. Charlotte Corday probably was one of many peasants who longed to free France by killing the insolent tyrant. We feel sure that many an incipient poet, too obedient and docile, or too overwhelmed with work to let her light shine, was a mute, inglorious Milton in petticoats, and went to her grave unwept, unhonored and unsung. Time was when the most fitting epitaph for the average wife was that of the bereaved farmer: "She was such a good woman to work!" Chance songsters, modest and timid, who sometimes had their verses collected by some old gentleman after their death, were but types of many housewives who saw Italian glory in the sunsets from their kitchen window, and felt a thrill at the yellow primrose by the river's brim, as they rinsed the clothes of the family washing; but whose songs perished on their lips.

The very docility of woman has been a vital factor in retarding her development. It is the unusual woman, the path-breaker, the fighter, if you please, who has met the eternal opposition of man (and the weak echo of many women) and martyred herself to overcome it. But there was this difference in the struggle: whereas man's persistence sprang from the motive of selfish appropriation of life's best, woman's was born of the legitimate desire for growth.

One other fact explains the fewness of women geniuses. Not only were they suppressed and forbidden expression, but their actual fruits were appropriated by their male relatives! The most shocking example of this, *known, is* that of the Mendelssohns Some of Felix Mendelssohn's finest compositions were the work of his sister Fanny. By contemporaries she was regarded as fine a piano performer as he, yet her music and fame have been absorbed in. his. He was educated under celebrated masters, was feted throughout Germany, patronized by the emperor, adored in England, while poor Fanny, with exactly the same God-given talents, had her compositions appropriated wholesale, and is not even mentioned in the cyclopedia!

Gradually, step by step, grudgingly, man has yielded what was never morally his to yield, but was originally won by brute force, and then held by laws of his own making. Woman never has struggled to supersede man, merely to occupy a place by his side in the world's work.

What are the gains that once were timid, half-suppressed sat longings of feminine pioneers, which were fought step by step, but now are accepted joyfully?

(1) Education—lower, higher, professional.

(2) Employment—industrial, commercial, (with financial returns for labor)

(3) Recognition—legal and civil.

Each of these has a long, pathetic history, as harrowing in detail as any of the world's battles. Every gain has been made at the sacrifice for the path-breakers of much that woman holds dear. Nothing is so precious to woman as reputation—the opinion of society; it almost precedes self esteem. She shrinks in terror from ridicule and disapprobation. Yet, these have been the portion of the new women who have sought to abolish the most flagrant abuses, even the existence of which the present century marvels at!

Too much stress cannot be laid upon the universal and democratic educating of women. The very elements of our ideal republic are involved in the raising of the level. The successful women are those that have learned co-operation while men are still in the throes of competition! Our new women are the result of new conditions, which they in turn are creating. Through the efforts of the pioneers, within a. century, girls have passed from no educational privileges to highest collegiate opportunities. In 1809, seven industries were open to women, (sewing, cooking, etc.); now three hundred and seventy-one offer employment. At that time, thirty-five women in the United States were working in factories; now, nearly four million are earning money. This shows the vast increase in industrial life, in the evolution of the new woman; and who shall say that the bright, self-supporting girl, who is not forced to marry to be supported, thus degrading marriage almost to prostitution, or the widow who supports her family, is not as fine a product of humanity as the helpless domestic woman of the past.

Who does not know the inestimable value of the woman physician? It is amazing that delicacy has been so deadened by years of custom as to admit of women patronizing men physicians when there is any opportunity of securing a woman doctor.

Why the desperate fight against the feminine minister, when woman (whether justly or not) has been extolled for ages as the moral and spiritual superior of man?

Time was when woman, although considered fit for nothing but the rearing of children, was not thought fitted for teaching them. Now, four-fifths of the teachers of the country are women.

The finest achievement of the new woman has been personal liberty. This is the foundation of civilization; and as Long as any one class is watched suspiciously, even fondly guarded, and protected, so long will that class not only be weak, and treacherous, individually, but parasitic, and a collective danger to the community. Who has not heard wives commended for wheedling their husbands out of money, or joked because they are hopelessly extravagant? As long as caprice and scheming are considered feminine virtues, as long as man is the only wage-canter, doling out sums of money, or scattering lavishly, long will women

be degraded, even if they are perfectly contented, and men are willing to labor to keep them in idleness!

Although *individual* women from pre-historic times have accomplished much, as a class they have been set aside to minister to men's come fort. But when once the higher has been tried, civilization repudiates the lowers Men have come to see that no advance can be made with one half- humanity set apart merely for the functions of sex; that children are quite liable to inherit from the mother, and should have opportunities to inherit the accumulated ability and culture and character that is produced only by intellectual and civil activity. The world has tried to move with men for dynamos, and "clinging" women impeding every step of progress, —in arts, science, industry, professions, they have been a thousand years behind men because forced into seclusion. They have been *over-sexed*. They have naturally not been impressed with their duties to society, in its myriad needs, or with their own value as individuals.

The new woman, in the sense of the best woman, the flower of all the womanhood of past ages, has come to stay—if civilization is to endure. The sufferings of the past have but strengthened her, maternity has deepened. her, education is broadening her—and she now knows that she must perfect herself if she would perfect the race, and leave her imprint upon immortality, through her offspring or her works.

FOCUS QUESTIONS:

1. Why does the author say "The new woman is only the old woman with new opportunities"?
2. According to Cooley, what are the chief gains made by women?
3. In what ways might Cooley consider the term "the new woman" historically inaccurate?

12-2 The Change in the Feminine Ideal

Margaret Deland (1857-1945) was a writer. Her views on the new woman contrast with those of Winnifred Harper Cooley. Deland worked against the achievement of suffrage for women. Note

Source: Margaret Deland "The Change in the Feminine Ideal", *Atlantic Monthly* 105 (March 1910): 287-291.

Of the *prevailing discontent among women* I shall speak very briefly, and I must not go into certain industrial and economic conditions which have forced stern and inevitable discontents upon us all; nor shall I refer to the discontents of foolish or second-rate minds — those vacant minds that are discontented unless they *dope* themselves with amusement — novel-reading, bridge-playing, theatre-going. It is women, with minds of this quality who have put their sex to shame in the last year or two by the wild vulgarity of their silly, and hideous, and selfish hats (these adjectives will, I think, be analysis); but happily such women are, generally too indolent or too ridiculous to do much harm to the community—their example being really a warning and their precepts too uninteresting be listened to. It is the discontents the woman of privilege, the woman of sane and sheltered life, which have real significance.

I am sometimes amused to have the response made by some mild-eyed, domestic creature, in her comfortable home, with her little children about her knees, "Why, I don't believe women are discontented. I'm not discontented!" and so ending the subject; for women must, it seems, always be personal. It is recorded that a husband, discussing tendency with his wife, said oracularly, "You women make everything personal." And the lady, aggrieved , r e sponded, "I don't. "Yeteven thi s satisfied and sheltered woman can hardly venture outside the warm and narrow circle of her own content, without hearing a shrill feminine chatter and clamor, a more or less petulant criticism of life as it is lived; a demand, — often intelligent but sometimes extremely silly and devoid of any economic basis, — a loud demand for the reconstruction of many things: government, business, the laws of property, the education of children. This contented woman (who has to be told by her husband whether she is a Re publican or a Democrat), whose property never troubles her because her dear and honest men-creatures take such affairs from her shoulders, whose children are admirably well and good, — even this happy and contented woman must know that all women are not so satisfied as she. Even while she thanks God that her girls are not as other mothers' girls, she is aware of her neighbor's daughter's discontent.

This young person — a wholesome, lovable creature with surprisingly bad manners—has gone to college, and when she graduates she is going to earn her own living. She declines to be dependant upon a father and mother amply able to support her. She will do settlement work; she won't go to church; she has views upon marriage and the birth-rate, and she utters them calmly, while her mother blushes with embarrassment she occupies herself, passionately, with everything except the things chat used to occupy the minds of girls. Restlessness! Restlessness! And as it is with the young woman, so it is with the, older woman. Countless Woman's Clubs, largely composed of middle-aged women, have sprung into eager existence in the last twenty years: they are admirable and helpful organizations, but they all express in one way another the restlessness of growth, a restlessness infinitely removed from the old content of a generation ago. The "club-woman," as she likes to call herself, has none of her mother's placid content with things as they are, any more than she has the pretty little accomplishments of her mother's youth, or her small conventional charities, or her sweet and gracious and dutiful living.

FOCUS QUESTIONS:

1. Compare the view of "contentment" in the first two excerpts. How do Cooley and Deland value women's contentment?

2. What are Deland's principle concerns about young women of her age?

3. Deland contrasts the "satisfied and sheltered woman" with the clamoring women outside her door. Which does Deland prefer?

12-3 Letter Discussing Women Ministers (1896)

The following excerpt was written from Susan B. Anthony to Adelaide Johnson (1859-1955). Johnson was an activist for women's rights, but above all a sculptor. She created the portrait monument depicting the great suffragists that sits in the Capitol Rotunda, given in the name of the National Woman's Party. The following letter concerns the latter's marriage earlier that year to Frederick Jensen by a woman minister. The letter also mentions the bust, and the individual portrait busts from which it was derived. The original busts had indeed served as "bridesmaids" at the marriage ceremony.

Source: Letter from Susan B. Anthony to Adelaide Johnson, <http://memory.loc.gov/mss/mcc/063/0001.jpg>

NATIONAL-AMERICAN
WOMAN SUFFRACE ASSOOIATION.
Honorary President:
ELIZABETH CADY STANTON, 26 West 61st
Street New York
OFFICE OF THE PRESIDENT

Rochester, N.Y., February 8, 1896

Mrs. Adelaide Johnson,

Washington, D.C.

By dear friend:

Your letter of the 6th come yesterday. The inclosed letter to the President of the Washington Theosophical Society from Mrs. Sumner proves her to be capable of making a most logical statement. You did not inclose the newspaper report of that gentleman's saying, but no matter. He showed himself exceedingly ignorant as to what constitutes 'legal' marriage. According to his saying, a Quaker marriage, which has neither priest nor magistrate to sanction it, must be illegal, ant yet nobody has ever questioned the morality of Quakers in their mode of marrying simply by the twain clasping hands and repeating their determination to be loyal husband and wife respectively. These marriages usually have the certificate witnessed by the friends present, and, as I said, nobody has ever called Quaker marriages Immoral. Then, certainly, your marriage with the 15 or 20 witnesses present and an authorized person performing the ceremony must be not only moral, out legal also. The man must be next doer to en idiot when be says a marriage ceremony performed by a woman is immoral. Of course neither you nor your good husband will mind all of this gossip. I am glad you were married by a woman, and I am glad that for the first time in the history of marriages of our woman's rights women, one man has at last been found to give up his own name cheerfully end accept that of the woman he married. At any rate, he and you have a perfect right to make your arrangements as to name, residence and mode of living to please yourselves, and I trust neither of you will have one moment's worry over what any sectarian, Theosophist or other, shall have to say about you.

I hope Mr. Cummings' bill will be carried through Congress. If you want testimony as to the faithful likeness of the bust, you can easily get the names of everybody who looked at it standing by the fountain in that great hail of the Woman's Building. I have never heard any one say that it was other than a good likeness of me. I do hope Congress can be induced to buy it, and it ought also to buy the busts of Mrs. Stanton and Mrs. Mott to pot into that great library, for those two women were the originators of the woman suffrage movement as an organized force in this country, and their busts ought to stand in some of the niches in that mammoth building, the taxes to build which have been wrung from the hard earnings of the women of this nation as well as from those of the men. If the bill gets into the hands of the committee, let me know at once and I will write to the librarlan, Mr. Spofford, telling him that I think the bust is not only a good likeness of me, but a most flattering one. Mr. Cummings is an old friend of mine, of thirty years ago, when be was on the New York Sun, and I don't know but he is a member of that staff still.

I sin very grateful for your letter, and also that you gave me an opportunity to see Mrs. Sumner's letter to Mr. Coffin.

Very affectionately,

Focus Questions:

1. What arguments does Anthony use in legitimizing Johnson's marriage? What traditions does she invoke?

2. What elements of Johnson's marriage were considered unusual?

12-4 Letter from Eliza Anna Grier to Susan B. Anthony (1890)

The history of Eliza Anna Grier (1864-1902) is sufficiently detailed in the following letters. She graduated from medical college in 1898. Susan B. Anthony was unable to help Grier, but forwarded her letter to the dean of the Woman's Medical College.

Source: Letter of Eliza Anna Grier to Susan B. Anthony, in *We Are Your Sisters: Black Women in the Nineteenth Century*, Dorothy Sterling, ed., New York: W. W. Norton, 1984, 446-447.

To The Proprietor of The Woman's Med. College, Philadelphia, Pa.
Dear Friend:
Fisk University, Nashville, Tennessee,
December 6, 1890

It is with some hesitation I attempt to write you. I am a Negro woman—a fair representative of my race. I have been attending this school for seven years and God willing I hope to complete the Advanced Normal Course of Study next June. I desire to be of the most possible benefit to my race and to my fellow creatures. I think I can accomplish more by having a Medical Education. Few of our colored girls have dared to enter the Medical Science I presume for several reasons. Viz: on account of timidity—on account of means whereby to pursue such a course. I have no money and no source from which to get it only as I work for every dollar. I desire a thorough Med. education and I desire to enter the school to which I write now or some other good school. What I want to know from you is this. How much does it take to put one through a year in your school. Is there any possible chance to do any work that would not interfere with one's studies. Do you know of any possible way that might be provided for an emancipated slave to receive any help into so lofty a profession. If you cannot do otherwise than give me a chance—a fair chance—I will begin with that.

Please let me bear from you at once or as soon as you have had time to think.
I am yours truly
Miss Eliza A. Grier

FOCUS QUESTIONS:

1. What appear to be the greatest challenges to Grier in obtaining her medical education?
2. Why do you think Grier chose to write to Susan B. Anthony for help?

12-5 Teaching School in Franklin, Virginia

Della Irving Hayden (1854-1924), graduated from teaching college in 1877. Her education was interrupted because she worked as a teacher for two years to earn her tuition (see Chapter 10.) The following excerpt describes the beginning of the school she founded, the Franklin Normal and Industrial Institute. "Normal" in this context simply indicates a teaching college.

Source: Letter of Della Irving Hayden, in *We Are Your Sisters: Black Women in the Nineteenth Century*, Dorothy Sterling, ed., New York: W. W. Norton, 1984, 379-380.

I rented a little room 15 by 20 feet, bought two dozen chairs, gota blackboard, stove, table and broom. I had twenty-one students the first month. We had five acres of land donated to us by Mrs. Marriage Allen of London, England. I taught school in the week and went on Sundays and begged money at the churches, so we were finally able to put up a building with four classrooms that cost about $1,000.

The first year I was alone, but now I have three teachers besides myself. In addition to this building we have a dormitory for the girls, with 22 rooms, costing $6,000. We borrowed the money for ten years, and we still owe $3,800 of it. Eight hundred fifty students have at-tended this school and 4o have graduated. Some are teaching, others are in business, and several have gone to other schools.

FOCUS QUESTIONS:

1. How was Hayden's school funded?
2. What was the role of schools such as the one founded by Hayden?

12-6 Report on Social Economics

What follows is an excerpt from the Social Affairs Committee of the Boston Women's Educational and Industrial Union. It give an insight into the kinds of work undertaken by such organizations.

Source: Melissa Chamberlin "Report of Social Affairs Committee" *Report of the Women's Educational and Industrial Union, for the Year Ending May 7, 1879,.* Boston: 1879, 16-26 (http://pds.lib.harvard.edu/pds/view/2577566)

Report of the Women's Educational and Industrial Union for the Year Ending May 7, 1789

Report of Social Affairs Committee.

This Committee consists of five members, who have met every Monday afternoon to receive the Reports of its Sub- Committees, including Reception, Reading Room, Library, Entertainment, Lecture and Class, Agency of Direction and Protective Work, appointing new members and filling vacancies when required, submitting its work each month to the action of the Board. The Reading has been in charge of a Reception Committee, of seventeen members, who have served three hours a day each, thus dividing the time through the week. The duties of this Committee are to receive strangers, explain the work, take membership fees, and attend to such matters as properly come under their supervision. One member has regularly taken the hours from the close of the morning services upon Sunday until the commencement of the afternoon meetings, that women from out of town might have the privilege of resting in the rooms. The Union has reason to be thankful to these ladies for the interest they have shown, and the faithful manner in which they have discharged their offices. The report of the Chairman, Miss Caroline P. Pierce, gives an average daily attendance of ten who come to rest and enjoy the advantages of the Room.

During the winter the means of the society were so limited, it accepted the services of an attendant, who kindly volunteered to take care of the rooms and serve during the hours the Committee were not present. Upon her resignation it was decided that in the future, this was not advisable, as the position was one of much responsibility, and should command an ample salary, which it is hoped the Union will be able to pay the coming year.

The Reading-Room has been supplied with four monthly magazines, seven weekly and three daily papers, all presented by the publishers. For these the Committee would express their thanks, as well as for stationery, several articles of furniture, and four pictures, all of which have much to the comfort and attractions of the rooms. The Library has only been in use for the Reading-Room. It is still small, as it has been obliged to depend entirely upon the contributions of friends. The Chairman, Miss McLean, reports seventy-seven volumes added this year, gifts from Lee & Shepard, Estes & Lauriat, Mrs. Maria L. Porter, and others, making a total of one hundred and ninety-three volumes. Social gatherings under the charge of the Committee of Entertainments, have been held nearly every Wednesday evening since November 13th. These have been varied by music, vocal and instrumental, and recitations, besides " the fact giving " "William Henry Letters," which have formed not the least agreeable features. These gatherings have been free to members, each ticket holder having the privilege of inviting a friend. This Committee has given an exhibition of the Phonograph, two Concerts, a Costume-Party, and an Entertainment at Wesleyan Hall. The proceeds from these, besides paying expenses, including a the rent of a piano for six months, have brought to the Treasury $85.90.

All the Entertainments have been contributed by friends interested in the work. to whom the Union would here take occasion to return its grateful acknowledgement.

The Lecture and Class Committee reports a series of talks upon Astronomy by Mr. Geo. P. Bradford, a Lecture upon "Goethe " by Mr. Arnold Zueligg, another upon "Life in the South" by Mr. Thos. Morang, and a Talk upon "Growth in Italian Art" by Miss Harriet S. Tolman. A course of evening lectures was proposed, conducted upon the plan of the Sunday Meetings, to be open to ladies and gentlemen, but was abandoned for want of time. It is hoped that another winter will see it in successful operation. This Committee has done much service in distributing circulars throughout the shops and places where women are employed, besides securing the free insertions of the advertisements of the work in many papers both in and out of the city. The Classes have all been in a flourishing condition.

The English Grammar Class, with Miss Dudley as teacher, has had sixteen pupils, and been regularly attended, the members keeping up their interest to the last. The class in Political Economy, with Dr. C. E. Hastings as Chairman, has had an average attendance of twenty-five. In Feburary, its members resolved themselves into a Debating Club, which has continued with out any decrease through the whole season.

Miss Wilson has had three Classes in French, in all numbering twenty-six pupils. Madame Büttner in German has taught every Wednesday and Saturday afternoon, her numbers varying from twelve to fifteen. In Italian, Miss Langa has had but six pupils, as she began late in the season. These Classes have been free to members when teachers volunteered their services, and in French, German and Italian, they have been offered at a much lower rate than the ordinary terms for teaching. The Union has a per cent. of all money taken for teaching, and has received this year, after defraying contingent expenses, $44.80.

The Agency of Direction has not made as much progress as other Committees, as the first appointed Chairman found herself unable to attend to the work, and was obliged to resign. Later in the season, Mrs. Lousia A. Morrison took the chair. This Committee has collected much valuable information, which is being compiled, and will be ready for reference during the summer. A list of summer boarding places, where board can be obtained at reasonable rates, can be seen in the rooms.

The only work of Practical Philanthropy yet attempted is the Department of Protection to Women, which will be given in a separate report.

M. CHAMBERLIN, Chairman.

FOCUS QUESTIONS:

1. What kinds of work did these women undertake, and what services did they provide.
2. What kinds of services seem to have been most in demand by the women using these facilities?

12-7 Part of the Working Class

Rose Pastor Stokes (1879-1933) was born in Russia. She and her family emigrated in 1881, and moved to Cleveland in 1891. She became very active in the Socialist Party, and later the Communist Party. Her autobiography was cut short by her death. The following excerpt describes her first job at a cigar factory.

Source: Rose Pastor Stokes, Herbert Shapiro, David L. Sterling, I *Belong to the Working Class: The Unfinished Autobiography of Rose Pastor Stokes*, University of Georgia Press, 1992, 38-

Two days later Jennie, a tall dark raw-boned girl of thirteen, started out for the job in the cigar factory, and I went with her.

As we were leaving Jennie's kitchen in the cold and the dark, my mother kissed me, and my stepfather patted my head and gave mea dime.

They both laughed with forced gaiety:

"Look! Our little breadwinner," my mother chuckled, through tears. And my stepfather too, with a catch in his voice: "Our Rosalie, already a working woman!"

****

We start out at dawn to be there before others fill the places.

The air is sharp with early frost. My thin jacket is like a sieve against the wind. I hold it tightly—with both hands to my chest and throat—as if the clutch of my hands could protect me.

Jennie too must be cold. She shivers.

"Come on, we must hurry!" She grips me by the hand. She is taller than I, and takes longer strides. Every few steps, I run to keep up with her.

The long way seems endless. Down the muddy unpaved street at right angles to Liberal Street. A turn to the right, then to the left down Orange Street. Down Broadway, on to the end of Ontario Street. Across the Public Square, dodging a confusing network of street-cars. Then left, for several blocks to the viaduct, and down—steeply, to a street under it. We've walked miles and miles, it seems.

Near the end of this street Jennie finds the number she has on a slip of paper. We enter the big loft building, our hearts pounding. We hold hands and climb two flights of stairs.

There are two doors: Maybe it's this one. Timidly, we push open a heavy metal door. The suffocating effluvium of tobacco dust strikes us in the face.

I want to run away from the unexpected offense. But I stand still beside Jennie, and continue to hold her hand.

There are many workers here—at work—benches all of new wood. A row each, facing the two long walls of the narrow left; in the middle, two rows facing each other built as of one piece. The bodies of the workers move in short sharp rhythm as the hands roll dark brown sticks on a board, or cut dark brown leaves into patterned pieces, or chop the ends off the sticks with a small cutting-tool.

A man comes out of a newly-partitioned office near the door. A very comfortable-looking man. I have never before been talked-to by anyone so comfortable-looking—not even Mr. Cohen of the Princess Theatre.

"I'm Mr. Wertheim," he says. "Do you want work?"

"Yes, please."

Turning to Jennie: "How old are you?"

"Fourteen," and Jennie gets very red in the face.

"A fine big girl for fourteen," Mr. Wertheim says, placing a hand on her broad, square shoulders.

"And you?"

"Eleven." "You're tall for your age, but—" he trails off.

Does he mean not to give me work? My heart beats! And something pounds in my throat and tightens it.

"What do you say to going right to work?"

He is including us both in his look! The blood that was pounding through my heart and clutching at my throat goes to my head.

We nod our yes, and at the same moment I think of the two troubled voices from the kitchen, and go dizzy with joy in the thought of being able to help.

"Oh, Jake, two more new ones," he calls to a large heavy-featured man.

The man leaves a bench where he is teaching a young worker, and comes to the door.

"The foreman," Mr. Wertheim explains. "He'll teach you stogie-rolling."

As we go with the foreman, Mr. Wertheim offers tersely:

"Two weeks to learn. After that half-pay for six weeks, then full pay. All right?"

Had he announced six months without pay we would have nodded our heads just the same. At the end of the third week I get three silver quarters and two copper pennies—my first week's pay.

I run home with the treasure.

My mother takes it from me, looks long at the coins in the open palm of her hand, and with a bitter cry throws them on the table.

"The blood of a child! Look," she says, "look what it will bring!"

On a Friday morning, Mr. Wertheim came and stood behind my chair.

"Rose Pastor, how would you like to go home today, and help your mother? I'll bet she needs you.

I'm sure she works very hard. You can come back Monday morning, and it will be all right.

"Who would have thought a boss could be so kind! I thanked him and hurried home, glad to be of help to my mother.

She always had a burden of work to do, especially on Fridays. I scrubbed the kitchen floor, and ran errands to the grocer's, and filled the oil lamps, and brought up coal, and washed the baby's things down by the yard pump; and all the time I did my chores, I overflowed with gratitude toward the boss who spoke so feelingly of my poor overburdened mother.

On Monday morning, when I came to my work-bench, I said to the girl on my right

"Wasn't Mr. Wertheim kind?"

"Kind?" The girl on my right chuckled, "It's a good thing you were sent home Friday morning.

The factory inspector came in the afternoon. Some of the young ones can sit on two extra blocks, and look over fourteen. But not you."

Jennie too never told me till Monday:

"Oh, I passed. I look old. Mr. Wertheim didn't

want to lose you, I guess, so he sent you home."

"Lose me?" I asked.

"Yeah!" said the girl on my right, "Lose ye, is what she said. The younger and quicker ye are, the more money the boss makes on ye—see?"

FOCUS QUESTIONS:

1. What are Stokes' feelings on having work?

2. Does the term "new woman" apply to Stokes? Compare Stokes' experience with the description of the new woman by Winnifred Harper Cooley.

THE WOMAN MOVEMENT, 1880–1900

13-1 American Methodist Episcopal Church Review (1902)

The following is from the 'Women's Department", a regular feature of the American Methodist Episcopal Church Review. The author reports back from the biennial meeting of the General Federation of Women's Clubs (GFWC) in Los Angeles, earlier in 1902.

Source: "The Colored Woman and the Woman's Clubs", *The A.M.E. Church Review*, Vol. 91, No.1, July, 1902, 469-470 (http://dbs.ohiohistory.org/africanam/page.cfm?ID=2278)

The colored woman of to-day occupies, one may say, a unique position in this country. In a period of itself transitional and unsettled, her status seems one of the least ascertainable and definitive of all the forces which make for our civilization. She is confronted by both a woman question and a race problem, and is as yet an unknown or an unacknowledged factor in both. While the women of the white race can with calm assurance enter upon the work they feel by nature appointed to do, while their men give loyal support and appreciative countenance to their efforts, recognizing in most avenues of usefulness the propriety and the need of woman's distinctive co-operation, the colored woman too often finds herself hampered and shamed by a less liberal sentiment and a more conservative attitude on the part of those for whose opinion she cares most. That this is not universally true I am glad to admit. There are to be found both intensely conservative white men and exceedingly liberal colored men. But as far as my experience goes the average man of our race is less frequently ready to admit the actual need among the sturdier forces of the world for woman's help or influence. That great social and economic questions await her interference, that she could throw any light on problems of national import, that her intermeddling could improve the management of school systems, or elevate the tone of public institu-

tions, or humanize and sanctify the far reaching influence of prisons and reformatories and improve the treatment of lunatics and imbeciles,—that she has a word worth hearing on mooted questions in political economy, that she could contribute a suggestion on the relations of labor and capital, or offer a thought on honest money and honorable trade, I fear the majority of "Americans of the colored variety" are not yet prepared to concede. It may be that they do not yet see these questions in their right perspective, being absorbed in the immediate needs of their own political complications. A good deal depends on where we put the emphasis in this world; and our men are not perhaps to blame if they see everything colored by the light of those agitations in the midst of which they live and move and have their being. The part they have had to play in American history during the last twenty-five or thirty years has tended rather to exaggerate the importance of mere political advantage, as well as to set a fictitious valuation on those able to secure such advantage. It is the astute politician, the manager who can gain preferment for himself and his favorites, the demagogue known to stand in with the powers at the White House and consulted on the bestowal of government plums, whom we set in high places and denominate great. It is they who receive the hosannas of the multitude and are regarded as leaders of the people. The thinker and the doer, the man who solves the problem by enriching his country with an invention worth thousands or by a thought inestimable and precious is given neither bread nor a stone. He is too often left to die in obscurity and neglect even if spared in his life the bitterness of fanatical jealousies and detraction.

And yet politics, and surely American politics, is hardly a school for great minds. Sharpening rather than deepening, it develops the faculty of taking advantage of present emergencies rather than the insight to distinguish between the true and the false, the lasting and the ephemeral advantage. Highly cultivated selfishness rather than consecrated benevolence is its passport to success. Its votaries are never seers. At best they are but manipulators—often only jugglers. It is conducive neither to profound statesmanship nor to the higher type of manhood. Altruism is its *mauvais succes* and naturally enough it is indifferent to any factor which cannot be worked into its own immediate aims and purposes. As woman's influence as a political element is as yet nil in most of the commonwealths of our republic, it is not surprising that with those who place the emphasis on mere political capital she may yet seem almost a nonentity so far as it concerns the solution of great national or even racial perplexities.

There are those, however, who value the calm elevation of the thoughtful spectator who stands aloof from the heated scramble; and, above the turmoil and din of corruption and selfishness, can listen to the teachings of eternal truth and righteousness. There are even those who feel that the black man's unjust and unlawful exclusion temporarily from participation in the elective franchise in certain states is after all but a lesson "in the desert" fitted to develop in him insight and discrimination against the day of his own appointed tune. One needs occasionally to stand aside from the hum and rush of human interests and passions to hear the voices of God. And it not unfrequently happens that the All-loving gives a great push to certain souls to thrust them out, as it were, from the distracting current for awhile to promote their discipline and growth, or to enrich them by communion and reflection. And similarly it may be woman's privilege from her peculiar coigne of vantage as a quiet observer, to whisper just the needed suggestion or the almost for-

gotten truth. The colored woman, then, should not be ignored because her bark is resting in the silent waters of the sheltered cove. She is watching the movements of the contestants none the less and is all the better qualified, perhaps, to weigh and judge and advise because not herself in the excitement of the race. Her voice, too, has always been heard in dear unfaltering tones, ringing the changes on those deeper interests which make for permanent good. She is always sound and orthodox on questions affecting the well-being of her race. You do not find the colored woman selling her birthright for a mess of pottage. Nay, even after reason has retired from the contest, she has been known to cling blindly with the instinct of a turtle dove to those principles and policies which to her mind promise hope and safety for children yet unborn. It is notorious that ignorant black women in the South have actually left their husbands' homes and repudiated their support for what was understood by the wife to be race disloyalty or "voting away," as she expresses it, the privileges of herself and little ones.

FOCUS QUESTIONS:

1. How did the GFWC's decision keep black women from being involved at the national level?

2. What do you think prompted the GFWC's decision to leave the decision on race to the state Federations?

3. According to the author, what is the attitude of black women towards the GFWC's policy?

13-2 Anna Julia Cooper, From A Voice from the South: By a Black Woman of the South (1892)

Born in Raleigh, North Carolina, Anna Julia Cooper was the daughter of a slave. Anna was educated at St. Augumne Normal School and Collegiate Institute, and in 1877 she married one of her teachers, George A. C. Cooper. By 1881, Cooper (a widow since her husband's death in 1879) was attending Oberlin College in Ohio. Earning a degree in 1884, she accepted a position in Ohio at Wilberforce University, but she stayed only a year, leaving to take a position at St. Augustine. After being awarded an MA from Oberlin College, she relocated to Washington, D.C., to teach at M Street School, where she served as principal from 1901 to 1906. Her speeches and essays were collected in A Voice from the South: By a Black Woman of the South (1892). She advocated civil

rights, women's rights, suffrage for women, and an American literature that would be more inclusive and would render respectful images of African Americans. Believing in the importance of education for black Americans, she became one of the first African American women to receive a Ph.D. when she earned a doctorate from the Sorbonne at age 65. Cooper gave a voice to the disenfranchised black women of the nineteenth century while anticipating the feminist movement of the twentieth century.

Source: A Voice From the South, Anna Julia Cooper. Xenia, Ohio: The Aldine Printing House, 1892.

The Status of Woman in America

Just four hundred years ago an obscure dreamer and castle builder, prosaically poor and ridiculously insistent on the reality of his dreams, was enabled through the devotion of a noble woman to give to civilization a magnificent continent.

What the lofty purpose of Spain's pure-minded queen had brought to the birth, the untiring devotion of pioneer women nourished and developed. The dangers of wild beasts and of wilder men, the mysteries of unknown wastes and unexplored forests, the horrors of pestilence and famine, of exposure and loneliness, during all those years of discovery and settlement, were braved without a murmur by women who had been most delicately constituted and most tenderly nurtured.

And when the times of physical hardship and danger were past, when the work of clearing and opening up was over and the struggle for accumulation began, again woman's inspiration and help were needed and still was she loyally at hand. A Mary Lyon, demanding and making possible equal advantages of education for women as for men, and, in the face of discouragement and incredulity, bequeathing to women the opportunities of Holyoke.

A Dorothea Dix, insisting on the humane and rational treatment of the insane and bringing about a reform in the lunatic asylums of the country, making a great step forward in the tender regard for the weak by the strong throughout the world.

A Helen Hunt Jackson, convicting the nation of a century of dishonor in regard to the Indian.

A Lucretia Mott, gentle Quaker spirit, with sweet insistence, preaching the abolition of slavery and the institution, in its stead, of the brotherhood of man; her life and words breathing out in tender melody the injunction

Have love. Not love alone for one

But man as man thy brother call;

And scatter, like the circling sun,

Thy charities on all.

And at the most trying time of what we have called the Accumulative Period, when internecine war, originated through man's love of gain and his determination to subordinate national interests and black men's rights alike to considerations of personal profit and loss, was drenching our country with its own best blood, who shall recount the name and fame of the women on both sides the senseless strife,—those uncomplaining souls with a great heart ache of their own, rigid features and pallid cheek their ever effective flag of truce, on the battle field, in the camp, in the hospital, binding up wounds, recording dying whispers for absent loved ones, with tearful eyes pointing to man's last refuge, giving the last earthly hand clasp and performing the last friendly office for strangers whom a great common sorrow had made kin, while they knew that somewhere—somewhere a husband, a brother, a father, a son, was being tended by stranger hands—or mayhap those familiar eyes were even then being closed forever by just such another ministering angel of mercy and love.

But why mention names? Time would fail to tell of the noble army of women who shine like beacon lights in the otherwise sordid wilderness of this accumulative period—prison reformers and tenement cleansers, quiet unnoted workers in hospitals and homes, among imbeciles, among outcasts—the sweetening, purifying antidotes for the poisons of man's acquisitiveness,—mollifying and soothing with the tenderness of compassion and love the wounds and bruises caused by his overreaching and avarice.

The desire for quick returns and large profits tempts capital ofttimes into unsanitary; well nigh inhuman investments,—tenement tinder boxes, stilling, stunting, sickening alleys and pestiferous slums; regular rents, no waiting, large percentages,—rich coffers coined out of the life-blood of human bodies and souls. Men and women herded together like cattle, breathing in malaria and typhus from an atmosphere seething with moral as well as physical impurity; reveling in vice as their native habitat and then, to drown the whisperings of their higher consciousness and effectually to hush the yearnings and accusations within, flying to narcotics and opiates—rum, tobacco, opium, binding hand and foot, body and soul, till the proper image of God is transformed into a fit associate for demons,—a besotted, enervated, idiotic wreck, or else a monster of wickedness terrible and destructive.

These are some of the legitimate products of the unmitigated tendencies of the wealth-producing period. But, thank Heaven, side by side with the cold, mathematical, selfishly calculating, so-called practical and unsentimental instinct of the business man, there comes the sympathetic warmth and sunshine of good women, like the sweet and sweetening breezes of spring, cleansing, purifying, soothing, inspiring, lifting the drunkard from the gutter, the, outcast from the pit. Who can estimate the influence of these "daughters of the king," these lend-a-hand forces, in counteracting the selfishness of an acquisitive age?

To-day America counts her millionaires by the thousand; questions of tariff and questions of currency are the most vital ones agitating the public mind. In this period, when material prosperity and well earned ease and luxury are assured facts from a national standpoint, woman's work and woman's influence are needed as never before; needed to bring a heart power into this money getting, dollar-worshipping civilization; needed to bring a moral force into the utilitarian motives and interests of the time; needed to stand for God and Home and Native Land versus gain and greed and grasping selfishness.

There can be no doubt that this fourth centenary of America's discovery which we celebrate at Chicago, strikes the keynote of another important transition in the history of this nation; and the prominence of woman in the management of its celebration is a fitting tribute to the part she is destined to play among the forces of the future. This is the first congressional recognition of woman in this country, and this Board of Lady Managers constitute the first women legally appointed by any government to act in a national capacity. This of itself marks the dawn of a new day.

Now the periods of discovery, of settlement, of developing resources and accumulating wealth have passed in rapid succession. Wealth in the nation as in the individual brings leisure, repose, reflection. The struggle with nature is over, the struggle with ideas begins. 'We stand then, it seems to me, in this last decade of the nineteenth century, just in the portals of a new and untried movement on a higher plain and in a grander strain than any the past has called forth. It does not require a prophet's eye to divine its trend and image its possibilities from the forces we see already at work around us; nor is it hard to guess what must be the status of woman's work under the new regime.

In the pioneer days her role was that of a camp-follower, an additional something to fight for and be burdened with, only repaying the anxiety and labor she called forth by her own incomparable gifts of sympathy and appreciative love; unable herself ordinarily to contend with the bear and the Indian, or to take active part in clearing the wilderness and constructing the home.

In the second or wealth producing period her work is abreast of man's, complementing and supplementing, counteracting excessive tendencies, and mollifying over rigorous proclivities.

In the era now about to dawn, her sentiments must strike the keynote and give the dominant tone.

And this because of the nature of her contribution to the world.

Her kingdom is not over physical forces. Not by might, nor by power can she prevail. Her position must ever be inferior where strength of muscle creates leadership. If she follows the instincts of her nature, however, she must always stand for the conservation of those deeper moral forces which make for the happiness of homes and the righteousness of the country. In a reign of moral ideas she is easily queen.

There is to my mind no grander and surer prophecy of the new era and of woman's place in it, than the work already begun in the waning years of the nineteenth century by the America, an organization which has even now reached not only national but international importance, and seems destined to permeate and purify the whole civilized world. It is the living embodiment of woman's activities and woman's ideas, and its extent and strength rightly prefigure her increasing power as a moral factor.

The colored woman of to-day occupies, one may say, a unique position in this country. In a period of itself transitional and unsettled, her status seems one of the least ascertainable and definitive of all the forces which make for our civilization. She is confronted by both a woman question and a race problem, and is as yet an unknown or an unacknowledged factor in both. While the women of the white race can with calm assurance enter upon the work they feel by nature appointed to do, while their men give loyal support and appreciative countenance to their efforts, recognizing in most avenues of usefulness the propriety and the need of woman's distinctive co-operation, the colored woman too often finds herself hampered and shamed by a less liberal sentiment and a more conservative attitude on the part of those for whose opinion she cares most. That this is not universally true I am glad to admit. There are to be found both intensely conservative white men and exceedingly liberal colored men. But as far as my experience goes the average man of our race is less frequently ready to admit the actual need among the sturdier forces of the world for woman's help or influence. That great social and economic questions await her interference, that she could throw any light on problems of national import, that her intermeddling could improve the management of school systems, or elevate the tone of public institutions, or humanize and sanctify the far reaching influence of prisons and reformatories and improve the treatment of lunatics and imbeciles,—that she has a word worth hearing on mooted questions in political economy, that she could contribute a suggestion on the relations of labor and capital, or offer a thought on honest money and hon¬orable trade, I fear the majority of "Americans of the colored variety" are not yet prepared to concede. It may be that they do not yet see these questions in their right perspective, being absorbed in the immediate needs of their own political complications. A good deal depends on where we put the emphasis in this world; and our men are not perhaps to blame if they see everything colored by the light of those agitations in the midst of which they live and move and have their being. The part they have had to play in American history during the last twenty-five or thirty years has tended rather to exaggerate the importance of mere political advantage, as well as to set a fictitious valuation on those able to secure such advantage. It is the astute politician, the manager who can gain preferment for himself and his favorites, the demagogue known to stand in with the powers at the White House and consulted on the bestowal of government plums, whom we set in high places and denominate great. It is they who receive the hosannas of the multitude and are regarded as leaders of the people. The thinker and the doer, the man who solves the problem by enriching his country with an invention worth thousands or by a thought inestimable and precious is given neither bread nor a stone. He is too often left to die in obscurity and neglect even if spared in his life the bitterness of fanatical jealousies and detraction.

And yet politics, and surely American politics, is hardly a school for great minds. Sharpening rather than deepening, it develops the faculty of taking advantage of present emergencies rather than the insight to distinguish between the true and the false, the lasting and the ephemeral advantage. Highly cultivated self¬ishness rather than consecrated benevolence is its passport to success. Its votaries are never seers. At best they are but manipulators—often only jugglers. It is con¬ducive neither to profound statesmanship nor to the higher type of manhood. Altruism is its *mauvais succes* and naturally enough it is indifferent to any factor which cannot be worked into its own immediate aims and purposes. As woman's influence as a political element is as yet nil in most of the commonwealths of our republic, it is not surprising that with those who place the emphasis on mere political capital she may yet seem almost a nonentity so far as it concerns the solution of great national or even racial perplexities.

There are those, however, who value the cairn elevation of the thoughtful spectator who stands aloof from the heated scramble; and, above the turmoil and

din of corruption and selfishness, can listen to the teachings of eternal truth and righteousness. There are even those who feel that the black man's unjust and unlawful exclusion temporarily from participation in the elective franchise in certain states is after all but a lesson "in the desert" fitted to develop in him insight and discrimination against the day of his own appointed tune. One needs occasionally to stand aside from the hum and rush of human interests and passions to hear the voices of God. And it not unfrequently happens that the All-loving gives a great push to certain souls to thrust them out, as it were, from the distracting current for awhile to promote their discipline and growth, or to enrich them by communion and reflection. And similarly it may be woman's privilege from her peculiar coigne of vantage as a quiet observer, to whisper just the needed suggestion or the almost forgotten truth. The colored woman, then, should not be ignored because her bark is resting in the silent waters of the sheltered cove. She is watching the movements of the contestants none the less and is all the better qualified, perhaps, to weigh and judge and advise because not herself in the excitement of the race. Her voice, too, has always been heard in dear unfaltering tones, ringing the changes on those deeper interests which make for permanent good. She is always sound and orthodox on questions affecting the well-being of her race. You do not find the colored woman selling her birthright for a mess of pottage. Nay, even after reason has retired from the contest, she has been known to ding blindly with the instinct of a turtle dove to those principles and policies which to her mind promise hope and safety for children yet unborn. It is notorious that ignorant black women in the South have actually left their husbands' homes and repudiated their support for what was understood by the wife to be race disloyalty or "voting away," as she expresses it, the privileges of herself and little ones.

It is largely our women in the South today who keep the black men solid in the Republican party. The latter as they increase in intelligence and power of discrimination would be more apt to divide on local issues at any rate. They begin to see that the Grand Old Party regards the Negro's cause as an outgrown issue, and on Southern soil at least finds a too intimate acquaintanceship with him a somewhat unsavory recommendation. Then, too, their political wits have been sharpened to appreciate the fact that it is good policy to cultivate one's neighbors and not depend too much on a distant friend to fight one's home battles. But the black woman can never forget—however lukewarm the party may to-day appear—that it was a Republican president who struck the manacles from her own wrists and gave the possibilities of manhood to her helpless little ones; and to her mind a Democratic Negro is a traitor and a time-server. Talk as much as you like of venality and manipulation in the South, there are not many men, I can tell you, who would dare face a wife quivering in every fiber with the consciousness that her husband is a coward who could be paid to desert her deepest and dearest interests.

Not unfelt, then, if unproclaimed has been the work and influence of the colored women of America. Our list of chieftains in the service, though not long, is not inferior in strength and excellence, I dare believe, to any similar list which this country can produce.

Among the pioneers, Frances Watkins Harper could sing with prophetic exaltation in the darkest days, when as yet there was not a rift in the clouds overhanging her people:

Yes, Ethiopia shall stretch

Her bleeding hands abroad;

Her cry of agony shall reach the burning throne of God.

Redeemed from dust and freed from chains

Her sons shall lift their eyes,

From cloud-capt hills and verdant plains

Shall shouts of triumph rise.

Among preachers of righteousness, an unanswerable silencer of cavilers and objectors, was Sojourner Truth, that unique and rugged genius who seemed carved out without hand or chisel from the solid mountain mass; and in pleasing contrast, Amanda Smith, sweetest of natural singers and pleaders in dulcet tones for the things of God and of His Christ.

Sarah Woodson Early and Martha Briggs, planting and watering in the school room, and giving off from their matchless and irresistible personality an impetus and inspiration which can never die so long as there lives and breathes a remote descendant of their disciples and friends.

Charlotte Forten Grimke, the gentle spirit whose verses and life link her so beautifully with Americas great Quaker poet and loving reformer.

Hallie Quinn Brown, charming reader, earnest, effective lecturer and devoted worker of unflagging zeal and unquestioned power.

Fannie Jackson Coppin, the teacher and organizer, pre-eminent among women of whatever country or race in constructive and executive force.

These women represent all shades of belief and as many departments of activity; but they have one thing in common—their sympathy with the oppressed race in America and the consecration of their several talents in whatever line to the work of its deliverance and development.

Fifty years ago woman's activity according to orthodox definitions was on a pretty clearly cut "sphere," including primarily the kitchen and the nursery, and rescued from the barrenness of prison bars by the womanly mania for adorning every discoverable bit of china or canvass with forlorn looking cranes balanced idiotically on one foot. The woman of to-day finds herself in the presence of responsibilities which ramify through the profoundest and most varied interests of her country and race. Not one of the issues of this plodding, toiling, sinning, repenting, falling, aspiring humanity can afford to shut her out, or can deny the reality of her influence. No plan for renovating society, no scheme for purifying politics, no reform in church or in state, no moral, social, or economic question, no movement upward or downward in the human plane is lost on her. A man once said when told his house was afire: "Go tell my wife; I never meddle with household affairs." But no woman can possibly put herself or her sex outside any of the interests that affect humanity. All departments in the new era are to be hers, in the sense that her interests are in all and through all; and it is incumbent on her to keep intelligently and sympathetically en rapport with all the great movements of her time, that she may know on which side to throw the weight of her influence. She stands now at the gateway of this new era of American civilization. In her hands must be moulded the strength, the wit, the statesmanship, the morality, all the psychic force, the social and economic intercourse of that era. To be alive at such an epoch is a privilege, to be a woman then is sublime.

In this last decade of our century; changes of such moment are in progress, such new and alluring vistas are opening out before us, such original and radical suggestions for the adjustment of labor and capital, of government and the governed, of the family, the church and the state, that to be a possible factor though an infinitesimal in such a movement is pregnant with hope and weighty with responsibility. To be a woman in such an age carries with it a privilege and an opportunity never implied before. But to be a woman of the Negro race in America, and to be able to grasp the deep significance of the possibilities of the crisis, is to have a heritage, it seems to me, unique in the ages. In the first place, the race is young and full of the elasticity and hopefulness of youth. All its achievements are before it. It does not look on the masterly triumphs of nineteenth century civilization with that blasé world-weary look which characterizes the old washed out and worn out races which have already, so to speak, seen their best days.

Said a European writer recently: "Except the Sclavonic, the Negro is the only original and distinctive genius which has yet to come to growth—and the feeling is to cherish and develop it."

Everything to this race is new and strange and inspiring. There is a quickening of its pulses and a glowing of its self-consciousness. Aha, I can rival that! I can aspire to that! I can honor my name and vindicate my race! Something like this, it strikes me, is the enthusiasm which stirs the genius of young Africa in America; and the memory of past oppression and the fact of present attempted repression only serve to gather momentum for its irrepressible powers. Then again, a race in such a stage of growth is peculiarly sensitive to impressions. Not the photographer's sensitized plate is more delicately impressionable to outer influences than is this high strung people here on the threshold of a career.

What a responsibility then to have the sole management of the primal lights and shadows! Such is the colored woman's office. She must stamp weal or woe on the coming history of this people. May she see her opportunity and vindicate her high prerogative.

FOCUS QUESTIONS:

1. What is the black woman's "unique position", according to Cooper?

2. What is Cooper's feeling on reflecting that women's political influence is "nil"?

3. What role or roles does Cooper envision as influential or important for black women?

13-3 Solitude of Self, Elizabeth Cady Stanton (1892)

Elizabeth Cady Stanton (1815-1902) was one of the great leaders of the woman's movement. The following speech was first delivered at the National American Women's Suffrage Association at its 1892 convention in Washington, D.C.

Source: Solitude of Self : Address Delivered by Mrs. Stanton Before the Committee of the Judiciary of the United States Congress, Monday, January 18, 1892., http://hdl.loc.gov/loc.rbc/rbnawsa.n8358

Address delivered by Elizabeth Cady Stanton before the Committee of the Judiciary of the United States Congress, Monday, January 18, 1892

Mr. Chairman and gentlemen of the committee: We have been speaking before Committees of the Judiciary for the last twenty years, and we have gone over all the arguments in favor of a sixteenth amendment which are familiar to all you gentlemen; therefore, it will not be necessary that I should repeat them again.

The point I wish plainly to bring before you on this occasion is the individuality of each human soul; our Protestant idea, the right of individual conscience and judgment-our republican idea, individual citizenship. In discussing the rights of woman, we are to consider, first, what belongs to her as an individual, in a world of her own, the arbiter of her own destiny, an imaginary Robinson Crusoe with her woman Friday on a solitary island. Her rights under such circumstances are to use all her faculties for her own safety and happiness.

Secondly, if we consider her as a citizen, as a member of a great nation, she must have the same rights as all other members, according to the fundamental principles of our Government.

Thirdly, viewed as a woman, an equal factor in civilization, her rights and duties are still the same-individual happiness and development.

Fourthly, it is only the incidental relations of life, such as mother, wife, sister, daughter, that may involve some special duties and training. In the usual discussion in regard to woman's sphere, such as men as Herbert Spencer, Frederic Harrison, and Grant Allen uniformly subordinate her rights and duties as an individual, as a citizen, as a woman, to the necessities of these incidental relations, some of which a large class of woman may never assume. In discussing the sphere of man we do not decide his rights as an individual, as a citizen, as a man by his duties as a father, a husband, a brother, or a son, relations some of which he may never fill. Moreover he would be better fitted for these very relations and whatever special work he might choose to do to earn his bread by the complete development of all his faculties as an individual.

Just so with woman. The education that will fit her to discharge the duties in the largest sphere of human usefulness will best fit her for whatever special work she may be compelled to do.

The isolation of every human soul and the necessity of self-dependence must give each individual the right, to choose his own surroundings.

The strongest reason for giving woman all the opportunities for higher education, for the full development of her faculties, forces of mind and body; for giving her the most enlarged freedom of thought and action; a complete emancipation from all forms of bondage, of custom, dependence, superstition; from all the crippling influences of fear, is the solitude and personal responsibility of her own individual life. The strongest reason why we ask for woman a voice in the government under which she lives; in the religion she is asked to believe; equality in social life, where she is the chief factor; a place in the trades and professions, where she may earn her bread, is because of her birthright to self-sovereignty; because, as an individual, she must rely on herself. No matter how much women prefer to lean, to be protected and supported, nor how much men desire to have them do so, they must make the voyage of life alone, and for safety in an emergency they must know something of the laws of navigation. To guide our own craft, we must be captain, pilot, engineer; with chart and compass to stand at the wheel; to match the wind and waves and know when to take in the sail, and to read the signs in the firmament over all. It matters not whether the solitary voyager is man or woman.

Nature having endowed them equally, leaves them to their own skill and judgment in the hour of danger, and, if not equal to the occasion, alike they perish.

The appreciate the importance of fitting every human soul for independent action, think for a moment of the immeasurable solitude of self. We come into the world alone, unlike all who have gone before us; we leave it alone under circumstances peculiar to ourselves. No mortal ever has been, no mortal over will be like the soul just launched on the sea of life. There can never again be just such environments as make up the infancy, youth and manhood of this one. Nature never repeats herself, and the possibilities of one human soul will never be found in another. No one has ever found two blades of ribbon grass alike, and no one will never find two human beings alike. Seeing, then, what must be the infinite diversity in human, character, we can in a measure appreciate the loss to a nation when any large class of the people in uneducated and unrepresented in the government. We ask for the complete development of every individual, first, for his own benefit and happiness. In fitting out an army we give each soldier his own knapsack, arms, powder, his blanket, cup, knife, fork and spoon. We provide alike for all their individual necessities, then each man bears his own burden.

Again we ask complete individual development for the general good; for the consensus of the competent on the whole round of human interest; on all questions of national life, and here each man must bear his share of the general burden. It is sad to see how soon friendless children are left to bear their own burdens before they can analise their feelings; before they can even tell their joys and sorrows, they are thrown on their own resources. The great lesson that nature seems to teach us at all ages is self-dependence, self-protection, self-support. What a touching instance of a child's solitude; of that hunger of heart for love and recognition, in the case of the little girl who helped to dress a christmas tree for the children of the family in which she served. On finding there was no present for herself she slipped away in the darkness and spent the night in an open field sitting on a stone, and when found in the morning was weeping as if her heart would break. No mortal will ever know the thoughts that passed through the mind of that friendless child in the long hours of that cold night, with only the silent stars to keep her company. The mention of her case in the daily papers moved many generous hearts to send her presents, but in the hours of her keenest sufferings she was thrown wholly on herself for consolation.

In youth our most bitter disappointments, our brightest hopes and ambitions are known only to otherwise, even our friendship and love we never fully share with another; there is something of every passion in every situation we conceal. Even so in our triumphs and our defeats.

The successful candidate for Presidency and his opponent each have a solitude peculiarly his own, and good form forbide either in speak of his pleasure or regret. The solitude of the king on his throne and the prisoner in his cell differs in character and degree, but it is solitude nevertheless.

We ask no sympathy from others in the anxiety and agony of a broken friendship or shattered love.

When death sunders our nearest ties, alone we sit in the shadows of our affliction. Alike mid the greatest triumphs and darkest tragedies of life we walk alone. On the devine heights of human attainments, eulogized land worshiped as a hero or saint, we stand alone. In ignorance, poverty, and vice, as a pauper or criminal, alone we starve or steal; alone we suffer the sneers and rebuffs of our fellows; alone we are hunted and hounded thro dark courts and alleys, in by-ways and highways; alone we stand in the judgment seat; alone in the prison cell we lament our crimes and misfortunes; alone we expiate them on the gallows. In hours like these we realize the awful solitude of individual life, its pains, its penalties, its responsibilities; hours in which the youngest and most helpless are thrown on their own resources for guidance and consolation. Seeing then that life must ever be a march and a battle, that each soldier must be equipped for his own protection, it is the height of cruelty to rob the individual of a single natural right.

To throw obstacle in the way of a complete education is like putting out the eyes; to deny the rights of property, like cutting off the hands. To deny political equality is to rob the ostracised of all self-respect; of credit in the market place; of recompense in the world of work; of a voice among those who make and administer the law; a choice in the jury before whom they are tried, and in the judge who decides their punishment. Shakespeare's play of Titus and Andronicus contains a terrible satire on woman's position in the nineteenth century-"Rude men" (the play tells us) "seized the king's daughter, cut out her tongue, out off her hands, and then bade her go call for water and wash her hands." What a picture of woman's position. Robbed of her natural rights, handicapped by law and custom at every turn, yet compelled to fight her own battles, and in the emergencies of life to fall back on herself for protection.

The girl of sixteen, thrown on the world to support herself, to make her own place in society, to resist the temptations that surround her and maintain a spotless integrity, must do all this by native force or superior education. She does not acquire this power by being trained to trust others and distrust herself. If she wearies of the struggle, finding it hard work to swim upstream, and allow herself to drift with the current, she will find plenty of company, but not one to share her misery in the hour of her deepest humiliation. If she tried to retrieve her position, to conceal the past, her life is hedged about with fears last willing hands should tear the veil from what she fain would hide. Young and friendless, she knows the bitter solitude of self.

How the little courtesies of life on the surface of society, deemed so important from man towards woman, fade into utter insignificance in view of the deeper tragedies in which she must play her part alone, where no human aid is possible.

The youngwife and mother, at the head of some establishment with a kind husband to shield her from the adverse winds of life, with wealth, fortune and position, has a certain harbor of safety, occurs against the ordinary ills of life. But to manage a household, have a deatrable influence in society, keep her friends and the affections of her husband, train her children and servants well, she must have rare common sense, wisdom, diplomacy, and a knowledge of human nature. To do all this she needs the cardinal virtues and the strong points of character that the most succesful stateman possesses.

An uneducated woman, trained to dependence, with no resources in herself must make a failure of any position in life. But society says women do not need a knowledge of the world, the liberal training that experience in public life must give, all the advantages of collegiate education; but when for the lock of all this, the woman's happiness is wrecked, alone she bears her humiliation; and the attitude of the weak and the ignorant in indeed pitiful in the wild chase for the price of life they are ground to powder.

In age, when the pleasures of youth are passed, children grown up, married and gone, the hurry and hustle of life in a measure over, when the hands are weary of active service, when the old armchair and the fireside are the chosen resorts, then men and women alike must fall back on their own resources. If they cannot find companionship in books, if they have no interest in the vital questions of the hour, no interest in watching the consummation of reforms, with which they might have been identified, they soon pass into their dotage. The more fully the faculties of the mind are developed and kept in use, the longer the period of vigor and active interest in all around us continues. If from a lifelong participation in public affairs a woman feels responsible for the laws regulating our system of education, the discipline of our jails and prisons, the sanitary conditions of our private homes, public buildings, and thoroughfares, an interest in commerce, finance, our foreign relations, in any or all of these questions, here solitude will at least be respectable, and she will not be driven to gossip or scandal for entertainment.

The chief reason for opening to every soul the

doors to the whole round of human duties an pleasures is the individual development thus attained, the resources thus provided under all circumstances to mitigate the solitude that at times must come to everyone. I once asked Prince Krapotkin, the Russian nihilist, how he endured his long years in prison, deprived of books, pen, ink, and paper. "Ah," he said, "I thought out many questions in which I had a deep interest. In the pursuit of an idea I took no note of time. When tired of solving knotty problems I recited all the beautiful passages in prose or verse I have ever learned. I became acquainted with myself and my own resources. I had a world of my own, a vast empire, that no Russian jailor or Czar could invade." Such is the value of liberal thought and broad culture when shut off from all human companionship, bringing comfort and sunshine within even the four walls of a prison cell.

As women of times share a similar fate, should they not have all the consolation that the most liberal education can give? Their suffering in the prisons of St. Petersburg; in the long, weary marches to Siberia, and in the mines, working side by side with men, surely call for all the self-support that the most exalted sentiments of heroism can give. When suddenly roused at midnight, with the startling cry of "fire! fire!" to find the house over their heads in flames, do women wait for men to point the way to safety? And are the men, equally bewildered and half suffocated with smoke, in a position to more than try to save themselves?

At such times the most timid women have shown a courage and heroism in saving their husbands and children that has surprise everybody. Inasmuch, then, as woman shares equally the joys and sorrows of time and eternity, is it not the height of presumption in man to propose to represent her at the ballot box an the throne of grace, do her voting in the state, her praying in the church, and to assume the position of priest at the family alter.

Nothing strengthens the judgment and quickens the concience like individual responsibility. Nothing adds such dignity to character as the recognition of one's self-sovereignity; the right to an equal place, every where conceded; a place earned by personal merit, not an artificial attainment, by inheritance, wealth, family, and position. Seeing, then that the responsibilities of life rests equally on man and woman, that their destiny is the same, they need the same preparation for time and eternity. The talk of sheltering woman from the fierce sterns of life is the sheerest mockery, for they beat on her from every point of the compass, just as they do on man, and with more

fatal results, for he has been trained to protect himself, to resist, to conquer. Such are the facts in human experience, the responsibilities of individual. Rich and poor, intelligent and ignorant, wise and foolish, virtuous and vicious, man and woman, it is ever the same, each soul must depend wholly on itself.

Whatever the theories may be of woman's dependence on man, in the supreme moments of her life he can not bear her burdens. Alone she goes to the gates of death to give life to every man that is born into the world. No one can share her fears, on one mitigate her pangs; and if her sorrow is greater than she can bear, alone she passes beyond the gates into the vast unknown.

From the mountain tops of Judea, long ago, a heavenly voice bade His disciples, "Bear ye one another's burdens," but humanity has not yet risen to that point of self-sacrifice, and if ever so willing, how few the burdens are that one soul can bear for another. In the highways of Palestine; in prayer and fasting on the solitary mountain top; in the Garden of Gethsemane; before the judgment seat of Pilate; betrayed by one of His trusted disciples at His last supper; in His agonies on the cross, even Jesus of Nazareth, in these last sad days on earth, felt the awful solitude of self. Deserted by man, in agony he cries, "My God! My God! why hast Thou forsaken me?" And so it ever must be in the conflicting scenes of life, on the long weary march, each one walks alone. We may have many friends, love, kindness, sympathy and charity to smooth our pathway in everyday life, but in the tragedies and triumphs of human experience each moral stands alone.

But when all artificial trammels are removed, and women are recognized as individuals, responsible for their own environments, thoroughly educated for all the positions in life they may be called to fill; with all the resources in themselves that liberal though and broad culture can give; guided by their own conscience an judgment; trained to self-protection by a healthy development of the muscular system and skill in the use of weapons of defense, and stimulated to self-support by the knowledge of the business world and the pleasure that pecuniary independence must ever give; when women are trained in this way they will, in a measure, be fitted for those hours of solitude that come alike to all, whether prepared or otherwise. As in our extremity we must depend on ourselves, the dictates of wisdom point of complete individual development.

In talking of education how shallow the argument that each class must be educated for the special work it proposed to do, and all those faculties not needed in this special walk must lie dormant and utterly wither for want of use, when, perhaps, these will be the very faculties needed in life's greatest emergies. Some say, Where is the use of drilling serie in the languages, the Sciences, in law, medicine, theology? As wives, mothers, housekeepers, cooks, they need a different curriculum from boys who are to fill all positions. The chief cooks in our great hotels and ocean steamers are men. In large cities men run the bakies; they make our bread, cake and pies. They manage the laundries; they are now considered our best milliners and dressmakers. Because some men fill these departments of usefulness, shall we regulate the curriculum in Harvard and Yale to their present necessities? If not why this talk in our best colleges of a curriculum for girls who are crowding into the trades and professions; teachers in all our public schools rapidly hiling many lucrative and honorable positions in life? They are showing too, their calmness and courage in the most trying hours of human experience.

You have probably all read in the daily papers of the terrible storm in the Bay of Biscay when a tidal wave such havoc on the shore, wrecking vessels, unroofing houses and carrying destruction everywhere. Among other buildings the woman's prison was demolished. Those who escaped saw men struggling to reach the shore. They promptly by clasping hands made a chain of themselves and pushed out into the sea, again and again, at the risk of their lives until they had brought six men to shore, carried them to a shelter, and did all in their power for their comfort and protection.

What especial school of training could have prepared these women for this sublime moment of their lives. In times like this humanity rises above all college curriculums and recognises Nature as the greatest of all teachers in the hour of danger and death. Women are already the equals of men in the whole of ream of thought, in art, science, literature, and government. With telescope vision they explore the starry firmament, and bring back the history of the planetary world. With chart and compass they pilot ships across the mighty deep, and with skillful finger send electric messages around the globe. In galleries of art the beauties of nature and the virtues of humanity are immortalized by them on their canvas and by their inspired touch dull blocks of marble are transformed into angels of light.

In music they speak again the language of Mendelssohn, Beethoven, Chopin, Schumann, and are worthy interpreters of their great thoughts. The poetry and novels of the century are theirs, and they have touched the keynote of reform in religion, politics, and social life. They fill the editor's and professor's chair, and plead at the bar of justice, walk the wards of the hospital, and speak from the pulpit and the platform; such is the type of womanhood that an enlightened public sentiment welcomes today, and such the triumph of the facts of life over the false theories of the past.

Is it, then, consistent to hold the developed woman of this day within the same narrow political limits as the dame with the spinning wheel and knitting needle occupied in the past? No! no! Machinery has taken the labors of woman as well as man on its tireless shoulders; the loom and the spinning wheel are but dreams of the past; the pen, the brush, the easel, the chisel, have taken their places, while the hopes and ambitions of women are essentially changed.

We see reason sufficient in the outer conditions of human being for individual liberty and development, but when we consider the self dependence of every human soul we see the need of courage, judgment, and the exercise of every faculty of mind and body, strengthened and developed by use, in woman as well as man.

Whatever may be said of man's protecting power in ordinary conditions, mid all the terrible disasters by land and sea, in the supreme moments of danger, alone, woman must ever meet the horrors of the situation; the Angel of Death even makes no royal pathway for her. Man's love and sympathy enter only into the sunshine of our lives. In that solemn solitude of self, that links us with the immeasurable and the eternal, each soul lives alone forever. A recent writer says:

I remember once, in crossing the Atlantic, to have gone upon the deck of the ship at midnight, when a dense black cloud enveloped the sky, and the great deep was roaring madly under the lashes of demoniac winds. My feelings was not of danger or fear (which is a base surrender of the immortal soul), but of utter desolation and loneliness; a little speck of life shut in by a tremendous darkness. Again I remember to have climbed the slopes of the Swiss Alps, up beyond the point where vegetation ceases, and the stunted conifers no longer struggle against the unfeeling blasts. Around me lay a huge confusion of rocks, out of which the gigantic ice peaks shot into the measureless blue of the heavens, and again my only feeling was the awful solitude.

And yet, there is a solitude, which each and every one of us has always carried with him, more inaccessible than the ice-cold mountains, more profound than the midnight sea; the solitude of self. Our inner being, which we call ourself, no eye nor touch of man or angel has ever pierced. It is more hidden than the caves of the gnome; the sacred adytum of the oracle; the hidden chamber of eleusinian mystery, for to it only omniscience is permitted to enter.

Such is individual life. Who, I ask you, can take, dare take, on himself the rights, the duties, the responsibilities of another human soul?

FOCUS QUESTIONS:

1. What is Stanton's thesis? How does it differ from other arguments for suffrage, and for woman rights?

2. Why would Stanton chose to address Congress members in this way, relying on philosophical arguments, and not legal ones?

13-4 Work among workingwomen in Baltimore (1889)

Herbert B. Adams (1850-1901) was an historian and professor at Johns Hopkins University. The following excerpt is from a study he published in 1889. His approach to the subject was that of sociology, a discipline that was first taught in an American university in 1890.

Source: Adams, Herbert Baxter. *Work among workingwomen in Baltimore.* Baltimore: Johns Hopkins University Press, 1889 (at http://nrs.harvard.edu/urn-3:FHCL:489234)

In the year 1883 was incorporated the Young Women's Christian Association, "for the improvement and education of young women, having in view the improvement of the condition of the workingwomen of Baltimore, by providing for them a reading-room, and such other departments as may be found necessary." This institution has now been in successful operation for six years. A brief review of its work is not without educational and sociological interest.

The Association was organized by thoughtful - Christian ladies of Baltimore, with an advisory board of gentlemen. Besides the usual executive officers, there were standing committees for the lunch-room, library, entertainment, educational and religious instruction, increase of membership, visiting, fresh-air excursions, etc. The annual reports of these various committees are suggestive sources of information concerning the character and progress of the various lines of work. A careful study of these reports has been supplemented by personal conference with members of the Association.

The first practical work done by the Young Women's Christian Association in Baltimore was to rent two rooms over a shop in Lexington street, one of the business thoroughfares, along which are numerous stores employing saleswomen. A kitchen and a lunch-room were at once established, and here the wife of a university professor made the first soup. It was originally intended to provide every day a simple lunch of soup, tea or coffee, bread and butter; but gradually such simple meats and vegetables as could be sold for five cents a portion were added to the bill of fare. The first day the lunch-room was opened it was patronized by only four persons. The second day there were ten. At the end of the first week there had been ninety-three meals served; at the end of the second week, 163; at the end of the first year, 17,865; at the end of the third year, 21,297; at the end of the fourth year, 29,009; at the end of the fifth year, 43,020.

Among the first results noticed by the committee were the gratitude of the girls, their improved health and appearance. Some of the girls spoke of the comfort of leaving the store for a half-hour and getting a warm meal. Others spoke of "the nervous headaches kept off by the soup or cup of coffee and the little rest in the parlor afterwards."

The means for supporting the lunch-room came partly from the girls, who cheerfully paid the small charges for what they took, and partly from generous donations by friends of the enterprise. Gentlemen connected with the Corn and Flour Exchange sent barrels of flour, etc. The committee on the lunch-room never ran into debt. They kept the prices of food as low as possible, and their enterprise is now practically self-sustaining, which is a gratifying economic result. The patronage of the lunchroom by working girls has been so great that the Association has twice been compelled to change its quarters in order to secure more commodious dining-rooms. The present building, 221 Liberty street, is neat and attractive, but evidently too small for the growing and helpful work which the Association has undertaken. Good food is, and always has been, a good physical basis for social work. It promotes good-will and healthful, cordial co-operation among members of any society.

The supply of home-cooked food to working girls for their midday meal naturally led to a demand for temporary board and lodgings on the part of girls who had been thrown out of work, or who had come to the city from a distance seeking employment, but with little ready money. Next to food, shelter and security are social necessities. These the lodging-house committees endeavored to supply, with the aid of a competent and trust worthy matron. Upon application, any respectable young woman was admitted to one night's lodging for fifteen cents. If she wished to stay longer, she was required to furnish references, and promise conformance to the rules of the house.

The few rooms at command in the early experience of the Association made it impossible to shelter more than six persons at a time. The third year the committee furnished 1,044 nights' lodgings. There were, how ever, only 139 different lodgers. The fourth year, in the new Home on

Liberty street, where there is room for 27 guests, 3,465 lodgings were afforded, but the total number of individual guests was only 100. In 1887 there was 114 transient and 47 permanent boarders, the cost of board being $250 per week. These facts indicate a tendency on the part of the girls to take up their abode at the Home of the Association, a fact manifestly explained by its economy and general attractiveness. Cheerful surroundings, marks of good taste in furniture and adornment-these things have a positive educational value. Great care, however, should be taken, on the one hand, not to allow an abuse of privilege, and, on the other, to develop higher standards of living among working girls outside the Home.

One interesting feature of the lodging-rooms is that they have been furnished by contributions from young ladies' schools, by industrial associations, or in memory of good women whose influence lives on in the Young Women's Christian Association. Speaking of the attractions of the Home on Liberty street, the managers once said: "We deem it no little thing that our friends have made it beautiful, and that its memorial rooms grace it with tender associations. In a home a pure sentiment is ever a fitting guest, and with us whatever inspires a home feeling and tends to create a softening and elevating influence becomes an educational force of significant value."

Very attractive are the rooms devoted to literary and social purposes. The library, which was begun by a donation of books from a now discontinued night

school, is well supplied with books and magazines. The library is furnished in memory of Miss White, a young lady who from the first was actively engaged in promoting the interests of the Association. The parlor also is a memorial room, and opens directly into the library. The walls of both rooms are hung with good pictures, and the furniture is suggestive of quiet comfort. When the writer visited these rooms, accompanied by one of the lady managers, he saw a shop-girl practising upon the piano in the parlor. She told the lady, in answer to a question, that she had finished her work early that day in the straw-shop, and had chosen this form of recreation quite by herself. A utilitarian might perhaps have suggested a more profitable form of enjoyment during leisure hours; hut is there really any finer pleasure than music for the working classes? Surely they need it, and perhaps appreciate it quite as much as do those who neither toil nor spin. Even the slaves on the old plantations were not denied the use of the banjo and the violin. Shall not women who were born free cultivate all the musical talent which they possess?

In the use of the library it is said that there is a decided preference for fiction. This fact only goes to show that working girls are not altogether different from other girls. Compared with fiction, history and biography and other forms of literature will forever occupy a lower place in popular favor. Good stories, and good music are at once the joy, solace, and inspiration of modern democracy. Good taste in the choice of novels, as in other reading, is one of the best criterions of intellectual and moral progress. In this regard it is said that there has been marked improvement among those who frequent the Association rooms. A member of the library committee is present every day to advise and assist the girls in their selection of literature, in no way, perhaps, can cultivated ladies render more valuable educational service to their sex than in developing higher standards of literary taste and in providing well-selected libraries for clubs of working girls.

FOCUS QUESTIONS:

1. According to Adams, how does the WYCA best serve working girls?

2. What do you consider the best features of the early WYCA?

3. What was the chief role or function of the WYCA in these years?

13-5 Women's Clubs

The following article appeared in The Arena, *a periodical devoted to reform. Ellen Henrotin (1847-1922) was the second president of the General Federation of Women's Clubs.*

Source: Henrotin, Ellen M. "The State Federations," *The Arena,* 16(1896):120-126

Six years ago, when the General Federation of Women's 'Clubs was organized, about fifty clubs joined as members. The original conception of the General Federation was a federation of literary clubs to compare methods of work, prepare programmes and, as far as possible, establish a high standard of literary work for the women's clubs.

The clubs responded to the invitation to join the Federation in far greater numbers than at first was anticipated. Over two hundred clubs sent delegates to the first biennial meeting, held in Chicago in 1892, the Women's Club of that city being hostess. All sections of the country, north, south, east and west, were represented and a large number of club women of Chicago and suburbs were present. The greatest interest was evinced in the proceedings. Every meeting that was held in Central Music Hall was crowded and the occasion was signalized by many social functions. From that time on the usefulness of the Federation was an established fact.

****

The membership of the State Federations has grown with the same rapidity as that of the General Federation. Ohio has one hundred and thirty-five club memberships; New York, according to last report, one hundred and sixteen; Illinois, one hundred and twenty-five; Massachusetts, nearly one hundred Pennsylvania, thirty-three, with a total membership of over six thousand women; New Jersey has sixty-two; New Camp shire, twenty-eight; Nebraska, seventy-five; Minnesota, fifty-four; and new clubs are being organized all over the country and joining the State Federations. It is estimated that the General Federation has about five hundred clubs in membership, and the State Federations about one thousand. The interesting features of the meetings of the State Federations have been, the enthusiasm which has characterized these meetings, and the social atmosphere and perfect good breeding of the delegates in attendance. It is invidious to mention one where all have reached such a high standard, but having recently returned from the Minnesota State Federation, I must speak of that programme as it embodies several interesting features. First, the report of the town and country clubs. These clubs are formed in the towns for the benefit of country women. The Northfield Town and Country Club has sixty members, forty from the country and twenty in the town. A room was secured as a restroom for the women who came in to do their shopping; arrangements were made to have a custodian in charge who would serve tea, and the visitors were at liberty to bring their own luncheon, every facility being provided to render it a pleasant meal. The country members pay twenty-five cents a year. This club was formed through the exertions of a small committee of town women who visited the different stores, physicians, and druggists, and ascertained the addresses of about eighty country women within an easy driving distance of the town of Northfield. They addressed letters to these ladies, asking them if they would be interested informing such a club. They received about fifty answers, and the singular part of it is that each woman answered that she would greatly enjoy the literary part, but felt that that was all that was necessary to her as she had a sister or some relative in town where she usually went for lunch. The ladies, however, engaged their quarters, hired the custodian, opened the club and sent out notices with fear and trembling for their new departure. They had over thirty visitors the first day, and in the year since the club was first formed, they have moved three times, each time into larger quarters. A literary meeting is held once a month regularly, summer and winter, and on other occasions. A book was selected (the first one being Reade's "Put Yourself in His Place") and at the next meeting the book was discussed, some lady being the leader. This plan was pursued for thefirst year with the best results. The club bought inexpensive copies of the book and placed them on sale with the leading booksellers. All the copies were bought, and at the end of the year not only had each member her delightful experience, but her family had twelve good books that she had read, heard discussed, and was able to interest them in. Northfield itself is a most interesting community; Carlton College, a coeducational institution, is situated in the town, with about five hundred pupils in attendance. The presiding genius of the town is Miss Margaret J. Evans, president of the Minnesota State Federation. She is the inspiration of much of the club work and of the Village Improvement Associations, which are being organized in Minnesota, and of which Northfield is so beautiful an example. A very valuable paper was read on the forests of Minnesota, and a description given of how much one club had accomplished toward pre-serving the forests and also by planting trees. The Ohio State Federation met in Cleveland, and most interesting reports were given on the public libraries which are being fostered by the clubs and on travelling libraries. A bill to provide for these libraries has just passed the Ohio legislature, fostered by the Ohio Federation of Women's Clubs and the powerful cooperation of Governor Bushnell. The Illinois State Federation, which met at Springfield in the capitol by the invitation of Governor Altgeld, was a notable gathering. The subject of many of the papers and discussions was state education, and the part which the women's clubs could take in fostering a high standard of education and providing ways and means to meet the growing demands of the primary, as well as the higher education. The Women's Club of Chicago has taken the initiative in organized charity, civics, and all the grave social questions which naturally come to the front in a metropolis. The West End Club of Chicago has been greatly interested in the subject of wage-earners, while the South Side clubs and the Woodlawn Club have been most sympathetic and energetic in dealing with the sweat-shop system and in studying social problems.

FOCUS QUESTIONS:

1. What do you think was the greatest strength of the women's clubs?

2. What kinds of work was undertaken by the clubs?

3. Reading between the lines, what might explain the rapid growth of these clubs? Why would women join in such large numbers?

13-6 Report of the National Woman Suffrage Convention (1900)

The following excerpt from a newspaper article gives a personal view of the 1900 suffrage convention.

Source: "Report of the National Woman Suffrage Convention held at Washington Feb. 14, 1900 By a New York State Delegate", *The Geneva [New York] Advertiser,* March 6, 1900 (at http://hdl.loc.gov/loc.rbc/rbcmil.scrp1006001)

Geneva Advertiser.

TUESDAY, MARCH 6, 1900.

Report of the—National Woman Suffrage Convention held at Washington Feb. 14, 1900.

———

By a New York state delegate.

....

No doubt you have all read the excellent reports of our convention which appeared from day to day in the Rochester papers, and I dare say some of you may know more of its details and business transactions than do I; at the same time, I hope you will be glad to hear a few personal impressions and experiences. Every one agreed that the convention was the best, in all respects, that had ever been held, and I, who could make no comparisons, felt that whatever other conventions may have been, this one was a pronounced success. It seems to me there are four evident signs of a successful convention : First the number and quality of its delegates; second the size and quality of its public audiences; third the amount of money it raises; and last but not least the election of efficient officers who are to guide the course of the association for the coming year. In every one of these four particulars the recent convention reached a high level of excellence-for instance, the N, Y. State delegation, entitled to 26 members, was complete, the only absentee being Miss E. B. Curtis who fully intended to come, and who failed only at the last moment to appear. Her place in the delegation was tilled at once by Miss Margaret Chanler, the well known nurse at Porto Rico during our late war. Miss Chanler sat beside me when we voted for Mrs. Chapman Catt, who, to our great satisfaction, was elected President by an overwhelming majority. As to financial results $10,000 was raised in one session.

I seem to have jumped into the middle of the convention in my attempt to give you evidences of its claim to success. But was it not a success, when you remember that our delegation was complete, the election went the way we wanted it to go? the money and the public came the way we wanted them to come?

The Church of Our Father, which has a large seating capacity was well filled both on floor and in its several galleries, at all the sessions, and in the evenings many persons stood during the two hours program, and on the last evening several hundred persons were turned away, Mrs. Stanton-Blatch, who was to have been the first speaker that evening, had great difficulty in effecting an entrance. She gave an amended, enlarged and up to date version of her Geneva lecture on "War and the work of women," and in opening said she had intended to begin by contrasting the peaceful proclivities of women with the opposite in men, but her experience of the past few moments had spoiled the point of her opening paragraph-for in endeavoring to reach the platform she had encountered at the outer walls of the church an army of women besieging the doors through which she was obliged to fight her way.

Mrs. Blatch was preceded by Hon. John C. Hall, member of congress from Colorado, who gave a glowing account of the woman's vote in that state. He had lived in Colorado before and after the introduction of woman into many public activities, including the casting of ballots, and he considers her a beneficial and important factor everywhere. As a voter she is especially individual, and he says the men of Colorado honor the independence of their women and admire them for voting as they individually choose to do, No broken families on record.

Mr. Bell said: "You must bear in mind that the extending of the elective franchise to women not only elevates and broadens the women but the men as well. Again, it is asked if the husbands and wives don't vote alike. Not by any means. During the past two years in the town where I live the only issue has been for or against the saloons. Almost every large property holder among the men was determinedly for the saloons, and was a most earnest electioneer for a license, and generally his wife was just as determinedly electioneering against the saloons, and for two years the women have voted the town dry against the greatest efforts and protests of their husbands."

Following Mrs. Blatch came Mrs. Caroline Halowell Miller, of Maryland, one of Miss Anthony's Quaker Friends. Mrs. Miller's personality is quaint and magnetic, From her first word the huge audience were with her. Her intense earnestness and absolute simplicity place her at once in the first rank of orators. She gave a few basic principles of true life and government and was so happy in her choice of similes, and her manner was so original, she kept the audience in almost continuous laughter and applause. Her closing sentences were addressed to Miss Anthony, to whom she turned in making them. The audience lost a word or, two and at once clamored. "Louder, louder!" Mrs. Miller stopped and turning to the multitude said in the simplest and most courteous way possible, "I was speaking to Miss Anthony; I told her that I had asked for 60 seconds on the program of her birthday celebration, that I might say a few words and was told that I could take my 60 seconds this evening." Then Mrs. Miller began her tribute to Miss Anthony by saying that in her life she had known two heroes, Abraham Lincoln and Susan Anthony; both lives were devoted to freedom. Each of Mrs. Miller's sentences were followed by loud applause which seemed somewhat to annoy her because she had prepared her speech for Miss Anthony's rather than for the public. She suddenly stopped and appealing directly to Miss Anthony, who was presiding, said, in a clear voice "Susan, can't you stop this applause! It spoils the effect," Miss Anthony came at once to the rescue of the popular orator and explained that Mrs. Miller being; a Quaker, was accustomed to silent meetings, and requested that there be no further demonstrations or approval while she was speaking. After this the audience was absolutely still until the last word was said when Mrs. Miller gracefully acknowledged round after round of applause.

FOCUS QUESTIONS:

1. What does the correspondent consider the goals of the conference?

2. Why was the Colorado representative given the chance to speak? Why the quip about "no broken families on record"?

13-7 Frances E. Willard, Christian Temperance (1893)

Frances Willard (1839-1898) was an activist in the woman suffrage and temperance movement. She was elected the first president of the International Council of Women in 1888 and as the president of the Woman's Christian Temperance Union advanced the "do-everything" policy. In the following passage, she describes the success of the White Ribbon program.

Source: Willard, Frances E. "Address Before The Second Biennial Convention of the World's Woman's Christian Temperance Union, and the Twentieth Annual Convention of The National Woman's Christian Temperance Union, World's Columbian Exposition, Chicago, Illinois, U.S.A. October 16-21, 1893."

So far as the White Ribbon movement is concerned, this has been its best and brightest year from the outlook of the World's W.C.T4U., and that is the only point of view that is adequate. How little did they dream, chose devoted women of the praying bands. who with their patient footsteps bridged the distance between borne and saloon, and in their little despised groups poured out their souls to God, and their pitiful plea into the ears of men, that the "Movement" would be systematized twenty years later into an organization known and loved by the best men and women in every civilized nation on the earth; and that its heroic missionaries would be obliged to circumnavigate the globe in order to visit the outposts of the Society. How little did they dream that in the year of the World's Columbian Exposition well nigh half a million of children would send their autographs on the triple pledge cards of our Loyal Temperance Legions, and Sunday School Department; that we should have a publishing house, owned and conducted by the Society itself; from which more than a hundred million pages of the literature of light arid leading should go forth this year; how little could they have conceived of the significance that is wrapt up in the lengthening folds of the Polyglot Petition, signed and circulated in fifty languages, and containing the signatures and attestations of between three and four million of the best people that live, praying for the abolition of the alcohol traffic, the opium traffic, and the licensed traffic in degraded women. How little they dreamed of that great movement by which the study of physiology and hygiene were to bring the arrest of thought to millions of young minds concerning the true inwardness of all narcotic poisons in their effects on the body and the brain How "far beyond their thought" the enfranchisement of women in New Zealand and Wyoming, Kansas and "Michigan, ray Michigan" How inconceivable to them the vision of our House Beautiful reared in the heart of the world's most electric city, and sending forth its influence to the furthest corner of the globe. How little did they dream that the echo of their hymns should yet he heart and heeded by a woman whose lineage, and the prowess of whose historic name may be traced through centuries,— and that not alone from the cottage and the homestead, but from the emblazoned walls of splendid castles, should be driven the cup that seems to cheer, but at the last inebriates. But w must remember that1 after all, these are but the days of small beginnings compared with what ac more years shall show. Doubtless if we could see the power to which this movement of women's hearts for the protection of their heart-stones shall attain in the next generation, the inspiration of that knowledge would exhilarate us beyond that which is good for such steady patient workers as we have been, are, and wish to be; but I dare prophesy that twenty years from now woman will be fully panoplied in the politics and government of all English-speaking nations; she will find her glad footsteps impeded by no artificial barriers, but whatever she can do well she will he free to do in the enlightened age of worship, helpfulness and brotherhood, toward which we move with steps accelerated far beyond our ken. The momentum of the centuries is in the widening, deepening current of 19th century reform; the 20th century's dawn shall witness our compensations and reprisals, and as these increase humanity shall pay back into the mother-heart of woman its unmeasured penitence and unfathomed regret for all that she has missed (and through her, every son and daughter that she has brought into the world), by reason of the awful mistake by which, in the age of force, man substituted *his* "thus far and no farther," in place of the "thus far and no farther" of God; one founded in a selfish and ignorant view of woman's powers, the other giving her what every sentient being ought to have—a fair field and a free course to run and be glorified.

FOCUS QUESTIONS:

1. What were some of the tools used by the temperance movement?

2. What were the goals of the WCTU besides fighting against alcohol consumption?

3. In reading this passage, what are the points of convergence of the temperance and woman's suffrage movements?

13-8 Women as Conservators of Public Health (1896)

The following is part of a paper presented to the General Federation of Women's Clubs in 1896, in one of the sessions of the Social Economics Department. It examines the role of women in maintaining public health. Perry concludes her address" Home interests and public interests, now and forever, one and inseparable, is the fact that confronts us everywhere" (p. 301)

Source: Belle M. Perry, "Women as Conservators of Public Health", report from the Third Biennial, General Federation of Women's Clubs / by invitation of the Woman's Club of Louisville, Ky., May, 1896, 295-296 (http://nrs.harvard.edu /urn-3:FHCL:135492)

Third Biennial General Federation of Women's Clubs, Louisville KY, May, 1896

Women as Conservators of Public Health

Women are inevitably, in a larger sense than they know, conservators of public health. Let us look at our ground. What is public health? The public are the people. Public health, then, is the people's health Women are, themselves, one-half the people. They are the mothers of all the people. They are the care-takers of all the children from birth till school age. It is women, then, mainly, who supplement the care of mothers during the six, eight or a dozen years of school life. It is women who plan and prepare the daily food for the world. It is women who oversee the sanitary conditions of the homes. It is the mothers who are the instructors of the children in regard to the mystery of life, or who ought to be, and who will be when they know what infinite crime and suffering might be saved by teaching the children wisely of the sacred powers of the gift of potential parenthood, and the far-reaching dangers and inevitable injury attending its misuse.

In health and in sickness it is the women of the world who are looking after and taking care of the people of the world.

Women, then, have a mighty power and responsibility as conservators of the public health, both physical and moral, even in their time-honored, world-conceded sphere. This much granted, it follows, inevitably, that any cause of ill-health, or indeed any cause of any ill whatsoever that affects human beings, is of legitimate, vital and immediate interest to women. Whether that danger lies in her own ignorance, her neighbor's ignorance, an unsanitary schoolroom, impure water supply, foul alleys or basements in her immediate neighborhood, or in the heart of the city, if the menace to the people's health exists, the interest and the duty are hers to know about it and to have it corrected.

The laws of health emphasize the unity of humanity, the oneness of of the great human family, the inseparableness of home interests from civic interests.

We must be our "brothers' keepers" if we would keep ourselves. The slums are a perpetual menace to the palace. Cholera in Hamburg means danger in Chicago.

What mean these mighty truths? Woman's responsibility and the unity of humanity. They mean that the crying need of the world is for awakened and enlightened womanhood and motherhood. They mean a sacred obligation on the part of those who are beginning to comprehend to evolve ways and means to arouse and enlighten the rest, and to see to it that the coming generations of mothers are better and better fitted for ithe high responsibility which will be theirs.

FOCUS QUESTIONS:

1. How has the author expanded the notion of the woman's sphere?

2. What arguments does Perry use in arguing that living conditions should be improved?

13-9 Suffragist Convention at Dunkirk (1899)

The following newspaper notice announces the arrival of distinguished suffragists in Dunkirk, Massachusetts. The venue for the convention gives yet another idea of the role of the Educational and Industrial Unions.

Source: "Women Suffragists Began Their State Convention Here Today", Dunkirk [Massachusetts] ***Evening Observer,*** November 1, 1899 (at http://hdl.loc.gov/loc.rbc/rbcmil. scrp1005001)

DUNKIRK EVENING OBSERVER,

Women suffragists

_____

Began Their State Convention Here Today.

l_____

MANY DELEGATES ARE HERE

_____

And More Are Expected on Evening Trains. Work of the Convention to Begin in Earnest Tomorrow Public Reception Tonight.

_____

The thirty-first annual convention of the State of New York Woman Suffrage Association opened today, at the Women's Educational and Industrial Union This morning, and in fact all day, the chairmen of the reception and other committees were in the Union rooms receiving the delegates and otherwise serving them.

Lunch was served to the delegates at noon in the dining room of the Union building. Lunch and supper will be served at the Union rooms every day luring the convention. The assembly hall and other rooms of the Union building were tastefully ornamented with plants and flowers.

Up to noon the following delegates had arrived and had been assigned to the following ladies who will entertain them during their visit in Dunkirk: Miss Susan B. Anthony, Rochester, president of the National Suffrage Association— Mrs. Julien T. Williams, Rev. Anna H. Shaw, Philadelphia, Vice president National Suffrage Association-Mrs. John W. Babcock, 627 Washington avenue. The executive committee of the State Association held a private meet-Ing from 3:30 p. m. to 5:30.

[.....]

This evening from 8 to 10 o'clock a public reception will be given in the Women's Union tomorrow's program.

Morning, 9:30 12. Women's Union Hall.

Minutes ....Mrs. Mary Thayer Sanford

Announcement of Committees Credentials

Resolutions, Finance, Courtesies.............

Roll Call of Counties............................

Report of Executive Committee.................. Mrs. Mariana W. Chapman.

Report of Corresponding Secretary............. Miss Isabel Howland.

Report of Treasurer. Mrs. Priscilla D. Hackstaff

Report of Finance Committee................... Mrs. Zobedia Allemau, Chairman.

Introduction of Fraternal Delegates............

County Reports................................

Afternoon, 2 4:30. Women's Union Hall.

Minutes...

Report of Credential Committee...............

Election of Officers..........................

Report of Press Committee..................... Mrs. Elnora M. Babcock.

County Reports................................

Evening, 8 10. Academy Hall. (Admission free. Silver collection.)

Music Vocal Solo (Selected)..................... Miss Libbie Wilson.

Prayer.......................Rev. J. T. Badgley

Address of Welcome......................,........ Mayor Alex. Williams, for City of Dunkirk.

Mrs. Ellen Cheney, for Chautauqua County Political Equality Club.

Response... Mrs. Mariana W. Chapman, President New York State Woman Suffrage Association.

Address—Politics and the Home..............Mrs. Liliie

Devereux Blake, President New-York City Woman Suffrage League.

Address.. Harriet May Mills. Chairman Organization Committee, New York State W.S.A.

Address...............Mrs. Carrie E. S, Twing

Address....................Susan B. Anthony

FOCUS QUESTIONS:

1. What does this document tell you about the relationship between the national and state suffragist associations?

2. Given the organization apparent in such conventions and the organizations that called them, what kinds of experience could the women involved claim?

13-10 Mary Church Terrell, "What the National Association [of Colored Women] has Meant to Colored Women"

The life of Mary Church Terrell (1863-1954) was born a slave, but lived to see the passage of Brown v. Board of Education. She founded the National Association of University Women, and was elected the first president of the National Association of Colored Women's Clubs. The following undated essay reflects on the role of the organization in black women's lives.

Source: (http://memory.loc.gov/cgi-bin/query/r?ammem /aaodyssey:@field(NUMBER+@band(mssmisc+ody0706))

What the National Association Has Meant to Colored Women. It would be hard to overestimate the splendid contribution which the National Association of Colored. Women has made to the development of the group for which it was formed in 1896. When two national organizations in Washington, D.C. and solidified the women into one large body a new day for them had dawned. Their eyes were turned to duties which women alone can perform as they had never been turned before. They were pressed into doing certain kinds of work end were advised concerning the best methods with which to proceed. They were urged to interest themselves in civic affairs— to study the conditions under which they lived in their respective cities and towns and to do everything they could to put the right men into places of trust and power long before the amendment granting suffrage to women was passed.

And yet, it would misrepresent the facts to s that colored women bad done little or nothing for themselves or their race until the National Association of Colored Women was formed. The rapidity with which colored women strode forward as soon as they were enfranchised would sound like a fairy tale if it were told. Unfortunately, it has not been written yet, but when it is, it will amaze the world.

Colored women have always had high aspirations for themselves end their race. From the day when shackles fell from their fettered limbs till to day, as individuals they have often struggled single handed and alone against the most desperate and discouraging odds, in order to secure for themselves and their loved ones that culture of the head and heart for which they had hungered end thirsted so long invain. But it dawned upon them finally that individuals working alone, or scattered here and there in small companies, might be never so honest in purpose, so indefatigable in labor, so conscientious about methods and so wise in projecting plans, they would nevertheless accomplish little compared with the possible achievements of many individuals, all banded strongly together throughout the entire land, with heeds and hearts fixed on the same high purpose, and hands joined in united strength.

As the result of a general realization of this fact the National Association of Colored Women was born. It soon gave an impressive object lesson in the necessity for and the efficacy of organization, proved its reason for existence and its right to live. Even though it has been seriously handicapped both because of lack of experience in some particulars end leek of funds, the efforts it has made have for the most part been crowned with success.

In her first address delivered at the first convention which was belt in Nashville, Tennessee, September, 15,16 and 17, 1897 the first president commented upon the name of the organization end the purpose for which it was organized as follows: "Acting upon the principle of organization an union the colored women of the United States have banded themselves adapted together to fulfill a mission to which they feel peculiarly and especially celled. We have become "National", because from the Atlantic to the

Pacific, from Maine to the Gulf we wish to set in motion influences and forces that shall stop the ravages made by practices that sap our strength and preclude the possibility of advancement which under other circumstances could easily be made.

We called ourselves an "Association" to signify that we have joined hands one with another to work together in a common cause; to proclaim to the world that the women of our race have become partners in the great firm of progress and reform.

We denominate ourselves "Colored", not because we are narrow, and wish to let special emphasis upon the color of the skin, for which no one is responsible, which of itself is a proof neither of an individual's virtue nor of his vice, which is a stamp neither of one's intelligence nor of his ignorance, but we refer to the fact that this is an Association of Colored Women, because our peculiar status in this country at the present time seems to demand that we stand by ourselves in the special work for which we have been organized. For this reason and for no other it was thought best to invite the attention of the world to the fact that colored women feel their responsibility as a unit and together have clasped hands to assume it.

Special stress is laid upon the fact that our Association is composed or women, no because we wish to deny tights and privileges to our brothers in imitation of the example which they have sometimes set us, but because the work which we hope to accomplish can be done better, we believe, by the mothers, wives, daughters and sisters of the race than by the fathers husbands, brothers and sons.

The crying need of en organization of colored women is questioned by one conversant with our peculiar trials and perplexities and acquainted with the almost insurmoutable obstacles in our path to those attainments and acquisitions to which it is the right and privilege of every member of every race to aspire."

From the very first the National Association has adopted the slogan "Raise the standard and purify the atmosphere of the home." Women were told that so long as any race calls that place "home" in which the air is foul, the manners had and the morals worse, just so long would such a home be a menace to health, the breeder of vice and the abode of crime. An effort has been consistently made to impress upon the members of the Association their duty to those less favored than themselves." Not only upon the inmates of these hovels will the awful consequences of their filth and immorality be visited," warned the first president, "but upon the heads of those of us who make no effort to

stem the tide of disease and vice will vengeance as surely fall."

To the women who belong to the Association membership has meant a constant reminder of their duty to the children, They have been urged to listen to the cry of the children, particularly to those little waifs and strays whose better natures are dwarfed and whose higher impulses are throttled by the very atmosphere which they breathe, The more closely I study the relation of the Association to the race , the more clearly defined becomes its duty to the young that reason from the very beginning of the organization with all the earnestness the first president could commend she urged the establishment of kindergartens and day nurseries as fast as it could be done. There are more wage earners among colored women than can be found among the women of any other race in the United States. For that reason special effort has been made and should in the future be made to establish day nurseries, so that wage-earning mothers may have some place to leave their children while they go out to do a day's work. Even though the cost of founding and supporting either a day nursery or a kindergarten seemed so great at first as to be almost prohibitive, nevertheless not a few of these institutions have been established and successfully maintained.

Looking back over the thirty three years that have elapsed is very gratifying to recall that the very first fund established by the flat ional Association was the Kindergarten Fund—something to be used for the benefit of children. A speech entitled "The Progress of Colored Women" which had been delivered by the first president of the National Association at the National American Women Suffrage Association Biennial in Washington, D.C. in 1898 was printed in pamphlet form and sold at the Chicago Biennial in August 1899 and the money thus raised was the nucleus of the Kindergarten Fund. Surely no offense will be taken because the first president in a reminiscent mood dares to state that if the Chicago Biennial of 1899 has ever been equaled it has certainly never been surpassed by any other from any point of view.

An effort ha been made to impress upon the women that the real solution of the race problem, of which we hear so much, lies in the children, both so far as those who are handicapped are concerned and those o fail to obey the golden rule. Of course it would have been a great mistake to try to make a large organization like the National Association of Colored Women a body of one idea. With no thoughts, plans or purposes except that which centers about the children. And this has not been done. The women have been encouraged to enter various channels of generosity and beneficence whenever it seemed to be their duty and wherever they had a chance.

It was pointed out that as a race our needs are many while those able and willing to meet them are comparitively few. Homes for the orphaned and aged had to be established; Sanatoriums hospitals and training schools for nurses had to be founded; The duty of helping unfortunate women and tempted girls who have been (and still are) so sadly neglected was emphasized; It was suggested that if they were encircled by the loving arms of those who tried to turn them back to the path of rectitude, many of them might be saved. In many communities where the educational facilities were inferior or lacking members of the Association classes might be formed and were reminded that teachers might be found willing either to give their services or accept small a fee which their pupils could pay. When the national Association was first organized there were comparitively few schools of Domestic Science for colored women and girls, so that the members were urged to establish them whenever they had a chance. But in connection with such work they were entreated neither to neglect not to forget the children. They were asked to follow the example of the Great Teacher of men who could not offer himself as a sacrifice, until he had made an eternal plea for the innocence arid helplessness of child hood.

Members of the Association have been encouraged to study the Labor question , as it directly affects their group. For years their attention has been called to the alarming manner in which the race has been losing ground in their efforts to secure positions and get jobs. Such a condition affects nobody more directly and more disastrously than the women. Fair that reason the mothers, teachers or guardians of children and the youth have been strongly advised to teach the dignity. of labor to boys and girls, to young women and to young men to impress upon them the necessity of fitting themselves properly for the trade or vocation by which they expect to earn their daily bread and to establish a reputation for racial reliability and proficiency.

Membership in the National Association has meant an increase of self respect for every woman who has joined. And this spreads through the households to which they respectively belong. Sometimes colored children seem to have but little self respect. They are ashamed because they are descended from slaves. But these children should be taught that in being descended from the proud Anglo-Saxon once bowed under a yoke of bondage as bitter and as galling as that under which their African ancestors groaned. If history teaches one lesson more than another, it is that races wax and wane. The conqueror may laud it over his subject for a while, but he is himself conquerred in the end. So far as I have been able with one possible exception, perhaps, to ascertain no race has ever lived upon the face of this earth which has not at some time been the subject of a stronger. In being descended from slaves, therefore, the colored people of this country are no exception to a general rule.

The lives of the members of the Association have been broadened and deepened in a various ways. any of them have literally done with their might what their hands found to do. Some of them have worked with their 1es favored sisters on the plantations of the South and taught them the A.B.C. of living, so far as they could. Mothers meetings have been held here, there and every-concerning the management of households and the rearing of children where and much useful information has been disseminated to women who needed it most.

FOCUS QUESTIONS:

1. What indeed has the Association meant to black women, according to Terrell?

2. Why does Terrell say an organization based on skin color and sex is necessary?

THE NEW MORALITY, 1880–1920

14-1 Elizabeth Cady Stanton, The Need of Liberal Divorce Laws (1884)

The following article was written by Elizabeth Cady Stanton to consider the objections against more liberal divorce laws.

Source: Elizabeth Cady Stanton, "The Need of Liberal Divorce Laws". *The North American Review*, Vol. 139, Issue 334, Sept 1884] pp. 234-245.

THE NEED OF LIBERAL DIVORCE LAWS.

Within the past few years a new interest has been awakened in questions relating to marriage and divorce, many of the ablest men in England, France, and America taking part in the discussion. In the prolonged debate on "the deceased wife's sister's bill," in the British Parliament, we have had the opinions of the leading men of England as to what constitutes marriage, and the best conditions to insure the happiness and stability of home life. In the French Chamber of Deputies, where a divorce bill has been pending for years, the social relations have been as exhaustively discussed. And now, the proposition to secure a general law of divorce in the United States, by an amendment to the national constitution, must necessarily arouse a wide-spread agitation in this country.

When a distinguished Judge of the Supreme Court of New York, in an able article in one of our most liberal reviews, suggests important changes that should be made in our laws regulating the marriage relation, it is time for every good citizen to give a candid consideration to this subject. With many points made by Judge Noah Davis most thoughtful minds must agree, viz., the wisdom of having uniform laws in every State;

more stringent laws against early marriages; the same moral code for men and women; that marriage should be regulated by the State, by the civil and not the canon law, wholly independent of church interference, unless the parties desire to solemnize the contract with its ceremonies. Thus far I agree with Judge Davis; but there are a few other equally vital points that I would suggest to him for reconsideration.

In common with the British Parliament, the Chamber of Deputies, and the general spirit of our laws, he regards marriage too much as a physical union, wholly in its material bearings, and from the mans stand-point. He says: Restrictions ought to be imposed on the marriage of infants. The common-law rule of twelve years for females and fourteen for males is not a fit or decent one for this country. The age should be at least fifteen and eighteen years. On what principle, I would ask, should the party on whom all the inevitable hardships of marriage must fall, be the younger to enter the relation? Girls do not get their full growth until twenty-five, and are wholly unfit at fifteen for the trials of maternity. Both mother and child are enfeebled in such premature relations, and the girl robbed of all freedom and sentiment just as she awakes to the sweetest dreams of life. Few fathers or mothers would consent to the marriage of a daughter of fifteen, and the state, by wise laws, should reflect the common sense of the people. What knowledge can a girl of fifteen have of the great problems of social life, of the character of a husband, of the friendship and love of which the true marriage should be an outgrowth?

The state not only views marriage as a physical union and a civil contract, but seemingly as of inferior importance to all other contracts. A legal contract for a section of land requires that the parties be of age and of sound mind; that there be no flaw in the title, no liens or mortgages thereon not specified; and that the agreement be in writing, with the names of parties and witnesses duly affixed, stamped with the seal of the state, and recorded in the office of the county clerk. But a legal marriage, in most of the states, may be contracted between a boy of fourteen and a girl of twelve, without the consent of parents or guardians, without publication of banns, without witnesses, without even the signatures of the parties, the presence of a priest, or of any officer of the state.

Though we are taught to regard France, of all European nations, most lax in social morals, yet her legislation on marriage is far more stringent than ours. By French law the husband must be eighteen, the wife fifteen. The consent of the parents or guardians of both parties is required, and, in case of their refusal, the contract cannot be made until the man is twenty-five, and the woman twenty-one. The marriage must be preceded by the publication of the banns, and the ceremony performed by a public official, at his office, in the presence of four witnesses. It is, moreover, recorded in two special registers, one of which is deposited in the archives of the state. Yet, while this contract may be formed so ignorantly, thoughtlessly, and irreverently in the United States, the whole power of law, religion, and public sentiment are now about to be summoned to enforce its continuance, without regard to the happiness or misery of the parties.

Judge Davis speaks of divorce as the foe of marriage. He makes this mistake throughout his article. Divorce is not the foe of marriage. Adultery, intemperance, licentiousness are its foes. One might as well speak of medicine as the foe of health. Again, in subordinating the individual to the state, the premises of Judge Davis are unsound. He says, the interests of society are first and paramount, those of individuals secondary and subordinate. We have so often heard the declaration that the individual must be sacrificed to society that we have come to think their interests lie in different directions; whereas, the reverse of this proposition is true. Whatever promotes the best interests of the individual promotes the best interests of society, and vice versa. The normal condition of adult men and women is one of individual independence, of freedom, and of equality; their first duty, the full, development of their own faculties and powers, with a natural right to life, liberty, and happiness, and of resistance to all artificial contrivances that endanger life, curtail liberty, or destroy happiness. The best interests of the individual are the primal consideration; individual happiness, the only true basis of a happy home, a united church, a peaceful state, a well organized society. "We must first have units," says Emerson, "before we can have unions." We must have harmoniously developed men and women before we can have happy marriages. The central idea of barbarism has ever been the family, the tribe, the nation, never the individual. The Roman idea, the pagan idea, was, that the individual was made for the state. The Christian idea is the sacredness of the individual, superior to all human institutions. It was this central truth, taught by the great founder of our religion, that gave Christianity such a hold on the people, slowly molding popular thought to the higher idea, culminating at last in the Protestant Reformation and a Republican Government, alike based on individual rights, on individual conscience and judgment.

In regard to Judge Davis's proposition for an amendment to the national constitution, to make the laws homogeneous from Maine to Texas, the question naturally suggests itself.

On what basis should this general law be enacted? On the progressively freer divorce laws that the true American sovereign of the West will surely demand, or on more restrictive legislation? It is evident that Judge Davis inclines to the latter; but in selecting South Carolina as his standard of "peace, purity, and felicity" in family life, because no divorce laws have existed there, he is most unfortunate alike in his philosophy and his statistics. From 1872 to 1878, divorces were obtainable for adultery in South Carolina, but none were granted. In 1878 the law was repealed. Judge Davis indicates, in a very indefinite manner, the result of having no divorce law in South Carolina; he says: "I am greatly misinformed if in that State the peace, purity, and felicity of families do not maintain a far higher standard than in States where divorces are the chronic mischief and misery of domestic life." I will prove by judicial evidence the disastrous effect that the want of a divorce law has had on the family life of South Carolina, the only State in the Union in which a divorce has never been granted. "The Legislature has found it necessary to regulate, by statute, how large a proportion of his property a married man may give to his concubine."

This fact proves that where divorces are not permitted, meretricious connections will be formed. The above-mentioned law would not have been passed unless there had been subject-matter for it to operate upon. But listen to the words of wisdom from the judicial bench of South Carolina:

In this country, where divorces are not allowed for any cause whatever, we sometimes see men of excellent character unfortunate in their marriages, and virtuous women abandoned or driven away houseless by their husbands, who would be doomed to celibacy and solitude if they did not form connections which the law does not allow, and who make excellent husbands and virtuous wives still. Yet they are considered as living in adultery, because a rigorous and unyielding law, from motives of policy alone, has ordained it so. (Nott, J., in Cusack vs. White, 2 Mill, 279, 292.)

This is the system that a Judge of the Supreme Court upholds and praises, and is sustained by the Supreme Court of Georgia, which says: "In South Carolina, to her unfading honor, a divorce has not been granted since the Revolution." I would refer the learned judges of New York and Georgia to the case in South Carolina of Jelinean vs. Jelinean, 2 Des., p. 45, where a man took his negro slave woman to his bed and board, and with brutal punishment compelled the unoffending wife to eat with his colored concubine. To her unfading honor, the powers of the State of South Carolina compelled this family to live on in peace, purity, and felicity. One of the ablest writers on this subject, Joel P. Bishop, says:

That the judges should themselves praise the legislation of their own State is no more than we ought to expect; since all men esteem what is their own more highly than what is anothers. Thus it is remarked by ONeal, J.: 'The most distressing cases, justifying divorce even upon Scriptural grounds, have been again and again presented to the Legislature, and they have uniformly refused to annul the marriage tie.' They have nobly adhered to the injunction, 'Those whom God has joined together, let not man put asunder.' The working of this stern policy of 'nobly' refusing redress even in the 'most distressing cases, where Scripture joined with reason in crying for redress, has been to the good of the people and the State in every respect.' And another of her judges exclaims: 'The policy of this State has ever been against divorces. It is one of her boasts that no divorce has ever been granted in South Carolina.' Could South Carolina truly declare that no husband within her borders had ever proved unfaithful to the marriage vow, and no wife had been false to her husband; that the observation judicially made by one of her judges concerning marriages in this State is in no part true, namely, 'all marriages almost are entered into on one of two considerations, love or interest and the Court is induced to believe the latter is the foundation of most of them' (Thompson, J., in Devall vs. Devall, 4 Des., 79); that no judge of hers had from the judicial bench proclaimed it a virtue to commit the legal felony of polygamy, and to live in adultery; that no class of men existed in the State calling for legislation to regulate their connections with their concubines, then, indeed, might the people of the other States talk of 'unfading honor,' which had settled as a halo, or as a crown of glory about her brow!"

Another view of the domestic virtue and felicity of South Carolina law can be had by reference to the United States Census of 1880, which shows the number of mulattoes, or the mixed races, in that State. Where concubinage is recognized, there is no pressing need for liberal divorce laws. Judge Davis says: "In the colonial history of the State of New York, for more than a century, divorces were unknown." The Patroon Courts granted divorces in 1630, and other divorces were granted in 1655. In Massachusetts divorces were granted before 1674. In Connecticut, before 1655. I am informed that the declaration by Judge Davis, that a legal divorce can be obtained in New York in twelve hours, is incorrect. In case of a default, the plaintiff cannot get judgment in less than twenty days. If the defendant answers, the motion for judgment must be made at the regular Special Term, in accordance with the accurate interpretation of rule 77 by Judge A. R. Lawrence. In this latter case, the plaintiff cannot get judgment in less than one month. It usually takes at least two months to get judgment in the simplest divorce case. But if it be true in the case specified by Judge Davis, where the crime is adultery and the parties are agreed, that a legal divorce and marriage can occur within twelve hours, the question is, Who is responsible for such laws? and can we safely trust legislators who have placed the marriage institution on such uncertain foundations to draw up a constitutional amendment giving general laws to all the States? Again, Judge Davis's inferences from his facts are not logical. He says the percentage of divorces is largest in States furnishing the readiest facilities for dissolving the union. True, but it is not because the inhabitants of that State are made fickle and faithless by the laws, as he suggests, but because large numbers of persons come from States having rigid divorce laws into those furnishing the readiest facilities for their purpose. The number of divorces granted in a given State is no indication of the general discontent of its own citizens.

Judge Davis is equally unfortunate in his facts of ecclesiastical history. He calls monogamy "an Hebraic Christianized idea." The Hebraic part of that idea was pure polygamy; the Christianized part was the unchanged polygamy of the early Christian church, except where and until it came in contact with the monogamic Greek and Roman civilizations omitting, the Germanic and Norse monogamy from the account, only because Christianity reached them after its modification by Roman civilization. Neither Christ nor his disciples ever attempted to change polygamous into monogamic marriage, any more than they attempted to change absolute political despotism into constitutional or republican government, or to abolish slavery where they found it.

The Catholic Church early seized the control of marriage, as she did of every institution that would give her a hold on mankind, and administered its ordinances in the most tyrannical form as regards the masses, her instinct ever being restrictive; though she always claimed for herself the right of divorce, and exercised it for what she deemed sufficient cause. One of the prominent features of the Reformation was the demand of its great leaders for free divorce, in the interests of morality, in view of the licentiousness of Catholic Europe. And to-day the only hope for the purification of manners and morals is in free divorce; in elevating the ideal of marriage so that it shall consist of the spiritual as well as the physical element. Where unfitness exists, it would be for the interest of society for the state to step in (supposing authority in the matter an admitted fact), and insist on annulling the contract, instead of impeding a separation. The popular objections to divorce are unsound and contradictory.

First. It is said, to make divorce respectable is to break up all family relations, which is to say that human affections are the result of church canons and statute laws. The love of men and women for each other and for their children existed long before human governments were established, and will survive when all these artificial arrangements shall have passed away. Did the happy wives in this State ever suppose that the regret they felt in leaving home, husband, and children, and the joy in returning, were due to the stringent divorce laws of New York and that without these they would have been wanderers on the face of the earth? To open the door of escape to those who live in contention, would not necessarily embitter the relations of those who are happy. On the contrary, freedom in all relations strengthens the bond of union. When husbands and wives do not own each other as property, marriage will be a life-long courtship, not a weary yoke, from which both may sometimes long for deliverance. Many a tyrannical husband, knowing that public sentiment would protect his wife in leaving him, might become gracious and reasonable; and many a peevish wife, knowing that her husband, could honorably sunder the tie, would soon change her manners.

Second. It is said that the fickle would separate for trifling causes, and that unprincipled men, from love of change, would take a new wife every Christmas, if they could legally rid themselves in season of the old one. As the centripetal forces in the material world are strong enough to hold matter to a common center against all outside attractions, so, in the moral world, the love of change is subordinate to the stronger love of the familiar objects and conditions about them. All experience proves the truth of the historical maxim, "Mankind are more disposed to suffer while evils are sufferable, than to right themselves by abolishing the forms to which they have been accustomed." This objection is based on the idea that woman will always remain the helpless victim of every man she meets. But a new type of womanhood is developing under our free institutions, demanding higher conditions. Educated to self-support, with a profitable place in the world of work, with land under her feet and a shelter over her head, the political equal of the man by her side, she will not clutch at every offer of marriage, like a drowning man at the floating straw. Though men should remain just what they are, the entire revolution in woman's position, now begun, will force a new moral code in social life. But the virtue and independence of women must evolve a higher type of manhood, also.

Third. Some claim that the interests of children require an indissoluble tie. It is a great blessing to be well born, to be welcomed on the threshold of time, and to be reared in an atmosphere of peace and love. No amount of care and education can ever compensate a child for the morbid conditions of its organization, resulting from coldness, indifference, or disgust in the parents for one another. Next to the misfortune of such a birth, is the demoralizing influence on children trained in an atmosphere of discord and dissatisfaction, such as a false marriage relation inevitably creates. One of the strongest reasons for demanding the release of unhappy wives and husbands is the evil effects on the children.

Fourth. Men and women, it is said, would not exercise the deliberation they now do, if to marry ill were not considered a crime, and the parties doomed to suffer a life-long penalty. Nothing could be more reckless than what is done legally every day, under the present system when to be seen merely walking together may be taken as evidence in court of intent to marry, and going through the ceremony in jest may seal the contract. The fear of transient conditions would make the parties far more careful in making their family arrangements. Women, acting on the faith of a life-long relation, a permanent home, are very apt to surrender all their earthly possessions into the hands of husbands who spend their substance and then abandon them to self-support. The theory of the indissoluble marriage never was and never can be practicable, except for the best organized men and women, in happy relations, and they are a law to themselves. For others, legal divorces are far better than discord or erratic relations outside of law. Impulsive people, under the influence of strong passions, pay little attention, in any circumstances, to laws or future consequences; and very few know what the laws are, or the penalty for their violation.

Fifth. It is said that the Bible is against divorce. When those who are opposed to all reforms can find no other argument, their last resort is the Bible. It has been interpreted to favor intemperance, slavery, capital punishment, and the subjection of women; and now, in the face of the most pronounced declarations, and the example of "men after Gods own heart" and his chosen people for centuries, we are told that it condemns divorce. The one form of marriage recognized in the Bible is polygamy, both in the Old Testament and the New. It was at a Jewish polygamous wedding that Jesus performed his first miracle, and polygamy was practiced by Christians for centuries. It would be rather a difficult task for one thoroughly versed in Scripture to prove the monogamic marriage and the indissoluble tie by any fair interpretation of Hebrew or Greek texts.

As the great majority of divorces are asked for by women, release and divorce are of vital importance to them. No words can describe the infinite outrages to which women are subject in compulsory relations for which the law gives no redress. The decisions of judges in many cases show that the subjection of woman is the very essence of the law of marriage; and how could it be otherwise when the contract and all the statutes governing it have been made by one of the parties, while the other has been profoundly ignorant of its provisions and specifications. How many women in this republic know anything of the spirit or letter of the civil or canon law on this whole question of marriage and divorce? Not until they feel its iron teeth in their own flesh do they awake to the helplessness of their position. Thus far this vital question has been discussed by man; he has spoken in Scripture, and he has spoken in law; from the beginning he has had the whole and sole regulation of the matter. In all history, sacred and profane, woman has never been recognized as an equal party to the contract. Will the remedy that Judge Davis proposes, a general law on the basis of the code in South Carolina, bring new liberties to woman? No, no; in justice to the daughters of this republic there should be no such final settlement of this question as a constitutional amendment involves until woman has a direct voice in the legislation of the country. For the past half century, those who understand our system of jurisprudence have been constantly protesting against the spirit and letter of the common law of England on which our system is based, until many of the old statutes so degrading and oppressive to married women have been, one after another, swept away. Finding the marriage relation theoretically a condition of slavery, and practically so when tyrannical husbands chose to avail themselves of their legal rights, women early began to ask release from their yoke of bondage, and here and there humane legislators, roused with a sense of woman's wrongs, began to open the door of escape through liberal divorce laws. But at first it required great courage and self-respect for wives, however miserable, in the face of time-honored laws, religion, and public sentiment, to avail themselves of these new privileges. Now, with higher light and knowledge of the true marriage, and all the responsibilities that grow out of it, they begin to feel themselves more degraded by remaining with unworthy and unloved partners than by sundering the unholy ties that bind them in such unions. When we appreciate the fact that the vast majority of applications for divorce are made by women, that liberal divorce laws for oppressed wives are what Canada was for Southern slaves, it is clearly a work of supererogation for learned men to demand "more stringent laws for women's protection!"—protection, such as the eagle gives the lamb he carries to his eyrie! Alas, for the wrongs that woman has suffered under the specious plea of protection!

If the marriage institution is of divine origin, we may safely trust him who ordained it to see that those whom he hath joined together will never be put asunder. It is not necessary to reenact the laws of God. Liberal divorce laws are intended to enable those only whom God has not joined together to be put asunder. Such laws, so far from being barbarous and degrading, indicate the growing independence, intelligence, and virtue of American womanhood. Our decreasing families, so far from being an evidence of the dying out of maternal love, indicate a higher perception of the dignity and responsibility of motherhood. With woman's keen sense of moral principles, she begins to appreciate the awful waste of human force as she contemplates the panorama of our social life: the unhappy inmates of our jails and prisons, of our asylums for the insane, the deaf, the dumb, the blind, the orphan and pauper, the innumerable standing army of drunkards, the multitudes of children whom nobody owns, and for whom nobody cares—cold, hungry, their feet in slippery places, sleeping at night in all our cities, like rats, in any hole they can find. In view of these appalling facts, the mothers of the race may well pause and put the question to themselves, Is it for such as these we give the heyday of our lives? For such as these we ever and anon go down to the very gates of death? Is this a life-work worthy our highest ambition, a religious duty for our best powers? The answering echo from every mountain-top is, No! Above the thunders of Sinai, a warning voice, loud and clear, rings through the centuries: "The sins of the fathers shall be visited upon the children, to the third and fourth generations."

Before claiming that marriage is a divine institution, before binding women by further restrictive legislation, let the high-priests at the family altars purify themselves, body and soul, and make themselves fit to be the creators of immortal beings. Science has vindicated the right to discuss freely whether our ancestors were apes; let it be as free to ask whether our posterity shall be idiots, knaves, and lunatics; and if not, by what changes such wretched results may be avoided.

Judge Davis's picture of the general upheaval in our social life, under liberal divorce laws, is, indeed, a sad presentation of the possible future; but a change in the civil code will not destroy all natural affections. Is family life with the mass of mankind so satisfactory that it calls for no improvement? Change is not death, neither is progress destruction. We have shifted governments from despotisms, empires and monarchies, to republics, without giving up the idea of national life; and we Americans believe that greater peace and prosperity are enjoyed in a republic than under any other form of government. True, these changes from the lower to the higher have involved hot debates, violence, and war; but the free institutions we enjoy more than compensate for the struggles we have endured. We have changed the foundations of the church, too, without destroying the religious sentiment in the human soul. The dissensions in the church have filled the world with despair for ages and deluged nations in blood; but the right of individual conscience and judgment, against all authority, is the result. Though the cardinal points of our faith have been changed again and again, yet we have a church still. So we shall have the family, that great conservator of national strength and morals, after the present restrictive divorce laws are all swept from the statute-books. To establish a republican form of government in the family must of necessity involve discussion and division; but more satisfactory relations will be the result of the transition evils that we now see and deplore. The same law of equality that has revolutionized the state and the church is now reorganizing the home. The same process of evolution that has given us a state without a king and a church without a Pope, will give us a family without a divinely ordained head, in which the interests of father, mother, and child will be equally represented.

ELIZABETH CADY STANTON.

FOCUS QUESTIONS:

1. What do you think of both the arguments against more liberal divorce law, and Stanton's attacks on these arguments?

2. What assumptions about family and marriage does Stanton make?

3. What new conception of the household and family does Stanton imagine would accompany greater availability of divorce for women?

14-2 The Comstock Act of 1873

The Act for the Suppression of Trade In and Circulation of Obscene Literature and Articles of Immoral Use were popularly named the Comstock Act for Anthony Comstock.

The Comstock Law (1873)

Be it enacted...That whoever, within the District of Columbia or any of the Territories of the United States...shall sell...or shall offer to sell, or to lend, or to give away, or in any manner to exhibit, or shall otherwise publish or offer to publish in any manner, or shall have in his possession, for any such purpose or purposes, an obscene book, pamphlet, paper, writing, advertisement, circular, print, picture, drawing or other representation, figure, or image on or of paper or other material, or any cast instrument, or other article of an immoral nature, or any drug or medicine, or any article whatever, for the prevention of conception, or for causing unlawful abortion, or shall advertise the same for sale, or shall write or print, or cause to be written or printed, any card, circular, book, pamphlet, advertisement, or notice of any kind, stating when, where, how, or of whom, or by what means, any of the articles in this section...can be purchased or obtained, or shall manufacture, draw, or print, or in any wise make any of such articles, shall be deemed guilty of a misdemeanor, and on conviction thereof in any court of the United States...he shall be imprisoned at hard labor in the penitentiary for not less than six months nor more than five years for each offense, or fined not less than one hundred dollars nor more than two thousand dollars, with costs of court.

FOCUS QUESTIONS:

1. What is the scope of the Comstock Act? Was it enforceable?
2. Who would interpret the meaning of such terms as "immoral" and "obscene" used in this act?

14-3 Jane Addams, "An Analogy" (1912)

The problem of prostitution was one of many which reformers hoped to remedy. The following excerpt is from a book by Jane Addams (1860-1935) at the height of the "white slavery panic".

Source: Jane Addams, "An Analogy" from *A New Conscience and an Ancient Evil.* New York: The MacMillan Company, 1912, 3-8.

In every large city throughout the world thousands of women are so set aside as outcasts from decent society that, it is considered an impropriety to speak the very word which designates them. Lecky calls this type of woman "the most mournful and the most awful figure in history": he says that "she remains, while creeds and civilizations rise and fall, the eternal sacrifice of humanity, blasted for the sins of the people." But evils so old that they are imbedded in man's earliest history have been known to sway before an enlightened public opinion and in the end to give way to a growing conscience, which regards them first as a moral affront and at length as an utter impossibility. Thus the generation just before us, our own fathers, uprooted the enormous up as of slavery, "the tree that was literally as old as the race of man," although slavery doubtless had its beginnings in the captives of man's earliest warfare, even as this existing evil thus originated.

Those of us who think we discern the beginnings of a new conscience in regard to this twin of slavery, as old and outrageous as slavery itself and even more persistent, find a possible analogy between certain civic, philanthropic and educational efforts directed against the very existence of this social evil and similar organized efforts which preceded the overthrow of slavery in America. Thus, long before slavery was finally declared illegal, there were international regulations of its traffic, state and federal legislation concerning its extension, and many extra legal attempts to control its abuses; quite as we have the inter-national regulations concerning the white slave traffic, the state and interstate legislation for its repression, and an extra legal power in connection with it so universally given to the municipal police that the possession of this power has become one of the great sources of corruption in every American city.

Before society was ready to proceed against the institution of slavery as such, groups of men and women by means of the underground rail road cherished and educated individual slaves; it is scarcely necessary to point out the similarity to the rescue homes and preventive associations which every great city contains.

It is always easy to overwork an analogy, and yet the economist who for years insisted that slave labor continually and arbitrarily limited the wages of free labor and was therefore a detriment to national wealth was a forerunner of the economist of to-day who points out the economic basis of the social evil, the connection between low wages and despair, between over-fatigue and the demand for reckless pleasure.

Before the American nation agreed to regard slavery as unjustifiable from the standpoint of public morality, an army of reformers, lecturers, and writers set forth its enormity in a never-ceasing flow of invective, of appeal, and of portrayal concerning the human cruelty to which the system lent itself. We can discern the scouts and outposts of a similar army advancing against this existing evil: the physicians and sanitarians who are committed to the task of ridding the race from contagious diseases, the teachers and lecturers who are appealing to the higher morality of thousands of young people; the growing literature not only biological and didactic, but of a popular type more closely approaching "Uncle Tom's Cabin."

Throughout the agitation for the abolition of slavery in America, there were statesmen who gradually became convinced of the political and moral necessity of giving to the freedman the protection of the ballot. In this current agitation there are at least a few men and women who would extend a greater social and political freedom to all women if only because domestic control has proved so ineffectual.

We may certainly take courage from the fact that our contemporaries are fired by social compassions and enthusiasms, to which even our immediate predecessors were indifferent. Such compunctions have ever manifested themselves in varying degrees of ardor through different groups in the same community. Thus among those who are newly aroused to action in regard to the social evil are many who would endeavor to regulate it and believe they can minimize its dangers, still larger numbers who would eliminate all trafficking of unwilling victims in connection with it, and yet others who believe that as a quasi-legal institution it may be absolutely abolished. Perhaps the analogy to the abolition of slavery is most striking in that these groups, in their varying points of view, are like those earlier associations which differed widely in regard to chattel slavery. Only the so-called extremists, in the first instance, stood for abolition and they were continually told that what they proposed was clearly impos-

sible. The legal and commercial obstacles, bulked large, were placed before them and it was confidently asserted that the blame for the historic existence of slavery lay deep within human nature itself. Yet gradually all of these associations reached the point of view of the abolitionist and before the war was over even the most lukewarm unionist saw no other solution of the nation's difficulty. Some such gradual conversion to the point of view of abolition is the experience of every society or group of people who seriously face the difficulties and complications of the social evil. Certainly all the national organizations—the National Vigilance Committee, the American Purity Federation, the Alliance for the Suppression and Prevention of the White Slave Traffic and many others—stand for the final abolition of commercialized vice. Local vice commissions, such as the able one recently appointed in Chicago, although composed of members of varying beliefs in regard to the possibility of control and regulation, united in the end in recommending a law enforcement looking towards final abolition. Even the most sceptical of Chicago citizens, after reading the fearless document, shared the hope of the com-mission that "the city, when aroused to the truth, would instantly rebel against the social evil in all its phases." A similar recommendation of ultimate abolition was recently made unanimous by the Minneapolis vice commission after the conversion of many of its members. Doubtless all of the national societies have before them a task only less gigantic than that faced by those earlier associations in America for the suppression of slavery, although it may be legitimate to remind them that the best-known anti-slavery society in America was organized by the New England abolitionists in 1836, and only thirty-six years later, in 1872, was formally disbanded because its object had been accomplished.

FOCUS QUESTIONS:

1. What analogy does Addams make? Do you consider the analogy legitimate?

2. Why does Addams view prostitution as an evil?

3. What is the "new conscience" that Addams writes of? How does she use this notion to find comfort in the fact that prostitution was still prevalent?

14-4 Advertisement for Contraceptives From Late Nineteenth Century Newspaper.

The ads below were commonly found in the last pages of newspapers and magazines from the late nineteenth century on.

Source: Reprinted in D'Emilio, John and Estelle B. Freedman, *Intimate Matters: A History of Sexuality in America.* New York: Harper & Row, Publishers, 1988, 112.

RUBBER GOODS

RUBBER GOODS Gent's latest improved rubber Protectors, best material, pliable and easily adjusted, $.25 each, 4 for $.50, 10 for $1. Ladies' patent shields, very durable, $.50, 3 for $1. Rubber Bulb Syringes, double neck, $1 each. Address H.B. Williams, Boston, Mass.

RUBBER GOODS for Ladies or Gents; good service, pliable, secure; try ours once you will use no other. Gent's $.25 each; 4 for $.50; 9 for $1. Ladies' $.50 each; 3 for $1. Secret helper, either sex, $.25, H.R. Chestonok, Providence, R.I.

RUBBER GOODS Latest improved, gents, $1 per doz.—NO LESS SOLD, Ladies' Shields, $1 each, best material, pliable, durable, safe, and will last for years with careful usage.

M.W. Veronica, Box 3,502, New York, N.Y.

Special Gentlemen's New **Silk Rubber Goods**; Superior Quality, Absolutely Reliable; Prices—$.25, 4 for $.50, 10 for $1.00, Special low rates in large quantities to dealers.

Harris Specialty Co., Box No. 57, Cleveland O.

RUBBER GOODS Pliable, safe and durable; never fail; affording absolute security. By mail, $.25 each; 3, $.50; 7, $1. QUEEN CITY SUPPLY AGENT Toronto, Canada.

GENTS send 15 cents for useful Rubber article. Best made, 3 for $.25, W.J. McFadden, Chicago, Ill.

MEDICAL
THE GREAT FRENCH REMEDY, KAVA FOURNIER

FOR GONORRHOEA Over 30,000 cases successfully treated in the leading Paris hospitals.

Used in daily practice by all French physicians.

Medals and Diploma of Honor, Paris Expositions.

Acts with magical rapidity in new cases.

Cures absolutely those chronic case which other remedies only relieve.

Full package remedies sent C.O.D. express, prepaid, $5.00. Handsome pamphlet free.

KAVA FOURNIER AGENCY, 38 East 13th Street, New York.

LADIES SHOULD USE FRENCH MEDICATED PARTICLES

Safe, sure relief when Pills entirely fail. No obstructions can stand against them. Easily used; failure impossible, Quickest regulators in the world. Ladies using them delighted. Particulars free. Mrs. Clara Boswell, Boston , Mass., Box 2977

FOCUS QUESTIONS:

1. Considering the passage of the Comstock Act in 1873, why were such ads still being printed?

14-5 Birth Control in the Feminist Program

Crystal Eastman (1881-1928) was a lawyer, activist and journalist. She was one of the founding members of both the Woman's Peace Party and the National Woman's Party. The following is from her collected writings.

Source: Crystal Eastman, Blanch Wiesen Cook, *Crystal Eastman on Women and Revolution*, Oxford University Press, 1978

Feminism means different things to different people, I suppose. To women with a taste for politics and reform it means the right to vote and hold office. To women physically strong and adventuresome it means freedom to enter all kinds of athletic contests and games, to compete with men in aviation, to drive racing cars, to get up Battalions of Death, to enter dangerous trades, etc. To many it means social and sex freedom, doing away with exclusively feminine virtues. To most of all it means economic freedom —not the ideal economic freedom dreamed of by revolutionary socialism, but such economic freedom as it is possible for a human being to achieve under the existing system of competitive production and distribution,—in short such freedom to choose one's way of making a living as men now enjoy, and definite economic rewards for one's work when it happens to be "home-making." This is to me the central fact of feminism. Until women learn to want economic independence, i.e., the ability to earn their own living independently of husbands, fathers, brothers or lovers,—and, until they work out a way to get this independence without denying themselves the joys of love and motherhood, it seems to me feminism has no roots.. Its manifestations are often delightful and stimulating but they are sporadic, they effect no lasting change in the attitude of men to women, or of women to themselves. Whether other feminists would agree with me that the economic is the fundamental aspect of feminism, I don't know. But on this we are surely agreed, that Birth Control is an elementary essential in all aspects of feminism.

Whether we are the special followers of Alice Paul, or Ruth Law, or Ellen Key, or Olive Schreiner, we must all be followers of Margaret Sanger. Feminists are not nuns. That should be established. We want to love and to be loved, and most of us want children, one or two at least. But we want our love to be joyous and free—not clouded with ignorance and fear. And we want our children to be deliberately, eagerly called into being, when we are at our best, not crowded upon us in times of poverty and weakness. We want this precious sex knowledge not just for ourselves, the conscious feminists; we want it for all the millions of unconscious feminists that swarm the earth,—we want it for all women.

Life is a big battle for the complete feminist even when she can regulate the size of her family. Women who are creative, or who have administrative gifts, or business ability, and who are ambitious to achieve and fulfill themselves in these lines, if they also have the normal desire to be mothers, must make up their minds to be a sort of supermen, I think. They must develop greater powers of concentration, a stronger will to "keep at it," a more determined ambition than men of equal gifts, in order to make up for the time and energy and thought and devotion that child-bearing and rearing, even in the most "advanced" families, seems inexorably to demand of the mother. But if we add to this handicap complete uncertainty as to when children may come, how often they come or how many there shall be, the thing becomes impossible. I would almost say that the whole structure of the feminist's dream of society rests upon the rapid extension of sci-

entific knowledge about birth control.

This seems so obvious to me that I was astonished the other day to come upon a group of distinguished feminists who discussed for an hour what could be done with the woman's vote in New York State and did not once mention birth control.

As the readers of this magazine well know, the laws of this state, instead of establishing free clinics as necessary centers of information for the facts about sex hygiene and birth control, actually make it a crime, even on the part of a doctor, to tell grown men and women how to limit the size of their families. What could be a more pressing demand on the released energies of all these valiant suffrage workers than to repeal that law?

This work should especially commend itself, now in wartime when so many kinds of reform are outlawed. There is nothing about Birth Control agitation to embarrass the President or obstruct the prosecution of the war. If limited to the New York State laws it need not even rouse the indignation of Mr. Burleson. It is a reform absolutely vital to the progress of woman and one which the war does not interfere with. While American men are fighting to rid the old world of autocracy let American women set to and rid the new world of this intolerable old burden of sex ignorance. It should not be a difficult task.

I don't believe there is one woman within the confines of this state who does not believe in birth control. I never met one. That is, I never met one who thought that *she* should be kept in ignorance of contraceptive methods. Many I have met who valued the knowledge they possessed, but thought there were certain other classes who would be better kept in ignorance. The old would protect the young. The rich would keep the poor in ignorance. The good would keep their knowledge from the bad, the strong from the weak, and so on. But never in all my travels have I come on one married woman who, possessed of this knowledge would willingly part with it, or who not yet informed, was not eager for knowledge. It is only hypocrisy, and here and there a little hard-faced puritanism we have to overcome. No genuine human interest will be against the repeal of this law. Of course capitalism thrives on an over-supplied labor market, but with our usual enormous immigration to be counted on as soon as the war, is over, it is not likely that an organized economic opposition to birth control will develop.

In short, if feminism, conscious and bold and intelligent, leads the demand, it will be supported by the secret eagerness of all women to control the size of their families, and a suffrage state should make short work of repealing these old laws that stand in the way of birth control.

FOCUS QUESTIONS:

1. Why does Eastman say "we must all be followers of Margaret Sanger"?

2. What are the laws that should be repealed, according to Eastman?

3. The article was written towards the end of World War I. What impact does this have on Eastman's goals?

14-6 Mary to Helena (1869, 1870)

Source: Hallock, Mary, to Helena, 1869 or 1870, *Mary Hallock Foote Letters,* Manuscript Divison, Stanford University. Excerpted in Smith-Rosenberg, Carroll. "The Female World of Love and Ritual: Relations between Women in Nineteenth Century America."

During the same years that Jeannie and Sarah wrote of their love and need for each other, two slightly younger women began a similar odyssey of love, dependence and—ultimately—physical, though not emotional, separation. Molly and Helena met in 1868 while both attended the Cooper Institute School of Design for Women in New York City. For several years these young women studied and explored the city together, visited each other's families, and formed part of a social net-work of other artistic young women. Gradually, over the years, their initial friendship deepened into a close intimate bond which continued throughout their lives. The tone in the letters which Molly wrote to Helena changed over these years from "My dear Helena," and signed "your attached friend," to "My dearest Helena," "My Dearest," "My Beloved," and signed "Thine always" or "thine Molly."

The letters they wrote to each other during these first five years permit us to reconstruct something of their relationship together. As Molly wrote in one early letter:

I have not said to you in so many or so few words that I was happy with you during those few so incredibly short weeks but surely you do not need words to tell you what you must know. Those two or three days so dark without, so bright with firelight and contentment within I shall always remember as proof that, for a time, at least—I fancy for quite a long time—we might be sufficient for each other. We know that we can amuse each other for many idle hours together and now we know that we can also work together. And that means much, don't you think so?

She ended: "I shall return in a few days. Imagine yourself kissed many times by one who loved you so dearly."

The intensity and even physical nature of Molly's love was echoed in many of the letters she wrote during the next few years, as, for instance in this short thank-you note for a small present: "Imagine yourself kissed a dozen times my darling. Perhaps it is well for you that we are far apart. You might find my thanks so expressed rather overpowering. I have that delightful feeling that it doesn't matter much what I say or how I say it, since we shall meet so soon and forget in that moment that we were ever separated. . . . I shall see you soon and be content."

At the end of the fifth year, however, several crises occurred. The relationship, at least in its intense form, ended, though Molly and Helena continued an intimate and complex relationship for the next half-century. The exact nature of these crises is not completely clear, but it seems to have involved Molly's decision not to live with Helena, as they had originally planned, but to remain at home because of parental insistence. Molly was now in her late twenties. Helena responded with anger and Molly became frantic at the thought that Helena would break off their relationship. Though she wrote distraught letters and made despairing attempts to see Helena, the relationship never regained its former ardor—possibly because Molly had a male suitor." Within six months Helena had decided to marry a man who was, coincidentally, Molly's friend and publisher. Two years later Molly herself finally married. The letters toward the end of this period discuss the transition both women made to having male lovers—Molly spending much time reassuring Helena, who seemed depressed about the end of their relationship and with her forthcoming marriage."

It is clearly difficult from a distance of 100 years and from a post-Freudian cultural perspective to decipher the complexities of Molly and Helena's relationship. Certainly Molly and Helena were lovers—emotionally if not physically. The emotional intensity and pathos of their love becomes apparent in several letters

Molly wrote Helena during their crisis: wanted so to put my arms round my girl of all the girls in, the world and tell her. . . . I love her as wives do love their husbands, as *friends* who have taken each other for life—and believe in her as I believe in my God. . . . If I didn't love you do you suppose I'd care about anything or have ridiculous notions and panics and behave like an old fool who ought to know better. I'm going to hang on to your skirts. . . .You can't get away from [my] love." Or as she wrote after Helena's decision to marry: "You know dear Helena, I really was in love with you. It was a passion such as I had never known until I saw you. I don't think it was the noblest way to love you." The theme of intense female love was one Molly again expressed in a letter she wrote to the man Helena was to marry: "Do you know sir, that until you came along I believe that she loved me almost as girls love their lovers. *I know I loved her so.* Don't you wonder that I can stand the sight of you." This was in a letter congratulating them on their forthcoming marriage."

Several factors in American society between the mid-eighteenth and the mid-nineteenth centuries may well have permitted women to form a variety of close emotional relationships with other women. American society was characterized in large part by rigid gender-role differentiation within the family and within society as a whole, leading to the emotional segregation of women and men. The roles of daughter and mother shaded imperceptibly and ineluctably into each other, while the biological realities of frequent pregnancies, childbirth, nursing, and menopause bound women together in physical and emotional intimacy. It was within just such a social framework, I would argue, that a specifically female world did indeed develop, a world built around a generic and unself-conscious pattern of single-sex or homosocial networks. These supportive networks were institutionalized in social conventions or rituals which accompanied virtually every important event in a woman's life, from birth to death. Such female relationships were frequently supported and paralleled by severe social restrictions on intimacy between young men and women. Within such a world of emotional richness and complexity devotion to and love of other women became a plausible and socially accepted form of human interaction.

FOCUS QUESTIONS:

1. How would we characterize such a relationship today, or does it defy modern categories?

2. According to the author, what was the role of close friendships between women in this period?

14-7 Family Planning (1926)

Margaret Sanger was a controversial figure in her day. She introduced the term birth control to American couples, she encouraged people to explore the pleasures of passionate and sexual love, and she wrote frankly about the topic. She advocated the use of contraceptives for working class people, to control family growth at an economically manageable level, and also to the middle class, to postpone the arrival of children so the couple could build their relationship on the pleasure of intimate knowledge of each other.

Source: Margaret Sanger, *Happiness in Marriage* (1926) pp. 191-203.

PREMATURE PARENTHOOD AND WHY TO AVOID IT

Coming together with widely differing likes and dislikes, varying inheritances and often with widely divergent training and ideals, the two young people who marry will not be long in discovering that they may have much less in common than they had ever dreamed possible.

When Society has tossed them a marriage certificate and the Church has concluded the ceremony which has legally united them, they are then forced back upon their own resources. Society, so to speak, has washed its hands of the young couple, or cast this man and this woman into the deep waters of matrimony, where they are left to sink or swim as best they may.

The certificate of marriage solves nothing. Rather it accentuates the greater and more complex problems of life. To find a solution to this great problem of living together and growing together requires all the combined intelligence and foresight both man and woman can command. Drifting into this relation will offer no solution, for very often those who drift into marriage, drift out of it in the same aimless fashion.

Others, who have not realized that the marriage of a man and woman is not merely a legal sanction for parenthood, but that it is an important relation in itself—the most important one in human life—often find themselves defeated and forced into an accidental and premature parenthood for which they are not financially or spiritually prepared.

Two years at least are necessary to cement the bonds of love and to establish the marriage relation. Parenthood should therefore be postponed by every young married couple until at least the third year of marriage.

Why is this advisable?

When the young wife is forced into maternity too soon, both are cheated out of marital adjustment and harmony that require time to mature and develop. The plunge into parenthood prematurely with all its problems and disturbances, is like the blighting of a bud before it has been given time to blossom.

Even in the fully matured healthy wife pregnancy has a disturbing physiological and nervous reaction. Temporarily the whole character and temperament of the woman undergoes profound changes. Usually nausea, headaches, irritability, loss of appetite, ensue. At the beginning of this period there develop temporary eccentricities that do not belong to the woman in her normal condition.

If the bride is enforced into an unwilling or accidental pregnancy during the honeymoon or the early stages of their marital love, the young husband is deprived of the possible opportunity of knowing his wife during one of the most interesting stages of her development. He has known her in the exciting days of courtship and during the heightened though brief period of the honeymoon, and now, alas, she enters all too soon the ominous days of early pregnancy. Never under such conditions can he know her in the growing beauty and ripening of mature womanhood. He has known her as a romantic girl before marriage—and now as a mother-to-be, frightened, timorous, and physically and nervously upset by the great ordeal she must go through.

Here often begins a spiritual separation between husband and wife. Conscious of his own helplessness, likewise of his own responsibility, the young husband feels it his duty to leave her alone. This enforced separation is spiritual rather than physical. Outwardly the relation may seem the same. It may be a separation only in the sense that no real unity or welding has been attained. Engrossed by this new problem, the young wife may resign herself to the inevitable and enters a state of passive resignation that is deadening to her love-life. She is in no condition to enjoy companion-ship. Beneath the superficial and conventional expression of happiness at the approaching parenthood, there may rankle a suppressed resentment at the young husband's careless pride in becoming a father. The young bride knows that she is paying too great a price for the brief and happy days of her honeymoon. She has been swept too rapidly from girlhood to motherhood. Love and romance, as many young wives have confessed to me, were but traps leading her to endless travail and enslavement. And this hidden rankling is often directed toward the husband, whom the wife holds responsible for her accidental pregnancy.

This unhappy condition would not have occurred if they had time to become one, if there were a period of two years during which the bonds of love might be firmly cemented, for time alone can produce this unity. It is a process of growth. Married love does not spring full grown into life. It is a delicate plant and it grows from the seed. It must be deeply and firmly rooted, nourished by the sunlight of tenderness, courtship and mutual consideration, before it can produce fine flowers and fruits. This period is as essential for human development as the period of body-building and adolescence.

It is a period of mutual adjustment. It is a period of spiritual discovery and exploration, of finding one's self and one's beloved. It is a period for the full and untroubled expression of passionate love. It is a period for cultural development. It thrusts forward its own complex problems-problems, let it be understood, intricately complex in themselves.

Husband and wife must solve many problems only by *living through them*, not by any cut and dried rules and regulations. For marriage brings with it problems that are individual and unique for each couple.

If instead of solving these problems of early parenthood, in which the life of a third person is immediately involved, a child thrusts itself into the lives of young husband and wife, these fundamental problems of marriage are never given the attention they deserve. A new situation arises, and in innumerable cases, love, as the old adage has it, flies out of the window.

We must recognize that the whole position of womanhood has changed today. Not so many years ago it was assumed to be a just and natural state of affairs that marriage was considered as nothing but a preliminary to motherhood. A girl passed from the guardianship of her father or nearest male relative to that of her husband. She had no will, no wishes of her own. Hers not to question why, but merely to fulfill duties imposed upon her by the man into whose care she was given.

Today women are on the whole much more individual. They possess as strong likes and dislikes as men. They live more and more on the plane of social equality with men. They are better companions. We should be glad that there is more enjoyable companionship and real friendship between men and women.

This very fact, it is true, complicates the marriage relation, and at the same time enables it. Marriage no longer means the slavish subservience of the woman to the will of the man. It means, instead, the union of two strong and highly individualized natures. Their first problem is to find out just what the terms of this partnership are to be. Understanding full and complete cannot come all at once, in one revealing flash. It takes time to arrive at a full and sympathetic understanding of each other, and mutually to arrange lives to increase this understanding. Out of the mutual adjustments, harmony must grow and discords gradually disappear.

These results cannot be obtained if the problem of parenthood is thrust upon the young husband and wife before they are spiritually and economically prepared to meet it. For naturally the coming of the first baby means that all other problems must be thrust aside. That baby is a great fact, a reality that must be met. Preparations must be made for its coming. The layette must be prepared. The doctor must be consulted. The health of the wife may need consideration. The young mother will probably prefer to go to the hospital. All of these preparations are small compared to the regime after the coming of the infant.

In the wife who has lived through a happy marriage, for whom the bonds of passionate love have been fully cemented, maternal desire is intensified and matured. Motherhood becomes for such a woman not a penalty or a punishment, but the road by which she travels onward toward completely rounded self-development. Motherhood thus helps her toward the unfolding and realization of her higher nature.

Her children are not mere accidents, the outcome of chance. When motherhood is a mere accident, as so often it is in the early years of careless or reckless marriages, a constant fear of pregnancy may poison the days and nights of the young mother. Her marriage is thus converted into a tragedy. Motherhood becomes for her a horror instead of a joyfully fulfilled function.

Millions of marriages have been blighted, not because of any lack of love between the young husband and wife, but because children have come too soon. Often these brides become mothers before they have reached even physical maturity, before they have completed the period of adolescence. This period in our race is as a rule complete around the age of twenty-three. Motherhood is possible after the first menstruation. But what is physically possible is very often from every other point of view inadvisable. A young woman should be fully matured from every point of view—physically, men-tally and psychically before maternity is thrust upon her.

Those who advise early maternity neglect the spiritual foundation upon which marriage must inevitably be built. This takes time. They also ignore the financial responsibility a family brings.

The young couple begin to build a home. They may have just enough to get along together. The young wife, as in so many cases of early marriage these days, decides to continue her work. They are partners in every way—a commendable thing. The young man is just beginning his career—his salary is probably small. Nevertheless, they manage to get along, their hardships are amusing, and are looked upon as fun. Then suddenly one day, the young wife announces her pregnancy. The situation changes immediately. There are added expenses. The wife must give up her work. The husband must go into debt to pay the expenses of the new and joyfully received arrival. The novelty lasts for some time. The young wife assumes the household duties and the ever growing care of the infant. For a time the child seems to bring the couple closer together. But more often there ensues a concealed resentment on the part of the immature mother at the constant drudgery and slavery to the unfortunate child who has arrived too early upon the scene, which has interfered with her love life.

For the unthinking husband, the "proud papa," the blushing bride is converted at once into the "mother of my children." It is not an unusual occurrence to find that three months after the birth of the baby, the parents are thinking and speaking to each other as "mumsy" and "daddy." The lover and sweetheart relation has disappeared forever and the "mamma-papa" relation has taken its place.

Instead of being a self-determined and self-directing love, everything is henceforward determined by the sweet tyranny of the child. I know of several young mothers, despite a great love for the child, to rebel against this intolerable situation. Vaguely feeling that this new maternity has rendered them unattractive to their husbands, slaves to deadly routine of bottles, baths and washing, they have revolted. I know of innumerable marriages which have been wrecked by premature parenthood.

Love has ever been blighted by the coming of children before the real foundations of marriage have been established. Quite aside from the injustice done to the child who has been brought accidentally into the world, this lamentable fact sinks into insignificance when compared to the injustice inflicted by chance upon the young couple, and the irreparable blow to their love occasioned by premature or involuntary parenthood.

For these reasons, in order that harmonious and happy marriage may be established as the foundation for happy homes and the advent of healthy and desired children, premature parenthood must be avoided. Birth Control is the instrument by which this universal problem may be solved.

FOCUS QUESTIONS:

1. How does Sanger define "premature parenthood"? What are the problems that come with it?
2. According to Sanger, what is the best way for marriage to develop?

14-8 Margaret Sanger, *Women Rebel* and *The Fight for Birth Control* (1916)

The following is from a short pamphlet written by Margaret Sanger to accompany her nationwide tour in 1916. The publication highlights not only Sanger's ideas, but her focus on disseminating information.

Source: http://hdl.loc.gov/loc.rbc/rbcmisc.awh0004

"The Woman Rebel" and The Right for Birth Control

During fourteen years experience as a trained nurse, I found that great percentage of women's disease were due to ignorance of the means to prevent conception. I found that quackery was thriving on this ignorance, and that thousands of abortions were, being performed each year—principally upon the women of the working class. Since the laws deter reliable and expert surgeons from performing abortions, working women have always been thrown into the hands of the incompetent, with fatal results. The deaths from abortions mount very high.

I found that physicians and nurses were dealing with these symptoms rather than their causes, and I decided to help remove the chief cause by imparting knowledge to prevent conception, in defiance of existing laws and their extreme penalty. I sent out a call to the proletarian women of America to assist me in this work, and their answers came by the thousands. I started *The Woman Rebel* early in 1914. The first issue of the magazine was suppressed. Seven issues out of nine were suppressed, and although sent out as first-class mail, the editions were confiscated. The newspapers—even the most radical—declined to give this official tyranny any publicity.

In August, 1914 Federal Grand Jury returned three indictments against me, based on articles in the March, May and July issues of *The Woman Rebel*. The articles branded as "obscene" merely discussed the question and contained no information how to prevent conception. But the authorities were anxious to forestall the distribution of this knowledge and knew that this could only be done by imprisoning me. I decided to avoid the imprisonment, at least until I had given out the information. One hundred thousand copies of a pamphlet, *Family Limitation*, were prepared and distributed, and I sailed for England.

I studied the question in England, Holland, France and Spain, and prepared three other pamphlets: *English Methods of Birth Control*, *Dutch Methods of Birth Control* and *Magnetation Methods of Birth Control*.

After these had been mailed to the United States, I returned to take up the fight with the authorities. The latter had, in the meantime set a Comstock trap for William Sanger and railroaded him to jail for 30 days. Nevertheless they postponed my case time and again, although I was anxious to face the issue and get the decision of a jury. They noted the wide spread agitation in favor of birth control. They saw that interest had been thoroughly aroused. Never had there been an issue that had so aroused the entire country. Letters at the rate of 40 to 50 a day poured in upon the authorities and educated them.

Finally, it was decided by Federal Judge Dayton, United States District Attorney Marshall and Assistant United States District Attorney Content to acquit me, instead of allowing a jury to do it. This decision is fully as important a precedent for future work as the decision of a jury would have been.

Hundreds of requests have been made to me to revive *The Woman Rebel*; but I feel that it has already accomplished its purpose—to arouse interest. Now more constructive work is needed, in meeting the people directly and interesting them in establishing free clinics in those sections where women are overburdened with large families.

MARGARET SANGER,

163 Lexington Avenue,

New York, N.Y.

FOCUS QUESTIONS:

1. What is Sanger's approach to birth control? Why is she so adamant in spreading knowledge of birth control methods?

2. What means has Sanger used to spread her ideas?

THE PROGRESSIVE ERA, 1890–1920

15-1 Jane Addams, Twenty Years at Hull House (1910)

In Twenty Years at Hull House, Jane Addams reviewed her work at the famous settlement house. The following excerpts describe her search for the best location, and some of the work she undertook.

Source: Jane Addams, *Twenty Years at Hull House*, New York, Macmillan, 1911.89-93; 283-287.

CHAPTER V

FIRST DAYS AT HULL-HOUSE

THE next January found Miss Starr and myself in Chicago, searching for a neighborhood in which we might put our plans into execution. In our eagerness to win friends for the new undertaking, we utilized every opportunity to set forth the meaning of the settlement as it had been embodied in Toynbee Hall, although in those days we made no appeal for money, meaning to start with our own slender resources. From the very first the plan received courteous attention, and the discussion, while often skeptical, was always friendly. Professor Swing wrote a commendatory column in the Evening Journal, and our early speeches were reported quite out of proportion to their worth. I recall a spirited evening at the home of Mrs. Wilmarth, which was attended by that renowned scholar, Thomas Davidson, and by a young Englishman who was a member of the then new Fabian society and to whom a peculiar glamour was attached because he had scoured knives all summer in a camp of high-minded philosophers in the Adirondacks. Our new little plan met with criticism, not to say disapproval, from Mr. Davidson, who, as nearly as I can remember, called it "one of those unnatural attempts to understand life through cooperative living."

It was in vain we asserted that the collective living was not an essential part of the plan, that we would always scrupulously pay our own expenses, and that at any moment we might decide to scatter through the neighborhood and to live in separate tenements; he still contended that the fascination for most of those volunteering residence would lie in the collective living aspect of the Settlement. His contention was, of course, essentially sound; there is a constant tendency for the residents to "lose themselves in the cave of their own companionship," as the Toynbee Hall phrase goes, but on the other hand, it is doubtless true that the very companionship, the give and take of colleagues, is what tends to keep the Settlement normal and in touch with "the world of things as they are." I am happy to say that we never resented this nor any other difference of opinion, and that fifteen years later Professor Davidson handsomely acknowledged that the advantages of a group far outweighed the weaknesses he had early pointed out. He was at that later moment sharing with a group of young men, on the East Side of New York, his ripest conclusions in philosophy and was much touched by their intelligent interest and absorbed devotion. I think that time has also justified our early contention that the mere foothold of a house, easily accessible, ample in space, hospitable and tolerant in spirit, situated in the midst of the large foreign colonies which so easily isolate themselves in American cities, would be in itself a serviceable thing for Chicago. I am not so sure that we succeeded in our endeavors " to make social intercourse express the growing sense of the economic unity of society and to add the social function to democracy." But Hull-House was soberly opened on the theory that the dependence of classes on each other is reciprocal; and that as the social relation is essentially a reciprocal relation, it gives a form of expression that has peculiar value.

. . .

Three weeks later, with the advice of several of the oldest residents of Chicago, including the ex-mayor of the city, Colonel Mason, who had from the first been a warm friend to our plans, we decided upon a location somewhere near the junction of Blue Island Avenue, Halsted Street, and Harrison Street. I was surprised and overjoyed on the very first day of our search for quarters to come upon the hospitable old house, the quest for which I had so recently abandoned. The house was of course rented, the lower part of it used for offices and storerooms in connection with a factory that stood back of it. However, after some difficulties were overcome, it proved to be possible to sublet the second floor and what had been the large drawing-room on the first floor.

...

On the 18th of September, 1889, Miss Starr and I moved into it, with Miss Mary Keyser, who began by performing the housework, but who quickly developed into a very important factor in the life of the vicinity as well as in that of the household, and whose death five years later was most sincerely mourned by hundreds of our neighbors. In our enthusiasm over "settling," the first night we forgot not only to lock but to close a side door opening on Polk Street, and were much pleased in the morning on Polk Street, and were much pleased in the morning to find that we possessed a fine illustration of the honesty and kindliness of our new neighbors.

Our first guest was an interesting young woman who lived in a neighboring tenement, whose widowed mother aided her in the support of the family by scrubbing a downtown theater every night. The mother, of English birth, was well bred and carefully educated, but was in the midst of that bitter struggle which awaits so many strangers in American cities who find that their social position tends to be measured solely by the standards of living they are able to maintain.

Our guest has long since married the struggling young lawyer to whom she was then engaged, and he is now leading his profession in an eastern city.

...

CHAPTER XIII

PUBLIC ACTIVITIES AND INVESTIGATIONS

ONE of the striking features of our neighborhood twenty years ago, and one to which we never became reconciled, was the presence of huge wooden garbage boxes fastened to the street pavement in which the undisturbed refuse accumulated day by day. The system of garbage collecting was inadequate throughout the city but it became the greatest menace in a ward

such as ours, where the normal amount of waste was much increased by the decayed fruit and vegetables discarded by the Italian and Greek fruit peddlers, and by the residuum left over from the piles of filthy rags which were fished out of the city dumps and brought to the homes of the rag pickers for further sorting and washing.

The children of our neighborhood twenty years ago played their games in and around these huge garbage boxes. They were the first objects that the toddling child learned to climb; their bulk afforded a barricade and their contents provided missiles in all the battles of the older boys; and finally they became the seats upon which absorbed lovers held enchanted converse. We are obliged to remember that all children eat everything which they find and that odors have a curious of Hull-House can understand their own early enthusiasm for the and intimate power of entwining themselves into our tenderest memories, before even the residents of Hull-House can understand their own early enthusiasm for the removal of these boxes and the establishment of a better system of refuse collection.

It is easy for even the most conscientious citizen of Chicago to forget the foul smells of the stockyards and the garbage dumps, when he is living so far from them that he is only occasionally made conscious of their existence but the residents of a Settlement are perforce constantly surrounded by them. During our first three years on Halsted Street, we had established a small incinerator at Hull-House and we had many times reported the untoward conditions of the ward to the city hall. We had also arranged many talks for the immigrants, pointing out that although a woman may sweep her own doorway in her native village and allow the refuse to innocently decay in the open air and sunshine, in a crowded city quarter, if the garbage is not properly collected and destroyed, a tenement-house mother may see her children sicken and die, and that the immigrants must therefore, not only keep their own houses clean, but must also help the authorities to keep the city clean.

Possibly our efforts slightly modified the worst conditions but they still remained intolerable, and the fourth summer the situation became for me absolutely desperate when I realized in a moment of panic that my delicate little nephew for whom was guardian, could not be with me at Hull-House at all unless the sickening odors were reduced. I may well be ashamed that other delicate children who were torn from their families, not into boarding school but into eternity, had not long before driven me to effective action. Under the direction of the first man who came as a resident to Hull-House we began a systematic investigation of the city system of garbage collection, both as to its efficiency in other wards and its possible connection with the death rate in the various wards of the city.

The Hull-House Woman's Club had been organized the year before by the resident kindergartner who had first inaugurated a mothers' meeting. The members came- together, however, in quite a new way that summer when we discussed with them the high death rate so persistent in our ward. After several club meetings devoted to the subject, despite the fact that the death rate rose highest in the congested foreign colonies and not in the streets in which most of the Irish American club women lived, twelve of their number undertook in connection with the residents, to carefully investigate the condition of the alleys.

During August and September the substantiated reports of violations of the law sent in from Hull-

House to the health department were one thousand and thirty-seven. For the club woman who had finished a long day's work of washing or ironing followed by the cooking of a hot supper, it would have been much easier to sit on her doorstep during a summer evening than to go up and down ill-kept alleys and get into trouble with her neighbors over the condition of their garbage boxes. It required both civic enterprise and moral conviction to be willing to do this three evenings a week during the hottest and most uncomfortable months of the year. Nevertheless, a certain number of women persisted, as did the residents and three city inspectors in succession were transferred from the ward because of unsatisfactory services. Still the death rate remained high and the condition seemed little improved throughout the next winter. In sheer desperation, the following spring when the city contracts were awarded for the removal of garbage, with the backing of two well-known business men, I put in a bid for the garbage removal of the nineteenth ward. My paper was thrown out on a technicality but the incident induced the mayor to appoint me the garbage inspector of the ward.

The salary was a thousand dollars a year, and the loss of that political "plum" made a great stir among the politicians. The position was no sinecure whether regarded from the point of view of getting up at six in the morning to see that the men were early at work ; or of following the loaded wagons, uneasily dropping their contents at intervals, to their dreary destination at the dump; or of insisting that the contractor must increase the number of his wagons from nine to thir-

teen and from thirteen to seventeen, although he assured me that he lost money on every one and that the former inspector had let him off with seven; or of taking careless landlords into court because they would not provide the proper garbage receptacles ; or of arresting the tenant who tried to make the garbage wagons carry away the contents of his stable.

With the two or three residents who nobly stood by, we set up six of those doleful incinerators which are supposed to burn garbage with the fuel collected in the alley itself. The one factory in town which could utilize old tin cans was a window weight factory, and we deluged that with ten times as many tin cans as it could use — much less would pay for. We made desperate attempts to have the dead animals removed by the contractor who was paid most liberally by the city for that purpose but who, we slowly discovered, always made the police ambulances do the work, delivering the carcasses upon freight cars for shipment to a soap factory in Indiana where they were sold for a good price although the contractor himself was the largest stockholder in the concern. Perhaps our greatest achievement was the discovery of a pavement eighteen inches under the surface in a narrow street, although after it was found we triumphantly discovered a record of its existence in the city archives. The Italians living on the street were much interested but displayed little astonishment, perhaps because they were accustomed to see buried cities exhumed. This pavement became the casus belli between myself and the street commissioner when I insisted that its restoration belonged to him, after I had removed the first eight inches of garbage. The matter was finally settled by the mayor himself, who permitted me to drive him to the entrance of the street in what the children called my "garbage phaeton" and who took my side of the controversy.

A graduate of the University of Wisconsin, who had done some excellent volunteer inspection in both Chicago and Pittsburg, became my deputy and performed the work in a most thoroughgoing manner for three years. During the last two she was under the regime of civil service for in 1895, to the great joy of many citizens, the Illinois legislature made that possible.

FOCUS QUESTIONS:

1. What was Addams' goal in opening Hull House? How did she chose her location?

2. Why did Addams undertake garbage collection? Does such work have anything to do with her original goals?

15-2 Protective Legislation

Below is an example of the protective legislation that limited the hours of work, especially for women and children. These are the Massachusetts laws that were amended in 1911, leading to the Lawrence Textile Strike in 1912.

Source: *Protective Legislation, The Revised Laws of the Commonwealth of Massachusetts,* vol. 1, chap. 106. Boston: Wright & Potter Printing Co., State Printers, 1902, pp. 920-921. http://memory.loc.gov/cgi-bin/query/r?ammem/awhbib:@field(DOCID+@lit(awh0026))

HOURS OF LABOR.

SECTION 19. Nine hours shall constitute a day's work for all laborers, workmen and mechanics who are employed by or on behalf of the commonwealth or of any county, city or town therein, except as provided in the following section.

SECTION 20. In a city or town which by a vote taken by ballot at an annual election accepts the provisions of this section or has accepted the corresponding provisions of earlier laws, eight hours slush constitute a day's work far all laborers, workmen and mechanics who arc employed by such city or town. If a petition for such vote, signed by such hundred or more registered voters of a city, or twenty-five or more registered voters of a town, is filed with the city or town clerk, respectively, thirty days or more before an annual election, such vote shall be taken at such election.

SECTION 21. Contracts by or on behalf of the commonwealth, requiring the employment of manual labor, shall provide that persons employed in manual labor there under shall not be required to work more than nine hours in each day and that said nine how's shall constitute a day's work.

SECTION 22. A day's work fur all conductors, drivers and motormen who are employed by or on behalf of a sheet railway company shall not exceed ten hours, and shall be so arranged by the employer that it may lie performed within twelve consecutive hours. No officer or agent of any such company shall require from said employees more than ten hours' work for a day's labor but on 1ega1 holidays, on days when the company is required to provide for extraordinary travel, and in case of accident or unavoidable delay, extra labor may be performed for extra compensation. The provisions of this section shall not affect written contracts existing the twenty-second day of July in the year eighteen hundred and ninety-four.

SECTION 23. No child under eighteen years of age amid no woman shall be employed in laboring in a mercantile establishment more than fifty-eight hours in a week; but the provisions of this section shall not apply during December to persons who are employed in shops for the sale of goods at retail. Every employer shall post in a conspicuous place in every room in which such persons are employed a printed notice stating the number of hours' work which are required of them on each day of the week, the hours of commencing and stopping such work, and the our when the time or times allowed for dinner or other meals begin and end. The printed form of such notice shall be furnished by the chief of the district police and shall be approved by the attorney general.

The employment of any such person for a longer time in any day titan that so stated shall be deemed a violation of the provisions of this section. An employer, superintendent, overseer or other agent of a mercantile establishment who violates any of the provisions of this section shall ho punished by a fine of not less than fifty nor more than one hundred dollars.

SECTION 24. No child under eighteen years of age and no woman shall be employed in laboring in a manufacturing or mechanical establishment more than ten hours in any one day, except as hereinafter provided in this section, unless a different apportionment of the hours of labor is made for the sole purpose of making a shorter day's work for one day of the week; and in no case shall the hours of labor exceed fifty-eight in a week. Every employer shall post in a conspicuous place in every room in which such persons are employed a printed notice stating the number of hours' work required of them on each day of the week, time hours of commencing and stopping work, and the hours when the time allowed for meals begins and ends or, in the ease or establishments exempted from the provisions of sections thirty-six and thirty-seven, the time, if any, allowed for meals. The printed firms of such notices shall he provided by the chief of the district police, after approval by the attorney general. The employment of such person for a longer time in a day than that so stated shall be deemed a violation of the provisions of this section unless it appears that such employment was to make up time lost on a previous day of the cone week in consequence of the stopping of machinery upon which lie was employed or dependent for employment; but no stopping of machinery for less than thirty consecutive minutes shall justify such overtime employment, nor shall such overtime employment be authorized until a written report of the day and hour of its occurrence and its duration is sent to the chief of the district police or to an inspector of factories and public buildings.

FOCUS QUESTIONS:

1. How do these laws differentiate between women, men and children? In what ways are they treated equally?

2. What was the impetus behind such legislation, and why was it opposed?

15-3 Muller v. Oregon (1908)

The Supreme Court case of Muller v. Oregon upheld the Oregon law limiting women's work to ten hours per day. When a supervisor in a laundry forced a worker to exceed ten hours' work, the case eventually went to trial, and finally to the U.S. Supreme Court.

BREWER, J., Opinion of the Court

SUPREME COURT OF THE UNITED STATES

208 U.S. 412

Muller v. Oregon

ERROR TO THE SUPREME COURT OF THE STATE OF OREGON

No. 107 Argued: January 15, 1908 — Decided: February 24, 1908

MR. JUSTICE BREWER delivered the opinion of the court:

On February 19, 1903, the legislature of the State of Oregon passed an act (Session Laws 1903, p. 148) the first section of which is in these words:

SEC. 1. That no female [shall] be employed in any mechanical establishment, or factory, or laundry in this State more than ten hours during any one day. The hours of work may be so arranged as to permit the employment of females [p417] at any time so that they shall not work more than ten hours during the twenty-four hours of any one day.

Sec. 3 made a violation of the provisions of the prior sections a misdemeanor subject to a fine of not less than $10 nor more than $25. On September 18, 1905, an information was filed in the circuit court of the State for the County of Multnomah, charging that the defendant on the 4th day of September, A.D. 1905, in the county of Multnomah and State of Oregon, then and there being the owner of a laundry, known as the Grand Laundry, in the city of Portland, and the employer of females therein, did then and there unlawfully permit and suffer one Joe Haselbock, he, the said Joe Haselbock, then and there being an overseer, superintendent, and agent of said Curt Muller, in the said Grand Laundry, to require a female, to-wit, one Mrs. E. Gotcher, to work more than ten hours in said laundry on said 4th day of September, A.D. 1905, contrary to the statutes in such cases made and provided, and against the peace and dignity of the State of Oregon.

A trial resulted in a verdict against the defendant, who was sentenced to pay a fine of $10. The Supreme Court of the State affirmed the conviction, *State v. Muller*, 48 Oregon 252, whereupon the case was brought here on writ of error.

FOCUS QUESTIONS:

1. What Justice Brewer's approach to the case?

2. What attitudes towards women supported Brewer's finding?

3. In what ways is the judgment restricted?

15-4 Laws Affecting Women and Children in Various States (1917)

The excerpt below is from a book comparing the laws of the states in areas of concern to the woman suffrage movement. Note the stated purpose of the book, and consider its effectiveness.

Source: Annie G. Porritt, *Laws Affecting Women and Children in the Suffrage and Non-suffrage States*, New York: National Woman Suffrage Publishing Co., 1917. 5; 8; 89 (http://hdl.loc.gov/loc.rbc/rbnawsa.n3563)

FORWARD

The National Woman Suffrage Publishing Co., Inc., in offering to the public this digest of the laws of the various states relating to matters of greatest interest to women, wishes to state that its purpose is to give the Suffrage workers and speakers a ready reference book containing a general statement of the statutory law of the various states, relating to the particular subjects covered by the book, in such form that the laws of the various states may be quickly grasped and compared.

This book has been prepared by our editor, Mrs. Annie G. Porritt, with the greatest care, and we believe the book to be an accurate statement, in condensed form, of the statutory law of the various states at the present time upon the subjects which it purports to cover. The book, however, is not a law treatise, and it has been thought not only impossible, but undesirable, to go into the various questions arising under the different statutes, relating to their interpretation and enforcement. Whenever there is any doubt, the careful student should consult the statutes and the decisions of the courts.

With this warning against relying upon this book except as the statement of the general statutory law, we trust that it may be found of use to a large number of workers who need in their speaking or writing, such general, comparative statements of the laws of the various states as are here contained.

....

PREFACE

The National Woman Suffrage Publishing Co., Inc., in offering to the public this digest of the laws of the various states relating to matters of greatest inter-est to women, wishes to state that its purpose is to give the Suffrage workers and speakers a ready reference book containing a general statement of the statutory law of the various states, relating to the particular subjects covered by the book, in such form that the laws of the various states may be quickly grasped and compared.

This book has been prepared by our editor, Mrs. Annie G. Porritt, with the greatest care, and we believe the book to be an accurate statement, in condensed form, of the statutory law of the various states at the present time upon the subjects which it purports to cover. The book, however, is not a law treatise, and it has been thought not only impossible, but undesirable, to go into the various questions arising under the different statutes, relating to their interpretation and enforcement. Whenever there is any doubt, the careful student should consult the statutes and the decisions of the courts.

With this warning against relying upon this book except as the statement of the general statutory law, we trust that it may be found of use to a large number of workers who need in their speaking or writing, such general, comparative statements of the laws of the various states as are here contained.

....

MOTHER'S PENSIONS

State laws providing pensions for mothers in order to enable them to keep their children with them after the loss of the bread-winner, belong entirely to the last six years. The first mothers' pension law was passed in Missouri and went into effect in June, 1911. Its operation was limited to Jackson County, where Kansas City is situated; but later in 1911 a law was passed giving St. Louis power to establish a board of children's guardians by city ordinance. This board had authority to board out children with their own mothers, and St. Louis entered upon this experiment in 1912. Before this, Illinois had passed a "Funds to Parents Act," much more comprehensive than the first Missouri law. The Illinois law which went into operation on July 1, 1911, was quickly copied by other states, and at the beginning of 1917 there were 29 states which had passed mothers' pension laws.

The mothers' pension law of Arizona was submitted by initiative petition and received popular endorsement at the polls in 1914. It was, however, pronounced unconstitutional in the Superior Court of Maricopa County in 1915, and the case was appealed to the State

Supreme Court where the decision was upheld. It provides that:—

All widows who are mothers of dependant children, and also wives whose husbands are confined in state institutions who have children under 16 looking to them for support, shall be entitled to $15 a month for one child and if there are more children, to $15 for the first child and an additional $6 for each other child in their keeping under the age of 16.

Under a provision of the California Constitution, the state had been paying for every orphan, $100, and for every half-orphan $75 a year to institutions in which needy orphans were cared for. A liberal construction of the law had permitted the payment of this sum to the mothers of such orphans when the children remained at home. An act of 1913 amended the older law by providing that "in addition to the amount paid by the State for each orphan maintained at home by its mother, the county, city and county, city, or town may pay for the support of such half-orphan an amount equal to the sum paid by the State." In case such aid be refused, the mother , backed by five reputable citizens, is given the right of direct appeal to the State Board of Control.

To enjoy the benefit of the act the children must be under 14, and the parent or parents must have resided in the state for at least three years, or have become citizens of the State.

A mothers' pension act was adopted by popular vote in Colorado 1912. It became law upon proclamation by the Governor in 1913. The law provides that:—

If the parent or parents of such child are poor and unable to properly care for such child, but otherwise are proper guardians, and it is for the welfare of such child to remain at home, the court may enter an order fixing the amount of money necessary for the case of such child, and it shall be the duty of the commissioners vested with power for the relief of the poor to pay the money to the parent or parents. Children for whom such payments are made must not be over 16 years old.

The act also provides for the establishment of facilities for the detention and employment of men convicted of nonsupport. The money earned by these men goes into the fund for the carrying out of the act, and it is specifically stated that "this act shall be liberally construed for the protection of the child, the home and the State, and in the interest of public morals and for the prevention of crime."

Idaho passed a mother's pension law in 1913. The chief provisions of the act are as follows:—

The probate judge of each country is given power to make provision for the partial support of women whose husbands are dead, or confined in the penitentiary or in an insane asylum, when such women are poor and are mothers of children under 15 years old, and such mothers and children reside in the country.

The allowance must not exceed $10 a month for one child, and five dollars in addition for each of the other children under 15 years of age.

The child or children must be living with the mother; and the allowance shall be made only if without it the mother would be obliged to work regularly away from home, while with it she is enabled to remain at home with her children. The mother must in the judgment of the probate court be a fit person to bring up her children, and she must have been a resident of the county for two years before applying for aid.

FOCUS QUESTIONS:

1. Note the publisher and the introductory material. What do you think of the woman suffrage organization by this period? Note that passage of the Nineteenth Amendment is only two years away by this stage.

2. How do you imagine this book may have been used by those in the suffrage movement?

3. What conditions are placed on mothers' pensions?

15-5 Women and the Republic (1897)

Helen Kendrick Johnson's Woman and the Republic, first published in 1897, comprehensively examines the arguments in favor of suffrage, with the purpose of refuting them. It came out in response to the monumental History of Woman Suffrage by Elizabeth Cady Stanton, Susan B. Anthony and Matilda Joslyn Gage, completed in 1885.

Source: Helen Kendrick Johnson, *Woman and the Republic: a survey of the woman suffrage movement in the United States and a discussion of the claims and arguments of its foremost advocates.* New York: Guidon Club, 1913. (http://hdl.loc.gov/loc.rbc/rbnawsa.n8334) pp. 314-319

Woman and the Republic

Chapter XII: Conclusion

In the opening of this volume I have given it as my opinion that the movement to obtain the elective franchise for woman is not in harmony with those through which woman and government have made progress. I have spoken of the marvellous forward impulse that has marked the passage of the last half-century, and have mentioned the growth of religious liberty, the founding of foreign and home missions, the extinction of slavery, the temperance movement, the settlement of the West, the opening of the professions and trades to women, the progress of mechanical invention, the sudden advance of science, the civil war, and the natu-

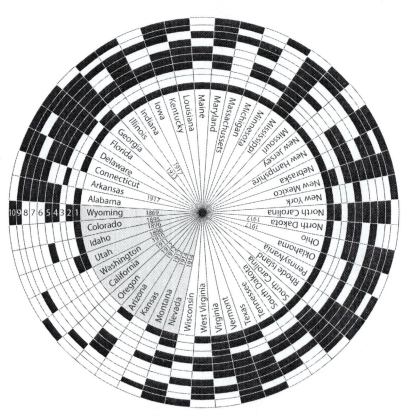

IMPORTANT LEGISLATION IN THE UNITED STATES AFFECTING WOMEN AND CHILDREN

WHITE SPACES INDICATE GOOD LEGISLATION
BLACK SPACES INDICATE POOR LEGISLATION OR NONE AT ALL

In regard to the following:
Circle 1. Industrial Welfare Commissions to regulate hours, wages and working conditions of women and children.
Circle 2. Child Labor—14 year limit. Guarded exemptions during vacations are allowed and poverty exemptions when these are neutralized by Mother's Pensions laws.
Circle 3. Compulsory education—State wide.

Circle 4. Eight or nine hour day for women.
Circle 5. Minimum wage.
Circle 6. Mothers' pensions.
Circle 7. Equal guardianship.
Circle 8. Age of consent, 18 years—chaste or unchaste.
Circle 9. Red Light Abatement.
Circle 10. Prohibition.

ral play of free conditions, us among the causes of this impulse. I have pointed out the fact that the Suffrage movement has nearly reached its semi-centennial year, and has made a record by which its relation to these progressive forces can be judged, and I have a appealed from the repetition of its claims to the verdict of its accomplishment.

In the second chapter I have considered the growth of republican forms the world over, and endeavored, to show that the dogma of Woman Suffrage is fundamentally at war with true democratic principles, and that, practically, woman suffrage has been allied with despotism, monarchy, and ecclesiastical oppression on the one hand, and with the powers of license and misrule that assail republican government on the other.

In the third chapter I attempt to prove this further by a study of the origin of the Suffrage movement, and by its relation of the Government of the United States. I try to refute the two propositions which it has put forth as solid resting-ground for woman's claim to the elective franchise in this land—"Taxation without representation is tyranny," and "There is no just government without the consent of the governed." I have also set forth the different between municipal and constitutional suffrage, and shown that the extension of school suffrage, so far from being stepping-stone to full suffrage, affords another evidence that such full suffrage is unprogressive and undemocratic. It is held that regulated, universal manhood suffrage is the natural and only safe basis of government.

In the fourth chapter I consider the early relation of the Suffrage movement to the causes of anti-slavery and temperance. I also discuss the attitude of the Suffrage leaders during the civil war, and indicate that the Suffrage movement was not patriotic, and was a hindrance to emancipation and reform.

The fifth chapter treats of the connection of the Suffrage movement with the change that has taken place in the laws, and it contains a synopsis of the present laws of New York regarding women. From this study it appears that the Suffrage movement did not originate the change in the laws; that many changes most vigorously urged by its associations never have been enacted; and that change of laws has not been so much sought as a voice upon change of laws—the fact being, that the vote *per se* has been urged as the panacea for all woman's wrongs.

The sixth chapter deals with Woman Suffrage and the trades. It shows that this movement was not instrumental in opening the trades to women; that the conditions of industrial life are not changed in such essentials as would involve a change of sex relation to Government; and that, so far from altering the basis of government, industrialism has introduced new problems of such gave import that security in the enforcement of law is doubly necessary. It shows, furthermore, that socialistic labor has been naturally the friend of Woman Suffrage, while the safer and sounder organizations have extended sympathetic help to woman.

The seventh chapter discusses the connection of Woman Suffrage with the professions. It aims to show that here, too, suffrage has not been necessary to gain, for women who were fitted to hold it, an honorable place; and, in regard to the places they have not yet entered, it is held that the impulse must come from within. It is argued that, in the professions, as in the trades, Suffrage effort has hindered more than it has helped, and that in the West its practical working is the most damaging thing that has attended woman's real progress.

The eight chapter considers the connection of Woman Suffrage with education. Its conclusions are, that not education, but coeducation, was the persistent demand of Suffragists, and that woman's advancement in college and university was wrought out by the impulse gained from women who opposed the Suffrage idea, and made practical by men to who also that idea was repugnant. It is suggested that women who could prepare and defend the ignorant Suffrage Woman's Bible have no right to utter a syllable in protest of the educational ideas of men and women who are competent to speak on the subject, and whose verdict has been, on the whole, for separate study during collegiate age, wherever such could be afforded, while it is not disputed that coeducation has its place and its uses.

The ninth chapter presents Woman Suffrage in its relation to the church. It first discusses, briefly, a few points in the Suffrage Woman's Bible, published in New York in 1895. This is a commentary on such passages in the Pentateuch as relate to women, and the title "Rev." is prefixed to four names of editors on its title-page. This book, or rather a book of which this is the first instalment, was promised by Suffrage writers and speakers from the beginning. It is considered to contain the consummate blossom of the mind that first expounded the Suffrage theory—the mind that grasped it as a whole, in its full meaning and intent, and never has wavered in expression as to its ultimate object and the means by which that objects is to be sought. This chapter sets forth, in few words, the present writer's view of woman in the creation, and of St.

Paul's attitude toward woman. The chapter further discusses woman's early preaching in this country, and shows that it has not been such as to build up religion or the state, but has been such as to suggest that, while the possibilities of her nature tend to make her supreme in capacity to point the way to higher regions, it also contains qualities that may render her peculiarly dangerous as a public leader.

The tenth chapter, entitled "Woman Suffrage and Sex," alludes briefly to the social evil, and then discusses the Suffrage ideas in regard to sex as explained by both their older and more recent writers. It discusses the disabilities of sex in relation to the suffrage—the difficulties in the way of jury duty, police duty, and office-holding —and draws the conclusion that the fulfillment of such necessary work of the voting citizen is practically an impossibility for woman, and has been formed to be so in the Western States.

The eleventh chapter has for its title "Woman Suffrage and the Home." It sets forth the belief that the Suffrage movement strikes a blow squarely at the home and the marriage relation, and that the ballot is demanded by its most representative leaders for the purpose of making woman independent of the present social order. It argues that communism is the natural ally of Suffrage, and that, as homes did not spring out of the ground, they will not remain where men and women alter the mutual relations out of which the institution of home has slowly grown.

The general conclusion of the book is, that woman's relation to the Republic is as important as man's. Woman deals with the beginnings of life; man, with the product made from those beginnings; and this fact marks the difference in their spheres, and reveals woman's immense advantage in moral opportunity. It also suggests the incalculable loss in case her work is not done or ill done. In a ruder age the evident value of power that could deal with developed force was most appreciated; but such is not now the case. It lies with us to prove that education, instead of causing us to attempt work that belongs even less to the cultivated woman than to the ignorant, is fitting us to train up statesmen who will be the first to do us honor. The American Republic depends finally for its existence and its greatness upon the virtue and ability of American womanhood. If our ideals are mistaken or unworthy, then there will be ultimately no republic for men to govern or defend. When women are Buddhists, the men build up an empire of India. When women are Mohammedans, the men construct an Empire of Turkey. When women are Christians, men can conceive and bring into being a Republic like the United States. Woman is to implant the faith, man is to cause the Nation's faith to show itself in works. More and more these duties overlap, but they cannot become interchangeable while sex continues to divide the race into the two halves of what should become a perfect whole. Woman Suffrage aims to sweep away this natural distinction, and make humanity a mass of individuals with an indiscriminate sphere. The attack is now bold and now subtle, now malicious and now mistaken; but it is at all times an attack. The greatest danger with which this land is threatened comes from the ignorant and persistent zeal of some of its women. They abuse the freedom under which they live, and to gain an impossible power would fain destroy the Government that alone can protect them. The majority of women have no sympathy with this movement; and in their enlightenment, and in the consistent wisdom of our men, lies hope of defeating this unpatriotic, unintelligent, and unjustifiable assault upon the integrity of the American Republic.

New York, *March*, 1897.

FOCUS QUESTIONS:

1. Are you convinced by Johnson's arguments against woman suffrage?

2. Was it true that the majority of women were unsympathetic to woman suffrage?

3. Why did Johnson refer to the Republic in her title? What is woman's role in the American Republic, according to the author?

15-6 Justice David J. Brewer (1909)

More information about Brewer's opinions are found in the following pamphlet created by The Equal Franchise Society, extracted from an article by Brewer in Ladies World.

Source: Equal Franchise Society Legislative Series: Extract of article by Justice David J. Brewer, December 1909; Women and the Law; Judge Sets Aside Their Legal Equality with Men (at http://hdl.loc.gov/loc.rbc/rbcmil.scrp6013101)

Equal Franchise Society, Legislative Series (Extract from an article on Woman Suffrage in the *Ladies' World*, December, 1909, by JUSTICE DAVID J. BREWER of the United States Supreme Court.)

"How does woman suffrage work when tried? In this nation, four States-Colorado, Utah, Wyoming and Idaho, have granted full suffrage, and in at least the first three of them it has been in existence long enough for substantial results. The conditions of life in them differ, and doubtless that difference may effect the full significance of the results. One thing is true of all: There has been no organized effort to repeal the grant. Whatever may be isolated opinions, the general mass of the voters are satisfied. Indeed few have antagonistic views. * * * If the citizens of these States find nothing objectionable in woman a natural conclusion is that no injury has resulted therefrom. * * * Doubtless some opposition may come from personal ambition and expectations defeated by the action of the women voters. * * * It would be strange if the defeated candidates did not feel and express themselves against woman suffrage*** "Woman has not forced her way into politics, though she has held some minor offices and discharged their duties acceptably. According to the best information I can get, her influence on political life has been mainly in the way of restraint, preventing the nomination of unworthy persons, and demanding, as in the case of Judge Lindsay, the election of the best man. She has not hesitated to take her part in school matters, and her insistence has caused many improvements in the administration of city affairs. She has not improved everything. Intemperance still prevails and the social evil abounds. But large changes like these cannot be accomplished solely by legislation or in a day. If the tendency of her efforts is in the right direction it is can be expected. * * *

"Female suffrage will come. Not everywhere at once, but by varying steps. Woman's broader education, her increasing familiarity with business and pub-lic affairs, will lead to it. And why not? The chief reply is the home. But female suffrage will not debase the home or lessen its power and influence. On the other hand, it will introduce a refining and uplifting power into our political life." FRANCHISE SOCIETY,

Albany Headquarters,

The Ten Eyck.

WOMEN AND THE LAW

JUDGE SETS ASIDE THEIR LEGAL EQUALITY WITH MEN.

(From Our Own Correspondent.)

NEW YORK, Wednesday.

"Woman is the ward of the State. She must be protected from the greed as well as from the passion of man." Such is the momentous decision just handed down by Justice Brewers of the Supreme Court of the United State8, in a ease of fundamental importance to the political status of the weaker sex.

Mr. Curt Müller, a wealthy manufacturer, appealed against a statute of Oregon State forbidding the employment of women in any factory, mechanical establishment or laundry for more than ten hours in any one day. He declared that the law was unoontitutiona1 inasmuch as it limited the right of contract, and supported his appeal by reference to a verdict delivered by the Supreme Court of New York last June, affirming "under our laws men and women now stand alike in constitutional rights. There is no warrant for making any discrimination between them with respect to liberty of the person or contract."

Justice Brewer, however, decided that though woman legally stands absolutely on an equal plane with man, vet &he is so differently constituted that different legislation is justified, both in the interests of her own welfare and that of the human race generally. In his verdict, which is to-day being discussed throughout the country alike by sociologists, politicians, and suffragists, Justice Brewer finally lays down that woman must be compensated by law for the burdens which her sex obliges her to assume.

FOCUS QUESTIONS:

1. How does Brewer feel about woman suffrage?

2. How can one reconcile Brewer's opinions in this pamphlet with his opinion in *Muller v. Oregon*?

3. Consider the nature of this source. Why was it circulated?

15-7 Carrie Chapman Catt (1916)

Carrie Chapman Catt (1859-1947) was in her second term as president of the National American Woman Suffrage Association. Her concerns about dissension in the organization, though well founded, did not prevent her overseeing the passage of the Nineteenth Amendment in 1920, after which Catt retired.

Source: Catt, C.C."Report of Survey Committee to Board of Officers." March 1916. Excerpted in Eleanor Flexner. *Century of Struggle: The Woman's Rights Movement in the United States.* New York: Atheneum, 1972, 274-275.

A serious crisis exists in the suffrage movement. A considerable number of women in the various states have turned to the Federal Amendment as the most promising avenue. The victory of the Federal Amendment especially appeals to the women of those states with constitutions which make a successful referendum well-nigh impossible. A consider-able number of women in the South are dead set against the Federal Amendment. The first anti-suffrage organization of importance to be effected in the South has been formed in Alabama with the slogan: "Home Rule, States Rights, and White Supremacy." A considerable number of other women wish to work exclusively for suffrage within their own states. The Congressional Union is drawing off from the National Association those women who feel it is possible to work for suffrage by the Federal route only. Certain workers in the South are being antagonized because the National is continuing work for the Federal Amendment. The combination has produced a great muddle from which the National can be freed only by careful action.

FOCUS QUESTIONS:

1. What crisis does Catt describe?
2. Was this division entirely new, or was it rooted in older conflicts?
3. From our vantage point, was the crisis as serious as Catt feared?

15-8 Nineteenth Amendment (1920)

This remarkable short document is the Nineteenth Amendment to the U.S. Constitution.

Amendment XIX Passed by Congress June 4, 1919. Ratified August 18, 1920

The right of citizens of the United States to vote shall not be denied or abridged by the United States or by any State on account of sex.

Congress shall have power to enforce this article by appropriate legislation.

FOCUS QUESTIONS:

1. Why does this landmark legislation apply only to voting? Was further legislation necessary?
2. Summarize the arguments against this amendment that made woman suffrage so hard to obtain.
3. Why did this version of the amendment pass so quickly? Was it ratified by all the states?

15-9 Letters from Mary Church Terrell (1924-1925)

The following letters are from the correspondence between Mary Church Terrell and members of President Coolidge's administration. Terrell sought a political appointment, but was advised to enter the government through the civil service examination process. She was not successful in gaining a position in Coolidge's administration.

Source: http://hdl.loc.gov/loc.mss/amrlm.mc22

December 10, 1924.

My dear Mr. Henning:

I am sending you, herewith, an office memorandum relating to the desire of Mrs. Mary Church Terrell to be appointed as head of a colored woman's section of the Woman's Bureau of the Department, together with the folders referred to.

Sincerely yours,

C.B. Slemp

Secretary to the President.

Hon. E.J. Henning,

Acting Secretary of Labor.

THE WHITE HOUSE

December 10, 1924.

Memorandum for the Secretary:

During your absence from the city, Mrs. Mary Church Terrell, of this city, called at the Executive Office and stated that she thought it very desirable to have in the woman's Bureau of the Department of Labor a division devoted to colored women and that she was very anxious to be appointed at the head of such a division. She left the attached folder to show some of her work during the campaign and another to show some of the comments on her work as a lecturer in the educational field.

[Presidential office staff]

DEPARTMENT OF LABOR

OFFICE OF THE ASSISTANT SECRETARY

WASHINGTON

December 11, 1924.

My dear Mr. Secretary:

This is to acknowledge receipt of your letter of the 10th instant, transmitting memorandum relating to the desire of Mrs. Mary Church Terrell to be appointed head of a colored women's section in the Woman's Bureau of this Department, together with a folder descriptive of Mrs. Terrell's work.

I am taking up this subject with the Chief of the Woman's Bureau and will be glad to communicate to you whatever may develop from these negotiations.

Very sincerely yours,

E.J. Henning,

Acting Secretary.

Hon. C. B. Slemp,

Secretary to the President.

The White House.

EJH/C

THE WHITE HOUSE

WASHINGTON

December 11, 1924.

My dear Mr. Henning:

Since I wrote you on yesterday, I have seen Mrs. Mary Church Terrell and she would very much prefer to have a place in the Children's Bureau as she has been interested in that line of work for a number of years. Mrs. Terrell is the wife of one of the Municipal Judges here in the District, and is a woman of considerable ability, and I am sure that if it is found possible to give her a place in either the Woman's Bureau or the Children's Bureau, she would render valuable service to the Department.

Sincerely yours,

C. B. Slemp

Secretary to the President,

Hon. E. J. Henning,

Acting Secretary of Labor

U. S. DEPARTMENT OF LABOR

WOMEN'S BUREAU

WASHINGTON

December 12, 1924.

To: E. J. Henning, Acting Secretary of Labor

From: The Director of the Women's Bureau

Subject: A suggested division for colored women in the Women's Bureau.

When the Women in Industry Service was created during the war we instituted in this Service a division of colored women which consisted of one colored woman investigator and a stenographer. The report made by this woman was later published in the report issued by Dr. Haynes of the Division of Negro Economics in the Department. This woman investigator, Mrs. Irvin, left the Women's Bureau and in order that we might have a real report on the Negro women in industry, we again employed a colored woman investigator by the name of Miss Emma Shields and she made investigations and issued a report which is our bulletin No. 20, Negro Women in Industry.

Since then we have had no colored women investigator but in eight of our state reports we have treated the colored women as a separate unit. Colored women in industry are not a very large factor and while Mrs. Terrell has done a great deal of work, particularly along humanitarian lines, her greatest effort has been spent in the League for Peace sad Freedom and I do not feel Mrs. Terrell has the special qualifications which we require of our investigators. She is a speaker and her work has not given her the qualifications and the technical knowledge which are essential in our work. I doubt very much if she could pass the special examination which our investigators have to pass.

Because of the small amount of money the Women's Bureau has at its disposal it would be impossible to establish a division of colored women at the present time. As you will remember, in the recommendation of the Budget of the Congress, we have a decrease in our appropriation instead of an increase. The only way we could handle this question at this time is when a special emergency arises to employ a colored woman, a trained investigator, to do emergency work. We are hoping, however, to issue a bulletin on the occupational progress of colored women, which will be material secured from the Bureau of the Census.

MA:L

Mary Anderson, Director.

DEPARTMENT OF LABOR

OFFICE OF THE ASSISTANT SECRETARY

WASHINGTON

December 13, 1924.

My dear Mr. Secretary:

Referring further to your letter of the 10th instant, with reference to the desire of Mrs. Mary Church Terrell to be appointed as head of a colored women's section of the Women's Bureau of this Department, I beg to inclose, herewith, for your information, a memorandum just received from the chief of the Women's Bureau on this subject.

Apparently, it is not feasible, at this time, to comply with Mrs. Terrell's request.

I am, my dear Mr. Secretary,

    Very sincerely yours.

    E.J. Henning,

    Acting Secretary.

Hon. C. B. Slemp,

Secretary to the President,

The White House.

Inc.

EJH:C

December 13, 1924.

My dear Mrs. Terrell:

Referring to your recent call at the Executive office I beg to send you the accompanying copy of a memorandum which has just been received from the Department of Labor. It explains itself.

I have taken up further with the acting Secretary of Labor the matter of the Children's Bureau.

    Sincerely yours,

    C. B. Slemp

    Secretary to the President.

Mrs. Mary Church Terrell,

1615 S Street, N. W.,

Washington, D. C.

enclosure

Woman's Republican League

Mr. C. Bascom Slemp

Secretary to the President,

My dear Mr. Slemp:

Thank you very much for your letter and enclosure. I myself had a very pleasant interview with Miss Anderson a few days ago and she told me that no one could be appointed to the Women's Bureau without passing a techni-[cal] examination. I want first to call special attention to a mistake which Miss Anderson made with reference to myself. She says "While Mrs. Terrell has done a great deal of work particularly along humanitarian lines, her greatest effort has been spent in the League for Peace and Freedom." I have been a member of that League for only a few years and am not actively connected with it now. Since there is no organization of colored women connected with it, I have had very little opportunity to do any effective work. I was invited by the League to represent colored women, when the members held a meeting in Switzerland a few years ago and I delivered an address on that occasion. That represents practically all the work I have ever done except attend meetings.

My greatest efforts have been exerted to help the women and children of my race. As I have told you I was one of the first two women appointed on the Board of Education in this city, when it was publicly declare that no white men and certainly no white women could be found here who would be willing to work with any colored women. That prophesy was so far wrong that I was reappointed so many times that I surged eleven years-a longer period than anybody else has ever served whether white or black. I finally resigned of my own free will and accord and was given on ovation by both white and colored patrons of the public schools.

I was the first president of the National Association of colored women and I have studied the problems of our women from all angles.

When Miss Anderson says"I do not feel that Mrs. Terrell has the special qualifications which we require of our investigators," she expresses that opinion without knowing anything about the work I have done except the few efforts I have put forth in behalf of a League composed practically of white women.

I should be willing to try to do any work which the Women's Bureau would require us to do. If I failed in that effort, it would be the first time I have ever failed in any work I have attempted.

I had a pleasant interview with Miss. Abbott, director of the Children's Bureau, and she also told me that an examination was necessary. Miss Abbott told me that no one but college graduates should be appointed. I have both an A. B. and A. M. degree from Oberlin college. In addition to that I studied abroad three years in France, Germany and Italy. I have been invited twice by organizations of white women to represent my race abroad and I have done so in Berlin, Germany and in Zurich. White women do not invite a colored woman to represent her race, if she knows nothing about its problems, has done no work for it and can do nothing but talk. I hope the requirements will not be so great that no colored women can be appointed either in the Women's Bureau or the Children's Bureau. I should like to have a chance to serve in either.

I can not tell you how grateful I am to you for the interest you have manifested in me and I am depending upon you to let me serve in some capacity commensurate with my training and experience.

Very gratefully and sincerely yours,

Mary Church Terrell

DEPARTMENT OF LABOR

OFFICE OF THE ASSISTANT SECRETARY

WASHINGTON

December 19, 1924.

My dear Mr. Secretary:

This is to acknowledge receipt of your letter of today, transmitting letter of Mrs. Terrell.

I do not know the nature of the Civil Service examination for employment in the Children's Bureau or in the Women's Bureau. I understand the Children's Bureau has been declared a professional bureau by the Reclassification Board. Just what that many mean, I do not know, except that it would indicate that technical training is required. I will make inquiry and advise you.

I might suggest that Mrs. Terrell call on Mr. Karl Phillips, Room 415, Department of Labor Building. Mr. Phillips has been doing work there with special reference to the needs of the negro and is a negro of good education and broad experience. Mrs. Terrell writes such a splendid letter that it does seem some way should be found to make use of her talents.

As soon as I can secure the information with reference to the qualifications for the Women's and Children's Bureau, I shall advise you.

Mrs. Terrell's letter is, herewith, returned to you.

I am my dear Mr. Secretary,

Very sincerely yours,

E. J. Henning,

Hon. C. B. Slemp,

Secretary to the President,

The white House.

Inc.

EJH:C

December 19, 1924.

My dear Mr. Henning:

I am sending you, herewith, for consideration with my previous correspondence with you, another letter from Mrs. Mary Church Terrell.

Sincerely yours,

C. B. Slemp

Secretary to the President.

Hon. E. J. Henning,

Acting Secretary of Labor.

enclosure.

December 19, 1924.

My dear Mrs. Terrell.

I shall bring your letter of December 17th to the attention of Acting Secretary Henning for consideration in connection with your previous correspondence with him.

Sincerely yours,

C. B. Slemp

Secretary to the President.

Mrs. Mary Church Terrell,

1615 S Street, N. W.,

Washington, D. C.

December 20, 1924.

My dear Mrs. Terrell.

With reference to your letter of December 17th, I am sending you, herewith, a copy of a letter which has just been received from the Acting Secretary of Labor. I think that it might be well for you to follow Mr. Henning's suggestion and see Mr. Phillips.

Sincerely yours,

C. B. Slemp

Secretary to the President.

Mrs. Mary Church Terrell,

1615 S Street, N. W.,

Washington, D. C.

DEPARTMENT OF LABOR

OFFICE OF THE ASSISTANT SECRETARY

WASHINGTON

December 27, 1924.

My dear Mr. Secretary:

Reference is made to your letter of the 19th instant, by which you transmitted a letter from Mrs. Mary Church Terrell, of this city, who has expressed the desire to be appointed as head of a colored women's section in the Women's or Children's Bureau of this Department.

Under date of the 19th instant, I wrote you on this subject advising you that I would inquire of these Bureaus, as well as of the Civil Service Commission as to the nature of the special qualifications required for those seeking employment in these Bureaus. I made this request of each of the Chiefs of these Bureaus on the 19th instant and also of the Civil Service Commission.

The Civil Service Commission some days ago sent me, by way of response, the inclosed. I have not yet received any word from either the Women's Bureau or the Children's Bureau.

I am, my dear Mr. Secretary,

Very sincerely yours,

E. J. Henning,

Acting Secretary.

Hon. C. B. Slemp,

Secretary to the President,

The White House.

Inc.

EJH:C

COPY

DEPARTMEMT OF LABOR

Office of the Chief Clerk

Washington

December 27, 1924.

MEMORANDUM FOR MRS. HENNING:

Referring to the communication from the Director of the Women's Bureau concerning educational tests required for certain positions, the data contained in the notices of examinations sent therewith is summarized as follows:

Special Agent, $1500 to $1800 a year, calls for grammar school education or its equivalent and at least one year's experience in industry; educational training equivalent to that required for a bachelor's degree from a college or university.

Assistant in Information, $1500 to $1800 a year calls for graduation from a college or university of recognized standing and at least one year's experience as writer and editor or assistant editor on a newspaper or periodical, or for persons lacking such college education at least an additional year of experience for each lacking such college course.

Assistant Editor, Women in Industry, $2100 to $2700 a year requires graduation from a college or university of recognized standing and at least two year's experience; or completion of two years of college and three years of practical experience; or the completion of a four year's high school course or equivalent education, and one year's training in a recognized school of social service and three years of practical experience.

(signed) S. J. Gompers

Chief Clerk.

Washington, D. C., January 26, 1925.

Remarks: (Mrs. Mary Church Terrell)

1. Wife of Robert H. Terrell, Roosevelt-Taft-Wilson appointee, Judge of the Municipal Court, Washington, D. C. Present term expires June, 1925.

2. Graduated of Oberlin College, Ohio; lecturer, educator in higher academic branches; writer; forceful orator; no practical experience in industrial work.

3. Non-voter.

4. Strongly aligned with minority (class) group of Negroes; stays aloof from the messes of Negro workers.

5. From a political standpoint among Negroes, her appointment would probably bring forth murmurs of displeasure because of two appointments in some "family;" non-voting status; and pronounced removal from the rank and file of Negroes. This demeanor, during the Harding campaign, was most harmful in the New York district.

6. Splendid character; outstanding literary attainments; fair organizing ability; no practical experience other than as teacher.

7. Does not work well with others.

FOCUS QUESTIONS:

1. Was there support for Terrell's desire to work in the administration?

2. What were Terrell's reasons for seeking a position in the Women's Bureau or Children's Bureau?

15-10 Helen M. Todd, "Getting Out the Vote" (1911)

The movement for woman suffrage began in the mid-nineteenth century. By the early 1900s, several western states had granted women the right to vote, but no success was achieved on the national level. Womans suffrage groups maintained efforts to pass a constitutional amendment giving women the right to vote.

On a June day last year, six or eight insurgent women met in the library of the Chicago Women's Club and decided to add the Sixteenth Amendment to the Constitution of the United States. . . .

It would be untrue to leave the impression that we found this fraternal feeling toward woman suffrage readymade. It was only achieved in many instances by effort and experience.

The men were sometimes obviously thankful their women folks were incapable of going gallivanting through the country making speeches. Often, as our automobile, covered with banners, stopped in front of the blacksmith shop or on the street corner where we were scheduled to speak, we realized that the temper of the audience was not one of unmixed approval; but

they were interested, and above all they were there. The rest was for us to do. Every type of man was represented in these down-State audiences, and every kind of vehicle. The stores were left in charge of whoever was unfor-tunate enough to have to stay, generally the errand boy, and the rest of the village turned out to "hear the women talk."

We opened our plea for women by showing our audience that the mother and wife could not long protect herself and her children unless she had a vote. That the milk the city mother gave her baby; the school her children were educated in; the purity of the water they drank; the prices she paid for meat and clothes; the very wages her husband received; the sanitary and moral condition of the streets her children passed through were all matters of politics. When once we had clearly established the fact that women wanted to vote to protect their homes we had won a large part of our audience.. .

When we reached Warren the place was decorated with flags and yellow banners. The big street meeting had already gathered. "Let me take up all the time," Mrs. McCulloch said, "because we have only a thirty minutes' stop here." "With all your banners and welcome," she said, getting energetically upon the seat of the automobile, "the man that you have sent to represent you in the Legislature has knifed our Suffrage bill every time it came up. I am just going to tell you your Representative's history and ask you to keep him at home," and she did.

Mixed with the arraignment of Representative Gray was the pathos and wit of the story of the struggles of the women of Illinois in the Legislature to protect its children. When she had finally finished the story of Mr. Gray's part in this struggle you could feel the audience with her. They came crowding about the machine. "All right, we will get some-body else; we never knew about all this. We cannot do much for you ladies because he has got another year to serve," was suggested. This seemed final, and just as the automobile was beginning to move, a crowd of men and women pushing for-ward a central figure that was half laughing and half resisting bore down upon us and called for the chauffeur to stop. "Here he is!" they shouted. "We went to his house and got him. You just ask him whether he is going to stand for that Suffrage bill this fall and we'll stand back and see what he says. This is Representative Gray." Mrs. McCulloch who had become acquainted with him in the Legislature looked coldly at him. The Rev. Kate Hughes, who had also had the pleasure of meeting him in the same place, sniffed, I might almost say snorted, audibly and looked absently over his head. Dr. Blount greeted him with friendly interest as one would a sinner in whom there were possibilities of repentance. And I, being nearest on the outside, hastily assumed my most ingratiating and feminine air and held out my hand. "Well, Mr. Gray," I said, "will you promise us to stand for our Woman's Suffrage bill this time?" "It looks as if I would have to," he said, disengaging himself with difficulty from the press of the crowd in order to take off his hat. "I have always thought women were about the best things there were in the world, but I never thought you were so in earnest about this voting. If you have really set your hearts on it why there is nothing for me to do but give in. I can't fight against a woman's campaign. I'm for you," he shouted as we drove off amid the laughter and cheers of the crowd.

On the Fourth of July we spoke in the city square. Truths, familiar to city men through a prevalence of speakers, are sometimes new to a down-State audience. We told them that in a country that boasted of its representative government half the population of women were not represented at all, that they were classed with the criminal and insane even though they had given their sons to make a Fourth of July possible.

When we had finished, an old man pushed his way to the auto-mobile and gave us some money. He had an old, weather-beaten face and instead of week-day overalls wore a stiff suit of "store" clothes in honor of the Fourth; his trousers guiltless of any crease looked like two sections of stovepipe. So serious and almost forbidding was the expression that we waited for him to speak before making any overtures of friendship. Accustomed as we were to the more mobile city face, we often could not tell from the faces of our audience what they were feeling. This old man might have been going to say, "I hate what you are saying; I wish you would go away," but he handed us a two-dollar bill and leaning over the machine squeezed each of our hands with a grip that brought tears to our eyes. "I would just give anything in the hull world if my wife had been well enough to come along, but she's been poorly all this winter and couldn't stand the long drive. I'm giving you this two dollars for her. The idea," he continued, gazing angrily at us, "of a woman like my wife bein' put along with imbeciles and criminals. Why, she came out with me from New York in the pioneer days when Illinois was nothing but woods and bears and swamps and we drove the hull way in a mover's wagon and took our three children too." . . .

Power and confidence are as valuable assets to a woman as a man; and as one of our party remarked, it is not only the people we have reached on this trip that matters, but we have learned how to do it.

After all, with women, isn't it largely a question of learning how?

There is a comradeship which only comes from working together for a common cause. Although most men know the pleasure of this, comparatively few women have experienced it, and although we were as tired as any pioneer women who had crossed the country in a mover's wagon after this last meeting and our week's campaign, yet our party was loath to break up.

It had been inspiring to depend upon the honesty, personal kindness, the spirit of fair play and neighborliness, the quick response to anyone in sorrow or need, which were characteristics of our country audiences. And we lingered taking to each other and to members of the crowd who were seeing us home until it was very late when I entered the farm-house where I was to spend my last night down State.

Late as it was, the old bed-ridden mother was awake and called softly for me to come in and tell her about the meetin'. "I knew it would be a fine meetin'," she said. "I had my bed turned 'round to the window. I seen the wagons coming in from out of town since morning. I knew you'd be leaving for Chicago early, and I just thought I would wait up for you so's I could hear all about it and tell Lucy. You see," she explained, "Daughter Lucy and the hired girl couldn't both go and leave me alone, since I have had my stroke. Lucy, she was born and brought up to woman's rights, bein' my daughter; but our hired girl's new in our family and she's real ignorant about it. So Lucy she felt it was her duty to send our girl to get converted, and stay to home herself. I'm a believer," she said, "and Maggie ain't. But Lucy she felt terrible put out about it though she didn't let on to me of course, and I made up my mind I'd ask you to just say over what you said so's I could tell it to her. I had hoped," she added, "that I'd last to see the day when women would vote in Illinois, but if Susan B. Anthony can die without seem' it, I guess I can. It's a comfort to see you young women back keepin' up the same fight that we started back East when we was young and spry. It makes us feel as if we hadn't educated you for nothing, for we did educate you. 'What, educate shes!' the men said when we wanted the girls to go to school. 'What's the use spendin' money on educatin' shes?' Well I guess we've showed them what the use was. I've seen that done anyhow."...

No words can better express the soul of the woman's movement, lying back of the practical cry of "Votes for Women," better than this sentence which had captured the attention of both Mother Jones and the hired girl, "Bread for all, and Roses too." Not at once; but woman is the mothering element in the world and her vote will go toward helping forward the time when life's Bread, which is home, shelter and security, and the Roses of life, music, education, nature and books, shall be the heritage of every child that is born in the country, in the government of which she has a voice.

There will be no prisons, no scaffolds, no children in factories, no girls driven on the street to earn their bread, in the day when there shall be "Bread for all, and Roses too."

To help to make such a civilization possible is the meaning of "Votes for Women." It was the power of this idea which sent the women of Illinois "down State" on their automobile campaign.

FOCUS QUESTIONS:

1. What arguments did the supporters of woman suffrage use to promote a constitutional amendment giving women the right to vote?

2. What tactics did the supporters of the amendment use and how successful were they? Why were they successful?

THE JAZZ AGE, 1920 –1930

16-1 Alice Drysdale Vickery, "The Place of Birth Controlin the Woman's Movement" (1925)

This essay, is by Alice Drysdale-Vickery (1844-1929), who, along with her husband Charles Drysdale, founded the Malthusian league, and a journal, The Malthusian.

Source: *"Alice Drysdale Vickery. The Place of Birth Control in the Woman's Movement. 1925."* In *Major Problems in American Women's History.* 2nd edition. Mary Beth Norton and Ruth M. Alexander, editors. Lexington, MA: D.C. Heath and Company, 1996, 327-329.

This seems to me a very critical period in the world's history. Either the world's in-habitants must face the problem of controlling the numbers of suc-ceeding genera-dons in proportion to the supply of necessaries, or the struggle between the various races and nations will become intensified and lead to world-wide disaster.

This is a time in which it is of the utmost impor-tance that women shall learn to realize their responsi-bility, in view of the fact that the peopling of the world belongs to them. It is essential then that women shall come to the front and insist that they will no longer consent to be deprived of the knowledge which will allow them to fulfill their function in the way which will reflect credit upon themselves individually and collectively, and benefit the world at large. Sir Arbuthnot Lane has written of "the crass stupidity of man," and when we recall the obstacles which have been placed in the way of women's education general-ly, and education in physiology, biology, and all that concerns the reproduction of the human species in particular, we cannot think the phrase misplaced. The church has always looked with disfavor on the educa-tion of young people, more particularly women, in sex matters. Men also have very largely desired ignorance

in their mates. The legal profession have placed obsta-cles in the way of woman's power of acting on her own judgment, by making her in the past so largely dependent on the husband as to feel it impossible to form or take any action of which he might not approve. The subject which above all others craves the woman's outlook is that of maternity and reproduction. As woman did not know how to control reproduction and as she naturally, as did man, desired a mate in the early days of maturity, she fell, almost of necessity, into a state of dependence, and that dependence has been fruitful of evil results. But with the knowledge of con-traception, of Birth Control, there is no longer the same reason why she should accept a position of depend-ence. The young girl like the young man should find the same opportunities for employment and self-dependence open to her. She can postpone marriage until she meets with a suitable partner. And when she does meet with an apparently suitable partner (say at 21 years of age) she will not be faced with the necessi-ty of forfeiting her independent position for fear of the premature arrival of offspring. She will by means of birth control methods be able to maintain a position of self-dependence for some years. There is much to be said for a temporary postponement of parentage after marriage. First as the age of physiological maturity is 25, it will doubtless be granted that parentage should be delayed to that age in order that maturity and not immaturity should produce the next generation. Again, is it not well that the young couple should be able to enjoy to the full (say from 21 to 25 years) the delight of intimate companionship, until they can feel assured that they are well suited to one another, that their characters and ideals are likely to develop along mutu-ally sympathetic lines; also that their career (industrial or otherwise) may not be hampered by the premature arrival of another mouth to feed and care for, obliging the young mother to cease her independent employ-ment. The young couple owe to each other fidelity and companionship, mutual solace and assistance, They will learn in this period of experience to understand each other more fully, not merely trusting to the more or less superficial attraction which brought them together. They will besides be more able to assure their future, to build up the home and create and develop the little capital which will enable them to face the responsibility of parentage without alarm. The prospective mother, with health assured, will be willing to cease her contribution to the family budget at a suitable period, having laid by what she deems sufficient for the time being. She will be prepared to give to the new-comer her time, her strength, her thoughts, so that together the young parents will mutually enjoy the delights of parentage, and by the careful use of contraceptive methods will feel assured that no second birth will come to cut short prematurely the mother-care due to the first comer. Think what all this power of direction means to the young couple in their early married life. The power to go slow, to adjust their expenses to their means to avoid all the overstrain of

being always a little behind. Poverty is held at bay. Slums are not being created. The child will enjoy its childhood. He will have time for play, for education. If accidents happen, if ill-health supervene, the strain is materially lessened. Woman with efficient knowledge of birth control can practically abolish poverty in the home. Collectively she will learn how to abolish poverty in the town, the city, the village, the nation. There need be no sex-promiscuity either for men or women. Rational early marriage laws will allow for needful changes.

Focus Questions:

1. What are Drysdale-Vickery's main arguments in favor of birth control?

2. Why does the author argue that birth control will allow women to "practically abolish poverty in the home"?

16-2 Carlton C. Frederick, M.D., "Nymphomania as a Cause of Excess Venery" (1907)

The following is one of the clearest statements of accepted ideas of women's sexuality. Compare his views on "normal" practices among "normal" women with the study of Katherine Bement Davis in the textbook.

Source: Transactions of the American Association of Obstetricians and Gynecologists for the year 1907, v.20. New York: Federal Printing Company, 1908. pp. 237-238.

THE sexual instinct is not so common in woman as it is in man. With the latter it is, under normal conditions of health and vigor, an ever-present, powerful impulse to procreation. Sexual desire is entirely absent in a much larger number of women than is generally supposed. If present it is ordinarily not so strong as it is in man. If a woman has in her makeup the sexual instinct to the ordinary degree, that impulse is only aroused by the man she loves, and for no other has she that feeling. There is a small percentage of women in whom it is very strong, but relatively to the whole number the percentage is small.

Woman naturally is a monogamous, and man by nature a polygamous animal. Among many prostitutes the feeling of coitus with men in general is one of disgust. A small proportion of them are led to the life by

their strong sexual desires. I have been told by many that their only reason for continuing it is that they are unable to earn a livelihood otherwise after having the stain upon their character due to their nefarious occupation. Otherwise they would gladly leave it for a purer life. Generally every such woman has some one man friend whom she chooses to call her lover, with whom there is sexual desire and gratification. Fortunate it is for the morals of humanity that woman generally is not so constituted sexually as is man, otherwise, as has been aptly said, this world would be one vast brothel. Surely, to the influence of woman we must look for the standard of moral tone, however high that may be. This being the sexual status of women, we turn to those individuals in whom nyphomania and the resulting excesses and perversions exist.

Nymphomania is an excessive development of sexual desire in the female, manifesting itself in various ways dependent upon the mental status, moral sense, environment, or social scale of the individual. Masturbation is probably one of its most prominent manifestations. Masturbation in normally constituted girls and women is relatively infrequent. I have seen but very few cases in my whole experience. Among women physicians of large experience with whom I have conversed, with the object of obtaining material for this paper, the verdict has been the same, and naturally a mother would take her daughter, in whom she discovered such a habit, to a woman rather than to a man for advice. Constituted as most women are in their sexual instincts, there must be an exciting cause for masturbation in those who are physically and nervously normal. It is doubtful if the habit is acquired simply by the bad example of schoolmates or other companions who are addicted to the habit. I have personally never seen a case for which some cause other than bad associations was not found, and such also has been the experience of other competent observers.

FOCUS QUESTIONS:

1. Would you say Frederick's findings are typical for his time? Were they accurate?

2. How does Frederick's understanding of women's sexuality fit in with other ideas current in the early 1900s about family, morality and the woman's sphere?

16-3 Elizabeth Blackwell, M.D., on Female Sexuality (1902)

Elizabeth Blackwell (1821-1910) was the first woman to qualify as a doctor in the U.S. She was also very active in the women's rights movement. She and her sister opened the New York Infirmary for Indigent Women and Children in 1857. The following excerpt draws on her long experience as a doctor.

Source: Elizabeth Blackwell Essays in *Medical Sociology*, published by Bell, 1902 Item notes: v.1 Original from Harvard University Digitized May 23, 2008. pp. 51-56.

This mental element of sex exists in major proportion in the vital force of women, and justifies the statement that the compound faculty of sex is as strong in woman as in man. Those who deny sexual feeling to women, or consider it so light a thing as hardly to be taken into account in social arrangements, confound appetite and passion; they quite lose sight of this immense spiritual force of attraction, which is distinctly human sexual power, and which exists in so very large a proportion in the womanly nature. The impulse towards maternity is an inexorable but beneficent law of woman's nature, and it is a law of sex.

The different form which physical sensation necessarily takes in the two sexes, and its intimate connection with and development through the mind (love) in women's nature, serve often to blind even thoughtful and painstaking persons as to the immense power of sexual attraction felt by women. Such one-sided views show a misconception of the meaning of human sex in its entirety.

The affectionate husbands of refined women often remark that their wives do not regard the distinctively sexual act with the same intoxicating physical enjoyment that they themselves feel, and they draw the con-clusion that the wife possesses no sexual passion. A delicate wife will often confide to her medical adviser (who maybe treating her for some special suffering) that at the very time when marriage love seems to unite them most closely, when her husband's welcome kisses and caresses seem to bring them into profound union, comes an act which mentally separates them, and which may be either indifferent or repugnant to her. But it must be under-stood that it is not the special act necessary for parentage which is the measure of the compound moral and physical power of sexual passion; it is the profound attraction of one nature to the other which marks passion, and delight in kiss and caress — the love-touch — is physical sexual expression as much as the special act of the male.

It is well known that terror or pain in either sex will temporarily destroy all physical pleasure. In married life, injury from childbirth, or brutal or awkward conjugal approaches, may cause unavoidable shrinking from sexual congress, often wrongly attributed to absence of sexual passion. But the severe and compound suffering experienced by many widows who were strongly attached to their lost partners is also well known to the physician, and this is not simply a mental loss that they feel, but an immense physical deprivation. It is a loss which all the senses suffer by the physical as well as moral void which death has created.

Although physical sexual pleasure is not attached exclusively, or in woman chiefly, to the act of coition, it is also a well-established fact that in healthy, loving women, uninjured by the too frequent lesions which result from childbirth, increasing physical satisfaction attaches to the ultimate physical expression of love. A repose and general well-being results from this natural occasional intercourse, whilst the total deprivation of it produces irritability.

On the other hand, the growth in men of the mental element in sexual passion, from mighty wifely love, often comes like a revelation to the husband. The dying words of a man to the wife who, sending away children, friends, every distraction, had bent the whole force of her passionate nature to holding the beloved object in life — ' I never knew before what love meant ' — indicates the revelation which the higher element of sexual passion should bring to the lower phase. It is an illustration of the parallelism and natural harmony between the sexes. The prevalent fallacy that sexual passion is the almost exclusive attribute of men, and attached exclusively to the act of coition — a fallacy which exercises so disastrous an effect upon our social arrangements — arises from ignorance of the distinctive character of human sex — viz., its powerful mental element. A tortured girl, done to death by brutal soldiers, may possess a stronger power of human sexual passion than her destroyers.

The comparison so often drawn between the physical development of the comparatively small class of refined and guarded women, and the men of worldly experience whom they marry, is a false comparison. These women have been taught to regard sexual passion as lust and as sin — a sin which it would be a shame for a pure woman to feel, and which she would die rather than confess. She has not been taught that sexual passion is love, even more than lust, and that its ennobling work in humanity is to educate and transfigure the lower by the higher element. The growth and indications of her own nature she is taught to condemn, instead of to respect them as foreshadowing that mighty impulse towards maternity which will place her nearest to the Creator if reverently accepted.

But if the comparison be made between men and women of loose lives — not women who are allowed and encouraged by money to carry on a trade in vice, but men and women of similar unrestrained and loose life — the unbridled impulse of physical lust is as remarkable in the latter as in the former. The astounding lust and cruelty of women uncontrolled by spiritual principle is a historical fact.

The most destructive phase of fornication is promiscuous intercourse. This riotous debauchery introduced the devastating scourge of syphilis into Western Europe in the fourteenth century. Promiscuous intercourse can never be made ' safe.' The resort of many men to one woman, with its results, is against nature.

The special structures of the female body, which are endowed with the elasticity necessary for the passage of a child, rich in secreting glands, in folds, in power of absorption, cannot be treated as a plane surface, to be washed out and labelled ' safe.' Physical danger will always be connected with unnatural use of the body; neither party engaged in promiscuous intercourse can be pronounced clean.

This is not the place to speak of the moral danger inseparable from a corrupt bargain which debases the highest function, the creative, to the low status of trade competition, but the Christian physician is bound to consider this.

Some medical writers have considered that women are more tyrannically governed than men by the impulses of physical sex. They have dwelt upon the greater proportion of work laid upon women in

the reproduction of the race, the prolonged changes and burden of maternity, and the fixed and marked periodical action needed to maintain the aptitude of the physical frame for maternity. They have drawn the conclusion that sex dominates the life of women, and limits them in the power of perfect human growth. This would undoubtedly be the case were sex simply a physical function.

The fact in human nature which explains, guides, and should elevate the sexual nature of woman, and mark the beneficence of Creative Force, is this very mental element which distinguishes human from brute sex. This element, gradually expanding under religious teaching and the development of true religious sentiment, becomes the ennobling power of love. Love between the sexes is the highest and mightiest form of human sexual passion.

The mental element in human sex, although as distinctly a part of sexual passion as the physical element, does not necessarily imply good use. The woman who employs the arts of dress to bring the physical peculiarities of sex into prominence, and uses every method of coquetry and flirtation to excite the attention and awaken the physical impulses of men, is abusing her sexual power. The degree in which she employs these arts, measures the extent to which her own nature is dominated by brute sexual instinct, and the unworthiness of the use to which she puts this instinct.

This power of sex in women is strikingly shown in the enormous influence which they exert upon men for evil. It is not the cold beauty of a statue which enthrals and holds so many men in terrible fascination; it is the living, active power of sexual life embodied in its separate overpowering female phase. The immeasurable depth of degradation into which those women fall, whose sex is thoroughly debased, who have intensified the physical instincts of the brute by the mental power for evil possessed by the human being, indicates the mighty character of sexual power over the nature of woman for corruption. It is also a measure of what the ennobling power of passion may be.

Happily in all civilized countries there is a natural reserve in relation to matters which indicates the reverence with which this high social power of our human nature should be regarded. It is a sign of something wrong in education, in the social state, when matters which concern the subject of sex are discussed with the same freedom and boldness as other matters. This subject should neither be a topic of idle gossip, of unreserved publicity, nor of cynical display. . . .

FOCUS QUESTIONS:

1. Compare the perspectives of Frederick and Blackwell, What are the main points of disagreement?
2. To what cause or causes does Blackwell attribute lack of passion in women?
3. What does Blackwell mean by the "power of sex in women"?

16-4 The Physical Education of Girls (1852)

Elizabeth Blackwell wrote this short treatise, drawing on lectures she had delivered the year before, in 1852, just after qualifying as a doctor. In this book, she explained both the principles and practices which she hoped might improve the lives of young women. In it she advocates strongly for exercise for children and young adults.

Source: Elizabeth Blackwell, *The Laws of Life With Special Reference to the Physical Education of Girls*, New York: George P. Putnam, 1852, 57-59; 171-172.

Having thus found the first division which our subject clearly presents, you will readily perceive that my remarks on " The Laws of Life, with special reference to the Physical Education of Girls," will chiefly refer to the related life of the body, towards which we have so important a part to perform; but we have already seen that there is no such thing as simple isolated life in the universe, and that our will may powerfully influence the organic life of the body, its connection being so intimate with every part of our human nature, that I must first call your attention to this division of our subject before we shall be prepared to take up the important second branch.

Let us now consider, therefore, the Organic Life of the body, and the way in which we can aid this life. We have seen that each organ has its own special work to do, and understands, better than we can do, the best method of doing it. In the organic life of the body we are not called upon either to furnish an object, or to educate any part to the attainment of an object. Our part lies solely in placing the body in a position to work ; in other words, our duty to the organic life consist in

furnishing the following conditions, viz., 1st, freedom to work ; and 2dly, materials to work with. In these two rules lie our most important duties to the body. Our first duties, — for, before education is possible, the observance of these laws is essential to the life of the infant; our last duties, — for, when the aim of human life has been accomplished, when the related life of the body having finished its work, grows weak, and the period of separation approaches, it is by diligent observation of these rules that we can most effectually cheer declining life. Indeed, throughout the whole period of our earthly existence, of infancy, youth, manhood, and old age, if we would prevent sickness, promote well-being, and prolong life, we must never cease to perform our first grand duty to the body, the securing to it of freedom to work and materials to work with.

Let us examine more in detail the application of these principles, and see how clear a light they shed upon the relation of our will to every period of existence.

Look at the first faint gleam of life, the life of the embryo, the commencement of human existence. We see a tiny cell, so small that it may easily be overlooked; the anatomist may examine it with scalpel or microscope, and what does he discover? Nothing but a delicate, transparent membrane, containing one drop of clear water; the chemist may analyze it with the most scrupulous care, and find nothing but the trace of some simple salts. And yet there is in that simple germ-cell something most wonderful — life ! — it is a living cell; it contains a power of progressive growth, according to law, towards a definite type, that we can only regard with reverent admiration.

Leave it in its natural home, tended by the healthy life of the maternal organization, and it will grow steadily in the human type ; in no other by any possibility. Little by little faint specks will appear in the enlarging cell, marking the head, the trunk, the budding extremities; tiny channels will groove themselves in every direction, red particles of inconceivable minuteness will appear in these channels, and will move towards one central spot, where a little channel has become enlarged, has assumed a special form, has already begun to palpitate; the living blood in the small arteries now joins that in the heart, and the circulation is established. From every delicate incomplete part shoot forth minute nerve-threads, which tend inevitably towards their centres, joining the brain, the spinal marrow, the ganglia. The nervous system is formed. The cell rapidly enlarges; its attachments to the maternal, organism become more powerful, for increasing amounts of fresh nourishment must be conveyed to the growing being, and as the work advances to perfection, each organ is distinctly formed, and placed in the cavities of head, chest, and abdomen, which are now completely closed ; the human type is surely attained, and after a brief period of consolidation the young existence, created from that simple cell, will awake to a further development of independent life.

.....

The paramount importance of physical development should never be lost sight of in any arrangements for the education of the young. No pursuit should place the child under unfavorable conditions of position, atmosphere, &c., and direct physical exercise should constantly terminate the short periods of mental application. Lofty, well ventilated halls, and a large piece of ground partly shaded by trees, should be essential elements of every establishment for education.

Such changes could easily be introduced into schools. It only needs that public opinion should be roused to the necessity of an ample provision for the physical education of the young ; that mothers should lay to heart the immense mischief that is done to their daughters by neglecting the body and overtasking the mind, and that they should resolve, as a duty of primary importance, to ensure for them a strong physical organization. When public sentiment shall thus demand the conditions of a sound and true education, its wants will soon be met by the establishment of the necessary institutions, and intelligent teachers will gladly welcome the change, for they clearly perceive the evils of the present system, though they are unable, alone, of themselves, to remedy them.

I cannot now enlarge on the condition, wants and duties of the young lady, who has left school, nor on the many evils of adult life; for the plan of the present lectures is limited to a consideration of the physical necessities of girlhood.

I will only in closing most earnestly entreat you as wise mothers, as responsible human beings, to be faithful to the trust committed to you, as the educators of the young, and to remember the one great truth, which I have constantly endeavored to enforce, viz., that there is a Divine Order of Growth appointed for the human being, which we dare not neglect without violating our duty as parents and as Christians ; a Divine Order which, if we observe faithfully through every period of life, will bring health and beauty, and happiness amongst us. Glorious indeed is the duty confided to mothers; the duty of training to perfection, to the ideal of our human nature, the young beings committed to their care; a most sacred duty, to be accomplished with religious devotion, and the deepest sense of responsibility. In this spirit let us meet the trust committed to us as women, and we shall then see our children growing up around us in strength and grace, and fulfilling in after life the promise of their childhood. The beauty of Adam and Eve will then no longer be a tradition, for the Divine Image shall again be stamped upon our race.

FOCUS QUESTIONS:

1. How does Blackwell's medical knowledge add to her ideas about raising children?

2. Considering the date of this publication, was Blackwell's writing in the mainstream of thought of the time?

3. Blackwell's "facts of life" are rather tame in some ways, but what are the implications of her ideas about "the organic life of the body"?

16-5 Florence Kelley Explains Her Opposition to Full Legal Equality (1922)

Florence Kelley (1859-1932) was active in working for children's rights. The following excerpt, written just two years after women gained voting rights, addresses her concerns for the impact of abolishing distinctions between men and women on legal protections for working women.

Source: in *Major Problems in American Women's History*: Documents and Essays, edited by Mary Beth Norton, Ruth M. Alexander, Boston, Houghton Mifflin, 2003, 325-326

"The removal of all forms of subjection of women is the purpose to which the National Woman's Party is dedicated."

A few years ago the Woman's Party counted disfranchisement the form of subjection which must first be removed. Today millions of American women, educated and uneducated, are kept from the polls in bold defiance of the Suffrage Amendment. Every form of subjection suffered by their white sisters they also suffer. Deprivation of the vote is theirs alone among native women. Because of this discrimination all other forms of subjection weigh a hundred fold more heavily upon them. In the family, in the effort to rent or to buy homes, as wage-earners, before the courts, in getting education for their children, in every relation of life, their burden is greater because they are victims of political inequality. How literally are colored readers to understand the words quoted above?

Sex is a biological fact. The political rights of citizens are not properly dependent upon sex, but social and domestic relations and industrial activities are. All modern-minded people desire that women should have full political equality and like opportunity in business and the professions. No enlightened person desires that they should be excluded from jury duty or denied the equal guardianship of children, or that unjust inheritance laws or discriminations against wives should be perpetuated.

The inescapable facts are, however, that men do not bear children, are freed from the burdens of maternity, and are not susceptible, in the same measures as women, to poisons now increasingly characteristic of certain industries, and to the universal poison of fatigue. These are differences so far reaching, so fundamental, that it is grotesque to ignore them. Women cannot be made men by act of the legislature or by amendment of the Federal Constitution. This is no matter of today or to-morrow. The inherent differences are permanent. Women will always need many laws different from those needed by men.

The effort to enact the blanket bill in defiance of all biological differences recklessly imperils the special laws for women as such, for wives, for mothers, and for wage-earners...

Why should wage-earning women be thus forbidden to get laws for their own health and welfare and that of their unborn children? Why should they be made subject to the preferences of wage-earning men? Is not this of great and growing importance when the number of women wage-earners, already counted by millions, in-creases by leaps and bounds from one census to the next? And when the industries involving exposure to poisons are increasing faster than ever? And when the over-work of mothers is one recognized cause of the high infant death rate? And when the rise in the mortality of mothers in childbirth continues?

If there were no other way of promoting more perfect equality for women, an argument could perhaps be sustained for taking these risks. But why take them when every desirable measure attainable through the blanket bill can be enacted in the ordinary way? ... .

Is the National Woman's Party for or against protective measures for wage-earning women? Will it publicly state whether it is for or against the eight-hour day and minimum-wage commissions for women? Yes or No?

FOCUS QUESTIONS:

1. Kelley ends her essay with a question for the National Woman's Party. How does this question illustrate an important division in the woman movement that continued after women obtained suffrage?

2. For Kelley, what should the main legislative goals of women be?

3. Why does Kelley say that women are still kept from the polls?

16-6 "Two Doctors Describe a Case of Perverted Sexual Instinct in a Young Female" (1883)

Source: Reprinted in Mary Beth Norton, Ruth M. Alexander, *Major Problems in American Women's History: Documents and Essays,* Boston, Houghton Mifflin, 1996, 220-221.

Case. 5 – A Jewish servant-girl, twenty-eight years old, went of her own free will to an asylum; said she felt sick and miserable, and wished to die. She had a great passion for a female friend; recognized the same as abnormal, but could not repress it; wished to be helped. Patient's mother died of consumption and in her later years had been quite demented. No further hereditary history obtained. As a child she was careless, mischievous; did not learn readily; played almost exclusively with boys; menstruated at twelve and a half years irregularly, profusely, and with pain. About this time experienced a preference for girls, particularly ones who attracted her by the expression of their eyes; followed the hosen ones all over; blushed when she spoke to them; was jealous when they spoke to others; when she kissed them, experienced a voluptuous sensation in her genital organs. This desire occurred shortly before and after the menses; when masturbating, thought of the loved girl. As she grew older, was shown some attention by men; had offers of marriage, but she

would have nothing to do with them; was not interested in men, and at times experienced a real disgust for them. But her love for girls increased in intensity; was not content to kiss and hug them, but wished to sleep with them and handle their sexual organs. When resisted by them became very much excited; finally recognized the fact that they did not feel as she did, and began to think she was sick; neglected her work; would stand still gazing in one direction; became very unhappy; attempted to drown herself. The suppression of her desire made her finally so unhappy that medical advice was sought. Physically, patient corresponded to the female type: breasts well developed, genital organs quite normal, uterus in normal position; some asymmetry of the face. Patient complains of headache, dizziness, backache, pain in pit of stomach, and loss of sleep and appetite. In the institution was restless, depressed, worked but little; fell in love with a nurse and a childish patient; wished to embrace them and sleep with them; menstruated twice without trouble; improved very much; went home; did fairly well after another short exacerbation during which she attempted to drown herself.

FOCUS QUESTIONS:

1. What factors does the author seem to think are significant in analyzing this case?
2. Reading between the lines, what is the doctors' attitude towards this girl?

16-7 Ida B. Wells-Barnett, from *A Red Record* (1895)

The rise of racial segregation was accompanied by racial violence that went punished by the law, including lynching. Journalist Ida B. Wells-Barnett emerged as the strongest voice against lynching.

Source: Ida B. Wells-Barnett, The Red Record: Tabulated Statistics and Alleged Causes of Lynching in the United States, 1895

A word as to the charge itself. In considering the third reason assigned by the Southern white people for the butchery of blacks, the question must be asked, what the white man means when he charges the black man with rape. Does he mean the crime which the statutes of the states describe as such? Not by any means. With the Southern white man, any misalliance existing between a white woman and a colored man is a sufficient foundation for the charge of rape. The

southern white man says that it is impossible for a voluntary alliance to exist between a white woman and a colored man, and therefore, the fact of an alliance is a proof of force. In numerous instances where colored men have been lynched on the charge of rape, it was positively known at the time of lynching, and indisputably proven after the victim's death, that the relationship sustained between the man and the woman was voluntary and clandestine, and that in no court of law could even the charge of assault have been successfully maintained.

It was for the assertion of this fact, in the defense of her own race, that the writer hereof became an exile; her property destroyed and her return to her home forbidden under penalty of death, for writing the following editorial which was printed in her paper, the *Free Speech,* in Memphis, Tenn., May 21, 1892:

"Eight Negroes lynched since last issue of the *Free Speech*: one at Little Rock, Ark., last Saturday morning where the citizens broke (?) into the penitentiary and got their man; three near Anniston, Ala., one near New Orleans; and three at Clarksville, Ga.; the last three for killing a white man, and five on the same old racket-the new alarm about raping white women. The same programme of hanging, then shooting bullets into the lifeless bodies was carried out to the letter. Nobody in this section of the country believes in the old thread-bare lie that Negro men rape white women. If Southern white men are not careful, they will over-reach themselves and public sentiment will have a reaction; a conclusion will then be reached which will be very damaging to the moral reputation of their women."

But threats cannot suppress the truth, and while the Negro suffers the soul deformity, resultant from two and a half centuries of slavery, he is no more guilty of this vilest of all vile charges than the white man who would blacken his name.

During all the years of slavery, no such charge was ever made, not even during the dark days of the rebel-lion.... While the master was away fighting to forge the fetters upon the slave, he left his wife and children with no protectors save the Negroes themselves. . . .

Likewise during the period of alleged "insurrec-tion," and alarming "race riots," it never occurred to the white man that his wife and children were in dan-ger of assault. Nor in the Reconstruction era, when the hue and cry was against "Negro Domination," was there ever a thought that the domination would ever contaminate a fireside or strike toward the virtue of womanhood. . . .

It is not the purpose of this defense to say one word against the white women of the South. Such need not be said, but it is their misfortune that the . . . white men of that section . . . to justify their own bar-barism . . . assume a chivalry which they do not pos-sess. True chivalry respects all womanhood, and no one who reads the record, as it is written in the faces of the million mulattos in the South, will for a minute con-ceive that the southern white man had a very chival-rous regard for the honor due the women of his race, or respect for the womanhood which circumstances placed in his power.. . . Virtue knows no color line, and the chivalry which depends on complexion of skin and texture of hair can command no honest respect.

When emancipation came to the Negroes . . . from every nook and corner of the North, brave young white women... left their cultured homes, their happy associ-ations and their lives of ease, and with heroic determi-nation went to the South to carry light and truth to the benighted blacks.... They became the social outlaws in the South. The peculiar sensitiveness of the southern

white men for women, never shed its protecting influ-ence about them. No friendly word from their own race cheered them in their work; no hospitable doors gave them the companionship like that from which they had come. No chivalrous white man doffed his hat in honor or respect. They were "Nigger teachers"-unpardonable offenders in the social ethics of the South, and were insulted, persecuted and ostracized, not by Negroes, but by the white manhood which boasts of its chivalry toward women.

And yet these northern women worked on, year after year. . . Threading their way through dense forests, working in schoolhouses, in the cabin and in the church, thrown at all times and in all places among the unfortunate and lowly Negroes, whom they had come to find and to serve, these northern women, thousands and thousands of them, have spent more than a quar-ter of a century in giving the colored people their splendid lessons for home and heart and soul. Without protection, save that which innocence gives to every good woman, they went about their work, fearing no assault and suffering none. Their chivalrous protectors were hundreds of miles away in their northern homes, and yet they never feared any "great dark-faced mobs." . . . They never complained of assaults, and no mob was ever called into existence to avenge crimes against them. Before the world adjudges the Negro a moral monster, a vicious assailant of womanhood and a menace to the sacred precincts of home, the colored people ask the consideration of the silent record of gratitude, respect, protection and devotion of the mil-lions of the race in the South, to the thousands of northern white women who have served as teachers and missionaries since the war. . . .

These pages are written in no spirit of vindictive-ness. . . We plead not for the colored people alone, but for all victims of the terrible injustice which puts men and women to death without form of law. During the year 1894, there were 132 persons executed in the United States by due form of law, while in the same year, 197 persons were put to death by mobs, who gave the victims no opportunity to make a lawful defense. No comment need be made upon a condition of pub-lic sentiment responsible for such alarming results.

FOCUS QUESTIONS:

1. What does the author have to say regarding the charges of rape that are leveled against African Americans?

2. Explain the author's opinion of the "chivalry" of Southern men. What evidence does the author use to question it?

16-10 Lynch Law in Georgia: A Six-Weeks' Record

Lynch law in Georgia : by Ida B. Wells-Barnett ; a six-weeks' record in the center of southern civilization, as faithfully chronicled by the "Atlanta journal" and the "Atlanta constitution" ; also the full report of Louis P. Le Vin, the Chicago detective sent to investigate the burning of Samuel Hose, the torture and hanging of Elijah Strickland, the colored preacher, and the lynching of nine men for alleged arson.

Source: http://hdl.loc.gov/loc.rbc/lcrbmrp.t1612

CONSIDER THE FACTS.

During six weeks of the months of March and April just past, twelve colored men were lynched in Georgia, the reign of outlawry culminating in the torture and hanging of the colored preacher, Elijah Strickland, and the burning alive of Samuel Wilkes, alias Hose, Sunday, April 23, 1899.

The real purpose of these savage demonstrations is to teach the Negro that in the South he has no rights that the law will enforce. Samuel Hose was burned to teach the Negroes that no matter what a white man does to them, they must not resist. Hose, a servant, had killed Cranford, his employer. An example must be made. Ordinary punishment was deemed inadequate. This Negro must be burned alive. To make the burning a certainty the charge of outrage was invented, and added to the charge of murder. The daily press offered reward for the capture of Hose and then openly incited the people to burn him as soon as caught. The mob carried out the plan in every savage detail.

Of the twelve men lynched during that reign of unspeakable barbarism, only one was even charged with an assault upon a woman. Yet Southern apologists justify their savagery on the ground that Negroes are lynched only because of their crimes against women.

The Southern press champions burning men alive, and says, "Consider the facts." The colored people join issue and also say, "Consider the fact." The colored people of Chicago employed a detective to go to Georgia, and his report in this pamphlet gives the facts. We give here the details of the lynching as they were reported in the Southern papers, then follows the report of the true facts as to the cause of the lynchings, as learned by the investigation. We submit all to the sober judgment of the Nation, confident that, in this cause, as well as all others, "Truth is mighty and will prevail."

IDA B. WELLS-BARNETT.

2939 Princeton Avenue, Chicago, June 20, 1899.

NINE MEN LYNCHED ON SUSPICION.

In dealing with all vexed questions, the chief aim of every honest inquirer should be to ascertain the facts. No good purpose is subserved either by concealment on the one hand or exaggeration on the other. "The truth, the whole truth and nothing but the truth," is the only sure foundation for just judgment.

The purpose of this pamphlet is to give the public the facts, in the belief that there is still a sense of justice in the American people, and that it will yet assert itself in condemnation of outlawry and in defense of oppressed and persecuted humanity. In this firm belief the following pages will describe the lynching of nine colored men, who were arrested near Palmetto, Georgia, about the middle of March, upon suspicion that they were implicated in the burning of the three houses in February preceding.

The nine suspects were not criminals, they were hard-working, law-abiding citizens, men of families. They had assaulted no woman, and, after the lapse of nearly a month, it could not be claimed that the fury of an insane mob made their butchery excusable. They were in the custody of law, unarmed, chained together and helpless, awaiting their trial. They had no money to employ learned counsel to invoke the aid of technicalities to defeat justice. They were in custody of a white Sheriff, to be prosecuted by a white State's Attorney, to be tried before a white judge, and by a white jury. Surely the guilty had no chance to escape.

Still they were lynched. That the awful story of their slaughter may not be considered overdrawn, the following description is taken from the columns of the Atlanta Journal, as it was written by Royal Daniel, a staff correspondent. The story of the lynching thus told is as follows:

Palmetto. Ga., March 16.—A mob of more than 100 desperate men, armed with Winchesters and shotguns and pistols and wearing masks, rode into Palmetto at 1 o'clock this morning and shot to death four Negro prisoners, desperately wounded another and with deliberate aim fired at four others, wounding two, believing the entire nine had been killed.

{Begin page no. 2}

The boldness of the mob and the desperateness with which the murder was contemplated and executed, has torn the little town with excitement and anxiety.

All business has been suspended, and the town is under military patrol, and every male inhabitant is armed to the teeth, in anticipation of an outbreak which is expected to-night.

Last night nine Negroes were arrested and placed in the warehouse near the depot. The Negroes were charged with the burning of the two business blocks here in February.

At 1 o'clock this morning the mob dashed into town while the people slept.

They rushed to the warehouse in which the nine Negroes were guarded by six white men.

The door was burst open and the guards were ordered to hold up their hands.

Then the mob fired two volleys into the line of trembling, wretched and pleading prisoners, and to make sure of their work, placed pistols in the dying men's faces and emptied the chambers.

Citizens who were aroused by the shooting and ran out to investigate the cause were driven to their homes at the point of guns and pistols and then the mob mounted their horses and dashed out of town, back into the woods and home again.

None of the mob was recognized, as their faces were completely concealed by masks. The men did their work orderly and coolly and exhibited a determination seldom equaled under similar circumstances.

The nine Negroes were tied with ropes and were helpless.

The guard was held at the muzzle of guns and threatened with death if a man moved.

Then the firing was deliberately done, volley by volley.

The Negroes now dead are: Tip Hudson, Bud Cotton, Ed Wynn, Henry Bingham.

Fatally shot and now dying: John Bigby.

Shot but will recover: John Jameson.

Arm broken: George Tatum.

Escaped without injury: Ison Brown, Clem Watts.

The men who were guarding the Negroes are well know and prominent citizens of Palmetto, and were sworn in only yesterday as a special guard for the night.

. . . . .

REPORT OF DETECTIVE LOUIS P. LEVIN.

The colored citizens of Chicago sent a detective to Georgia, and his report shows that Samuel Hose, who was brutally tortured at Newman, Ga., and then burned to death, never assaulted Mrs. Cranford and that he killed Alfred Cranford in self-defense.

The full test of the report is as follows:

About three weeks ago I was asked to make an impartial and thorough investigation of the lynchings which occurred near Atlanta, Ga., not long since. I left Chicago for Atlanta, and spent over a week in the investigation. The facts herein were gathered from interviews with persons I met in Griffin, Newman, Atlanta and in the vicinity of these places.

I found no difficulty in securing interviews from white people. There was no disposition on their part to conceal any part they took in the lynchings. They discussed the details of the burning of Sam Hose with the freedom which one would talk about an afternoon's advertisement in which he had very pleasantly participated.

Who was Sam Hose? His true name was Samuel Wilkes. He was born in Macon, Ga., where he lived until his father died. The family, then consisting of his mother, brother and sister, moved to Marshall, where all worked and made the reputation of hard-working, honest people. Sam studied and was soon able to read and write, and was considered a bright, capable man. His mother became an invalid, and as his brother was considered almost an imbecile, Sam was the mainstay of the family. He worked on different farms, and among the men he worked for was B. Jones, who afterward captured him and delivered him over to the mob at Newman.

Sam's mother partly recovered, and as his sister married, Sam left and went to Atlanta to better his condition. He secured work near Palmetto for a man named Alfred Cranford, and worked for him for about two years, up to the time of the tragedy. I will not call it a murder, for Samuel Wilkes killed Alfred Cranford in self-defense. The story you have read about a Negro stealing into the house and murdering the unfortunate man at his supper has no foundation in fact. Equally untrue is the charge that after murdering the husband he assaulted the wife. The reports indicated that the murderer was a stranger, who had to be identified. The fact is he had worked for Cranford for over a year.

Was there a murder? That Wilkes killed Cranford there is no doubt, but under what circumstances can never be proven. I asked many white people of Palmetto what was the motive. They considered it a useless question. A "nigger" had killed a white man, and that was enough. Some said it was because the young "niggers" did not know their places, others that they were getting too much education, while others declared that it was all due to the influence of the Northern "niggers." W.W. Jackson, of Newman, said: "If I had my way about it I would lynch every Northern "nigger" that comes this way. They are at the bottom of this." John Low of Lincoln, Ala., said: "My negroes would die for me simply because I keep a strict hand on them and allow no Northern negroes to associate with them."

FOCUS QUESTIONS:

1. What is Wells-Barnett's strategy in publishing this pamphlet?
2. Why did the citizens of Chicago hire a detective to report on the lynchings?
3. What special role did Wells-Barnett play in this struggle to end lynchings?

16-11 United States Women's Bureau Bulletin No. 20 Negro Women in Industry (1922)

The Women's Bureau published this bulletin in 1922,

Source: Bulletin of the Women's Bureau, No. 20. Negro Women in Industry. Washington: Government Printing Office, 1922.

In "A New Day for the Colored Woman Worker," " it is stated that—

An effort was made to discover what employers thought of the success or failure of their experiment. As was to be expected, their testimony was contradictory. In many instances colored women have made good. In other cases they have not. About half of the employers considered them as efficient as their white workers. These found them well-mannered and more courteous than the white girls, and found them steadier, although slower in movements. The other half considered them lazy, stupid, and unreliable, and declared that they would not have them if white girls were obtainable.

The following extracts from an article which appeared in Life and Labor" have the same tenor:

There has been a lot of theorizing regarding colored working women. but the testimony of their worth has far outweighed the unfavorable criticism. "More loyal. More cheerful and more intelligent than foreign girls." are some of the reports.

So far as efficiency is concerned, there have been numerous cases where colored girls, given equal conditions, far excelled their white sisters. In the cartridge factory at Newark, N. J., the colored women working nights averaged fifteen hundred more shells per eight-hour shift than the white women who worked in the day.

At Decatur, Ill., a tent and awning company engaged in making bags for the Government hired colored girls to take the place of white. According to rate at which the white girls had been turning out the work, it is estimated that it would take the sew force until February to complete the contract. The colored girls worked so much faster than their white predecessors that the contract was completed early in December. These examples have no significance as to the comparative superiority of white or colored girls, but they do show that as many examples can be given of the Colored girl's efficiency as of her inefficiency. It has been suggested that colored girls, realizing that they were on trial, should have taken pains to be extra efficient. But isn't this expecting too much vision from a poor working girl?

These bits of expert testimony from authorities who were in contact with the industrial situation during the war give ground for believing that the Negro woman in spite of the handicaps which surrounded her did make a record in the work which it fell to her lotto do. The majority of the criticisms directed against Negro women may be traced directly or indirectly to some of the living or working conditions surrounding them. They are slow, unreliable, inexperienced? Long hours and low wages, menial, undesirable work, unhealthy working conditions, with a lack of welfare facilities—conditions which colored women as marginal workers had to face—underlie much of this criticism.

The salient facts concerning the Negro woman in industry during the war may be very briefly summarized:

1. Labor shortage due to the mobilization of men for the Army, cessation of immigration, the drafting of white women from the traditional woman-employ-

ing industries into new occupations, and the war's demand for varied, increased production made necessary the employment of Negro women.

2. Although recruited for many industries, opportunity on the more skilled processes came to the largest numbers of Negro women in the traditional woman-employing industries from which white women had advanced into those industries which men had monopolized during the prewar period.

3. Considerable statistics point to the fact that large numbers of Negro women were employed on varied, semiskilled, and skilled processes in many industries not heretofore employing them.

4. Negro women migrated into remote industrial centers in their search for opportunity, but they were the marginal workers and had to fill the gap, either in domestic or industrial openings, wherever they were needed.

5. Skepticism about her utility on the one hand and her industrial ignorance and inexperience on the other, presented barriers to the success of the Negro woman in industry.

6. Examination of available data shows that the Negro woman was as successful as could reasonably be expected in view of her handicaps, the discrimination against her, and the dearth of industrial incentives.

7. In many cases the criticisms against her may be traced in the last analysis to the conditions under which she has lived and worked more than to the Negro woman herself.

FOCUS QUESTIONS:

1. According to this information, what was the situation for black women in industry? How had the war impacted their work?

2. What barriers hindered black working women in the period between the wars?

THE GREAT DEPRESSION, 1930-1940

17-1 Betty Burke, "Interview with Mary Siporin"

The following interview was conducted by Betty Burke, as part of the WPA Life Histories Project. Burke spoke to packing house workers in Chicago, as well as workers in many other industries. In the following text, Burke interviews Mary Siporin about her work in the packing house.

Source: WPA Life Histories Project, http://memory.loc.gov/ cgibin/query/D?wpa:41:./temp/~ammem_3Iz8::

FORM C

Text of Interview (Unedited)

CHICAGO FOLKSTUFF

FOLKLORE

CHICAGO

STATE Illinois

NAME OF WORKER Betty Burke

ADDRESS 1339 South Troy Street

DATE April 19, 1939

SUBJECT Packing house worker's job

NAME OF INFORMANT Mary Siporin

I'm in the sliced bacon. The work is very simple but very fast. They brought a lot of new machinery in. The man who makes all that detailed machinery is only a worker. He gets paid a little more and the girls who lost their jobs because of his junk, Jesus Christ you couldn't count 'em. In sliced bacon where there were 20 girls working there's 6 now. Once I went up to that guy, he was on the floor, and I asked him how much the machinery was stepping up production. My God, kid, you should have seen the superintendent rush up and tell him not to talk to me and for me to mind my own business and get back to my table. Then for instance here's one thing you ought to put down about sliced bacon department in Swift's. I used to think Swift's was the cream. You know, they pat you on the back and make out you're just one of the family, a great big happy family. Lots of the girls go for that. And then they start laying them off right and left and some of these girls even then will say 'well, they were nice about it, they said they were sorry to have to do it.' Anyway, in sliced bacon, that's supposed to be the cleanest, lightest place to work in, why they wouldn't take on a Negro girl if she was a college graduate. There's plenty of them doing all kinds of dirty jobs in the yards but sliced bacon, oh, that's too good to give a colored girl. In Swift's now, they're laying off this way too. Say if a married couple work there they lay off one of them. There's many like that, you know.

Reminds me of Wilson's. Boy, what a craphole! In '34 they had me going like a clock 10 and 12 hours a day. I used to get home so tired I'd just sit down at the table and cry like a baby. That's where I was blacklisted. Some spy found out I was friendly to the union, you know. It took me a long time to catch on to why they kept laying me off. They broke up my seniority that way, see, and then finally they wouldn't put me back at all. Well, I went to see the head employment manager, I didn't waste my time fooling around with the foremen and the small time guys around the office. I asked him how it was that I wasn't put on when I knew other girls were working, girls in my department. He just looked at me a while. Then he said 'We've got the girls in that department like this,' and he clenched his fist. 'That's the way we'll keep them. You couldn't do a thing with them, even if you had the chance—which you won't have. Of course, you van go out and sit in the employment office and wait. Come very day if you want to. That's all he said, didn't mention union, organizing, not in so many words, but I knew I was through as far as Wilson's was concerned.

Here's the psychology of a girl at the yards. She

tries to forget she works in the yards after work. She'll tell people she works in an office, at best, she'll say she's an office worker in the yards. She'll go around with everyone except yards girls. That's the single ones. Married ones are different. Of course the union has changed that attitude to a certain extent. But say like in Swift's, see, Swift beat the union to the draw. They raised the wages before the union got established there and so the workers think Swift's is the nuts. The fail to realize that if it hadn't been for the union they wouldn't have got that in the first place. And if the union don't catch hold there they'll get out so fast they won't know what struck them.

FOCUS QUESTIONS:

1. What distinctions exist between workers, according to Siporin?

2. What tools are at Siporin's disposal in fighting for better work and better conditions?

3. Why does Siporin say that after work, women lie about where they work?

17-2 Seymour D. Buck, "Interview with Minnie Caranfa"

The following interview, part of a project that led to the publication of These Are Our Lives in 1939, includes a reference to the 1939 WPA sewing strike.

Source: lcweb2.loc.gov/wpa/14030312.html

ORIGINAL MSS. OR FIELD NOTES (CHECK ONE)

PUB. THESE ARE OUR LIVES

TITLE MINNIE CARANFA

WRITER SEYMOUR BUCK

DATE July 22, 1939 WDS. PP. 12

CHECKER

SOURCES GIVEN (?)

COMMENTS

Date: July 22, 1939

Submitted by: Seymour D. Buck - Newburyport, Mass.

WPA Workers (Mrs.) Minnie Caranfa

Consulted 139 Merrimac Street

WPA Occupation: Worker on WPA Household-Aid Project.

Hell with it? I want work, - and I got all the time a telephone to answer, if there is any. That goddam thing don't ring, now, one week t'the next, 'less it's a wrong number. There aint any work - not in this town. Christ, I can't work in the shoe shops. The smell of the cement just gets me - all through here." Minnie rubbed pudgy hands across her breasts and down over her protruding abdomen.

"Only thing I know is housework, - and theyaint enough of that, anymore. I only know I'm not going to go hungry, - and I'm not going to wait until I've hocked every goddam piece of furniture I got before they gotta help me, either. That's old stuff, boy.

"Lawrie? Oh, he can't work - inside. It'd kill him. You see, ever since about ten, he's been sick alla time with asthma. It's something wicked, sometimes. Doctor coming in the middle of the night, and everything. No, he's gotta be outdoors about all the time. That stuff costs extra too, you know. Jeez, it's a wonder I got two dimes to rub together, - my friend says he don't see how I manage. I watch the pennies," Minnie stated proudly, "and I'm not one of them kind to throw my money around on a good time, like some.

"Worry? Jesus, do I! Nights I can't sleep, - just lie there and watch my goddam legs twitch. It's terrible! Next day, you'll be in somebody's house, - and you'll see things so tough it makes you figure they's others lots worse over than you are.

"The real trouble with everything? Christ, tell me! I don't read much but the papers, - and I gotta admit they're mostly crap somebody wants to put in, - not read. Hell, I got eyes, but I get so sick, mostly, what I see, I just go on minding my own business. Trouble coming, though, if this WPA business all goes to Hell.

"You can't make other people understand all the different kinds there are on it," Minnie stated firmly. "If they'd just take a goddam good look at everybody, - see all the kinds, - old and young, smart and dumb, - all banged together - it's some pitcher!

"What with these strikes, now, I'm afraid we got a black eye, all over. I don't see why it's any fairer for them guys who are striking to work only half time and get paid's much as we do, anyway. Who the Hell are they's what I'd like to know. Aint we all in the same trough? Hell, - give us grub enough and what we got to have, and let us all push our own way, I say.

"Now, though, those guys in the new gov'ment are mad! They figure we're striking against them! Hell, we aint the only ones. If you're asking me, it's like my friend says, he says, "Minnie, big business's pullin' the strike, - and it's a permanent one, 'slong as you WPA bums hold out.' Aint that swell, now.

FOCUS QUESTIONS:

1. What is Caranfa's attitude towards the WPA?
2. What is Caranfa's work.

17-3 The Problem of Married Women

Paul Douglas worked briefly on Franklin Roosevelt's National Recovery Administration, His education was in economics, and he worked as economic advisor to Roosevelt as governor of New York. In the following excerpt from his treatise, Douglas considers issues surrounding unemployment insurance for married women.

Source: Douglas, Paul. *Standards of Unemployment Insurance.* Chicago: University of Chicago Press, 1933, 57-59

2. *The problem of married women.*—Some very ticklish problems arise in the case of married women. Women who are and will be customarily employed in industry should of course be compensated for unemployment irrespective of whether or not they are married. But there would seem to be no legitimate claim for benefit in the two following cases:

(a)Where a married woman customarily supported by her husband's earnings entered industry for a brief period of time in order to meet some temporary emergency and after having acquired eligibility under the act, then retired to strictly family life. Such a person would not in fact be at that time a member of the real army of potential wage-workers and should not, therefore, be a charge upon industry. Many of these claims could be weeded out by the officials if in their judgment, these women refused "suitable employment." But since such officers naturally tend to be somewhat liberal in the standards which they impose on women with families, some added administrative power would seem from the British experience, to be necessary.

(b)Where a woman who was a genuine member of the labor supply marries and upon leaving industry claims unemployment benefit although she in fact does not wish to continue in employment. Such a case becomes especially plausible where the woman upon

marriage moves to a new locality where there are not many openings in her former line of work, and where, though she is ostensibly seeking work, it is in reality almost impossible for her to be so placed.

The passage of the Anomalies Act by the Labour Government in Great Britain and its enforcement by the judicial committees attached to the employment offices has disclosed a large number of abuses in the case of married women who were drawing benefits. Somewhere around 150,000 were dropped from the benefit roll as a result of this combing out and while the tests were per-haps too severe in some cases, the fact that apparently the majority of the women who were so dropped did not take the trouble to re-register for employment at the free public labor exchanges seems to furnish sufficient proof that these, at least, were not genuinely seeking work. While most of the difficulties in England arose from the fact that the requisite period of prior contributions had been greatly reduced because of the depression to one of only 8 weeks in the two preceding years, or 30 weeks through-out the past history of the claimant, it is still true that some such cases would arise even with the requirement which has been suggested of 36 weeks in the two preceding years or of 22 weeks in the last year. It would be well, therefore, to give the administrative authorities specific power 'to deal with such cases of married women and to exclude them if they really were no longer genuine members of the labor supply, and were not actually seeking employment. This power should not, however, be used as a cloak to discriminate against married women who are *bonafide* seekers for work.

FOCUS QUESTIONS:

1. According to Douglas, what is the "problem of married women"?
2. What remedy does Douglas consider for this problem?

17-4 Crude Birthrate by Race (1889–1998)

This chart follows birth rates in the U.S. over almost two centuries.

Source: *Historical Statistics of the United States;* Millenial Online Edition, 2008

FOCUS QUESTIONS:

1. What biases are apparent in this chart?
2. How do you explain the peaks and troughs in the birth rates for the 1900s?

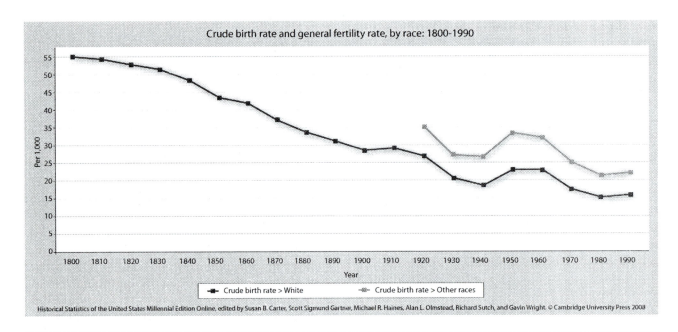

Crude birth rate and general fertility rate, by race: 1800-1990

Historical Statistics of the United States Millennial Edition Online, edited by Susan B. Carter, Scott Sigmund Gartner, Michael R. Haines, Alan L. Olmstead, Richard Sutch, and Gavin Wright. © Cambridge University Press 2008

17-5 Zora Neale Hurston Letters (1930, 1934)

Zora Neale Hurston (1891-1960) was an author and prominent figure in the Harlem Renaissance. Her training as an anthropologist led to her interest in folklore. These letters are from Hurston during her college years. Mules and Men is a reference to a collection of folklore she published the next year, in 1935.

Source: Kaplan, Carla. Editor. *Zora Neale Hurston: A Life in Letters.* New York: Doubleday, 2002, 194-195; 326-327.

TO CHARLOTTE OSGOOD MASON

2109 Springwood Ave

Asbury Park, N.J.

Nov. 25, 1930

Darling Godmother,

Perhaps my silence has been terrible, but I have been trying to get something done while resting. That is, I have been trying to find the gate to the future. I don't want to commit myself at this moment, but the quest does no seem hopeless. I held utterly silent to hold my spiritual forces together.

Now, I think I must hurry back to town to see about certain things I am sure you dont mind my silence at this stage of the game.

I am feeling fine. I have done a few local trips. Knowing all that I do, I didnt want to get too far from base now, so that I would be too hard to reach. I wanted to be so that I could be on the scene within a few hours after I got any word, good or bad.

You see, Darling Godmother, I am trying to get some bone in legs so that you can see me standing so that I shall cease to worry you. I dont want all your worry and generosity to go in vain. Thus I fee lthat I must let no grass grow under my feet. I dont need to call upon your ebbing strength for every little thing. So

I shall wrassle me up a future or die trying. I have spent the last four days re-writing the first act and polishing it up a bit. I am going after things. Because your behavior of love makes you willing to give your life, is no reason why I should be willing to take it. You love me. You have proved it. It is up to me now to let you see what my behavior of love looks like. So watch your sun-burnt child do some scuffling. That is the thing that I have lacked—the urge to push hard and insist on a hearing.

I shall be back in town immediately and see what a certain person has to say to me. Then I shall proceed on down in Va. That is, if I am not held on business. I shall call immediately on reaching town.

You remember that we talked about selling the car. I have gotten a few appraisals. Whooeee!! They dont think so much of it. The Chevrolet Company put out their new car this year two months ahead of time to help the unemployment. Then they added so many improvements and are selling it for much less than mine cost that I am afraid we are not going to get the $500.00 I had in mind. Nothing like that has been offered, except as a turn-in, and that isnt in our plans.

Until I see you in town, all, all my love.

Most devotedly yours,

Zora

TO FRANZ BOAS

4559 So. Parkway [YWCA] Chicago, Ill.

Dec. 14, 1934

Dr. Franz Boas

Columbia U.

New York City

Dear Dr. Boas,

Great news! I think that I have secured a Rosenwald scholarship to return to Columbia and work for my doctorate. If all goes well I shall be entering immediately after the holidays. I have wanted the training very keenly and tried very hard to get Mrs. Mason to do it for me. She would give money for everything else but that. I have been so concerned to get more training so that I might work out two projects that I have in mind. Is it all right for me to enter at this time of year?

Now I realize that this is going to call for rigorous routine and discipline, which every body seems to feel that I need. So be it. I want to do it. I have always wanted to do it and nobody will have any trouble about my applying myself I wonder if it ought not to be taken into consideration that I have been on my own since fourteen years old and went to high school, college and everything progressive that I have done because I wanted to, and not because I was being pushed? All of these things have been done under most trying circumstances and I stuck. I have had two or three people say to me, why dont you go and take a master's or a doctor's degree in Anthropology since you love it so much? They never seem to realize that it takes money to do that. I had such a hard time getting the money to take my bachelor's that I could appreciate what it meant to attempt to attend a college on nothing. Another thing, it is hard to apply ones self to study when there is no money to pay for food and lodging. I almost never explain these things when folks are asking me why dont I do this and that. I have to make a living, and consequently I have to do the jobs that will support me. But oh, Dr. Boas, you dont know how I have longed for a chance to stay at Columbia and study. Otherwise there would be no point to my using evry thing possible to get this scholarship.

Hoping that all goes well with you and yours, I am

Most sincerely, [unsigned carbon]

P.S. Do you remember Miguel Covarrubias, the Mexican artist that you met one Sunday night with me when we went to the Sanctified church? He has just returned from four years study in Bali and is to do all the illustrations for MULES AND MEN.

FOCUS QUESTIONS:

1. What challenges does Hurston face, and what help has she had in her academic career?
2. What perspective and training did Hurston bring to the flowering of the Harlem Renaissance?

17-6 Frances Perkins, Speech to the 1936 Democratic Convention

The following is a brief excerpt from a speech by Frances Perkins (1882-1965), in which she spoke of the leadership of Eleanor Roosevelt. Perkins was the Secretary of Labor from 1933 to 1945, the first woman to hold a cabinet position. By the time Franklin Roosevelt was elected president in 1933, Perkins already had worked with him for some years.

Source: In Cook, Blanche Wiesen. *Eleanor Roosevelt.* Vol. 2, 1933-1938. New York: Viking, 1999. p. 367.

The Democratic women considered ER their leader. Even Frances Perkins, who was closer to the president, considered ER the heart of the Democratic women's movement. At one breakfast, "the loudest cheers" arose when Perkins departed from her prepared speech to pay tribute to the First Lady. According to *The New York Times*, Perkins celebrated ER with "deep feeling":

I want to speak of a prominent woman Democrat who is not here. She is kept away by convention—not political, but social convention, although she is not a woman to be bound by convention.

Her genius is the capacity to love the human race and to hear and understand the misery and wants and aspirations of people. . . .

If ever there was a gallant and courageous and intelligent and wise woman, she is one.

I know that many women . . . when they go to vote in November for Franklin Roosevelt will be thinking with a choke in their throats of Eleanor Roosevelt.

Upon Perkins's last words, a spontaneous demonstration of prolonged enthusiasm erupted throughout the ballroom.

FOCUS QUESTIONS:

1. What does this excerpt tell you about Eleanor Roosevelt's standing among Democratic women?
2. What role does Perkins give Eleanor Roosevelt in the upcoming election?

17-7 Eleanor Roosevelt, Anti-lynching Letter (1936)

Among the many causes for which Eleanor Roosevelt campaigned was the fight against lynching.

Source: http://memory.loc.gov/mss/mcc/015/0001.jpg

PERSONAL AND CONFIDENTIAL

THE WHITE HOUSE

WASHINGTON

March 19, 1936

My dear Mr. White:

Baton I received your letter today I had been in to the President, talking to his about your letter enclosing that of the Attorney General. I told him that it seemed rather terrible that one could get nothing done and that I did not blame you is the least for feeling there was no interact in this very serious question. I asked him if there were any possibility of getting even one step taken, and he said the difficulty is that it is unconstitutional apparently for the federal Government to step in in the lynching situation. The Government has only been allowed to do anything about kidnapping because of its interstate aspect, and even that has not as yet been appealed so they are not sure that it will be declared constitutional.

The President feels that lynching is a question of education in the states, rallying good citizens, and creating public opinion so that the localities themselves will wipe it out. However, if it were done by a Northerner, it will have an antagonistic effect. I will talk to him again about the Van Nuys resolution and will try to talk also to senator Byrnes and get his point of view. I am deeply troubled about the whole situation as it seems to be a terrible thing to stand by and let it continue and feel that one cannot speak out as to his feeling. I think your next step would be to talk to the more prominent members of the Senate.

Very sincerely yours,

Eleanor Roosevelt

FOCUS QUESTIONS:

1. What does this letter tell you about Roosevelt's activity within her husband's administration?
2. How does Roosevelt (or the president) suggest attacking the problem of lynching?

17-8 Interview with Mary Smith (1938)

Another WPA Writer's Project interview, this time in North Carolina, follows.

Source: American Life Histories: Manuscripts from the Federal Writers' Project, 1938. http://memory.loc.gov/cgi-bin/query/D?wpa:1:./temp/~ammem_KMuw::

When she was eleven the family income was supplemented by group participation in a relatively new industry. Smoking tobacco was gaining in popularity and the manufacturers of the product needed many small bags in which to pack it for distribution. The bag factories which grew up in answer to this need sent the bags out by the thousands into the surrounding countryside to be strung and tagged. During periods of slack in farm work Mary and her young brother walked the five miles into Durham and took back to their home two large sacks, each containing ten thousand small bags. She can remember sitting up all night on occasion during the rush season, each member of the family working as hard as he could to string these sacks for which they received thirty cents a thousand. When sleep laid such a heavy claim on her that she felt she could no longer stand it her mother sent her out on the back porch to dash cold water on her face that she might keep her eyes open yet a little longer. The year she was twelve her skill increased so that she raised the family income by several dollars, and her parents out of appreciation of her industry bought her two percale dresses instead of one.

By the time she was fifteen years old her father had decided his family would have a better living at a cotton mill than they could ever make for themselves on another man's farm. They sold the mule and the cow but they kept the twenty-six chickens for a while after moving to town. The nice fresh eggs came in handy because wages weren't so high that such things could be bought in plenty.

Mary began work at twenty-five cents a day. Her hours were from six to six but she will tell you that she doesn't believe the twelve hours then were any harder than eight hours now what with the speed-up system they have. Her man Jim comes in clean wore out at the end of a day, but of course she knows he's not a young man any longer. In fact, his working days are almost over because he's not so far from sixty and his body is none too stout.

When she married at eighteen she was making four dollars a week and Jim four dollars and a half. If it hadn't been for the installment plan she wonders if they ever could have bought the two beds and stove with which they began housekeeping. Nighttimes Jim made four chairs and a table. With so much furniture in their house they decided to take a couple of boarders to help with the installments still to be paid. The furniture wasn't more than paid for when Mary had to have an operation which cost Jim fifty dollars. That was three months before her first baby was born and another baby was on its way before the debt was finally paid.

Sometimes when her health was too bad to work in the mill Mary took up her old occupation of stringing bags. The wage had increased to fifty cents a thousand and with steady use of her spare time she could do a thousand a day. In the course of time five children were born to Mary Smith and four of them managed to live past babyhood. Mary's last child was born in 1912. It didn't live but three days and the Smiths had to borrow the money to bury it. "That year was one of the hardest in my life," Mary told me that afternoon. "The doctor started comin' to see me in early May and there wasn't a day from then on until the middle of September that he didn't come to our house. *{Begin inserted text} {Begin handwritten} ({End handwritten} {End inserted text}* As soon as I was out of bed Jim took sick with the typhoid fever and for six solid weeks he wasn't able to work. Two of the younguns took the fever from him. If we couldner got credit we woulder starved. It was many a year before we ever caught up again. We was in such bad shape that the two younguns was forced to go in the mill though I'd hoped to keep 'em out until they'd had a little more chance for schoolin'."

The oldest boy entered the mill at twelve and the oldest girl at thirteen. The boy has been there since except for sick leaves in the past few years when he has been bothered with hemorrhages of the lung. He was such a scrawny, pale, little fellow that many a time when Mary went to rouse him on a cold winter morning she felt like turning away from the bed and letting him rest through the day. But she knew he might lose his job, and the money he made was badly needed. Sometimes now she wonders if his health wouldn't have held out better if she could have kept him out of the mill a few years longer until his body had been given more chance to grow. *{Begin inserted text}{Begin handwritten}){End handwritten}{End inserted text}*

This son married after thirty and he has three children, all too young to work, and a wife whose health is so poor she cannot work. He was brought home from the mill with another hemorrhage the other day and Mary is wondering how she can help him. It seems to her that the fourteen dollars a week Jim is making cannot be stretched over another need.

Mary paused at this point in her story and sat with her hands folded in her lap. Janie looked first at her mother and then at me. "If it hadn't been for Mama my younguns wouldner had no clothes atall the past year," she said. "The mill where my husband works aint give its help but four days' work a week in over a year. Tom makes eleven dollars and its all I can do to feed, let along cloths, my crowd on that. *{Begin inserted text}{Begin handwritten}({End handwritten}{End inserted text}* My children is pretty good about not complainin'. They'll set down one day right after another to dried beans and potatoes without raisin' a row. Of course, that oldest one has got all manner of pride and she caused me a sight of trouble for awhile when she had to wear a old coat to school that never fit her nowhere. *{Begin inserted text}{Begin handwritten}){End handwritten}{End inserted text}* The worst hurt I ever seen her, though, was along 'bout the last of school when her teacher tried to collect rent for the school books she'd been usin' all the year. I thought the State was furnishin' 'em free but they say everybody is supposed to pay rent on 'em. Emma Lee kept after me but I never had the money to give her. One day she broke down in school and cried and told her teacher they wasn't a penny at her home to pay for book rent. The teacher told her to stop worryin' then, and she never bothered her any more. Emma Lee says she's not goin' to stop until she goes clear on through high school."

FOCUS QUESTION:

1. What is the role of child labor in this extended family?

2. What kinds of work has Mary done?

WORLD WAR II HOME FRONTS, 1940-1945

18-1 Married Women Who Work

The Women's Bureau of the U.S. Department of Labor published a monthly journal, The Woman Worker, highlighting issues and trends in women's employment. This article from September, 1939, describes a recent Massachusetts ruling that curtailed employment discrimination against married women, and analyzes press coverage from around the country on the subject of married women who work.

Source: The United States Department of Labor. *The Woman Worker,* Vol. XIX, September 1939. pp. 3-5.

THE Supreme Court of Massachusetts has become the first to declare it illegal to bar married women from public-service jobs. In a five to two decision on June 29 the Court said that the legislature cannot "arbitrarily discriminate against any class of citizens," adding that "women married or unmarried are members of the State * * *and like other citizens they are entitled to the benefit of the constitutional guaranties against arbitrary discrimination." Replying to questions asked by the legislature, the Court decreed that

The prohibition of the employment of married women in the in the public service while such employment is open to men and to unmarried women would violate the Massachusetts Constitution. The removal from public employment of all unmarried women upon marriage, in the absence of any provision for the removal of unmarried men upon marriage, would violate both the Massachusetts and the Federal Constitutions.

The Court further stated that

The bill providing that husband and wife shall not at the same time be employed in the service of the Commonwealth discriminates between a particular class of married persons and all other persons married or un-married, though under the Constitution all citizens have the right to equal opportunity for employment in the public service.

A subsequent effort to pass a law that would meet these constitutional objections and still would bar employment of married women was decisively defeated in the legislature.

This subject has been widely dealt within popular magazines, so-called polls have been taken on it, and it has been discussed on popular programs such as that of the Chicago University forum. In considering the matter, it is well to remember the following pertinent facts:

In 1930, the date of the latest census, married women constituted only about 6 percent of all employed persons.

Three-fourths of the married women's work were in stores or factories or in domestic and personal service. A *very small minority* were in the professional jobs or in public types of work on which the publicity is focused.

Considerably smaller proportions of working married than of the working unmarried women, as a rule, are in clerical or professional occupations.

Men seeking jobs ordinarily look for entirely different types of jobs than those now filled by married women.

The movement against married working women quickly spreads into an attack against employed women, married and single, *definitely opposed to the advancement of women on the job.*

. . . It is uncertain whether the public could have enough data to decide on such strictly personal matters, and reasoning from a few known cases may prove false and dangerous. As to the employer's authority, the president of a large New York department store states:

We employ people not because they are married; not because they are single; but because we believe they are the best people for the particular job that needs filling at the time.

The school board in Concord, N. H., took the same attitude recently when it passed a resolution to select teachers "on a merit basis alone."

Protesting against the policy of the Vermont Old Age Assistance Commission to end a woman's employment within a year after marriage, Rev. Kendall B. Burgess, of Waterbury, declared:

Wedlock suffers already under a sufficient number of financial handicaps, without adding more problems in the way of such arbitrary rulings.

In discussing his statement, the Burlington *Free Press* said editorially: "It seems a dangerous principle for any governmental agency to attempt to determine who should work and who should not. * * * Few married women care to continue working if they have adequate support without it."

A group of women's organizations in Washington State reported that the dismissal Of married women from the pay roll of King County would create only a few more than 50 vacancies, whereas there were83,000 unemployed persons in the county. A questionnaire bringing 660 replies from all parts of this State showed that (not counting spouses of the married persons)married women had more dependents than married men, and single women 20 percent more dependents than single men (in both cases, living at home). The married women give four times as much employment to others as the married men.

A large section of the press would help rather than hinder these married women(and helping them means helping all employed women). This is evidenced by editorials from such papers as the Asheville (N. C.) *Times*, the Wisconsin *News-Herald*, the Pittsburgh *Press*, the Hartford *Times*, New Haven (Conn.) *Journal-Courier-Times*, the Washington (D. C.) *Times-Herald*, the Columbus (Ohio) *Dispatch*, the Lafayette(Ind.) *Journal and Courier*, and so forth.

The Women's Bureau receives many letters from employed married women them-selves, or their families, that testify to their actual need of jobs. Factory workers from two Ohio cities write as follows:

. . . married women . . . would rather earn their own way in life than live off the State or Government. Because I am married, I am criticized by one in whose family six members have had work all through the depression. Yet I have spent the whole of my married life caring for someone who was ill, including her husband; the husband's father, who was helpless 4 years after a broken hip; her father, who died with but 34 cents in his pocket; her mother ill with cancer; and the husband's mother who had tuberculosis.

My husband works part time, but not enough to live on. As we have a family, I sure do hope I can get work till they are through school. We real poor ones need to work so bad. I can't see why we' married women don't have as much right to work as three and four in one family.

A Missouri wife writes:

I am just one of the families with five or more children that have some troubles. I have seven children. I don't want to leave them, but when the husband can't make enough to take care of family even though he has tried very hard, the wife will help if she can. My reason for going to work is that we have had a lot of sickness.

Following are a few of the many letters from Massachusetts women who have written the Bureau, a number of them in professional work:

To throw a woman out of work simply because she is married is putting a penalty on marriage itself. It would rob Peter to pay Paul, . . . destroy one family and build another on the ashes of its despair. . . . Most of the married women who are working, whether in public or private positions, find it necessary to work. If thrown out of their employment, many of them, still paying for their homes, would be unable to meet the payments, and would lose their homes—the savings of a lifetime. I am one of that group, and know this is true, and I personally know many others. I happen to be the mother of seven children and for the past 26 years I have been obliged to teach school in order to support them; even the combined incomes of my husband and myself are not sufficient.

It was necessary that I go back to work after several years at home. "We had two to educate and my mother to care for. My husband's pay was cut . . . sometime she received nothing-in the week. . . . I see no reason why I should stop and be cared for when I am willing to work. After several years' experience I can give the public better service than a young girl just starting.

FOCUS QUESTIONS:

1. What types of work are women portrayed as doing?

2. Why are married women working?

3. What are the benefits of work to married women and their families? Are any disadvantages discussed? What benefits or disadvantages to society are suggested?

18-2 Women in Labor Unions (1947)

Women's participation in the formal labor market increased dramatically during the war years. Women's membership in labor unions spiked even more. Gladys Dickason, research director of the Amalgamated Clothing Workers of America and assistant chairman of the CIO Committee for the Organization of the South, put these trends in context in a 1947 article for a scholarly journal.

Source: Gladys Dickason, "Women in Labor Unions," Annals of the American Academy of Political and Social Science, Vol. 251, Women's Opportunities and Responsibilities (May, 1947), pp. 70-78 Published by: Sage Publications, Inc. in association with the American Academy of Political and Social Science Stable URL: http://www.jstor.org/stable/1024881 Accessed: 17/09/2008 18:12

In Alabama recently a farmer's wife, who was also a shirtmaker in a small-town clothing factory, visited the Governor of the state with a union delegation to report a case of mob violence against union organizers. After hearing her story, the Governor ordered an investigation and issued a statement emphasizing that union members possessed the same rights under the law as other people.

This woman in the office of the Governor of her state epitomizes the progress that working women have made through union organization. We have come a long way since 1831, when the Boston Transcript denounced the efforts of the tailoresses of New York to form a union as an instance of woman's "clamorous and unfeminine declarations of personal rights which it is obvious a wise Providence never destined her to exercise."

A double issue is involved in the organization of women—the rights of women and the rights of labor. These were two of the focal points of the nineteenth-century struggle to extend democracy; and in our own century they have been among the first victims of such counter democratic movements as nazism and fascism. Both the labor movement and the "woman" movement have had to wage a stubborn fight against the practice which seeks to grade human beings arbitrarily, by race or sex or class, into superiors and inferiors, into the elite few who give orders and the many who accept them with unquestioning obedience. Both movements are based on the principle that a healthy society depends upon equal opportunities for all men and women to participate actively in shaping the conditions of their lives.

Today it is evident that the survival of democracy, and perhaps of civilization itself, depends on the ability of people everywhere to understand their world and take their full share of responsibility in it. It is against this background that we must consider the work unions are doing in organizing women, in improving their economic status, and in enabling them to play their part as responsible members of society.

WOMEN IN THE LABOR FORCE AND IN UNIONS

The organization of women workers has assumed increasing importance during the past several decades as more and more women have entered the labor market and as it has become evident that they constitute a permanent factor in the total labor force. This trend is shown in Table 1.

TABLE 1—TREND IN EMPLOYMENT OF WOMEN, 1910-46

Year	Number of women in Labor Force	Per Cent of All Persons in Labor Force
1910	7,789,000	20.9
1920	8,430,000	20.4
1930	10,679,000	22.0
1940	13,015,000	24.4
1944 (July)	19,110,000	34.7
1946 (Nov.)	17,020,000	28.9

Among the chief factors responsible for the entrance of women into the labor force have been: (1) inadequacy of in come of male members of family for a proper standard of living; (2) inadequacy of public provision for families deprived of male breadwinners; (3) insufficiency of available male workers (especially during war periods); (4) development of service and distributive functions in our economy; (5) simplification of mechanical jobs; (6) change in traditional attitudes towards women in industry and professions; and (7) the opportunity presented to employers to obtain cheaper labor, especially after mass immigration was halted.

The number of women in trade unions has increased notably in the past fifty years, and particularly within the past decade. No accurate statistics are available, but estimates that have been made (summarized in Table 2) provide a satisfactory picture of the progress achieved in the organization of women. However, in spite of the progress made in extending unionization to women workers, they are still organized to a much smaller extent than are men. For example, in 1910 there were 7 men in labor unions for every 100 men in the labor force, but only 1 woman for every 100 women in the labor force. By the summer of 1944, at the peak of female employment and union membership, the figures had risen to 30 and almost 16 respectively.

TABLE 2—TREND IN UNION MEMBERSHIP OF WOMEN, 1910—44

Year	Estimated Number of Women in Unions	Per cent of All Union Members
1910	76,750	3.6
1920	397,000	7.9
1930	260,000	7.7
1940	800,000	9.4
1944	3,000,000	21.8

OBSTACLES TO UNIONIZATION

The substantial discrepancy that exists results from the types of work which women have been forced, or permitted, to perform; the fact that women workers, as individuals, have been considered a temporary factor in the labor force; traditional ideas about the abilities and status of women; and policies of organizations adopted in the past. In most of these respects the situation has changed in the past decade, but the concentration of women workers in unskilled, semiskilled, and white-collar jobs, and in nonmanufacturing industries such as laundries, restaurants, beauty parlors, domestic service, and the like, still remains the major obstacle to their rapid unionization.

The recent war caused a significant change in the pattern of employment. In 1940 only one out of every four women wage earners worked in manufacturing industries; in 1945 the proportion had risen to one out of three. Since the war the proportion of women in manufacturing industries has declined but is still well above the prewar level; the proportion in service industries has increased but is still below the prewar level.

The spectacular increase in women membership

in unions during the war can undoubtedly be ascribed to the type of jobs they entered, yet in the decade before the war the number of women union members tripled under the labor legislation of the first two Roosevelt administrations which put collective bargaining on a firmer basis. This in turn made possible the new organizational policy adopted by the American labor movement in the later thirties, that of organizing workers on an industrial instead of a craft basis. As a result large numbers of unskilled, semiskilled and white-collar workers were unionized, and it was to these groups that the majority of women workers largely belonged.

Traditional prejudices about the abilities and status of women have played a part in retarding the organization of women workers. Among the unions themselves there has been in the past some distrust of women's loyalty as union members and a tendency to look upon them as an unstable and unreliable factor in the union—a "blithering liability" as one male unionist put it. On the side of society there has been an idea that the participation of women in union activities, and especially in strikes, was unfeminine and improper. Striking women garment workers in 1924 were arrested and sent to jail after being called "low women, a disgrace to their sex." Official government guarantees, after 1932, of the right' to organize helped to remove the stigma of "disorderly" and "unfeminine" conduct from the union activities of women.

In the past some unions have had restrictions barring women from membership. Today all CIO unions and most AFL unions admit women without regard to skill, color or creed. In contrast to the common practice of twenty years ago, there is only one union today, the International Brotherhood of Bookbinders, which has a separate woman's organization—the Bindery Women's Local Unions.

The unions having the largest number of women members in 1945 included the United Automobile Workers of America, CIO, with 280,000 women members, constituting 28 per cent of its total membership; the United Electrical, Radio and Machine Workers of America, CIO, with 280,000 women members, or 40 per cent of its total membership; the International Ladies' Garment Workers' Union, AFL, with 225,000 women members, or 75 per cent of its total membership; the Amalgamated Clothing Workers of America, CIO, with 200,000 women members, or 66 per cent of its total membership; and the Textile Workers Union of America, CIO, with 180,000 women members, making up 40 per cent of its total membership.

WHAT UNIONISM MEANS TO WOMEN

The problem of raising the economic status of women workers is, of course, a part of the larger problem of raising the economic status of all workers, but, for a number of reasons, the utilization of unions to raise wage levels and improve working conditions is of particular importance in the case of women workers and involves special problems. The most important of these are that the majority of women workers belong to the most depressed economic groups; most women workers have household and family responsibilities to attend to outside of working hours; woman's physical constitution involves special problems of health and welfare; and finally, traditional ideas as to women's "place" and abilities have led to discrimination against them in wages and job opportunities. All this means that any program for improving the conditions of women workers must involve, on the one hand, the elimination of various forms of unwarranted discrimination against them, and, on the other hand, special measures of protection or adjustment to meet their special needs. Unions have done and are doing much to solve the special problems of women workers, not only through collective bargaining but by drawing public attention to these problems and pressing for legislative action. And in the process of dealing with the economic problems of women, they have found it necessary to deal with the wider problem of enabling women to play their full part as citizens.

FOCUS QUESTIONS:

1. What trend or trends do you find most surprising?
2. What is Dickason's attitude regarding women in the workforce? Regarding unionization?
3. Do unions serve different purposes for women than they do for men?

18-3 Dr. Leslie Hohman Asks, "Can Women in War Industry Be Good Mothers?" (1942)

Even in the twenty-first century, many commentators worry that children's well-being will be diminished in some way or another if their mothers work outside the home. In this 1942 article, psychiatrist Dr. Leslie Hohman turns the issue around, suggesting that at least some children would be better-adjusted if their mothers were employed. He proposes that the way mothers spend time with their children is more important than how much time they spend together – a concept that led, late in the twentieth century, to an emphasis on "quality time."

Source: In *Major Problems in American Women's History.* 2ⁿᵈ edition. Mary Beth Norton and Ruth M. Alexander, editors. Lexington, MA: D.C. Heath and Company, 1996. pp. 363-365.

The task of working women who are mothers, too, involves unquestionable difficulties which we must face squarely. Yet it gives women and their husbands a chance to prove dramatically and quickly where their deepest interests are.

If I had had any doubts on the question, my trip to the Hartford home of Fred and Mary Berckman would have converted me. Their whole household teems with evidence that their children are to them the most important consideration in the world. Their unflagging interest is the solid foundation for the first of the specific rules to be drawn from their highly successful experience.

The first rule is that mothers who are working must deliberately and determinedly plan to spend ample time with their children. To Mary this is not in the least burden-some. She delights in helping with the lessons of all her merry brood — second-grader son Junie, and the daughters Eileen, Fredrica and the eldest, Catherine, in the fifth grade. Mary sings with them, laughs with them, tells them stories in her fine Irish brogue of County Mayo, where she was born and lived until she came to America nineteen years ago.

"We make things interesting in this house," Mary said — an excellent boost for girls and boys along the road to happiness and security.

With all her fondness for her children, Mary could not accomplish so much time with them if both she and Fred had not organized their days carefully with that very purpose in mind. Her early shift at the Colt arms plant brings her home in the afternoons about the time the children arrive from school. She mixes them a malted milk, does preliminary work on dinner, then lies down for an hour until the children call out that their father is home from work. Fred is there at noon, too, from the Royal Typewriter plant just across the street, to help the youngsters prepare the lunch that has been arranged by Mary before she left for work.

Not much is to be gained by a detailed study of the exact schedule Fred and Mary use. Each working mother will have to arrange a schedule according to her individual working hours and her individual problems. We can be sure in advance that those who haven't the will to succeed will seek excuses for not doing so well as Fred and Mary — such as, "Neither my husband nor I can come home at noon." We can be equally sure that those who sincerely try will find some way to make certain that their children are well cared for while they are at work.

One mother I know who has an important executive position and commutes every working day to her desk rises much earlier every morning than she otherwise would have to, so that she can have breakfast and a long chat with her daughter. In the evenings, also, she always manages to spend some time with the child. They talk gaily of topics which interest the little girl. Their companionship is far closer than that of most daughters with mothers who haven't any outside work to do.

A writing assistant on a daily radio program who has few unfilled hours at home during the week still arranges to find brief and happy intervals for her young son every day. The main feature of her admirable plan comes every Sunday. The entire day is her son's. Any reasonable suggestion he makes on how they shall spend his day, she follows merrily. They have grand fun. The scheme often means that she and her husband decline weekend invitations, but they hold to their plan and enjoy them-selves more than they would on the missed parties. The result is that the son is held to his parents by the strongest possible bonds of wholesome affection.

The general attitude of mothers — and fathers too — is a more powerful influence than the actual number of hours they spend with their children. Couples who want to act childless and who find association with their children irksome and dull, do not fool their children by staying home and snapping at them. Fewer hours and more companionship would be much better.
'

A child's sense of security is fostered psychologically by stability in his environment. Despite all protestations of love at odd moments, young children in a harum-scarum household are likely to develop unstable emotional habits and a feeling of insecurity.

I am convinced that jobs for mothers outside the home generally help to create the stability of environment that is so essential. The gain usually more than offsets the loss of the hours in which the mother has to be away. Besides the scheduling of household routine imposed by regular employment, there is the added advantage for children that the inefficient mothers whose home management is hit-or-miss and disturbingly unreliable will learn to be more efficient by working where efficiency is required.

The skill and willingness in housework which Fred acquired when he took it over completely while his heart would not permit more strenuous exertion, makes him an ideal partner for a working wife. This suggests still another flat rule:

If children are to be reared successfully in families with employed mothers who haven't enough money for nursemaids and servants, it is absolutely necessary for husbands to help their wives with home duties and with the children's training. . .

Even when father knuckles down to do his share, there will be plenty of chores left for children in homes where both parents have outside jobs and abundant assistance cannot be hired. That is a great good fortune for the children. If we had enough working mothers, there would be a reinstatement of work training and early feeling for useful accomplishment. Too many young boys and girls are missing this valuable training.

Watching the Berckman children, I thought how much more fortunate they were than the ten-year-old son of an idle, prosperous mother who recently sought my ad-vice because she saw, at last, that something was going wrong with him. Something had been going wrong since infancy. His mother and nursemaid and later his whole family waited on him hand and foot. An important part of my prescription was that useful chores be found for him. The family is having a hard time following the prescription after its long habit of spoiling the boy.

The troubles of mothers who have jobs will be greatly lessened if they and their husbands enforce good training while they are at home. Mary and Fred established a cornerstone by affectionate discipline from infancy, not shying from occasional punishment when it was necessary to stop the development of traits that would handicap their children.

Merely the presence of a mother in the house will not make children behave —as harried neighbors can testify. Mothers cannot incessantly watch children old enough to go out and play, and it would be harmful to the children's self-reliance if they could. The best guaranty is the trained-in reliability and independence that enable Mary to say confidently: "My children never have done anything I told them not to do. I can trust them completely."

War or no war, outside work should never be undertaken by mothers until adequate care and training of their young children are assured. The arrangements frequently are hard to make, but rarely impossible. Where there is money enough, a qualified woman can be paid to come in and take charge. In most neighborhoods where money is not too plentiful, some woman who has proved her skill with her own children will be glad to augment the family income a little by taking care of one or two more for eight or nine hours a day.

No story of the problems and difficulties that working mothers meet could give a complete picture without prominent mention of the intangible gain that is nearly always overlooked. With few exceptions, women are made more interesting to their girls and

boys by an outside job. Mary Berckman is a shining example. She is in brisk step with the world of today. She has sorted out her values under the test of stern realities. She has no time to be bored, no time for gossip. She always has time for companionship. It is not surprising that she, with Fred's excellent help, fills her children's lives with happiness.

FOCUS QUESTIONS:

1. What costs and benefits are described for children of working mothers? What costs and benefits are described or implied for the women themselves? For their husbands?

2. What assumptions does Hohman make about gender divisions in housework and childcare? What assumptions does he believe his readers will make?

18-4 Executive Order 9066

The Japanese attack on Pearl Harbor concerned the government that a Japanese invasion of the west coast was imminent. The War Department urged Roosevelt to order the evacuation of all Japanese and Japanese-Americans on the west coast to relocation centers. This action was debated openly in government and in California before it was implemented with the full knowledge of the American people.

Source: http://www.ourdocuments.gov/doc.php?flash=true&doc=74&page=transcript

Executive Order No. 9066

The President

Executive Order

Authorizing the Secretary of War to Prescribe Military Areas

Whereas the successful prosecution of the war requires every possible protection against espionage and against sabotage to national-defense material, national-defense premises, and national-defense utilities as defined in Section 4, Act of April 20, 1918, 40 Stat. 533, as amended by the Act of November 30, 1940, 54 Stat. 1220, and the Act of August 21, 1941, 55 Stat. 655 (U.S.C., Title 50, Sec. 104);

Now, therefore, by virtue of the authority vested in me as President of the United States, and Commander in Chief of the Army and Navy, I hereby authorize and

direct the Secretary of War, and the Military Commanders whom he may from time to time designate, whenever he or any designated Commander deems such action necessary or desirable, to prescribe military areas in such places and of such extent as he or the appropriate Military Commander may determine, from which any or all persons may be excluded, and with respect to which, the right of any person to enter, remain in, or leave shall be subject to whatever restrictions the Secretary of War or the appropriate Military Commander may impose in his discretion. The Secretary of War is hereby authorized to provide for residents of any such area who are excluded therefrom, such transportation, food, shelter, and other accommodations as may be necessary, in the judgment of the Secretary of War or the said Military Commander, and until other arrangements are made, to accomplish the purpose of this order. The designation of military areas in any region or locality shall supersede designations of prohibited and restricted areas by the Attorney General under the Proclamations of December 7 and 8, 1941, and shall supersede the responsibility and authority of the Attorney General under the said Proclamations in respect of such prohibited and restricted areas.

I hereby further authorize and direct the Secretary of War and the said Military Commanders to take such other steps as he or the appropriate Military Commander may deem advisable to enforce compliance with the restrictions applicable to each Military area hereinabove authorized to be designated, including the use of Federal troops and other Federal

Agencies, with authority to accept assistance of state and local agencies.

I hereby further authorize and direct all Executive Departments, independent establishments and other Federal Agencies, to assist the Secretary of War or the said Military Commanders in carrying out this Executive Order, including the furnishing of medical aid, hospitalization, food, clothing, transportation, use of land, shelter, and other supplies, equipment, utilities, facilities, and services.

This order shall not be construed as modifying or limiting in any way the authority heretofore granted under Executive Order No. 8972, dated December 12, 1941, nor shall it be construed as limiting or modifying the duty and responsibility of the Federal Bureau of Investigation, with respect to the investigation of alleged acts of sabotage or the duty and responsibility

of the Attorney General and the Department of Justice under the Proclamations of December 7 and 8, 1941, prescribing regulations for the conduct and control of alien enemies, except as such duty and responsibility is superseded by the designation of military areas hereunder.

Franklin D. Roosevelt

The White House,

February 19, 1942.

FOCUS QUESTIONS:

1 Why is this order vaguely worded?

2. Why would American citizens permit this to happen?

18-5 Hitler Gets Fanny Christina Hill Out of the Kitchen

Many African-American women used wartime defense-industry jobs to work their way into the middle class. Fanny Christina Hill left Texas for Los Angeles in 1940, when she was twenty-one. At first, she worked as a domestic helper, in jobs similar to those she had held in Texas – but better paid. By 1943, she was working for North American Aviation, her employer – with a few breaks – for close to 40 years.

Source: Gluck, Sherna Berger. "Interview with Fanny Christina Hill." *Rosie the Riveter Revisited.* Boston: Twayne, 1987. In Robert D. Marcus and David Burner. *America Firsthand: Volume Two, Readings from Reconstruction to the Present.* 4th edition. Boston: Bedford Books, 1997, 222-229.

The war made me live better, it really did. My sister always said that Hitler was the one that, got us out of the white folks' kitchen.

This comment—attributed to her sister but repeated with sufficient relish to make the real authorship suspicious—captures the spirit of Fanny Christina ("Tina") Hill. ... Tina is both an actor and an observer. Her oral history not only richly details her life experiences but is sprinkled with commentaries on them. Determined to acquire the better things in life and to live the American dream, Tina is wryly self-mocking as she describes her ascent to the middle class.

For Tina, and for many black women, the war was a turning point. The expansion of jobs in the defense industries, coupled with Roosevelt's executive order prohibiting discrimination in hiring, helped black women get out of the white women's kitchens. In Los Angeles, for instance, in 1940, over 55 percent of non-white women workers were in private household service. Ten years later, this figure was down 15 percent. Tina was one of those who were able to leave domestic service permanently. And the money she earned during the war years paved the way for a new life.

That new life is reflected in her home, which is filled with the material goods she has acquired. She points to these as an indicator of what the job at North American Aircraft meant to her. But her home also symbolizes the past and her own family history. The bowl that Tina's great-grandmother was given by her owner when the slaves were emancipated is proudly displayed on a shelf. Tina's quilting frame is set up in the middle of her living room. The embroidered decorations and the garden outback both reflect Tina's commitment to preserve the traditions handed down by the generations of women in her family. She feels that it is her turn to pass down these skills and this history to the next two generations—her daughter and granddaughter.

[In 1943, Tina applied for a manufacturing job with North American Aviation.]

[FOLLOWING TEXT QUOTED FROM HILL]

I don't remember what day of the week it was, but I guess I must have started out pretty early that morning. When I went there, the man didn't hire me. They had a school down here on Figueroa and he told me to go to the school. I went down and it was almost four o'clock and they told me they'd hire me. You had to fill out a form. They didn't bother too much about your experience because they knew you didn't have any experience in aircraft. Then they give you some kind of little test where you put the pegs in the right hole.

There were other people in there, kinda mixed. I assume it was more women than men. Most of the men was gone, and they weren't hiring too many men unless they had a good excuse. Most of the women was in my bracket, five or six years younger or older. I was twenty-four. There was a black girl that hired in with me. I went to work the next day, sixty cents an hour.

I think I stayed at the school for about four weeks. They only taught you shooting and bucking rivets and how to drill the holes and to file. You had to use a hammer for certain things. After a couple of whiles, you worked on the real thing. But you were supervised so you didn't make a mess.

When we went into the plant, it wasn't too much different than down at the school. It was the same amount of noise; it was the same routine. One difference was there was just so many more people, and when you went in the door you had a badge to show and they looked at your lunch. I had gotten accustomed to a lot of people and I knew if it was a lot of people, it always meant something was going on. I got carried away: "As long as there's a lot of people here, I'll be making money." That was all I could ever see.

I was a good student, if I do say so myself. But I have found out through life, sometimes even if you're good, you just don't get the breaks if the color's not right. I could see where they made a difference in placing you in certain jobs. They had fifteen or twenty departments, but all the Negroes went to Department

17 because there was nothing but shooting and bucking rivets. You stood on one side of the panel and your partner stood on this side, and he would shoot the rivets with a gun and you'd buck them with the bar. That was about the size of it. I just didn't like it. I didn't think I could stay there with all this shooting and a'bucking and a'jumping and a'bumping. I stayed in it about two or three weeks and then I just decided I did *not* like that. I went and told my foreman and he didn't do anything about it, so I decided I'd leave.

While I was standing out on the railroad track, I ran into some-body else out there fussing also. I went over to the union and they told me what to do. I went back inside and they sent me to another department where you did bench work and I liked that much better. You had a little small jig that you would work on and you just drilled out holes. Sometimes you would rout them or you would scribe them and then you'd cut them with a cutters.

I must have stayed there nearly a year, and then they put me over in another department, "Plastics." It was the tail section of the B-Bomber, the Billy Mitchell Bomber. I put a little part in the gun-sight. You had a little ratchet set and you would screw it in there. Then I cleaned the top of the glass off and put a piece of paper over it to seal it off to go to the next section. I worked over there until the end of the war. Well, not quite the end, because I got pregnant, and while I was off having the baby the war was over.

FOCUS QUESTIONS:

1. Would similar opportunities have been available to Hill in the absence of World War II?
2. What steps did Hill take to improve her situation?
3. Does Hill ever imply that her situation would have been better if she had been a man? Do you believe her situation would have been better?

18-6 Jeanne Wakatsuki Houston, A Schoolgirl at Manzanar

In accordance with Executive Order 9066 (see document), Japanese-Americans and Japanese residents of the western United States were detained in one of ten concentration camps. Over 10,000 were interned at Manzanar, a hot and desolate camp in southeastern California. Jeanne Wakatsuki Houston's autobiographical Farewell to Manzanar provides a schoolgirl's perspective on the relocation experience and life in the camp.

NOTE: Nisei refers to the American-born children of immigrants from Japan.

Source: Houston, James D. and Jeanne Wakatsuki Houston. *Farewell to Manzanar.* New York: Houghton Mifflin Co., 1973. pp. 89-92.

Once we settled into Block 28 that ache I'd felt since soon after we arrived at Manzanar subsided. It didn't entirely disappear, but it gradually submerged, as semblances of order returned and our pattern of life assumed its new design.

For one thing, Kiyo and I and all the other children finally had *a school*. During the first year, teachers had been volunteers; equipment had been makeshift; classes were scattered all over camp, in mess halls, recreation rooms, wherever we could be squeezed in. Now a teaching staff had been hired. Two blocks were turned into Manzanar High, and a third block of fifteen barracks was setup to house the elementary grades. We had blackboards, new desks, reference books, lab supplies. That second, stable school year was one of the things *Our World* commemorated when it came out in June of 1944.

My days spent in classrooms are largely a blur now, as one merges into another. What I see clearly is the face of my fourth-grade teacher—a pleasant face, but completely invulnerable, it seemed to me at the time, with sharp, commanding eyes. She came from Kentucky. She wore wedgies, loose slacks, and sweaters that were too short in the sleeves. A tall, heavyset spinster, about forty years old, she always wore a scarf on her head, tied beneath the chin, even during class, and she spoke with a slow, careful Appalachian accent. She was probably the best teacher I've ever had—strict, fair-minded, dedicated to her job. Because of her, when we finally returned to the outside world I was, academically at least, more than prepared to keep up with my peers.

I see her face. But what I hear, still ringing in my mind's ear, is the Glee Club I belonged to, made up of girls from the fourth, fifth, and sixth grades. We rehearsed every day during the last period. In concert we wore white cotton blouses and dark skirts. Forty voices strong we would line up at assemblies or at talent shows in the firebreak and sing out in unison all the favorites school kids used to learn: *Beautiful Dreamer, Down By the Old Mill Stream, Shine On Harvest Moon, Battle Hymn of the Republic.*

Outside of school we had a recreation program, with leaders hired by the War Relocation Authority. During the week they organized games and craft activities. On weekends we often took hikes beyond the fence. A series of picnic groups and camping sites had been built by internees—clearings, with tables, benches, and toilets. The first was about half a mile out, the farthest several miles into the Sierras. As restrictions gradually loosened, you could measure your liberty by how far they'd let you go—to Camp Three with a Caucasian, to Camp Three alone, to Camp Four with a Caucasian, to Camp Four alone. As fourth- and fifth-graders we usually hiked out to Camp One, on the edge of Bair's Creek, where we could wade, collect rocks, and sit on the bank eating lunches the mess hall crew packed for us. I would always take along a quart jar and a white handkerchief and sit for an hour next to the stream, watching it strain through the cloth, trickling under the glass. Water there was the clearest I've ever seen, running right down off the snow.

One of our leaders on these excursions was a pretty young woman named Lois, about twenty-five at the time, who wore long braids, full skirts, and peasant blouses. She was a Quaker, like so many of the Caucasians who came in to teach and do volunteer work. She also had a crush on a tall, very handsome and popular Nisei boy who sometimes sang and danced in the talent shows. His name was Isao. In order to find a little free time together, Lois and Isao arranged an overnight camping trip for all the girls in our class. We took jars for water, potatoes to roast, and army blankets and hiked up Bair's Creek one Friday afternoon to a nice little knoll at the base of the mountains.

All the girls were tittering and *giggling* at the way Isao and Lois held hands and looked at each other. They built us a big driftwood fire that night, and told us ghost stories until they figured we had all dozed off. Then they disappeared for a while into the sagebrush. I was still awake and heard their careful footsteps snapping twigs. I thought how hard it would be to walk around out there without a flashlight. It was years later that I remembered and understood what that outing must have been for them. At the time I had my own escape to keep me occupied. In truth, I barely noticed their departure. This was the first over-night camping trip I'd ever made. For me it was enough to be outside the barracks for a night, outside the square mile of wire, next to a crackling blaze and looking at stars so thick and so close to the ground I could have reached up and scooped out an armful.

FOCUS QUESTIONS:

1. What developments helped Houston regain a sense of normalcy?

2. What imagery does Houston provide that counteracts the impression of normalcy?

3. Why are both of the Caucasians described in this passage female?

18-7 Hortense Johnson: What My Job Means to Me (1943)

Women war workers were employed by private industry (such as airplane manufacturers) and by the government. African-American women were among the workers at the Picatinny Arsenal in Dover, NJ, a major producer of munitions for the U.S. Army in World War II. Hortense Johnson recorded her thoughts on the significance of her work at Picatinny, both to herself and to her nation.

Source: Johnson, Hortense. "What My Job Means to Me," *Opportunity* 21 (April 1943):50-51.

Of course I'm vital to victory, just as millions of men and women who are fighting to save America's changes for Democracy, even if they never shoulder a gun nor bind a wound. It's true that my job isn't so exciting or complicated. Perhaps there are millions of girls who could do my job as well as I – certainly there are thousands. I am an inspector in a war plant. For eight hours a day, six days a week, I stand in line with five other girls, performing a routine operation that is part of our production schedule. We inspect wooden boxes that are to hold various kinds of munitions, and that range in size from eight inches to six feet. When we approve them they are ready to be packed with shells, bombs, fuses, parachutes– and other headaches for Hitler and Hirohito.

Not much to that, you say. Well, that all depends on the way you look at it. A missing or projecting nail, a loose board or hinge–these are some of the imperfections that we watch for. If we miss them, they may be checked later on, or they may not. If they are not, they may mean injury for a fellow worker on a later operation or an explosion in another part of the plant with dozens of lives lost–or they might even spell disaster for American soldiers in a tight spot in North Africa.

Did I say my job isn't exciting or complicated? I take that back. It may be a simple matter to inspect one box or dozens, but it's different when you are handling them by the hundreds. The six of us in my crew sometimes inspect as many as fourteen or fifteen hundred boxes during one shift. That means two hundred and fifty apiece–an average of one every two minutes, regardless of size and not counting any rest periods. Try sometime and see if it's a simple job. You stand at your bench all say long, with rest periods sometimes seeming years apart. You fight against the eye fatigue that might mean oversight. You probe with your fingers and tap here and there. Your back aches, your legs get weary, your muscles scream at you sometimes–groan at you all the time. But the dozens and one little operations must be carried on smoothly and efficiently if our work output is to keep up. It's exciting all right, and it's plenty complicated–in the same way that jungle warfare must be, hard and painstaking and monotonous–until something goes off with a bang!

And then when your shift is finished, you stalk off stiffly to the washroom and hurry to get ready for the bus that brings you forty miles back from the plant to your home in the city. You slip on an extra sweater and heavy woolen socks, because the unheated bus is apt to be cold and damp. Even when you get into the bus your day's jobs isn't over, for you work almost as hard as the driver. You strain with him to see through the heavy winter fog that blankets the highway. You watch with him for the tricky ice that waits at curves to throw you into dangerous skids. When sleet has covered the road and made all travel seem suicidal, you sit ready to get out at the worst spots and walk with the rest of your crowd until the bus pulls across to safety.

So when you get back home, you're glad to jump in to bed and die until morning– or until your alarm-clock tells you it's morning, no matter how black it is. Then your two-hour experience of traveling back to the job begins all over again, because in spite of rain, snow, cold or illness, the job is there to be done, and you're expected to do your share. It never occurs to you to figure out how much money you're making, because it isn't enough anyhow– after you've had your victory tax deducted, paid for your war bond, set aside money for your bus commutation ticket. By the time you've given grandmother the food and rent money, and paid the doctor for helping you to fight off your frequent colds, and bought the extra-heavy clothes the job calls for, you're just about where the boys in New Guinea are. Don't let Senator Wheeler fool you with his talk about "high wages for war workers!"

So if it's as tough as all that–and it is! –why do you stick on the job? Why did you leave the comfortable job you held with a city business house? Why don't you go back to it and make as much money as you're now? Why? Because it's not that easy to leave, and it's not that tough to stay here! Of course the work is hard and sometimes dangerous, but victory in this war isn't going to come the easy way, without danger. And we brown women of America need victory so much, so desperately. America is a long way from perfect. We resent the racial injustices that we meet every day of our lives. But it's one thing to resent and fight racial injustices; it's another thing to let them break your spirit, so that you quit this struggle and turn the country over to run this country if Hitler wins. America can't win this war without us, and we know it. We must prove it to white Americans as well–that our country can't get along without the labor and sacrifice of her brown daughters, can't win unless we *all* fight and work and save.

So the hardships of war work becoming willing sacrifices to victory, not to victory for Democracy, but to victory by a country that some day, please God, will win Democracy. In such a spirit, even some of the hardships are forgotten in the daily rewards of the job. After all, we *are* working today and drawing regular pay checks. And there is fun on the bus trips, even when you're half-dozing. There is a comradeship that comes from working and traveling together, expressed in jokes and singing and laughter on the return trip. Sometimes we have parties on the bus, sharing candy or sandwiches, and even cutting birthday cake bought from a roadside bakery. Frayed nerves and short tempers show themselves sometimes, and that's understandable, but real quarrel seldom develops. Ill –tempered remarks are usually understood, and passed over without comeback.

I imagine that our boys at the front develop the same kind of tolerance, the same kind of partnership, for the same reason. Wouldn't it be great if the white workers who are fellow-fighters with us in war productions, would develop more of the same spirit and partnership? What can we do to make them realize that colored people must be given equal opportunity in every walk of life to make that partnership real–to build an impregnable, free, and democratic America.

Well, that's why I stay on this job, and that's what this job means to me. I might shift plants if I get a good chance. I haven't been very well, and the constant strain and exposure have put me into bed too often for my doctor's satisfaction and my own comfort. But one thing is sure; if I leave this job I'll get another one in war work. Victory is vital and I'm vital to victory. It's going to take courageous deeds at the front, and in the Navy and the Merchants Marine to win this war, but it's also going to take top speed production in the war plants at home–and that's my assignment.

I'm not fooling myself about this war. Victory won't mean victory for Democracy–yet. But that will come later, because most of us who are fighting for victory today will keep on fighting to win the peace–maybe a long time after the war is over, maybe a hundred years after. By doing my share today, I'm keeping a place for some brown women tomorrow, and for the brown son of that woman the day after tomorrow. Sterling Brown once wrote, "The strong men keep a-comin' on," and millions of those men have dark skins. There will be dark women marching by their side, and I like to think that I'm one of them.

FOCUS QUESTIONS:

1. What does Johnson present as the goals of her work?
2. In the statement, "Victory is vital and I'm vital to victory," what constitutes victory for Johnson?
3. How does Johnson's description dignify herself and her colleagues?

18-9 Ruth Fujii's Service in the Women's Army Corps

Ruth Fujii, a Nisei from Hawaii, joined the Women's Army Corps. She served both on the U.S. mainland, and in the Pacific theater during World War II.

Souce: Moore, Brenda L. "Interview with Ruth Fujii." In *Serving Our Country: Japanese American Women in the Military during World War II.* New Brunswick: Rutgers University Press, 2003, 115-117.

From basic training, Ruth Fujii went to advanced training in clerical work at fort Des Moines. Later she was assigned as a secretary to an executive officer at Camp Hood, Texas. Fujii did not like her assignment:

It was miserable at Camp Hood. . . . no ocean, no mountains. I was so uncomfortable and it wasn't pleasant in the office. . . . That's the only time I faced some racial discrimination. I don't know [if it was because] I was a Wac or because I was Japanese. . . . But the colonel I was assigned to had just come back from Europe and then I replaced this man's secretary. And so he made it rough for me, but I didn't say anything. He called me in for dictation so I went in with my pad. . . .He used all the big words that others [other secretaries] wouldn't understand, but I took it all.. ... And then I sat down and ran it off. And then I gave it to the office manager . . . and covered my type-writer. I walked out, back to my barracks. I didn't say goodbye or anything. . . . Later the office manager called me and said the colonel wanted to see me. So I said "Okay, I'll come over after I take a shower. . . " So I took a shower and I went in and you know what he asked me?

"Where did you learn English?"

Fujii did not bother to explain to the colonel that English was the primary language in Hawaiian schools. She resented his ignorance.

In March 1945, the first Wacs arrived in Manila. After serving only a few months at Camp Hood, Fujii applied for overseas duty and was stationed there, in the Southwest Pacific Area (SWPA):

I got assigned to General Marshall's group.. . . There were about nine of us girls. It was a small outfit they used to call MAGIC—Military Advisory Group In China. . . . I was a secretary to four colonels .[and] each had locked files. I had four files: personnel, intelligence, training and plants with pits, and supply ... and had to memorize all four.

Fujii explained that the office in which she worked was under heavy security "Nobody was supposed to go behind the railing in our office. . . . They could sit outside but could not cross the bar."

During our interview, Fujii recalled that an officer from Japan with the same last name as hers was on trial while she was stationed in the Philippines:

Being of Japanese parentage and bearing a typical Japanese name, I was certain that I would be attacked because the Filipino people despised the Japanese. And I didn't blame them. But a Filipino boy said to me, "You're Japanese, but from Hawaii. That's different." He and I were good friends after that.

U.S. military officials saw to it that Fujii was protected with a bodyguard: "Everybody took precautions and made sure that I had an escort wherever, I went. . . . When I went to town or anyplace, to the opera or anything, [there was [always a male soldier] sitting in a jeep with a gun. . . . If I was called at night to take dictation, they'd send a jeep over to pick me up and take me wherever I was supposed to go. . . I'd have a jeep driver and a soldier sitting in front with a gun."

On February 12, 1946, after spending eleven months in the Philippines, Fujii received orders to report to the China theater. She spent two weeks in Shanghai before traveling with a special group of Wacs assigned to Nanking. Everyone she was assigned with in Asia seemed to get along: "Everybody 'treated me well. My officers and fellow servicemen and women, we always did things together; I got to go all over the place." The living condition the Philippines, however, were somewhat less than desirable: "We had no sheets; only army cots, army blankets, and that's it. . . . And then when I went; to China, it was different. We had service—linen tablecloths, . . . and all because the Wacs were living in the same building as the [male] officers, only on a different floor."

FOCUS QUESTIONS:

1. What is Fujii's attitude towards the U.S. military as an institution? What are her attitudes towards particular officers?

2. Do her attitudes seem justified?

3. Do you think Fujii would say that her experiences were shaped more by her gender, or her ethnicity? Why? What is your own perspective on her experiences, as described here?

18-9 Kiyo Hirano at the Amache Relocation Center

Like Jeanne Wakatsuki Houston (see document), Kiyo Hirano was interned during World War II. As an adult sent to the Amache Relocation Center, in southeastern Colorado, Hirano had a different perspective than Houston.

Source: Hirano, Kiyo, *Enemy Alien.* San Francisco: JAM Publications, 1983. pp. 11-14.

A day in August was decided as the departure date for Colorado. With little to pack, the preparation was simple. We hoped to live nearby to a family from San Rafael and a family from Tiburon with whom we had become good friends, so we were relieved when the numbers on our registration tags to be worn on our chests were not too far apart. When leaving, we three families stood together in the same spot and were pushed as a group with our baggage onto the open truck which had come to take us to the station. Waiting there was a small old train.

Black blinds had been pulled over all the windows. We boarded and sat down. Immediately, helmeted soldiers with rifles took their stands before each entrance, as though we were prisoners. The train began to move, making a great noise. How it must have spurted black smoke! When one man tried to pull up a blind, he was faced with a pointed rifle.

"Hey you! No one looks outside!"

In dismay I realized that enjoying the mountain

landscape had been only a thought of "luxury."

At lunch time, people began to go in groups to the dining car. Here too, there were black blinds. At times, the train stopped. Could it be a station? Each time I heard many voices. Probably they wanted to take a look at the Japanese who had been removed from California. Perhaps all human beings have a sense of curiosity. With every stop, the train got hotter. A small fan on the ceiling did little good. Since bringing in newspapers or magazines was prohibited, we heard continuous complaints and yawns. Not feeling up to going for dinner, and thinking of going to sleep, I asked a soldier, "Is it okay to fold out the bed up there?"

He replied, "No, sleep leaving the back of your seat up."

Someone said, "Goddamn!"

The soldier again pointed his rifle and yelled, his eyes glaring, "Who said that?"

He had to work standing all day, so I sympathized a little with him.

The lights went out. In the darkness, the grinding of teeth and snoring was heard. I was impressed that there were people who could actually sleep in that place. I could not sleep at all. Finally it appeared to be morning. Were we going to live this day again inside a box? I wanted to go outside, no matter where it was and just breathe in the air as hard as I could. The children must have been feeling the same way, for I could sense their irritation. Poor things, just for being born a Japanese American. I wanted to apologize to them. The train, perhaps having entered the midst of the mountains, made no stops and went on running, making groaning noises. The faces of those on the train were covered with soot and our throats hurt. Such great heat! We had no appetite. We did not even want to move. The children, however, seemed to healthily eat their fill during mealtimes. They would bring some food for me when they came back from the dining car.

At last the train stopped, though not at the camp but at a hastily-made train station. We got off there in the middle of a prairie. How good it felt to fill my entire body with air! I breathed in deeply. It was a rare, marvelous feeling! As if risen from the dead, every soot-covered face laughing, we three families gathered together and waited to be taken to the Center. In a while, two or three trucks came to pick us up and we were taken to the Center.

On the truck, people seemed too tired to talk. We went over rural roads, then through the gates of Amache Relocation Center. Was this the desert? Light brown sand as far as we could see and sagebrush that I had only seen in movies.

"Here I stand on desert land," I found myself saying dramatically. Lined up far away were pinkish-brown houses. "Those must be our homes," I murmured to myself as we were led to the inspection room.

With the large number of people, the inspection took longer, but our *new homes* were assigned. All three families were to be placed in 8F Block and again in the larger room of the barracks. We were overjoyed that all three families could live in quarters facing each other. The barracks here could be called more or less *homes*. The outward appearance was a little better than the barracks at Merced.

In each barrack six families, large or small, were to live. There were three front doors in each barrack which, when opened, split to the left and right for each family. Such barracks were lined into five horizontal rows, to the side of which ran a road wide enough for two cars. Across from the road lay another group of barracks in five rows, the same as those described above. By the road was a large building with the laundry room, shower room, and toilet, next to which stood the mess hall. These buildings formed one block of the Amache camp. The blocks were named alphabetically. Blocks A, B and C were apparently administrative offices and the barracks were from Blocks E to K A Buddhist church was built in Block K and Block G. The hospital was at the edge of Block H, an inconvenient spot.

Next to Block 8F was an open lot on which later the PX was built, which made shopping convenient. However, when we first entered camp, when even schools had not been built yet, the lot served as a storage area for lumber. We had our eyes on that lumber! Since there were no shelves, tables or benches inside the room, we needed wood.

The floor was of brick and comfortable. On it sat a large iron stove, reminding us of the winter cold. Just like America! Was not the use of steel forbidden in Japan? I felt the contrast in the two countries' conditions. The exterior of the houses were reddish-brown. It was quite nice. Apparently small pebbles had been mixed with reddish-brown cement, then pressed onto a compressed piece of cardboard about one inch thick. The always important beds here were quite miserable. Wooden frames merely covered by a thick canvas-like cloth. There were also seven thin army blankets. The toilet here was located in the same wing as the shower room and had regular toilets but no doors, so that three partitioned areas faced each other. It was uncomfortable. Showers were also three on each side and without doors. It was fun to talk and yell across to people while taking a shower. After washing away a day's worth of exhaustion in the showers and going to sleep on the awkward beds, we all woke up complaining of body aches. Sleep was impossible in a springless bed of canvas which bent our bodies almost in two!

The Japanese here established a system of self-government which was to be under the authority of the Caucasians. In the salaried system, the highest pay was nineteen dollars a month. The highest pay was given to doctors, teachers, and directors. A pay of sixteen dollars was for regular labor and twelve for student work, dishwashing, and waitressing. Those desiring employment were recruited. I applied for the job of hospital *traygirl*. The job was to place meals on trays according to the hospital patient list such as O.B., Isolation, Regular, or Soft. After the trays were placed accordingly on separate carts, the nurses would distribute them to the patients. It was hard until I became used to the job. Once I was reprimanded by the nurse for feeding regular meals to those requiring soft meals. The nurse was probably criticized by the doctor, and I was on the final receiving end. The job was in a three-person shift. Sixteen dollars a month. It was an interesting job.

In between work there was fixing up the living quarters. With no wood, no hammers, no nails, no knives, no saws, there was just nothing! To create something out of nothing is quite a challenge.

However, after two months we had made a desk, a bench, a shelf, and beds on which, though hard, one could at least lie straight. The lumber in the open lot disappeared as though dragged away by ants! I would go with my son and say, as I had been taught, to the soldiers on guard, "Please keep your eyes closed. Close your eyes please." They would laugh and leave. And then we would hurry. This could not be done at night because search lights would be shining from all directions. Should we be found inside a lighted spot, at once we would have been bombarded by bullets. The above process was how we acquired the lumber we needed. I felt really guilty, but I followed the old saying that the spine of principle cannot replace the stomach of need. I quickly ordered carpentry tools from Sears Roebuck. I waited in great anticipation for the package to arrive.

From September, school instruction was to start. As for teachers, there were excellent ones interned from all over the state of California, so the school was rumored to be better than the California public schools.

FOCUS QUESTIONS:

1. How did Hirano and her family establish a sense of normalcy for themselves?

2. Why does Hirano cite what she calls an "old saying," "the spine of principle cannot replace the stomach of need?"

3. What can you gather from this passage about Hirano's role in the family?

THE FEMININE MYSTIQUE, 1945-1965

19-1 Women's Bureau, Handbook of Facts on Women Workers

The Women's Bureau of the U.S. Department of Labor periodically collected data on women's employment rate, occupations, marital status, and other aspects of labor. This group of tables shows changes in various aspects of women's workforce participation between 1940 and 1949.

Source: Women's Bureau, 1950. *Handbook of Facts on Women Workers*, Bulletin No. 237.

CHIEF OCCUPATION GROUPS EMPLOYING WOMEN

CHANGES IN NUMBERS EMPLOYED, 1940 TO 1949

In most occupation groups the number of women increased from1940 to 1949. The greatest increases were those of more than 2 million among clerical and kindred workers and of over 1 million among operatives and kindred workers. The number of sales workers and of service workers (except domestic) increased each by more than 1/2 million, farm workers by about 1/3 million. Two relatively small occupation groups also showed increases-proprietors, managers, and officials (except farm), and craftsmen and foremen.

The number of women decreased from 1940 to 1949 in three occupation groups. The greatest decline, approaching 1/2 million, occurred among the domestic service workers. The professional and semiprofessional group also showed some decline, and the small group of laborers declined.

DISTRIBUTION IN OCCUPATION GROUPS

In 1949 nearly half the women workers were in the clerical and operative groups, nearly a fourth were in service groups, and almost a tenth were in the pro-fessional and semiprofessional group. Smaller fractions were in each of the other groups. The proportion who were in the clerical and in the operative groups combined increased from 39 percent of all women workers in 1940 to 48percent in 1949. The proportion in the combined service groups declined from 29 percent of the total in 1940 to 22 percent in 1949. A smaller proportion than in 1940 was in the professional group in 1949, and a slightly larger proportion than in 1940 was in the group of sales-women, as well as in that of proprietors and managers. Farm workers were in the same proportion-both years, as was the craftsmen group.

PROPORTION OF WORKERS IN EACH OCCUPATION GROUP WHO ARE WOMEN

Women constituted over 90 percent of the domestic service workers in 1949, over 60 percent of the clerical workers, about 40 percent each of the professional, of the sales, and of the service (other than domestic) workers, and nearly 30 percent of the operatives. In other groups smaller proportions of the workers were women. During World War II the proportion of workers who were women increased in all occupation groups save that of domestic service workers, and in some groups increased quite markedly. After the war, the proportion of workers who were women declined in every occupation group, but in most groups still remained larger than in the prewar period. The excepted groups were the domestic service, the professional, and the small group of craftsmen, foremen, and laborers; each of these had a smaller proportion of women among its workers after than before the war.

MARITAL STATUS OF WOMEN WORKERS

WOMEN OF EACH MARITAL STATUS GROUP WHO ARE WORKERS

In 1949 over half the single women in this country were in the labor force, as were more than a third of the widowed and divorced women, and nearly a fourth of the married women.

MARITAL STATUS OF ALL WOMEN AND OF WOMEN WORKERS

Single women constituted 20 percent of the woman population in1949 but were 33 percent of the women in the labor force. Married women were 66 percent of the adult female population and 51 percent of the women in the labor force. Widows and divorced women were 14 percent of the woman population, 16 percent of the female labor force.

FOCUS QUESTIONS:

1. In what types of work are women employed?
2. What trends are mentioned in the report? Can you notice any other trends or interesting points in the data?

Table 2.-Changes in number of women in each occupation group, 1940 to 1949

Occupation group	Number of women		Change, 1940 to 1949	
	1940[1]	1949	Number	Percent
All groups -	11,920,000	16,356,000	+4,436,000	+37
Clerical, kindred workers - - - - - - - - - - - - - - -	2,530,000	4,542,000	+2,012,000	+80
Operatives, kindred workers - - - - - - - - - - - - - -	2,190,000	3,199,000	+1,009,000	+46
Domestic service workers - - - - - - - - - - - - - - -	2,100,000	1,666,000	-434,000	-21
Professional, semiprofessional workers - - - - - - - - -	1,570,000	1,477,000	-93,000	-6
Service workers (except domestic) - - - - - - - - - - -	1,350,000	1,911,000	+561,000	+42
Sales workers -	830,000	1,386,000	+556,000	+67
Farmers, farm workers - - - - - - - - - - - - - - - - -	690,000	1,057,000	+367,000	+53
Proprietors, managers, officials (except farm) - - - - -	450,000	867,000	+417,000	+93
Craftsmen, foremen, kindred workers - - - - - - - - - -	110,000	165,000	+55,000	+50
Laborers (except farm) - - - - - - - - - - - - - - - - -	100,000	85,000	-15,000	-15

[1] Employed women whose occupations were not reported, a small proportion of all employed women, were apportioned according to the distribution of those whose occupations were reported.

Source: U. S. Bureau of the Census reports.

Table 3.—Status of women in each occupation group before, during, and after World War II

Occupation group	Women employed							
	Percent. of all persons in the occupation group				Percent distribution			
	1940	1945	1947	1949	1940	1945	1947	1949
All groups -	26	36	28	28	100	100	100	100
Clerical, kindred workers - - - - - - - - - - - - - -	53	70	59	61	21	25	26	28
Operatives, kindred workers - - - - - - - - - - - - -	26	38	28	28	18	24	22	20
Domestic service Workers - - - - - - - - - - - - - -	94	94	92	92	18	9	11	10
Professional, semiprofessional workers - - - - - - - -	45	46	40	37	13	8	10	
Service workers (except domestic) - - - - - - - - - -	40	48	44	44	11	10	11	12
Sales workers -	28	54	40	38	7	8	8	8
Farmers, farm workers - - - - - - - - - - - - - - - -	8	22	12	14	6	10	6	
Proprietors, managers, officials (except farm) - - - -	12	17	14	14	4	4	5	5
Craftsmen, foremen, kindred; laborers (except farm) -	3	5	2	2	2	2	1	2

Source: U. S. Bureau of the Census reports.

Table 7.—Changes in number and distribution of women in each marital status group, in population and in labor force, 1940 to 1949

Marital status	Number of women		Percent change, 1940 to 1949	Percent distribution	
	1940	1949		1940	1949
POPULATION					
All groups - - - - - - - - - - - - - - - - - - -	50,140,000	56,001,000	+12	100	100
Single -	13,733,000	11,174,000	-19	27	20
Married -	29,973,000	37,013,000	+23	60	66
Widowed and divorced - - - - - - - - - - - - - -	6,434,000	7,815,000	+21	13	14
LABOR FORCE					
All groups - - - - - - - - - - - - - - - - - - -	13,810,000	17,167,000	+24	100	100
Single -	6,710,000	5,682,000	-15	49	33
Married -	5,040,000	8,739,000	+73	36	51
Widowed and divorced - - - - - - - - - - - - - -	2,090,000	2,746,000	+31	15	16

19-2 Louise Alcott, Combining Marriage and Nursing

Louise Alcott's article describes her experiences as a private duty nurse – a nurse who works directly for an infirm person, usually in the person's home, rather than being employed in a hospital or other institution. Note that Alcott takes pains to assure her readers that her son and husband are well cared for, despite Alcott's job responsibilities.

Source: Alcott, Louise. "Combining Marriage and Nursing." *American Journal of Nursing.* November 1955, 1344.

Many nurses practice their profession and rear their families at the same time. A private duty nurse discusses her approach to her dual role....

How to combine a career with marriage successfully is a vital problem for about 55 percent of the women who do private duty nursing, especially those who have children. I suppose there are many ways to measure success, but it seems to me that if all members of the family are happy, if they are well cared for both physically and emotionally, if the atmosphere at home is suited to their temperaments, and if mother, father, and the children can go to their jobs and schools with the assurance that all is well, then there is a full measure of success.

The most important factor contributing to success in my family is a spirit of friendly cooperation. Each of us is interested in the activities of the others-on the job and off. Everyone assumes a share of home responsibilities. The system we have evolved is largely self-propelled and is adaptable to changes in my case assignments. Sometimes I have worked for just a few days, and on other occasions a case has lasted for many months. The situation is not always easy, and everything does not always run smoothly, but we have learned to be patient if some of the things we have planned must be postponed or eliminated entirely.

We try to make our work just as easy as possible for ourselves while maintaining certain standards of living. For example, I don't think we could get along without the washing machine and some of the other household appliances which make house- work easier. We all have a double supply of washable clothing so, if the laundry is delayed, no one needs to fret. I hire someone to do the ironing because it is not only one of the most time-consuming chores that I have but, if I am interrupted by a call to go on a case, a basket of mildewed clothes and a bundle of frayed nerves may result.

To get the housekeeping done, I plan to do a little every day, and on one or two evenings a week we all pitch in for a heavy session. When I am "between cases," the first item to chalk off the list is cleaning the house. If I don't get this out of the way, it seems that nothing proceeds very efficiently. A cleaning woman is the answer when I find myself on a long assignment; then the things which need my personal attention just wait for me.

Planning meals is not a major problem, because the pantry shelves, refrigerator, and the freezer are kept well stocked. If the day has complications, it is an easy matter to switch from a menu which takes lengthy preparation to one that can be pre- pared in a jiffy. Between cases I cook and bake for the future.

My son, Richard, goes to school before my husband leaves for his office, and I am home before he returns. We are fortunate to have Granddaddy living with us, so Richard is not without supervision even when he is not in school. We plan in advance what Richard may do when he is not in school. He has a well-defined program for the day, and we are most willing to hear him tell about it each evening. Dependable and competent care for children must be provided. This often poses quite a problem for private duty nurses, because the working schedule does not follow a regular pattern.

It seems that private duty nursing has been particularly adaptable to my family situation. We have always been able to meet emergencies, such as a sudden illness in the family, by relinquishing my case to another nurse. I can do this without feeling that I have worked a hardship on the organization of a ward or that the patient is not receiving adequate care. My husband cannot always plan his vacation time in advance, but I can usually conform-at least within a few days—to his plans.

We cooperate with our long-range plans just as we do with our day-to- day plans. Our family knows the goal that we are all working toward, and when the going gets a little rough this knowledge keeps us facing in the right direction. I am sure there are times when I would not feel justified in leaving my home for a big portion of the day if I were doing so solely to satisfy my desire to continue with my career. But when my family feels that I am making a worthwhile contribution toward future goals, that adds the satisfaction of corporate accomplishment.

Our family has not forgotten individual and common interests outside of home and careers, although they may be somewhat curtailed. A private duty nurse makes a dreadful mistake when she does not plan to have time off between cases or time off during long assignments so that she may take part in a reasonable amount of family, social, church, and professional activity. Not working a prescribed 5-day week, is no excuse for staying on the job so steadily that all we can do is go to work, keep house, and sleep, to the exclusion of all else. That is not success unless one measures success only in dollars.

The result of our scheme of living seems to me to be a successful combination of marriage and a career in private duty nursing. I enjoy my family, my home, friends, outside activities, and my career. I believe my family does too, for they are keenly interested in my activities.

FOCUS QUESTIONS:

1. What is Alcott's definition of success? How does it compare to your own definition of success?
2. What are Alcott's roles, as she describes them? What are the roles of Alcott's husband? Are there others, in or outside of the family, whose help or support she specifically cites?

19-3 The Kinsey Report (1948)

Alfred C. Kinsey's scientific study on sexual behavior in humans arrested public attention. Humans – male and female – were described as highly sexual and sexually complex beings. The 12,000 subjects reported seeking a variety of outlets for sexual satisfaction; they engaged in a variety of sexual activities, and often did so outside of marriage.

Source: Alfred C. Kinsey, et al., *Sexual Behavior in the Human Male* (Philadelphia: W. B. Sanders, 1948), pp. 263-273.

MARITAL STATUS AND SEXUAL OUTLET

Among the social factors affecting sexual activity, marital status is the one that would seem most likely to influence both the frequencies and the sources of the individual's outlet. The data, however, need detailed analyses.

Social and Legal Limitations

In Social and religious philosophies, there have been two antagonistic interpretations of sex. There have been cultures and religions which have inclined to the hedonistic doctrine that sexual activity is justifiable for its immediate and pleasurable return; and there have been cultures and religions which accept sex primarily as the necessary means of pro-creation, to be enjoyed only in marriage, and then only if reproduction is the goal of the act. The Hebrews were among the Asiatics who held this ascetic approach to sex; and Christian sexual philosophy and English-American sex law is largely built around these Hebraic interpretations, around Greek ascetic philosophies, and around the asceticism of some of the Roman cults

(Angus 1925, May 1931).

A third possible interpretation of sex as a normal biologic function, acceptable in whatever form it is manifested, has hardly figured in either general or scientific discussions. By English and American standards, such an attitude is considered primitive, materialistic or animalistic, and beneath the dignity of a civilized and educated people. Freud has contributed more than the biologists toward an adoption of this biologic viewpoint.

Since English-American moral codes and sex laws are the direct outcome of the reproductive interpretation of sex, they accept no form of socio-sexual activity outside of the marital state; and even marital intercourse is more or less limited to particular times and places and to the techniques which are most likely to result in conception. By this system, no socio-sexual outlet is provided for the single male or for the widowed or divorced male, since they cannot legally procreate; and homosexual and solitary sources of outlet, since they are completely without reproductive possibilities, are penalized or frowned upon by public opinion and by the processes of the law.

Specifically, English-American legal codes restrict the sexual activity of the unmarried male by characterizing all pre-marital, extra-marital, and post-marital intercourse as rape, statutory rape, fornication, adultery, prostitution, association with a prostitute, incest, delinquency, a contribution to delinquency, assault and battery, or public indecency—all of which are offenses with penalties attached. However it is labelled, all intercourse outside of marriage (non-marital intercourse) is illicit and subject to penalty by statute law in most of the states of the Union, or by the precedent of the common law on which most courts, in all states, chiefly depend when sex is involved. In addition to their restrictions on hetero-sexual intercourse, statute law and the common law penalize all homosexual activity, and all sexual contacts with animals; and they specifically limit the techniques of marital intercourse. Mouth-genital and anal contacts are punishable as crimes whether they occur in heterosexual or homosexual relations and whether in or outside of marriage. Such manual manipulation as occurs in the petting which is common in the younger generation has been interpreted in some courts as an impairment of the morals of a minor, or even as assault and battery. The public exhibition of any kind of sexual activity, including self masturbation, or the viewing of such activity, is punishable as a contribution to delinquency or as public indecency.

There have been occasional court decisions which have attempted to limit the individual's right to solitary masturbation; and the statutes of at least one state (Indiana Acts 1905, ch. 169, & 473, p. 584) rule that the encouragement of self masturbation is an offense punishable as sodomy. Under a literal interpretation of this law, it is possible that a preacher, biologist, psychologist, physician or other person who published the scientifically determinable fact that masturbation does no physical harm might be prosecuted for encouraging some person to "commit masturbation." There have been penal commitments of adults who have given sex instruction to minors, and there are evidently some courts who

TOTAL SEXUAL OUTLET

The mean frequencies of total sexual outlet for the married males are always, at all age levels, higher than the total outlets for single males; but, as already pointed out (Chapter 6), essentially all single males have regular and usually frequent sexual outlet, whether before marriage, or after being widowed, separated, or divorced. Of the more than five thousand males who have contributed to the present study, only 1 per cent has lived for as much as five years (after the onset of adolescence and outside of old age) without orgasm.

As previously recorded, the mean frequency of the total outlet for the single males between 16 and 20 is (on the basis of the U. S. Corrections) about 3.3 per week (Table 60, Figures 50-52). The mean frequency of total outlet for the married male is about 4.8 per week, which is 47 per cent above the average outlet of the single male. At 30, the frequencies for the married males are about 18 per cent above those of the single males, and approximately this relation holds for some period of years. Beyond 40 years of age, the single

males may actually exceed the married males in their sexual frequencies. In adolescent years, the restrictions upon the sexual activity of the unmarried male are greatest. He finds it more difficult to locate sources of outlet and he has not learned the techniques for approaching and utilizing those sources when they are available. Nevertheless, his frequency between adolescence and 16 does average about 3.0 per week and between16 and 20 it amounts to nearly 3.4 per week. This represents arousal that leads to orgasm on an average of about every other day. By the time he is 30, the single male has become much more efficient in his social approaches and does not lag far behind the married individual in his performance. Considering the physical advantage which the married individual has in securing intercourse without going outside of his own home, it is apparent that the older single male develops skills in making social approaches and finding places for sexual contacts which far exceed the skills of married persons. Beau Brummels and Casanovas are not married males. A few of the married males who are involved in promiscuous extra-mar-ital activity are the only ones whose facilities begin to compare with those found among unmarried groups. It is notable that in the male homosexual, where long-term unions are not often maintained and new partners are being continually sought, there are many persons who preserve this same facility for making social contacts for long periods of years.

The differences that exist between the total activities of the younger married male and the younger unmarried male are, to some degree, a measure of the effectiveness of the social pressures that keep the single male's performance below his native capacity; although the lower rates in the single males may depend, in part, upon the possibility that less responsive males may not marry so young, or may never marry. On the other hand, the fact that the single male, from adolescence to30 years of age, does have a frequency of nearly 3.0 per week is evidence of the ineffectiveness of social restrictions and of the imperativeness of the biologic demands. For those who like the term, it is clear that there is a sexual drive which cannot be set aside for any large portion of the population, by any sort of social convention. For those who prefer to think in simpler terms of action and reaction, it is a picture of an animal who, however civilized or cultured, continues to respond to the constantly present sexual stimuli, albeit with some social and physical restraints...

In addition to the differences in frequencies of total outlet between married and single males, there are minor differences in incidence and in range of variation in the groups. Between adolescence and 15 years of age, 95 per cent of the unmarried boys have some sort of sexual outlet. From 16 to 35 years of age, 99 per cent or more of these males are engaging in some form of sexual activity (Table 60). Among the married males, a full 100 per cent is sexually active between 16 and 35 years of age. Beyond 35, the incidence figures drop for single males, and at a somewhat faster rate than for married males. The differences are not great.

The range of variation in frequency of outlet in any particular age group is also nearly identical for single and married males. In both populations (Table 49), there are individuals who engage in sexual activity only a few times a year, and there are some who engage in sexual activities regularly 3 or 4 or more times per day (29 or more per week). The lower average rates for single males are not dependent upon the fact that there are no high-rating individuals in that group, but upon the fact that there is a large number of the single males who have lower rates, and a larger number of married males who have higher rates. At least half of the younger married males have outlets which average 3 or more per week, whereas only a third of the single males fall into that category. Throughout both single and married histories, there is a steady decline in total sexual outlet in successive age groups (Chapter 7). After 30 years of age this decline in any 5-year period (Figures 50-52) is very nearly as great as the differences between married and single males of the same age group. Age is eventually as important as all of the social, moral, and legal factors which differentiate single from married histories.

FOCUS QUESTIONS:

1. Is the behavior Kinsey documents likely to reflect a sudden change in human sexual and social conduct? What changes occurred in American society to make this research and its publication possible?
2. Are women's sexual urges and behaviors portrayed as fundamentally different from men's in this excerpt?

19-4 Audre Lorde on Lesbian Love

Audre Lorde was born in 1934 in New York City; her parents were immigrants from the Caribbean. She became a renowned poet and a potent activist, criticizing the mainstream American feminist movement for focusing on the experiences of middle-class white women.

Source: Lorde, Audre. "Love Poem." *Chosen Poems – Old and New.* New York: W.W. Norton & Company, 1982, p. 77.

Love Poem

Speak earth and bless me with what is richest
make sky flow honey out of my hips
rigid as mountains
spread over a valley
carved out by the mouth of rain.

And I knew when I entered her I was
high wind in her forests hollow

fingers whispering sound
honey flowed
from the split cup
impaled on a lance of tongues
on the tips of her breasts on her navel
and my breath
howling into her entrances
through lungs of pain.

Greedy as herring-gulls
or a child
I swing out over the earth
over and over
again.

FOCUS QUESTIONS:

1. Could Lorde's unabashed sexuality have been discussed in polite company without the Kinsey Report and the sexual revolution?
2. What is specifically female about this poem?
3. Is this poem political?

19-5 *The Group*

Mary McCarthy's 1962 novel follows eight Vassar College friends (Class of '33) in their first decade after graduation. The story relentlessly satirizes their pretensions, and the fundamental inadequacies of the privileged society in which they find themselves.

Source: McCarthy, Mary. *The Group*. New York: Harcourt, Brace & World, Inc, 1954, pp. 95-99.

Harald and Kay were giving a party to celebrate Harald's having sold an option on his play to a producer. It was Washington's Birthday, and Kay had the day off from the store. The group had made a point of coming, in their nicest winter dresses and hats. Harald, poor fellow, had been out of work for months, it seemed, ever since September when, according to Polly Andrews, a director had molested him. They had not paid the rent for months either; the real-estate people were "carrying" them. When they got the check for the option ($500), the telephone was about to be shut off. It was a mystery what they had been living on, even with Kay's salary. On faith, hope, and charity, Kay said, laughing: Harald's *faith* in himself gave his creditors *hope*, which made them extend *charity*. And she told how Harald had proposed that they invite a select group of their creditors to the party: the man from the real-estate office, the man from the telephone company, Mr. Finn from the Internal Revenue, and their dentist, Dr. Mosenthal—wouldn't that have been a howl?

Kay had been showing the apartment to everyone who hadn't seen it. Two rooms, plus dinette and kitchen, plus a foyer, plus Kay's pride and joy, a darling little dressing room, so compact, with closets and cupboards and bureau drawers built in. Pure white walls and woodwork and casement windows, a whole row of them, looking out on a sunny court with young trees and shrubs. The latest models of stove, sink, and icebox; built-in cupboards for dishes, broom closet, linen closet. Every stick of furniture was the latest thing: blond Swedish chairs and folding table (made of birch with natural finish) in the dinette, which was separated from the kitchen by a slatted folding door; in the living room, a bright-red modern couch and armchairs to match, a love seat covered in striped gray-and-white mattress ticking, steel standing lamps, a coffee table that was just a sheet of glass that Harald had had cut at the glazier's and mounted on steel legs, built-in bookcases that Harald had painted canary yellow. There were no rugs yet and, instead of curtains, only white Venetian blinds at the windows.

Instead of flowers, they had ivy growing in white pots. In the bedroom, instead of a bed, they had a big innerspring mattress with another mattress on top of it; Harald had nailed red pegs to the bottom one to keep it off the floor.

Instead of a dress, Kay was wearing a cherry-red velvet sleeveless hostess gown (Harald's Christmas present) from Bendel's; they had an old colored maid from Harlem passing canapes in a modern sectioned hors d'oeuvre tray. Instead of cocktails, they had had Fish House Punch, made from One Dagger Rum, in a punch bowl with twenty-four matching glass cups they had borrowed from Priss Hartshorn Crockett, who had got it for a wedding present when she was married in Oyster Bay in September.

On *that* occasion, only four of the group had been able to make it. Today, *mirabile dictu*, the only one missing was Lakey, who was now in Spain. Pokey Prothero had flown down from Cornell Agricultural in a helmet and goggles; Helena Davison, who had spent the summer and fall in Europe, was in town from Cleveland. Dottie Renfrew had come back from Arizona, where her family had sent her for her health, with a marvelous tan and an engagement ring—a diamond almost as big as her eyes; she was going to marry a mining man who owned half the state.

This was quite a change from Dottie's modest plans for working in a settlement house and living at home in Boston. "You'd miss the concerts and the theatre," Helena had remarked dryly. But Dottie said that Arizona had a great deal to offer too. There were lots of interesting people who had gone there because of T.B. and fallen in love with the country—musicians and painters and architects, and there was the riding and the incredible wild flowers of the desert, not to mention the Indians and some fascinating archaeological digs that attracted scientists from Harvard.

The party was almost over; only one mink coat was left in the bedroom. At the high point, there had been five—Harald had counted them. Kay's supervisor's, Harald's producer's wife's, Connie Storey's, Dottie's, and a mink-lined greatcoat belonging to Connie's fiance, that apple-cheeked boy who worked on *For-tune*. Now Dottie's lay in solitary state, next to Helena's ocelot and a peculiar garment made of old gray wolf that belonged to Norine Schmittlapp Blake, another member of the Vassar contingent. Harald's producer had left after half an hour, with his wife (who had the money) and a star who had replaced Judith Anderson in *As You Desire Me*, but the Class of '33 had practically held a reunion, there was so much news to keep up with: Libby MacAusland had sold a poem to

Harper's; Priss was pregnant; Helena had seen Lakey in Munich and met Miss Sandison in the British Museum; Norine Schmittlapp, who was there withher husband (the one in the black shirt), had been to the Scottsboro trial; Prexy (bless his heart!) had had lunch on a tray with Roosevelt in the White House. . . .

Helena, who was Class Correspondent, took a *few* terse mental notes. "At Kay Strong Petersen's," she foresaw herself inditing for the next issue of the *Alumnae Magazine*, "I saw Dottie Ren-frew, who is going to marry Brook Latham and live in Arizona. 'The Woman Who Rode Away'—how about it, Dottie? Brook is a widower—see the Class Prophecy. Kay's husband, Harald, has sold his play, *Sheepskin*, to the producer, Paul Bergler-watch out, Harald. The play is slated for fall production; Walter Huston is reading the script. Norine Schmittlapp's husband, Putnam Blake (Williams '30), has started an independent fund-raising organization for labor and left-wing causes. Volunteer workers take note. His partner is Bill Nickum (Yale '29). Charles Dickens take note. Polly Andrews reports that Sis Farnsworth and Lely Baker have started a business called 'Dog Walk.' It keeps them outdoors, Polly says, and they're swamped with applications from people who don't have butlers any more to take their canines walking in the Park. . . ."

Helena puckered her little forehead. Had she mastered (mistressed?) the idiom of the *Alumnae Magazine* Class Notes? She and Dottie were in the living room, waiting tactfully to get their coats to leave. Harald and Kay were in the bedroom with the door closed, having "words," she supposed. The party, to quote the host, had laid an egg. The main body of guests had decamped just as the old colored maid had appeared, all smiles, with a Washington's Birthday cake she had brought for a present. Harald, reddening, had shooed her back to the kitchen, so as not to let people see, presumably, that they had been expected to stay longer. But Kay, who had always been a blurter, had let the cat out of the bag. "But Harald was going to read his play!" she cried sadly after the departing guests. The whole party had been planned around that, she confided. Now the maid had gone home with her satchel, and the only guests remaining, besides Helena herself and Dottie, were a radio actor, who was helping himself copiously at the punch bowl, the two Blakes, and a naval officer Harald had met in a bar, whose sister was married to a famous architect who used ramps instead of stairs. The actor, who had wavy hair in a pompadour, was arguing with Norine about Harald's play. "The trouble is, Norine, the line of the play is sheer toboggan. I told Harald that when he read it to me. It's very

interesting, the way you've done it, but I wonder: is it a *play*?'" He gestured, and some punch from his cup fell on his suit. "If the audience identifies with a character, they want to feel he has a chance to win. But Harald's view of life is too blackly logical to give them that sop." Across the room, Putnam Blake, a thin, white-faced young man with a close collegiate haircut, an unsmiling expression, and a low, tense voice, was explaining what he called his "Principle of Accumulated Guilt" to the naval officer.

"Mr. Blake," said Dottie with a twinkle, "has a system for finding rich people to give money to Labor. He was telling about it earlier. It sounds terribly interesting," she added warmly. Glancing at their watches, at Norine and the actor, and at the closed bedroom door, the two girls drew near to listen. Putnam ignored them, dividing his attention between his pipe and the naval officer. Using Gustavus Myers' *Great American Fortunes*, Poor's *Register of Directors*, and Mendel's Law, he was able to predict, he said, when a wealthy family was "due." As a rule, this occurred in the third generation. "What I've done," he said, "is take the element of chance out of fund-raising and put it on a scientific basis. I'm simplifying, of course, but roughly speaking the money guilt has a tendency to skip a generation. Or if it crops out in the second generation, as with the Lamont family, you will find it in a younger son rather than in the first-born. And it may be transmitted to the females while remaining dormant in the males. This means that the guilt tends to separate from the chief property holdings, which are usually transmitted from first-born male to first-born male. Thus the guilt, being a recessive character, like blue eyes, may be bred out of a family without any profit to the Left." A ghostly quiver, the phantom of a smile, passed across his lips; he appeared eager to take the naval officer into his confidence, like some crazy inventor, thought Helena, with a patent, and it was as if some bashful ectoplasmic joke hovered in the neighborhood of his Principle. "I'm working now," he continued, "on the relation between mental deficiency and money guilt in rich families. Your ideal contributor (the Communists have found this), scion of a for-tune, has a mental age of twelve." Without altering his expression, he gave a quick parenthetic little laugh.

FOCUS QUESTIONS:

1. How are the social roles of women defined here? What about their economic roles?

2. Would a male participant in this scene likely have described it differently? If so, in what way(s)?

19-6 "What's Become of Rosie the Riveter?"

As war-time manufacturing wound down, and veterans returned home, the many women – symbolized by "Rosie the Riveter" – who had found work at defense industry factories, found themselves out of their jobs. This was a difficult adjustment, both economically and in terms of identity. Frieda S. Miller, director of the women's bureau at the U.S. Department of Labor, wrote an article for the New York Times Magazine discussing this transition.

Source: Miller, Frieda. "What's Become of Rosie the Riveter?" *New York Times Magazine.* May 5, 1946, 21

What's Become of Rosie the Riveter?

Her numbers reduced by millions since July, she is involved in a tremendous reshuffling.

By Frieda S. Miler

Director, Women's Bureau, United State Department of Labor

When a character captures the imagination of the American public, his ups and downs are followed with an interest that sometimes surpasses avidity. Thus it is with Rosie the Riveter, who symbolized to America the effort of all women workers toward winning the war.

Today, there is little doubt that Rosie and her industrial sisters are fading from the scene of heavy manufacturing. Since V-E Day, about a million women production workers have left that nation's aircraft plants, shipyards, ammunitions factories and other industries that produced so prodigiously for war. The sharpest decline, of course, followed victory over Japan, but the trend had started even before V-E Day in the shipyards and aircraft plants, large wartime employers of women among the durable goods industries.

As a result of this exodus of women factory workers, the public is asking: Where have Rosie and the rest of the heroines of the war production front gone? What are they planning to do now that men are taking over? Is it true that these women, despite their gallant war service, are finding factory doors to heavy industry closed to them?

Positive answers to all of these questions are not easy in a period of readjustment. Rosie and her sisters, like millions of men and women, have become involved in the most tremendous reshuffling of human resources, both occupationally and geographically, that the country ever has know. Some answers, however, have emerged with a certain clarity, and one of these is the whereabouts of Rosie the Riveter and the women for whom she became a wartime symbol.

Some of the former riveters and other industrial workers, wearied by the long grind of forty-eight hours and more per week and the exacting task of producing for war, are taking well-earned rests before putting out feelers about post –war jobs. Still others, particularly a number of the young women whose husbands have been demobilized from the armed services, they are waiting to see how their veteran husbands fare in the readjustments to civilian life.

If the ex-GI can bring home enough pay in his weekly envelope to support a wife and establish a home, the form Rosie will at least have the chance to devote their entire time to homemaking and some of them are sure to take it. One the other hand, if the husband wishes to continue his education, start in business for himself, or for some reason or another does not immediately resume his breadwinning role, the wife may find her pay check badly needed. In that even, she probably will seek another job, though the job in all likelihood will not be similar to her wartime occupation, as disappointing as that fact will be–and has been to other displaced women war workers.

Some of the wartime factory workers, of course, already have new jobs–in consumer goods plants, laundries, stores, restaurants, hotels, beauty shops and other civilian services. From records of employment, however, this number is not large, for the employment of women in all types of work has decreased by more than 4 million since last July or dropped from about 19 1/2 million to around 15 1/2 million. In view of this large decline, the number of women looking for work –about half a million, according to the latest estimate–is surprisingly small, only 40,000 more than last July.

In the light of the long-time trend of women's increasing participation in the work life of the nation, this appears to be accounted for not by the fact that women as workers are showing a tendency to withdraw from paid employment but by certain characteristics of the present transitional period. Important among these are: (1) The reabsorption of returning service men; (2) the indecision of some worker, both men and women concerning their future plans; (3) the lack of job opportunities commensurate with the skills and wages of displaced women; (4) the desire of some places workers to take a rest before looking for jobs; and (5) the expected voluntary withdrawal of large numbers of women who were duration workers. Other factors contributing to the decline in the number of women workers during the period from last July to the present were the withdrawal of seasonal workers and teenagers.

Much has been written and said about the fact that reconverted heavy industries are closing their doors, for the most part, to the very women they depended on during the war. This frequently has been referred to as marking "the end of industry's courtship of women workers." Undoubtedly, heavy industry no longer is courting the riveters, the welders and machine operators who help to make victory possible and in this fact may be reflected some of the prejudice that always has been leveled at women by certain sections of industry. The inference, however, that prejudice alone accounts for this trek of women from the war plants is both unfair and unsound.

Prior to the war, women were less that 1 per cent of the wage-earners in the shipbuilding industry. Women riveters, welders or crane operators would have been considered by some employers as fanciful as a tale from the "Arabian Nights." Yet, during the war, women production worker in commercial and Navy yards reached about 150,000. In the aircraft industry, which had only 4,000 women factory workers the week before the Pearl Harbor attack, the numbers rose to over 350,000, and women became more than a third of all workers producing such giants of the air as Liberators, B-29's, and the swift fighters that help to spell victory.

Today with peace at hand, our nation no longer needs these ships of war or the vast army of men and women who produce them. Women, relatively speaking, were newcomers to the shipyard and aircraft plants and, as such, were the first to feel the impact of cutbacks. Additionally, there were scores of factories that owed their very existence to war. Foremost among these were the ammunition plants, in which women formed more that 41 per cent of all workers. Obviously, many of these factories have no peacetime future.

Women workers themselves, for the most part, are cognizant of the workings of the seniority system under which American industry operates. Since they generally were that last to come, it came as no surprise to them that they were the first to go. Most of them,

however, liked the new and shining factories of which they became a part. They liked the up-to-date equipment, the comfortable dressing rooms, the music that came to them through the loudspeaker system.

But more than the refinements, they liked the regular and higher pay that came in their weekly envelopes. It is in the pay that is being offered them with the current openings that they are most disappointed. This interest in the pay check is not peculiar to their sex. It is, as one woman riveter put it, "just the plain American desire to get ahead."

Women workers do not want to get ahead at the expense of veterans. In fact, they never have regarded their work as a substitute for that of men. Their own record of achievement over a long period of years obviates that need or desire. Even before the war, they were a fourth of all the nation's employed persons, and a half or more of those engaged in domestic service, medical and other health services, educational services, telephone services, hotels and lodging places, limited price variety stores, general merchandise stores and in the manufacture of apparel and accessories, tobacco, knit goods and miscellaneous products made from textiles.

Contrary to the opinion held by many persons, even during the height of our spectacular war production, the bulk of the nation's employed women were hard at work on the kinds of jobs women always had performed. Unsung and unheralded, millions of women did their part for victory by staffing the stores, laundries, restaurants, consumer-goods plants and other establishments and industries that gave necessary underpinning to war production. The needs of these women, as well as those of the displaced war workers, must be taken into account in the various plans that were made for women.

ROSIE THE RIVETER and her industrial coworkers, as it was pointed out at a recent Women's Bureau conference on the post-war employment problems of women, upgraded themselves during the war. They would like to retain some, if not all, of the gains. Because expanding opportunities for women appear to be in the extension of established services and in the development of new services that post-war America will want and need rather than in the old-line industries in which men have predominated, the industrial worker's gains may not be measured in terms of retaining their war-acquired skills. If America accepts the challenge, they can be measured in other terms: Wages that permit them to maintain the standards of living they already have achieved, hours of work that are conducive to health and decency standards, and working environments that are a far cry from those of some pre-war establishments.

Closely related to the question of wages is the matter of equal pay, or objective rates based on the content of the job rather than on the sex of workers. As Senator Wayne Morse, co-author of the pending Federal equal-pay legislation, has pointed out, the principles of equal pay goes far beyond being a matter of plain justice to women. Because it rests on a sound economic basis, such a practice promotes the general welfare of the community and the nation by promoting wage levels and sustaining the purchasing power of all concerned. Women's awareness of this fact is one of the reasons why they feel that we cannot afford the treat that unequal pay to them involves. They have a deep, natural interest in the welfare of their families and realize that every time a working man's income is reduced through the competition of workers who can be hired at lower rates than those prevailing, the family of the man inevitably suffers a lower standard of living.

These needs of women workers have long existed, and for just as many years they have been recognized by individuals and agencies interested in wages earning woman. Through concerted action notable gains have been made in minimum wage legislation, in State equal-pay laws, and through other measures sponsored by unions and progressive employers. A great deal, however, remains to be done before Rosie the Riveter, Winnie the Welder, and other women of the war sorority of industrial workers will be content to return to the women-employing fields that are characterized by substandard wages and unreasonably long hours.

These changes are needed not only for the sake of Rosie and other returning war workers but for the benefit of the thousands of women who stuck to their jobs in the service industries throughout the war. The plight of Rosie and her highly praised war companies may serve, however, to focus public attention on the issue, Club women, unions and other champions of women already have made considerable progress in the direction and a few individual communities–though not nearly enough–are including women in their programs for post-war workers.

Secretary of Labor Schwellenbach, in an address before key representatives of more than 70 organizations who attended a recent Women's Bureau conference on the employment problems of women, summed up the needs of women workers and issued a challenge to post-war American when he said:

"Certain artificial restrictions that belong to a past age should not be allowed to handicap the contribution women can make… for instance, no bars should be erected against the employment of women married or single, in work they can do under physically healthful conditions… no pay scale should discriminate against them. As members of a free society, women should be enabled to choose the way of life that permits them to make their fullest contribution to the world's upbuilding."

FOCUS QUESTIONS:

1. For what audience did Miller write in this piece? Is she simply reporting, or is she advocating any policy or agenda?

2. Why, according to Miller, did women enjoy their wartime defense-industry jobs? Does Miller believe they are likely to again find work that is as satisfying, or remunerative?

19-7 Lorraine Hansberry, Under the Impression that Negroes are People

Lorraine Hansberry's successful Broadway play A Raisin in the Sun presented issues of racism and segregation through the experiences of a black Chicago family. The 1959 play was followed by numerous film and theater adaptations. Hansberry wrote speeches and essays supporting the Civil Rights Movement, before dying in 1965.

Source: Nemiroff, Robert. *To Be Young, Gifted, and Black: Lorraine Hansberry in Her Own Words.* Englewood Cliffs, N.J.: Prentice-Hall, Inc, 1969. pp. 113-114.

INTERVIEWER

The question, I'm sure, is asked you many times—you maybe tired of it—someone comes up to you and says: "This is not really a Negro play; why, this could be about anybody! It's a play about people!" What is your reaction? What do you say?

L. H.

Well, I hadn't noticed the contradiction because I'd always been under the impression that Negroes are people. But actually it's an excellent question, because invariably that has been the point of reference. And I do know what people are trying to say. People are trying—what they are trying to say is that this is not what they consider the traditional treatment of the Negro in the theater. They're trying to say that it isn't a propaganda play, that it isn't something that hits you over the head; they are trying to say that they believe the characters in our play transcend category. However, it is an unfortunate way to try and say it, because I believe that one of the most sound ideas in dramatic writing is that in order to create the universal, you must pay very great attention to the specific. Universality, I think, emerges from truthful identity of what is. In other words, I have told people that not only is this a Negro family, specifically and definitely culturally, but it's not even a New York family or a southern Negro family. It is specifically Southside Chicago. . . . that kind of care, that kind of attention to detail. In other words, I think people, to the extent we accept them and believe them as who they're supposed to be, to that extent they can become everybody. So I would say it is definitely a Negro play before it is anything else. . . .

FOCUS QUESTIONS:

1. Is Hansberry's point convincing? Do you find it in any way controversial?

2. Why does Hansberry begin her reply with humor?

19-8 Working Mothers, Pro and Con

The circumstances under which mothers should work (if any) have been debated in various media for decades. The first of these two letters was prompted by a radio call-in program.

Source: "Letters – Pro and Con." *American Journal of Nursing.* October 1955, 1160.

Women's Place

Dear Journal:

I heard something over the radio recently that worries me. It was one of those problems put before an audience for solution.

The problem was that of a 36-year-old woman, married to a farmer, with three children, the youngest being one year old. She asked whether she should leave the farm and the children and go to school to become a teacher so that she would help her husband and children financially. It would take her three to four years to get her degree. Both a hospital nurse and a public health nurse advised this woman to go and complete her education.

Is this what we are training our nurses for? Have we put such emphasis on education ourselves that members of the profession can stand up in public and advocate that a woman leave her children? Is a distant-future security more important than a very present need of growing children? The school teachers in the audience were against that mother leaving her children. They can recognize the difference in children reared by a mother and those that rear themselves. Are nurses any less interested in the well-being of the younger generation?

Many nurses are leaving their own children without proper supervision while they go out and earn the almighty dollar. Aren't nurses taught child development so that they can use it in their own lives? Some nurses work until they deliver their babies during the coffee break. Do we advocate such activity for the pre- and postpartum woman? Are we in the category of people who do not practice what they preach? Joy DeLeon, R.N., Wisconsin.

Women's Place

Dear Journal:

I write in opposition to the letter on "Women's Place" in the July Journal.

I am a married woman with two children. One is eight and a half and one is six years old. I had to leave my husband and children for nine months to complete my nursing education two years ago. But I did not leave them until I was certain that they could be well taken care of.

As a result of my nursing experience we have

become a closer family unit than we were before. I am now practicing nursing with no ill effects to my family; in fact, they are proud and pleased that I am a nurse. They do not feel that I am neglecting them in any way. My husband and children fully understand the need for nurses and also the effort and time involved in ministering to the sick. They learn a great deal through my nursing experience about public health and the general aspects of health problems which they in turn share with their friends. – Elinor Quandt, R.N., NJ

FOCUS QUESTIONS:

1. Are both letters equally clear and logical?

2. Does it matter that the work under discussion is nursing? Do the letter-writers believe it matters?

3. Why does this topic continue to excite strong opinions, both pro and con?

19-9 Ladies Home Journal, "Young Mother" (1956)

The post-World War Two years witnessed a tremendous baby boom that led to great interest in family life. The mother was seen as the person responsible for maintaining the house, raising the children, and caring for the husband. In some cases, the mother not only received little or no help, but often was an unequal partner in the family and received little recognition for the work she did.

Mrs. Gould: As editors and parents we are extremely interested in this whole problem. The welfare of our society depends upon the type of children you young mothers and others like you are able to bring up. Anything that affects the welfare of young families is most crucial, and I do feel that the young mother, any young mother in our day, should get far more general recognition and attention than she does-not so much for her own sake as for society as a whole, or just out of sheer common sense.

Miss Hickey: And understanding. I think there is a lack of understanding, too. Since it would take all day to tell what a busy woman does all day . . . how about your high points?

Mrs. Petry: I would say in the morning-breakfast and wash time. I put the breakfast out, leave the children to eat it and run into the bathroom-that is where the washer is-and fill it up. I come back into the kitchen and shove a little in the baby's mouth and try to keep

the others eating. Then I go back in the bathroom and put the clothes in the wringer and start the rinse water. That is about the end of the half-hour there. I continue then to finish the wash, and either put them out or let them see one program they like on television, and then I go out and hang the wash up.

Miss Hickey: You put that outside?

Mrs. Petry: Yes. Then I eat.

Mrs. Gould: Can you sit down and eat in peace? Are the children outdoors at that time or watching television?

Mrs. Petry: They are supposed to be outside, but they are usually running in and out. Somebody forgot something he should have eaten, or wants more milk, or a toy or something. Finally I lock the screen door. I always read something while I'm eating-two meals a day I read. When my husband isn't there, and if I am alone, or maybe just one child at the table, I read something quick. But I time it. I take no more than half an hour for eating and reading.

Miss Hickey: You work on schedule quite a bit. Why do you do that?

Mrs. Petry: Because I am very forgetful. I have an orange crayon and I write "defrost" on the refrigerator every now and then, or I forget to defrost it. If I think of something while I am washing, I write it on the mirror with an eyebrow pencil. It must sound silly, but that is the only way I can remember everything I have to do. . . .

Miss Hickey: Mrs. Ehrhardt, your quietest half-hour?

Mrs. Ehrhardt: I would say . . . that when I go out to take the wash in. There is something about getting outdoors-and I don't get out too often, except to hang out the wash and to bring it in. I really enjoy doing it. If it is a nice day, I stand outside and fold it outdoors. I think that is my quietest hour.

Miss Hickey: How often do you and your husband go out together in the evening?

Mrs. Ehrhardt: Not often. An occasional movie, which might be every couple of months or so, on an anniversary. This year is the first year we celebrated on the day we were married. We were married in June. We always celebrated it, but it might be in July or August.

It depends on our babysitter. If you cannot get anyone, you just cannot go out. I am not living near my family and I won't leave the children with teenagers. I would be afraid it might be a little hectic, and a young girl might not know what to do. So we don't get out very often. . . .

Miss Hickey: Let us hear about Mrs. Petry's recreation.

Mrs. Petry: Oh, I went to work in a department store that opened in Levittown. I begged and begged my husband to let me work, and finally he said I could go once or twice a week. I lasted for three weeks, or should I say he lasted for three weeks.

Mrs. Gould: You mean you worked in the daytime?

Mrs. Petry: Three evenings, from six until nine, and on Saturday.

Mrs. Gould: And your husband took care of the children during that time?

Mrs. Petry: Yes, but the third week, he couldn't stand it anymore, Saturday and all. In fact, I think he had to work that Saturday, so I asked if I could just come in to the store during the week. My husband was hoping they would fire me, but they didn't. But I could see that it wasn't really fair to him, because I was going out for my own pleasure.

Mrs. Gould: In other words, your working was your recreation.

Mrs. Petry: Yes, and I enjoyed it very much.

Miss Hickey: Why did you feel you wanted to do this?

Mrs. Petry: To see some people and talk to people, just to see what is going on in the world. . . Miss Hickey: How about your shopping experiences?

Mrs. McKenzie: Well, I don't go in the evening, because I cannot depend on Ed being home; and when

he is there, he likes to have me there too. I don't know. Usually all three of the children go shopping with me. At one time I carried two and dragged the other one along behind me in the cart with the groceries. It is fun to take them all. Once a man stopped me and said, "Lady, did you know your son is eating hamburger?" He had eaten a half- pound of raw hamburger. When corn on the cob was so expensive, my oldest one begged me to buy corn on the cob, so I splurged and bought three ears for thirty-nine cents. When I got to the check-out counter, I discovered he had eaten all three, so he had to pay for the cobs.

Miss Hickey: You go once a week?

Mrs. McKenzie: Once a week or every ten days now, depending on how often I have the use of the car. That day we usually go to the park, too. . . .

Miss Hickey: Tell us about your most recent crisis.

Mrs. McKenzie: I had given a birthday party for fifteen children in my little living room, which is seven by eleven. The next morning my son, whose birthday it had been, broke out with the measles, so I had exposed fifteen children to measles, and I was the most unpopular mother in the neighborhood.

He was quite sick, and it snowed that day. Ed took Lucy sleigh riding. Both of them fell off the sled and she broke both the bones in her arm.

Mrs. Gould: Did she then get the measles?

Mrs. McKenzie: She did, and so did the baby. . . . My main problem was being in quarantine for a month. During this time that all three had measles and Lucy had broken her arm, we got a notice from the school that her tuberculin test was positive-and that meant that one of the adults living in our home had active tuberculosis. It horrified me. I kept thinking, "Here I sit killing my three children with tuberculosis." But we had to wait until they were over their contagion period before we could all go in and get x-rayed.

Miss Hickey: And the test was not correct?

Mrs. McKenzie: She had had childhood tuberculosis, but it was well healed and she was all right. About eight often have had childhood tuberculosis and no one knows it.

Mrs. Gould: It is quite common, but it is frightening when it occurs to you. Were your children quite sick with measles?

Mrs. McKenzie: Terribly ill.

Mrs. Gould: They had high temperatures?

Mrs. McKenzie: My children are a great deal like my

father. Anything they do, they do to extreme. They are violently ill, or they are as robust as can be. There is no in-between. . . .

Dr. Montagu: There is one very large question I would like to ask. What in your lives, as they are at present, would you most like to see changed or modified?

Mrs. Ehrhardt: Well, I would like to be sure my husband's position would not require him to be transferred so often. I would like to stay in place long enough to take a few roots in the community. It would also be nice to haves someone help with the housework, but I don't think I would like to have anyone live in. The houses nowadays are too small. I think you would bump into each other. Of course, I have never had any one in, so I cannot honestly, give an opinion.

Mrs. Townsend: At the present time, I don't think there is anything that I would like to change in the household. We happen to be very close, and we are all very happy. I will admit that there are times when I am a little overtired, andI might be a little more than annoyed with the children, but actually it doesn't last too long. We do have a problem where we live now. There aren't any younger children for my children to play with. Therefore, they are underneath my heels just constantly, and I am not able to take the older children out the way I would like to, because of the two babies.

Miss Hickey: You have been in how many communities?

Mrs. Townsend: I have lived in Louisiana, California, New York, and for a short period in Columbia, South Carolina. . . .

Miss Hickey: Mrs. Petry, what would you change?

Mrs. Petry: I would like more time to enjoy my children. I do take time, but if I do take as much time as I like, the work piles up. When I go back to work I feel crabby, and I don't know whether I'm mad at the children, or mad at the work or just mad at everybody sometimes.

I would also like to have a little more rest and a little more time to spend in relaxation with my husband. We never get to go out together, and the only time we have much of a conversation is just before we go to bed. And I would like to have a girl come and do my ironing.

I am happy there where we live because this is the first time we have stayed anywhere for any length of time. It will be two years in August, and it is the first home we have really had. That is why my husband left the Navy. I nearly had a nervous collapse, because it seemed I couldn't stand another minute not having him home and helping, or not helping, but just being there.

FOCUS QUESTIONS:

1. What vision of Suburban American life is formed from these accounts?

2. What seems to be the prescribed roles for women in these accounts?

19-10 The Feminist Mystique (1963)

Journalist Betty Freidan wrote The Feminine Mystique to expose the social mechanisms used to oppress women. In theory, middle class women were provided with the same opportunities as men, but social expectations regarding men and women were not equal and did not change significantly overtime. More than at any other time in recent history, the 1950s were a period during which women were assaulted with articles and images that defined their existence in the domestic sphere and required them to register supine contentment with that status. As Friedan undertook to define "the problem that has no name," she launched a new era in the movement for women's rights.

Source: Betty Friedan, *The Feminine Mystique*, (New York: Norton, 1963), pp. 15-32.

THE PROBLEM THAT HAS NO NAME

The problem lay buried, unspoken, for many years in the minds of American women. It was a strange stirring, a sense of dissatisfaction, a yearning that women suffered in the middle of the twentieth century in the United States. Each suburban wife struggled with it alone. As she made the beds, shopped for groceries, matched slipcover material, ate peanut butter sandwiches with her children, chauffeured Cub Scouts and Brownies, lay beside her husband at night—she was afraid to ask even of herself the silent question—"Is this all?"

For over fifteen years there was no word of this yearning in the millions of words written about women, for women, in all the columns, books and articles by experts telling women their role was to seek fulfillment as wives and mothers. Over and over women heard in voices of tradition and of Freudian sophistication that they could desire no greater destiny than to glory in their own femininity. Experts told them how to catch a man and keep him, how to breastfeed children and handle their toilet training, how to cope with sibling rivalry and adolescent rebellion; how to buy a dishwasher, bake bread, cook gourmet snails, and build a swimming pool with their own hands; how to dress, look, and act more feminine and make marriage more exciting; how to keep their husbands from dying young and their sons from growing into delinquents. They were taught to pity the neurotic, unfeminine, unhappy women who wanted to be poets or physicists or presidents. They learned that truly feminine women do not want careers, higher education, political rights—the independence and the opportunities that the old-fashioned feminists fought for. Some women, in their forties and fifties, still remembered painfully giving up those dreams, but most of the younger women no longer even thought about them. A thousand expert voices applauded their femininity, their adjustment, their new maturity. All they had to do was devote their lives from earliest girlhood to finding a husband and bearing children.

* * *

By the end of the fifties, the United States birthrate was overtaking India's. The birth-control movement, renamed Planned Parenthood, was asked to find a method whereby women who had been advised that a third or fourth baby would be born dead or defective might have it anyhow. Statisticians were especially astounded at the fantastic increase in the number of babies among college women. Where once they had two children, now they had four, five, six. Women who had once wanted careers were now making careers out of having babies. So rejoiced *Life* magazine in a 1956 paean to the movement of American women back to the home.

In a New York hospital, a woman had a nervous breakdown when she found she could not breastfeed her baby. In other hospitals, women dying of cancer refused a drug which research had proved might save their lives: its side effects were said to be unfeminine. "If I have only one life, let me live it as a blonde," a larger-than-life-sized picture of a pretty, vacuous woman proclaimed from newspaper, magazine, and drugstore ads. And across America, three out of every ten women dyed their hair blonde. They ate a chalk called Metrecal, instead of food, to shrink to the size of the thin young models. Department-store buyers reported that American women, since 1939, had become three and four sizes smaller. "Women are out to fit the clothes, instead of vice-versa," one buyer said.

Interior decorators were designing kitchens with mosaic murals and original paintings, for kitchens were once again the center of women's lives. Home sewing became a million-dollar industry. Many women no longer left their homes, except to shop, chauffeur their children, or attend a social engagement with their husbands. Girls were growing up in America without ever having jobs outside the home. In the late fifties, a sociological phenomenon was suddenly remarked: a third of American women now worked, but most were no longer young and very few were pursuing careers. They were married women who held part-time jobs, selling or secretarial, to put their husbands through school, their sons through college, or to help pay the mortgage. Or they were widows supporting families. Fewer and fewer women were entering professional work. The shortages in the nursing, social work, and teaching professions caused crises in almost every American city. Concerned over the Soviet Union's lead in the space race, scientists noted that America's greatest source of unused brainpower was women. But girls would not study physics: it was "unfeminine." A girl refused a science fellowship at Johns Hopkins to take a job in a real-estate office. All she wanted, she said, was what every other American girl wanted—to get married, have four children and live in a nice house in a nice suburb.

The suburban housewife—she was the dream image of the young American women and the envy, it was said, of women all over the world. The American housewife—freed by science and labor-saving appliances from the drudgery, the dangers of childbirth and the illnesses of her grandmother. She was healthy, beautiful, educated, concerned only about her husband, her children, her home. She had found true feminine fulfillment. As a housewife and mother, she was respected as a full and equal partner to man in his world. She was free to choose automobiles, clothes, appliances, supermarkets; she had everything that women ever dreamed of.

In the fifteen years after World War II, this mystique of feminine fulfillment became the cherished and self-perpetuating core of contemporary American culture. Millions of women lived their lives in the image of those pretty pictures of the American suburban housewife, kissing their husbands goodbye in front of the picture window, depositing their station wagonsful of children at school, and smiling as they ran the new electric waxer over the spotless kitchen floor. They baked their own bread, sewed their own and their children's clothes, kept their new washing machines and dryers running all day. They changed the sheets on the beds twice a week instead of once, took the rug-hooking class in adult education, and pitied their poor frustrated mothers, who had dreamed of having a career. Their only dream was to be perfect wives and mothers; their highest ambition to have five children and a beautiful house, their only fight to get and keep their husbands. They had no thought for the unfeminine problems of the world outside the home; they wanted the men to make the major decisions. They gloried in their role as women, and wrote proudly on the census blank: "Occupation: housewife."

* * *

If a woman had a problem in the 1950's and 1960's, she knew that something must be wrong with her marriage, or with herself. Other women were satisfied with their lives, she thought. What kind of a women was she if she did not feel this mysterious fulfillment waxing the kitchen floor? She was so ashamed to admit her dissatisfaction that she never knew how many other women shared it. If she tried to tell her husband, he didn't understand what she was talking about. She did not really understand it herself. For over fifteen years women in America found it harder to talk about this problem than about sex. Even the psychoanalysts had no name for it. When a women went to a psychiatrist for help, as many women did, she would say, "I'm so ashamed," or "I must be hopelessly neurotic." "I don't know what's wrong with women today," a suburban psychiatrist said uneasily. "I only know something is wrong because most of my patients happen to be women. And their problem isn't sexual." Most women with this problem did not go to see a psychoanalyst, however, "There's nothing wrong really," they kept telling themselves. "There isn't any problem."

But on an April morning in 1959, I heard a mother of four, having coffee with four other mothers in a suburban development fifteen miles from New York, say in a tone of quiet desperation, "the problem." And the others knew, without words, that she was not talking about a problem with her husband, or her children, or her home. Suddenly they realized they all shared the same problem, the problem that has no name. They began, hesitantly, to talk about it. Later, after they had picked up their children at nursery school and taken them home to nap, two of the women cried, in sheer relief, just to know they were not alone.

Gradually I came to realize that the problem that has no name was shared by countless women in America

* * *

Just what was this problem that has no name? What were the words women used when they tried to express it? Sometimes a woman would say "I feel empty somehow . . . incomplete." Or she would say, "I feel as if I don't exist." Sometimes she blotted out the feeling with a tranquilizer. Sometimes she thought the problem was with her husband, or her children, or that what she really needed was to redecorate her house, or move to a better neighborhood, or have an affair, or another baby. Sometimes, she went to a doctor with symptoms she could hardly describe: "A tired feeling . . . I get so angry with the children it scares me . . . I feel like crying without any reason." (A Cleveland doctor called it "the house-wife's syndrome.") A number of women told me about great bleeding blisters that break out on their hands and arms. "I call it the housewife's blight," said a family doctor in Pennsylvania. "I see it so often lately in these young women with four, five and six children who bury themselves in their dishpans. But it isn't caused by detergent and it isn't cured by cortisone."

* * *

In 1960, the problem that has no name burst like a boil through the image of the happy American housewife. In the television commercials the pretty housewives still beamed over their foaming dishpans and *Time's* cover story on "The Suburban Wife, an American Phenomenon" protested: "Having too good a time . . . to believe that they should be unhappy." But the actual unhappiness of the American housewife was suddenly being reported—from the *New York Times* and *Newsweek* to *Good Housekeeping* and CBS Television ("The Trapped Housewife"), although almost everybody who talked about it found some superficial reason to dismiss it. It was attributed to incompetent appliance repairmen (*New York Times*), or the distances children must be chauffeured in the suburbs (*Time*), or too much PTA (*Redbook*). Some said it was the old problem—education: more and more women had education, which naturally made them unhappy in their role as housewives. "the road from Freud to Frigidaire, from Sophocles to Spock, has turned out to be a bumpy one," reported the *New York Times* (June 28, 1960). "Many young women—certainly not all—whose education plunged them into a world of ideas feel stifled in their homes. They find their routine lives out of joint with their training. Like shut-ins, they feel left out. In the last year, the problem of the educated housewife has provided the meat of dozens of speeches made by troubled presidents of women's colleges who maintain, in the face of complaints, that sixteen years of academic training is realistic preparation for wifehood and motherhood."

There was much sympathy for the educated housewife. ("Like a two-headed schizophrenic . . . once she wrote a paper on the Graveyard poets; now she writes notes to the milkman. Once she determined the boiling point of sulphuric acid; now she determines her boiling point with the overdue repairman. . . . The housewife often is reduced to screams and tears. . . . No one, it seems, is appreciative, least of all herself, of the kind of person she becomes in the process of turning from poetess into shrew.")

* * *

A bitter laugh was beginning to be heard from American women. They were admired, envied, pitied, theorized over until they were sick of it, offered drastic solutions or silly choices that no one could take seriously. They got all kinds of advice from the growing armies of marriage and child-guidance counselors, psychotherapists, and armchair psychologists, on how to adjust to their role as housewives. No other road to fulfillment was offered to American women in the middle of the twentieth century. Most adjusted to their role and suffered or ignored the problem that has no name. It can be less painful, for a woman, not to hear the strange, dissatisfied voice stirring within her.

It is no longer possible to ignore that voice, to dismiss the desperation of so many American women. This is not what being a woman means, no matter what the experts say. For human suffering there is a reason; perhaps the reason has not been found because the right questions have not been asked, or pressed far enough. I do not accept the answer that there is no problem because American women have luxuries that women in other times and lands never dreamed of; part of the strange newness of the problem is that it cannot be understood in terms of the age-old material problems of man: poverty, sickness, hunger, cold. The women who suffer this problem have a hunger that food cannot fill. It persists in women whose husbands are struggling interns and law clerks, or prosperous doctors and lawyers; in wives of workers and executives who make $5,000 a year or $50,000. It is not caused by lack of material advantages; it may not even be felt by women preoccupied with desperate problems of hunger, poverty or illness. And women who think it will be solved by more money, a bigger house, a second car, moving to a better suburb, often discover it gets worse.

It is no longer possible today to blame the problem on loss of femininity: to say that education and independence and equality with men have made American women unfeminine. I have heard so many women try to deny this dissatisfied voice within themselves because it does not fit the pretty picture of femininity the experts have given them. I think, in fact, that this is the first clue to the mystery: the problem cannot be understood in the generally accepted terms by which scientists have studied women, doctors have treated them, counselors have advised them, and writers have written about them. Women who suffer this problem, in whom this voice is stirring, have lived their whole lives in the pursuit of feminine fulfillment. They are not career women (although career women may have other problems); they are women whose greatest ambition has been marriage and children. For the oldest of these women, these daughters of the American middleclass, no other dream was possible. The ones in their forties and fifties who once had other dreams gave them up and threw themselves joyously into life as housewives. For the youngest, the new wives and mothers, this was the only dream. They are the ones who quit high school and college to many, or marked time in some job in which they had no real interest until they married. These women are very "feminine" in the usual sense, and yet they still suffer the problem.

* * *

If the secret of feminine fulfillment is having children, never have so many women, with the freedom to choose, had so many children, in so few years, so willingly. If the answer is love, never have women searched for love with such determination. And yet there is a growing suspicion that the problem may not be sexual, though it must somehow be related to sex. I have heard from many doctors evidence of new sexual problems between man and wife—sexual hunger in wives so great their husbands cannot satisfy it. "We have made women a sex creature," said a psychiatrist at the Margaret Sanger marriage counseling clinic. "She has no identity except as a wife and mother. She does not know who she is herself. She waits all day for her husband to come home at night to make her feel alive. And now it is the husband who is not interested. It is terrible for the women, to lie there, night after night, waiting for her husband to make her feel alive." Why is there such a market for books and articles offering sexual advice? The kind of sexual orgasm which Kinsey found in statistical plentitude in the recent generations of American women does not seem to make this problem go away.

On the contrary, new neuroses are being seen among women—and problems as yet unnamed as neuroses—which Freud and his followers did not predict, with physical symptoms, anxieties, and defense mechanisms equal to those caused by sexual repression. And strange new problems are being reported in the growing generations of children whose mothers were always there, driving them around, helping them with their homework—an inability to endure pain or discipline or pursue any self-sustained goal of any sort, a devastating boredom with life. Educators are increasingly uneasy about the dependence, the lack of self-reliance, of the boys and girls who are entering college today. "We fight a continual battle to make our students assume manhood," said a Columbia' dean.

* * *

Can the problem that has no name be somehow related to the domestic routine of the housewife? When a woman tries to put the problem into words, she often merely describes the daily life she leads. What is there in this recital of comfortable domestic detail that could possibly cause such a feeling of desperation? Is she trapped simply by the enormous demands of her role as modern housewife: wife, mistress, mother, nurse, consumer, cook, chauffeur; expert on interior decoration, child care, appliance repair, furniture refinishing, nutrition, and education? Her day is fragmented as she rushes from dishwasher to washing machine to telephone to dryer to station wagon to supermarket, and delivers Johnny to the Little League field, takes Janey to dancing class, gets the lawnmower fixed and meets the 6:45. She can never spend more than 15 minutes on any one thing; she has no time to read books, only magazines; even if she had time, she has lost the power to concentrate. At the end of the day, she is so terribly tired that sometimes her husband has to take over and put the children to bed.

This terrible tiredness took so many women to doctors in the 1950's that one decided to investigate it. He found, surprisingly, that his patients suffering from "housewife's fatigue" slept more than an adult needed to sleep—as much as ten hours a day—and that the actual energy they expended on housework did not tax their capacity. The real problem must be something else, he decided—perhaps boredom. Some doctors told their women patients they must get out of the house for a day, treat themselves to a movie in town. Others prescribed tranquilizers. Many suburban housewives were taking tranquilizers like cough drops. "You wake up in the morning, and you feel as if there's no point in going on another day like this. So you take a tranquilizer because it makes you not care so much that it's pointless."

It is easy to see the concrete details that trap the suburban housewife, the continual demands on her time. But the chains that bind her in her trap are chains in her own mind and spirit. They are chains made up of mistaken ideas and misinterpreted facts, of incomplete truths and unreal choices. They are not easily seen and not easily shaken off.

How can any women see the whole truth within the bounds of her own life? How can she believe that voice inside herself, when it denies the conventional, accepted truths by which she has been living? And yet the women I have talked to, who are finally listening to that inner voice, seem in some incredible way to be groping through to a truth that has defied the experts.

* * *

I began to see in a strange new light the American return to early marriage and the large families that are causing the population explosion; the recent movement to natural childbirth and breastfeeding; suburban conformity, and the new neuroses, character pathologies and sexual problems being reported by the doctors. I began to see new dimensions to old problems that have long been taken for granted among women: menstrual difficulties, sexual frigidity, promiscuity, pregnancy fears, childbirth depression, the high incidence of emotional breakdown and suicide among women in their twenties and thirties, the menopause crises, the so-called passivity and immaturity of American men, the discrepancy between women's tested intellectual abilities in childhood and their adult achievement, the changing incidence of adult sexual orgasm in American women, and persistent problems in psychotherapy and in women's education.

If I am right, the problem that has no name stirring in the minds of so many American women today is not a matter of loss of femininity or too much education, or the demands of domesticity. It is far more important than anyone recognizes. It is the key to these other new and old problems which have been torturing women and their husbands and children, and puzzling their doctors and educators for years. It may well be the key to our future as a nation and a culture. We can no longer ignore that voice within women that says: "I want something more than my husband and children and my home."

FOCUS QUESTIONS:

1. What is "the problem that has no name"?
2. What similarities are there between the problem that has no name and the advertising goals of those who wrote Workingman's. Wife?
3. What were the roots of this problem?

CIVIL RIGHTS AND LIBERAL ACTIVISM, 1945–1975

20-1 Postwar Unionism and Feminism

As described in the "What's Become of Rosie the Riveter?" document (see chapter 19), the postwar period saw significant changes in women's employment patterns. But the picture is more complicated than a simple withdrawal of women from unionized labor, as this excerpt from a scholarly analysis suggests.

Source: Cobble, Dorothy Sue. "Recapturing Working-Class Feminism: Union Women in the Postwar Era. In *Not June Cleaver: Women and Gender in Postwar America, 1945-1960*. Joanne Meyerowitz. Editor. Philadelphia: Temple University Press, 1994, pp. 58-60.

The historian Nancy Gabin has suggested that once the experience of working-class women is incorporated into the history of American feminism, unions will emerge as crucial organizational vehicles for gender-based protest. My research confirms this notion. Indeed, in the 1940s and 1950s, labor organizations may have spurred feminism among wage-earning women much as civil rights and New Left organizations did for a very different group of women in the 1960s and 1970s. This emerging portrait of unionism as a vehicle for feminist aspirations stands in marked contrast to earlier scholarship on World War II and the immediate postwar era that viewed the relation between working women and unions as problematic. The first research monographs, for example, documented the poor treatment wartime "Rosies" received at the hands of the craft union brotherhoods and held the newer industrial unions responsible for the wholesale layoffs of women after the war and their subsequent rehire into lower grade classifications. Writers depicted the powerful union institutions of the 1940s and 1950s as bureaucratic, male-dominated organizations with little sensitivity or interest in their now-diminished female constituency. In part, scholars reached such negative assessments because they focused almost exclusively on male-dominated craft unions and unions in mass production. In part, the dismissal flowed from the widespread assumption that unions historically have been bastions of male power and unwavering agents of patriarch impulses.

Along with the new institutional labor history, more recent scholarship had to reassess the relation between female activism and unions. Ruth Milkman's 1987 study of the auto, and electrical industries in the 1940s, for e)ample, argued that management must shoulder a major share of the blame f(the job discrimination women suffered; critical management decisions involving layoff and rehiring of workers were not yet subject to union control. In her 1991 book, *Feminism in the Labor Movement*, Nancy Gabin carried this reassessment into the 1950s and 1960s , contending that the new prominence given to women's issues during World War II by such progressive CIO unions as the United Auto Workers (UAW) was institutionalized after the war. Recent theses on women unionists within the United Electrical Workers (UE) and the United Packinghouse Workers of America support Gabin's work. The UAW women were not atypical: Working-class female activism survived and even flourished in the 1950s. This essay offers a framework within which to place the, many excellent case studies of female activism in manufacturing union that have emerged; it also extends and complicates the revisionist scholarship by analyzing the experience of women in service-sector unions.

Unions representing female-dominated industries not only experienced a surge of membership during wartime, but in contrast to the UAW, for example, their ranks continued to expand once the war ended. As women were laid off from jobs in auto plants and shipyards, they returned to the "pink collar" ghetto, swelling the membership of unions such as the AFL-affiliated Hotel Employees and Restaurant Employees (HERE), the National Federation of Telephone Workers

(NFTW), and others. By 1950, more than two hundred thousand female food-service workers were organized, for example, and they constituted 45 percent of the union's membership, almost double the prewar figure. Women also constituted 40 percent or more of organized telephone workers, department store employees, and bakery and confectionary workers, and they composed the majority of union members in such older female-dominated industries as garment and textile.

Even within manufacturing, certain industries and shops maintained their wartime female majorities. Between 1946 and 1958, approximately 40 percent of all UE workers were female, slightly below their wartime peak of 49 percent, but certainly above their prewar numbers. Depending on the electrical product being manufactured, "women constituted from 25 to 75 percent of the workforce in any given shop.

Overall, then, despite the wholesale layoffs of women in manufacturing during reconversion, women emerged in a much stronger position within the labor movement than before the war. Less than a tenth of union members (some eight hundred thousand) were female before 1940. Although female membership sky-rocketed to 3 million (or 22 percent of organized workers) during wartime and then fell abruptly at the war's end, the number of union women throughout the late 1940s and 1950s still vastly exceeded its prewar level. By 1954, for example, close to 3 million women belonged to unions—some 17 percent of all union members. Of equal importance, with their shift out of male-dominated organizations into unions in which women made up a large if not majority constituency, women union members now wielded considerable power at local and even national levels. They used this newfound power to reshape the labor movement along more gender-conscious lines and to win significant victories for wage-earning women.

FOCUS QUESTIONS:

1. Are there examples from earlier in U.S. history of women organizing and gaining rights in the workplace? Are there new factors at play after the mid-1940s?

2. What seems to be the author's perspective on unionized women?

20-2 The Civil Rights Act of 1964

Partially in response to the march on Washington, Congress passed a civil rights act that attempted to provide African Americans with the rights they had been granted them ninety years earlier. One of the provisions included ensuring voting rights for African Americans.

TITLE I

Voting Rights

Sec. 101 (2). No person acting under color of law shall-

(A) in determining whether any individual is qualified under State law or laws to vote in any Federal election, apply any standard, practice, or procedure different form the standards, practices, or procedures applied under such law or laws to other individuals within the same county, parish, or similar political subdivision who have been found by State officials to be qualified to vote; . . . .

(C) employ any literacy test as a qualification for voting in any Federal election unless (i) such test is administered to each individual wholly in writing; and (ii) a certified copy of the test and of the answers given by the individual is furnished to him within twenty-five days of the submission of his request made within the period of time during which records and papers are required to be retained and preserved pursuant to Title III of the Civil Rights Act of 1960. . . .

TITLE II

Injunctive Relief Against Discrimination in Places of Public Accommodation

Sec. 201. (a) All persons shall be entitled to the full and equal enjoyment of the goods, services, facilities, privileges, advantages, and accommodations of any place of public accommodation, as defined in this section, without discrimination or segregation on the ground of race, color, religion, or national origin.

(b) Each of the following establishments which serves the public is a place of public accommodation within the meaning of this title if its operations affect commerce, or if discrimination or segregation by it is supported by State action:

(1) any inn, motel, or other establishment which provides lodging to transient guests, other than an establishment located within a building which contains not more than five rooms for rent or hire and

which is actually occupied by the proprietor of such establishment as his residence;

(2) any restaurant, cafeteria, lunch room, lunch counter, soda fountain, or other activity principally engaged in selling food for consumption on the premises. . . .

(3) any motion picture house, theater, concert hall, sports arena, stadium, or other place of exhibition or entertainment. . . .

(d) Discrimination or segregation by an establishment is supported by State action within the meaning of this title if such discrimination or segregation (1) is carried on under color of any law, statute, ordinance, or regulation; or (2) is carried on under color of any custom or usage required or enforced by officials of the State or political subdivision thereof. . . .

Sec. 202. All persons shall be entitled to be free, at any establishment or place, from discrimination or segregation of any kind on the ground of race, color, religion, or national origin, if such discrimination or segregation is or purports to be required by any law, statute, ordinance, regulation, rule, or order of a State or any agency or political subdivision thereof. . . .

Sec. 206. (a) Whenever the Attorney General has reasonable cause to believe that any person or group of persons is engaged in a pattern of practice of resistance to the full enjoyment of any of the rights secured by this title, the Attorney General may bring a civil action in the °appropriate district court of the United States by filing with it a complaint . .requesting such preventive relief, including an application for a permanent or temporary injunction, restraining order or other order against the person or persons responsible for such pattern or practice, as he deems necessary to insure the full enjoyment of the rights herein described.

TITLE IV

Nondiscrimination in Federally Assisted Programs

Sec. 601. No person in the United States shall, on the ground of race, color, or national origin, be excluded from participation in, be denied the benefits of, or be subjected to discrimination under any program or activity receiving Federal financial assistance.

FOCUS QUESTIONS:

1. What provisions are stipulated in this act regarding voting rights?

2. What practical impact does this act have in regard to access to "public accommodation"?

20-3 Sex and Caste

Mary King and Casey Hayden, both Southern white women, were early activists in the Student Nonviolent Coordinating Committee (SNCC), among other organizations. They noted that, even in organizations devoted to ending racial inequality, they were expected to perform clerical work and other menial labor simply because they were women. Though they were ridiculed when they publicly raised this issue at the 1964 SNCC annual conference, in the summer of 1965 they wrote this broadside and mailed it to 40 female leaders of anti-racism campaigns. Many scholars see this as the founding document of the modern feminist movement.

Source: Casey Hayden and Mary King, "A Kind of Memo ... to a Number of Other Women in the Peace and Freedom Movements," reprinted in Mary King, *Freedom Song* (New York: William Morrow,1987), pp. 571-574.

Sex and caste: There seem to be many parallels that can be drawn between treatment of Negroes and treatment of women in our society as a whole. But in particular, women we've talked to who work in the movement seem to be caught up in a common-law caste system that operates, sometimes subtly, forcing them to work around or outside hierarchical structures of power which may exclude them. Women seem to be placed in the same position of assumed subordination in personal situations too. It is a caste system which, at its worst, uses and exploits women.

This is complicated by several facts, among them: (1) The caste system is not institutionalized by law (women have the right to vote, to sue for divorce, etc.); (2) Women can't withdraw from the situation (a la nationalism) or over-throw it; (3) There are biological differences (even though these biological differences are usually discussed or accepted without taking present and future technology into account so we probably can't be sure what these differences mean). Many people who are very hip to the implications of the racial caste system, even people in the movement, don't seem to be able to see the sexual caste system and if the question is raised they respond with: "That's the way it's supposed to be. There are biological differences." Or with other statements which recall a white segregationist confronted with integration.

Women and problems of work: The caste-system

perspective dictates the roles assigned to women in the movement, and certainly even more to women outside the movement. Within the movement, questions arise in situations ranging from relationships of women organizers to men in the community, to who cleans the Freedom house, to who holds leadership positions, to who does secretarial work and to who acts as spokesman for groups. Other problems arise between women with varying degrees of awareness of themselves as being capable as men but are held back from full participation, or between women who see themselves as needing more control of their work than other women demand. And there are problems with relationships between white women and black women.

Women and personal relations with men: Having learned from the movement to think radically about the personal worth and abilities of people whose role in society had gone unchallenged before, a lot of women in the movement have begun trying to apply those lessons to their own relations with men. Each of us probably has her own story of the various results, and of the internal struggle occasioned by trying to break out of very deeply learned fears, needs, and self-perceptions, and of what happens when we try to replace them with concepts of people and freedom learned from the movement and organizing.

Institutions: Nearly everyone has real questions about those institutions which shape perspectives on men and women: marriage, child-rearing patterns, women's (and men's) magazines, etc. People are beginning to think about and even to experiment with new forms in these areas. . . .

Lack of community for discussion: Nobody is writing, or organizing or talking publicly about women in any way that reflects the problems that various women in the movement come across and which we've tried to touch above. . . .

Objectively, the chances seem nil that we could start a movement based on anything as distant to general American thought as a sex-caste system. Therefore, most of us will probably want to work full time on problems such as war, poverty, race. The very fact that the country can't face, much less deal with, the questions we're raising means that the movement is one place to look for some relief. Real efforts at dialogue within the movement and with whatever liberal groups, community women, or students might listen are justified. That is, all the problems between men and women and all the problems of women functioning in society as equal human beings are among the most basic that people face. We've talked in the movement about trying to build a society which would see basic human problems (which are now seen as private troubles), as public problems and would try to shape institutions to meet human needs rather than shaping people to meet the needs of those with power. To raise questions like those above illustrates very directly that society hasn't dealt with some of its deepest problems and opens discussion of why that is so. . . . The second objective reason we'd like to see discussion begin is that we've learned a great deal in the movement and perhaps this is one area where a determined attempt to apply ideas we've learned there can produce some new alternatives.

Focus Questions:

1. How do King and Hayden link racial injustice and gender-based injustice?

2. What do they mean by a "common-law caste system"? Does such a system still exist for women today? Does it exist for other groups in American society?

20-4 Sit-In

Anne Moody's autobiography, Coming of Age in Mississippi, *recounts both dramatic moments in the Civil Rights Movement and the process of personal transformation experienced by the author, an African-American who grew up poor in rural Mississippi. While attending Tougaloo College in Jackson, Mississippi, on a scholarship, Moody became active in the Congress of Racial Equality (CORE), the Student Nonviolent Coordinating Committee (SNCC), and the National Association for the Advancement of Colored People (NAACP). The NAACP organized this sit-in to protest segregation at a Woolworth's in Jackson in 1963.*

Source: Moody, Anne. *Coming of Age in Mississippi.* New York: The Dial Press, Inc., 1968, 264-267

To divert attention from the sit-in at Woolworth's, the picketing started at J. C. Penney's a good fifteen minutes' before. The pickets were allowed to walk up and down in front of the store three or four times before they were arrested. At exactly 11 A.M., Pearlena, Memphis, and I entered Woolworth's from the rear entrance. We separated as soon as we stepped into the store, and made small purchases from various counters. Pearlena had given Memphis her watch. He was to let us know when it was 11:14. At 11:14 we were to join him near the lunch counter and at exactly 11:15 we were to take seats at it.

Seconds before 11:15 we were occupying three seats at the previously segregated Woolworth's lunch counter. In the beginning the waitresses seemed to ignore us, *as* if they really didn't know what *was* going on. Our waitress walked past us a couple of times before she noticed we had started to write our own orders down and realized we wanted ser-vice. She asked us what we wanted. We began to read to her from our order slips. *She* told us that we would be served at the back counter, which was for Negroes.

"We would like to be served here," I said.

The waitress started to repeat what she had said, then stopped in the middle of the sentence. She *turned* the lights out behind the counter, and she and the other waitresses almost ran to the back of the store, deserting all their white customers. I guess they thought that violence would start immediately after the whites at the counter realized what was going on. There were five or six other people at the counter. A couple of them just got up and walked away. A girl sitting next to me finished her banana split before leaving. A middle-aged white woman who had not yet been served rose from her seat and came aver to us. "I'd like to stay here with you," she said, "but my husband is waiting."

The newsmen came in just as she was leaving. They must have discovered what was going on shortly after some of the people began to leave the store. One of the newsmen ran behind the woman who spoke to us and asked her to identify herself. She refused to give her name, but said she was a native of Vicksburg and a former resident of California. When asked why she had said what she had said to us, she replied, "I am in sympathy with the Negro movement" By this time a crowd of cameramen and re-porters had gathered around us taking pictures and asking questions, such as Where were we from? Why did we sit-in? What organization sponsored it? Were we students? From what school? How were we classified?

I told them that we were all students at Tougaloo College, that we were represented by no particular organization, and that we planned to stay there even after the store closed. "All we want is service," was my reply to one of them. After they had finished probing for about twenty minutes, they were almost ready to leave.

At noon, students from a nearby white high school started pouring in to Woolworth's. When they first saw us they were sort of surprised. They didn't know how to react. A few started to heckle and the newsmen became interested again. Then the white students started chanting all kinds of anti-Negro slogans. We were called a little bit of everything. The rest of the seats except the three we were occupying had been roped off to prevent others from sitting down. A couple of the boys took one end of the rope and made it into a hangman's noose. Several attempts were made to put it around our necks. The crowds grew *as* more students and adults came in for lunch.

We kept our eyes straight forward and did not look at the crowd except for occasional glances to see what was going on. All of a sudden I saw a face I remembered—the drunkard from the bus station sit-in. My eyes lingered on him just long enough for us to recognize each other. To-day he was drunk too, so I don't think he remembered where he had seen me before. He took out a knife, opened it, put it in his pocket, and then began to pace the floor. At this point, I told Memphis and Pearlena what was going on. Memphis suggested that we pray. We bowed our heads, and all hell broke loose. A man rushed forward, threw Memphis from his seat, and slapped my face. Then another man who worked in the store threw me against an adjoining counter.

Down on my knees on the floor, I saw Memphis lying near the lunch counter with blood running out of the corners of his mouth. As he tried to protect his face, the man who'd thrown him down kept kicking him against the head. If he had worn hard-soled shoes instead of sneakers, the first kick probably would have killed Memphis. Finally a man dressed in plain clothes identified himself as a police officer and arrested Memphis and his attacker.

Pearlena had been thrown to the floor. She and I got back on our stools after Memphis was arrested. There were some white Tougaloo teachers in the crowd. They asked Pearlena and me if we wanted to leave. They said that things were getting too rough. We didn't know what to do. While we were trying to make up our minds, we were joined by Joan Trumpauer. Now there were three of us and we were integrated. The crowd began to chant, "Communists, Communists, Communists." Some old man in the crowd ordered the students to take us off the stools.

"Which one should I get first?" a big husky boy said.

"That white nigger," the old man said.

The boy lifted Joan from the counter by her waist

and carried her out of the store. Simultaneously, I was snatched from my stool by two high school students. I was dragged about thirty feet toward the door by my hair when someone made them turn me loose. As I was getting up off the floor, I saw Joan coming back inside. We started back to the center of the counter to join Pearlena. Lois Chaffee, a white Tougaloo faculty member, was now sitting next to her. So Joan and I just climbed across the rope at the front end of the counter and sat down. There were now four of us, two whites and two Negroes, all women. The mob started smearing us with ketchup, mustard, sugar, pies, and everything on the counter. Soon Joan and I were joined by John Salter, but the moment he sat down he was hit on the jaw with what appeared to be brass knuckles. Blood gushed from his face and someone threw salt into the open wound. Ed King, Tougaloo's chaplain, rushed to him.

At the other end of the counter, Lois and Pearlena were joined by George Raymond, a CORE field worker and a student from Jackson State College. Then a Negro high school boy sat down next to me. The mob took spray paint from the counter and sprayed it on the new demonstrators. The high school student had on a white shirt; the word "nigger" was written on his back with red spray paint.

We sat there for three hours taking a beating when the manager decided to close the store because the mob had be-gun to go wild with stuff from other counters. He begged and begged everyone to leave. But even after fifteen minutes of begging, no one budged. They would not leave until we did. Then Dr. Beittel, the president of Tougaloo College, came running in. He said he had just heard what was happening.

About ninety policemen were standing outside the store; they had been watching the whole thing through the windows, but had not come in to stop the mob or do anything. President Beittel went outside and asked Captain Ray to come and escort us out. The captain refused, stating the manager had to invite him in before he could enter the premises, so Dr. Beittel himself brought us out. He had told the police that they had better protect us after we were outside the store. When we got outside, the policemen formed a single line that blocked the mob from us. How-ever, they were allowed to throw at us everything they had collected. Within ten minutes, we were picked up by Reverend King in his station wagon and taken to the NAACP headquarters on Lynch Street.

After the sit-in, all I could think of was how sick Mississippi whites were. They believed so much in the segregated Southern way of life, they would kill to preserve it. I sat there In the NAACP office and thought of how many times they had killed when this way of life was threatened. I knew that the killing had just begun. "Many more will die before it is over with," I thought. Before the sit-in, I had always hated the whites in Mississippi. Now I knew it was impossible for me to hate sickness. The whites had a disease, an incurable disease in its final stage. What were our chances against such a disease? I thought of the students, the young Negroes who had just begun to protest, as young interns. When these young interns got older, I thought, they would be the best doctors in the world for social problems.

FOCUS QUESTIONS:

1. What happened at Woolworth's?
2. Why do these events cause Moody to stop hating whites?

20-5 Voting Rights in Mississippi

Born into a life of poverty and dreadful conditions as the twentieth child of a Mississippi sharecropper, Fannie Lou Hamer found the moral courage to challenge an unjust system. On August 31, 1962, Hamer and seventeen others braved the twenty-six mile trip to the county courthouse in Indianola to register to vote. African-American voters comprised only 5 percent of the voting-age pool in 1960, largely due to intimidation and Mississippi's literacy test, which Hamer failed on her first two attempts. She continued to work for voting rights and was one of the leaders in the Mississippi Freedom Democratic Party (MFDP).

Denied participation in the political process, the MFDP held elections and sent 64 delegates to the Democratic National Convention to challenge the all-white Democratic delegation.

Source: "Testimony," July 22, 1964; Speech given at the Democratic National Convention in 1964.

Testimony of Fannie Lou Hamer

Mr. Chairman, and the Credentials Committee, my name is Mrs. Fannie Lou Hamer, and I live at 626 East Lafayette Street, Ruleville, Mississippi, Sunflower

County, the home of Senator James O. Eastland, and Senator Stennis.

It was the 31st of August in 1962 that 18 of us traveled 26 miles to the country courthouse in Indianola to try to register to try to become first-class citizens.

We was met in Indianola by Mississippi men, Highway Patrolmens and they only allowed two of us in to take the literacy test at the time. After we had taken this test and started back to Ruleville, we was held up by the City Police and the State Highway Patrolmen and carried back to Indianola where the bus driver was charged that day with driving a bus the wrong color.

After we paid the fine among us, we continued on to Ruleville, and Reverend Jeff Sunny carried me four miles in the rural area where I had worked as a time-keeper and sharecropper for 18 years. I was met there by my children, who told me that the plantation owner was angry because I had gone down to try to register.

After they told me, my husband came, and said that the plantation owner was raising cain because I had tired to register, and before he quit talking the plantation owner came, and said, "Fannie Lou, do you know—did Pap tell you what I said?"

And I said, "yes, sir."

He said, "I mean that," he said, "If you don't go down and withdraw your registration, you will have to leave," he said, "Then if you go down and withdraw," he said, "You will—you might have to go because we are not ready for that in Mississippi."

And I addressed him and told him and said, "I didn't try to register for you. I tried to register for myself."

I had to leave that same night.

On the 10th of September 1962, 16 bullets was fired into the home of Mr. and Mrs. Robert Tucker for me. That same night two girls were shot in Ruleville, Mississippi. Also Mr. Joe McDonald's house was shot in.

And in June the 9th, 1963, I had attended a voter registration workshop, was returning back to Mississippi. Ten of us was traveling by the Continental Trailway bus. When we got to Winona, Mississippi, which is in Montgomery County, four of the people got off to use the washroom, and two of the people—to use the restaurant—two of the people wanted to use the washroom.

The four people that had gone in to use the restaurant was ordered out. During this time I was on the bus. But when I looked through the window and saw they had rushed out I got off of the bus to see what had happened, and one of the ladies said, "It was a State Highway Patrolman and a Chief of Police ordered us out."

I got back on the bus and one of the persons had used the washroom got back on the bus, too.

As soon as I was seated on the bus, I saw when they began to get the four people in a highway patrolman's car, I stepped off of the bus to see what was happening and somebody screamed from the car that the four workers was in and said, "Get that one there," and when I went to get in the car, when the man told me I was under arrest, he kicked me.

I was carried to the county jail, and put in the booking room. They left some of the people in the booking room and began to place us in cells. I was placed in a cell with a young woman called Miss Ivesta Simpson. After I was placed in the cell I began to hear the sound of kicks and horrible screams, and I could hear somebody say, "Can you say, yes, sir, nigger? Can you say, yes, sir?"

And they would say other horrible names.

She would say, "Yes, I can say yes, sir."

"So say it."

She says, "I don't know you well enough."

They beat her, I don't know how long, and after a while she began to pray, and asked God to have mercy on those people.

And it wasn't too long before three white men came to my cell. One of these men was a State Highway Patrolman and he asked me where I was from, and I told him Ruleville, he said, "We are going to check this."

And they left my cell and it wasn't too long before they came back. He said, "You are from Ruleville all right," and he used a curse work, and he said, "We are going to make you wish you was dead."

I was carried out of that cell into another cell where they had two Negro prisoners. The State Highway Patrolmen ordered the first Negro to take the blackjack.

The first Negro prisoner ordered me, by orders from the State Highway Patrolman for me, to lay down on a bunk bed on my face, and I laid on my face.

The first Negro began to beat, and I was beat by the first Negro until he was exhausted, and I was holding my hands behind me at that time on my left side because I suffered from polio when I was six years old.

After the first Negro had beat until he was exhausted the State Highway Patrolman ordered the second Negro to take the blackjack.

The second Negro began to beat and I began to work my feet, and the State Highway Patrolman ordered the first Negro who had beat me to sit upon my feet to keep me from working my feet. I began to scream and one white man got up and began to beat me my head and told me to hush.

One white man—since my dress had worked up high, walked over and pulled my dress down and he pulled my dress back, back up.

I was in jail when Medgar Evers was murdered

All of this is on account of us wanting to register, to become first-class citizens, and if the freedom

Democratic Party is not seated now, I question America, is this America, the land of the free and the home of the brave where we have to steep with our telephones off of the hooks because our lives be threatened daily because we want to live as decent human beings, in America?

Thank you.

FOCUS QUESTIONS:

1. What happened to Hamer after she registered to vote?

2. How did Mississippi and other southern states deny African Americans participation in the political process?

3. How do you account for the violence that Hamer and other civil rights leaders experienced?

4. What impact did Hamer and the MFDP have on the Democratic convention and voting rights?

20-6 The Birth of NOW

Lawyer and activist Pauli Murray described several formative moments in the U.S. feminist movement in her autobiography, Song in a Weary Throat. *She was influential in the establishment of the National Organization for Women in 1966, as described below.*

NOTE: Title VII is the portion of the Civil Rights Act of 1964 that prohibits employment discrimination on the basis of race, color, religion, sex and national origin.

Source: Murray, Pauli. *Song in a Weary Throat, An American Pilgrimage,* Harper and Row, New York, 1987. pp. 366-368.

By the time the Third National Conference of State Commissions on the Status of Women convened at the Washington Hilton Hotel in June1966, Betty Friedan was just about convinced that a new action group should be set up. Sponsored by the Interdepartmental Committee and Citizens' Advisory Council on the Status of Women and bringing together prominent women commission members from virtually every state, the conference seemed the logical setting in which to test the idea among abroad cross-section of women. As a writer-observer covering the conference, Betty was in a position to sound out leading representatives free state commissions around the country. I was to speak on the panel "Sex Discrimination—

Progress in Legal Status," held on the final morning of the conference, and other members of our network were there to support Betty in exploring possibilities.

By June 29, the second day of the conference, there were enough rumblings of dissatisfaction among activists in attendance to suggest the time was ripe. Betty was encouraged to invite a few women who might be interested in organizing a new group to join an informal discussion II]her hotel room that evening, the only opportunity we would have for meeting before the closing sessions next day.

Some fifteen women met in Betty Friedan's room at about ten o'clock. Many of us were strangers to one another; I knew only five of those present—Betty herself, Mary Eastwood, Dorothy Haener of the Women's Department of the United Automobile Workers, Catherine Conroy of the Communications Workers of America, and Kathryn Clarenbach, chair of the Wisconsin Commission on the Status of Women. Everyone present felt the general frustration over the issue of women's employment rights under Title VII. Each conference participant had been furnished with a copy of Congresswoman Martha Griffiths' angry speech of June 20, delivered on the floor of the House, in which she charged "The whole attitude of the EEOC toward discrimination based on sex is specious, negative and arrogant." Working women were outraged over a guideline issued by the EEOC in April, permitting employers to advertise jobs open to both sexes in segregated "Help Wanted, Male" or "Help Wanted,

Female" newspaper columns in blatant contradiction of Title VII's prohibition of any want ad expressing a preference or limitation based on race, religion, sex, or national origin. Griffiths found the Commission's interpretation of the statute "nothing more than arbitrary arrogance, disregard of law, and a manifestation of flat hostility to the human rights of women." Conference delegates were also angry over the impending expiration of EEOC Commissioner Richard Graham's term on July 1 and the strong rumors that he would not be reappointed. Since he was the one male member of the Commission who had shown sensitivity in dealing with issues of sex bias in employment, Commissioner Graham's imminent departure was seen as calamitous. Our only differences were over strategies to meet what we all saw as an ominous situation.

But those differences were deep. The discussion quickly developed into a heated debate over the need for a new organization. Kay Clarenbach, the commissioner from Wisconsin, and Catherine Conroy of the Communications Workers union, in particular questioned the idea and argued that the issues which immediately concerned us could be handled through the existing machinery of state commissions. Kay suggested that since the theme of the conference was "Targets for Action," it would be appropriate for conference delegates to adopt strong resolutions at the closing luncheon next day, urging the enforcement of the sex provisions of Title VII and the reappointment of Commissioner Graham. Those of us who felt the time had come for action independent of government sponsorship could make little headway against the state commission approach. Tempers flared and we wrangled until after midnight without resolving the basic disagreement. The meeting finally broke up after we agreed—some of us halfheartedly—to Kay's proposal that she draft the resolutions and bring them before the entire conference the following day.

I left Betty Friedan's room that night thoroughly discouraged: it seemed to me that we had fumbled a major opportunity to begin mobilizing women nationally to press for their civil rights. I was so depressed that I seriously considered leaving for New York immediately after my panel presentation next morning, without attending the closing luncheon. But I had not reckoned with the persistent power of an idea whose time had clearly come, and I had not anticipated the radicalization of Kay Clarenbach and Catherine Conway when their plans for moderate action through existing channels were frustrated. In the morning, when Kay approached conference officials to arrange

to introduce her resolutions, she was told that "government commissions cannot take action against other departments." Kay and Catherine were so outraged by this rebuff that they had an immediate change of heart. By noon, word had been passed that we were going ahead with the new organization.

During the luncheon about twenty of us gathered at two tables near the rostrum, and while conference dignitaries were making speeches just above our heads, we carried on whispered conversations and set in motion a temporary body to be called the National Organization for Women. Betty Friedan hastily scribbled its purpose on a paper napkin: "to take the actions needed to bring women into the mainstream of American society *now* . .. in fully equal partnership with men." We urged others at the luncheon to join us in a brief meeting to form the new organization.

Before the conference ended that afternoon, twenty-eight women had signed up and paid five dollars each for immediate expenses. A telegram bearing the names of the twenty-eight founding members went to the White House, urging the reappointment of Richard Graham to the Equal Employment Opportunity Commission, and night letters were sent to each EEOC commissioner, urging that the discriminatory guideline approving sex-segregated "help wanted" ads be rescinded. Kay Clarenbach was named temporary coordinator of NOW, and along with Caroline Ware, I was elected to a "temporary coordinating committee" of six to assist Kay over the summer in developing the framework for a permanent organization. The birth of NOW had happened so quickly and smoothly that most of the delegates left the conference unaware that a historic development in the women's movement had begun. Three months later, at an organizing conference held in Washington on October 29 and 30.1966, thirty-two of us set up the permanent organization of NOW, never dreaming that within less than two decades it would have more than 200,000 members and become a potent force in American politics.

FOCUS QUESTIONS:

1. What were the immediate issues of concern NOW's founders? What was it about the general climate that concerned them?

2. What surprised Murray about the way the organization came into being?

20-7 NOW Statement of Purpose

As described by Pauli Murray (see document, "The Birth of NOW"), the founding of the National Organization of Women grew out of dissatisfaction with employment law and policies. The organization's 1966 Statement of Purpose put that issue into a much broader political and social context.

National Organization for Women, Statement of Purpose (1966)

The civil rights movement stimulated other groups to seek improvement of their conditions. In 1966, a group of feminist leaders founded NOW to fight for equal rights with men.

We, men and women who hereby constitute ourselves as the National Organization for Women, believe that the time has come for a new movement toward true equality for all women in America, and toward a fully equal partnership of the sexes, as part of the worldwide revolution of human rights now taking place within and beyond our national borders.

The purpose of NOW is to take action to bring women into full participation in the mainstream of American society now, exercising all the privileges an responsibilities thereof in truly equal partnership with men.

WE BELIEVE the time has come to move beyond the abstract argument, discussion, and symposia over the status and special nature of women which have raged in America in recent years; the time has come to confront, with concrete action, the conditions that now prevent women from enjoying the equality of opportunity and freedom of choice which is their right, as individual Americans, and as human beings.

NOW is dedicated to the proposition that women, first and foremost, are human beings, who, like all other people in our society, must have the chance to develop their fullest human potential. We believe that women can achieve such equality only by accepting to the full the challenges and responsibilities they share with all other people in our society, as part of the decision-making mainstream of American political, economic, and social life.

WE ORGANIZE to initiate or support action, nationally, or in any part of this nation, by individuals or organizations, to break through the silken curtain of prejudice and discrimination against women in government, industry, the professions, the churches, the political parties, the judiciary, the labor unions, in education, science, medicine, law, religion, and every other field of importance in American society. . . .

Despite all the talk about the status of American women in recent years, the actual position of women in the United States has declined, and is declining, to an alarming degree throughout the 1950's and 1960's. . . . Working women are becoming increasingly-not less-concentrated on the bottom of the job ladder. As a consequence full-time women workers today earn on the average only 60% of what men earn, and that wage gap has been increasing over the past twenty-five years in every major industry group. . . .

Further, with higher education increasingly essential in today's society, too few women are entering and finishing college or going on to graduate or professional school. . . .

In all the professions considered of importance to society, and in the executive ranks of industry and government, women are losing ground. Where they are present it is only a token handful. . . .

Official pronouncement of the advance in the status of women hide not only the reality of this dangerous decline, but the fact that nothing is being done to stop it. The excellent reports of the President's Commission on the Status of Women and of the State Commissions have not been fully implemented. Such Commissions have power only to advise. They have no power to enforce their recommendations; nor have they the freedom to organize American women and men to press for action on them. The reports of these commissions have, however, created a basis upon which it is now possible to build.

Discrimination in employment on the basis of sex is now prohibited by federal law, in Title VII of the Civil Rights Act of 1964. . . . Until now, too few women's organizations and official spokesmen have been willing to speak out against these dangers facing women. Too many women have been restrained by the fear of being called "feminist."

There is no civil rights movement to speak for women, as there has been for Negroes and other victims of discrimination. The National Organization for Women must therefore begin to speak.

WE BELIEVE that the power of American law, and the protection guaranteed by the U.S. Constitution to the civil rights of all individuals, must be effectively applied and enforced to isolate and remove patterns of sex discrimination, to ensure equality of opportunity in employment and education, and equality of civil and political rights and responsibilities on behalf of women, as well as for Negroes and other deprived groups.

WE REALIZE that women's problems are linked to many broader questions of social justice; their solution will require concerted action by many groups. . . .

WE DO NOT ACCEPT the token appointment of a few women to high-level positions in government and industry as a substitute for a serious continuing effort to recruit and advance women according to their individual abilities. To this end, we urge American government and industry to mobilize the same resources of ingenuity and command with which they have solved problems of far greater difficulty than those now impeding the progress of women.

WE BELIEVE that this nation has a capacity at least as great as other nations, to innovate new social institutions which will enable women to enjoy true equality of opportunity and responsibility in society, without conflict with the irresponsibilities as mothers and homemakers. . . . . . .

WE REJECT the assumption that these problems are the unique responsibility of each individual woman, rather than a basic social dilemma which society must solve. . . .

WE BELIEVE that it is an essential for every girl to be educated to her full potential of human ability as it is for every boy-with the knowledge that such education is the key to effective participation in today's economy and that, for a girl as for a boy, education can only be serious where there is expectation that it will be used in society. . . .

WE REJECT the current assumptions that a man must carry the sole burden of supporting himself, his wife, and family, and that a woman is automatically entitled to lifelong support by a man upon her marriage, or that marriage, home, and family are primarily woman's world and responsibility-hers to dominate-his to support. We believe that a true partnership between the sexes demands a different concept of marriage, and equitable sharing of the responsibilities of home and children and of the economic burdens of their support. We believe that proper recognition should be given to the economic and social value of homemaking and child care. . . .

WE BELIEVE that women must now exercise their political rights and responsibilities as American citizens. They must refuse to be segregated on the basis of sex into separate-and-not-equal ladies' auxiliaries in the political parties, and they must demand representation according to their numbers in the regularly constituted party committees-at local, state, and national levels-and in the informal power structure, participating fully in the selection of candidates and political decision making, and running for office themselves . . .

NOW WILL HOLD ITSELF INDEPENDENT OF ANY POLITICAL PARTY in order to mobilize the political power of all women and men intent on our goals.. .

WE BELIEVE that women will do most to create a new image of women by acting now, and by speaking out in behalf of their own equality, freedom, and human dignity-not in pleas for special privilege, nor in enmity toward men, who are also victims of the current, half-equality between the sexes-but in an active, self-respecting partnership with men. By so doing, women will develop confidence in their own ability to determine actively, in partnership with men, the conditions of their life, their choices, their future, and their society.

FOCUS QUESTIONS:

1. What is the status of women in American Society according to this document? How has this status changed in the decades previous to this document?

2. What steps must be taken to rectify what is seen as inequality between the sexes in terms of opportunity and self-actualization?

20-8 Womanpower

The costs and benefits of women participating in the formal workforce continued to occupy both social commentators and bureaucrats. Here, the National Manpower Council proposes ways for government agencies and employers to facilitate women's work.

Source: National Manpower Council. *Womanpower.* New York: Columbia University Press, 1957, 4-6.

. . . National Manpower Council recommends that:

1. School and college officials, boards of education, and Federal, state, and local governments expand and improve educational and vocational guidance

in order to help young women make sound decisions with respect to their self-development, the growing and changing employment opportunities open to them, and the probability that paid employment will occupy a significant place in their adult lives

2. The Federal and state governments, employers, unions, and voluntary organizations cooperate to increase occupational guidance and placement services for mature women who want to work, in order to help them make sound decisions in the light of their individual interests, capacities, and employment opportunities

3. The Federal and state governments, employers, labor unions, voluntary groups, and individuals expand their support of scholarship and fellowship programs, in order to enable more young women of high ability to continue their formal education in college or in professional or graduate school,

4. State governments, in cooperation with local communities, educational institutions, employers, and labor unions, initiate surveys to determine whether existing training facilities are adequate to meet the needs of mature women who want to work, and in what ways mature women can be helped to meet the requirements for employment in professional or semiprofessional occupations where manpower shortages exist.

With respect to expanding the opportunities for the effective utilization of womanpower, the National Manpower Council recommends that:

1. Employers hire, assign, train, and promote all individuals regardless of sex on the basis of their personal qualifications; labor unions strive to implement for all individuals the principle of equality of opportunity in employment; and both employers and unions take additional steps to apply the principle of equal pay for equal work

2. Employers review their hiring, assignment, training, and promotion practices in light of the changes which have taken place in the education, skill, age composition, and work interests of women in the labor force, in order to insure that they make effective use of their women employees

3. Employers experiment further with part-time and flexible work arrangements, so that they can draw upon the potential supply of women who want to work, but are not available for regular, full-time employment

4. Management associations and personnel groups undertake studies for the purpose of appraising the experiences of business organizations which have developed new practices for utilizing their women workers more effectively and make their findings broadly available for use by employers

5. The Secretary of Defense direct the Secretaries of the Army, Navy, and. Air Force to review jointly their experiences with the utilization of women in uniform and to make their significant findings available for use by employers.

With respect to increasing knowledge about the effective development and utilization of womanpower, the National Manpower Council recommends that:

1. Universities, foundations, and government encourage and support research dealing with the impact of the increased employment of women upon family life, the rearing of children, and the self-development of women; upon the process of occupational choice among both younger and older women; upon the prosperity of the economy and living standards; and upon the availability of volunteer workers for community service functions

2. The Secretary of Labor initiate a comprehensive study the maximum use which could be made of the actual and potential resources of womanpower in the event of a national emergency

3. The Secretary of Labor take the initiative in establishing a commission to review, in the light of recent changes in technology and the economy and in the composition of the female labor force, the consequences and adequacy of existing Federal and state laws which have a direct bearing on the employment of women.

FOCUS QUESTIONS:

1. Is there anything in these recommendations that appears controversial?

2. What obligations or aspirations of women does the council seem to believe might be threatened by women's participation in the workforce?

3. What benefits does the council seem to believe women can gain through working? What benefits might society gain?

THE PERSONAL IS POLITICAL, 1960-1980

21-1 SNCC Position Paper

In the ongoing struggles of women for recognition and responsibility within the Student Nonviolent Coordinating Committee, this document stands out for its concise and specific examples of the problems faced by women.

Source: In Evans, Sara Margaret. *Personal Politics: The Roots of Women's Liberation in the Civil Rights Movement and the New Left.* New York: Vintage Books, 1980. pp. 153-155.

SNCC POSITION PAPER
(Women in the Movement)

Name Withheld by Request, November 1964

1. Staff was involved in crucial constitutional revisions at the Atlanta staff meeting in October. A large committee was appointed to present revisions to the staff. The committee was all men.

2. Two organizers were working together to form a farmers league. Without asking any questions, the male organizer immediately assigned the clerical work to the female organizer although both had had equal experience in organizing campaigns.

3. Although there are women in Mississippi project who have been working as long as some of the men, the leadership group in COFO is all men.

4. A woman in a field office wondered why she was held responsible for day to day decisions, only to find out later that she had been appointed project director but not told.

5. A fall 1964 personnel and resources report on Mississippi projects lists the number of people in each project. The section on Laurel, however, lists not the number of persons, but "three girls."

6. One of SNCC's main administrative officers apologizes for appointment of a woman as interim project director in a key Mississippi project area.

7. A veteran of two years' work for SNCC in two states spends her day typing and doing clerical work for other people in her project.

8. Any woman in SNCC, no matter what her position or experience, has been asked to take minutes in a meeting when she and other women are outnumbered by men.

9. The names of several new attorneys entering a state project this past summer were posted in a central movement office. The first initial and last name of each lawyer was listed. Next to one name was written: (girl).

10. Capable, responsible, and experienced women who are in leader-ship positions can expect to have to defer to a man on their project for final decision making.11.A session at the recent October staff meeting in Atlanta was the first large meeting in the past couple of years where a woman was asked to chair. Undoubtedly this list will seem strange to some, petty to others, laugh-able at most. The list could continue as far as there are women in the movement. Except that most women don't talk about these kinds of incidents, because the whole subject is [not] discussable—strange to some, petty to others, laughable to most. The average white person finds it difficult to understand why the Negro resents being called "boy," or being thought of as "musical" and "athletic," because the average white person doesn't realize that *he assumes he is superior.* And naturally he doesn't understand the problem of paternalism. So too the average SNCC worker finds it difficult to discuss the woman problem because of the assumption of male superiority. Assumptions of male superiority are as widespread and deep rooted and every much as crippling to the woman as the assumptions of white supremacy are to the Negro. Consider why it is in SNCC that women who are competent, qualified, and experienced, are automatically assigned to the "female"

kinds of jobs such as typing, desk work, telephone work, filing, library work, cooking, and the assistant kind of administrative work but rarely the "executive" kind. The woman in SNCC is often in the same position as that token Negro hired in a corporation. The management thinks that it has done its bit. Yet, every day the Negro bears an atmosphere, attitudes and actions which are tinged with condescension and paternalism, the most telling of which are when he is not promoted as the equally or less skilled whites are. This pa-per is anonymous. Think about the kinds of things the author, if made known, would have to suffer because of raising this kind of discussion. Nothing so final as being fired or outright exclusion, but the kinds of things which are killing to the insides—insinuations, ridicule, over-exaggerated compensations. This paper is presented anyway because it needs to be made know [n]that many women in the movement are not "happy and contented" with their status. It needs to be made known that much talent and experience are being wasted by this movement when women are not given jobs commensurate with their abilities. It needs to be known that just as Negroes were the crucial factor in the economy of the cotton South, so too in SNCC, women are the crucial factor that keeps the movement running on a day-to-day basis. Yet they are not given equal say-so when it comes today-to-day decision making. What can be done? Probably nothing right away. Most men in this movement are probably too threatened by the possibility of serious discussion on this subject. Perhaps this is because they have recently broken away from a matriarchal framework under which they may have grown up. Then too, many women are as unaware and insensitive to this subject as men, just as there are many Negroes who don't understand they are not free or who want to be a part of white America. They don't understand that they have to give up their souls and stay in their place to be accepted. So too, many women, in order to be accepted by men, or men's terms, give themselves up to that caricature of what a woman is— unthinking, pliable, an ornament to please the man. Maybe the only thing that can come out of this paper is discussion—amidst the laughter—but still discussion. (Those who laugh the hardest are often those who need the crutch of male supremacy the most.) And maybe some women will begin to recognize day-to-day discriminations. And maybe sometime in the future the whole of the women in this movement will become so alert as to force the rest of the movement to stop the discrimination and start the slow process of changing values and ideas so that all of us gradually come to understand that this is no more a man's world than it is a white world.

FOCUS QUESTIONS:

1. How are the roles of women and of African Americans linked in this document?

2. Do the scenarios described here seem "laughable"? Why does the author claim that "most" contemporary readers will find them laughable?

21-2 Black, Feminist, and Lesbian

Named after the South Carolina locale of a mass liberation led by Harriet Tubman that freed more than 700 slaves, the Combahee River Collective was a group of African-American women – many of them lesbian – who met and wrote collectively, mostly in the Boston area.

Source: From Combahee River Collective, "A Black Feminist Statement," in *Capitalist Patriarchy and the Case for Socialist Feminism*, ed. Zillah Eisenstein. Copyright © 1979 by Monthly Review Press. Reprinted by permission of Monthly Review Foundation.

The Combahee River Collective
A Black Feminist Statement

We are a collective of black feminists who have been meeting together since 1974.[1] During that time we have been involved in the process of defining and clarifying our politics, while at the same time doing political work within our own group and in coalition with other progressive organizations and movements. The most general statement of our politics at the present time would be that we are actively committed to struggling against racial, sexual, heterosexual, and class oppression and see as our particular task the development of integrated analysis and practice based upon the fact that the major systems of oppression are interlocking. The synthesis of these oppressions creates the conditions of our lives. As black women we see black feminism as the logical political movement to combat the manifold and simultaneous oppressions that all women of color face.

We will discuss four major topics in the paper that

follows: (1) The genesis of contemporary black feminism; (2) what we believe, i.e., the specific province of our politics; (3) the problems in organizing black feminists, including a brief history of our collective; and (4) black feminist issues and practice.

1. THE GENESIS OF CONTEMPORARY BLACK FEMINISM

Before looking at the recent development of black feminism, we would like to affirm that we find our origins in the historical reality of Afro-American women's continuous life-and-death struggle for survival and liberation. Black women's extremely negative relationship to the American political system (a system of white male rule) has always been determined by our membership in two oppressed racial and sexual castes. As Angela Davis points out in "Reflections on the Black Woman's Role in the Community of Slaves," black women have always embodied, if only in their physical manifestation, an adversary stance to white male rule and have actively resisted its inroads upon them and their communities in both dramatic and subtle ways. There have always been black women activists-some known, like Sojourner Truth, Harriet Tubman, Frances E. W. Harper, Ida B. Wells Barnett, and March Church Terrell, and thousands upon thousands unknown-who had a shared awareness of how their sexual identity combined with their racial identity to make their whole life situation and the focus of their political struggles unique. Contemporary black feminism is the outgrowth of countless generations of personal sacrifice, militancy, and work by our mothers and sisters.

A black feminist presence has evolved most obviously in connection with the second wave of the American women's movement beginning in the late 1960s. Black, other Third World, and working women have been involved in the feminist movement from its start, but both outside reactionary forces and racism and elitism within the movement itself have served to obscure our participation. In 1973 black feminists, primarily located in New York, felt the necessity of forming a separate black feminist group. This became the National Black Feminist Organization (NBFO).

Black feminist politics also have an obvious connection to movements for black liberation, particularly those of the 1960s and 1970s. Many of us were active in those movements (civil rights, black nationalism, the Black Panthers), and all of our lives were greatly affected and changed by their ideology, their goals, and the tactics used to achieve their goals. It was our experience and disillusionment within these liberation

movements, as well as experience on the periphery of the white male left, that led to the need to develop a politics that was antiracist, unlike those of white women, and antisexist, unlike those of black and white men.

There is also undeniably a personal genesis for black feminism, that is, the political realization that comes from the seemingly personal experiences of individual black women's lives. Black feminists and many more black women who do not define themselves as feminists have all experienced sexual oppression as a constant factor in our day-to-day existence.

Black feminists often talk about their feelings of craziness before becoming conscious of the concepts of sexual politics, patriarchal rule, and, most importantly feminism, the political analysis and practice that we women use to struggle against our oppression. The fact that racial politics and indeed racism are pervasive factors in our lives did not allow us, and still does not allow most black women, to look more deeply into our own experiences and define those things that make our lives what they are and our oppression specific to us. In the process of consciousness-raising, actually life-sharing, we began to recognize the commonality of our experiences and, from that sharing and growing consciousness, to build a politics that will change our lives and inevitably end our oppression.

Our development also must be tied to the contemporary economic and political position of black people. The post-World War II generation of black youth was the first to be able to minimally partake of certain educational and employment options, previously closed completely to black people. Although our economic position is still at the very bottom of the American capitalist economy, a handful of us have been able to gain certain tools as a result of tokenism in education and employment which potentially enable us to more effectively fight our oppression.

A combined antiracist and antisexist position drew us together initially, and as we developed politically we addressed ourselves to heterosexism and economic oppression under capitalism.

2. WHAT WE BELIEVE

Above all else, our politics initially sprang from the shared belief that black women are inherently valuable, that our liberation is a necessity not as an adjunct to somebody else's but because of our need as human persons for autonomy. This may seem so obvious as to sound simplistic, but it is apparent that no other ostensibly progressive movement has ever considered our specific oppression a priority or worked seriously for the ending of that oppression. Merely naming the pejorative stereotypes attributed to black women (e.g., mammy, matriarch, Sapphire, whore, bulldagger), let alone cataloguing the cruel, often murderous, treatment we receive, indicates how little value has been placed upon our lives during four centuries of bondage in the Western hemisphere. We realize that the only people who care enough about us to work consistently for our liberation is us. Our politics evolve from a healthy love for ourselves, our sisters, and our community which allows us to continue our struggle and work.

This focusing upon our own oppression is embodied in the concept of identity politics. We believe that the most profound and potentially the most radical politics come directly out of our own identity, as opposed to working to end somebody else's oppression. In the case of black women this is a particularly repugnant, dangerous, threatening, and therefore revolutionary concept because it is obvious from looking at all the political movements that have preceded us that anyone is more worthy of liberation than ourselves. We reject pedestals, queenhood, and walking ten paces behind. To be recognized as human, levelly human, is enough.

We believe that sexual politics under patriarchy is as pervasive in black women's lives as are the politics of class and race. We also often find it difficult to separate race from class from sex oppression because in our lives they are most often experienced simultaneously. We know that there is such a thing as racial-sexual oppression which is neither solely racial nor solely sexual, e.g., the history of rape of black women by white men as a weapon of political repression.

Although we are feminists and lesbians, we feel solidarity with progressive black men and do not advocate the fractionalization that white women who are separatists demand. Our situation as black people necessitates that we have solidarity around the fact of race, which white women of course do not need to have with white men, unless it is their negative solidarity as racial oppressors. We struggle together with black men against racism, while we also struggle with black men about sexism.

We realize that the liberation of all oppressed peoples necessitates the destruction of the political-economic systems of capitalism and imperialism as well as patriarchy. We are socialists because we believe the work must be organized for the collective benefit of those who do the work and create the products and not for the profit of the bosses. Material resources must be equally distributed among those who create these resources. We are not convinced, however, that a socialist revolution that is not also a feminist and antiracist revolution will guarantee our liberation. We have arrived at the necessity for developing an understanding of class relationships that takes into account the specific class position of black women who are generally marginal in the labor force, while at this particular time some of us are temporarily viewed as doubly desirable tokens at white-collar and professional levels. We need to articulate the real class situation of persons who are not merely raceless, sexless workers, but for whom racial and sexual oppression are significant determinants in their working/economic lives. Although we are in essential agreement with Marx's theory as it applied to the very specific economic relationships he analyzed, we know that this analysis must be extended further in order for us to understand our specific economic situation as black women.

A political contribution which we feel we have already made is the expansion of the feminist principle that the personal is political. In our consciousness-raising sessions, for example, we have in many ways gone beyond white women's revelations because we are dealing with the implications of face and class as well as sex. Even our black women's style of talking/testifying in black language about what we have experienced has a resonance that is both cultural and political. We have spent a great deal of energy delving into the cultural and experiential nature of our oppression out of necessity because none of these matters have ever been looked at before. No one before has ever examined the multilayered texture of black women's lives.

As we have already stated, we reject the stance of lesbian separatism because it is not a viable political analysis or strategy for us. It leaves out far too much and far too many people, particularly black men, women, and children. We have a great deal of criticism and loathing for what men have been socialized to be in this society: what they support, how they act, and how they oppress. But we do not have the misguided notion that it is their maleness, per se-i.e., their biological maleness-that makes them what they are. As black women we find any type of biological determinism a particularly dangerous and reactionary basis upon which to build a politic. We must also question whether lesbian separatism is an adequate and progressive political analysis and strategy, even for those who practice it, since it so completely denies any but the sexual sources of women's oppression, negating the facts of class and race.

3. PROBLEMS IN ORGANIZING BLACK FEMINISTS

During our years together as a black feminist collective we have experienced success and defeat, joy and pain, victory and failure. We have found that it is very difficult to organize around black feminist issues, difficult even to announce in certain contexts that we are black feminists. We have tried to think about the reasons for our difficulties, particularly since the white women's movement continues to be strong and to grow in many directions. In this section we will discuss some of the general reasons for the organizing problems we face and also talk specifically about the stages in organizing our own collective.

The major source of difficulty in our political work is that we are not just trying to fight oppression on one front or even two, but instead to address a whole range of oppressions. We do not have racial, sexual, heterosexual or class privilege to rely upon, nor do we have even the minimal access to resources and power that groups who possess any one of these types of privilege have.

The psychological toll of being a black woman and the difficulties this presents in reaching political consciousness and doing political work can never be underestimated. There is a very low value placed upon black women's psyches in this society, which is both racist and sexist. As an early group member once said, "We are all damaged people merely by virtue of being black women." We are dispossessed psychologically and on every other level, and yet we feel the necessity to struggle to change our condition and the condition of all black women. In "A Black Feminist's Search for Sisterhood," Michele Wallace arrives at this conclusion:

We exist as women who are black who are feminists, each stranded for the moment, working independently because there is not yet an environment in this society remotely congenial to our struggle-because, being on the bottom, we would have to do what no one else has done: we would have to fight the world.[2]

Wallace is not pessimistic but realistic in her assessment of black feminists' position, particularly in her allusion to the nearly classic isolation most of us face. We might use our position at the bottom, however, to make a clear leap into revolutionary action. If black women were free, it would mean that everyone else would have to be free since our freedom would necessitate the destruction of all the systems of oppression.

Feminism is, nevertheless, very threatening to the majority of black people because it calls into question some of the most basic assumptions about our existence, i.e., that gender should be a determinant of power relationships. Here is the way male and female roles were defined in a black nationalist pamphlet from the early 1970s.

We understand that it is and has been traditional that the man is the head of the house. He is the leader of the house/nation because his knowledge of the world is broader, his awareness is greater, his understanding is fuller and his application of this information is wiser.... After all, it is only reasonable that the man be the head of the house because he is able to defend and protect the development of his home.... Women cannot do the same things as men-they are made by nature to function differently. Equality of men and women is something that cannot happen even in the abstract world. Men are not equal to other men, i.e., ability, experience, or even understanding. The value of men and women can be seen as in the value of gold and silver-they are not equal but both have great value. We must realize that men and women are a complement to each other because there is no house/family without a man and his wife. Both are essential to the development of any life.[3]

The material conditions of most black women would hardly lead them to upset both economic and sexual arrangements that seem to represent some stability in their lives. Many black women have a good understanding of both sexism and racism, but because of the everyday constrictions of their lives cannot risk struggling against them both.

The reaction of black men to feminism has been notoriously negative. They are, of course, even more threatened than black women by the possibility that black feminists might organize around our own needs. They realize that they might not only lose valuable and hard-working allies in their struggles but that they might also be forced to change their habitually sexist ways of interacting with and oppressing black women. Accusations that black feminism divides the black struggle are powerful deterrents to the growth of an autonomous black women's movement.

Still hundreds of women have been active at different times during the three-year existence of our group. And every black women who came, came out of a strongly felt need for some level of possibility that did not previously exist in her life.

When we first started meeting early in 1974 after

the NBFO first eastern regional conference, we did not have a strategy for organizing, or even a focus. We just wanted to see what we had. After a period of months of not meeting, we began to meet again late in the year and started doing an intense variety of consciousness-raising. The overwhelming feeling that we had is that after years and years we had finally found each other. Although we were not doing political work as a group, individuals continued their involvement in lesbian politics, sterilization abuse and abortion rights work. Third World Women's International Women's Day activities, and support activity for the trials of Dr. Kenneth Edelin, Joan Little, and Inez Garcia. During our first summer, when membership had dropped off considerably, those of us remaining devoted serious discussion to the possibility of opening a refuge for battered women in a black community. (There was no refuge in Boston at that time.) We also decided around that time to become an independent collective since we had serious disagreements with NBFOs bourgeois-feminist stance and their lack of a clear political focus.

We also were contacted at that time by socialist feminists, with whom we had worked on abortion rights activities, who wanted to encourage us to attend the National Socialist Feminist Conference in Yellow Springs. One of our members did attend and despite the narrowness of the ideology that was promoted at that particular conference, we became more aware of the need for us to understand our own economic situation and to make our own economic analysis.

In the fall, when some members returned, we experienced several months of comparative inactivity and internal disagreements which were first conceptualized as a lesbian-straight split but which were also the result of class and political differences. During the summer those of us who were still meeting had determined the need to do political work and to move beyond consciousness-raising and serving exclusively as an emotional support group. At the beginning of 1976, when some of the women who had not wanted to do political work and who also had voiced disagreements stopped attending of their own accord, we again looked for a focus. We decided at that time, with the addition of new members, to become a study group. We had always shared our reading with each other, and some of us had written papers on black feminism for group discussion a few months before this decision was made. We began functioning as a study group and also began discussing the possibility of starting a black feminist publication. We had a retreat in the late spring which provided a time for both political discussion and working out interpersonal issues. Currently we are

planning to gather together a collection of black feminist writing. We feel that it is absolutely essential to demonstrate the reality of our politics to other black women and believe that we can do this through writing and distributing our work. The fact that individual black feminists are living in isolation all over the country, that our own numbers are small, and that we have some skills in writing, printing, and publishing makes us want to carry out these kinds of projects as a means of organizing black feminists as we continue to do political work in coalition with other groups.

4. BLACK FEMINIST ISSUES AND PRACTICE

During our time together we have identified and worked on many issues of particular relevance to black women. The inclusiveness of our politics makes us concerned with any situation that impinges upon the lives of women, Third World, and working people. We are of course particularly committed to working on those struggles in which race, sex, and class are simultaneous factors in oppression. We might, for example, become involved in workplace organizing at a factory that employs Third World women or picket a hospital that is cutting back on already inadequate health care to a Third World community, or set up a rape crisis center in a black neighborhood. Organizing around welfare or daycare concerns might also be a focus. The work to be done and the countless issues that this work represents merely reflect the pervasiveness of our oppression.

Issues and projects that collective members have actually worked on are sterilization abuse, abortion rights, battered women, rape, and health care. We have also done many workshops and educationals on black feminism on college campuses, at women's conferences, and most recently for high school women.

One issue that is of major concern to us and that we have begun to publicly address is racism in the white women's movement. As black feminists we are made constantly and painfully aware of how little effort white women have made to understand and combat their racism, which requires among other things that they have a more than superficial comprehension of race, color, and black history and culture. Eliminating racism in the white women's movement is by definition work for white women to do, but we will continue to speak to and demand accountability on this issue.

In the practice of our politics we do not believe that the end always justifies the means, many reactionary and destructive acts have been done in the name of achieving "correct" political goals. As feminists we do not want to mess over people in the name of politics. We believe in collective process and a nonhierarchical distribution of power within our own group and in our vision of a revolutionary society. We are committed to a continual examination of our politics as they develop through criticism and self-criticism as an essential aspect of our practice. As black feminists and lesbians we know that we have a very definite revolutionary task to perform and we are ready for the lifetime of work and struggle before us.

1-This statement is dated April 1977.

2-Michele Wallace, "A Black Feminist's Search for Sisterhood," *The Village Voice.* 28 July 1975, pp. 6-7.

3-Mumininas of Committee for Unified Newark, *Mwanamke Mwanancbi (The Nationalist Woman),* Newark, N.J., c. 1971, pp. 4-5

FOCUS QUESTIONS:

1. For whom do the authors appear to be writing?
2. What are their main points?
3. How do they connect the personal and the political?

21-3 The Equal Rights Amendment (1972)

Various amendments to the U.S. Constitution, to explicitly guarantee equal rights to women, were proposed in the 20th century. This 1972 resolution came closest to passage: 38 state legislatures were required to pass the resolution within seven years for it to become an amendment, but only 35 did so.

Source: http://www.equalrightsamendment.org/overview.htm

Joint Resolution Proposing an Amendment to the Constitution of the United States Relative to Equal Rights for Men and Women

Resolved by the Senate and House of Representatives of the United States of America in Congress assembled (two-thirds of each House concurring therein), That the following article is proposed as an amendment to the Constitution of the United States, which shall be valid to all intents and purposes

as part of the Constitution when ratified by the legislatures of three-fourths of the several States within seven years from the date of its submission by the Congress:

"Article—

"Section 1. Equality of rights under the law shall not be denied or abridged by the United States or by any State on account of sex.

"Section. 2. The Congress shall have the power to enforce, by appropriate legislation, the provisions of this article.

"Section. 3. This amendment shall take effect two years after the date of ratification."

FOCUS QUESTIONS:

1. Does any part of this resolution appear controversial?
2. Why do you think this bill failed to pass the necessary number of state legislatures?

21-4 Women's Shitwork

As the various Civil Rights Movement and student-led organizations grew, women found it increasingly difficult to find venues for addressing their own concerns. The distribution of menial tasks and leadership roles continued to follow gender lines, so more women became disillusioned and, in some cases, angry.

Source: Evans, Sara. *Personal Politics: The Roots of Women's Liberation in the Civil Rights Movement & The New Left.* New York: Vintage Books, 1979. pp. 175-177.

Students were becoming more introspective in general. The fringe subculture of folk music lovers that had, nurtured the early new left had blossomed into a self-identified counterculture greatly concerned with personal life and lifestyle. Self-consciously alienated and political in varying degrees, these "hippies," as they came to be called, declared them-selves with long hair, beards, sandals, and jeans. They glorified gentleness, love, community, and cooperation, and spurned competitiveness, polished professionalism in work, and materialism. Later on their trademarks became events like "be-ins," "love-ins," and phrases like "getting your head together" and "do your own thing." Crucial ingredients for the future of women's liberation lay in this counterculture's rejection of middle-class standards and lifestyles and its focus on personal issues. It called into question basic defining institutions for women like marriage and the family, asserting in fact that communal living was superior. And it pushed into reality the potential sexual freedom inherent in the pill.

Out of the new themes and the focus on organizing students there emerged a highly personalized technique, which again presaged the consciousness-raising of the feminist movement. Dubbed the "Guatemala Guerrilla approach," the method required an SDS campus organizer to begin any meeting with local members or potential members by talking about himself or herself, his or her background, and the process of his or her radicalization. Then the organizer would encourage the others to do the same. According to SDS vice-president Carl Davidson:

You'd be astonished at the reception this gets, when people realize that they aren't alone, that the failures and the problems they ascribed to themselves stem in large part from the society in which they live and the images of themselves they accepted from society.

At the same time other countercurrents made it more and more necessary for women to step out on their own. As the student movement and its counterculture swelled after 1965, the spaces that had nurtured women's strength and self-assertion contracted. The size of the movement rendered women invisible. Meetings of hundreds, rallies of thousands, marches of hundreds of thousands, did not constitute arenas conducive to female leadership, except for those already exceptionally strong and self-confident. Now there were movement "groupies," both male and female, who hung around to be near the action, vicariously involved and anonymous. Stardom was increasingly defined by glamour and rhetorical verbal skills, and the talents that could prove effective in small groups or in community organizing had little place in the broader movement. A Bettina Aptheker here, a Jane Adams there, stood out as highly unusual anomalies to the general pattern of male leadership.

In Berkeley all the tendencies of the movement became exaggerated. Vivian Leburg finally went to Mississippi in 1965 after two years of participation in the massive Oakland civil rights movement because she wanted more control over her activity. As time went on, many others may have felt the same but there were no longer other options. Campus SDS chapters became exaggerated versions of the male clique-dominated chapter at Harvard described earlier by Barbara Easton. Betty Chewning attended only a few meetings at the University of Chicago. She found them so alienating that she came away feeling that while she would participate in marches, she would avoid any further involvement in such organizations:

It made me feel like other people were making decisions for me and were making assumptions about me, as to who I was and what my political views were. And some of those assumptions were right, but, the fact that the group was moving without my [input] really bothered me a lot. . . . In some instances I felt used . . . [be-cause of] the kinds of things which I had to do in the organization, which included mimeoing, typing, secretarial types of things, but when it came to making real decisions about marches, when and where, what would be the content of speeches . . . the decisions were already reached by the time I was involved in it.

In such experiences lay the roots of the fury and pain articulated by Marge Piercy in 1970:

If the rewards are concentrated at the top, the shit-work is concentrated at the bottom. The real basis is the largely unpaid, largely female labor force that does the daily work. Reflecting the values of the larger capitalist society, there is no prestige whatsoever attached to actually working. Workers are invisible. It is writers and talkers and the actors of dramatic roles who are visible and respected. The production of abstract analysis about what should be done and the production of technical jargon are far more admired than what is called by everybody shitwork. . . ."

FOCUS QUESTIONS:

1. What tensions are described here? Are they based more on class, gender, politics, or some other factor(s)?

2. Is Piercy's anger (in the quoted passage) justified?

21-5 The Personal is Political

In this 1969 essay, radical feminist Carol Hanisch popularized both the phrase and the idea that, "the personal is political." (Hanisch, however, claims not to have authored the phrase itself.) Among other accomplishments, Hanisch also organized an "action" (demonstration) against the Miss American Pageant in 1968.

Source: Hanisch, Carol, "The Personal is Political", in *Feminist Revolution, An Abridged Edition with Additional Writings.* New York: Random House, 1978.

THE PERSONAL IS POLITICAL

Carol Hanisch

For this paper I want to stick pretty close to an aspect of the Left debate commonly talked about—namely "therapy" vs. "therapy and politics." Another name for it is "personal" vs. "political" and it has other names, I suspect, as it has developed across the country. I haven't gotten over to visit the New Orleans group yet, but I have been participating in groups in New York and Gainesville for more than a year. Both of these groups have been called "therapy" and "personal" groups by women who consider themselves "more political." So I must speak about so-called therapy groups from my own experience.

The very word "therapy" is obviously a misnomer if carried to its logical conclusion. Therapy assumes that someone is sick and that there is a cure, e.g., a personal solution. I am greatly offended that I or any other woman is thought to need therapy in the first place. Women are messed over, not messed up! We need to change the objective conditions, not adjust to them. Therapy is adjusting to your bad personal alternative.

We have not done much trying to solve immediate personal problems of women in the group. We've mostly picked topics by two methods: in a small group it is possible for us to take turns bringing questions to the meeting (like, Which do/did you prefer, a girl or a boy baby or no children, and why? What happens to your relationship if your man makes more money than you? Less than you?). Then we go around the room answering the questions from our personal experiences. Everybody talks that way. At the end of the meeting we try to sum up and generalize from what's been said and make connections.

I believe at this point, and maybe for a long time to come, that these analytical sessions are a form of political action. I do not go to these sessions because I need or want to talk about my "personal problems." In fact, I would rather not. As a movement woman, I've been pressured to be strong, selfless, other-oriented, sacrificing, and in general pretty much in control of my own life. To admit to the problems in my life is to be deemed weak. So I want to be a strong woman, in movement terms, and not admit I have any real problems that I can't find a personal solution to (except those directly related to the capitalist system). It is at this point a political action to tell it like it is, to say what I really believe about my life instead of what I've always been told to say.

So the reason I participate in these meetings is not to solve any personal problem. One of the first things we discover in these groups is that personal problems are political problems. There are no personal solutions at this time. There is only collective action for a collective solution. I went, and I continue to go to these meetings because I have gotten a political understanding which all my reading, all my "political discussions," all my "political action," all my four-odd years in the movement never gave me. I've been forced to take off the rose-colored glasses and face the awful truth about how grim my life really is as a woman. I am getting a gut understanding of everything as opposed to the esoteric, intellectual understandings and *noblesse oblige* feelings I had in "other people's" struggles.

This is not to deny that these sessions have at least two aspects that are therapeutic. I prefer to call even this aspect "political therapy" as opposed to personal therapy. The most important is getting rid of self-blame. Can you imagine what would happen if women, blacks, and workers (my definition of worker is anyone who *has* to work for a living as opposed to those who don't. All women are workers) would stop blaming ourselves for our sad situations? It seems to me the whole country needs that kind of political therapy. That is what the black movement is doing in its own way. We shall do it in ours. We are only starting to stop blaming ourselves.

We also feel like we are thinking for ourselves for the first time in our lives. As the cartoon in *Lilith* puts it, "I'm changing. My mind is growing muscles." Those who believe that Marx, Lenin, Engels, Mao, and Ho have the only and last "good word" on the subject and that women have nothing more to add will, of course, find these groups a waste of time.

The groups that I have been in have also not gotten into "alternative life-styles" or what it, means to be a "liberated" woman. We came early to the conclusion that all alternatives are bad under present conditions. Whether we live with or without a man, communally or in couples or alone, are married or unmarried, live with other women, go for free love, celibacy, or lesbianism, or any combination, there are only good and bad things about each bad situation. There is no "more liberated" way; there are only bad alternatives.

This is part of one of the most important theories we are beginning to articulate. We call it "the prowoman line." What it says basically is that women are really neat people. The bad things that are said about us as women are either myths (women are stupid), tactics women use to struggle individually (women are bitches), or are actually things that we want to carry into the new society and want men to share too (women are sensitive, emotional). Women as oppressed people act out of necessity (act dumb in the presence of men), not out of choice. Women have developed great shuffling techniques for their own survival (look pretty and giggle to get or keep a job or man) which should be used when necessary until such time as the power of unity can take its place. Women are smart not to struggle alone (as are blacks and workers). It is no worse to be in the home than in the rat race of the job world. They are both bad. Women, like blacks, workers, must stop blaming ourselves for our "failures."

It took us some ten months to get to the point where we could articulate these things and relate them to the lives of every woman. It's important from the standpoint of what kind of action we are going to do. When our group first started, going by majority opinion, we would have been out in the streets demonstrating against marriage, against having babies, for free love, against women who wore makeup, against housewives, for equality without recognition of biological differences, and god knows what else. Now we see all these things as what we call "personal solutionary." Many of the actions taken by "action" groups have been along these lines. The women who did the antiwoman stuff at the Miss America Pageant were the ones who were screaming for action without theory. The members of one group want to set up a private day-care center without any real analysis of what could be done to make it better for little girls, much less any analysis of how that center hastens the revolution.

That is not to say, of course, that we shouldn't do action There may be some very good reasons why women in the group don't want to do anything at the moment. One reason that I often have is that this thing is so important to me that I want to be very sure that we're doing it the best way we know how, and that it is a "right" action that I feel sure about. I refuse to go out and produce for the movement. We had a lot of conflict in our New York group about whether or not to do action. When the Miss America Protest was proposed there was no question but that we wanted to do it. I

think it was because we all saw how it related to *our* lives. We *felt* it was a good action. There were things wrong with the action, but the basic idea was there.

This has been my experience in groups that are accused of being "therapy" or "personal." Perhaps certain groups may well be attempting to do therapy. Maybe the answer is not to put down the method of analyzing from personal experiences in favor of immediate action, but to figure out what can be done to make it work. Some of us started to write a handbook about this at one time and never got past the outline. We are working on it again.

It's true we all need to learn how to better draw conclusions from the experiences and feelings we talk about and how to draw all kinds of connections. Some of us haven't done a very good job of communicating them to others.

One more thing: I think we must listen to what so-called apolitical women have to say—not so we can do a better job of organizing them but because together we *are* a mass movement. I think we who work full-time in the movement tend to become very narrow. What is happening now is that when nonmovement women disagree with us, we assume it's because they are "apolitical," not because there might be something wrong with *our* thinking. Women have left the movement in droves. The obvious reasons are that we are tired of being sex slaves and doing shit work for men whose hypocrisy is so blatant in their political stance of liberation for everybody (else). But there is really a lot more to it than that. I can't quite articulate it yet. I think "apolitical" women are not in the movement for very good reasons, and as long as we say, "You have to think like us and live like us to join the charmed circle," we will fail. What I am trying to say is that there are things in the consciousness of "apolitical" women (I find them very political) that are as valid as any political consciousness we think we have. We should figure out why many women don't want to do action. Maybe there is something wrong with the action or something wrong with why we are doing the action or maybe the analysis of why the action is necessary is not clear enough in our minds.

March, 1969

FOCUS QUESTIONS:

1. When there are no good options, what does Hanisch propose women should do?

2. What is "political therapy"?

3. Why is Hanisch interested in "apolitical" women?

21-6 *Roe v. Wade* (1973)

Voting 7-2 in 1973, the Supreme Court struck down state laws preventing abortion in the first trimester of pregnancy. The decision also set guidelines for abortion in the second and third trimesters. Roe v. Wade was based on the grounds that extant state laws prohibiting abortion were unconstitutional, as they violated the right to privacy implicitly guaranteed in the 9th and 14th amendments

Source: Henry Steele Commager, Roe v. Wade, Documents of American History (New York: Appleton-Century-Crofts, 1965), pp. 798-800.

BLACKMUN, J .... We forthwith acknowledge our awareness of the sensitive and emotional nature of the abortion controversy, of the vigorous opposing views, even among physicians, and of the deep and seemingly absolute convictions that the subject inspires. One's philosophy, one's experiences, one's exposure to the raw edges of human existence, one's religious training, one's attitudes toward life and family and their values, and the moral standards one establishes and seeks to observe, are all likely to influence and to color one's thinking and conclusions about abortion.

In addition, population growth, pollution, poverty, and racial overtones tend to complicate and not to simplify the problem.

Our task, of course, is to resolve the issue by constitutional measurement free of emotion and of predilection. We seek earnestly to do this, and, because we do, we have inquired into, and in this opinion place some emphasis upon, medical and medical-legal history and what that history reveals about man's attitudes toward the abortive procedure over the centuries ....

The Texas statutes that concern us here are Arts. 1191-1194 and 1196 of the State Penal Code. These make it a crime to "procure an abortion," as therein defined, or to attempt one, except with respect to "an abortion procured or attempted by medical advice for the purpose of saving the life of the mother." Similar statutes are in existence in a m<Dority of the states ....

The principal thrust of appellant's attack on the Texas statutes is that they improperly invade a right, said to be possessed by the pregnant women, to choose to terminate her pregnancy. Appellant would discover this right in the concept of personal "liberty" embodied in the Fourteenth Amendment's Due Process Clause; or in personal, marital, familial, and sexual privacy said to be protected by the Bill of Rights or its penumbras, see *Griswold v. Connecticut*, 381 U. S. 479 (1965); *Eisenstadt v. Baird*, 405 U. S. 438 (1972); id., at 460 (White, J., concurring); or among those rights reserved to the people by the Ninth Amendment, *Griswold v. Connecticut*, 381 U. S., at 486 (Goldberg, J., concurring) ....

The Constitution does not explicitly mention any right of privacy. In a line of decisions, however, going back perhaps as far as *Union Pacific R. Co. v. Botsford, 141 U. S. 250,251 (1891)*, the Court has recognized that a right of personal privacy, or a guarantee of certain areas or zones of privacy, does exist under the Constitution ....

This right of privacy, whether it be founded in the Fourteenth Amendment's concept of personal liberty and restrictions upon state action, as we feel it is, or, as the District Court determined, in the Ninth Amendment's reservation of rights to the people, is broad enough to encompass a women's decision whether or not to terminate her pregnancy. The detriment that the state would impose upon the pregnant woman by denying this choice altogether is apparent. Specific and direct harm medically diagnosable even in early pregnancy may be involved. Maternity, or additional offspring, may force upon the woman a distressful life and future. Psychological harm may be imminent. Mental and physical health may be taxed by child care. There is also the distress, for all concerned, associated with the unwanted child, and there is the problem of bringing a child into a family already unable, psychologically and otherwise, to care for it. In other cases, as in this one, the additional difficulties and continuing stigma of unwed motherhood may be involved. All these are factors the woman and her responsible physician necessarily will consider in consultation.

On the basis of elements such as these, appellants and some amici argue that the woman's right is absolute and that she is entitled to terminate her pregnancy at whatever time, in whatever way, and for whatever reason she alone chooses. With this we do not agree. Appellants' arguments that Texas either has no valid interest at all in regulating the abortion decision, or no interest strong enough to support any limitation upon the woman's sole determination, is unpersuasive. The Court's decisions recognizing a right of privacy also acknowledge that some state regulation in areas protected by that right is appropriate. As noted above, a state may properly assert important interests in safeguarding health, in maintaining medical standards, and in protecting potential life. At some point in pregnancy, these respective interests become sufficiently compelling to sustain regulation of the factors that govern the abortion decision. The privacy right involved, therefore, cannot be said to be absolute ....

We therefore conclude that the right of personal privacy includes the abortion decision, but that this right is not unqualified and must be considered against important state interests in regulation.

We note that those federal and state courts that have recently considered abortion law challenges have reached the same conclusion ...

The appellee and certain amici argue that the fetus is a "person" within the language and meaning of the Fourteenth

Amendment. In support of this they outline at length and in detail the well-known facts of fetal development. If this suggestion of personhood is established, the appellant's case, of course, collapses, for the fetus' right to life is then guaranteed specifically by the Amendment. The appellant conceded as much as reargument. On the other hand, the appellee conceded on reargument that no case could be cited that holds that a fetus is a person within the meaning of the Fourteenth Amendment.

The Constitution does not define "person" in so many words. Section 1 of the Fourteenth Amendment contains three references to "person." The first, in defining "citizens," speaks of "persons born or naturalized in the United States." The word also appears both in the Due Process Clause and in the Equal Protection Clause. "Person" is used in other places in the Constitution .... in nearly all these instances, the use of the word is such that it has application only postnatally. None indicates, with any assurance, that it has any possible pre-natal application.

Texas urges that, apart from the Fourteenth Amendment, life begins at conception and is present throughout pregnancy, and that, therefore, the state has a compelling interest in protecting that life from and after conception. We need not resolve the difficult question of when life begins. When those trained in the respective disciplines of medicine, philosophy, and theology are unable to arrive at any consensus, the judiciary, at this point in the development of man's knowledge, is not in a position to speculate as to the answer ....

In areas other than criminal abortion the law has been reluctant to endorse any theory that life, as we recognize it, begins before live birth or to accord legal rights to the unborn except in narrowly defined situations and except when the rights are contingent upon live birth ....

In short, the unborn have never been recognized in the law as persons in the whole sense ....

In view of all this, we do not agree that, by adopting one theory of life, Texas may override the rights of the pregnant woman that are at stake. We repeat, however, that the state does have an important and legitimate interest in preserving and protecting the health of the pregnant woman, whether she be a resident of the state or a nonresident who seeks medical consultation and treatment there, and that it has still another important and legitimate interest in protecting the potentiality of human life. These interests are separate and distinct. Each grows in substantiality as the woman approaches term and, at a point during pregnancy, each becomes "compelling."

With respect to the state's important and legitimate interests in the health of the mother, the "compelling" point, in the light of present medical knowledge, is at approximately the end of the first trimester. This is so because of the now established medical fact, referred to above ... , that until the end of the first trimester mortality in abortion is less than mortality in normal childbirth. It follows that, from and after this point, a state may regulate the abortion procedure to the extent that the regulation reasonably relates to the preservation and protection of maternal health ....

With respect to the state's important and legitimate interest in potential life, the "compelling" point is at viability.

This is so because the fetus then presumably has the capability of meaningful life outside the mother's womb. State regulation protective of fetal life after viability thus has both logical and biological justifications. If the state is interested in protecting fetal life after viability, it may go so far as to proscribe abortion during that period except when it is necessary preserve the life or health of the mother.

Measured against these standards, Art. 1196 of the Texas Penal Code, in restricting legal abortions to those "procured or attempted by medical advice for the purpose of saving the life of the mother," sweeps too broadly. The statute makes no distinction between abortions performed early in pregnancy and those performed later, and it limits to a single reason, "saving" the mother's life, the legal justification for the procedure. The statute, therefore, cannot survive the constitutional attack made upon it here ....

To summarize and to repeat:

1. A state criminal abortion statute of the current Texas type, that excepts from criminality only a life saving procedure on behalf of the mother, without regard to pregnancy stage and without recognition of the other interests involved, is violative of the Due Process Clause of the Fourteenth Amendment.

(a) For the stage prior to approximately the end of the first trimester, the abortion decision and its effectuation must be left to the medical judgment of the pregnant woman's attending physician.

(b) For the stage subsequent to approximately the end of the first trimester, the state, in promoting its interest in the health of the mother, may, if it chooses, regulate the abortion procedure in ways that are reasonably related to maternal health. (c) For the stage subsequent to viability the state, in promoting its interest in the potentiality of human life, may, if it chooses, regulate, and even proscribe, abortion except where it is necessary, in appropriate medical judgment, for the preservation of the life or health of the mother ....

FOCUS QUESTIONS:

1. What ramifications does this law have for women's rights?
2. On what elements did the court base its decision?
3. What is the role of the state in this matter? At what point does the interest of the state begin? Why?

21-7 Mirta Vidal: New Voice of La Raza

Mirta Vidal was a Chicana and a socialist, and author and an activist. In her writings and her political actions, she worked to find a path that would uphold the progressive elements of her heritage, while also allowing her full opportunities as a woman.

Source: Vidal, Mirta. Women: *New Voices of La Raza.* Pathfinder Press, 1971.

At the end of May 1971, more than 600 Chicanas met in Houston, Texas, to hold the first national conference of Raza women. For those of us who were there it was clear that this conference was not just another national gathering of the Chicano movement. Chicanas came from all parts of the country inspired by the prospect of discussing issues that have long been on their minds and which they now see not as individual problems but as an important and integral part of a movement for liberation. The resolutions coming out of the two largest workshops, "Sex and the Chicana" and "Marriage Chicana Style," called for "free, legal abortions and birth control for the Chicano community, controlled by *Chicanas.*" As Chicanas, the resolution stated, "we have a right to control our own bodies." The resolutions also called for "24-hour child-care centers in Chicano communities" and explained that there is a critical need for these since "Chicana motherhood should not preclude educational, political, social and economic advancement." While these resolutions articulated the most pressing needs of Chicanas today, the conference as a whole reflected a rising consciousness of the Chicana about her special oppression in this society. With their growing involvement in the struggle for Chicano liberation and the emergence of the feminist movement, Chicanas are beginning to challenge every social institution which contributes to and is responsible for their oppression, from inequality on the job to their role in the home. They are questioning "machismo," discrimination in education, the double standard, the role of the Catholic Church, and all the backward ideology designed to keep women subjugated. This growing awareness was illustrated by a survey taken at the Houston conference. Reporting on this survey, an article in the Los Angeles magazine *Regeneracion* stated: "84% felt that they were not encouraged to seek professional careers and that higher education is not considered important for Mexican women . . . 84% agreed that women do not receive equal pay for equal work." The article continued: "On one question they were unanimous. When asked: Are married women and mothers who attend school expected to also do the housework, be responsible for childcare, cook and do the laundry while going to school, 100% said yes. 88% agreed that a social double standard exists." The women were also asked if they felt that there was discrimination toward them within La Raza: 72% said yes, *none* said no and 28% voiced no opinion. While polls are a good indicator of the thoughts and feelings of any given group of people, an even more significant measure is what they are actually doing. The impressive accomplishments of Chicanas in the last few months alone are a clear sign that Chicanas will not only play a leading role in fighting for the liberation of La Raza, but will also be consistent fighters against their own oppression as Chicanas, around their own specific demands and through their own Chicana organizations. Last year, the women in MAPA (Mexican-American Political Association) formed a caucus at their annual convention. A workshop on women was also held at a Latino Conference in Wisconsin last year. All three Chicano Youth Liberation Conferences held in 1969, 1970, and 1971 in Denver, Coloradohave had women's workshops.In May of this year, women participating at a Statewide Boycott Conference called by the United Farm Workers Organizing Committee in Castroville, Texas, formed a caucus and addressed the conference, warning men that sexist attitudes and opposition to women's rights can divide the farmworker's struggle. Also in May, Chicanas in Los Angeles organized a regional conference attended by some 250 Chicanas, in preparation for the Houston conference and to raise funds to send representatives from the Los Angeles area.Another gathering held last year by the Mexican American National Issues Conference in Sacramento, California, included a women's workshop that voted to become the Comision Feminil Mexicana (Mexican Feminine Commission) and function as an independent organization affiliated to the Mexican American National Issues Conference. They adopted a resolution which read in part:"The effort of Chicana/Mexican women in the Chicano movement is generally obscured because women are not accepted as community leaders either by the Chicano movement or by the Anglo establishment."In Pharr, Texas, women have organized pickets and demonstrations to protest police brutality and to demand the ousting of the city's mayor. And even in Crystal City, Texas, where La Raza Unida Party has won major victories, women have had to organize on their own for the right to be heard. While the men constituted the decision-making body of Ciudadanos Unidos (United Citizens) the organization of the Chicano community of Crystal Citythe women were organized into a women's auxiliaryCiudadanas Unidas. Not satisfied with this role, the women got together, stormed into one of the meetings, and demanded to be recognized as members on an equal basis. Although the vote was close, the women won.The numerous articles and publications that have appeared recently on La Chicana are another important sign of the rising consciousness of Chicanas. Among the most outstanding of these are a special section in *El Grito del Norte*, an entire issue dedicated to and written by Chicanas published by *Regeneracion*, and a regular Chicana feminist newspaper put out by Las Hijas de Cuahtemoc in Long Beach, California. This last group and its newspaper are named after the feminist organization of Mexican women who fought for emancipation during the suffragist period in the early part of this century.These developments, by no means exhaustive of what Chicanas have done in this last period, are plainly contradictory to the statement made by women participat-ing in the 1969 Denver Youth Conference. At that time a workshop held to discuss the role of women in the movement reported to the conference:"It was the consensus of the group that the Chicana woman does not want to be liberated." Although there are still those who maintain that Chicanas not only do not want to be liberated, but do not *need* to be liberated, Chicanas themselves have decisively rejected that attitude through their actions. **"Machismo"** In part, this awakening of Chicana consciousness has been prompted by the "machismo" she encounters in the movement. It is adequately described by one Chicana, in an article entitled "Macho Attitudes":When a freshman male comes to MECHA [Movimiento Estudiantil Chicano de Aztlana Chicano student organization in Californial he is approached and welcomed. He is taught by observation that the Chicanas are only useful in areas of clerical and sexual activities. When something must be done there is always a Chicana there to do the work. "It is her place and duty to stand behind and back up her Macho!" . . . Another aspect of the MACHO attitude is their lack of respect for Chicanas. They play their games, plotting girl against girl for their own benefit.... They use the movement and Chicanismo to take her to bed. And when she refuses, she is a vendida [sell-out] because she is not looking after the welfare of her men. This behavior, typical of Chicano men, is a serious obstacle to women anxious to play a role in the struggle for Chicano liberation.The oppression suffered by Chicanas is different from that suffered by most women in this country. Because Chicanas are part of an oppressed nationality, they are subjected to the racism practiced against La Raza. Since the overwhelming majority of Chicanos are workers, Chicanas are also victims of the exploitation of the working class. Hut in addition, Chicanas, along with the rest of women, are relegated to an inferior position because of their sex. Thus, Raza women suffer a triple form of oppression: as members of an oppressed nationality, as workers, *arid* as women. Chicanas have no trouble understanding this. At the Houston conference 84 percent of the women surveyed felt that"there is a distinction between the problems of the Chicana and those of other women."On the other hand, they also understand that the struggle now unfolding against the oppression of women is not only relevant to them, but is their struggle.Because sexism and male chauvinism are so deeply rooted in this society, there is a strong tendency, even within the Chicano movement, to deny the basic right of Chicanas to organize around their own concrete issues. Instead they are told to stay away from the women's liberation movement because it is an "Anglo thing."We need only analyze the origin of male supremacy to expose this false position. The inferior role of women in society does not date back to the beginning of time. In fact, before the Europeans came to this part of the world women enjoyed a position of equality with men. The submission of women, along with institutions such as the church and the patriarchy, was imported by the European colonizers, and remains to this day part of Anglo society. Machismoin English, "male chauvinism"is the one thing, if any, that should be labeled an "Anglo thing."When Chicano men oppose the efforts of women to move against their oppression, they are actually opposing the struggle of every woman in this country aimed at changing a society in which Chicanos themselves are oppressed. They are saying to 51 percent of this country's population that they have no right to fight for their liberation.Moreover, they are denying one half of La Raza this basic right. They are denying Raza women, who are triply oppressed, the right to struggle around their specific, real, and immediate needs.In essence, they are doing just what the white male rulers of this country have done. The white male rulers want Chicanas to accept their oppression because they understand that when Chicanas begin a movement demanding legal abortions, child care, and equal pay for equal work, this movement will pose a real threat to their ability to rule.Opposition to the struggles of women to break the chains of their oppression is not in the interest of the oppressed but only in the interest of the oppressor. And that is the logic of the arguments of those who say that Chicanas do not want to or need to be liberated.The same problem arose when the masses of people in this country began to move in opposition to the war in Vietnam. Because Black people did not until recently participate in massive numbers in antiwar demonstrations, the bourgeois media went on a campaign to convince us that the reason Blacks were not a visible component of these demonstrations was because the antiwar movement was a "white thing." Although, for a while, this tactic was successful in slowing down the progress of the Black nationalist movement, for whom the question of the war is of vital importance, Black antiwar activity is now clearly rising.But once again the white males who run this country are up to their old tricks. Only this time around it is the women's liberation movement which is a "white thing."Again, the bourgeois media is a key tool for perpetrating this myth. As one Chicana explains, in an article entitled "Chicanes Speak Out" in *Salsipuedes*, published in Santa Barbara, California: "The real issue of the women's liberation movement is fighting the established female role in society which has kept women enslaved as human beings. But the news

media portrays women's liberation people as karate-chopping, man-hating hippies."Among the many distortions about the feminist movement is the argument that women are simply fighting against men. One such statement appeared in an article by Enriqueta Vasquez some months ago in *El Grito del Norte*. Vasquez wrote:In looking at women's lib [sic] we see issues that are relevant to that materialistic, competitive society of the Gringo. This society is only able to function through the sharpening of wits and development of the human instinct of rivalry. For this same dominant society and mentality to arrive at a point where there is now a white women's liberation movement is dangerous and cruel in that that social structure has reached the point of fracture and competition of the male and female.Thus, since the feminist movement is "anti-male," when Chicanas attempt to organize against their own oppression they are accused of trying to divide the Chicano movement.The appeal for "unity" based on the continued submission of women is a false one. While it is true that the unity of La Raza is the basic foundation of the Chicano movement, when Chicano men talk about maintaining La Familia and the"cultural heritage"of La Raza, they are in fact talking about maintaining the age-old concept of keeping the woman barefoot, pregnant, and in the kitchen. On the basis of the subordination of women there can be no real unity.This attitude is vividly illustrated in an article entitled"El Movimiento and the Chicana"which explains:The political and economical struggle of the Chicana is the universal question of women. The difference between the liberation of Chicana women and other Third World women is cultural. The Chicano culture has very positive effects and very bad ones. We have to fight a lot of Catholic ideas in our homes and in the movement. For example, the idea of large families is very Catholic. The Pope says no birth control, abortions, lots of kids (and make me richer). So what do the guys say in the movement, have lots of kids, keep up the traditional Chicano family. The point is made even clearer by Francisca Flores in the issue of *Regeneracion* cited earlier when she says: "The issue of birth control, abortions, information on sex and the pill are considered 'white' women's lib issues and should be rejected by Chicanas according to the Chicano philosophy which believes that the Chicana women's place is in the home and that her role is that of a mother with a large family. Women who do not accept this philosophy are charged with betrayal of 'our culture and heritage.' OUR CULTURE HELL!"Far from turning their anger and frustrations against individual men, what Chicanas, and all women, are saying is that men should support their struggles. This, too, has been repeatedly expressed by Chicanas. For example, an editorial in *Regeneracion* says in part:It is hoped that women who disagree with any aspect of the new role of the Chicana will be willing to discuss the issue or the difference of opinion within the group. This is the only way many of the questions will be dealt with. Primarily . . . that the Chicana feminist movement is not anti-men! The Comision Femenil Mexicana in California welcomes men membersbut the men who have joined to date are men not threatened by women. Rather, they represent a small but growing nucleus who recognize and appreciate the power of women in action.The only real unity between men and women is the unity forged in the course of struggle against their oppression. And it is by supporting, rather than opposing, the struggles of women that Chicanos and Chicanas can Genuinely unite.Stripped of all rationalizations, when Chicanos deny support to the independent organization of Chicanas, what they are saying is simply that Chicanas are not oppressed. And that is the central question we must ask: are Chicanas oppressed?All other arguments aside, the fact is that Chicanas *are* oppressed and that the battles they are now waging and will wage in the future, are for things they need: the right to legal abortions, the right to adequate child care, the right to contraceptive information and devices, the right to decide how many children they do or do not want to have. In short, the right to control their own bodies. As Flores points out:Mexican women who bear (large) families beyond the economic ability to support them, suffer the tortures of damnation when their children die of malnutrition, of tuberculosis and other illnesses which wipe out families in poverty stricken or marginal communities in the Southwest.... IF A WOMAN WANTS A LARGE FAMILY ... NO ONE WILL INTERFERE WITH HER RIGHT TO HAVE ONE . . . even if they cannot personally afford it . . . that is their right. However, to stipulate this right as a tenet of La Causa for all women of La Raza is to play a dangerous game with the movement. It meansstripped of its intellectual romanticismthat Chicanas are being condemned to wash diapers and stay home all of their youth. She goes on to say, "As stated before, the question of large families is the choice each person or family will make for themselves. That is their inalienable right. A woman who wants a large family should not be denied. *What we are saying is that the woman should have the right to participate in making that decision.*"At the National Abortion Action Conference held in New York in July, a Third World Women's Workshop, attended by close to fifty Blacks, Asian-Americans, Chicanas, and Latinas, voted unanimously to support the national abortion campaign and passed a resolution which reads in part:There is a myth that Third World women do not want to control our bodies, that we do not want the right to contraception and abortion. But we know that Third World women have suffered the most because of this denial of our rights and will continue to suffer as long as the antiabortion laws remain on the books. We know that more Third World women die every year from illegal back-street abortions than the rest of the female population. We know that Third World women are the first victims of forced sterilization. And we know that we intend to fight for our freedom as women.Coupled with this campaign to repeal all abortion laws, women are fighting to end all forced sterilizations, a campaign in which Chicanas will play a central role. This demand is of key importance to Chicanas who are the victims of forced sterilizations justified by the viciously racist ideology that the problems of La Raza are caused by Raza women having too many babies.In line with other brutal abuses of women, Chicanas have been used as guinea pigs for experimentation with contraception. This was done recently in San Antonio by a doctor who wanted to test the reaction of women to birth control pills. Without informing them or asking their opinion, he gave some of the women dummy pills (placebos) that would not prevent conception, and as a result some of the women became pregnant. When questioned about his action, his reply was: "If you think you can explain a placebo test to women like these you never met Mrs. Gomez from the West Side."The feminist movement today provides a vehicle for organizing against and putting an end to such racist, sexist practices. And that is what women are talking about when they talk about women's liberation.Another essential fight that Chicanas have begun is around the need for adequate child care. While billions of dollars are spent yearly by this government on war, no money can be found to alleviate the plight of millions of women who, in addition to being forced to work, have families to care for.The following figures poignantly demonstrate the seriousness of this problem and the pressing need for adequate child-care facilities. Nancy Hicks, writing in the November 30, 1970, *New York Times*, reports: "There are more than 11.6 million working mothers in the country today, more than 4 million of these with children under 6 years old. However, only 640,000 licensed daycare spaces are available. More than one-third of these are privately run." These figures do not include the women who, because of lack of child care, are unable to work and are therefore pushed onto the welfare rolls. In addition, although such figures are not available for Raza women specifically, it is safe to assume that they are much higher.Demands such as twenty-four hour child-care centers financed by the government and controlled by the community, are the kinds of concrete issues that Chicanas are fighting for. As Chicanas explain in "A Proposal for Childcare," published in *Regeneracion,* "Child care must be provided as a public service, like public schools, unemployment insurance, social security, and so forth. The potential for a mass movement around this initiative is clear." An important aspect of the struggles of Chicanas is the demand that the gains made through their campaigns be *controlled by Chicanas.* The demand for community control is a central axis of the Chicano liberation struggle as a whole. Thus, when Chicanas, as Chicanas, raise demands for child-care facilities, abortion clinics, etc., controlled by Chicanas, their fight is an integral part of the Chicano liberation struggle. When Chicanas choose to organize into their own separate organizations, they are not turning away from La Causa or waging a campaign against men. They are saying to Chicanos: "We are oppressed as Chicanas and we are moving against our oppression. Support our struggles." The sooner that Chicanos understand the need for women to struggle around their own special demands, through their own organizations, the further La Raza as a whole will be on the road toward liberation. It is important to keep in mind that many of the misunderstandings that have arisen so far in the Chicano movement regarding Chicanas are due primarily to the newness of this development, and many will be resolved through the course of events. One thing, however, is clear Chicanas are determined to fight. As Flares states, the issue of equality and freedom for the Chicana "is *not negotiable.* Anyone opposing the right of women to organize into their own form of organization has no place in the leadership of the movement. FREEDOM IS FOR EVERYONE." In the spirit of Las Adelitas, Las Hijas de Cuahtemoc, and all the unrecognized Mexican women who fought valiantly for their rights, who formed their own feminist organizations, and who fought and died in the Mexican revolution, Chicanas in this country will take the center stage in the advances of La Raza. The struggle for women's liberation is the Chicana's struggle, and only a strong independent Chicana movement, as part of the general women's liberation movement and as part of the movement of La Raza, can ensure its success.

FOCUS QUESTIONS:

1. What is the evidence for "the rising consciousness of Chicanas"?

2. Does Vidal see any substantive difference between the condition of Chicanas and women from other ethnic groups?

3. Does she believe Chicanas should ally themselves with a universal women's rights movement, or with a general struggle for Chicana/o rights – or does she have a different perspective altogether?

ENDINGS AND BEGINNINGS, 1980 TO 2008

22-1 Defining Feminist Activism

Issues are rarely simple, but in our wired world – where all kinds of information about causes, institutions, and individuals is just a few keystrokes away – it is easy to become paralyzed by fear of either acting hypocritically, or of not doing 'enough.' Jennifer Baumgardner and Amy Richards take these fears head-on in their consideration of what constitutes a feminist activist, and why a feminist activist is a worthwhile thing to be.

Source: Baumgardner, Jennifer and Amy Richards. *Grassroots: A Field Guide for Feminist Activism.* New York: Farrar, Strauss and Giroux, 2005, xix, xxii-xxiii.

Since we ended up committing to activism as a term as well as a process, we want to make sure readers know what we personally mean by the word. The two of us define activism as consistently expressing one's values with the goal of making the world more just. We use feminism as our philosophy for that value system; that is, we try to take off the cultural lens that sees mostly men and filters out women and replace it with one that sees all people. We ask: "Do our lifestyles reflect our politics?" "How can we make sure that we all receive the same breaks—and basic necessities—traditionally awarded to white males?" An activist is anyone who accesses the resources that he or she has as an individual for the benefit of the common good. With that definition, activism is available to anyone. By asserting that anyone can be an activist, we aren't trying to weaken or water down its power. We believe that activism is by definition profound, a big deal, revolutionary. However, we are challenging the notion that there is one type of person who is an activist—someone serious, rebellious, privileged, and unrealistically heroic. . . .

***

. . . it's not who you are but what you do. We came to this understanding through our years of traveling across the country in support of our first book, *Manifesta: Young Women, Feminism, and the Future.* One of the most popular questions we were asked points to this truth. The question almost always came from a young woman, some- one who reports she has taken her first women's studies class the year before and it changed her life. "I see the world through feminist-colored glasses now. Issues make so much more sense. I am electrified!" she'd gush. "I'm volunteering at a battered women's shelter and I can't wait to do more and . . . urn, I wear a thong. Can I still be a feminist?" At first we laughed, and answered that her underwear neither qualified nor disqualified her feminism. After getting this question at several schools, though, we realized that the woman wasn't asking for clothing advice. She was saying, "Can I be myself and care about these issues?" And the questions in that vein kept coming. *Am I good enough? Am I pure enough? If I don't eat red meat, do I also have to forgo leather? Can I never shop at the Gap again? Do I have to give up my religion? I think I'm a feminist but . . . I diet. I listen to rap. I'm pro-life.* We realized that one of the main barriers to seeing oneself as someone who could truly make change in the world is that we feel trapped in our own contradictions. As Amy says, "Can I wear Nike running shoes and still protest their labor practices in Indonesia?" There is a huge fear that we'll be revealed as hypocrites so, in search of moral perfection, we're paralyzed from doing anything.

The two of us are not advising people to deck themselves out in Nike gear and get a bikini wax every week—or even to disavow careful reflection about the challenges of participating in a capitalist economy. We are advocating, quite simply, that if you wait until you are perfect and free of conflicts, you will never change anything in the world. In fact, all of our most-loved social justice superstars have lives that are riddled with contradictions. "Mother of Modern Feminism" Betty Friedan had a husband who used to give her black eyes, yet Friedan didn't complain publicly, nor did she report him to the police or leave him flat. Inspiring civil rights activist Al Sharpton took Republican funding for his radical bid for the 2004 Democratic nomination for President. Beloved feminist author bell hooks advocates a Marxist critique of capitalist society but nonetheless has been known to love her red BMW and charge large speaking fees. The filmmaker Michael Moore advocates workers' rights but we've met a few disillusioned former employees who note he doesn't apply the same pro-labor standards to his own workplaces. The Center for Third World Organizing eviscerates major corporations like Levi's in its magazine *Colorlines* and yet takes money from Levi's foundation. We're not telling people's dirty secrets but demonstrating that these accomplished, effective, respected

activists still have issues to work out—just like the rest of us. Each of us has to begin where we are to address the slew of inequities that present themselves in our lives.

FOCUS QUESTIONS:

1. How do Baumgardner and Richards define activism? Do you agree with their definition?

2. Is the kind of activism they describe "enough"? Would society actually change if a subset of individuals became feminist activists, as defined by Baumgardner and Richards?

22-2 Asma Gull Hasan: *American Muslim Women, Between Two Worlds*

The Muslim population in the United States is growing rapidly due to both immigration and conversion. It is also very diverse. Asma Gull Hasan's parents immigrated to the United States from Pakistan; she is a feminist author, who often writes about the issues affecting Muslim women.

Source: Hasan, Asma Gull. "American Muslim Women: Between Two Worlds." In *American Muslims: The New Generation.* Continuum, 2000. pp. 107-111.

I was debating with my extended family once during a family gathering whether Muslim women and men should be allowed to pray in the same room. I reasoned that on Judgment Day men and women will stand equally before God with no gender preference. My grandfather piped up, "No, men are superior in Islam!" We were in my uncle's normally quite noisy Suburban, which had now gone silent at my grandfather's words. My family members waited a moment, and then said things like, "Oh no!" and "You're in for it now, grandfather!" They were saying all this because I am known in my family for responding vehemently to such statements. I stayed levelheaded, however, and asked my grandfather, "You mean in the Qur'an?"

"Yes!" he said.

"I don't think so," I said.

"No, it says it!" he retorted.

After a few minutes of this yes-no business we finally got to the merits of the argument. My grandfather felt that since God's messengers were all male,

men must then be superior in God's eyes. I countered that a woman, Khadijah, Muhammad's wife, was the first convert to Islam.

Without her faith in Muhammad, no **Muslims would exist.**

I offered other arguments proving gender equality in Islam, but something told me that my points were falling on deaf ears. I joked that my grandfather must have received the Taliban version of the Qur'an. The Taliban are the Islamic revolutionaries who took over the Afghanistan government and banned women from working because they said that was against their interpretations of the Qur'an. The country came to a near stand-still as half the professional population—doctors, teachers—were not allowed to work. Obviously, the Taliban had to modify some of their policies to keep the country functioning. The Taliban validly has pronounced that they put an end to Afghanistani tribal practices which hurt women. They were forced to marry and had no right to property or divorce. So as unenlightened as the Taliban is, they have actually elevated Afghanistan's rural population.

Though I tried to make light of the situation, I was saddened that *my own grandfather* would say such a thing, even if he believed it. Does he really think that I, as a woman, am inferior to my brother, merely because he's male? I see in my grandfather the effects of South Asian culture, which is patriarchal, on his interpretation of the Qur'an. Sure, there are a few passages that taken out of context, interpreted from a patriarchal perspective, or not updated for our times (which the Qur'an instructs us to do) imply women's inferiority. They are by no means passages on which to build tenets of Islam, however. When I asked my grandfather to show me where in the Qur'an it says that women are inferior to men, he replied that it would take him some time to find the passage. As he has still not found it, I presume it doesn't exist or isn't clear in its meaning.

But this is what it came to—my own grandfather, a product of his society and prejudices, saying that women are inferior to men. This despite the fact that women outnumber men in his own family. He has five granddaughters and three grandsons—it's in his interest to see women as equal to men! It hurts, but I understand that we all have to read the Qur'an and make our own interpretation. This is *my jihad* with my grandfather. Who knows—maybe someday my grandkids will disagree with me on a belief, emphasized by my American culture, on something similar.

The debate over the status of women in Islam is probably the best example of how culture affects interpretation. Men like my grandfather have taken a few Qur'anic passages and, coupled with a patriarchal culture, have interpreted them in the most literal and self-serving way. It happens in all cultures, not just among Muslims, and such chauvinism existed before Islam, perhaps even before organized religion itself. There is no Islamic basis for demeaning women or oppressing them. Culture is the culprit here, and no one really is immune from that.

American culture often favors men and holds women back. Women are paid less than men for similar jobs. We have yet to elect a female president. We're still arguing over a woman's right to control her body. Sexual harassment and rape are very difficult to prosecute. Office politics, sometimes on a subliminal level, keep women from rising to top positions. However, no one sees the American woman as being as severely oppressed as the Muslim woman. Women *are* oppressed in *some* countries where the majority of the population is Muslim. There, women's literacy rates are often quite low, among many other disadvantages for advancement.

However, such oppression is not mandated by the Qur'an. It is in fact condemned by it. Furthermore, strong Muslim women are all over the place. Benazir Bhutto became the prime minister of Pakistan twice, which is more than we can say for a female politician in the United States. Muhammad's wife Khadijah, was one of the most successful business people in Mecca. Fatima Mernissi is one of the most intelligent Islamic scholars and a prominent thinker, and she is a woman. My own mother runs the lives of our family as well as being a dynamic volunteer worker and fundraiser. My dad calls her "the boss" and sometimes a tyrant. Here I am writing a book on Islam in America. Do I seem oppressed to you?

The challenge women like my mom and I face is to overcome the cultural baggage that haunts American Muslim women. Though women in Islamic countries are often oppressed, Islam as a philosophy is very pro-woman. However, as with all philosophies, societies, and cultures, contradictions occur in the journey from paper (Qur'an) to practice (my grandfather). Because of these contradictions, Muslim women all over the world are being pulled in two different directions: one is to fulfill the traditional expectations for a Muslim woman, like marriage at a young age and raising a family; the other to explore the new roles for women in the modern world by being career women and community activists.

The problems we face—in trying to express our feminism, become activists, and be independent–are acute versions of what American women in general are going through. As more American women convert to Islam and more young Muslim women like me grow up, it is in our interest, as Americans, not to be like my grandfather and rely on what we have heard through the grapevine, but to encourage all women to explore their identities and their strengths, and instill in them the belief that they can contribute to our society, our economy, our values as much as men can.

Who is the American-Muslim woman? The Islamic Council of New England Conference (ICNE) on "Women in Islam" said all Muslim women should be knowledgeable about Islam and become mothers. Women are also expected to be modest and keep interaction with males to a minimum, making activities outside the home difficult. According to Aminah McCloud, these aspects associated with the term "Muslim woman" arrived upon the American scene with Muslim immigrants in the later part of the twentieth century; these immigrant Muslim women wore strict Islamic dress and were committed to raising children as well as being obedient to their husbands.

These traditional views are not the only choices, however. Jane Smith, a scholar on Islam, presents a more open view in her essay "Islam" in the book *Women in World Religions*: "The new Islamic woman ... is morally and religiously conservative and affirms the absolute value of the true Islamic system for human relationships." This new Muslim woman disagrees with an interpretation of Islam that oppresses women. She is quite open to educational and professional advancement for herself, though she may think some professions are more appropriate for women than others. Additionally, she does not mind extending sole decision making power to a male member of her family in certain circumstances in return for security.

In reality, today's American Muslim female community is mix of all these models: educated and uneducated, married am unmarried, liberal and conservative, as diverse a population a American women in general. For example, I am educated, do not wear *hijab*, expect to have a career, a good marriage (possibly arranged), and kids. You're probably thinking that those expectations are not all that different from those of the average

American woman, with the exception of the *hijab* and arranged marriage.

For many Muslim girls, arranged marriage or semi-arranged to someone your parents introduced to you is no more odd than dating and marrying one of your older brother's friends, or someone you met at work. The same is true of *hijab*. Muslims have been

exposed to these traditional aspects of Islam for most of their lives.

American Muslim women are really between two worlds the old world of traditions, preserved and passed down by immigrant parents or older members of the indigenous community and the new world, as presented to us by the feminist movement, American emphasis on gender equality, and by the Qur'an, in a sense, too.

FOCUS QUESTIONS:

1. What does Hasan mean when she writes that "culture affects interpretation"? Is that a point that applies only to Muslim beliefs, or to any form of faith identity?

2. How does Hasan connect her struggles to those of other American women?

22-3 From the Consciousness-Raising Group to the Women's Studies Classroom

bell hooks is the pen-name of Gloria Watkins, an African-American woman who grew up in a working-class family in Kentucky. She is a professor of English at City College of New York, and has written many books and articles about feminism and class issues, among other topics.

Source: Hooks, bell. *Feminism is for Everybody: Passionate Politics.* Cambridge, MA: South End Press, 2000, 9-10.

The creation of women's studies as an academic discipline provided discipline another setting where women could be informed about feminist thinking and feminist theory. Many of the women who spearheaded the introduction of women's studies classes into colleges and uni- versities had been radical activists in civil rights struggles, gay rights, and early feminist movement. Many of them did not have doctorates, which meant that they entered academic institutions receiving lower pay and working longer hours than their colleagues in other disciplines. By the time younger graduate students joined the effort to legitimize feminist scholarship in the academy we knew that it was important to gain higher degrees. Most of us saw our commitment to women's studies as political action; we were prepared to sacrifice in order to create an academic base for feminist movement.

By the late '70s women's studies was on its way to

becoming an accepted academic discipline. This triumph overshadowed the fact that many of the women who had paved the way for the institutionalization of women's studies were fired because they had master's degrees and not doctorates. While some of us returned to graduate school to get PhDs, some of the best and brightest among us did not because they were utterly disillusioned with the university and burnt out from overwork as well as disappointed and enraged that the radical politics undergirding women's studies was being replaced by liberal reformism. Before too long the women's studies classroom had replaced the free-for-all consciousness-raising group. Whereas women from various backgrounds, those who worked solely as housewives or in service jobs, and big-time professional women, could be found in diverse consciousness-raising groups, the academy was and remains a site of class privilege. Privileged white middle-class women who were a numeric majority though not necessarily the radical leaders of contemporary feminist movement often gained prominence because they were the group mass media focused on as representatives of the struggle. Women with revolutionary feminist consciousness, many of them lesbian and from working-class backgrounds, often lost visibility as the movement received mainstream attention. Their displacement became complete once women's studies became entrenched in colleges and universities which are conservative corporate structures. Once the women's studies classroom replaced the consciousness-raising group as the primary site for the transmission of feminist thinking and strategies for social change the movement lost its mass-based potential.

Suddenly more and more women began to either call themselves "feminists" or use the rhetoric of gender discrimination to change their economic status. The institutionalization of feminist studies created a body of jobs both in the world of the academy and in the world of publishing. These career-based changes led to forms of career opportunism wherein women who had never been politically committed to mass-based feminist struggle adopted the stance and jargon of feminism when it enhanced their class mobility. The dismantling of consciousness-raising groups all but erased the notion that one had to learn about feminism and make an informed choice about embracing feminist politics to become a feminist advocate.

FOCUS QUESTIONS:

1. What does hooks claim differentiates women's studies in academia from consciousness-raising groups? Which does she prefer, and why? Do you think her differentiation is valid? Do you agree with her opinion?

2. What would you hope to see as the next step in the evolution of the feminist movement?

22-4 Restaurant Worker

Like many immigrants, Korean women are often unsure of their workplace rights in the United States. This oral history interview of Kim Chong Ok is part of a series of profiles of Korean-American workers in Los Angeles.

Source: Louie, Miriam Ching Yoon. *Sweatshop Warriors: Immigrant Women Workers Take on the Global Factory.* Cambridge, MA: South End Press, 2001. pp. 162-163.

I was a cook's helper when I started. I worked as a cook's helper for about seven months and then became a cook. I started out at $1,400 a month, working more than 12 hours a day, 6 days a week. After I became a cook I got $100 more. The restaurant ran a 24-hour shift. I worked four days on the night shift and two days on the day shift.

We couldn't negotiate about our wages. Whenever we tried to negotiate, as soon as the words came out of our mouths, the employer would start cussing us out, and go on and on for days after that. We didn't want to face them. I didn't want to quit working there. It's not good to switch jobs too often. I figured that it was like this everywhere so I needed to just bear the hardship and keep working there. During this process I grew close to my co-workers. There were about four or five people who had worked there around ten years like me. Our friendship grew and we decided to stick together. My wages increased to $1,800 a month. But in April 1998, the employer complained that the business was not doing well. She said the IMF crisis was affecting the business over here in the US, and that they had decided to cut our wages. The cooks' wages were cut to $1,400 a month. So we decided to walk out.

Since the restaurant ran 24 hours, there were three cooks to work the three different shifts. We used to have dishwashers and cook's helpers. We really need that help to cook, but the employer cut three people out. So the cooks had to do everything in the kitchen. It was very hard on us and we already worked long hours.

The owner kept oppressing us and acting like she was doing everything within the law on wages and hours. But when we calculated how much we should have been earning, the figures just didn't match up. So we confronted the employer. She kept saying if you don't like it, you can always leave. She started [paying me] for eight hours of work but did not reduce my hours to that amount. So the problems started there.

The wage cut was a problem, but the employer also laid off people—for example, I worked four peoples' jobs. The employer reduced the wages and also demanded that we do all of the work [of the people who were laid off]. That upset me and everyone else. We talked about what we could do about this situation and it led to us taking action. We eventually went to KIWA for consultation because my employer emphasized that she was doing things by the law. She kept on saying "The law is this and that." So the workers decided to find out what our rights were.

FOCUS QUESTIONS:

1. What is Ok's attitude toward work? Do you think her attitude or behavior might differ if she were a man?

22-5 If I Stop Trying, I Will be Deaf

Language differences can divide immigrant families along generational lines. Pat Mora is a Mexican-American author with a special interest in children's literacy. In this poem, she offers insight into a mother's fears of being separated from her children by language.

Source: Mora, Pat. "Elena," in *Chants*. Houston: Arte Publico Press, 1984. p. 58.

Elena

My Spanish isn't enough.

I remember how I'd smile

listening to my little ones,

understanding every word they'd say,

their jokes, their songs, their plots.

Vamos a pedirle dulces a mama. Vamos,

But that was in Mexico.

Now my children go to American high schools.

They speak English. At night they sit around

the kitchen table, laugh with one another.

I stand by the stove and feel dumb, alone.

I bought a book to learn English.

My husband frowned, drank more beer.

My oldest said, "*Mama*", he doesn't want you

to be smarter than he is." I'm forty,

embarrassed at mispronouncing words,

embarrassed at the laughter of my children,

the grocer, the mailman. Sometimes I take

my English book and lock myself in the bathroom,

say the thick words softly,

for if I stop trying, I will be deaf

when my children need my help.

FOCUS QUESTIONS:

1. What is being described here? What are the scenes, and what are the mother's emotions?

2. How is a male-female split demonstrated in this poem?

3. Is this a problem unique to Mexican-American women?

22-6 Crossing the Rio Grande

This interview with an illegal immigrant couple in El Paso, Texas, demonstrates the many strains on family life imposed by poverty and illegal status.

Source: Santoli, Al. "Crossing the Rio Grande." From *New Americans: An Oral History*. New York: Viking Press, 1988. pp. 267-268.

JOSE: The majority of the people in our apartment building have the same problem as my family. All of us are in El Paso without legal papers. I have been living here since 1981.

ROSA: I came in 1984, to find work. After Jose and I were married and we found a place to live, I brought my children from a previous marriage. We lived across the river, in Juarez. But I was born further south, in Zacatecas.

JOSE: My hometown is Juarez. Since I was nine years old, I've been coming to El Paso to work. At first I did gardening in people's yards, but I have stayed in El Paso constantly since 1981, going out to the fields to do farm work. I used to go to Juarez to visit my relatives at least one day each month. But in the last year, I haven't gone, because of the new immigration law. To visit Juarez I have to swim across the river. I can't cross the bridge or the "*migra*" [Border Patrol officers] can catch me right there.

During the past few months, the river has been very high and fast. That's one reason why not so many people have been crossing lately. I am not working now, because it isn't the growing or harvesting season on the big farms. On February 15, we usually begin to plant onions. That is when the main agricultural season begins. But during a three-month period between planting and harvesting, there is no work.

We haven't paid our rent since December. If we're lucky, I can find some part-time work to pay for food. Our baby, Jose Luis, is two months old. Because he was born in El Paso, he is an American citizen. We can only get food assistance for him. Once in a while, I find a job as a construction laborer, house painter, whatever is available. We use the money to buy food for the baby and the other three children first.

ROSA: I haven't been able to work lately, because the baby is so small. My other children are all in school. Lorenzo is twelve years old, Jose Ruben is ten, and Miriam is seven.

From the time I came to El Paso, I have worked as a housekeeper and minding homes for people. I am not used to staying in the apartment every day, but I have no other choice, because of my small baby.

I have known many changes in my life. I moved to Juarez from a farm in Zacatecas when I was seven years old. My mother and father were split up. After mother remarried, my stepfather took us to Juarez. We lived in an adobe house in the *colonias* [ramshackle housing projects] up in the hills.

When I was a teenager, I worked as a hairdresser in a beauty salon, cutting hair. My first husband was a mechanic, fixing cars. We made a good living. But my husband spent the money he made drinking in the *cantinas*. And after a while, he wouldn't let me work, because I had young children to take care of. When he died in 1984, he left me nothing at all. He drank too much and died from cirrhosis of his liver. I had no money . . nothing. My children were nine, seven, and three years old. I had to find a way to pay rent and feed them.

At that time, the economy in Mexico had become horrible. Inflation was going crazy. The peso jumped to 500 per dollar. Today it is still climbing at 1, 000 per dollar. I found a job working on an assembly line at a factory. We produced rubber gloves for hospitals and medical supplies like little caps for syringes. I would go into work at 4:30 in the afternoon and stay until 2:00 A. M. I was paid only 7,000 pesos [$14] each week. That was not enough to feed my kids. And I didn't have any relatives or friends to watch the kids while I worked. So I had no other choice but to put them in a special institution, like an orphanage, for children without parents. This upset me very much. But with my husband dead, and no other form of support, there was nothing I could do.

My only hope was to cross the river to the United States. If I could find a job that paid enough money, my children could join me. I wanted them to have an education and a proper life . . . to be someone.

After I made up my mind to cross the river, I met Jose Luis. It was like fate—we just found each other. You could say it was love at first sight. [Laughs] I had two young boys who needed a good man to learn from. When he asked me to live with him, I said yes.

FOCUS QUESTIONS:

1. What are Rosa's goals? What has she done to try to achieve her goals?

2. Why is Rosa poor? What is her attitude about her poverty?

22-7 Comparable Worth

Phyllis Schlafly is a white American conservative woman of firm convictions, and many apparent contradictions. She has opposed "feminism" for decades, but she has achieved fame and influence through the kinds of independent thinking and action that feminists have long fought for. She founded several conservative organizations, most notably the Eagle Forum, and the Eagle Forum Education and Legal Defense Fund. The second organization sponsored a conference on "comparable worth," the concept that work performed mostly by women should be compensated at the same rate as work performed mostly by men that requires similar levels of education, training, risk and commitment. Schlafly introduced the conference.

Source: Unequal Pay for Unequal Work, A Conference on Comparable Worth, Phyllis Schlafly, ed., Washington, D.C., The Fund, 1984. pp. vii–ix.

Introduction to the Comparable Worth Conference

National newsmagazines and legal journals have been running a public service ad. In big black letters, the ad is headlined: "It pays to be a man." The copy below states: "The statistics bear it out. For every dollar a man makes, a woman earns only 59¢. Yet we have already observed the 20th anniversary of the Equal Pay Act. . . . Today, a secretary is usually paid less than a truck driver. A teacher less than a liquor store clerk. And a nurse less than a pharmacist. Law or no law, it still pays to be a man. Isn't it time we made it pay just to do a good job?"

The ad doesn't mention the slogan "Equal Pay for Comparable Worth," but the ad is obviously designed to build public sentiment for that new concept.

Note that the ad does *not* compare the wages of male nurses with female nurses, or male truck drivers with female truck drivers, or male pharmacists with female pharmacists. The crux of the Comparable Worth concept is the comparing of wages paid for different job categories in which either males or females predominate — but who do different work, in different occupations, in different labor markets.

For example, in one highly-publicized lawsuit testing the Comparable Worth theory, the comparison was between nurses and tree-trimmers in Denver. The Federal judge who dismissed that case said the Comparable Worth theory is "pregnant with the possibility of disrupting the entire economic system" of the United States.

This Conference is designed to explore the issue of Comparable Worth — what it is, how to define it, whether it should or should not be a social or economic or legal goal of our society, and what it would cost to individuals, to business, and to society.

Much of the language of Comparable Worth is attractive. Who could be opposed to paying equal pay for work of Comparable Worth or comparable value? An attractive synonym often used for Comparable Worth is "pay equity." Isn't everybody for equitable pay? Who doesn't think he is worth more than he is being paid? Most everyone I know thinks he or she deserves a raise or a promotion.

But what is the best means of bringing about pay equity? Some believe that government regulation of labor markets is the best and perhaps the only way; others believe that private enterprise and free labor markets produce the best results.

We will examine the assumptions of the Comparable Worth doctrine. Are differences in the average wages of all men and all women the result of sex discrimination? Or are there other causes? Does the wage gap reflect the influence of a bias against women, or differences in productivity between men and women? We all share the goal of nondiscrimination in employment — and of equal pay for equal work. That is a very noncontroversial issue.

This Conference has been designed to raise the level of public debate on this issue by discussing the concerns raised by proposals for implementing Comparable Worth controls. An examination of the literature on this subject shows that the debate so far has been very one-sided. Very few groups have come forward to present criticisms of the Comparable Worth

goal. The 1982 Congressional hearings produced 1,829 pages of testimony, nearly all in favor of Comparable Worth. Perhaps this is because there are organized lobbying groups working to bring about Comparable Worth.

Senators Edward Kennedy and Alan Cranston are sponsors of the Senate bill on Comparable Worth. Eleanor Holmes Norton, former chair of the Equal Employment Opportunity Commission, has stated that this is the civil rights issue of the 1980s. Comparable Worth is a stated national goal of the American Federation of State, County and Municipal Employees. This union has already won one Comparable Worth lawsuit in the state of Washington (which is estimated to cost the state one billion dollars) and successfully negotiated a Comparable Worth contract in Minnesota.

There has been considerable activity to pass Comparable Worth legislation in various states and to implement the legislation that has already been passed in several states. None of these statutes defines any method for ascertaining Comparable Worth or the value of dissimilar jobs. It appears that some of this legislation was passed without adequate understanding or consideration of the issue and of its short-range costs and long-range economic consequences.

Many local governments and businesses, whose cost structures would be dramatically affected by Comparable Worth, do not seem to understand that Comparable Worth is radically different from Equal Pay for Equal Work.

We are indebted to Judith Finn, coordinator for this conference on Comparable Worth, for assembling a unique group of speakers to address this issue from their different perspectives, utilizing their different types of professional expertise. Mrs. Finn has done a brilliant job of bringing together knowledgeable and articulate spokesmen who can dissect the issue of Comparable Worth for the public to understand, as well as bring into focus this concept and its consequences.

FOCUS QUESTIONS:

1. What are Schlafly's views on "comparable worth"?
2. Does Schlafly provide evidence here to justify her position?